A Geography of
Urban Places

A Geography of Urban Places

Selected Readings

Edited by

Robert G. Putnam
Frank J. Taylor
Phillip G. Kettle

Methuen

Toronto   London   Sydney   Wellington

Library of Congress Catalog Card Number 77-116479
ISBN 0-458-90630-1 (hc)
ISBN 0-458-90620-4 (pb)

Design by Carl Brett
Illustrations by Gus Fantuz
Printed and Bound in Canada by
The Bryant Press Limited

74 73 72 71 2 3 4 5 6

Preface

The growth in the number of people who live in cities and the diffusion of urban life to every part of the habitable world is one of the outstanding characteristics of twentieth-century life. In Canada, nearly 75 per cent of the people reside in urban centres as defined by the census. Mississaga,* the great Southern Ontario conurbation, focussed around the western end of Lake Ontario, best illustrates the situation. In Mississaga there are five census metropolitan areas with populations of more than 100,000 each, and four other major cities, each with populations exceeding 50,000. Mississaga now contains more than 3,600,000 people, 92 percent of whom live in an urban environment. Growth has been rapid. Mississaga in 1951 contained about 2,100,000 people; between 1951 and 1966 it experienced a population increase of 75 per cent. Today the average population density is about 635 per square mile. In the densely populated areas, such as the City of Toronto, the population density exceeds 19,000 people per square mile.

How does a geographer evaluate and assess urban places such as Mississaga? What tools,

* For a discussion of the use of *Mississaga* see D. F. Putnam and R. G. Putnam, *Canada: A Regional Analysis* (Toronto, J. M. Dent and Sons, 1970), Chapter *111*.

techniques and theories are useful in understanding the geography of urban places? It is the intent of this book to provide a selection of readings that will help the geography student who is beginning to study the urban environment to realize the concepts and analytical techniques possible. The articles have been chosen to provide a wide range of ideas and levels of understanding about urban geography. Many of these ideas and concepts have been previously published only in professional journals and would not be readily available to students. These articles have not been modified from their original content. In all cases the original footnotes and references have been retained.

The book is divided into three major sections. The first is concerned with the definition of urban geography, the origin location characteristics of cities. In the second section, emphasis is placed upon the economic base of cities. How cities function, the role of the Central Business District and the intricate relationships that exist between cities and their hinterlands are all part of the economic base. The third section concentrates upon the effects of urbanization and examines closely the urban environment, and the ways in which this environment can be improved.

Contents

Contributors

Beecroft, Eric

*Formerly Director of the Community Planning Association of Canada. Now
Director of the Urban and Regional Studies Program, University of
Western Ontario, London, Ontario.*

Blumenfeld, Hans

*Formerly Assistant Director of Planning for the Metropolitan Toronto Planning
Board. Now Planning Consultant, Toronto, Ontario.*

Boal, Frederick W.

Department of Geography, The Queen's University of Belfast, Northern Ireland.

Borchert, John R.

Professor of Geography, University of Minnesota, Minneapolis, Minnesota.

Clawson, Marion

Resources for the Future, Inc., Washington, D.C.

Eaton, Leonard K.

Contributor to Landscape.

Epstein, Bart J.

Manager, Retail Real Estate, The B. F. Goodrich Co., Akron, Ohio.

Fountain, G. F.

Formerly Director of Planning for the City of Vancouver.

Gaffney, Mason

Resources for the Future, Inc., Washington, D.C.

Garner, Barry J.

Professor, Geographical Institute, University of Aarhus, Aarhus, Denmark.

Getis, Arthur

Rutgers, The State University, Brunswick, New Jersey.

Getis, Judith
Rutgers, The State University, Brunswick, New Jersey.

Goodwin, William
Associate Professor of Geography, University of Wisconsin, Milwaukee, Wisconsin.

Harris, Chauncy D.
Chairman of the Department of Geography, University of Chicago, Chicago, Illinois.

Horwood, Edgar M.
Professor of Urban Geography, University of Washington, Seattle, Washington.

Jacobs, Jane
Author of Downtown is for People, The Exploding Metropolis, The Death and Life of Great American Cities.

Kelley, Eugene J.
Director, Division of Business Administration of Clark University, Worcester, Massachusetts.

Kiang, Ying-Cheng
Professor of Geography, University of Chicago, Chicago, Illinois.

Kinsel, John
Contributor to Community Planning Review.

Kolosova, Yu A.
Moscow University, Moscow, U.S.S.R.

MacNair, Malcolm D.
The Office of the Urban Renewal Coordinator of the City of Seattle, Seattle, Washington.

Mayer, Harold M.
Professor of Geography, Kent State University, Kent, Ohio.

Murphey, Rhoads
Director, Center for Chinese Studies, University of Michigan, Ann Arbor, Michigan.

Nelson, Howard J.
Chairman of the Department of Geography, University of California, Los Angeles, California.

Reinemann, Martin W.

Professor of Earth Science, Northern Illinois University, DeKalb, Illinois.

Richardson, N. H.

Staff Consultant, City of Toronto Planning Board, Toronto, Ontario.

Rooney, John F., Jr.

Associate Professor of Geography, Southern Illinois University, Carbondale, Illinois.

Spelt, Jacob

Professor of Geography, University of Toronto, Toronto, Ontario.

Stafford, Howard A., Jr.

Professor, Head of the Department of Geography, University of Cincinnati, Cincinnati, Ohio.

Stanford, John H.

Contributor to Landscape.

Stokes, Charles J.

Charles Anderson Dana Professor, Chairman, Department of Economics, University of Bridgeport, Bridgeport, Connecticut.

Tanner, Ogden

Time-Life Books, New York, New York.

Thorsell, James

Contributor to Ontario Geography.

Ullman, Edward L.

Professor of Geography, University of Washington, Seattle, Washington.

Vance, James E., Jr.

Professor of Geography, University of California, Berkeley, California.

Voorhees, Alan M.

Westgate Research Park, MacLean, Virginia.

Wilson, L. H.

Formerly Chief Architect and Planning Officer for New Town of Cumbernauld. Now Planning Consultant, Glasgow, Scotland.

City Origin
and
Location

What is urban geography, and how do geographers study the urban landscape? Garner, in *Aspects and Trends of Urban Geography* suggests that urban geographers are concerned with towns as items in the general fabric of settlement and in the interaction that exists between these items. Towns can also be studied in terms of site, situation, layout and build. Internal structure, city interaction and city growth are all important. In *Cities and Urban Geography,* Mayer raises the problems associated with defining the area occupied by a city, for in most cases the urban area involved exceeds the official corporate limits. He also considers what is meant by the term *metropolis,* and points out some of the difficulties urban geographers have in dealing with the census metropolitan areas. The concept of megalopolis is also examined with the intention of showing how it has evolved since the time of the Greeks.

City Origin and Location

"The city is as old as civilization." Murphey, in *Historical and Comparative Urban Studies,* views the origins of cities as centres of exchange. Cities have possessed this important function right through history, from the early beginnings in Egypt, Mesopotamia and Asia, to the present day. It is his opinion that, as commercial and manufacturing functions evolve with the changes in technology, cities everywhere are becoming more like one another. Cities in North America, however, have not the long history of development of those in Eurasia. Most are less than two centuries old, and have evolved rapidly in response to the changing technology of the industrial revolution. As such, the origins and developments are traced in *American Metropolitan Evolution* by Borchert. He suggests that four epochs of development have occur-

red and that these reflect changes in the technology of transportation and industrial energy. The pattern of evolution that he suggests can be applied directly to Canada, and with some modifications is applicable elsewhere.

City location is important. Ullman, in his classic paper *A Theory for the Location of Cities,* suggests that urban places are not scattered illogically over the surface of the earth but that orderly spacing does occur. His comments on the settlement theory proposed by Christaller and others have been influential. More insight into Christaller's urban hierarchy system is found in the paper by Arthur and Judith Getis. Here the $k = 3$ network is explained, and some of the limitations to the theory are explored.

City Structure

The structure and form of cities are far from static. They evolve through time. In *Technology and Urban Form,* Frederick Boal makes the strong point that the city is characterized by flows — flows of people, commodities and information. The way these flows take place shapes the city, for they represent the interaction between various parts of the city. Transportation and construction technology have profound influences on the city because they are part of the "space adjusting" mechanism. He then shows the role of technology on urban form during three technological periods: the pedestrian city; the steam engine and wheel-track city; and the flexible city.

However, the structure of cities involves not only the build-up of urban uses within the city, but also the territorial expansion to areas that have become urbanized beyond the city limits. Voorhees, in *Urban Growth Characteristics,* illustrates how urban growth can be studied. An interesting viewpoint of city growth is provided by Kolosova of Moscow University in *The Territorial Expansion of American Cities and Their Population Growth*. He concentrates on the role that annexation has played in the growth of American cities.

Since it was published in 1945, *The Nature of Cities* by Harris and Ullman has been considered by many geographers to be a classic of its type. It reviews the reasons why cities form, what functions cities require, and how the internal structure of cities is arranged Attention is focussed on three generalizations of arrangement — concentric zone, sector, and multiple nuclei. These generalizations are expanded somewhat by Nelson's *The Form and Structure of Cities: Urban Growth Patterns*. Nelson also emphasizes the major elements in the urban structure of cities. One of these elements, which is very significant for city growth, is manufacturing. Reinemann, in *The Pattern and Distribution of Manufacturing in the Chicago Area,* carefully studies the dispersal of this land use between 1945 and 1960. While his conclusions regarding the outward movement of manufacturing to suburban areas are significant, the methods of analysis employed are also of considerable importance.

However, city structure also involves man. Within cities people live, work, and play in close proximity to one another. Many North American cities also benefit from the wide range of backgrounds possessed by their residents. One obvious characteristic is that of income, which has been mentioned earlier in the study by Harris and Ullman. Another is that of the ethnic origin of the people. Kiang, in *The Distribution of Ethnic Groups in Chicago, 1960,* outlines a procedure for studying the distribution of ethnic groups which could be applied to most cities in the world. He also documents the mobility of ethnic groups within a city, and shows the intra-urban migration pattern that has evolved.

1

Aspects and Trends of Urban Geography

Barry J. Garner

Perhaps the most general, although surely the least satisfactory, definition of geography is, "Geography is what geographers do." Accompanying the continuing trend toward urbanization in the world, an increasingly large part of contemporary geographical literature comprises studies of various aspects of the urban environment. Geographers are doing the city. But what are they doing in the city? What problems do they study? What are their concepts about the city? How do they, as distinct from sociologists, for example, approach the study of urban areas? Can the findings be useful in helping to improve the social and economic health of cities, which, it has been suggested, represents one of the gravest challenges in the twentieth century? This paper will answer some of these questions — perhaps not as fully as they deserve, but as adequately as space will allow.

It is often said that geographers are "Jacks-of-all-trades" since they seem to study a little of everything, much of which borders on other fields of study. One has only to glance at the table of contents of a geography textbook to see how true this is. In the same way, the subject matter of urban geography is a rich and varied potpourri. Moreover, there are many different approaches to the geographical study of towns, although perhaps two are most common. First, the town can be considered as forming a discrete phenomenon in the general fabric of settlement. Concepts and generalizations may be formed regarding their distribution, size, function, and growth. Areas served by urban places may be delimited and the spatial interaction between places may be studied. Second, the town may be studied in terms of its layout and build, which express its origin, growth, and function. Concepts and generalizations may be related to the character and intensity of land use within the urban area and to the spatial interaction between its constituent parts.

Perhaps the best way to understand the topics studied and the concepts used in urban geography is to imagine a town and view it through the eyes of an urban geographer and the studies he might undertake there. The first question he might ask is, "Where is it?" It has a *site*, the actual ground on which it stands. Why did it grow up here and not somewhere else? It also has a location, both

Reprinted from *Journal of Geography* (May, 1966), pp. 206-11 by permission.

an absolute and, more important, a relative location, a *situation* with respect to other physical and human things around about it. Today, many of the early site factors have ceased to be important. Similarly, relative locations have changed with improved communications. The communications have enabled distances to be covered more cheaply and in less time than ever before and have resulted in the intensification of interaction between places. Site and situation characteristics are thus constantly changing through time. The nature of these changes, the processes underlying them, and the effects they have on the changing spatial relationships between towns constitute one set of problems in urban geography.

The study of the town itself may be from an aggregative or an elemental viewpoint; that is, the geographer may consider the town as a discrete whole, as a collection of elements which distinguish it from others, or he may pay specific attention to some or all the constituent elements within it as separate parts that go to make up the whole. In both cases the studies may be cross-sectional in that they present the situation at a given point in time, or they may be time-oriented with emphasis on tracing the evolution of the present pattern. In fact, most studies contain elements of both of these approaches.

Most aggregative studies are concerned with form and function. In answer to questions about form or shape, concepts from biology have proved useful and various measures of shape have been attempted by geographers. In distinguishing towns by the functions they perform, analysis is usually in terms of the dominant activities revealed in census materials on employment and/or occupations, in terms of the presence or absence of functions difficult to quantify, such as government or universities, and in terms of their

roles, for example, as service centers or ports. The end product of these studies is the formulation of generic (type) classifications of towns, not only as ends in themselves, but also as a way of ordering information conveniently for the purpose of further analysis and investigation.

STUDIES OF INTERNAL CITY STRUCTURE

The town itself occupies an area of appreciable size, and activities are separated from one another within it. It has an internal structure which can most easily be expressed in terms of the differences in character and intensity of land uses at various locations. When the geographer recognizes residential areas, shopping districts, or industrial zones, he is also identifying different functions and forms, all of which give the basis for the recognition of uniform regions — areas which are homogeneous in terms of specified characteristics — within towns. He might say that it is the description of the nature of these urban regions, their disposition and their social interdependence, that constitutes a geographical analysis of the internal structure of the town.

Residential Land Use

A geographer may very well want to consider only one of the major functions or land uses within the town in isolation from all the others. Many studies are of this nature. For example, attention might be focused on residential land use, and questions pertaining to the patterns and the principles underlying those patterns would most surely be asked, for there is considerable internal variation in residential structure. The older, inner areas of the town are usually ones of high density, with old and multi-story buildings, whereas the outer and progressively newer parts are lower in density. He can view this as a surface of differing intensity and character of use and apply concepts of density gradients, decreasing outward from the core of the town, for purposes of analysis. Identifying the shapes of these gradients and studying the changes in them over time and in different-sized urban areas are increasingly important research topics.

Business and Commercial Structure

The commercial structure of towns has received much attention in recent investigations. The complex business structure of the town can be disaggregated into various component parts, such as ribbon development along arterials, into clusters or centers of activities of varying size and functional composition, and into specialized concentrations of similar types of function, such as printing or medical districts. A geographer would want to understand these patterns and would rely in part on the concepts of the *threshold size* (the minimum amount of support necessary for a business to survive in the economic landscape) and the *range of a good* (which defines the area from which this support can be obtained), for these help determine the spacing of business activities. He could use concepts of agglomeration of economic activity and of differences in shopping habits in the analysis of the location, functional composition, and interaction among activities.

He would most certainly recognize that part of the business structure consists of a hierarchy of vari-sized shopping centers — both newer, planned ones and older, unplanned nucleations — ranging from the smallest street corner cluster to the most complex concentration in the central business district, or the downtown area. Each level or center in

the hierarchy can be characterized by the numbers and types of activities it contains. The central business district alone furnishes ample study topics, ranging from its delimitation to an analysis of its internal structure and the interconnections existing within it. He would identify a *core*, comprising a number of highly interrelated functions, and a surrounding *frame* of loosely connected and less intensive land uses, and trace the connections between them.

Industrial Structure

Differences exist also in the nature and distribution of industries within and between towns. Some industrial types are highly concentrated in the inner, older parts of the city, while others are located in isolation toward the periphery. Clusters of similar types occur in some areas while others consist of apparently disparate kinds. Indeed, towns themselves are in many instances characterized by dominance of a single kind of industry or by the diversification of types. In the analysis of patterns of industrial location the geographer could use concepts of *scale economics* — which relate quantity of goods produced directly to costs of production — to understand the localization and grouping of industries within the town. He could also use the *economic base concept* (the idea that most cities exist primarily as centers of employment opportunities) to identify those activities which are *basic* to the town's existence, in that they bring money into the town from outside by trading with other areas, and those which are *nonbasic*, or city serving, in that they serve the people living within the area of the town itself. He would relate the town's growth and economic well-being to the basic industrial structure, since towns cannot exist without trade with other areas.

INTERACTION WITHIN THE CITY

We have asserted that activities occupy different locations within the city. For example, place of residence is separated by varying distances from place of work for most people. Linkages and movements between the various parts must therefore take place. People and goods must overcome distance in order to satisfy their demands, and in so doing they give rise to a variety of patterns of movement and flows, the most pronounced one being, of course, the daily commuting patterns. These interactions are reflected in the amount, direction, time, and character of movements between the various functional areas. Consequently, the study of urban transportation has become a major topic in urban geography. The town, in fact, comprises a complex system of overlapping functional areas and of nodes and foci about which human activity is organized. Concepts of *intervening opportunity,* of least-effort behavior resulting in minimizing distances traveled, and the principles relating trip generation to the character and intensity of land use afford partial explanations of these patterns.

Movement and focality are intimately connected with the concept of *accessibility*. Since activities have different needs from the viewpoint of accessibility, and since some locations are more accessible than others to the various parts of the urban area and its functions, there is competition for the use of land, and this competition affects its value. The economic concepts relating land values to differences in accessibility are fundamental to the analysis of the distribution and intensity of land uses within the urban area. Urban land can be represented as a rent surface, which, in general, resembles a contour map of a hill in that values and rents are highest in the core of the town, where accessibility is presumably greatest, and decrease by differing amounts in various directions to the periphery. Regularities exist in the relationship between this surface and the distribution of urban functions.

THE DYNAMIC NATURE OF CITIES

So far we have considered the town as static. In reality, however, its internal structure is constantly changing. New buildings replace old ones, and land uses are changed as functions move from one location to another or disappear altogether. Patterns are in a state of flux as adjustments are made to changing conditions. Centripetal forces of various kinds attracts activities to the centers of towns while centrifugal forces result in decentralization and dispersal. At the same time, areas of one kind of land use are invaded by other uses which eventually take over, resulting in change in function, in intensity of use, and in form.

An urban geographer would therefore be interested in the processes of residential decentralization, in the expansion of the suburbs at the town's periphery. He would note that the older, inner areas of the town, no longer meeting the requirements of the original users, decline and are taken over by alien uses. He would study slums and trace the evolution of uses at any given location by means of the concept of *sequent occupance*. He would study the changes in business structure as the quality of the market deteriorates and changes occur in the technology of retailing. He would note other changes — the growth of out-of-town shopping centers and the associated reductions in sales volumes and vacancy rates in the downtown area, the emergence of commercial blight as areas run down, and the trend toward industrial decentralization as older sites with their congestion, scarcity of land for expansion, and high costs become increasingly less suitable for most kinds of modern industry. He would want to know the effect of such changes as these on the patterns of movement within the city. In fact, he is interested in defining the relationships that exist and in identifying the processes underlying the changing internal structure of the town.

Towns do not exist only to serve the people living within their bounds; they are also intimately connected with the areas surrounding them. Another major group of study topics is thus concerned with the interaction between towns and the areas that comprise their hinterlands. The city has a sphere of influence, a trade area, in the same way that a magnet has a field of influence. People go to towns to purchase goods or attend a game and, through its function as a collecting and distributing center, the town serves the surrounding area in a variety of ways. The urban geographer would want to know what these relationships are. He would delimit the trade area, and analyze its character and size.

The extent of trade areas is directly related to the proximity and functional structure of other settlements. He would look at the size and spacing of towns in a region, asking questions about the degree of clustering or dispersal of settlement. He would find the ideas related to *central place theory** useful in understanding patterns. He would be concerned with the principles underlying distributions of towns and the evolution of patterns of town-spacing over time.

METHODS OF STUDY

Although the foregoing does not exhaust the

* See A. Getis and J. Getis, "Christaller's Central Place Theory," on p. 68.

concepts associated with urban geography, a word about methods and techniques is in order at this juncture. Much geographic representation is purely descriptive in character. The identification of patterns, their description, and the generation of classifications are the traditional and necessary prerequisites for geographical study. However, much of the recent work appears to be markedly different from this, although on closer inspection it will be found that the differences are mainly in the way research is undertaken rather than in the kinds of problems studied. Greater emphasis is being placed on the use of mathematics as an analytical techinque, and there is increased concern with the general rather than the specific. The subject is changing from an idiographic one, in which the emphasis was on the intensive study of individual cases, to the nomothetic approach, in which there is a search for general laws and spatial regularities.

We are really saying that the subject is becoming more scientific, with greater emphasis on the explanation and prediction of geographic phenomena. For, although description may be a logical starting point, it is inadequate by itself, since it can only lead to a rearrangement of the facts without adding principles from which to strike out anew. Moreover, once we emphasize explanation, we become engaged in the search for theories. It is in this connection that another interesting change has taken place in the approach to urban geography, namely, the increasing use that is being made of models.

The usual concept of a model is that of a miniature; for example, a model railroad set. This really is an analogue to the real thing. It is, in fact, not an exact replica but a likeness, since only the most salient features have

been represented. Models are just that —
abstractions or simplifications of the real
world in which the irrelevant material is discarded to lay bare the bones of what are considered to be the simplest and most significant
aspects of the problem under investigation.

Although models can be of various kinds,
those most widely used in urban geography
are mathematical ones, in which words are
replaced by mathematical symbols, and consist of a set of mathematical assertions from
which consequences can be derived by logical
mathematical argument. For example, in
studying the field of influence of a town, we
draw the analogy to the magnetic field. Phy-
sicists tell us that if two magnets are placed
near each other, the boundary of their magnetic fields is directly related to their size
or strength, and inversely related to the distance separating them. In the same way, the
boundary between the trade areas of towns
and the interaction between towns is also
related to their sizes and to the distances
between them. Translating this to symbols,
we can express the same thing simply as
P_aP_b/D where P_a and P_b stand for the size of
the two towns and D represents the spacing.
Using this very simple model, we can estimate the extent of trade area of say place *b*,
or the amount of interaction expected between towns *a* and *b*.

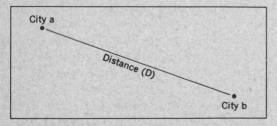

More complicated models have been developed recently to help in the study of journey-
to-work and journey-to-shop patterns. They
have been applied to the analysis and explanation of the distribution of land uses
within the city; for example, to residential
land use and to commercial structure. Much
effort is now being devoted to the development of models which can simulate entire
urban areas to aid in the formulation of
planning policies.

But the model gives us an artificial situation which must be compared to the findings
obtained from actual field observation. There
is, as a result, a problem of appraisal. It is in
the testing of theoretical results derived from
the use of a model that we find an added
departure from the traditional way of doing
things. The traditional way was largely to
use "eyeball" methods of direct visual comparison — methods which are both highly
subjective and generally inaccurate. In order
to gain greater objectivity and reliability,
more and more urban geographers are turning to the use of statistical methods of testing
hypotheses or in evaluating results.

Mathematical methods are also being used
now to describe phenomena (in the description of patterns, for example, or in the formulation of classifications) and in the identification and measure of relationships or
correlations between phenomena. Recent
work has therefore tended to become more
quantitative with (a) greater problem orientation, (b) hypothesis testing using mathematics, and (c) emphasis on the building of
models as an aid in the formulation of theory.

Once explanation is available, predictions
may become logical. It is here that urban
geography appears to be able to make an
even greater contribution to urban planning
than it has in the past. Continued search for
the understanding of the spatial structure of
the city can help in making decisions about
its future. It is the application of the findings

of geographical studies to this purpose that many urban geographers consider to be their most worthwhile goal. They are contributing in a large way to the understanding of the urban world and the eventual betterment of this environment for an increasingly urbanized society.

Further Reading

Dickinson, Robert E., *City and Region: A Geographical Interpretation* (London, Routledge and Kegan Paul, Ltd., 1964).
Mayer, Harold and Kohn, Clyde eds., *Readings in Urban Geography* (Chicago, University of Chicago Press, 1959).

2 Cities and Urban Geography

Harold M. Mayer

One of the most rapidly developing fields of geography during the generation which followed World War II has been that of urban studies. Currently, a very high proportion of the research effort and interests is in the phenomena of cities and metropolitan areas. In this, geography has shared with other social sciences many common concepts and methods, but has contributed a distinctive set of viewpoints and a unique focus: that which is primarily concerned with the organization of man's use of space and resources in the development and functioning of urban settlements. Research in urban

Reprinted from *Journal of Geography* (January, 1969), pp. 6-19 by permission.

geography has contributed to man's understanding of the complex of interrelated urban phenomena. In addition, the application of geographic concepts and viewpoints has produced substantial practical application in city and metropolitan planning.[1] In this paper some of these geographic concepts and contributions to urban studies will be outlined.

"City" and "Urban"

What is a city? What is meant by "urban"? Although there are many common definitions of these terms, the geographer seeks a definition which is unambiguous, definite, and clear. If we are to compare one city with another, or a metropolitan area or urban agglomoration with another, or if we wish to compare the extent and character of urban population in one country or region with that in another, we need some criteria which can be applied in the measurement of these phenomena. There have been many attempts by geographers and others to develop definitions that can be used in comparative measurement, but none is completely satisfactory for all such purposes. The difficulty lies in the nature of the phenomena themselves, for, in spite of some common characteristics, cities and urbanization, as spatial phenomena and process, exhibit many interregional and international differences, rendering comparative

studies of cities in different areas and at different times extremely difficult; yet the characteristics which all cities share render the attempts to compare them not entirely futile. There is a practical aspect to these attempts, as well as an academic: by learning of the successes and failures to solve urban problems in given cities, the probability of success or failure of similar solutions may be evaluated in terms of the extent to which the respective cities resemble, or do not resemble, each other with respect to the relevant characteristics. Solutions, for example, to the problems of housing in Swedish cities may not be entirely successful if applied to cities of the northeastern United States, because the political, cultural, racial, and economic backgrounds of the respective regions and countries differ in several important respects.

Nevertheless, cities throughout the world exhibit certain common characteristics which we identify as "urban," and which therefore help us to define the cities.

One of the definitions is administrative and legal. In most nations, and in each state in the United States, there is a set of criteria by which certain areas, called "cities" are designated by the sovereign power — the nation or state — to carry out certain functions and responsibilities, in return for which certain privileges are granted. In most of the British commonwealth countries, a City is such by royal decree, and the designation bears little, if any, relation to the population size of the place. Thus, the City of London, for example, embraces an area which constitutes only a very small portion of what in the United States would be considered a part of the central business district of the metropolitan complex. British usage of the term "City" thus is a purely historical and legal one; what Americans conceive of as a city is embraced in the British term "Town," while

---

[1] A general review of the main directions and trends in urban geography is contained in Philip M. Hauser and Leo F. Schnore, eds., *The Study of Urbanization* (New York, John Wiley & Sons, Inc., 1965), especially pp. 81-114, which include an extensive bibliography. Recent applications to planning are presented in Leo F. Schnore and Henry Fagin, eds., *Urban Research and Policy Planning* (Beverly Hills, Calif., Sage Publications, Inc., 1967), especially Chapter 8, "Urban Geography and City and Metropolitan Planning" by Harold M. Mayer, pp. 221-38.

the Town in America has different meanings in different parts of the country. British "town planning" has the same meaning as the American term "city planning," while some British geographers and planners refer to the urban landscape as a "townscape."

In most American states, a city is a municipality — a governmental unit embracing a proscribed area with definitely-located boundaries, and with a minimum population which, if reached, entitles the area to apply for city status. Smaller urban units of government, with smaller populations, or larger ones which choose not to apply for city status, may incorporate in most states as municipalities with lesser status, such as villages, towns, or boroughs, the various designations differing from state to state. In many states, municipalities may be further differentiated by "class," depending upon population size, each class being granted certain rights and obligations. Depending upon the amount of "home rule" permitted municipalities in each of the various states, state enabling legislation delegates authority over certain matters to municipalities in varying degrees, depending upon the class. Thus, for example, in Illinois the state does not pass legislation applying to any particular city, but it designates "cities of the first class," the only such city being Chicago.

Rarely do the boundaries of the municipalities correspond to the actual boundaries of the respective built-up areas; cities are virtually always "over-bounded" or "under-bounded," more usually the latter, depending upon whether, in the first instance, substantial areas of land which are not "urban" in character are included within the municipal boundaries, or, in the second instance, there is "overspill" of urban character beyond the municipal boundaries. Areas can, and frequently are, added to municipalities by an-

nexation, and most cities have expanded their extent many times as the population grows with the urbanization of land beyond the older boundaries. Thus, in 1854 Philadelphia city and county were consolidated, expanding the extent of the city severalfold, but there have been no annexations to Philadelphia since then. Other major American cities which once expanded by consolidating with their counties include St. Louis and San Francisco, and, more recently, Nashville, Tennessee, and, for certain functions, Miami (Dade County), Florida. Such consolidation is rare, however. More commonly, cities add territory by piecemeal annexation, usually in order to provide municipal services and controls to areas beyond the previous borders, or to take in commercial or industrial areas, existing or prospective, which would furnish an enhanced tax base while at the same time not requiring substantial expenditures for extension of municipal services, such as schools, which account for more costs in most urban areas than do any other municipal functions. Factories and shops do not produce children, but they do produce substantial shares of the municipal tax revenues.

Except in the Southwestern United States, where cities such as Dallas, Houston, El Paso, Phoenix, and Tucson have more than doubled their municipal areas by annexations in recent years, it has become increasingly difficult for most cities to expand their administrative boundaries by this means. One reason is that many people, business establishments, and industries have located, and continue to locate, outside of the areas of the central cities, but still within convenient reach of them, in order to escape some of the obligations of internal location, such as supporting the many services which central cities must supply for the respective metropolitan areas, and also to avoid the pressures of congestion, pollution, and social pathology associated with high central densities of population, traffic, and activity, including the high land values which reflect the mutual convenience of such high densities. In other words, a locational decision within an urban complex reflects the respective weights which, in each instance, are given to central convenience but high density on the one hand, and peripheral amenity and low density on the other; centripetal, or centralizing forces, and centrifugal, or decentralizing forces, are in balance, with the fulcrum at different locations for each function or establishment at the time the locational decision is made. Since there is a limit to the number and intensity of functions which can occupy any given area, beyond which "scale diseconomies" such as congestion and high land costs result, urban growth tends to take place at the outer edges of the built-up area, the result being peripheral expansion.[2]

As expansion takes place on the edges of the previously built-up urban area, it is not long before the need for services and facilities which are provided by local governments is manifest. Schools, paved streets, utilities, fire and police protection, and other services must be provided, and they cannot be provided efficiently if the population density is too low, or if effective municipal government does not cover the area. Thus, there is a lower limit, or threshold, under which "urban" conditions do not constitute characteristics of an area, and which is necessary for effective provision of many needed facilities and services.

This brings us to another form of definition of "city" and of "urban," based upon a minimum density.

As we drive through an urban complex, or inspect an air photo of one, we can readily identify variations in density of buildings, streets, and both working and residential population. In most "western" cities, the density drops off very sharply from the core or center, with the decline in density decreasing at a decreasing rate as we move outward; this typical pattern is described mathematically as a negative exponential curve.[3] At some distance from the city center, the density is so low that it can no longer be considered typically urban; here the urban area ends. We can draw contours of equal density around the city cores, and one of these contours can be used to describe the location of the outer limit of the urbanized area. For this purpose, we can use residential population — although with respect to this measure there tends to be a "crater" in the middle where intensive non-residential land uses tend to outbid the residential — or we can use some ratio of building volume or percent of land covered by structures, or,

[2] A classic statement of this principle in the geographic literature is that of Charles C. Colby, "Centrifugal and Centripetal Forces in Urban Geography," *Annals of the Association of American Geographers*, Vol. XXIII, no. 1 (March, 1933), pp. 1-20. In the literature of urban planning, an excellent statement of the process is: Hans Blumenfeld, "The Tidal Wave of Metropolitan Expansion," *Journal of the American Institute of Planners*, Vol. XX, no. 1 (Winter, 1954), pp. 3-14.

[3] There is extensive literature describing and documenting the negative exponential pattern of urban density. For example, Colin Clark, "Urban Population Densities," *Journal of the Royal Statistical Society*, Ser. A, Vol. CXIV (1951), pp. 490-96; Richard F. Muth, "The Spatial Structure of the Housing Market," *Papers and Proceedings of the Regional Science Association*, Vol. VII (1961), pp. 207-20; C. A. Doxiadis *et al.*, "Densities of Human Settlements," *Ekistics*, Vol. XXII, no. 128 (July, 1966), pp. 77-101; A critical review of some of the literature is Bruce E. Newling, "Urban Population Densities and Intra-urban Growth," *Geographical Review*, Vol. LIV, no. 3 (July, 1964), pp. 440-42.

perhaps, traffic volume, or land costs. In nearly every city, these various density measures are highly correlated; any one greatly influences all or most of the others, and the patterns which result are very similar.

The concept of the density threshold has been used by governmental agencies in defining, for example, the "urbanized areas" surrounding each central city with at least 50,000 population in 1950, and again, with some slight changes in measurement criteria, in 1960. Thus, it was found that, in the United States, there is a high correlation between the contours representing the outer limits of a typical "urban" density of streets (whether rectilinear or not), a housing density of about 500 units per square mile, or a residential population of roughly 2,000 per square mile. Lower than these limits indicates nonurban status, although, as mentioned previously, the administrative municipal limits rarely if ever coincide with these density contours.

The pre-industrial city, whether in the past or at present in some non-industrialized parts of the world, was perhaps more easily defined in physical and functional terms than the modern city. Before the advent of strong national governments, the city-state was common; in the middle ages the feudal estate was somewhat analogous. In each instance, the settlement was more or less economically self-contained, and it had to provide for its own defense. It was a center of government, of economic activity, and of defense. Not uncommonly, it was walled; within the walls and gates was urban, outside was not. With growth of population, not all citizens could locate within the walls, so "sub-urbs" developed outside, often performing trade functions as well as serving as residential locations for the population which could not be accommodated inside.

With industrialization and the advent of modern transportation, and especially the development of large national areas, the old concept of a dichotomy between "urban" and "nonurban" or rural has been breached. Figuratively, as well as literally, the walls have come down, and the distinctions between urban and rural are losing much of their former significance. Until the past few decades, urban development had to take place along lines of mass transportation of people and goods, and peripheral expansion of urban areas, along good transportation, was characterized by clear-cut distinctions between the areas which were urbanized and those which were not. Transportation made the difference; it not only permitted urban expansion, but it also permitted extremely high concentrations of activities and people to develop where the routes converged; this was a cause-and-effect relationship reciprocally. With the ubiquity of the automobile, truck, and modern highways, accessibility to good transportation is still important in the process of development of the urban pattern, but it takes different forms. Many industries no longer need to be located on navigable waterways, or alongside railroads to receive and ship goods; inter-model transportation, with break-of-bulk at intermediate transfer points or "interfaces," or, of increasing importance, the elimination of much goods handling at interfaces by development of containers interchangeable between highway, railroad, water, and even air carriers, has made locations much more footloose for most industries than was formerly the case. Similarly, shopping locations and residential development no longer need be entirely dependent upon large-scale mass transportation, so that many more locations are available for development. Densities, in the western world, are declining almost everywhere, and the cities are spreading out at an ever-increasing rate, but with no decrease in accessibility. The urbanized areas, therefore, are expanding at a rate even more rapid than the rapidly expanding urban population. In the United States, it is anticipated that if present trends continue, the amount of land occupied by urban settlement will double every twenty years.[4] The resulting urban "sprawl" represents a challenge to governments at all levels, from national to local, to find ways of guiding and controlling urban growth in order to maximize opportunities for all potential land uses to locate properly, and in the right amounts, for maximum efficiency and to provide for the maximum amenity and aesthetic satisfactions.[5]

The processes of guiding and controlling the patterns of urban land use have been the subject of much experimentation in recent decades, with the expansion of the concern of government with urban problems, the development of comprehensive city and metropolitan planning, and the adoption of various forms of regulation such as subdivision controls and zoning. None of these have been completely successful, and the problem still remains unsolved of how to provide a desirable degree of guidance and control of urban land development while at the same time retaining the maximum possible scope for the interplay of market forces in the traditional American free enterprise system. The guidance and control of patterns of urban growth, however, are enormously complicated by the proliferation of local governmental units and the fragmentation of the functional geographic urban areas into many local governmental jurisdictions. There are currently over 18,000 local governments in the United States — cities, towns, villages, and boroughs — most of them in the 230-odd metropolitan areas which are discussed later, in addition to special-purpose districts in at least equal number: school districts, park districts, sanitary districts, forest preserve districts, drainage districts, flood control districts, mosquito abatement districts, transit authorities, port authorities, housing authorities, and others.[6] Only school districts, among these, have decreased in number; for in the case of school districts it has been recognized that a certain minimum population and economic support, beyond reach of very small governmental units, is required in order to finance and operate adequate facilities with adequately qualified personnel. The study of the spatial aspects of inter-governmental relations and organization within urban areas is a field in which a few geographers have recently begun to produce significant studies, and it presents major opportunities for research and application in the future.

Thus, the problem of defining "urban" and "city" in areal or spatial terms is greatly complicated by the present patterns of government, with fragmentation of urban units in a geographic sense. On the other hand, these local governmental units, even though rarely coinciding with functional units in most geographic senses, are significant, for they represent organizational units which, in themselves, represent internal homogeneity with regard to certain policies, practices, and political and fiscal situations which are geographically significant, in spite of the fact that they

[4] Marion Clawson, R. Burnell Held, and Charles H. Stoddard, *Land for the Future* (Baltimore, The Johns Hopkins Press, 1960), especially pp. 109-14.

[5] Jean Gottmann and Robert A. Harper, eds., *Metropolis on the Move; Geographers Look at Urban Sprawl* (New York, John Wiley & Sons, Inc., 1967).

[6] *The Municipal Yearbook, 1967* (Chicago, The International City Managers' Association, 1967), pp. 11-17.

make more difficult the recognition of larger geographical units of which they are a part.

Metropolis

Geographers have long recognized that the concept of "city" cannot be exclusively concerned with the administrative or jurisdictional municipal unit, and that most cities, in a functional sense, transcend political boundaries. A major professional concern of some geographers has been to set up and apply criteria for delimiting and describing the functional city, as distinguished from the administrative city. In this process, the practical problems of collating statistics for various areas, with comparability of criteria and measurements among such urban areas from place to place and time to time, has been, and is, a major concern. The problem is complicated by the fact that, in most urban areas, a decreasing proportion of the population and economic activity is located in the central city, and in most central cities both are suffering an absolute decline. In a rapidly increasing proportion of the metropolitan areas, the suburbs and unincorporated fringe areas now contain larger residential populations than do the respective central cities, while at the same time commercial and industrial activities are increasing both relatively and absolutely in the suburban areas. These trends have been enormously accelerated by the ubiquity of highway transportation, with its flexibility, producing a much greater freedom of choice among locations than was ever before possible.

The metropolitan area, in some ways, constitutes the geographic city. These areas consist of one or more "central cities," together with suburban and fringe areas which are related functionally to the central city. The Federal agencies define Standard Metropolitan Statistical Areas, of which there are approximately 230, as consisting of a central city, or cities, with minimum population of 50,000, together with counties having functional inter-relations, as measured mainly by community patterns, with the county containing the central city. Thus, the concept of the labor-market area, or "commuter shed," is basic to the defining and delimitation of an urban unit. Such a unit contains the territory and population which is essentially dependent upon the central city for many services. In spatial terms, the component portions of metropolitan areas are mutually inter-related, and for many purposes the metropolitan area constitutes a more suitable unit for geographic study than does the central city alone.

A metropolitan area, then, is a geographic, functional city, and for many purposes may be regarded as the basic areal urban unit.

Yet the concept of the metropolitan area, too, like that of the administrative or municipal city, has certain serious shortcomings.

One set of shortcomings in defining metropolitan areas arises from the use of the statistical areal units. In the United States, the county is the basic areal unit for which statistics are compiled and tabulated; metropolitan areas are defined as consisting of one or more counties. In many instances, the urbanized area within a county may be located only in a small portion of the county, the rest of which has very little population or development, yet the entire county is included within the metropolitan area. Thus, the unit statistical area, the county, may be far from homogeneous with respect to the essential urban characteristics. This is a typical example of the use for geographic purposes of what has been called "modifiable units," or areas which, variously delimited and used in differing combinations, produce differing area definitions.[7] For example, the San Bernardino-Riverside-Ontario, California, Standard Metropolitan Statistical Area, the largest in the United States, consists of over 27,000 square miles, an area considerably larger than all of southern New England, because San Bernardino County, whose population is nearly entirely confined to the southwestern corner, the rest being virtually uninhabited desert, must, by definition, be included in its entirety. Similarly, St. Louis County, Minnesota, a part of the Duluth-Superior Standard Metropolitan Statistical Area, includes much wilderness and extends for about 150 miles northward from Lake Superior to the Canadian border.

By no stretch of the imgaination could the wilderness of the Mohave Desert or the northern Minnesota arrowhead be considered as urban or metropolitan in inherent characteristics, yet the rule that whole counties must be included within metropolitan areas if any part of them is metropolitan, produces such anomolous situations.

Recently, with the increased federal participation in the financing of many programs in urban areas, including highways, mass transit, open space land acquisition, urban renewal, and sewer and water facilities among others, the pressures to provide comprehensive metropolitan planning have increased. Since 1965, comprehensive plans prepared by metropolitan regional agencies, have been required as prerequisites for local assistance

[7] The problems of selecting suitable areal units are discussed in Otis Dudley Duncan, Ray P. Cuzzort, and Beverly Duncan, *Statistical Geography* (Glencoe, The Free Press, 1961), and by David Griff, "Regions, Models and Classes," *Models in Geography* by Richard J. Chorley and Peter Haggett (London, Methuen & Co., Ltd., 1967), pp. 461-509. The latter contains an extensive bibliography on the problem of geographically significant statistical units.

by the federal government, which has at the same time provided matching funds to set up and operate such metropolitan planning agencies. These agencies, however, are not substitutes for metropolitan government, which, in most parts of the United States, the electorate is unwilling, as yet, to accept. The lack of such acceptance springs largely from the pervasive trend of people and commercial and industrial establishments to move away from the central cities toward the suburbs and outer portions of the metropolitan areas. The vacuum thus created in the inner portions of cities tends to be filled by the recent in-migrants who, at least in many northern cities, tend to be members of minority groups, predominantly Negro. These in-migrants, having been long disadvantaged educationally and culturally, are least able to command the better and newer housing available on the outskirts of the respective urban areas, which, in turn, expand as the result of the peripheral growth of the city. Thus there tends to be a series of conflicts of interest between the inner city, or the central city, on the one hand, and the "middle class" areas on the edge of the city and in the suburbs beyond. This is commonly reflected in political differences, with the central cities tending to reflect the more liberal attitudes of the minorities as the proportion of central city population which they represent increases. It is not at all unexpected that Cleveland, Gary, and Washington have Negro mayors; in earlier generations many of the city governments were predominantly reflections of the succession of ethnic and national in-migration patterns. On the other hand, the suburbs tend, on the whole, to reflect the attitudes of those who have "arrived" economically and socially, and who resist the assimilation of the more recently urbanized in-migrant populations. Zoning, for example, as an instrument of land-use control, has frequently been misused as an instrument of economic segregation, and hence ethnic segregation in many suburban areas, by providing minimum lot sizes and density standards which only the more affluent could attain, thereby excluding people whose economic status tended to the lower.[8]

These city-suburban differences, of course, are reflected in resistance to metropolitan government and the continuation of proliferating local governments within metropolitan areas. In order to overcome some of the consequent inefficiencies and provide for the multiplicity of services and facilities which are the responsibilities of local governments, many devices short of comprehensive metropolitan government are being developed. One such device is the special-purpose government, in many instances functioning in a geographic area which does not coincide with any of the areas of local government, but dealing with problems of metropolitan scope beyond the ability of local governments. Among the early noteworthy examples are the Metropolitan Sanitary District of Greater Chicago and the Port of New York Authority, the latter representing an early noteworthy example of a government set up across state boundaries by interstate compact. Special-purpose governments, however, have certain shortcomings; among them are the lack of coincidence of boundaries with local governments and often with each other, the tendency to add to the proliferation of governmental units, and, in some instances, the interposition of an additional govern-

mental unit without direct control by the electorate. Many of the governmental and administrative problems of cities and metropolitan areas arise from an essentially geographic concern, namely, the determination of the nature and extent of those functions which are best dealt with locally and those which are of extra-local regional concern. For example, local access streets should be the responsibility of the local community, but regional expressways must be planned, built, and operated by a regional or larger unit of government. Similarly, local parks and regional parks must be differentiated. Schools constitute major problems in this regard; the different standards of inner-city and suburban schools have been adequately documented, and few people are unaware of the problems in this regard.[9] To the geographer, problems such as these constitute interesting and important challenges: to what extent should the planning, building, and operation of facilities and services be localized, and to what extent and in what manner — and especially within what area — should these facilities and services be the concern of the entire metropolitan region, or of major portions of it? How and by what criteria can determinations be made of the degree and areal extent of involvement of each level of government appropriate to the problem? How can local autonomy be preserved for matters of local concern and at the same time assure that regional and metropolitan concerns can be reconciled with the local ones?

Short of metropolitan government, and in addition to regional special-purpose governments, many official and unofficial devices are being tried to coordinate urban functions

[8] Richard F. Babcock, *The Zoning Game* (Madison, The University of Wisconsin Press, 1966); Sidney M. Wilhelm, *Urban Zoning and Land-Use Theory* (New York, The Free Press of Glencoe, 1962).

[9] One of the most widely known presentations of the disparities between city and suburban schools is James B. Conant, *Slums and Suburbs* (New York, McGraw-Hill Book Co., 1961).

in order that metropolitan areas may overcome the deficiencies of intergovernmental fragmentation and function as urban units. In the past two decades, many metropolitan areas have set up comprehensive transportation studies as prerequisite to planning of highway and transit systems; since 1965 these operations have been required, as previously mentioned, by the federal government. But it was soon realized that projections of traffic trends were inadequate, and that circulation patterns merely reflect land-use patterns, because it is the land uses which generate traffic. Many of the transportation study agencies thus evolved into comprehensive regional and metropolitan planning agencies, concerned not only with transportation and land-use patterns, but also with economic and social planning within the respective areas. The professional planners themselves, through such organizations as the American Institute of Planners, have formally recognized the broadening of their responsibilities and the scope of their profession, to include social and economic planning along with the physical. Geographers, likewise, are increasingly concerned with the spatial aspects of social and economic conditions and problems, many of which concentrate heavily in urban areas.

To coordinate planning and its effectuation, then, a variety of new organizational forms is evolving, and these constitute, in their spatial aspects, appropriate subjects for geographic investigation. Metropolitan comprehensive government is an ultimate solution in some instances, but, short of that, comprehensive regional and metropolitan planning agencies, special-purpose regional governments, informal and formal councils of government, and intergovernmental arrangements for purchasing or leasing of facilities and services, as well as pooling arrangements

are all effective in various situations. The analysis and planning of governmental and inter-governmental arrangements in their spatial aspects within urban areas constitute a set of challenges of great prospective opportunity to the geographer; very likely these problems will constitute a new frontier of geography in the near future.

Megalopolis: Inter-Metropolitan Coalescence

Just as the traditional concept of the city as a unit of spatial organization of urban areas has largely been superseded by the concept of the metropolitan area, so the metropolitan area is itself inadequate as a descriptive device for contemporary and prospective patterns of urbanization. With respect to many functions, the metropolitan areas are not discrete functional areal units; a more comprehensive and larger unit has had to be developed to describe groups of metropolitan areas with overlapping functions.

Modern transportation is largely responsible for the growth of super-metropolitan conurbations. Transportation and land use are but two sides of the same coin, one static, the other dynamic. Urban land is useful primarily because of its accessibility to other land. There is a complementarity[10] among land uses which gives rise to cities, and, at the local

[10] The principle of complementarity is effectively presented by Edward L. Ullman, "The Role of Transportation and the Bases for Interaction," *Man's Role in Changing the Face of the Earth*, edited by William L. Thomas, Jr. (Chicago, The University of Chicago Press, 1956), pp. 862-80. Complementarity is also related to the gravity analog in spatial interaction, the subject of many articles in the literature of both geography and planning. For example, Gunnar Olsson, *Distance and Human Interaction: A Review and Bibliography* (Philadelphia, Regional Science Research Institute, 1965).

scale, there is a complementarity among the component functional areas and establishments within cities and metropolitan regions. Transportation is one of two forms of mutual accessibility among land uses and establishments; it overcomes the friction of distance, but at a cost. The other form of accessibility is mutual proximity, which, at the cost of high-value land and high density, reduces or eliminates the necessity for providing transportation. Thus, the dichotomy of transport costs and land costs is reflected in the balance between centralizing and decentralizing forces, previously mentioned.[11] Geographers, land economists, sociologists, and others have evolved many idealized forms of spatial patterns to describe urban structure and growth, but all of them are based upon a balance between the two forms of accessibility: mutual proximity on the one hand and transportation on the other. Transportation — measured by traffic flows — depends, in turn, upon complementarity in which each area served produces specialized goods and/or services which are utilized elsewhere. In cities, the result is a functional differentiation of local areas; among cities, modern transportation and communication makes possible specialization, so that each city in a group or set of cities — such as a conurbation — does not need to perform all of the urban functions in equal degree, providing that inter-

change of people and services, as well as goods, can take place among the areas or cities within the group.[12] A common form of this in the modern city is the separation of working and residential areas, giving rise to the daily commuting between them.

As transportation improves — such as with the development of modern express highways — the area accessible within a given time-cost limit from any given point increases. This produces a greater flexibility

[11] The literature on relations between transportation and land use is enormous. A few examples: Lowdon Wingo, Jr., *Transportation and Urban Land* (Washington, Resources for the Future, Inc., 1961); Walter G. Hansen, "How Accessibility Shapes Land Use," *Journal of the American Institute of Planners*, Vol. XXV, no. 2 (May, 1959), pp. 73-76; numerous reports of the Highway Research Board (Washington), and the proliferating reports of the many comprehensive metropolitan transportation-land use studies, such as the *Final Report, Chicago Area Transportation Study* (Chicago, Chicago Area Transportation Study, 1959-61), 3 vols.

[12] Functional specialization among cities is the subject of a vast literature on "economic base". Among the more useful items are Ralph W. Pfouts, *The Techniques of Economic Base Analysis* (West Trenton, N.J., Chandler-Davis Publishing Co., 1960), selected readings; Charles M. Tiebout, *The Community Economic Base Study* (New York, Committee for Economic Development, 1962); John W. Alexander, "The Basic–Nonbasic Concept of Urban Economic Functions," *Economic Geography*, Vol. XXX, no. 3 (July, 1954), pp. 246-61; Walter Isard, "Interregional and Regional Input–Output Techniques," Chapter 8 of his *Methods of Regional Analysis* (Cambridge, Technology Press and New York, John Wiley & Sons, Inc., 1960), pp. 309-74; Edward L. Ullman and Michael Dacey, "The Minimum Requirements Approach to the Urban Economic Base," *Proceedings of the IGU Symposium in Urban Geography Lund 1960* Lund Studies in Geography Ser. B. Human Geography, no. 24, Lund, 1962), pp. 121-43. The differences among cities with respect to their economic functions also may serve as a basis for functional classification of cities, a subject of a proliferating literature, examples of which are Chauncy D. Harris, "A Functional Classification of Cities in the United States," *Geographical Review*, Vol. XXXIII, no. 1 (January, 1943), pp. 86-99; Howard J. Nelson, "A Service Classification of American Cities," *Economic Geography*, Vol. XXXI, no. 3 (July, 1955), pp. 189-210; Richard L. Forstall, "Economic Classification of Places over 10,000, 1960-1963," *The Municipal Yearbook 1967* (Chicago, The International City Managers' Association, 1967), pp. 30-65. Also R. H. T. Smith, "Method and Purpose in Functional Town Classification," *Annals of the Association of American Geographers*, Vol. LV, no. 3 (September, 1965), pp. 539-48.

of movement. Whereas a relatively short time ago, cities were highly concentrated, with radial transportation patterns focusing upon the core of the city, now the patterns of traffic flow and accessibility tend to be more diffuse and the densities of development lower, while the character of the urban functions within the cores is also changing. With respect to many activities, the central cores of the cities are rapidly becoming less important. At the same time, densities are becoming less, land is being absorbed by urbanization at an accelerating rate, and new nodes or foci of accessibility, such as regional shopping centers and industrial parks, are developing with reduced dependence upon access to the old city cores.

But even with modern transportation, equal access cannot be provided to all areas, and the form and shape of the urban pattern is still, no less than formerly, controlled in large measure by the pattern of transportation routes. Multiple nuclei, rather than a single dominant core, constitute the pattern of the modern city. Furthermore, the city does not spread with equal density or equal rapidity in all directions; those areas with best transportation access tend to develop more rapidly, and generally with higher densities than those less well provided with transportation access. Formerly, cities tended to develop a star-shaped pattern, with higher densities and earlier development along radial railroads, rapid transit lines, or trolley lines. More recently, with the ubiquity of highways, automobiles, and trucks, the interstitial areas between the older radial prongs of growth tended to fill in, generally, however, at somewhat lower densities than the older radial prongs. The outlines of the urbanized areas thus tended to depart from the star-shaped patterns characteristic of a few decades ago and to assume somewhat

more circular patterns. More recently, however, with the advent of the express highway, the tendency has been for the development of axial "corridors" along such routes of maximum accessibility, with higher density of development closest to such routes, and especially to the intersections of such routes. Indeed, the development of such "corridors of high accessibility" has been a major physical element in the recently-published comprehensive plans of a number of cities and metropolitan areas. Serving as the axes along which such corridors are expected to develop are efficient transportation routes, including various combinations of railroads, high-speed rail rapid transit lines, and express highways.[13]

Such corridors, however, are not confined to within the limits of individual metropolitan areas. With efficient high-speed transportation of people and goods, the expanding tentacles of urbanization of cities and metropolitan areas formerly separated by many miles tend to coalesce. The pressures for lower densities and consequent increasing amounts of urbanized land tend to expand along the lines of least resistance: the most efficient transportation routes. As the tentacles along these routes connecting adjacent cities and metropolitan areas extend toward each other, they eventually form more-or-less continuous chains of urban development.[14] Cross com-

[13] National Capital Regional Planning Council, "The Regional Development Guide 1966-2000, Washington, D.C.," (Washington, Government Printing Office, 1966); *Comprehensive Plan of Chicago* (Chicago, Department of Development and Planning, 1966); *The Comprehensive General Plan for the Development of the Northeastern Illinois* (Chicago, Northeastern Illinois Planning Commission, 1968).

[14] An interesting study of one such multi-nodal urban agglomoration is F. Stuart Chapin, Jr., and Shirley F. Weiss, eds., *Urban Growth Dynamics in a Regional Cluster of Cities* (New York, John Wiley & Sons, Inc., 1962).

muting, and functional specialization among the several or many cities forming such chains or clusters gives rise to common labor-market and housing-market areas; super-cities, transcending metropolitan area boundaries, thus tend to develop.

To this concept of the multi-nodal inter-metropolitan super-city, whether arranged as a cluster, or lineally along a corridor, the term Megalopolis has been applied.[15] The term is by no means a new one; it is derived from the Greek "mother city," and was first used a half-century ago by Patrick Geddes to describe an urbanized region.[16] Popularized as a generic term by Lewis Mumford,[17] it was adopted as a proper noun by Jean Gottmann[18] to describe the area between Boston and Washington, which, in fact, had developed even in colonial times as a chain of cities at the head of navigation for ocean-going vessels along the "fall line" marking the boundary between the Piedmont hard-rock area and the Atlantic coastal plain. When effective land transportation developed to replace coastal water transportation in the area during the late nineteenth century, the cities were linked by heavily-trafficked main-line railroads, and later by express highways and by shuttle airlines, all of which carry the heaviest volumes of inter-city traffic in North America. With these efficient transportation links, the urbanization spread along the axis, and the adjacent tentacles coalesced, eventually merging the older nodes into a lineal city.[19]

Many other "megalopolises," consisting of clusters or lineal arrangements of cities are recognized. Cross-commuting among cities fifty or more miles apart is now quite common, and a new form of urban structure is emerging. Meanwhile, the multi-nodal cluster type of super-city has its prototype in southern California, while the Boston-Washington axis constitutes the classic example of a lineal inter-city corridor. The federal government, in fact, now officially recognizes the new urban corridor form, for the so-called "Northeast Corridor" is the scene of a comprehensive series of experiments in high-speed intercity transportation.[20] Actually, this program springs directly from the work of Jean Gottmann, whom Senator Claiborn Pell, the author of the federal legislation, credits for the idea of the corridor.[21] Other corridor-like megalopoli exist in the area between Cleveland and Pittsburgh, Dallas and Fort Worth, Chicago and Milwaukee, Portland, Oregon and Vancouver, British Columbia, and in many other places, each of which is characterized by increased accessibility along a major axis of transportation. At a larger scale, the area between the Midwest and the Atlantic seaboard, long identified by geographers as the core urban-industrial area of the

[15] Jean Gottman, "Megalopolis, or the Urbanization of the Northeastern Seaboard," *Economic Geography*, Vol. XXXIII, no. 3 (July, 1957), pp. 189-200.

[16] Patrick Geddes, *Cities in Evolution* (London, 1915; reprinted London and New York, Oxford University Press, 1949).

[17] Lewis Mumford, *The Culture of Cities* (New York, Harcourt, Brace and Company, 1938), and *The City in History* (New York, Harcourt, Brace & World, Inc., 1961).

[18] Jean Gottmann, *Megalopolis* (New York, The Twentieth Century Fund, 1961).

[19] *The Region's Growth: A Report of the Second Regional Plan* (New York, Regional Plan Association, 1967).

[20] *Highway Travel in Megalopolis* (New York, Wilbur Smith and Associates, 1963).

[21] Robert A. Nelson, "A Quick Rundown on the Northeast Corridor Transportation Project," *A Report on the 1966 Conference on Mass Transportation*, University of Chicago Center for Continuing Education, March 4, 1966 (Cleveland, Brotherhood of Railroad Trainmen, 1967), pp. 117-22.

United States,[22] has recently been called by a planner the "Great Lakes Megalopolis,"[23] in which the east coast Megalopolis is at one end, the Chicago-Milwaukee conurbation at the other, and the Cleveland-Pittsburgh megalopolis in the center. Thus, just as geographers have identified a hierarchy of "central places," ranging from the crossroads hamlet to the world metropolis,[24] so there is emerging a concept of a hierarchy of conurbations, corridors, or megalopoli, constituting the framework of the pattern of urban development and urban functional organization.

The Nature of Urban Functions

Lewis Mumford has identified cities as "containers," since they contain the agglomeration of people and facilities which perform certain functions identified as urban.[25] What are the urban functions, in the performance of which the structural and spatial forms of organization discussed above have evolved?

The urban functions are predominantly, as indicated above, those which depend upon accessibility, whether by mutual proximity or transportation, or, most commonly, a combination of the two. Thus, in a sense, all basic urban functions are "central place" functions. Most urban geographers and economists differentiate functions as economic and non-economic, although even the essentially non-economic functions, such as education, religious shrines, and residence, have important economic aspects. The economic functions include, in one sense, the "central place" administrative and control functions, such as government, as well as the administration of business organizations. Many people differentiate economic functions into three or four categories. The primary functions are those which result in the exploitation or extraction of resources of the site, such as mining, forestry, and agriculture, whether or not the resources are renewable. Secondary functions are those involving the physical handling and processing of goods, including manufacturing, packaging, storage, and transportation. Tertiary functions involve transfer of title or ownership, and include retailing and wholesaling. Some writers include record-keeping among the tertiary functions; others designate them in a separate category as quaternary functions.[26]

The primary functions are not predominantly urban in character, although some give rise directly to urban settlements, such as fishing communities, mining camps, and others, but, invariably, other urban functions arise wherever numbers of people gather in

[22] This "core region," the American Manufacturing Belt, is identified in virtually all of the standard geographic texts on North America. For example: C. Langdon White, Edwin J. Foscue, and Tom L. McKnight, *Regional Geography of Anglo-America* (3rd ed., Englewood Cliffs, N.J., Prentice-Hall, Inc., 1964), pp. 32-66.

[23] C. A. Doxiadis, "The Great Lakes Megalopolis," *Ekistics*, Vol. XXII, no. 128 (July, 1966), pp. 14-31.

[24] The concept of the central-place hierarchy is one of the most intensively explored in the recent American literature of urban geography, and has attracted much world-wide attention. A comprehensive bibliography on the subject is Brian J. L. Berry and Allen Pred, *Central Place Studies: A Bibliography of Theory and Applications*, 2nd ed. (Philadelphia, Regional Science Research Institute, 1965). This bibliography contains annotations on over 1,000 items.

[25] Mumford, *op. cit.*

[26] William Goodwin, "The Management Center in the United States," *Geographical Review*, Vol. LX, no. 1 (January, 1965), pp. 1-16; William Applebaum, "Formation and Location of National Trade Associations in the United States," *The Professional Geographer*, Vol. XX, no. 1 (January, 1968), pp. 1-4; Sidney M. Robbins and Nestor F. Terleckyj, *Money Metropolis* (Cambridge, Harvard University Press, 1960).

mutual proximity. The locational patterns of the secondary functions depend upon relative access to raw materials, components, energy resources, manpower, markets, and site availability in varying proportions, and there is extensive literature on the factors of industrial location.[27] The tertiary and quarternary functions tend to locate at points of maximum accessibility to their respective service areas or "hinterlands," which are, in turn, "nested" in a hierarchical arrangement, giving rise to a hierarchy of central places or urban nodes within which the functions are concentrated.[28] A variation of the urban hierarchy in some areas is the "primate city" arrangement, in which one city dominates an extensive area, and several of the lower orders of urban places, between the dominant city on the one hand and the smaller places on the other, are absent. At the top of the hierarchy is the "world city," whose service area for some functions may be intercontinental.[29]

Cities are also centers for the orgination and diffusion of both material and non-material culture.[30] By providing concentrations of people, interaction and the development of new ideas and concepts is facilitated

in cities; the larger the city the more likely is it to be seat of new ideas and inventions, and the more attractive it becomes for the leaders in all fields. Thus, the gravitative pull of the city depends upon its mass, or population size and diversity, and the larger the city the more likely is it to attract additional population. This, in turn, creates more interaction and reinforces the role of the city as a center from which innovations diffuse outward. The increased diversity of the city, in turn, makes it more attractive, for maximum freedom of choice is available in the larger urban agglomerations. In larger metropolitan and megalopolitan agglomerations the greatest variety of economic, social, and cultural opportunities exist, as well as the greatest choice of housing accommodation and residential environments. Thus, there is a rural-urban migration, and a differential rate of growth, other factors being equal, favoring the larger urban concentrations over the smaller ones. The increased availability of the automobile, which releases urbanization from dependence upon a limited number of areas especially favored by mass transportation, is spreading the accessibility to the big-city advantages, homogenizing the culture, reducing the formerly sharp differences between urban and non-urban areas, and constituting new and abundant opportunities for geographers to investigate the changing relationships, in urban settings and beyond, between man and his culture on the one hand and the emerging spatial patterns and environmental challenges and opportunities on the other.

[27] Benjamin H. Stevens and Carolyn A. Brackett, *Industrial Location: A Review and Annotated Bibliography of Theoretical, Empirical and Case Studies* (Philadelphia, Regional Science Research Institute, 1967).

[28] A very useful recent statement is Brian J. L. Berry, *Geography of Market Centers and Retail Distribution* (Englewood Cliffs, N.J., Prentice-Hall, Inc., 1967).

[29] Peter Hall, *The World Cities* (New York, McGraw-Hill Book Co., 1966).

Historical and Comparative Urban Studies

3

Rhoads Murphey

The city is as old as civilization. The two words come from the same root, which originally meant city, suggesting an interrelation which was especially close in the early historical period, but which is still relevant. *Civilization* is generally equated with a literate tradition preserved by organized groups, or societies, living in permanently fixed clusters rather than in small, scattered units. These groups are also characterized by some *division of labor* or task specialization, which includes a variety of *secondary* and *tertiary* (trading, services, manufacturing) rather than merely *primary* (agriculture, fishing, hunting, and gathering) activities. Such a description also fits the city. Historically the first cities began to appear with the emergence of a division of labor. It seems reasonably certain that this development first took place somewhere in the hill country bordering the Tigris-Euphrates Valley, where the wild ancestors of wheat and barley were native, and where, well before the appearance of cities, goats, pigs, dogs, and cattle had been domesticated and permanent field agriculture had begun to produce consistent surpluses. Only when this stage was reached could a division of labor take place so that some members of the population could engage in non-food-producing activities and still be fed from surpluses produced by the remaining farmers.

Cities As Centers Of Exchange

There were obvious advantages in conducting most of these non-agricultural functions in a concentrated center — a city where trade goods, raw materials, and food could most conveniently be assembled and from which a set of goods and services could be made available to surrounding rural areas or to other cities as trading partners. The first cities profited in these ways from *economies of scale* (lower costs resulting from size and concentration of the enterprise) and demonstrated the universal function of all cities at every time and place — as *centers of exchange*. Some aspects of this function, as in nearly all cities now, may not have been strictly economic, for example, political administration, religious and ritual services, or the wider social and cultural rewards present in a large community, which is also more

Reprinted from *Journal of Geography* (May, 1966), pp. 212-19 by permission.

diverse than a farmers' village. From the time of its origin the city has been the chief engine of economic and institutional growth and change through specialization based on exchange.

But in order to perform every aspect of its function as a center of exchange, the city depended, as it still does, on good access to and from the areas served, the city's *hinterland.* Any city implies and is based on *spatial interaction,* or relations between places. It cannot exist as an isolated unit, but only as it can receive from outside the city, often from great distances, the materials and food which it needs, and can provide in return a set of goods and services to consumers in its hinterland. It must therefore be concerned with maximizing *transferability* (the means of moving goods from one point to another at bearable cost) by building artificial routes of easy movement, such as roads, and/or by selecting a site and a situation which make access to and from the city easy. *Site* refers to the actual ground on which a city is built, *situation* to the wider pattern of spatial interactions with other places. Situation is thus by definition a relative term rather than an absolute one. It describes the relation of a given place to other places in simple distance, or, more importantly, in cost or effort. It can, and usually does, change over time, especially as accessibility and spatial interaction are affected by changes in transport and transferability.

In this broad sense all cities are *central places.* They are nodes or nuclei of their respective hinterlands, performing in one concentrated and easily accessible (or central) place specialized functions on behalf of the wider area which they serve. A final essential basis of exchange, the city's universal function, is *complementarity* — the actual or potential relationship between places which possess different sets of goods or services and which therefore have a basis for mutually profitable exchange. No two places are alike, and each place tends to have its own set of *comparative advantages* for the production of different sets of goods. Complementarity results in trade, however, only if transferability between the places concerned is great enough to overcome the friction of distance at bearable cost, and if no *intervening opportunity* lies between them where either potential trade partner could satisfy its needs with less effort. These are universal conditions for and characteristics of cities in every area and at every historical period.

Early Cities Of Mesopotamia And Egypt

One of the results of historical or comparative urban studies is their demonstration of urban universals rather than differences. By about 4000 B.C., city building in the Middle East seems to have spread from its probable earlier hearth in the hill country of Syria, Palestine, and Iraq down onto the flood plain of the Tigris-Euphrates, and perhaps equally early to the lower Nile Valley in Egypt. These are both potentially productive areas where exchange was relatively easy and transferability great. The Nile and Tigris-Euphrates are both exotic rivers, rising in well-watered highlands and flowing across a desert to reach the sea. Their anual floods deposited highly fertile alluvium, especially in the deltas, and in addition provided semi-automatic irrigation. It was possible on this basis to produce large and reliable food surpluses and thus to enable a division of labor as well as to create a prosperous hinterland for cities to serve. But the advantages of both areas for the growth of large and numerous cities for the first time were at least as importantly derived from the relative ease with which goods could be moved and therefore centers of exchange could function. Both areas were level and largely or entirely treeless, so that movement overland was relatively easy. The cities which arose, however, made more important use of the rivers themselves as easy routes of spatial interaction where transferability was maximized. City sites were riparian (on the river banks) and their situational advantages meant that they could assemble by water transport and at low cost, large and bulky shipments of delta-grown grain, dates, and other food commodities, and could also bring in heavy materials like stone or metals from great distances in addition to trade goods, since they could use sea as well as river routes. Goods and services could be distributed from these cities in the same way. Transport costs tend to vary inversely with the capacity of the carriers, especially for heavy or bulky goods. For many millennia after the first cities arose and until the development of the railway, large cities could not be maintained except on navigable waterways.

The early cities of Mesopotamia and Egypt also depended, as all cities do, on complementarity as a basis for exchange. The fundamental complementary relationship is between the city itself and the non-urban agricultural or primary-producing areas in its hinterland. But even in the ancient period the lower Nile and Tigris-Euphrates were devoid of stone, wood, or metal, and these commodities had to be imported to the cities, which were thus involved in complementary exchange (finished goods or services in exchange for raw materials) with a variety of places by river and sea routes. Cedars came to Egypt by sea from Lebanon, stone in great quantities from quarries along the upper Nile, metals and ores from many distant sources. In the early cities of Mesopotamia, even nails and simple tools were originally made from sun-dried or kiln-fired clay until

exchange had been established with distant sources of ores and metals as well as wood and stone. There was thus a relatively rapid expansion of a commercial network, or field of spatial interaction, accompanying the rise of the first cities.

Urbanization In Asia

Connections of this sort were established with complementary areas as distant as India (to which the Mesopotamian urban model spread by at least 2500 B.C.). Cities of the Indus plain, notably Harappa and Mohenjo Daro, became trade partners with Mesopotamian cities in a mutually profitable exchange.

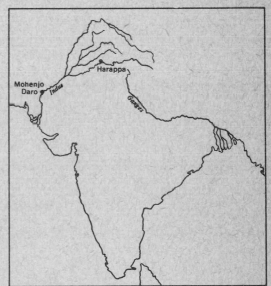

There was little or no exchange between these early Indian cities and Egypt, since urban Mesopotamia presented an intervening opportunity. Similarly trade and cultural exchange between Mesopotamia and China was apparently both late and weak, since the Indus cities intervened spatially and since transferability between Mesopotamia and India was much greater by sea routes along the shores of the Persian Gulf and Arabian

Sea. The flood plain of the Yellow River in north China was probably in historical terms the third major center of urbanization to develop (by about 2000 B.C.). It and the Indus plain shared the same set of physical characteristics as had earlier favored the rise of Mesopotamian and Egyptian cities — exotic river systems flowing across an arid but level and largely treeless plain where fertile alluvial soils and water for irrigation were combined with high transferability. Within each of these Asian areas urbanization spread first along the major rivers and their tributaries and distributaries, as avenues of easy access to and from productive agricultural areas. Asian urbanization is still heavily water-oriented.

With the rise of the first territorial empires in Asia, however, the dominant urban function became increasingly one of political administration and cultural synthesis. Trade did, of course, continue to grow in and from urban bases, but most traditional Asian cities were only secondarily involved in trade or manufacturing in terms of employment or investment, and were more importantly concerned with managing the administrative machinery of large bureaucratic states, including government trade monopolies. As with many modern political capitals, they also played an important cultural and ceremonial role as centers of the literate, intellectual, and artistic tradition in each area, and invested a large share of urban resources in monument building for both political and religious rather than strictly economic goals. City sites and situations had still, nevertheless, to maximize access, which is as important for an administrative city dealing in services as for a commercial city dealing in goods.

Urbanization In The West

From the beginning of the urban tradition of the West, however, the city was predominantly a commercial center. By the first millennium B. C., the dynamic centers of urbanization and expanding trade had for a variety of reasons shifted from Mesopotamia and the Nile into the Mediterranean Basin. A small enclosed sea, generally free of storms and with a highly indented coastline, the Mediterranean was one of the earliest hearths for the growth of navigation and ocean transport. Transferability within the basin was high, once the elementary techniques of navigation had been mastered. It is to Phoenician, Cretan, Greek, and Roman forms that the principal direct roots of modern Western urbanization extend, rather than to Luxor, Memphis, Ur, or Babylon. Tyre, Knossos, Athens, Syracuse (and Rome, to a degree) were centers of trade on a greatly increased scale and spatial spread. While it is true that

ancient urban Mesopotamia and Egypt show striking similarities to modern urbanism, confronted many of the same problems, and solved (or failed to solve) them in many of the same ways, the modern parallel with the pre-classical and classical Mediterranean is closer still, as part of a continuous Western urban tradition which stretches at least from Sidon and Carthage to Corinth, Rome, London, New York, and San Francisco. The great majority of Western cities has been and remains of dominantly commercial rather than administrative or symbolic, although, as in traditional Asia (where the proportions were reversed), most cities have performed both functions. The *polis*, or city-state of classical Greece, and the colonies which Greeks founded elsewhere along the Mediterranean shores as their trade by sea expanded, were primarily commercial centers involved in widely-extended spatial interaction patterns stretching from the Black Sea coasts and the Crimea to the Pillars of Hercules, where the Mediterranean joins the Atlantic. These sorts of cities, of which the Greek developments were prototypes, have been labelled *heterogenetic* — influenced by and involved with a variety of interactions with a great range of distant and different places — as opposed to the *orthogenetic* cities of the great Asian empires, which were proportionately more shaped by and involved in interactions within culturally homogeneous hinterlands and which functioned as urban pinnacles of the several Asian "Great Traditions."

Roman Cities

With the rise of the Roman Empire, the dominantly commercial nature of the Greek *polis* was overlaid by a new and wider set of administrative functions. The city of Rome, aided by its dual function in both trade and administration and by its central position within the Mediterranean for assembling and distributing food and other goods by sea, was probably the first city in history to reach or approach a population of one million. Its size was a reflection of the enormous extent and productivity of the hinterland it served. People and goods were transported by sea and by an impressive network of paved roads, all of which proverbially led to Rome and greatly augmented transferability and centrality. Cities founded or expanded by the Romans throughout their empire in Europe, North Africa, and the Middle East bore the imperial stamp of central authority. Many began as military camps or garrison towns, grew to provincial or regional capitals, and acquired some commercial functions as well. They were usually walled and in most instances carefully laid out on a gridiron plan, with major avenues leading from each of the gates at the four points of the compass. In this they resembled the administrative cities of the contemporary Chinese empire as its spatial extent also expanded and was marked by the establishment of walled regional centers of control laid out spatially on a uniform imperial plan.

The collapse of Roman control in the West was followed by a period of several centuries in which both the number and the size of cities shrank. Roman roads degenerated, transferability was everywhere lessened by brigandage and civil disorder, and commercial production was similarly affected. The basis for urban growth was thus sharply reduced as compared with the period of the *Pax Romana*, when exchange and transferability were maximized. The city of Rome itself may have shrunk to as few as 5,000 inhabitants at its lowest point, a dramatic illustration of what happens to a city when it loses its hinterland. No political or administrative functions remained, and economic functions were reduced to those of a tiny local exchange center for the immediate environs of the town. Elsewhere in the former empire urbanism was also in retreat. Many of the cities which survived the Dark Ages did so because they had become the seats of bishops (cathedral towns) or grew up in the shelter or even within the walls of the fortified castle of a feudal lord. As in Italy itself, lowland sites of easy access which had attracted cities under the *Pax Romana* were often abandoned, and nearly all cities sought the protection of elevated or defensible sites where accessibility was sacrificed for security.

Cities In The Middle Ages

Venice is the most notable example of a city which arose during the chaos following the Roman collapse as a protected refuge — in the marshes near the seaward edge of the Po River delta on the Adriatic — and was able to combine defensibility with high transferability by sea. With the combined advantages of its site and its situation at the northernmost extension of the Mediterranean, where it could serve the north European market and could assemble goods by sea from the Levant and the Orient, Venice became the biggest city in medieval Europe. Elsewhere in the West exchange was to a large extent provided by periodic fairs, as an adjustment to conditions of low transferability and limited commercial production. Fairs in effect brought the market to the hinterland on a rotating basis in the same way and for the same reasons that periodic fairs or markets still operate in areas of low transferability and restricted commercial production, such as large parts of North Africa or rural China.

Toward the close of the Middle Ages, and for a variety of reasons, larger and better-ordered political units began to grow, security and transferability began to increase, roads reappeared, barrier forests were removed, trade began to revive, and cities once more increased in numbers and size. The age of the great discoveries and the rapid improvements in shipping and navigation from the 15th cen-

tury on meant a further and enormous widening of the limits of spatial interaction by sea routes which soon encompassed the entire world. This, incidentally, meant the decline of Venice, since first its old rival Genoa and then the new port cities along the northwest coast of Europe now stood as a series of intervening opportunities between Venice and the new sea routes to world markets, which no longer flowed eastward through the Mediterranean but westward and southward in the Atlantic to the New World and to Asia around Africa. The Asian tropics, in particular, offered the basis for a strong complementarity with Europe as producers of spices and a growing variety of other goods which Europe demanded but could not produce. For the same reasons of complementarity and high transferability by sea, a large and profitable trade in sugar arose with the West Indies.

Commercial Centers And The Coming Of The Industrial Revolution

Booming urban commercial centers grew in northwest Europe to manage the expanded volume of trade, with the greatest advantages accruing to those cities with the most appropriate situations — ports in the Low Countries near the mouths of the Rhine which offered easy access to the variety of continental markets, and on the other side of the Channel, the city of London, well placed at the head of the Thames estuary to serve as a major *entrepôt* (center of assembly and distribution of goods by water) for the European market as a whole. This same urban model — the commercial city dominated by merchants — spread across the Atlantic and was reproduced in Boston, New York, Philadelphia, Baltimore, and other North American centers. It later spread to Australia-New Zealand and to parts of Latin America where commercial production of primary goods for export became prominent and required large urban centers of exchange and commercial services, such as Sydney, Melbourne, Buenos Aires, or Montevideo, whose shipments of grain and meat helped to feed the mushrooming urban populations of Europe and North America.

The coming of the industrial revolution reinforced the growth of most of the earlier-established commercial cities, for they were centers of investment capital and of cheap access for the assembly of raw materials and the distribution of finished goods. But there was also a new growth of manufacturing cities close to sources of the bulky materials which industrialization now required in enormous amounts and which therefore meant greatly increased sensitivity to transport costs. Manchester, Birmingham, Sheffield, Essen, Düsseldorf, Pittsburgh, Breslau, Magnitogorsk, Jamshedpur, Anshan, Yawata, and other virtually new cities arose in association with local deposits of coal or ore. The spread of railways did, however, make a greater degree of urban concentration possible. The railroad and other innovations, such as the steamship, and ultimately the truck and the pipeline, so heightened transferability at low cost that even the older commercial centers, far from raw material sources, could bring in what manufacturing required and could also bring in food to maintain urban populations of considerable size. One result of the rapid increase in the size of ocean carriers was that many of the harbors adequate for an earlier age could no longer accommodate them. *Outports* had to be developed, farther down the river or estuary on which the city lay, or harbors had to be artificially deepened or enlarged on the coast. Thus, for example, Le Havre came to serve as the outport for Paris, Southampton and Gravesend for London, Cuxhaven for Hamburg, and Kobe for Osaka.

As one consequence of the expansion of trade and the growth of a worldwide trade network, exchange between Europe and the Afro-Asian area greatly increased. In Asia there had in the past been few predominantly commercial cities, and in particular few coastal ports. The cities of the Great Tradition had been inland centers of administration. European traders and later colonial merchants had therefore to establish, or to expand from small indigenous nuclei, a whole set of new port cities to handle the new trade and to service the expanding commercial hinterlands from which they drew their export goods. From Karachi, Bombay, Madras, Colombo, and Calcutta through the major ports of Southeast Asia to Hong Kong, Shanghai, Tientsin, and Yokohama there arose a series of similarly organized cities which were either founded by Western traders where none had existed before or were largely developed by them (in Japan, by what were clearly Western methods). Not merely their coastal sites and their situations, which maximized access by sea, but their physical appearance and their institutions, which were designed to generate and safeguard the accumulation of commercial capital, the increase of trade, and the security of the private entrepreneur and his goods, were replicas of the urban models already developed by post-Renaissance Europe in the merchant cities of the modern West. With the coming of national independence in the wake of the second World War, many of these Western-developed colonial cities have also become political capitals. In every country of Asia (if Tokyo may be regarded as a city developed on Western lines, if not in Western hands), the colonial or semi-colonial (e.g., Bangkok) port became well before independence a strong or even over-whelming *primate* city, i.e., a city which is at least twice as populous as its nearest domestic rival. In the several small countries of Southeast Asia, in particular, the ex-colonial primate city almost monopolizes commercial and industrial as well as political functions for the entire state, and thus has no rational rivals as a national capital despite its alien origins. Urban development in parts of Africa during the past century has followed parallel lines. Colonial port cities were built by Europeans to handle the export of primary products and became much larger than the indigenous inland urban centers. Similarly, many of these ports, originally colonial, have become primate cities and, with national independence, political capitals.

The Growing Similarity Of Cities

With the creation of a global commercial network, the spread of industrialization, and the technological revolution in transport and transferability, cities everywhere are becoming more like one another. The urban differences which once distinguished various cultural and economic areas are lessening. The degree of urbanization, or the proportion of the total population living in cities, tends strongly to vary with the level of commercialization of the economy. Hence, for example, Australia, Uruguay, Germany, or Japan are much more highly urbanized than China, India, Mexico, or the Congo. But all cities are increasingly involved in spatial interaction with each other and with other parts of the world. This interaction involves what is more and more the same set of commercial and industrial functions dependent on the same kinds of techniques and confronting the same sorts of problems. The growing spatial spread of *conurbations* (city clusters and expanding metropolitan areas) is appearing in Asia and Africa and Latin America as in Europe and North America. The foreshadowings of *megalopolis* (literally, giant city, a growing together over a vastly extended urban area of what were orginally widely separated cities) are apparent not only in southern England or between Boston, Massachusetts, and Richmond, Virginia, but between Tokyo and Osaka-Kobe, along the Hooghly River, and along the Rio de la Plata. The growth of the city since urban-based civilization first developed some 6000 years ago is still continuing and the city still functions as the center of exchange which increasingly unites all areas of the world.

Further Reading

1 Chelde, V. G., *What Happened in History*, Rev. Ed. (Baltimore, Penguin Books, 1965).

2 Dickinson, R. E., *The West European City* (London, Routledge and Kegan Paul, Ltd., 1951).

3 Mumford, L., *The City in History* (New York, Harcourt, Brace, & World, 1961).

4 Murphey, Rhoads, "The City as a Centre of Change: Western Europe and China," *Annals of the Assoc. of Am. Geographers* (1954), pp. 349-62.

5 Pirenne, Henri, *Medieval Cities* (Princeton, N.J., Princeton University Press, 1925).

6 Ullman, E. L., "The Role of Transport and the Bases for Interaction," in *Man's Role in Changing the Face of the Earth*, ed. W. L. Thomas (Chicago, University of Chicago Press, 1956), pp. 862-80.

American Metropolitan Evolution

4

John R. Borchert

The landscapes of any American city reflect countless decisions and actions from the time of settlement to the present. The results are apparent not only in differences in land use but in the kaleidoscopic variety of building facades, street patterns, and lot sizes. Early actions precluded or frustrated many later locational decisions. The metropolitan physical plant has accumulated through various historical epochs, and clearly those epochs were distinguished from one another by different ideas and technologies. Increasingly, in proportion to its size and age, the metropolis is becoming a complicated puzzle of heterogeneous and anachronistic features.

The evolutionary nature of the metropolitan anatomy is, of course, widely recognized, and this fact is reflected in a wealth of studies of the historical-geographical development of individual cities and of the anachronistic legacies that make up much of the urban physical plant. Yet research on systems of cities, cities as central places, cities and transportation networks, internal spatial structure of cities, and rank-size distributions has

lacked a general historical context.[1] A structured urban history of the country or of its major regions, which would help to bring order to the mixture of historical-locational forces that generate the urban landscape,[2] has not yet appeared. Meanwhile, future populations are projected, and increasingly massive clearance and redevelopment proceed in the old central areas of metropolises without a fully developed theory of metropolitan

[1] See the excellent summary by Brian J. L. Berry, "Research Frontiers in Urban Geography," in *The Study of Urbanization* ed. by Philip M. Hauser and Leo F. Schnore (New York, John Wiley and Sons, 1965), pp. 403-30. For further comment see Fred Lukermann "Empirical Expressions of Nodality and Hierarchy in a Circulation Manifold," *East Lakes Geographer*, Vol. 2 (1966), pp. 17-44. A notable exception is the work of Allan Pred, "Industrialization, Initial Advantage, and American Metropolitan Growth", *Geogr. Rev.*, Vol. 55 (1965), pp. 158-85.

[2] This is the thesis of a detailed review of the literature of United States urban history by Charles N. Glaab, "The Historian and the American City: A Bibliographic Survey," in *The Study of Urbanization* (see footnote 1 above), pp. 53-80.

Adapted from *Geographical Review*, Vol. 57 (1967), pp. 301-32. Copyrighted by the America Geographical Society of New York. Reprinted by permission.

growth and form.[3] Stages of urban economic growth and social evolution have been postulated. Wilbur Thompson has observed that these are "highly impressionistic generalizations" and "leave much too strong a feeling of the inevitability of growth and development." And he has asked, "What are some of the dampening and restraining forces that surely must exist? We see all about us evidence of local economic stagnation and decay and even demise."[4]

Central questions relate to the factors that have influenced the location of relative growth and decline, the relationship of anachronistic regions within cities to the evolution of the national pattern of urban growth, the threads that run consistently through the evolutionary process, and the nature of future change as suggested by experience to date. These questions can be illuminated by examining the evolution of the present pattern of standard metropolitan statistical areas through a series of historical epochs, from the first census, in 1790, to the most recent, in 1960.

Major Innovations and Epochs

Most American metropolitan areas, throughout much of their history, have functioned chiefly as collectors, processors, and distributors of raw materials and goods. Consequently, it might be expected that changes in their growth rates would have been partic-

ularly sensitive to changes in (1) the size and resource base of the hinterland and (2) the technology of transport and industrial energy for the processing of primary resources. These two sets of variables are interrelated. The technology partly defines the resource base, and the transportation technology, in particular, strongly affects the size, and therefore the resources, of a city's hinterland. There is, of course, no implication that the technological changes have been independent variables or basic causes of growth. The presumptions are, rather, that within the given framework of values and institutions they were stimulated by the economic growth and geographical expansion of the nation and that they in turn not only further stimulated growth but also helped to differentiate it geographically.[5]

Among many possibilities, this paper emphasizes three relatively brief periods since the 1790 census in which major innovations appeared in the technology of transport and industrial energy.

THE INNOVATIONS

Steamboat and "Iron Horse"

The first of the innovations was the use of the steam engine in water and land transportation. The census year selected is 1830. To be sure, the early steamboats in America preceded that date, but the real buildup of steamboat tonnage on the Ohio-Mississippi-Missouri system begin in the 1830's (Figure 1),[6] and the main period of increase in the

[3] William Alonso, "The Historic and the Structural Theories of Urban Form: Their Implications for Urban Renewal," *Land Economics*, Vol. 40 (1964), pp. 227-31.

[4] Wilbur R. Thompson, "Urban Economic Growth and Development in a National System of Cities," in *The Study of Urbanization* (see footnote 1 above), pp. 431-90; reference on pp. 438-39. See also his "A Preface to Urban Economics" (Baltimore, 1965), pp. 12-17.

[5] For an excellent summary of the operation of contingent, interrelated variables in the growth process see Robert W. Fogel, *Railroads and American Economic Growth* (Baltimore, 1964), pp. 234-37 (section on "Implications for the Theory of Economic Growth").

[6] John W. Oliver, *History of American Technology* (New York, 1956), pp. 192-93 and 202.

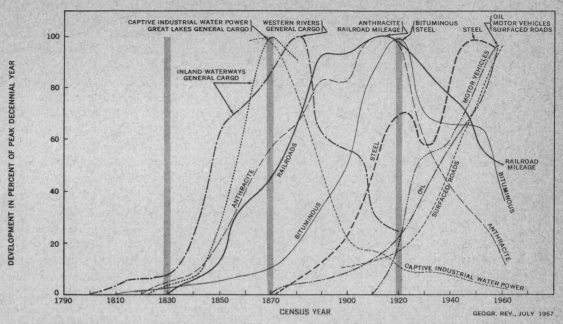

Figure 1. Rise and decline of ten indicators of the technology of transport and industrial energy. Peak values of past years concentrate around 1870 and 1920. Sources: "Historical Statistics of the United States," pp. 416-417, 427-429, 446, and 458; *Statistical Abstract of the United States 1965*, pp. 561, 569, 718, 729, and 811 (see text footnote for both); and "A Compendium of the Ninth Census" (U.S. Bureau of the Census, 1872), p. 706.

tonnage of general-cargo vessels on the Great Lakes also began in the 1830's and 1840's. Rail mileage, likewise, grew rapidly after initial development in 1829. By the end of the decade "the major mechanical features of the American locomotive were established," boxcars had been introduced, regular mail routes were in operation on the railroads, and the first transatlantic steamer had arrived in New York.[7]

The introduction of steam power created major transportation corridors on the western rivers and the Great Lakes and resulted in enlargement of the hinterlands of ports on both the inland waterways and the Atlantic. It made possible the development of a national transportation system through the

integration of these major waterways and regional rail webs. These changes favored the growth of ports with relatively large harbors and proximity to important resource concentrations. Simultaneously, however, they hurt the economy of nearby smaller ports.

Steam power was also applied in manufacturing, but its impact was apparently more localized because of the impracticality of long hauls of coal or other bulk commodities with the comparatively light equipment and iron rails of the time. As a result, local waterpower sites continued to influence industrial location. By 1870 waterwheels were still providing roughly half of the inanimate energy for manufacturing, especially in the major manufacturing region. About half of the entire inanimate power for industry was in the five

[7] *Ibid.*, pp. 184-85, 189, and 202.

states of Massachusetts, Connecticut, New York, Pennsylvania, and Ohio. Oliver observes that steam "was not universally used in cotton mills until the railroads were sufficiently developed to transport coal cheaply."[8] That ability came generally in the 1870's.

Steel Rails and Electric Power

The second major innovation was the appearance of abundant, and hence low-priced, steel. The census year chosen for this is 1870. The preceding decade had seen the first commercial output of Bessemer steel in America, and by the mid-1870's American steel products were breaking into the world market (Figure 1).

A number of related events, each with geographical ramifications of great importance, occurred in dramatic sequence in the decade of the 1870's. Steel rails replaced iron on both newly built and existing lines. Heavier equipment and more powerful locomotives permitted increased speed and the long haul of bulk goods. Rail gauge and freight-car parts were standardized[9] (there had been eleven gauges among the northern systems in 1860), so that interline exchange and coast-to-coast shipment were possible. Refrigerated

cars made their entry, ushering in a new era of regional specialization in agriculture and centralization of the packing industry at major rail nodes. Other ramifications favored industrial, hence urban, centralization. The practical length of coal haul was extended and the cost reduced. The effect was to open vast central Appalachian bituminous deposits and to facilitate the movement of coal to the great ports whose growth had been launched four decades earlier. The greater availability of coal was soon supplemented by the availability of central-station electric power, which followed in the 1880's.

For the first time massive forces were arrayed favoring market orientation of industry and the metropolitanization of America. At the same time there were negative impacts. The long rail haul spelled the doom of most passenger traffic and cargo movement on the inland waterways, especially the rivers. Small river ports were destined to become virtual museums. It is noteworthy that general-cargo shipping capacity on the western rivers peaked not on the eve of the Civil War but in the 1870's; thereafter it fell precipitously for half a century (Figure 1). The easier availability of coal and central-station electricity doomed the small waterpower sites. Most small industrial cities retained their function; many were rail nodes large and important enough to continue to grow with the national economy. But for subsequent decisions the decentralizing factor of many small waterpower sites had yielded to the centralizing force of the metropolitan rail centers, their giant markets, and their superior accessibility.[10]

---

[8] *Ibid.*, p. 160.

[9] The urgency of rebuilding existing lines with steel rails at standard gauge in the 1870's is related in Robert J. Casey and W. A. S. Douglas, *The Lackawanna Story* (New York, 1951), pp. 92-94. The impact of the introduction of the long haul on the geography of an existing system is described in Louis Jackson, *A Brief History of the Chicago, Milwaukee, and St. Paul Railway* (1900), pp. 6-8. See also Harlan W. Gilmore, *Transportation and the Growth of Cities* (Glencoe, Ill., 1953), p. 51. For a full account of the beginning of the steel era in the United States and for further references see Oliver, *op. cit.* (see footnote 6 above), pp. 319-425, especially pp. 416-25.

[10] Allan Pred has developed at length the fact that the period from the Civil War to World War I saw the major growth of large cities as industrial centers, *op. cit.* (see footnote 1 above), pp. 161-62.

Internal-Combustion Engine and Shift to Services

The third major innovation, and probably the least debatable, was the introduction of the internal-combustion engine in transportation and related technology. The census date chosen is 1920. To be sure, the automobile had entered the American scene in the 1890's, but motor-vehicle registration was insignificant before 1910, and road surfacing and petroleum production began their steep climb in the 1920's (Figure 1). The need for a national system of highways was recognized in 1916 with the first federal aid for road construction.

The impact of the internal-combustion engine on the geography of American cities needs little review. But some of the most profound changes affecting the city occurred in agriculture.[11] True, the new technology put the farmer in an automobile and thus encouraged the centralization of urban growth at the larger, diversified centers in all the commercial farming regions. But also, by putting the farmer on a tractor, it multiplied the land area he could work alone, initiated a revolution in family farm size, and sped the urbanization of much of rural America. In addition, air passenger transport helped to encourage centralization of the national business management function in a few cities,[12] and the auto stimulated the decentralization of most metropolitan functions. The internal-combustion engine had a profound and happy impact on the growth prospects of cities in

the oil fields, but the opposite effect on cities in the coal fields and at railroad division points.

Another change, of overriding importance, coincided with the beginning of the auto-air age. Throughout the nation's history the primary (agriculture, forests, fisheries, mining) and secondary (manufacturing) sectors of the economy had dominated the employment picture. Their share of total employment had been gradually diminishing, but in 1920 they still accounted for 56 percent. Since 1920, however, the share has been less than half and has been falling rapidly (Figure 2). The trend is, of course, a reflection of the combined technological advances that have been leading the nation gradually toward an era of automation.

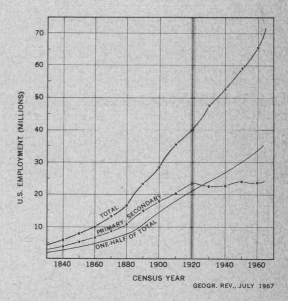

GEOGR. REV., JULY 1967

Figure 2. The changing relationship of employment in primary and secondary industries to total employment in the United States. Source: "Historical Statistics of the United States," p. 74; *Statistical Abstract of the United States 1965*, p. 220 (see text footnote 24 for both).

---

[11] See Chauncy D. Harris, "Agricultural Production in the United States, The Past Fifty Years and the Next," *Geogr. Rev.*, Vol. 47 (1957), pp. 175-93.

[12] See William Goodwin, "The Management Center in the United States," *Geogr. Rev.*, Vol. 55 (1965), pp. 1-16.

When employment was mainly in resource and processing industries, it was fair to look on cities mainly as assemblers and processors of the nation's resources. It was appropriate to assume that changes in the technology of transport and industrial energy would be crucial for the growth or decline of cities. In the auto-air age, when primary and secondary employment occupies only a decreasing minority of the labor force, such technological changes are of declining importance in the life and death of cities. Two new factors have come to the fore. One is the increase in service employment. With a fast-growing majority of new jobs since 1920 in the least mechanized and least automated part of our economy — the personal and professional services — the most likely locations for new employment growth have been the places where there were already large concentrations of people to be served. Hence in the auto-air age, even more than in the preceding epoch, growth breeds growth. The second factor is the large and growing amount of leisure time available. As Ullman pointed out some years ago, this has led to the great importance of amenities as an urban location factor, both for commuting workers and for retired people.[13] It had also led to an increase in the time available for, and, presumably, the need of, formal education. Hence educational centers as well as high-amenity locations have been blessed by the fruits of changing technology in this present age.

THE EPOCHS

In short, four epochs in American history can be identified that have been characterized by changes in technology crucial in the location

of urban growth and development: (1) Sail-Wagon, 1790-1830; (2) Iron Horse, 1830-1870; (3) Steel Rail, 1870-1920; (4) Auto-Air-Amenity, 1920-.[14]

Although emphasis here is on factors affecting the differential growth of American cities as entities, these periods are differentiated also by internal features of urban geography and morphology.[15] The railroad had many impacts on the structure and location of industrial and central business districts, and these districts changed with the entry of steel and the long haul. The coming of steel

[13] Edward L. Ullman, "Amenities as a Factor in Regional Growth," *Geogr. Rev.*, Vol. 44 (1954), pp. 119-32.

[14] This differentiation is somewhat related to Eric Lampard's formulation of three critical periods in the regional economic development of the United States up to 1910: (1) a period of initial resource exploitation in the historic eastern base region, from colonial time through the Civil War; (2) a period of "extension of accessibility" from the eastern base region to the rest of the country associated with an enlargement of the resource hinterland of the eastern base, from the Civil War to World War I; and (3) the era of "nationalization" of the economy, utilizing and improving on a virtually fully developed transportation system since World War I. See Eric E. Lampard, "Regional Economic Development, 1870-1950", in *Regions, Resources, and Economic Growth* by Harvey S. Perloff, Edgar S. Dunn, Jr., Eric E. Lampard, and Richard F. Muth (Baltimore, 1960), pp. 107-292 (Part 3). See also Constance McLaughlin Green, *American Cities in the Growth of the Nation* (New York, 1957), Chap. 10, and the works cited by Sjoberg in connection with his discussion of the Technological School (Gideon Sjoberg, "Theory and Research in Urban Sociology" in *The Study of Urbanization* (see footnote 1 above), pp. 157-89, reference on pp. 170-71).

[15] For an extensive discussion of urban evolution in relation to transportation technology and development in specific metropolitan areas see James E. Vance, Jr., "Labor-shed, Employment Field, and Dynamic Analysis in Urban Geography," *Econ. Geogr.*, Vol. 36 (1960), pp. 189-220, and his "Geography and Urban Evolution in the San Francisco Bay Area" (Berkeley, 1964).

and electric power made possible the sky-scraper and rapid transit. The auto and coincident developments in electronics need no elaboration. Each innovation brought major changes in land-use patterns, densities, lot sizes, nodality of the central business district, and other intraurban variables.

Reservations and qualifications apply, of course, to this fourfold historical division. The periods are not homogeneous. Even if they should stand up as useful divisions for the description and study of American metropolitan evolution, they contain many subdivisions, which vary from one region to another.

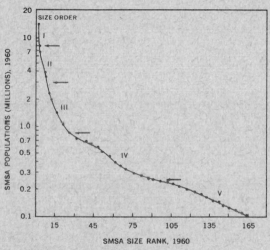

GEOGR. REV., JULY 1967

Figure 3. Population rank-size distribution and size-order limits for SMSA's in 1960. Except for the three largest metropolitan areas, dots represent only every fifth place in the sequence. The basis for this graph and for subsequent maps is a list of all 1960 SMSA's, with populations for the same counties or groups of counties for 1790, 1830, 1870, 1920, and 1960. The 212 census SMSA's on the list have been reduced to 178 by dropping areas with fewer than 80,000 inhabitants in 1960 and combining certain others, mainly in New England and several large multicentered complexes. Where SMSA's on the list differ in definition from those in the census, the differences are specified. Copies of the list are available from the author.

Furthermore, the boundaries between the epochs, although characterized by the near simultaneity of important innovations, are nevertheless complex transition periods. Some of the features of transition constitute little epochs of their own; examples might be the canal epoch (*ca.* 1810's to 1840's) and the electric interurban railway epoch (*ca.* 1900's to 1930's). Oliver[16] observes, "The canal was at best a temporary and an inadequate answer to the need for inland transportation." In a sense, it represented an attempt to adapt the technology of water transportation to the quickly growing need for tapping inland resources as the frontier advanced. Likewise, the rash of interurban electric rail lines that appeared about the turn of the present century may be viewed as a "temporary and inadequate" attempt to adapt rail-transport technology to the growing need for a flexible, rapid linkage between farm, small town, and city as the populations of large regions became commercialized and urban-oriented.[17]

Finally, throughout virtually all the first three epochs the settled area of the United States was expanding westward. The rate, timing, and direction of advance of the settlement frontier were in many ways quite independent of the major technological innovations that opened each of these epochs. On the other hand, the westward expansion helped to press the need for these innovations. More important from the viewpoint of this paper, cities were needed and built as

[16] Oliver, *op. cit.*, p. 180.

[17] See Mildred M. Walmsley, "The Bygone Electric Interurban Railway System," *Professional Geographer*, Vol. XVII, no. 3 (1965), pp. 1-6; and the detailed maps and descriptive data in G. W. Hilton and J. F. Due, *The Electric Interurban Railways in America* (Stanford, Calif., 1960).

new lands were opened. Hence the land pioneered during each of these epochs constitutes a region within which all city sites were chosen, and subsequent investments made, under a particular sequence of technological considerations.

Metropolitan Size Classes

In order to compare sizes and growth rates during the four historical epochs postulated

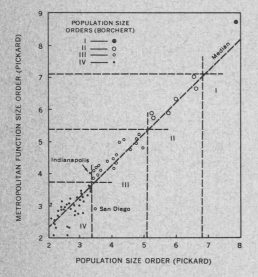

Figure 4. The 26 SMSA's defined as I, II, or III order in Figure 3 shown in their positions on Pickard's combined population and metropolitan-function scales. With only two exceptions, places that fall within the top three population size orders in Figure 3 also form discrete groups on the basis of metropolitan functions. "Metropolitan functions" in this case include measures of bank deposits, wholesale trade, Sunday newspaper circulation, federal-government employment, and manufacturing employment. The exceptions are San Diego, a third-order city based on population but weak in its metropolitan functions, and Indianapolis, a fourth-order city in Figure 3 (1960 SMSA definition of the Indianapolis SMSA) but with exceptional metropolitan strength. Graph modified from Pickard, Metropolitanization of the United States (see text footnote 18 for reference), Figure 21.

here, American cities were divided into five population size categories. First, the 212 standard metropolitan statistical areas of the 1960 census were reduced to 178 by combining some and dropping those under 80,000 population. The 178 were then ordered by size. A smoothed curve joining them in rank-size distribution is shown in Figure 3. A change in slope is noticeable at four points — at populations of about 250,000, 820,000, 3,000,000 and 8,000,000. Above each of these critical points lies a group of cities whose growth at some period in their history has been accelerated as compared with the places below the critical point. These division points break the 1960 SMSA's into five groups, which may be labeled as follows: first order, more than 8,000,000 (New York); second order, 2,300,000 to 8,000,000; third order, 820,000 to 2,300,000; fourth order, 250,000 to 820,000; and fifth order, less than 250,000. Although the divisions are somewhat arbitrary, they seem to identify significantly different groups of cities. The New York metropolis is, of course, in a class by itself no matter how the SMSA's are divided. The second and third groups appear as clusters on the graph that portrays Jerome Pickard's population and functional size orders (Figure 4).[18] The fifth group seems to match the primary wholesale-retail category identified, by the analysis of business functions, at the top level below Minneapolis-St. Paul in a regional hierarchy of trade centers in the northern Midwest and Great Plains.[19]

[18] Jerome P. Pickard, "Metropolitanization of the United States," *Urban Land Inst. Research Monograph*, Vol. 2 (Washington, D.C., 1959), Fig. 21, p. 67.

[19] John R. Borchert and Russell B. Adams, "Trade Centers and Trade Areas of the Upper Midwest," *Upper Midwest Economic Study Urban Rept. No. 3* (Minneapolis, 1963), pp. 36-39 and Figs. 1 (p. 4), 8 (p. 25), and 9 (p. 27).

For the earlier census years two definitions had to be formulated before the procedure could be applied. First, it was necessary to define "SMSA" for those years. In the 1960 census an SMSA by definition had to contain, in effect, a central city of at least 50,000 population. For the present study the minimum size of the central city was reduced to be commensurate with the smaller total population of the United States in the earlier census years. Hence the minimum-sized central city for an "emerging SMSA" in 1920 was 29,500; in 1870, 11,100; in 1830, 3600; and in 1790, 1100. The population of the county was used at each point in the time series. Where a county was split during the series, appropriate adjustments were made. But each SMSA or emerging SMSA that appears at any point in the time series is always defined by the same county or counties. To be sure, this is only one way of achieving a measure of consistency in dealing with a problem for which there is no entirely satisfactory solution at present.[20] Few of these counties in the early epochs were "metropolitan" in any modern sense. But they included the forty to fifty largest places in 1790 and 1830; and the definition identified, then as now, the nation's principal population clusters.

Second, it was necessary to define for the earlier census years the limits of the five size orders defined above for 1960. Again, each of the size-order limits was reduced to be commensurate with the smaller national population in the earlier years. These values, however, were then adjusted upward to account for the smaller proportion of a given "metropolitan" county covered by the smaller central city of earlier times.[21] The result was the set of limits shown in Table I.

Thus five size orders and four historical epochs were established. By comparing the numbers of newcomers, dropouts, and shifts in size order through the series of epochs it is possible to observe the evolution of the modern array of metropolitan areas. It is also possible to observe the impact of several major changes in technology and the expansion of resource base and metropolitan hinterlands that accompanied the westward movement. Figure 5 shows all the places included in these five size orders during at least one of the four historical epochs.

[20] See Karl Gustav Grytzell, "The Demarcation of Comparable City Areas by Means of Population Density," *Lund Studies in Geography*, Ser. B, Human Geography, no. 25 (1963), especially pp. 5-9.

[21] For the years before 1960 each size-order threshold, T_y, was first defined by the relationship $T_y = T_o (P_y/P_o)$ where T_o is the threshold population in 1960, P_o is the United States population in 1960, and P_y is the United States population in the earlier year. For thresholds under 100,000 "SMSA" population a further adjustment was made, using the relationship $T_r = T_y (F_y/F_o)$, where T_y is the threshold defined for the earlier year by the initial adjustment, T_r is the readjusted value, F_o is the percentage of United States population that was rural in 1960, and F_y is the percentage of United States population that was rural in the earlier year. Where the country population exceeded 100,000 it was assumed that rural (especially farm) population within the "SMSA" was negligible, and no second adjustment was made.

The net effect of this definition and procedure is to overstate the populations of urban areas in the earlier periods, especially before 1920 and especially in areas with populations under 100,000. Because of the second adjustment of threshold values, the size orders are roughly comparable throughout the series. Lukermann (see footnote 1 above) approximated urban-area populations for the eastern and central United States 1790-1890. Comparison of his rank sizes and geographical patterns with those in this paper shows no significant discrepancies resulting from the different definitions.

TABLE I

Limits of Size Orders for SMSA's in 1960 and Corresponding Areas in Earlier Years*

	Population Threshold (thousands)				
Size Order	1790	1830	1870	1920	1960
First	180	530	1,300	4,750	8,000
Second	90	160	400	1,480	2,300
Third	40	90	130	470	820
Fourth	15	35	750	150	250
Fifth	5	15	30	60	80
Central-city minimum	1.1	3.6	11.1	29.5	50.0

* The fifth order is truncated by the lower size limits for an SMSA; a number of urban areas not large enough to be defined as SMSA's are fifth-order centers.

Evolution of the Pattern[22]

Sail-Wagon Epoch, 1790-1830

At the time of the 1790 census almost all the major urban population clusters were ports on Atlantic bays or estuaries, or on the navigable reaches of the Connecticut, Hudson, Delaware, and Savannah Rivers, or on the Chesapeake Bay system (Figure 6). Among the centers of third or high order,

[22] This section is an attempt not to write history but to interpret briefly Figures 6 through 11 in the light of readily accessible secondary materials and historical census data. The regional framework and regional economic changes discussed are elaborated in Perloff and others (see footnote 14 above); in Ralph H. Brown, *Historical Geography of the United States* (New York, 1948); and in several standard regional geographies, notably J. Russell Smith, *North America* (New York, 1925); George J. Miller and Almon E. Parkins, *Geography of North America* (New York and London, 1928); and Harold Hull McCarty *The Geographic Basis of American Economic Life* (New York and London 1940). On the other hand, the detailed history and geography of specific cities within these regions, over time, are dispersed through myriad local studies. Important references appear in Harold M. Mayer, "Urban Geography" in *American Geography: Inventory & Prospect*, edited by Preston E. James and Clarence F. Jones (Syracuse, N.Y., 1954), pp. 142-66; and in Glaab, *op. cit.*, pp. 73-80.

only Worcester, Massachusetts, was not a port, and only Worcester and Pittsburgh were not on the Atlantic waterway. Lower-order centers also were mainly Atlantic ports, though they included inland centers of agricultural trade and local industry. There was no primate city or national metropolis; the Boston, New York, and Philadelphia areas were of about equal size. Lukermann has observed that the entire family of Atlantic ports was characterized by small hinterlands and a primary orientation toward the sea and Europe and could in fact be considered part of the West European urban system.[23]

Change was modest during the epoch (Figure 7). Virtually all places that rose in size order — that is, grew faster than the national growth rate — were in areas of westward expansion and accompanying development of new resources: the drift-filled valleys and drift-capped plateaus of western New York, the Ontario plain, the Great Valley, the Bluegrass, and the Nashville Basin. Other important resources lay within these new agricultural regions or adjacent to them — notably waterpower, the timber of the northern Appalachians and the Adirondacks,

[23] Lukermann, *op. cit.*

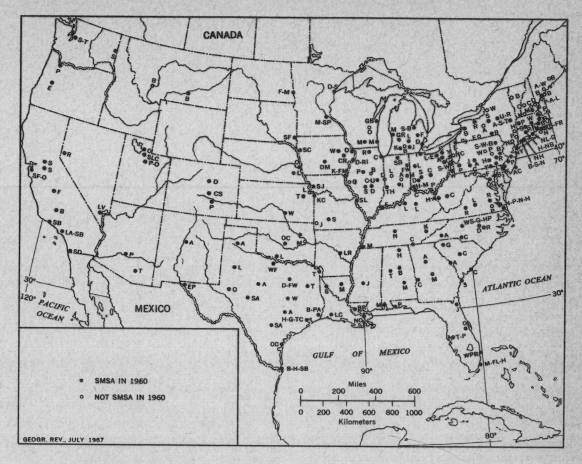

Figure 5. Places in the five size orders of SMSA's or "emerging metropolitan areas" in one or more of the census years 1790, 1830, 1870, 1920 or 1960. Names of the central cities are indicated by initials.

and the anthracite of northeastern Pennsylvania. The "boom" cities, those which rose two or more ranks, were mainly along the inland waterways that penetrated the new western lands — the Erie Canal, the lower Great Lakes, and the Ohio River system. Exceptions were the Great Valley cities near the anthracite fields.

As agricultural settlement expanded in western New York there was a relative decline in growth rate, and a drop in size order, at a number of small ports and inland centers serving agricultural areas in eastern New York and New England. Meanwhile, although the struggle for deeper hinterlands had begun, the absence of any major change in the technology of land transport permitted most Atlantic ports to retain essentially the same functions through most of the epoch and to register neither relative increase nor relative decrease in size order up to 1830.

Iron Horse Epoch, 1830-1870

At the beginning of this epoch all emerging metropolitan areas of third or higher order

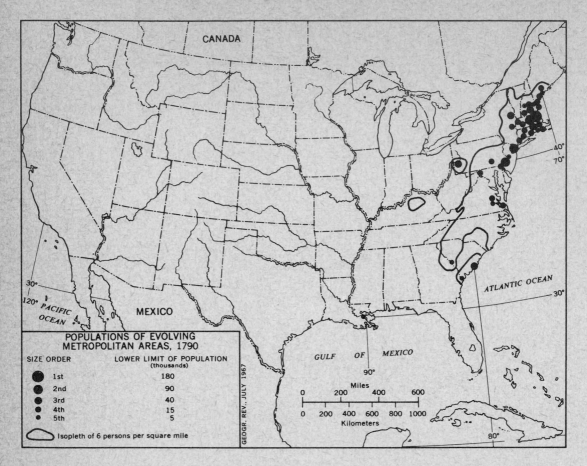

Figure 6.   Distribution of major towns and neighboring county populations by size order, 1790. Source of the population data for Figures 5 - 8, "A Compendium of the Ninth Census" (1872). Population-density isopleths generalized from Clifford L. Lord and Elizabeth H. Lord; Historical Atlas of the United States (New York, 1953), p. 46.

except Pittsburgh were east of the Appalachians or in western New York. The area of continuous settlement was spreading westward toward the Mississippi. But commercialization of the newly exploited land resources still awaited an effective network of transportation lines and cities.

The coming of the railroad brought drastic changes. A series of regional rail networks developed. The larger networks converged at critical port locations on the inland water-

ways that penetrated the vast agricultural land resource of the Interior Plains. Small networks or individual lines focused on the smaller ports. The emergence of these "great ports" of the Midwest accounted for most of the boom cities of the epoch (Figure 8) and laid the metropolitan base for an important part of the market-oriented industrial growth of the Steel-Rail Epoch. Limitations of technology made the rail networks generally tributary to the water-transport system; they

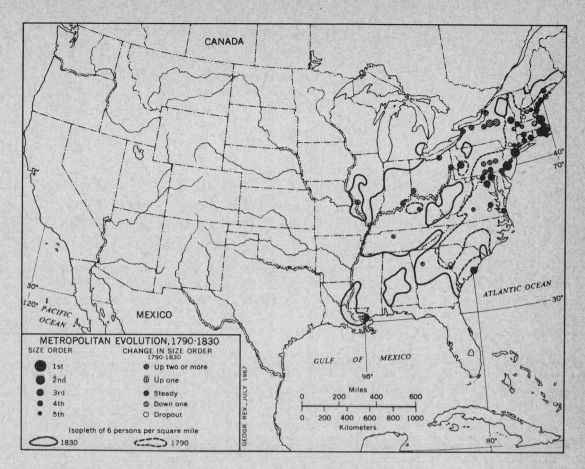

Figure 7. Changes in the order, major towns and neighboring counties, 1790-1830. Population-density isopleths generalized from Lord and Lord, *op. cit.* (see Figure 6), pp. 46 and 49.

were built outward from the major ports or to those ports from principal neighboring concentrations of farmland, mineral, or timber resources. In their initial effect they were therefore complementary to the waterways as long-haul general-freight carriers.

In the older settled areas of the North other important changes in the urban pattern emerged. Boom centers appeared in the anthracite fields, and Pittsburgh advanced to second order, where it would remain until the end of the Steel-Rail Epoch. These changes reflected the accelerated demand for coal

that came with the development of the railroad, the wider industrial application of steam, and accompanying changes in the iron industry. On the Atlantic seaboard New York became·a first-order center; it had been about the same size as Philadelphia at the beginning of the epoch, it was twice as large at the close.

Thus the urban pattern of the United States was revolutionized by the development of a national system of transportation, albeit a crude one. The epoch saw not only the emergence of a first-order center but also the

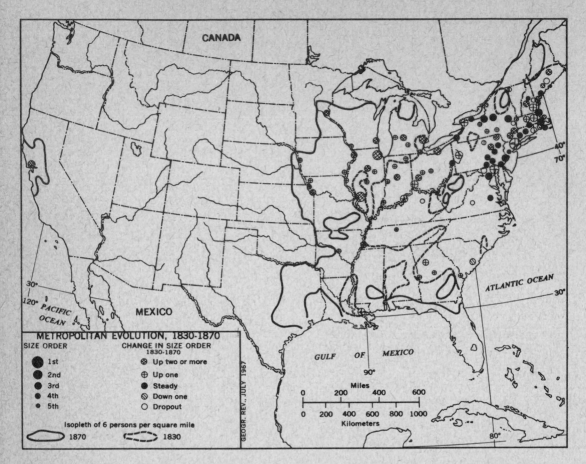

Figure 8. Changes in size order, major towns and neighboring counties, 1830-1870. Population-density isopleths generalized from Lord and Lord, *op. cit.*, pp. 49 and 104.

greatest increase, both relative and absolute, in the number of second- and third-order centers in the nation's history (Table II).

The map for this epoch (Figure 8) also reflects the aftermath of the Civil War and, probably more important, the slow rate of investment in urban, industrial, and transportation facilities in the South in the preceding decades. New Orleans was an exception. It was a critical point in the national transportation system that comprised the northern regional rail networks and the inland waterways. Before the Civil War it had risen to

third order and largest city in the South. Meanwhile Charleston, despite pioneer railroad building into its comparatively static agricultural hinterland, dropped to fourth order and began a prolonged relative decline.

Steel-Rail Epoch, 1870-1920

By 1870 major urban areas had arisen as far west as the Missouri River frontier, and one (Little Rock, Arkansas) had appeared west of the Mississippi in the South. Many resource concentrations remained unexploited

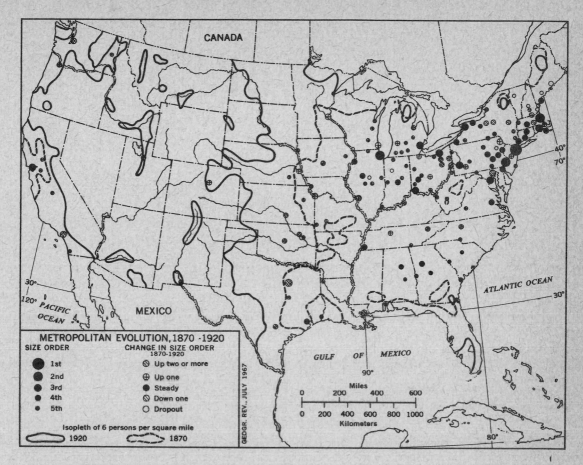

Figure 9. Emerging metropolitan areas in the Steel-Rail Epoch. Changes in size order of major cities, including neighboring county populations, 1870-1920. Population-density isopleths generalized from Lord and Lord, *op. cit.*, pp. 104 and 107-108. Sources of population data: "A Compendium of the Ninth Census" (1872) and "Abstract of the Fifteenth Census of the United States" (1933).

pending further improvement of the land transportation system and creation of a network of urban centers in the West and South. By the beginning of the following epoch all these regions had been knit together by a standardized, nationwide system of rail lines, and the modern pattern of major urban centers was beginning to emerge (Figure 9).

New urban centers reflected the opening or commercialization of the remaining important agricultural land resources of the West — the Texas and Oklahoma prairies, the Colorado piedmont, the Wasatch piedmont, the Central Valley and Southern California, the Puget Sound–Willamette lowland, and the Palouse. They also reflected the exploitation of hitherto isolated major mineral deposits, such as Butte copper, southwest Missouri lead and zinc, and Lake Superior iron ore, and of mineral and timber resources in the mountains adjoining the agricultural oases and valleys. Finally, they

TABLE II

Number of Centers and Total Population in Each Size Order

Size Order	1790	1830	1870	1920	1960
			Number of Centers		
First	0	0	1	1	1
Second	3	3	6	4	6
Third	8	8	14	16	19
Fourth	20	29	33	51	70
Fifth	8	12	37	75	82
Total	39	52	91	147	178
			Total Population (thousands)		
First	—	—	2,171	8,490	14,760
Second	514	1,120	3,301	10,364	28,826
Third	499	784	3,627	13,918	26,493
Fourth	530	1,812	2,533	12,829	30,473
Fifth	95	300	1,826	6,972	12,647
"SMSA" total	1,638	4,016	13,458	52,573	113,199
U.S. total	3,929	12,866	39,818	105,711	179,323

reflected the advance of the agriculture-timber-mineral frontier into Florida.

In the older settled areas the boom cities were associated mainly with the upward leap in the importance of coal — especially high-grade bituminous — that accompanied the growth of the modern iron and steel industry. A cluster of boom cities emerged on the western Pennsylvania coalfields and in the area between Pittsburgh and Lake Erie; and metropolitan Birmingham appeared on the map in the South. Other, but less spectacular, advances in rank occurred along the Norfolk-Toledo axis as long-haul technology opened the rich bituminous deposits of West Virginia and eastern Kentucky. Still others resulted from industrial growth based on the forest resources along the northern frontier of the agricultural Midwest and on the resources readily available for the hydroelectricity-based industrial development on the Piedmont in the South. Meantime, nearly all the great metropolitan commercial centers of the Midwest and Northeast, while establishing themselves as major industrial cities, retained their positions or advanced one level in the hierarchy.

Two groups of metropolitan areas accounted for most of the declines in size order in this epoch. The largest group comprised the towns along the Ohio–Mississippi–Missouri and principal tributaries. Smaller centers such as Dubuque and Quincy (Illinois) dropped out of the "metropolitan" ranks; St. Louis, Louisville, and Wheeling fell in the hierarchy, never to recover the relative positions they had held during the epoch of the steam packet and the iron horse. A second group consisted of a number of important industrial cities at historic waterpower sites along the Mohawk, the Merrimack, and the Blackstone and minor ports on the Hudson and the New England coast. None of these places was to regain the level it had held before the epoch of the steel rail and central-station electric power.

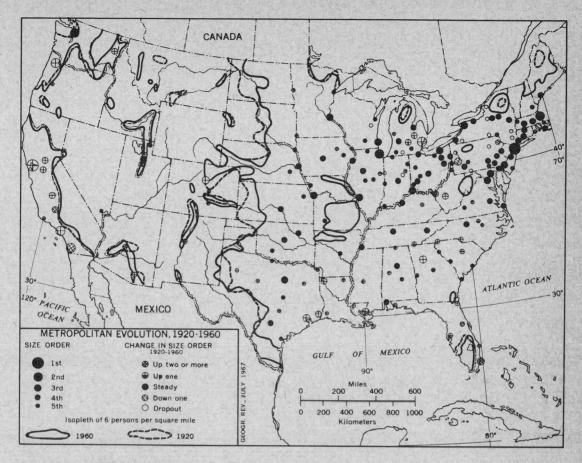

Figure 10. Changes in metropolitan-area size and distribution in the Auto-Air-Amenity Epoch, 1920-1960. Population-data source: *County and City Data Book, 1962*, U.S. Bureau of the Census. Population-density isopleths have been generalized from "Goode's World Atlas," 12th edit., 1964, p. 58.

The main shifts during the epoch are summarized in Table II. The new centralization of industry in major metropolitan areas was reflected in the growth of the five largest "SMSA's." That group increased its share of the national population faster than in any other epoch. The number of third- or higher-order centers, which had increased greatly in the Iron Horse Epoch, was stabilized, but their share of the nation's people rose sharply. The extension of national accessibility to isolated parts of the South and West augmented the number of lower-order metropolitan centers. The total number of fourth- and fifth-order cities registered its greatest growth in this epoch.

Auto-Air-Amenity Epoch, 1920-

By 1920 the present pattern of settled areas had been established, and subsequent metropolitan changes have taken place within that pattern. Nevertheless, new resources and

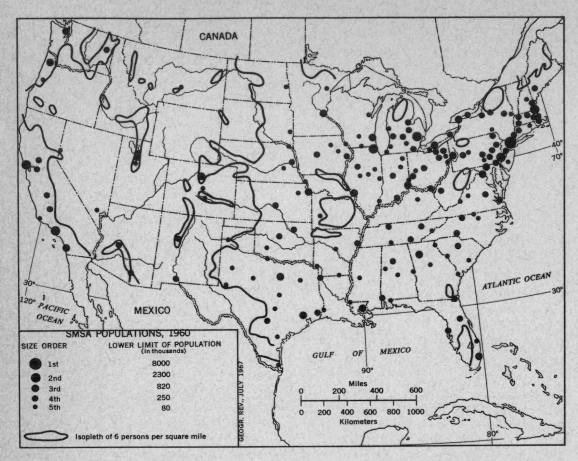

Figure 11. Geographic distribution of SMSA's by size order, 1960. Population-density isopleths have been generalized from "Goode's World Atlas," *op. cit.,* p. 58.

locations have been exploited and old ones abandoned (Figures 10 and 11).

The much smaller labor force required per unit of production in the extractive industries is reflected on the map in the relative decline of Butte and Joplin and, along with the shift from steam to internal combustion, in the decline of coal and railroad centers in the Appalachians and across the Midwest. The shift to internal combustion is, of course, largely behind the outbreak of new or higher-order metropolitan areas in the oil fields from central Kansas to western Texas and the western Gulf Coast and in the concentration of growth in the SMSA's of southern Michigan.

Regional and metropolitan dispersal, inherent in the shift to auto and truck and in the development of a dense highway network, is reflected on Figures 10 and 11 in two principal ways. One is the entry into the metropolitan ranks of numerous "satellite" cities on the fringes of the historic Manufacturing Belt and within 100 to 150 miles of great metropolitan industrial centers. The other is the effect of suburban dispersal on the definition of a metropolitan area. In the Appalachians, for example, half a dozen "SMSA's" have dropped out because their central cities failed to maintain a population equal to, or larger than, that of other metropolitan centers. In these cases it is typical to find a central city crowded on a valley floor, blighted by obsolescent buildings, air pollution, narrow streets, and rusty rail lines, and exposed to flood risk. Population and commercial growth have dispersed to the uplands to exploit the resources of open space, a dense rural road net, panoramic views, and relatively clean air. The result is that the metropolitan area has grown and ceased to be "metropolitan" by definition, and the central city has declined and ceased to be "central" in fact.

This diffusion of metropolitan structure is also evidence of the increasing importance of amenities in determining the growth pattern of individual cities and regions. The location of the boom centers is further evidence of the force of amenity on a national scale. All are in Florida, the desert Southwest, and Southern California. The migration to the Southwest and Florida in the Auto-Air-Amenity Epoch has been as massive as any in the earlier westward movement. There was a net migration of 11.4 million persons to California, Arizona, and Florida from other regions between 1920 and 1960. This equaled the total population[24] gain — and

[24] "Historical Statistics of the United States, Colonial Times to 1957" (U.S. Bureau of the Census, Washington, D.C., 1960), pp. 44-45 (1920-1960 migration data), p. 13 (1830-1870 population changes by states), and pp. 23-30 (early birth- and death-rate data); *Statistical Abstract of the United States 1965*, 86th edit., (Washington, D.C., 1965), U.S. Bureau of the Census, p. 34.

was probably double the immigration — for the twelve North Central States during the Iron Horse Epoch, 1830-1870.

At the regional scale the increase in importance of educational centers, related in part to the growing importance of amenity, is illustrated by two pairs of Midwestern cities. The coal-rail center of Danville, Illinois, dropped out of the "metropolitan area" group, and the nearby university center of Champaign-Urbana entered it. Among the urban centers of the old eastern Indiana gas belt, the industrial city of Anderson dropped out, and neighboring Muncie, with both industrial and university functions, entered.

Effects of Technological Change

Throughout the evolution of the present pattern of American metropolitan areas two factors, great migrations and major changes in technology, have particularly influenced the location of relative growth and decline. Both factors have repeatedly been given specific geographical expression through their relationship to resource patterns. Major changes in technology have resulted in critically important changes in the evaluation or definition of particular resources on which the growth of certain urban regions had previously been based. Great migrations have sought to exploit resources — ranging from climate or coal to water or zinc — that were either newly appreciated or newly accessible within the national market. Usually, of course, the new appreciation or accessibility had come about, in turn, through some major technological innovation.

Nor can one see the end of these changes in locational advantage due to technological change and migration. Speculate, for instances, on the possible outcome of three changes, quite conceivable within the next half-century whose seeds may well be lying in our midst at present. Assume the automation of, say, 80 percent of the office work heavily concentrated in the downtown skyscrapers of major metropolitan centers. Or assume the production of low-cost, mass-produced, single-family dwellings varied in style and superior in structure and maintenance to those now in use. Or assume the introduction and success of a lightweight family vehicle that requires neither steel to build nor oil to power. Clearly, the process of urban growth in an open system is open-ended. To be sure, the rate of change from any point in time is constrained by the existing physical plant and institutions. But there is unlikely to be any "end product" of the process. Each epoch will simply be succeeded by another.

VARYING PREDICTABILITY OF METROPOLITAN GROWTH

If metropolitan growth tends to be epochal and open-ended this suggests two probable characteristics of its predictability.

On the one hand, during any given epoch, similar conditions of paramount importance are likely to govern the rate and direction of growth over wide regions or types of location. Of course, countless short-term random effects are superimposed on the long-term trend. One might therefore expect the growth trend for a given metropolis during a given epoch to be regressive. That is, short-term spurts or declines will expectably be offset by succeeding short-term trends in the opposite direction. A regression line, fitted to the points representing these frequent ups and downs, describes the long-term trend. Thus the Upper Midwest Economic Study's urban research disclosed that past growth trends (during the automobile epoch) provided by

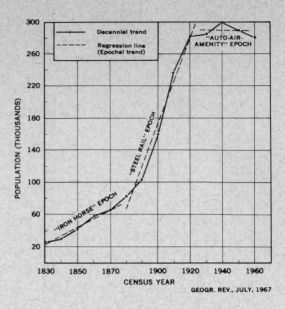

Figure 12. Population of the two counties comprising the Johnstown, Pa., SMSA (1960), by decades, 1830-1960. The depression of the 1930's, with its temporary decrease in mobility of a substantial economically "stranded" population, appears as a relatively short-term, low-amplitude event in the growth history in comparison with either the rise of the steel industry and dominance of steam-powered rail transportation or the advent of the internal-combustion engine.

far the most significant independent variable in a multiple regression equation to project 1950-1960 population growth rates of urban areas in its study region.[25]

On the other hand, when some basic component of the nation's society or economy or technology "turns a corner" and a new epoch opens, a new set of overriding and "long-term" forces goes into effect. Thereafter, one might expect past growth to cease to be a

25 John R. Borchert and Russell B. Adams, "Projected Urban Growth in the Upper Midwest: 1960-1975," *Upper Midwest Economic Study Urban Rept. No. 8,* (Minneapolis, 1964), pp. 1-2 and Appendix.

good predictor. At the least, its validity would have to be reestablished for a new set of conditions. The old regression line for a given metropolitan area would not necessarily represent the long-term growth trend in the new epoch. Short-term fluctuations would be less likely to regress toward the same line as in the preceding epoch (Figure 12).

As the new epoch unfolds, a new pattern of "initial advantage" also emerges; for certain advantages are created that could not have existed before.[26] Business and civic institutions must reorganize to meet new challenges. This seems to have been done most effectively in the places least tied to natural-resource exploitation or secondary production, and with the largest and most diversified hinterlands, hence the most important centers of circulation and management. Even some of the high-order centers have had to make massive adjustments from one epoch to the next; St. Louis and Pittsburgh are probably the outstanding cases so far.

INTERNAL DIFFERENTIATION OF METROPOLITAN AREAS

During each epoch a new increment of phy-

sical development has been added to each metropolitan area. Each increment is eventually differentiated from the adjoining ones not only by the age of its structures but also by their scale, design, use, degree of obsolescence, and, often, site or location. The successive increments form distinctive regions in the internal geography of any metropolitan area, and the regions have certain characteristics in common wherever they appear across the country.

But historically different increments tend to differentiate American cities at least as much as they tend to standardize them (Figure 13), because cities differ profoundly in their epoch of initial settlement and in their periods of boom or decline. For example, it is possible that a Chicago or a Los Angeles metropolitan area will someday be as populous as the present metropolitan area of New York. But both are most unlikely to have a physical structure similar to New York's, even aside from the differences among the natural settings. Chicago's growth so far belongs 47 percent to the Steel-Rail Epoch and 45 percent to the Auto-Air-Amenity Epoch; corresponding percentages for Los Angeles are 15 and 85 (Table III). Hence their historical increments have been markedly different, and their future increments will belong to a different technology from that which has built present-day New York.

If the system is indeed evolving and open-ended, it is patently incorrect to consider either Los Angeles or Chicago illustrative of a stage en route to the development of another New York or, for that matter, to consider any American city to be at any stage in any rigid model of development.

EXPLOITATION OF LAND

America's metropolitan centers grew initially

[26] This suggests a modification of Allan Pred's model of self-generating urban growth during a period of rapid industrialization (Pred, *op. cit.*) Innovation in a particular industry, because of its impact on the evaluation of a particular resource, may result in new or expanded industry at a place other than the one at which the innovation occurred. In that case, the flow of benefits may be diverted to a new location. The observed evolution also suggests that technological change may be considered an integral part of the basic process that generates an urban hierarchy. Although this was recognized by Walter Christaller in the section on "Dynamic Processes" in his *Central Places in Southern Germany* translated by Carlisle W. Baskin (Englewood Cliffs, N.J., 1966), pp. 84-132, technological change has generally been handled as a secondary "modifier" of the basic model.

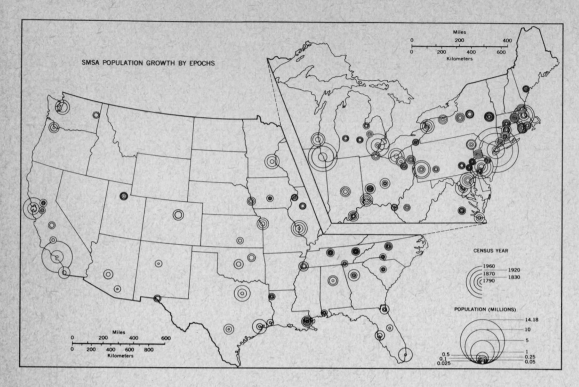

Figure 13. The varied historical layering of American SMSA's in 1960.

on land whose sites and locations were regarded as advantageous, given the contemporary technology and migration pattern. Improvement and use of the land made redevelopment or restoration much more costly, if not impossible. At first the land was "improved;" but as the improvements aged and grew obsolete the land appeared instead to have been "despoiled". New technologies hastened obsolescence and transferred the locational and site advantages to other land. Men moved to this new land and began again the sequence of improvement and abandonment: they abandoned the obsolete buildings, locations, or cities to those who remained behind to adapt and abandon in their turn.

This sequence of land selection in the light of existing technology, development, use,

despoliation, and abandonment has characterized in varying degree the past utilization of timber, soil, water, and mineral resources. It appears also to have characterized the use of land for urban purposes. The process can be visualized at three different scales on the accompanying maps. At the metropolitan scale it is illustrated by the partial abandonment of the central city for outlying areas during successive technological epochs; at the regional scale, by the shift of new development from mining towns to university towns, from railroad centers to recreational centers; at the national scale, by the shift from older cities in the Northeast to newer cities in the Southwest or Florida. It could be argued that, at any scale, the basic attitude toward the potential urban land resource has

TABLE III

Percentages of Populations of Selected 1960 SMSA's Attained in Major Historical Epochs

Size Order	SMSA[a]	Wagon-Sail Pre-1830	Iron Horse 1830-1870	Steel Rail 1870-1920	Auto-Air Amenity 1920-1960
First	New York[b]	3	11	44	42
Second	Philadelphia	9	15	38	38
	Boston[c]	9	18	48	25
	Chicago[b]	0	8	47	45
	Detroit	0	6	29	65
	San Francisco-Oakland and San Jose	0	7	27	66
	Los Angeles	0	0+	15	85
Third	Washington	5	5	19	71
	Pittsburgh	7	10	56	27
	St. Louis	2	21	34	43
	New Orleans	7	18	23	52
	Seattle-Tacoma	0	0+	42	58
	Denver	0	1	35	64
	Dallas and Fort Worth	0	3	30	67
	Miami and Fort Lauderdale	0	0	4	96
Fourth	Albany-Schenectady-Troy	23	25	23	29
	New Bedford and Fall River	13	12	65	10
	Scranton and Wilkes-Barre-Hazelton	4	20	63	13
	Birmingham	1	1	47	51
	Omaha	0	10	50	40
	Flint	0	7	27	66
	Jacksonville	0	3	22	75
	Phoenix	0	0	14	86
Fifth	Corpus Christi	0	2	8	90
	Altoona	0	21	72	7
	Charleston, S.C.	40	1	9	50
	Lubbock	0	0	7	93
	Las Vegas	0	0	4	96

[a]1960 SMSA except where noted to contrary.
[b]Standard consolidated area.
[c]Norfolk, Suffolk and Middlesex Counties.

been exploitive. There is no general provision for "recycling" the resource of developed land when the initial development has become obsolete.

The result is a gigantic, national "filter down" process with important geographical and historical dimensions. The nation's new construction has been concentrated, in any given epoch, not only in new neighborhoods and new suburbs but also in what have been, for all practical purposes, new cities (Table III). The residue of obsolescent physical plant has also become concentrated, not only in certain districts of most cities but in virtually the entire area of some. Vast big-city cores and nearly the whole of some smaller metropolitan areas are approaching the condition of inhabited ruins, and the residue of old structures continues to expand, thanks to the lagging national rate of replacement. Analysis of available historical housing data indicates that the construction of new dwelling units over the first sixty years of the twentieth century was enough to replace, on the average, only 4 percent of the units standing at the end of each decade.[27] For later generations the legacy of buildings, like the earlier "natural" endowment, has become an exploitable physical resource.

On the one hand, the traditional exploitive development of the land resource for urban purposes is understandable in view of the abundance of undeveloped land, the high costs of acquiring and clearing used land, and the high replacement costs under prevailing conditions.[28] On the other hand, the growing accumulation and low level of maintenance of obsolescent districts and cities suggest the inadequacy of the present approach.

ADAPTABILITY AND CONTROL

Two major problems seem to result from the

[27] John R. Borchert, Earl E. Stewart, and Sherman S. Hasbrouck, "Urban Renewal: Needs and Opportunities in the Upper Midwest," *Upper Midwest Economic Study Urban Rept. No. 5* (Minneapolis, 1963), pp. 1-4.

[28] Louis F. Winnick, "Housing and Urban Development: The Private Foundation's Role" (New York, The Ford Foundation, 1965), p. 3, makes the following observations: "No other important consumer good has been as inflation-prone as housing. Over the past seventy years the cost of a unit of housing space has risen twice as fast as other costs." Also, Chauncy D. Harris has pointed out the very small fraction of the land resource required by cities in "The Pressure of Residential-Industrial Land Use," in *Man's Role in Changing the Face of the Earth* edited by William L. Thomas, Jr., (Chicago, 1956), pp. 881-95, reference on p. 889.

nature of metropolitan evolution. First, long-term changes in size and physical character are highly uncertain. Second, the exploitation of new land and accompanying abandonment of old in successive periods lead to a gigantic accumulation of residual structures. This residue is a drag on both the improvement of the general health and welfare and the market for new, low-cost buildings.

It appears unlikely that the tendencies inherent in this evolutionary process will change significantly. To be sure, the fraction of the total number of metropolitan areas that changed size order diminished during the Steel-Rail and Auto-Air-Amenity Epochs. Also, there have been fewer booms (Table IV). This increasing stabilization was to be expected as the national transportation network was completed and improved and nearly every part of the country raised its level of participation in the national economy.[29] Nevertheless, metropolitan areas continue to grow at differential rates. There has been virtually no decrease over the past two epochs in the number of places that advanced one rank in the size order, and only a slight decrease in the number that declined one rank. At the beginning of each epoch a major change in technology registered its impact on the values of existing metropolitan locations and on the pattern of migration; and some new cities were also established. As long as America remains an open society, there will surely be unforeseen major changes affecting old cities and new alike — new rounds of initial advantage, reorganization, and adaptation, new reasons to exploit new land and abandon old.

Given the two problems of uncertainty and migration-abandonment, pressure is

[29] Lukermann, *op. cit.*

TABLE IV

Number of SMSA's and Emerging SMSA's Experiencing Shifts in Size Order

Shift in Size Order	1790-1830	1830-1870	1870-1920	1920-1960
Up one rank	7	37	66	65
Up two ranks	11	16	15	6
Up three ranks	2	4	3	1
Up four ranks	0	1	0	0
Down one rank	10	14	25	20
Down two ranks	2	2	2	0
Steady	26	24	49	103
New entries	19	47	69	48
Dropouts	6	8	13	17
Net increase	13	39	56	31

mounting to make the metropolitan settlement pattern more adaptable to change. For this purpose two types of development appear to be of great potential importance. One is the production, for the full range of urban functions, of soundly engineered and attractively designed structures that can be emplaced or removed at much lower costs than in the past.[30] The other is the improvement of information-education systems[31] to increase the extent, accuracy, and currency of knowledge of the changing metropolis. An important consequence of this might be the development of a degree of public objectivity that would permit more rapid adaptation of institutions, notably local government.[32]

On the other hand, one might expect mounting pressure to create new institutions and shift values in order to retard the rate of change and thereby reduce the need for rapid and massive adaptation. For example, in some cases truly comprehensive, long-range planning could lower the permissible rate of technological change throughout an urban or regional system to that of the least tractable, slowest-changing component of the system, in the interest of preserving orderly development.

The mounting pressures for greater adaptability and greater control may often conflict. Where and how to compromise them seems likely to be an important and recurring issue in the future course of American metropoli-

[30] For a concise recent summary of one aspect of this topic see William K. Wittausch, "New Concepts for the Housing Industry," *Urban Land*, Vol. XXV, no. 5 (1966), pp. 11-12.

[31] See Edward F. R. Hearle and Raymond J. Mason, *A Data Processing System for State and Local Governments* (Englewood Cliffs, N.J., 1963). Chapter 4 presents a long list of classes of data now generally noncomparable and incomplete in coverage that will inevitably be standardized and automated yet already form a vital body of information about the internal geography and other aspects of the structure of each metropolitan area. See also W. L. Garrison, "Urban Transportation Planning Models in 1975," *Journ. Amer. Inst. of Planners*, Vol. 31, (1965), pp. 156-58. This is an extension of the logic of Garrison's forecast of traffic planning that assumes more rapid adjustment to crises, through improved information systems and designs. See also Edward L. Ullman, "The Nature of Cities Reconsidered," *Papers and Proc. Regional Science Assn.*, Vol. 9 (1962), pp. 7-23.

[32] See Robert C. Wood, "1400 Governments," with Vladimir V. Almendinger, New York Metropolitan Region Study, Vol. 8 (Cambridge, Mass., 1961), especially the introductory and concluding chapters.

tan evolution. Furthermore, the issue is likely to be debated and resolved on many different grounds, since no one city is the evolutionary prototype for all others.

5

A Theory for the
Location of Cities

Edward L. Ullman

I

Periodically in the past century the location and distribution of cities and settlements have been studied. Important contributions have been made by individuals in many disciplines. Partly because of the diversity and un-coordinated nature of the attack and partly because of the complexities and variables involved, a systematic theory has been slow to evolve, in contrast to the advances in the field of industrial location.[1]

The first theoretical statement of modern importance was von Thünen's *Der isolierte Staat*, initially published in 1826, wherein he postulated an entirely uniform land surface

[1] CF. Tord Palander, *Beitragezur Standortstheorie* (Uppsala, Sweden, 1935), or E. M. Hoover, Jr., *Location Theory and the Shoe and Leather Industries* (Cambridge, Mass., 1937).

Reprinted from *American Journal of Sociology*, Vol. XLVI, (May, 1941), pp. 853-64 by permission of the author.

and showed that under ideal conditions a city would develop in the center of this land area and concentric rings of land use would develop around the central city. In 1841 Kohl investigated the relation between cities and the natural and cultural environment, paying particular attention to the effect of transport routes on the location of urban centers.[2] In 1894 Cooley admirably demonstrated the channelizing influence that transportation routes, particularly rail, would have on the location and development of trade centers.[3] He also called attention to break in transportation as a city-builder just as Ratzel had earlier. In 1927 Haig sought to determine why there was such a large concentration of population and manufacturing in the largest cities.[4] Since concentration occurs where assembly of material is cheapest, all business functions, except extraction and transportation, ideally should be located in cities where transportation is least costly. Exceptions are provided by the processing of perishable goods, as in sugar centrals, and of large weight-losing commodities, as in smelters. Haig's theoretical treatment is of a different type from those just cited but should be included as an excellent example of a "concentration" study.

In 1927 Bobeck[5] showed that German geographers since 1899, following Schlüter and others, had concerned themselves largely with the internal geography of cities, with the pattern of land use and forms within the urban limits, in contrast to the problem of location and support of cities. Such preoccupation with internal urban structure has also characterized the recent work of geographers in America and other countries. Bobeck insisted with reason that such studies, valuable though they were, constituted only half the field of urban geography and that there remained unanswered the fundamental geographical question: "What are the causes for the existence, present size, and character of a city?" Since the publication of this article, a number of urban studies in Germany and some in other countries have dealt with such questions as the relations between city and country.[6]

II

A theoretical framework for study of the distribution of settlements is provided by the work of Walter Christaller.[7] The essence of the theory is that a certain amount of productive land supports an urban center. The center exists because essential services must be performed for the surrounding land. Thus the primary factor explaining Chicago is the productivity of the Middle West; location at

[2] J. G. Kohl, *Der Verkehr und die Ansiedlungen der Menschen in ihrer Abhangikeit von der Gestaltung der Erdoberflache*, 2nd. ed., (Leipzig, 1850).

[3] C. H. Cooley, "The Theory of Transportation," *Publications of the American Economic Association*, Vol. IX (May, 1894), pp. 1-148.

[4] R. M. Haig, "Toward an Understanding of the Metropolis: Some Speculations Regarding the Economic Basis of Urban Concentration," *Quarterly Journal of Economics*, Vol. XL (1926), pp. 179-208.

[5] Hans Bobeck, "Grundfragen der Stadt Geographie," *Geographischer Anzeiger*, Vol. XXVIII (1927), pp. 213-24.

[6] A section of the International Geographical Congress at Amsterdam in 1938 dealt with "Functional Relations between City and Country." The papers are published in Vol. II of the *Comptes rendus* (Leiden: E. J. Brill, 1938). A recent American study is C. D. Harris, *Salt Lake City: A Regional Capital* (Ph.D. diss., University of Chicago, 1940). Pertinent also is R. E. Dickinson, "The Metropolitan Regions of the United States," *Geographical Review*, Vol. XXIV (1934), pp. 278-91.

[7] *Die zentralen Orte in Suddeutschland* (Jena, 1935); also a paper (no title) in *Comptes rendus du Congres international de geographie Amsterdam* (1938), Vol. II, pp. 123-37.

the southern end of Lake Michigan is a secondary factor. If there were no Lake Michigan, the urban population of the Middle West would in all probability be just as large as it is now. Ideally, the city should be in the center of a productive area.[8] The similarity of this concept to von Thünen's original proposition is evident.

Apparently many scholars have approached the scheme in their thinking.[9] Bobeck claims he presented the rudiments of such an explanation in 1927. The work of a number of American rural sociologists shows appreciation for some of Christaller's preliminary assumptions, even though done before or without knowledge of Christaller's work and performed with a different end in view. Galpin's epochal study of trade areas in Walworth County, Wisconsin, published in 1915, was the first contribution. Since then important studies bearing on the problem have been made by others. These studies are confined primarily to smaller trade centers but give a wealth of information[10] on distribution of settlements which independently substantiates many of Christaller's basic premises.

As a working hypothesis one assumes that normally the larger the city, the larger its tributary area. Thus there should be cities of varying size ranging from a small hamlet performing a few simple functions, such as providing a limited shopping and market center for a small contiguous area, up to a large city with a large tributary area composed of the service areas of many smaller towns and providing more complex services, such as wholesaling, large-scale banking, specialized retailing, and the like. Services performed purely for a surrounding area are termed "central" functions by Christaller,

---

[8] This does not deny the importance of "gateway" centers such as Omaha and Kansas City, cities located between contrasting areas in order to secure exchange benefits. The logical growth of cities at such locations does not destroy the theory to be presented — cf. R. D. McKenzie's excellent discussion in *The Metropolitan Community* (New York, 1933), pp. 4 ff.

[9] Cf. Petrie's statement about ancient Egypt and Mesopotamia: "It has been noticed before how remarkably similar the distances are between the early nome capitals of the Delta (twenty-one miles on an average) and the early cities of Mesopotamia (averaging twenty miles apart). Some physical cause seems to limit the primitive rule in this way. Is it not the limit of central storage of grain, which is the essential form of early capital? Supplies could be centralized up to ten miles away; beyond that the cost of transport made it better worth while to have a nearer centre" — W. M. Flinders Petrie, *Social Life in Ancient Egypt* (London, 1923; reissued, 1932), pp. 3-4.

[10] C. J. Galpin, "Social Anatomy of an Agricultural Community," University of Wisconsin Agricultural Experiment Station Research Bull. 34 (1915), and the restudy by J. H. Kolb and R. A. Polson, "Trends in Town-Country Relations, University of Wisconsin Agricultural Experiment Station Research Bull. 117 (1933); B. L. Melvin, "Village Service Agencies of New York State, 1925," Cornell University Agricultural Experiment Station Bull. 493 (1929), and "Rural Population of New York, 1855-1925, Cornell University Agricultural Experiment Station Memoir 116 (1928); Dwight Sanderson, *The Rural Community* (New York, 1932), esp. pp. 488-514, which contains references to many studies by Sanderson and his associates; Carle C. Zimmerman, "Farm Trade Centers in Minnesota, 1905-29," University of Minnesota Agricultural Experiment Station Bull. 269 (1930); T. Lynn Smith, "Farm Trade Centers in Louisiana 1905 to 1931," Louisiana State University Bull. 234 (1933); Paul H. Landis, "South Dakota Agricultural Experiment Station Bull. 274 (1932), and "The Growth and Decline of South Dakota Trade Centers, 1901-1933," Bull. 279 (1938), and "Washington Farm Trade Centers, 1900-1935," State College of Washington Agricultural Experiment Station Bull. 360 (1938). Other studies are listed in subsequent footnotes.

and the settlements performing them "central" places. An industry using raw materials imported from outside the local region and shipping its products out of the local area would not constitute a central service.

Ideally, each central place would have a circular tributary area, as in von Thünen's proposition, and the city would be in the center. However, if three or more tangent circles are inscribed in an area, unserved spaces will exist; the best theoretical shapes are hexagons, the closest geometrical figures to circles which will completely fill an area (Figure I).[11]

Christaller has recognized typical-size settlements, computed their average population, their distance apart, and the size and population of their tributary areas in accordance with his hexagonal theory as Table I shows. He also states that the number of central places follows a norm from largest to smallest in the following order: 1:2:6:18:54, etc.[12]

All these figures are computed on the basis of South Germany, but Christaller claims them to be typical for most of Germany and western Europe. The settlements are classified on the basis of spacing each larger unit

in a hexagon of next-order size, so that the distance between similar centers in the table above increases by the $\sqrt{3}$ over the preceding smaller category (in Figure I, e.g., the distance from A to B is $\sqrt{3}$ times the distance from A to C). The initial distance figure of 7 km. between the smallest centers is chosen because 4–5 km., approximately the distance one can walk in one hour, appears to be a normal service-area limit for the smallest centers. Thus, in a hexagonal scheme, these centers are about 7 km. apart. Christaller's maps indicate that such centers are spaced close to this norm in South Germany. In the larger categories the norms for distance apart and size of centers appear to be true averages; but variations from the norm are the rule, although wide discrepancies are not common in the eastern portion of South Germany, which is less highly industrialized than the Rhine-Ruhr areas in the west. The number of central places of each rank varies rather widely from the normal order of expectancy.

The theoretical ideal appears to be most nearly approached in poor, thinly settled farm districts — areas which are most nearly self-contained. In some other sections of Germany industrial concentration seems to be a more important explanation, although

---

[11] See August Lösch, "The Nature of the Economic Regions," *Southern Economic Journal*, Vol. V (1938), p. 73. Galpin (*op. cit.*) thought in terms of six tributary-area circles around each center. See also Kolb and Polson, *op. cit.*, pp. 30-41.

[12] Barnes and Robinson present some interesting maps showing the average distance apart of farmhouses in the driftless area of the Middle West and in southern Ontario. Farmhouses might well be regarded as the smallest settlement units in a central-place scheme, although they might not be in the same numbered sequence (James A. Barnes and Arthur H. Robinson, "A New Method for the Representation of Dispersed Rural Population," *Geographical Review*, Vol. XXX (1940), pp. 134-37).

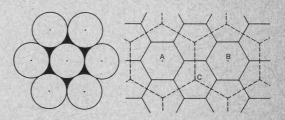

Figure 1. Theoretical shapes of tributary areas. Circles leave unserved spaces, hexagons do not. Small hexagons are service areas for smaller places, large hexagons (dotted lines) represent service areas for next higher-rank central places.

TABLE I

	Towns		Tributary Areas	
Central Place	Distance Apart (Km.)	Population	Size (Sq. Km.)	Population
Market hamlet (*Marktort*)	7	800	45	2,700
Township center (*Amtsort*)	12	1,500	135	8,100
County seat (*Kreisstadt*)	21	3,500	400	24,000
District city (*Bezirksstadt*)	36	9,000	1,200	75,000
Small state capital (*Gaustadt*)	62	27,000	3,600	225,000
Provincial head city (*Provinzhauptstadt*)	108	90,000	10,800	675,000
Regional capital city (*Landeshauptstadt*)	186	300,000	32,400	2,025,000

elements of the central-place type of distribution are present. Christaller points out that Cologne is really the commercial center for the Ruhr industrial district even though it is outside the Ruhr area. Even in mountain areas centrality is a more important factor than topography in fixing the distribution of settlements. Christaller states that one cannot claim that a certain city is where it is because of a certain river — that would be tantamount to saying that if there were no rivers there would be no cities.

III

Population alone is not a true measure of the central importance of a city; a large mining, industrial, or other specialized-function town might have a small tributary area and exercise few central functions. In addition to population, therefore, Christaller uses an index based on number of telephones in proportion to the average number per thousand inhabitants in South Germany, weighted further by the telephone density of the local subregion. A rich area such as the Palatinate supports more telephones in proportion to population than a poor area in the Bavarian Alps; therefore, the same number of tele-

phones in a Palatinate town would not give it the same central significance as in the Alps. He claims that telephones, since they are used for business, are a reliable index of centrality. Such a thesis would not be valid for most of the United States, where telephones are as common in homes as in commercial and professional quarters.

Some better measures of centrality could be devised, even if only the number of out-of-town telephone calls per town. Better still would be some measure of actual central services performed. It would be tedious and difficult to compute the amount, or percentage, of business in each town drawn from outside the city, but some short cuts might be devised. If one knew the average number of customers required to support certain specialized functions in various regions, then the excess of these functions over the normal required for the urban population would be an index of centrality.[13] In several states rural sociologists and others have computed the

13 In Iowa, e.g., almost all towns of more than 450 inhabitants have banks, half of the towns of 250-300, and 20 per cent of the towns of 100-150 (according to calculations made by the author from population estimates in *Rand McNally's Commercial Atlas for 1937*).

average number of certain functions for towns of a given size. With one or two exceptions only small towns have been analyzed. Retail trade has received most attention, but professional and other services have also been examined. These studies do not tell us actually what population supports each service, since the services are supported both by towns and by surrounding rural population, but they do provide norms of function expectancy which would be just as useful.[14]

A suggestive indicator of centrality is provided by the maps which Dickinson has made for per capita wholesale sales of cities in the United States.[15] On this basis centers are distributed rather evenly in accordance with regional population density. Schlier has computed the centrality of cities in Germany on

the basis of census returns for "central" occupations.[16] Refinement of some of our census returns is desirable before this can be done entirely satisfactorily in the United States, but the method is probably the most promising in prospect.

Another measure of centrality would be the number of automobiles entering a town, making sure that suburban movements were not included. Figures could be secured if the state-wide highway planning surveys in forty-six states were extended to gather such statistics.

IV

The central-place scheme may be distorted by local factors, primarily industrial concentration or main transport routes. Christaller notes that transportation is not an areally operating principle, as the supplying of central goods implies, but is a linearly working factor. In many cases central places are strung at short intervals along an important transport route, and their tributary areas do not approximate the ideal circular or hexagonal shape but are elongated at right angles to the main transport line.[17] In some areas the reverse of this normal expectancy is true. In most of Illinois, maps depicting tributary areas show them to be elongated

[14] See particularly the thorough study by B. L. Melvin, "Village Service Agencies, New York State 1925"; C. R. Hoffer, "A Study of Town-Country Relationships, Michigan Agricultural Experiment Station Special Bull. 181 (1928), (data on number of retail stores and professions per town); H. B. Price and C. R. Hoffer, "Services of Rural Trade Centers in Distribution of Farm Supplies," Minnesota Agricultural Experiment Station Bull. 249 (1938); William J. Reilly, "Methods for the Study of Retail Relationships," Bureau of Business Monographs, no. 4, University of Texas Bull. 2944 (1929), p. 26; J. H. Kolb, "Service Institutions of Town and Country," Wisconsin Agricultural Experiment Station Research Bull. 66 (1925) (town size in relation to support of institutions); Smith, *op. cit.*, pp. 32-40; Paul H. Landis, South Dakota Town-Country Trade Relations, 1901-1931," p. 20 (population per business enterprise), and pp. 24-25 (functions per town size); Zimmerman, *op. cit.*, pp. 16 and 51 ff.

For a criticism of population estimates of unincorporated hamlets used in many of these studies see Glenn T. Trewartha, "The Unincorporated Hamlet: An Analysis of Data Sources," (paper presented December 28 at Baton Rouge meetings, Association of American Geographers; forthcoming, probably, in March number of *Rural Sociology*, Vol. VI (1941).)

[15] *Ibid.*, pp. 280-81.

[16] Otto Schlier, "Die zentralen Orte des Deutschen Reichs," *Zeitschrift der Gesellschaft für Erdkunde zu Berlin* (1937), pp. 161-70. See also map constructed from Schlier's figures in R. E. Dickinson's valuable article, "The Economic Regions of Germany," *Geographical Review*, Vol. XXVIII (1938), p. 619. For use of census figures in the United States see Harris, *op. cit.*, pp. 3-12.

[17] For an illustration of this type of tributary area in the ridge and valley section of east Tennessee see H. V. Miller, "Effects of Reservoir Construction on Local Economic Units," *Economic Geography*, Vol. XV (1939), pp. 242-49.

parallel to the main transport routes, not at right angles to them.[18] The combination of nearly uniform land and competitive railways peculiar to the state results in main railways running nearly parallel and close to one another between major centers.

In highly industrialized areas the central-place scheme is generally so distorted by industrial concentration in response to resources and transportation that it may be said to have little significance as an explanation for urban location and distribution, although some features of a central-place scheme may be present, as in the case of Cologne and the Ruhr (p. 858).

In addition to distortion, the type of scheme prevailing in various regions is susceptible to many influences. Productivity of the soil,[19] type of agriculture and intensity of cultivation, topography, governmental organization, are all obvious modifiers. In the United States, for example, what is the effect on distribution of settlements caused by the sectional layout of the land and the regular size of counties in many states? In parts of Latin America many centers are known as "Sunday towns"; their chief functions appear to be purely social, to act as religious and recreational centers for holidays — hence the name "Sunday town."[20] Here social rather than economic services are the primary support of towns, and we should accordingly expect a system of central places with fewer and smaller centers, because fewer functions are performed and people can travel farther more readily than commodities. These underlying differences do not destroy the value of the theory; rather they provide variations of interest to study for themselves and for purposes of comparison with other regions.

The system of central places is not static or fixed; rather it is subject to change and development with changing conditions.[21] Improvements in transportation have had noticeable effects. The provision of good automobile roads alters buying and marketing practices, appears to make the smallest centers smaller and the larger centers larger, and generally alters trade areas.[22] Since good

[18] See, e.g., *Marketing Atlas of the United States* (New York, International Magazine Co., Inc.) or *A Study of Natural Areas of Trade in the United States* (Washington, D.C., U.S. National Recovery Administration, 1935).

[19] Cf. the emphasis of Sombart, Adam Smith, and other economists on the necessity of surplus produce of land in order to support cities. Fertile land ordinarily produces more surplus and consequently more urban population, although "the town . . . may not always derive its whole subsistence from the country in its neighborhood. . . ." Adam Smith, *The Wealth of Nations*, "Modern Library" edition, (New York, 1937), p. 357; Werner Sombart, *Der moderne Kapitalismus* (zweite, neugearbeitete Auflage, Munich and Leipzig, 1916), Vol. I, pp. 130-31).

[20] For an account of such settlements in Brazil see Pierre Deffontaines, "Rapports fonctionnels entre les agglomérations urbaines et rurales: un example en pays de colonisation, le Brésil," *Comptes rendus du Congrès internationale ae géographie Amsterdam*, Vol. II (1938), pp. 139-44.

[21] The effects of booms, droughts, and other factors on trade-centre distribution by decades are brought out in Landis' studies for South Dakota and Washington. Zimmerman and Smith also show the changing character of trade-center distribution (see footnote 10 of this paper for references). Melvin calls attention to a "village population shift lag"; in periods of depressed agriculture villages in New York declined in population approximately a decade after the surrounding rural population had decreased (B. L. Melvin, *Rural Population of New York, 1855-1925*, p. 120).

[22] Most studies indicate that only the very smallest hamlets (under 250 population) and crossroads stores have declined in size or number. The larger small places have held their own (see

roads are spread more uniformly over the land than railways, their provision seems to make the distribution of centers correspond more closely to the normal scheme.[23]

Christaller may be guilty of claiming too great an application of his scheme. His criteria for determining typical-size settlements and their normal number apparently do not fit actual frequency counts of settlements in

Landis for Washington, *op. cit.*, p. 37, and his *South Dakota Town-Country Trade Relations 1901-1931*, pp. 34-36). Zimmerman in 1930 (*op. cit.*, p. 41) notes that crossroads stores are disappearing and are being replaced by small villages. He states further: "It is evident that claims of substantial correlation between the appearance and growth of the larger trading center and the disappearance of the primary center are more or less unfounded. Although there are minor relationships, the main change has been a division of labor between the two types of centers rather than the complete obliteration of the smaller in favor of the larger" (p. 32).

For further evidences of effect of automobile on small centers see R. V. Mitchell, *Trends in Rural Retailing in Illinois 1926 to 1938*, University of Illinois Bureau of Business Research Bull., Ser. 59 (1939), pp. 31 ff., and Sanderson, *op. cit.*, p. 564, as well as other studies cited above.

[23] Smith (*op. cit.*, p. 54) states: "There has been a tendency for centers of various sizes to distribute themselves more uniformly with regard to the area, population, and resources of the state. Or the changes seem to be in the direction of a more efficient pattern of rural organization. This redistribution of centers in conjunction with improved methods of communication and transportation has placed each family in frequent contact with several trade centers. . . ."

In contrast, Melvin (*Rural Population of New York, 1855-1925*, p. 90), writing about New York State before the automobile had had much effect, states: "In 1870 the villages . . . were rather evenly scattered over the entire state where they had been located earlier in response to particular local needs. By 1920, however, the villages had become distributed more along routes of travel and transportation and in the vicinity of cities."

many almost uniform regions as well as some less rigidly deductive norms.[24]

Bobeck in a later article claims that Christaller's proof is unsatisfactory.[25] He states that two-thirds of the population of Germany and England live in cities and that only one-third of these cities in Germany are real central places. The bulk are primarily industrial towns or villages inhabited solely by farmers. He also declares that exceptions in the rest of the world are common, such as the purely rural districts of the Tonkin Delta of Indo-China, cities based on energetic entrepreneurial activity, as some Italian cities, and world commercial ports such as London, Rotterdam, and Singapore. Many of these objections are valid; one wishes that Christaller had better quantitative data and was less vague in places. Bobeck admits, however, that the central-place theory has value and applies in some areas.

The central-place theory probably provides as valid an interpretation of settlement distribution over the land as the concentric-zone theory does for land use within cities. Neither theory is to be thought of as a rigid framework fitting all location facts at a given moment. Some, expecting too much, would jettison the concentric-zone theory; others, realizing that it is an investigative hypothesis of merit, regard it as a useful tool for comparative analysis.

V

Even in the closely articulated national economy of the United States there are strong

[24] This statement is made on the basis of frequency counts by the author for several midwestern states (cf. also Schlier, *op. cit.*, pp. 165-69, for Germany).

[25] Hans Bobeck, "über einige functionelle Stadttypen und ihre Beziehungen zum Lande," *Comptes rendus du Congrès internationale de géographie Amsterdam*, Vol. II (1938), p. 88.

forces at work to produce a central-place distribution of settlements. It is true that products under our national economy are characteristically shipped from producing areas through local shipping points directly to consuming centers which are often remote. However, the distribution of goods or imports brought into an area is characteristically carried on through brokerage, wholesale and retail channels in central cities.[26] This graduated division of functions supports a central-place framework of settlements. Many nonindustrial regions of relatively uniform land surface have cities distributed so evenly over the land that some sort of central-place theory appears to be the prime explanation.[27] It should be worth while to study this distribution and compare it with other areas.[28] In New England, on the other hand,

[26] Harris, *op. cit.*, p. 87.

[27] For a confirmation of this see the column diagram on p. 73 of Lösch (*op. cit.*), which shows the minimum distances between towns in Iowa of three different size classes. The maps of trade-center distribution in the works of Zimmerman, Smith, and Landis (cited earlier) also show an even spacing of centers.

[28] The following table gives the average community area for 140 villages in the United States in 1930. In the table notice throughout that (i) the larger the village, the larger its tributary area in each region and (ii) the sparser the rural population density, the larger the village tributary area for each size class (contrast mid-Atlantic with Far West, etc.).

Community Area in Square Miles

Region	Small Villages (250-1,000 Pop.)	Medium Villages (1,000-1,750 Pop.)	Large Villages (1,750-2,500 Pop.)
Mid-Atlantic	43	46	87
South	77	111	146
Middle West	81	113	148
Far West	—	365	223

where cities are primarily industrial centers based on distant raw materials and extraregional markets, instead of the land sup-

Although 140 is only a sample of the number of villages in the country, the figures are significant because the service areas were carefully and uniformly delimited in the field for all villages (E. deS. Brunner and J. D. Kolb, *Rural Social Trends* (New York, 1933), p. 95; see also E. deS. Brunner, G. S. Hughes, and M. Patten, *American Agricultural Villages* (New York, 1927), chap. ii).

In New York 26 sq. mi. was found to be the average area per village in 1920. Village refers to any settlement under 2,500 population. Nearness to cities, type of agriculture, and routes of travel are cited as the three most important factors influencing density of villages. Since areas near cities are suburbanized in some cases, as around New York City, the village-density in these districts is correspondingly high. Some urban counties with smaller cities (Rochester, Syracuse, and Niagara Falls) have few suburbs, and consequently the villages are farther apart than in many agricultural counties (B. L. Melvin, *Rural Population of New York, 1855-1925*, pp. 88-89; table on p. 89 shows number of square miles per village in each New York county).

In sample areas of New York State the average distance from a village of 250 or under to another of the same size or larger is about 3 miles; for the 250-749 class it is 3-5 miles; for the 750-1,249 class, 5-7 miles (B. L. Melvin, *Village Service Agencies, New York, 1925*, p. 102; in the table on p. 103 the distance averages cited above are shown to be very near the modes).

Kolb makes some interesting suggestions as to the distances between centers. He shows the spacing is closer in central Wisconsin than in Kansas, which is more sparsely settled — J. H. Kolb, "Service Relations of Town and Country," Wisconsin Agricultural Experimental Station Research Bull. 58 (1923), see pp. 7-8 for theoretical graphs.

In Iowa, "the dominant factor determining the *size* of convenience-goods areas is distance" — *Second State Iowa Planning Board Report* (Des Moines, April, 1935), p. 198. This report contains fertile suggestions on trade areas for Iowa towns. Valuable detailed reports on retail trade areas for some Iowa counties have also been made by the same agency.

porting the city the reverse is more nearly true: the city supports the countryside by providing a market for farm products, and thus infertile rural areas are kept from being even more deserted than they are now.

The forces making for concentration at certain places and the inevitable rise of cities at these favored places have been emphasized by geographers and other scholars. The phenomenal growth of industry and world-trade in the last hundred years and the concomitant growth of cities justify this emphasis but have perhaps unintentionally caused the intimate connection between a city and its surrounding area partially to be overlooked. Explanation in terms of concentration is most important for industrial districts but does not provide a complete areal theory for distribution of settlements. Furthermore, there is evidence that "of late . . . that rapid growth of the larger cities has reflected their increasing importance as commercial and service centers rather than as industrial cen-

ters."[29] Some form of the central-place theory should provide the most realistic key to the distribution of settlements where there is no marked concentration — in agricultural areas where explanation has been most difficult in the past. For all areas the system may well furnish a theoretical norm from which deviations may be measured.[30] If might also be an aid in planning the development of new areas. If the theory is kept in mind by workers in academic and planning fields as more studies are made, its validity may be tested and its structure refined in accordance with regional differences.

[29] U.S. National Resources Committee, *Our Cities — Their Role in the National Economy: Report of the Urbanism Committee* (Washington, Government Printing Office, 1937), p. 37.

[30] Some form of the central-place concept might well be used to advantage in interpreting the distribution of outlying business districts in cities. cf. Malcolm J. Proudfoot, "The Selection of a Business Site," *Journal of Land and Public Utility Economics*, Vol. XIV (1938), esp. 373 ff.

6

Christaller's Central

Place Theory

Arthur Getis

Judith Getis

Much present-day research in urban geography has its roots in the work of Walter Christaller, a German scholar from Bavaria.* He was attempting to find the laws which determine the number, size, and distribution of towns. He was convinced, he wrote, that just as there are economic laws which determine the life of the economy, so are there special economic-geographic laws determining the arrangement of towns.

Since 1933, when his book on central places in southern Germany was published, many writers have praised and criticized, reformulated and expanded parts of Christaller's theory. Today very few accept all aspects of his work, but they realize that it stimulated some of the most advanced scientific work in geography. The following summary of the rudiments of central place theory is included here in order to acquaint the reader with the meaning of some of the terminology prevalent in urban geography today — a termin-

ology introduced into our literature by those dealing with Christaller's work. Hopefully this will be a reference when reading about urban geography.

No attempt is made to summarize all of Christaller's work. The emphasis is on Christaller's marketing principle or $k = 3$ network. Other networks were derived which had their foundation in principles of transportation and administration.

A Central Place

The chief function or characteristic of a town, Christaller said, is to be the center of a region. Settlements which are prevalently centers of regions he called *central places*. In contrast to these are dispersed places, i.e., all those places which are not centers. They might be areally-bound places (the inhabitants live from their agricultural activities), pointly-bound places (the inhabitants make their living from resources which occur at specific locations, such as mining settlements, customs places, and so on), or settlements which are indifferent with regard to their location (monastery settlements). Christaller was concerned with the central places only.

* Walter Christaller, *Die zentralen Orte in Suddeutschland*, trans. C. Baskin, (Jena, Gustave Fischer, 1933 and Charlottesville, University of Virginia, Bureau of Population and Urban Research, 1954).

Reprinted from *Journal of Geography* (May, 1966), pp. 220-26 by permission.

Some central places are more important than others — their central functions extend over regions in which other central places of less importance exist. Christaller devised a means of measuring the centrality of towns — their relative importance in regard to the surrounding region.

Central Goods and Services

Goods produced at a central place, and the services offered there, are called *central goods and services*. Dispersed goods and services, in contrast, are ubiquitous; they are offered and produced everywhere. Further, an industry using raw materials imported from outside the local region and shipping its products out of the local area would not constitute a central service. The goods must be produced for the surrounding region.

The Range Of A Good

This is the distance the dispersed population is willing to travel to buy a good offered at a central place. The good has both an upper and a lower limit to its *range*. The *upper limit* is the maximum radius of sales beyond which the price of the good is too high for it to be sold. The upper limit may be either an ideal or a real limit.

Ideal limit: the maximum radius results from the increase of price with distance until consumers will no longer purchase the good.

Real limit: the radius is determined by the proximity of an alternate center which can offer the good at a lower price at a certain distance from the first center. The *lower limit* of the range encloses the number of consumers necessary to provide the minimum sales volume required for the good to be produced and distributed profitably from the central place. This has been called the *threshold level* of the good. It should be noted that there is no fixed distance between the lower and upper limits of a range; sometimes the distance between the two is small, at other times it is great.

Each good will have its own range, due to the fact that the prices of various goods increase at different rates with increasing distances from the center, and to the fact that different goods have different thresholds. Further, Christaller notes that the range of any one good may be different at each central place and at each point in time.

The Complementary Region

This is the area enclosed about a central place by the range of a good. Christaller assumes that the central place has a monopoly in the supply of the good to its complementary region by virtue of the price at which it can offer the good.

Ideally, each central place would have a circular tributary (market) area, with itself at the center. However, either unserved places would exist, if this were the case, or the circles would overlap, in which case the condition of monopoly would not be fulfilled.

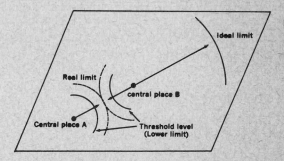

Figure 1. The range of a good, say a radio, offered at both A and B. Since the threshold level is less than the real limit, both central places will produce it. The real limit, halfway between the two central places, shows the trade area for radios for each place. Those living beyond the ideal limit must either do without radios or establish a new central place supplying the good.

Next to circles, hexagons are the most efficient figures both to serve an area (central places and distances traveled will be minimized) and to fill an area completely, as the figure below indicates. Therefore the complementary region of a central place assumes the form of a hexagon.

Using the terms defined above, and a set of assumptions and conditions, Christaller evolved a system of central places. The assumptions, which are listed below, tell us about the kind of landscape on which his system would be erected.

(1) An unbounded plain with soil of equal fertility everywhere and an uneven distribution of resources.

(2) An even distribution of population and purchasing power.
(3) A uniform transportation network in all directions, so that all central places of the same type are equally accessible.
(4) A constant range of any one central good, whatever the central place from which it is offered.

Given this landscape, we have to know what the desires of the people are — i.e., what constraints will exist on the system. These conditions follow:

(1) A maximum number of demands for the goods and services should be satisfied.
(2) The incomes of the people offering the goods and services should be maximized.
(3) Distances moved by consumers to purchase the goods and services should be minimized; i.e., goods are purchased from the closest point.
(4) The number of central places should be the minimum possible.

*The System Of Central Places:
The k = 3 Network*

Under the assumptions and conditions stated above, Christaller's system of central places may be derived. Let us assume first that there

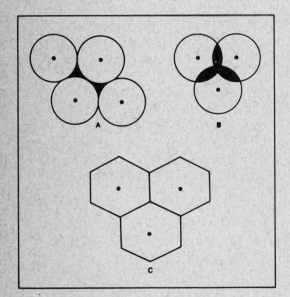

Figure 2. Three arrangements of complementary regions.

A. The unserved areas are shaded.

B. Shaded areas indicate places where the condition of monopoly would not be fulfilled.

C. Hexagons completely fill an area, with no overlap.

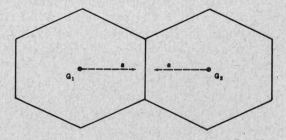

Figure 3. Real range of good 1 is shown by distance a.

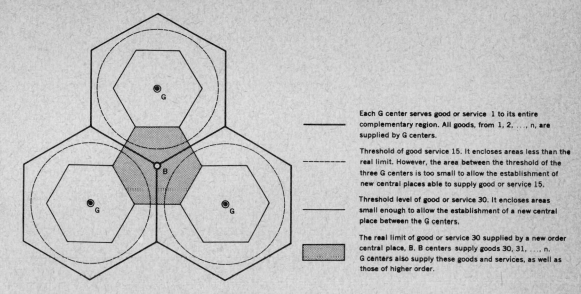

Each G center serves good or service 1 to its entire complementary region. All goods, from 1, 2, ..., n, are supplied by G centers.

Threshold of good service 15. It encloses areas less than the real limit. However, the area between the threshold of the three G centers is too small to allow the establishment of new central places able to supply good or service 15.

Threshold level of good or service 30. It encloses areas small enough to allow the establishment of a new central place between the G centers.

The real limit of good or service 30 supplied by a new order central place, B. B centers supply goods 30, 31, ..., n. G centers also supply these goods and services, as well as those of higher order.

Figure 4.

are two central places, called G centers, which offer all of the goods and services, from a good or service called order 1 with the highest threshold, to a good or service of order 100, with the lowest threshold. Of necessity, the two G centers have the largest market areas (complementary regions) of all central places. The "real" range of the highest order good demanded, good of order 1, defines the boundary between the two G centers. Therefore, the two hexagon-shaped complementary regions have one side in common.

As was noted above, the ranges of the goods decline successively; good of order 2 has a smaller range than that of order 1. As the ranges decline, larger and larger numbers of consumers are left between the two G centers. With some good, say good of order 30, there are enough "surplus" consumers over and above the thresholds of the G centers to allow the development of alternate centers. These are called B centers.

B centers supply goods, 30, 31, ..., 100 at lower prices than the G centers *in the areas*

between the threshold ranges of those goods from the G centers. B centers are located at the maximum economic distance from the G centers — i.e., on the outermost edges of the areas defined about G centers by the real range of good of order 1. In this way, consumer movements are kept to a minimum, and a maximum number of demands are satisfied from a minimum number of centers.

B centers in turn leave progressively larger numbers of surplus demands, and with some good, say good of order 50, these are large enough to permit the existence of a third rank of centers: K centers. K centers provide goods 50, 51, ..., 100. The existence of four other types of centers is accounted for in the same manner.

Besides its definite spatial pattern two things should be noted about Christaller's system. First, a very rigid class structure has been described. That is, each central place supplies all the goods and services — the *identical* goods and services — that the centers below it provide, plus some additional ones. It is due to this fact that Christaller was able to assume that discrete population levels could be assigned to centers of the same type. Since the population of a town depends upon the number and types of functions it performs, then centers performing similar functions will have similar populations. Further, since no centers not of the same type offer identical goods and services, the population levels will be unique.

Second, the system of central places and their complementary regions is characterized by interdependency. All centers except the smallest have other centers dependent upon them for the supply of certain goods. Thus, B centers have K centers and their complementary regions, and all centers of a lower

rank than K, dependent upon them for the supply of goods 30, 31, . . . , 49. In turn, B centers and their complementary regions depend on G centers for the supply of goods 1, 2, . . . , 29. Each complementary region of a B place is served with those goods by three G centers, and Christaller assumes that one-third of its trade goes to each. Each G center thus serves its own region for the supply of goods 1, 2, . . . , 29 as well as one-third of the complementary regions of the six B centers. In all, a G center serves three total B-type regions. This is called a k = 3 network, where k equals the total number of complementary regions of next lowest order served by the central place of next highest order. Likewise, of course, three complete K-type regions are served with goods 30, 31, . . . , 49 by a B center, and so on.

In summary, the chief contribution of Christaller to central place theory is, of course, its basic formulation. More specifically, his identification of concepts relevant to the location of cities, his logically-derived system of central places, and the conclusions following from it are to be noted. Further, it should once more be pointed out that there is much in the book which has not been mentioned here. Christaller recognizes certain deficiencies of his system and qualifies it whenever he deems necessary. In general, he noted that:

> The strict mathematical scheme developed previously is imperfect in some respects. It is even incorrect in this strictness. The scheme should approximate reality; therefore we should study the factors under whose influence it undergoes change (p. 217).

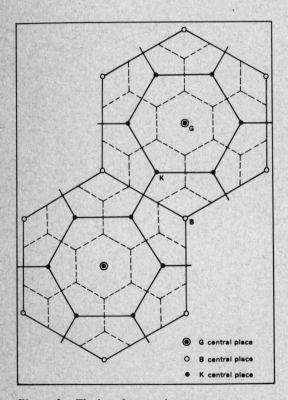

G central place
B central place
K central place

Figure 5.   The k = 3 network.

Berry, Brian J. L. and Pred, Allen, *Central Place Studies: A Bibliography of Theory and Applications* (Philadelphia, Pa., Regional Science Research Institute). A supplement through 1964 of central place studies is also available.

Christaller, Walter, trans. by Carlisle Baskin, *Central Places in Southern Germany, The Pioneer Work in Theoretical Geography* (Englewood Cliffs, N.J., Prentice-Hall, 1966).

Ullman, E. L., "A Theory of Location for Cities," *Am. Jour. of Sociology*, Vol. XLVI, no. 6 (1941), pp. 853-64.

Technology and Urban Form

7

Frederick W. Boal

. . . The "message" of any medium or technology is the change of scale or pace or pattern that it introduces into human affairs. The railway did not introduce movement or transportation or wheel or road into human society, but it accelerated and enlarged the scale of previous human functions, creating totally new kinds of cities and new kinds of work and leisure. — Marshall McLuhan, *Understanding Media*, p. 24.

Reprinted from *Journal of Geography*, (April, 1968), pp. 229-36 by permission.

Transportation and construction technology have profound influences on the internal geography of urban areas.[1] A city is characterized by flows — flows of people, commodities, and information. The way these flows take place shapes the city just as, in turn, the form of the developed city influences the ways in which the flows occur. These flows represent interaction between the various parts of the city, and at the present time they occur along a whole series of networks, such as streets, railroad tracks, pipelines, electricity and telephone lines, and even the channels for radio and television transmission.

Urban areas are also characterized by relatively intensive use of ground space. This is, of course, partly dependent on transportation technology, but it is also dependent on the nature of building construction. The taller a building, the greater the potential for intensive use of the piece of ground on which the structure is placed.

The impact of transportation and construction technology on the city is one of "space adjusting"[2] — in part of the adjustment of the spatial relationships between various areas by the development and use of various forms of transportation and communication, and in part the creation of additional space

by construction. In terms of "space adjusting," the city can be viewed at three technological periods, which we will call the period of the *Pedestrian City*, the period of the *Steam Engine and Wheel-Track City*, and the period of the *Flexible City*. Viewing the impact of technology on urban form through time clarifies the nature of the impact and also helps explain the form of existing cities, which in most cases have developed during more than one technological period. In a broader cultural context it is interesting to note that the three periods above closely parallel the three periods through which Marshall McLuhan suggests western society has moved — village society, mechanized society, and the electric era.[3]

The Pedestrian City

The urban areas of the pre-industrial period were dominated by movement on foot. This had a number of consequences. First, the distances that could be covered in a given time period were short and in so far as connection with the center of the town was important this set a strict limit to the radius of town development. Secondly, because movement was predominantly on foot, there could be a considerable number of routes and they could be narrow and quite irregular. The Swiss architect Le Corbusier suggested this when he wrote, "The pack-donkey meanders along, meditates a little in his scatter-brained and distracted fashion, he zigzags in order to avoid the larger stones, or to ease the climb, or to gain a little shade; he takes the line of least resistance. . . . The Pack Donkey's Way is responsible for the plan of every continental

[1] For discussion of certain aspects of these influences see John R. Borchert, "American Metropolitan Evolution," *Geographical Review*, Vol. 57 (July, 1967), pp. 301-32; A. Fleisher, "The Influence of Technology on Urban Forms," *Daedalus*, Vol. 90 (1961), pp. 48-60; and James E. Vance, Jr., "Labor-Shed, Employment Field, and Dynamic Analysis in Urban Geography," *Economic Geography*, Vol. 36 (July, 1960), pp. 189-220.

[2] E. A. Ackerman, *Geography as a Fundamental Research Discipline*, Research Paper No. 53 (Chicago, University of Chicago, Department of Geography, 1958), p. 24.

[3] Marshall McLuhan, *Understanding Media: The Extensions of Man* (New York, New American Library, 1966).

city."[4] E. A. Gutkind, though disagreeing with some of Le Corbusier's ideas, reinforces the concept of irregularity to street pattern which he claims was due to attaching more importance to the houses than to the streets.[5] In this sense the streets were almost relict space left between buildings. In addition, the whole street system was of equal importance, and ease of movement, with the exception of a few principal streets, developed along routes that joined the town to neighboring settlements. However, this was possible only in a pedestrian and animal transport dominated town. Transportation modes with higher space demands and lower directional flexibility would change all this.

A further feature of interest was the arrangement of the living areas of the various classes. Sjoberg has noted the universality of a pattern in which the well-to-do and powerful congregated in the city center while the poorer folks found what accommodation they could round the edge. The upper class needed ready access to the headquarters of the governmental, religious, and educational organizations and because "the feudal society's technology permits relatively little spatial mobility,"[6] this ready access could be obtained only by physical proximity. Interestingly, a mid-nineteenth century English proposal by John Silk Buckingham for a Utopian city to be called Victoria also had a layout of well-to-do in the middle and low income round the edge. This proposal was made just too early for recognition to be given to the significance of the railroad.

[4] Le Corbusier, *The City of Tomorrow* (London, The Architectural Press, 1947), pp. 23-24.

[5] E. A. Gutkind, *Urban Development in Central Europe* (New York, Free Press, 1964).

[6] G. Sjoberg, *The Pre-Industrial City* (New York, Free Press, 1960), p. 99.

The urban growth of this pedestrian period was achieved by creating new towns rather than adding area to existing ones. In this way the requirements of the pedestrian scale were not violated.

The Steam Engine and Wheel-Track City

The development by Watt of the steam engine in 1788 and the first tentative efforts of the steam locomotive in 1804 were to have revolutionary effects on urban areas.

The stationary steam engine can be characterized in three ways. First of all, up to a point, the larger the steam engine, the more efficient it was. Secondly, the steam engine burned bulky coal as fuel and was inefficent as a converter of energy. Thirdly, the energy made available by the steam engine could only be transferred to operate machinery by direct shaft and belt. Taken together these characteristics led to the development of large factory complexes with a very close locational association of coal mine, steam engine, and factory. Many factory buildings were developed to six or more stories, because, by so doing, the most efficient connections could be made between steam engine and factory machinery using short axles and belts.

The build-up of large industrial populations would not have been possible without the steam engine when used in long distance transport. However, the railroad had a profound effect, not only on the size of urban population concentrations, but also on the form of the urban areas themselves. The locomotive is capable of delivering great power while on the rails but is helpless and delivers no power off them. Its effectiveness is ribbon-like in form, introducing into an area relatively high mobility where railroad tracks exist. Because of the concomitant change in time-distance relationships where railroads were built, urban areas began to develop most markedly along the tracks. Thus the star-like form of the nineteenth century city began. However, the railroad does not improve accessibility all along its length but only at the stations, and because closely spaced stations would have led to excessive losses of energy in stopping and starting, the stations were spaced. In discussing London, Carter[7] has stated that "a steam train takes a long time to accelerate and draw up, so that for economy of operation the stations had to be fairly widely spaced. The urban units whose growth was stimulated by the railways remained well separated and maintained their identity." In this way main directions of urban growth developed, not, however, in a continuous fashion, but as a series of discrete beads (Figure 1). The developments around the suburban stations themselves were restricted and compact because foot travel was dominant within the suburban node. Later, the electrification of suburban lines enabled stations to be placed closer together, because of decreased energy losses in stopping and starting, and this in time led to fusion of the nodes.

The development of speedy transportation began to change fundamentally the social geography of cities. It was no longer necessary for the upper classes to congregate round the center. They could buy more space and seclusion for themselves on the now not-so-distant periphery. Robbins[8] has noted that "[the railroads] . . . enabled the wealthier and middle classes to live at some distance from the places of their daily work; this helped to create sharp differences of class between the

different parts of a city and its suburbs, which had not existed in the earlier age when 'good' town houses mostly lay close beside houses which were not so good."

While railroad transport in urban areas provided only a very coarse network of radial routes, urban street transport went some way towards providing a more finely articulated system. Like the railroad, it provided linear accessibility and only a limited number of points at which one could get on and off. Unlike the railroad, the number of generally radial routes was much greater, though still restricted because of minimum use levels below which it was uneconomical to provide public transport. In addition, of course, the stops were much closer together. As urban street transport developed from the stagecoach to the horse bus and the use of rails to the electrification of traction, so the distance that could be covered in a given time period was increased and fares per mile reduced, making the street-car a means of "mass" transport. In some cases the streetcar lines were constructed through pre-existing built-up areas, but frequently they were extended out into the rural fringe as a speculative measure to increase land values and

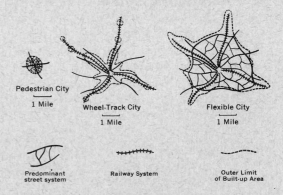

Figure 1. Urban shape and extent and predominant transportation networks.

[7] E. Carter, *The Future of London* (London, Penguin Books, 1962), p. 142.

[8] M. Robbins, *The Railway Age* (London, Penguin Books, 1965), pp. 48-49.

stimulate development. The "street-car" suburb of older American cities is a typical result of this. Together, the railroad and street-car made large areas available for urban development, producing, in both instances, a star like form, the "fingers" protruding out along the radial routes. Continual extension in this fashion led to the fusion of previously separate urban areas resulting in the conurbations, a term coined by Patrick Geddes in 1915.

The Flexible City

A number of technological innovations dating initially from the end of the nineteenth century are having very widespread effects on the form of urban areas today. In particular, the widespread use of electricity, the development of the internal combustion engine, telecommunications, and steel frame buildings must be given consideration.

Electricity as an energy form is unique in the variety of ways it can be applied and scales at which it can be used. In terms of its effect on urban form, the emphasis must be placed on flexibility. Economies of scale can be obtained by large scale generation, but unlike the nineteenth century steam engine-factory combination, the power can be used several hundred miles from where it is generated. Consequently industrial establishments can be located with much greater freedom than at any time since the introduction of large scale production units. Use of electrical power has also revolutionized factory layout. Each machine can have its individual power link, overhead belting and axles are unnecessary and highly developed forms of internal transportation can be utilized, whether they be conveyor, overhead crane, or small trucks (e.g. forklift). All these put a premium on horizontal, one floor layouts. The factory has thus changed from a multi-story mill to the one level structure, consequently increasing the demand for land. Locations on the urban periphery, where space is available and per acre land costs lower, become the most desirable.

We have noted previously the influence of electricity in transportation used in the spacing of suburban railroad stations. However, it is the internal combustion engine that has had the greatest effect of all on urban form. The car and the truck have introduced a combination of speed and flexibility previously unknown. Unlike fixed rail transportation, the car and the truck can move on almost any street in an urban area. Movement patterns are more complex, choice of route much wider. This has meant that the various functional parts of the city, whether industrial, residential, commercial, or any other, have to a considerable extent lost their dependence on close association with the railroad or the tramway. Public transport, in the form of the diesel bus, has greater route flexibility than the street-car, though bus routes are still overwhelmingly radial and deviate little from the previous street-car routes. To a large extent, the bus lacks the flexibility of the car, and the layout of bus routes makes it relatively easy to move from the periphery to the city center, but very difficult to move from one suburban area to another. The street-car in the past and the bus today reinforce the locational significance of the city center. The car and the truck are not affected by these route constraints. Lateral movement is relatively easy, though the previously developed predominantly radial road system does produce difficulties.

Car and truck transport opens up large areas for potential development. An all around increase in the effective radius for urban development from 3 to 12 miles increases the area available for development from 29 to 452 square miles. This in itself is an inbuilt mechanism to produce lower densities for urban areas than has been true in the past.

The dispersive effects of the internal combustion engine are also seen in the space demands generated by cars and trucks for movement and storage (parking). The high space demands of the motor vehicles have produced most of the urban planning problems associated with them. The vaunted flexibility of the motor car looks weak if you can't find anywhere to stop — "the pedestrian in the vehicle he cannot shed" as Fisher has put it.[9] The Table contrasts the space requirements of an individual with those of the car he may use.

However, the present day city is not entirely dominated by the motor vehicle. There still remain areas where the pedestrian scale is dominant, as in the central business district and in residential areas planned as "neighborhoods" in some European cities. In fact several recent studies have demonstrated that the horizontal dimensions of the commercial core of cities are internally conditioned by the distances people are willing to walk. These pedestrian dominated areas of the Flexible City have strong affinities with the Pedestrian City in terms of form.

While areal scales have been revolutionized by the use of internal combustion-engined vehicles, there are intriguing parallels with the Pedestrian City of the past, in that the whole street pattern is available for move-

TABLE

Space demands: One person and one car

Man standing comfortably	1 sq. ft.
Average car space	150 sq. ft.
Office worker	275 sq. ft.
Parked car of office worker	1500 sq. ft.
Space per person/mile	
Walk	3 sq. ft.
By car, assuming 1.5 persons per car	20-70 sq. ft.

* Assumes 1.5 persons per car.

In terms of space needed for movement, the car also contrasts with other forms of mechanical transport. Ritter refers to an estimate that during the peak period, using a nine foot wide traffic lane, 1,200 people per hour could be carried by car, 11,000 per hour using an 80 seater bus, and 40,000 per hour using "rapid track transport."

[9] H. T. Fisher, "Radials and Circumferentials," in T. H. William, *ed., Urban Survival and Traffic* (London, E. and F. N. Spon, 1962), p. 52.

ment and a restricted number of radial routes is no longer the predominant influence on urban form (Figure 1). Consequently many of the interstitial areas of the nineteenth century star-shaped city are being filled in while widespread development at low densities in the urban fringe is possible, unless, of course, there are legislative restraints. The only partial parallel with the railroad era is the freeway, which functions rather like a railroad in producing ribbon-like facilities for high-speed movement and critical points of high accessibility at the interchanges (stations), though the form of development associated with the interchanges will be very different from the pedestrian dominated beads of the nineteenth century suburban railroad station.

Telecommunications are also having important effects on urban form and function. Radio and television provide universal communication within an area, though, in terms of public systems, restricted in possible content and one-directional in flow. The telephone influences urban form more significantly in that it already acts as a substitute for certain forms of face-to-face communication. Thus information and instructions can flow between various parts of an industrial organization even though the parts may be in widely dispersed locations. Central area head offices can keep in contact with factory or warehouse in the periphery. Like the car, the telephone appears as a dispersive influence, though this may not be entirely true, because if a person makes a telephone call rather than an actual trip, transportation space is saved and higher densities may result. This is also true where people stay at home and watch television instead of going out to the movie theater. In fact, several aspects of modern technology are ambiguous in their effects on urban form. Overall, however, electricity, the internal combustion engine, and telecommunications have generally been conducive to urban spread. Equally important, they have tended to introduce greater flexibility into the use to which a given plot of land can be put. It has been suggested that, in this sense, urban land is being "homogenized."

The technology of building construction, while adapting to the demands for coverage of large ground areas (factories, stadiums, etc.), has been most noted for the development of the tall building.[10] The key technological breakthrough was the development by William Jenney of the iron frame building (Home Insurance Building, Chicago, 1885). Use of the iron frame meant that the walls ceased to be load bearing structures and became purely weather proofing. Thus thickness of wall and height of building did not need to bear any relationship to each other. However, as efficient functional units, tall buildings were not feasible without some means of rapid vertical transportation. This was provided by the elevator developed by Elisha Otis in 1857 with refinements through to 1889. It was said that Jenny's "skyscrapers" could be built just as high as Otis' "elevator" would go.

The development of the tall building enabled tremendous intensification of space use to take place. First in the United States, and now generally, central areas of large cities have become dominated by the tall commercial structure. This predominance is essentially a twentieth century constructional response to nineteenth century urban transportation/communication means in that, until recently, the city center was by far the most accessible point in any given urban complex. Under these conditions high land values justify the intensive use of space, or, as in this case, the actual creation of space.

The pressure on space in the centers of the largest cities has led to the development of subterranean transportation networks, which not only increase transportation capacity but also introduce route flexibility partially independent of the overlying street network. Recent proposals under the general head of "Traffic Architecture" further demonstrate

[10] James H. Johnson, "The Geography of the Skyscraper," *Journal of Geography,* Vol. LV (November, 1956), pp. 379-87.

the intensification of space use in central areas, partly associated with the need to segregate the motor vehicle and the pedestrian.

We have characterized the city as it is presently developing as flexible. It is increasingly flexible in terms of locational choice for various functions. It can be flexible in terms of social patterns. Thus the associations of an individual can be widely dispersed in a large urban area, linked by car and telephone. We can have "community without propinquity"[11] at least for all but the poor, the very young, and the very old. Flexibility is also seen in the multiplicity of different urban forms being proposed for new towns and cities in various parts of the world — dispersed grids, rings, linear cities, high density, low density, and so on. Technology provides this flexibility, but the profusion of proposed forms may suggest absence of adequate research as much as richness of alternatives.

[11] M. M. Webber, "Order in Diversity: Community without Propinquity," in L. Wingo, *ed., Cities and Space* (Baltimore, Johns Hopkins Press, 1963), pp. 23-54.

Conclusion

This paper has examined some aspects of the interaction of technology and urban form as it has occurred in the urban areas of the most highly developed countries. In the underdeveloped countries, public investment in transportation systems is low and private ownership and use of the car and telephone are generally restricted to a very small proportion of the total population. In addition, rates of population growth of the urban areas have been very high. Consequently it would be erroneous to conclude that urban form in the underdeveloped countries is similar to that in the developed. The vast low income shack areas on the edges of cities, such as Rio and Calcutta, make this only too clear. In addition, because of lack of resources, it is unrealistic to assume that the cities of Latin America, Africa, and South and East Asia represent, at present, stages of urban growth preliminary to the type of growth presently occurring in North America and Europe.

Urban Growth Characteristics

8

Alan M. Voorhees

New techniques have been developed to analyze growth characteristics of urban areas. These techniques have been applied in ten American cities — Hartford, Baltimore, Washington, and a group of Iowa cities including Des Moines, Sioux City, Council Bluffs, Waterloo, Cedar Rapids, Dubuque, and Davenport.

Although these communities may not be truly representative of all American cities, the findings show that former concepts of urban development are rapidly changing, along with social, economic, and technological changes, particularly as they relate to our rising standard of living.

The exact pattern of growth that materializes in a community is the result of many individual decisions — a manufacturer decides where to locate his next plant, a merchant decides which of his stores to expand, a government agency decides where to relocate, a family decides where to rent or buy a house. The final choice in all such cases depends upon the alternatives available at any given time.

In making such decisions many factors are weighed. For example, among other factors, a family will consider type, size and kind of house, financial cost arrangements, neighborhood amenities, distance to stores and schools, accessibility to jobs, and adequacy of governmental service.

The studies undertaken in the ten cities measured the importance people place on these and other factors in making their locational decisions. Though different individuals may weigh the same factors differently, on a group basis the most significant factors can be defined and measured. From the analysis, it was possible to develop mathematical formulas to indicate what weight people give to the various factors of location.

Use of formulas

In addition to serving as an analytical device to appraise past growth trends, formulas have other advantages. They can be used to estimate the potential impact of public policies or decisions. Thus a formula can be used to help

Reprinted from *Urban Land,* (December, 1961) by permission. Copyright 1961 by ULI-The Urban Land Institute, 1200 18th Street, N.W., Washington, D.C. 20036.

predict a pattern of growth that will be brought about by different urban plans or highway programs, as well as the influence that zoning plans might exert on urban growth. Cities like Hartford, Washington, and Baltimore have been employing such formulas to evaluate alternative schemes of land development.

Usually four or five formulas are developed to reflect aspects of urban growth. For example, in the Hartford area separate formulas were used to analyze manufacturing service and retail employment, as well as population.

To establish past growth trends of manufacturing employment in the Hartford area, nine variables were used in the analysis. The variables considered were highway accessibility, availability of industrial land, tax rate, sewer and water service, rail service, proximity of industrial land to airports, size of existing industrial activities, and promotional aspects.

With highway accessibility, tax rate, and proximity to airports, a quantitative measurement was fairly easy. However, for such things as promotional aspects subjective evaluations were necessary to develop a rating index.

The influence that the several variables had on urban growth was appraised by multiple correlation. In effect, a formula was developed by multiple correlation analysis which would give a growth index for a particular zone. This growth index, when compared with the sum of the indices for all the zones, reflects the amount of the growth that can be expected in a zone anticipating a certain amount of overall growth.[1, 2, 3]

This test indicated that the most important factors were *available land* and *sewer service*. Next in order of importance were accessibility to airport, highway access, and rail service. The other factors were of relatively minor significance in influencing community growth. Because this information can be of considerable value to developers and planners, a summary is presented based on the findings derived from these ten cities.

Population Patterns

In reviewing population and residential growth trends, the studies recognized that if builders are to build for the low-cost homes market, they must search for low-priced land. Doubtless, low land costs are probably the most influential factors affecting urban growth. The analysis in these cities reveals that, other things being equal, an area having low-priced land may develop up to three or four times as fast as it theoretically should, on the basis of accessibility and availability of land. Evansdale, Iowa, a small incorporated area outside Waterloo, grew at a rapid rate during the last decade because of inexpensive land. The pattern changed abruptly when FHA withheld mortgages in the town because of sewer problems.

However, as people rise in the income scale they tend to place more emphasis on the type of area in which their home is located. They ask: Is it an attractive neighborhood? Are the public services such as schools and police

[1] Charles F. Barnes, "Integrating Land Use and Traffic Forecasting (Washington, D.C., Highway Research Board, 1961).

[2] Rex H. Wiant, "A Simplified Method for Forecasting Urban Traffic" (Washington, D.C., Highway Research Board, 1961).

[3] *Baltimore-Washington Interregional Study* (Baltimore Regional Planning Council & National Capital Regional Planning Council, November, 1960).

protection adequate? Does the locality have any claim to distinction as a "prestige area?" Areas that meet these tests grow nearly twice as fast as those which do not. Notable examples of phenomenal growth of prestige areas are found in Montgomery County, Maryland, northwest of Washington, D.C. and in the Towson area, north of Baltimore.

But, as already indicated, there are many other elements involved in the rate of growth of a residential area. Lack of sewer or water service, for example, can hold growth rates to about one-third of normal, everything else being equal. An example of this is the southeast section of the Washington Metropolitan area. Otherwise attractive areas where land owners are deferring sale of property for tax advantages, or for capital gains, often have only half the growth that might be anticipated. A good example of this is Suffield, Connecticut, a town north of Hartford near the state line. This factor is much more prevalent than one might expect, particularly in the large metropolitan area.

Nevertheless, one of the prime growth factors is the availability of land. The extent and intensity of its use, of course, depend upon the zoning policy for the area.

Although accessibility of an area is an important consideration for a family, a family weighs other factors that have been cited. Most sections in a metropolitan area are served by highways. The difference in accessibility as between one place and another may be only a few minutes. Hence it is apparent that transportation facilities and services do not now exert the dominant influence on urban growth as formerly. *The automobile has freed the family transportation-wise so that it can afford to weigh other factors in the selection of a home.*

Employment Patterns

In considering the spatial distribution of employment, it was recognized that different types of work activities place varying emphasis on locational factors. Therefore, the various categories of employment were grouped by locational requirements in the studies cited here.

Manufacturing

As in residential selection, the employer in his choice of plant location also has been freed by the automobile. He now knows that he can locate a plant almost any place within an urban region and be assured of the necessary labor force. In short, today accessibility to the labor force is not the important factor to industrialists or other employers as in the past. More often the chief concern is in a specific site requirement such as water, sewer, freeway, port or rail service.

In the Baltimore area most of the largest manufacturing industries have gravitated to the corridor lying to the east and northeast of Baltimore City which has good rail and highway access as well as accessibility to water.

Only a few manufacturing activities are attracted to residential areas. Usually these are light industries looking for "prestige sites," as is particularly true in the area north of Baltimore where a number of smaller industrial plants have located. Overall, however, five-sixths of the industrial expansion that occurred in the Baltimore region was influenced largely by site requirements. Only one-sixth of the expansion was influenced primarily by the residence of population.

The studies also revealed a definite tendency for existing large employment centers to draw new industrial activities to their general vicinity. Similarly, greater growth was evidenced where there were promotional programs for industrial land development.

Certainly the availability of rail, port, and highway played a part in the location of some manufacturing plants. Areas with relatively low residential prestige often provided land to industrial developers at a price they could afford and, as a result, these areas had considerable growth. However, if the parcels of available land in such areas were too small, the growth was retarded.

An interesting sidelight in these studies is that industrialists are more interested in the capacity of the sewer system than in the cost of connecting to it. On the other hand, home builders are more interested in the cost of sewer service.

Retail

Retail employment trends in the study cities changed quite apparently with the changing pattern of population. As the families shifted to the suburbs, the neighborhood retail trade went along. However, retail expansion generally follows the first wave of residential development. Retailers like to have an "insured" market before they move out. The exact location of the store will depend largely upon the accessibilty factors.

The exact location of shopping centers and other commercial activities is largely dictated by street patterns. Most merchants want the point of highest accessibility. In various analyses made in these studies it was quite clear that commercial development will shift with changes in accessibility. For example, some of the older out-lying shopping areas were located at junctions of fairly narrow streets. When new and wider streets were built, new commercial areas developed along the new routes.

With the development of freeways in the area, the new commercial establishments located near the junctions of the freeways. Often these commercial areas were within a short distance of each other. All of these shifts were brought about by changes in the heightened level of transportation service, which in effect influenced the relative accessibility of the specific areas.

Shopping center location is also influenced by the accessibility factor. The location and size of existing centers have marked impact upon the location of new centers. Generally a new center is apt to locate within three or four miles of an existing center which does not have an adequate range of merchandise. But the pace of residential development will determine whether the old center is expanded or a new one is developed.

Other Employment

Service activities, such as dry cleaning outlets, hairdressers, banks, etc., have followed a pattern similar to that of retail establishments. They have moved to the suburbs to be closer to the people and industries they serve. Certain types of activity, however, still find the downtown area very attractive. These are organizations that depend upon accessibility to a large labor pool or specialize in certain lines. For example, in Baltimore the Commercial Industrial Trust located in the downtown area mainly because it needed a large pool of office workers. On the other hand, some of the more or less standardized office operations which do not require large labor forces will locate in the suburbs.

Governmental

In studying the location choice pattern for many government activities in the Washington area, it was clear that a strictly personal decision by the head of the agency was often involved. However, different factors of influence were noted. First, accessibility to the labor force is important. Thirty per cent of the governmental expansion between 1948 and 1957 occurred in the downtown area.

Certain governmental activities concentrate in outlying suburban zones where other governmental activities have already been located. On the basis of the analysis made in the study, nine zones in the suburban area received more than their share of growth.

In addition to increase in the number of Federal employees, an increase in employment by local governments took place. Most of this growth followed changes in population, since a large portion of it was aimed at serving the new people.

In general, the study has shown that many of the changes in employment patterns have followed population adjustments. Almost all retail and service employment has shifted with population. Many governmental and office activities have moved out to be closer to the people they serve. In effect, about two-thirds of the employment follows the migrating population.

Transportation No Longer Key Factor

The most important conclusion to be drawn from these studies is that transportation is not the key factor in shaping our cities today. With the universal use of the automobile and the development of metropolitan area street systems, the urban dweller has been given almost unlimited latitude in where to live or locate his business. Because of this, he gives considerable attention to factors other than transportation in making a final decision.

At first glance, this conclusion seems to be at odds with other recent research. For ex-

ample, the Bone and Wohl study[4] of the industrial expansion along Route 128 outside Boston has indicated that transportation was a very important factor in this growth. These results were based largely upon attitudes expressed by industrialists who have located along this freeway.

However, a further look at the replies by these industrialists reveals that they also were giving weight to other factors such as the attractiveness of the area and its advertising value. Though many of them did say that "commercial access" was very important to them, the fact remains that they could have obtained practically the same commercial access if they located one or two miles away from the expressway. A few minutes of travel would not have made that much difference.

Certainly the fact that the firm of Cabot, Cabot & Forbes was promoting the area along Route 128 increased its growth potential. In fact, the area along the route was not developing until Cabot, Cabot & Forbes were able to convince the first industrialist to locate along the route. The first venture began the wave of development found there today. The fact that industrialists follow "fads" just as people do was observed in most of the cities that were studied.

This would also hold with regard to the accessibility to the labor force. Perhaps, if overall employment patterns in the Boston area were analyzed, the findings would be similar to those found in the ten cities, mentioned earlier.

Also often cited, when discussing the influence of freeways on urban development, is the great expansion of residential development that occurred near the Gulf Freeway in

---

[4] A. J. Bone and Martin Wohl, *Massachusetts Route 128 Impact Study*, Highway Research Board Bulletin 227.

the southeast section of Houston.[5] It is true that when this facility was first opened there was a tremendous growth in its vicinity for a period of about five years. (See Figure 1.) However, recent growth trends in the Houston areas have swung to the southwest portion of the city, which is generally considered the prestige area. Furthermore, a new freeway has been built which serves a rather rundown section of Houston. This has had no apparent influence on the growth patterns.

Such illustrations show that the dynamic factors in urban growth must be considered together. When a change in transportation facilities is introduced it may modify the influence of the other factors. Improved accessibility, particularly at the beginning of a new development, if combined with other favorable factors may stimulate a great deal of growth. But, as in Houston, the other factors, like blight, may become dominant, and changes in accessibility are not enough to really stimulate growth.

Decisions, Alternatives, and Time

All of this tends to emphasize the basic point brought out at the beginning of this paper — namely, that urban growth depends not only upon many individual decisions, but on the alternatives offered at the time the decisions are made. If the expansion of large electronic activities in the Boston area had occurred before Route 128 was developed, these industries would have located in some other place. If Route 128 were being built today, it might not attract anywhere near the number of firms it has attracted there because the industries might not see the site advant-

[5] *Economic Evaluation of the Gulf Freeway* (City of Houston Department of Traffic and Transportation, July, 1949).

HOUSTON POPULATION INCREASES 1940-1957

1940-1950

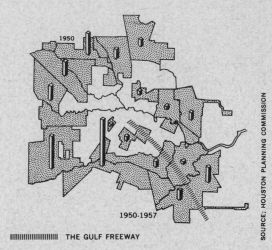

1950-1957

IIIIIIIIIIIIIIIIIIII   THE GULF FREEWAY

SOURCE: HOUSTON PLANNING COMMISSION

Figure 1.

ages in the same light today that they did a few years ago. Urban growth is sensitive to many factors modified by time.

In conclusion, this point should be strongly emphasized: it is quite obvious from the analysis of growth patterns in the ten American cities that our standard of living is becoming a major factor in our development patterns. The individual, whether home owner or industrialist, is becoming more and more concerned with other factors besides transportation. This change must be recognized in urban plans.

The Territorial Expansion of American Cities and their Population Growth

9

Yu A. Kolosova

.Any analysis of United States census data on the population growth of cities must not lose sight of the fact that one of the reasons for growth, and sometimes the principal reason, may be the expansion of the city area and changes in its limits. These changes are identified as annexations in the census reports. *The Municipal Yearbook* (1963) reports (p. 53) that 152 cities expanded their area in 1945, 382 in 1950, 526 in 1955, and 712 in 1960. (*The Municipal Yearbook* is the source for data in expansions of city areas in intercensal periods; each annual issue contains information on cities that expanded their area in the given year.) The data suggest that cities are expanding their area with increasing frequency, and annexations are assuming increasing importance as a factor in population growth. Because of this trend, the 1960 census data (series "Number of inhabitants," state volumes) included a separate table (No. 9) showing the population of cities within the annexed territories. The need for a proper assessment of factors resulting in population growth of the cities of the United States during the 1950-1960 period, a time when annexations assumed increasing importance, prompted us to analyze

these data. The principal results of that analysis are the subject of the present paper.

Before discussing the effect of annexation on city growth in the United States as a whole and in various regions, a few words should be said about the reasons for, and the essence of, this process. Judging from the paucity of information on the subject in the literature, Americans do not seem to have dealt with this question to any great extent.

Harland Bartholomew, author of *Land Uses in American Cities*, notes that the needs of a growing city for additional territory can be met in a variety of ways: (1) by peripheral expansion, (2) by redistribution of existing land uses, (3) by building up of empty lands, and (4) by more intensive use of existing lands and buildings (Harland Bartholomew, *Ispol'zovaniye territorii v amerikanskikh gorodakh*. Moscow: Gosstroyizdat, 1959 [Russian edition of: *Land Uses in American Cities*. Cambridge: Harvard University Press, 1955]). On the basis of his observations, he reports that the fourth approach is relatively little used in American cities because it is slower and more complicated. "More often community growth flows into areas offering the least physical

Reprinted by permission from *Soviet Geography: Review and Translation*. Translated by Theodore Shabad.

or economic resistance to expansion. Thus the predominant type of growth occurs in the form of lateral. expansion into surrounding agricultural areas where raw land is converted to urban purposes" (p. 33 in Russian edition; p. 13 in American edition). The first objective of city expansion is usually territory adjoining the city's periphery that is already being used for urban purposes but is still unincorporated.

Annexations involve a complex knot of contradictions. The actual annexation procedure is regulated in different ways in various states. In some states it is simpler, in others more complicated. In some states, Rhode Island for example, the law altogether prohibits changes in municipal boundaries; in eight states, annexations must be approved by state legislatures, and in others a local municipal ordinance is sufficient. Incorporation of a territory into a city may be initiated by residents of that particular territory in the form of a petition, on which the vote is restricted to property owners who reside permanently in the territory. (In 1962, 216 cities annexed new territory of at least one quarter square mile; only in 50 cases did the initiative stem from residents of the annexed territory.) Annexations may also be inspired by businessmen and politicians of the central city, interested in new land for industrial and residential construction. They also seek to control the course of development of territory adjoining the city, thus enhancing its importance. Another factor is the desire to gain additional taxpayers and thus reduce the deficit in the municipal budget so characteristic of many American cities.

The procedure is much simpler if the annexation does not require the approval of the residents of the area. There have been cases where annexation was inevitable because the central city had virtually surrounded a particular area, making its separate existence impractical. One such case is described in *Western City*, February, 1965, relating to North Sacramento, which was incorporated into Sacramento in 1964. As late as 1963, North Sacramento was still resisting annexation, but it gave in after it found itself surrounded by Sacramento territory. Similar cases are reported by Raymond Murphy in *The American City*, (New York, 1966). They are Hamtramck and Highland Park in the Detroit SMSA, [standard metropolitan statistical area], University Park and Highland Park in Dallas, and San Fernando in Los Angeles.

The annexation procedure may become more complex and may be frustrated by opposition on the part of the authorities of the county in which the particular territory is situated, or of residents of the county. According to the American literature, the system of representation in local legislatures does not reflect in some cases the extensive shifts in the distribution of population that have taken place as a result of urbanization. As a result rural areas sometimes carry weight out of proportion to their population. And it is their representatives who may frustrate city expansion plans. Opposition to annexation often is motivated by fear that the city may impose new local taxes and may gain control over land use. (*The Municipal Yearbook*, 1963, p. 52). The separate incorporation of territory is used as a countermeasure against annexation. In cases where unincorporated territory lies near two cities, competition between the two may also delay annexation.

Although annexation involves friction and aggravates relationships, the data cited earlier suggest that an increasing number of cities are making use of it. The 1960 Census notes that cities frequently expanded their territory through annexation in the 1950s, with some cities achieving substantial territorial expansion. In many cases this significantly affected both absolute and relative population growth.

In our analysis of the 1960 Census, we limited ourselves to cities with a population of at least 10,000 in 1960. There were 1899 such cities, of which 1080 (56.8%) had expanded their territory since 1950.

The distribution of cities that annexed territory in the 1950-1960 period is shown in Table I for various population classes and regions.

lion in the 1950-1960 period. Consequently, 71.8% of the total growth was the result of annexations. This factor must especially be borne in mind in cases where territorial expansion was the principal source of population growth, for example, the central cities of the 212 standard metropolitan statistical areas. Their combined population increased by 10.7% during the 1950-1960 period, with 9.3% of the increase stemming from annexations. Among the 58 million residents of these cities, 4.9 million lived in newly annexed territory. Annexation played a relatively

TABLE I

Distribution of cities that annexed territory in 1950-1960 by population classes and by regions

Population Class (in thousands)	Number of Cities that Expanded Their Territory			
	Total	North	South	West
10-25	627	294	216	117
25-100	363	156	120	87
100-500	80	27	34	19
500-1000	8	3	3	2
over 1000	2	1	—	1
Total	1080	481	373	226
Percentage share of cities of 10,000 or more in the total number of cities	56.8%	44.5%	75.9%	69.1%

The Census does not contain data on the size of the territory annexed by any particular city. *The Municipal Yearbook, 1963,* reports that the total area of annexations during 1951-1960 was 11,941.2 square kilometers. (In 1962, when 754 cities had annexations, the average territorial gain of large cities, according to the same source, was 1.5 square miles, or 3.9 square kilometers, and in the case of small cities 0.5 mi^2, or 1.3 km^2, but 15 cities acquired more than 10 mi^2, or 25.9 km^2, each.)

The total population of newly annexed territories was 8.5 million in 1960. The population of these cities increased by 11.8 mil-

minor role (only 0.4 million people) in the growth of population of the central cities of the largest SMSA (with more than 3 million). The central cities of the next group of SMSA (1 to 3 million) lost 2.2% of their population in their old territory, but annexations gave them an increase of 7.8%, and in the case of the smaller SMSA (under 1 million), more than two-thirds of the population growth stemmed from the expansion of city limits (U.S. Census of Population, 1960, *Number of Inhabitants, U.S. Summary.* Washington, 1961, p. XXVII).

In 1958 cities of 10,000 or more, the population of the newly annexed territory accounted for 25 to 50% of the city's total 1960 population (78 of these cities were in the South, 47 in the West and 33 in the North.) In 45 cities (21 in the South, 19 in the West and 5 in North), the annexed territory acounted for 50 to 75% of the population, and in six cities (three in the South, two in the West and one in the North) for more than 75%. For a list of cities with the most significant annexations, see U.S. Census of Population, 1960. *Number of Inhabitants, U.S. Summary*. Washington, 1961, pp. XXIV.)

Territorial expansion has been especially intensive in cities of the South and West. There are several reasons for this. The South, which used to lag behind other regions in the level of urbanization, has been accelerating its rate both because of major social-economic shifts in agriculture and the development of industry. Around the large cities of the South and its industrial centers, an urban fringe has arisen and, as time goes on, it becomes the first candidate for inclusion in the city limits. In Texas and some of the other southwestern states, annexation is also furthered by its relative juridical simplicity. There are quite a number of examples of substantial expansion in this region. Thus, 26.8% of the 1960 population of Houston lived in annexed territory, 28% in Dallas, 44.9% in El Paso and 63.7% in Odessa. Oklahoma City repeatedly expanded its city limits, and after its greatest expansion (354.2 km² in 1962) it extended into four counties and now has the largest area of any United States city — 1605.8 km² with 355,000 people (*The Municipal Yearbook,* 1963, p. 55. Oklahoma City and its environs contain 1800 oil wells; oil extraction and refining is the leading economic activity). Previously, Los Angeles had the largest city area, 1177.9 km² with a population of 2,479,000.

Territorial expansion of cities in the West is being furthered by the rapid growth of population in this region (mainly as a result of migration) and by intensive industrial development. Some cities registered virtually no population gain within their old limits, but annexed territory with a population far exceeding the former population. The outstanding example is Phoenix, Ariz. which had a population of 107,000 in 1950 and 439,000 in 1960, the difference (332,000) being equivalent to the population of the newly annexed territory. A similar situation is found in Tucson, Ariz., and Vallejo, San Jose, and San Leandro, Calif.

In the North, such great population growth as a result of annexations is much rarer and occurs mainly in the case of small cities. Among the larger cities in which population growth through annexation was significant are Milwaukee (17% of the total 1960 population), Wichita (33%), and Columbus, Ohio (16%). The presence of a dense network of incorporated places around a large city tends to block annexation attempts, as in the case of Cleveland and, to some extent, Chicago.

Despite annexations, some cities seem to be unable to maintain their former population level. Of the 481 cities of the North (with a population of 10,000 or more) which annexed territory in the 1950-60 period, 67 had a smaller population in 1960 within the enlarged territory than they had in 1950 within the smaller territory. Of these cities, 37 were small, 22 medium, and 8 large (including Chicago and Cincinnati). There are fewer such cities in the South (16) and they are not characteristic of the West (4), where the tendency toward suburbanization (the outflow of population to the suburbs) is less pronounced.

The Nature of Cities

10

Chauncy D. Harris

Edward L. Ullman

Cities are the focal points in the occupation and utilization of the earth by man. Both a product of and an influence on surrounding regions, they develop in definite patterns in response to economic and social needs.

Cities are also paradoxes. Their rapid growth and large size testify to their superiority as a technique for the exploitation of the earth, yet by their very success and consequent large size they often provide a poor local environment for man. The problem is to build the future city in such a manner that the advantages of urban concentration can be preserved for the benefit of man and the disadvantages minimized.

Each city is unique in detail but resembles others in function and pattern. What is learned about one helps in studying another. Location types and internal structure are repeated so often that broad and suggestive generalizations are valid, especially if limited to cities of similar size, function, and regional setting. This paper will be limited to a discussion of two basic aspects of the nature of cities — their support and their internal structure. Such important topics as the rise and extent of urbanism, urban sites, culture of cities, social and economic characteristics of the urban population, and critical problems will receive only passing mention.

THE SUPPORT OF CITIES

As one approaches a city and notices its tall buildings rising above the surrounding land and as one continues into the city and observes the crowds of people hurrying to and fro past stores, theaters, banks, and other establishments, one naturally is struck by the contrast with the rural countryside. What supports this phenomenon? What do the people of the city do for a living?

The support of a city depends on the services it performs not for itself but for a tributary area. Many activities serve merely the population of the city itself. Barbers, dry cleaners, shoe repairers, grocerymen, bakers, and movie operators serve others who are engaged in the principal activity of the city, which may be mining, manufacturing, trade, or some other activity.

Reprinted from *Annals of the America Academy of Political and Social Science,* Vol. 242 (1945), pp. 7-17 by permission of the author and the Academy.

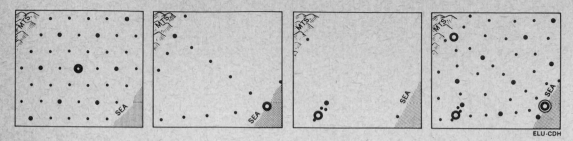

ELU-CDH

Figure 1. Theoretical distribution of central places. In a homogeneous land, settlements are evenly spaced; largest city in center surrounded by 6 medium-size centers which in turn are surrounded by 6 small centers. Tributary areas are hexagons, the closest geometrical shapes to circles which completely fill area with no unserved spaces.

Figure 2. Transport centers, aligned along railroad or at coast. Large center is port; next largest is railroad junction and engine-changing point where mountain and plain meet. Small centers perform break of bulk principally between rail and roads.

Figure 3. Specialized-function settlements. Large city is manufacturing and mining center surrounded by a cluster of smaller settlements located on a mineral deposit. Small centers on ocean and at edge of mountains are resorts.

Figure 4. Theoretical composite grouping. Port becomes the metropolis and, although off center, serves as central place for whole area. Manufacturing-mining and junction centers are next largest. Railroad alignment of many towns evident. Railroad route in upper left of Figure 2 has been diverted to pass through manufacturing and mining cluster. Distribution of settlements in upper right follows central-place arrangement.

The service by which the city earns its livelihood depends on the nature of the economy and of the hinterland. Cities are small or rare in areas either of primitive, self-sufficient economy or of meager resources. As Adam Smith stated, the land must produce a surplus in order to support cities. This does not mean that all cities must be surrounded by productive land, since strategic location with reference to cheap ocean highways may enable a city to support itself on the specialized surplus of distant lands. Nor does it mean that cities are parasites living off the land. Modern mechanization, transport, and a complex interdependent economy enable much of the economic activity of mankind to be centered in cities. Many of the people engaged even in food production are actually in cities in the manufacture of agricultural machinery.

The support of cities as suppliers of urban services for the earth can be summarized in three categories, each of which presents a factor of urban causation:[1]

1. Cities as central places performing comprehensive services for a surrounding area. Such cities tend to be evenly spaced throughout productive territory (Figure 1). For the moment this may be considered the "norm" subject to variation primarily in response to the ensuing factors.

2. Transport cities performing break-of-bulk and allied services along transport routes, supported by areas which may be remote in distance but close in connection because of the city's strategic location on transport channels. Such cities tend to be arranged in linear patterns along rail lines or at coasts (Figure 2).

3. Specialized-function cities performing

[1] For references see Edward Ullman, "A Theory of Location for Cities," *Am. Jour. of Sociology,* Vol. 46, no. 6 (1941), pp. 853-64.

one service such as mining, manufacturing, or recreation for large areas, including the general tributary areas of hosts of other cities. Since the principal localizing factor is often a particular resource such as coal, water power, or a beach, such cities may occur singly or in clusters (Figure 3).

Most cities represent a combination of the three factors, the relative importance of each varying from city to city (Figure 4).

Cities as central places

Cities as central places serve as trade and social centers for a tributary area. If the land base is homogeneous these centers are uniformly spaced, as in many parts of the agricultural Middle West (Figure 1). In areas of uneven resource distribution, the distribution of cities is uneven. The centers are of varying sizes, ranging from small hamlets closely spaced with one or two stores serving a local tributary area, through larger villages, towns, and cities more widely spaced with more special services for larger tributary areas, up to the great metropolis such as New York or Chicago offering many specialized services for a large tributary area composed of a whole hierarchy of tributary areas of smaller places. Such a net of tributary areas and centers forms a pattern somewhat like a fish net spread over a beach, the network regular and symmetrical where the sand is smooth, but warped and distorted where the net is caught in rocks.

The central-place type of city or town is widespread throughout the world, particularly in nonindustrial regions. In the United States it is best represented by the numerous retail and wholesale trade centers of the agricultural Middle West, Southwest, and West. Such cities have imposing shopping centers or wholesale districts in proportion to their size; the stores are supported by the trade of the surrounding area. This contrasts with many cities of the industrial East, where the centers are so close together that each has little trade support beyond its own population.

Not only trade but social and religious functions may support central places. In some instances these other functions may be the main support of the town. In parts of Latin America, for example, where there is little trade, settlements are scattered at relatively uniform intervals through the land as social and religious centers. In contrast to most cities, their busiest day is Sunday, when the surrounding populace attend church and engage in holiday recreation, thus giving rise to the name "Sunday town."

Most large central cities and towns are also political centers. The county seat is an example. London and Paris are the political as well as trade centers of their countries. In the United States, however, Washington and many state capitals are specialized political centers. In many of these cases the political capital was initially chosen as a centrally located point in the political area and was deliberately separated from the major urban center.

Cities as transport foci and break-of-bulk points

All cities are dependent on transportation in order to utilize the surplus of the land for their support. This dependence on transportation destroys the symmetry of the central-place arrangement, inasmuch as cities develop at foci or breaks of transportation, and transport routes are distributed unevenly over the land because of relief or other limitations (Figure 2). City organizations recognize the importance of efficient transportation, as witness their constant concern with freight-rate regulation and with the construction of new highways, port facilities, airfields, and the like.

Mere focusing of transport routes does not produce a city, but according to Cooley, if break of bulk occurs, the focus becomes a good place to process goods. Where the form of transport changes, as transferring from water to rail, break of bulk is inevitable. Ports originating merely to transship cargo tend to develop auxiliary services such as repackaging, storing, and sorting. An example of simple break-of-bulk and storage ports is Port Arthur-Fort William, the twin port and wheat-storage cities at the head of Lake Superior; surrounded by unproductive land, they have arisen at the break-of-bulk points on the cheapest route from the wheat-producing Prairie Provinces to the markets of the East. Some ports develop as entrepôts, such as Hong Kong and Copenhagen, supported by transshipment of goods from small to large boats or vice versa. Servicing points or minor changes in transport tend to encourage growth of cities as establishment of division points for changing locomotives on American railroads.

Transport centers can be centrally located places or can serve as gateways between contrasting regions with contrasting needs. Kansas City, Omaha, and Minneapolis-St. Paul serve as gateways to the West as well as central places for productive agricultural regions, and are important wholesale centers. The ports of New Orleans, Mobile, Savannah, Charleston, Norfolk, and others served as traditional gateways to the Cotton Belt with its specialized production. Likewise, northern border metropolises such as Baltimore, Washington, Cincinnati, and Louisville served as gateways to the South, with St. Louis a gateway to the Southwest. In recent years the South has been developing its own central places, supplanting some of the monopoly once held by the border gateways. Atlanta, Memphis, and Dallas are examples of the new southern central places and transport foci.

Changes in transportation are reflected in the pattern of city distribution. Thus the development of railroads resulted in a railroad alignment of cities which still persists. The rapid growth of automobiles and widespread development of highways in recent decades, however, has changed the trend toward a more even distribution of towns. Studies in such diverse localities as New York and Louisiana have shown a shift of centers away from exclusive alignment along rail routes. Airways may reinforce this trend or stimulate still different patterns of distribution for the future city.

Cities as concentration points for specialized services

A specialized city or cluster of cities performing a specialized function for a large area may develop at a highly localized resource (Figure 3). The resort city of Miami, for example, developed in response to a favorable climate and beach. Scranton, Wilkes-Barre, and dozens of nearby towns are specialized coal-mining centers developed on anthracite coal deposits to serve a large segment of the northeastern United States. Pittsburgh and its suburbs and satellites form a nationally significant iron-and-steel manufacturing cluster favored by good location for the assembly of coal and iron ore and for the sale of steel to industries on the coal fields.

Equally important with physical resources in many cities are the advantages of mass production and ancillary services. Once started, a specialized city acts as a nucleus for similar or related activities, and functions tend to pyramid, whether the city is a seaside resort such as Miami or Atlantic City, or, more important, a manufacturing center such as Pittsburgh or Detroit. Concentration of industry in a city means that there will be a concentration of satellite services and industries — supply houses, machine shops, expert consultants, other industries using local industrial by-products or waste, still other industries making specialized parts for other plants in the city, marketing channels, specialized transport facilities, skilled labor, and a host of other facilities; either directly or indirectly, these benefit industry and cause it to expand in size and numbers in a concentrated place or district. Local personnel with the know-how in a given industry also may decide to start a new plant producing similar or like products in the same city. Furthermore, the advantages of mass production itself often tend to concentrate production in a few large factories and cities. Examples of localization of specific manufacturing industries are clothing in New York City, furniture in Grand Rapids, automobiles in the Detroit area, pottery in Stoke-on-Trent in England, and even such a specialty as tennis rackets in Pawtucket, Rhode Island.

Such concentration continues until opposing forces of high labor costs and congestion balance the concentrating forces. Labor costs may be lower in small towns and in industrially new districts; thus some factories are moving from the great metropolises to small towns; much of the cotton textile industry has moved from the old industrial areas of New England to the newer areas of the Carolinas in the South. The tremendous concentration of population and structures in large cities exacts a high cost in the form of congestion, high land costs, high taxes, and restrictive legislation.

Not all industries tend to concentrate in specialized industrial cities; many types of manufacturing partake more of central-place characteristics. These types are those that are tied to the market because the manufacturing process results in an increase in bulk or perishability. Bakeries, ice cream establishments, ice houses, breweries, soft-drink plants, and various types of assembly plants are examples. Even such industries, however, tend to be more developed in the manufacturing belt because the density of population and hence the market is greater there.

The greatest concentration of industrial cities in America is in the manufacturing belt of northeastern United States and contiguous Canada, north of the Ohio and east of the Mississippi. Some factors in this concentration are: large reserves of fuel and power (particularly coal), raw materials such as iron ore via the Great Lakes, cheap ocean transportation on the eastern seaboard, productive agriculture (particularly in the west), early settlement, later immigration concentrated in its cities, and an early start with consequent development of skilled labor, industrial know-how, transportation facilities, and prestige.

The interdependent nature of most of the industries acts as a powerful force to maintain this area as the primary home of industrial cities in the United States. Before the war, the typical industrial city outside the main manufacturing belt had only a single industry of the raw-material type, such as lumber mills, food canneries, or smelters (Longview, Washington; San Jose, California; Anaconda, Montana). Because of the need for producing huge quantities of ships and airplanes for a two-ocean war, however, many cities along the Gulf and Pacific coasts have grown rapidly during recent years as centers of industry.

Applications of the three types of urban support

Although examples can be cited illustrating each of the three types of urban support, most American cities partake in varying proportions of all three types. New York City, for example, as the greatest American port is a break-of-bulk point; as the principal center of wholesaling and retailing it is a central-place type; and as the major American center of manufacturing it is a specialized type. The actual distribution and functional classification of cities in the United States, more complex than the simple sum of the three types (Figure 4), has been mapped and described elsewhere in different terms.[2]

The three basic types therefore should not be considered as a rigid framework excluding all accidental establishment, although even fortuitous development of a city becomes part of the general urban-supporting environment. Nor should the urban setting be regarded as static; cities are constantly changing, and exhibit characteristic lag in adjusting to new conditions.

Ample opportunity exists for use of initiative in strengthening the supporting base of the future city, particularly if account is taken of the basic factors of urban support. Thus a city should examine: (1) its surrounding area to take advantage of changes such as newly discovered resources or crops, (2) its transport in order to adjust properly to new or changed facilities, and (3) its industries in order to benefit from technological advances.

INTERNAL STRUCTURE OF CITIES

Any effective plans for the improvement

or rearrangement of the future city must take account of the present pattern of land use within the city, of the factors which have produced this pattern, and of the facilities required by activities localized within particular districts.

Although the internal pattern of each city is unique in its particular combination of details, most American cities have business, industrial, and residential districts. The forces underlying the pattern of land use can be appreciated if attention is focused on three generalizations of arrangement — by concentric zones, sectors, and multiple nuclei.

Concentric zones

According to the concentric-zone theory, the pattern of growth of the city can best be understood in terms of five concentric zones[3] (Figure 5).

1. *The central business district.* — This is the focus of commercial, social, and civic life, and of transportation. In it is the downtown retail district with its department stores, smart shops, office buildings, clubs, banks, hotels, theaters, museums, and organization headquarters. Encircling the downtown retail district is the wholesale business district.

2. *The zone in transition.* — Encircling the downtown area is a zone of residential deterioration. Business and light manufacturing encroach on residential areas characterized particularly by rooming houses. In this zone are the principal slums, with their submerged regions of poverty, degradation,

[2] Chauncy D. Harris, "A Functional Classification of Cities in the United States," *The Geographical Review*, Vol. 33, no. 1, (January, 1943), pp. 85-99.

[3] Ernest W. Burgess, "The Growth of the City," in *The City*, Robert E. Park, Ernest W. Burgess and Robert D. Mackenzie, *eds.* (Chicago, University of Chicago Press, 1925), pp. 47-62; Ernest W. Burgess, "Urban Areas," in *Chicago, an Experiment in Social Science Research*, T. V. Smith and Leonard D. White, *eds.* (Chicago, University of Chicago Press, 1929), pp. 113-38.

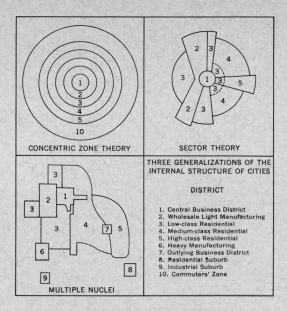

CONCENTRIC ZONE THEORY

SECTOR THEORY

THREE GENERALIZATIONS OF THE
INTERNAL STRUCTURE OF CITIES

DISTRICT

1. Central Business District
2. Wholesale Light Manufacturing
3. Low-class Residential
4. Medium-class Residential
5. High-class Residential
6. Heavy Manufacturing
7. Outlying Business District
8. Residential Suburb
9. Industrial Suburb
10. Commuters' Zone

MULTIPLE NUCLEI

Figure 5. Generalizations of internal structure
of cities The concentric-zone theory is a
generalization for all cities. The arrangement of the
sectors in the sector theory varies from city to city.
The diagram for multiple nuclei represents one
possible pattern among innumerable varions.

and disease, and their underworlds of vice.
In many American cities it has been inhabited
largely by colonies of recent immigrants.

3. *The zone of independent workingmen's
homes.* — This is inhabited by industrial
workers who have escaped from the zone in
transition but who desire to live within easy
access of their work. In many American
cities second-generation immigrants are important segments of the population in this
area.

4. *The zone of better residences.* — This
is made up of single-family dwellings, of exclusive "restricted districts," and of high-
class apartment buildings.

5. *The commuters' zone.* — Often beyond
the city limits in suburban areas or in satellite
cities, this is a zone of spotty development of

high-class residences along lines of rapid
travel.

Sectors

The theory of axial development, according
to which growth takes place along main
transportation routes or along lines of least
resistance to form a star-shaped city, is refined by Homer Hoyt in his sector theory,
which states that growth along a particular
axis of transportation usually consists of
similar types of land use[4] (Figure 5). The
entire city is considered as a circle and the
various areas as sectors radiating out from
the center of that circle; similar types of land
use originate near the center of the circle and
migrate outward toward the periphery. Thus
a high-rent residential area in the eastern
quadrant of the city would tend to migrate
outward, keeping always in the eastern quadrant. A low-quality housing area, if located
in the southern quadrant, would tend to extend outward to the very margin of the city
in that sector. The migration of high-class
residential areas outward along established
lines of travel is particularly pronounced on
high ground, toward open country, to homes
of community leaders, along lines of fastest
transportation, and to existing nuclei of buildings or trading centers.

Multiple nuclei

In many cities the land-use pattern is built
not around a single center but around several

[4] Homer Hoyt, "City Growth and Mortgage
Risk," *Insured Mortgage Portfolio*, Vol. I, nos.
6-10 (December 1936-April 1937), *passim*; U.S.
Federal Housing Administration, *The Structure
and Growth of Residential Neighborhoods in
American Cities*, Homer Hoyt (Washington,
Government Printing Office, 1939), *passim*.

discrete nuclei (Figure 5). In some cities these nuclei have existed from the very origins of the city; in others they have developed as the growth of the city stimulated migration and specialization. An example of the first type is Metropolitan London, in which "The City" and Westminster originated as separate points separated by open country, one as the center of finance and commerce, the other as the center of political life. An example of the second type is Chicago, in which heavy industry, at first localized along the Chicago River in the heart of the city, migrated to the Calumet District, where it acted as a nucleus for extensive new urban development.

The initial nucleus of the city may be the retail district in a central-place city, the port or rail facilities in a break-of-bulk city, or the factory, mine, or beach in a specialized-function city.

The rise of separate nuclei and differentiated districts reflects a combination of the following four factors:

1. Certain activities require specialized facilities. The retail district, for example, is attached to the point of greatest intracity accessibility, the port district to suitable water front, manufacturing districts to large blocks of land and water or rail connection, and so on.

2. Certain like activities group together because they profit from cohesion.[5] The clustering of industrial cities has already been noted above under "Cities as concentration points for specialized services." Retail districts benefit from grouping which increases the concentration of potential customers and makes possible comparison shopping. Financial and office-building districts depend

upon facility of communication among offices within the district. The Merchandise Mart of Chicago is an example of wholesale clustering.

3. Certain unlike activities are detrimental to each other. The antagonism between factory development and high-class residential development is well known. The heavy concentrations of pedestrians, automobiles, and streetcars in the retail district are antagonistic both to the railroad facilities and the street loading required in the wholesale district and to the rail facilities and space needed by large industrial districts, and vice versa.

4. Certain activities are unable to afford the high rents of the most desirable sites. This factor works in conjunction with the foregoing. Examples are bulk wholesaling and storage activities requiring much room, or low-class housing unable to afford the luxury of high land with a view.

The number of nuclei which result from historical development and the operation of localization forces varies greatly from city to city. The larger the city, the more numerous and specialized are the nuclei. The following districts, however, have developed around nuclei in most large American cities.

The central business district. — This district is at the focus of intracity transportation facilities by sidewalk, private car, bus, streetcar, subway, and elevated. Because of asymmetrical growth of most large cities, it is generally not now in the areal center of the city but actually near one edge, as in the case of lake-front, riverside, or even inland cities; examples are Chicago, St. Louis, and Salt Lake City. Because established internal transportation lines converge on it, however, it is the point of most convenient access from all parts of the city, and the point of highest land values. The retail district, at the point of maximum accessibility, is attached to the

---

[5] Exceptions are service-type establishments, such as some grocery stores, dry cleaners and gasoline stations.

sidewalk; only pedestrian or mass-transportation movement can concentrate the large numbers of customers necessary to support department stores, variety stores, and clothing shops, which are characteristic of the district. In small cities financial institutions and office buildings are intermingled with retail shops, but in large cities the financial district is separate, near but not at the point of greatest intracity facility. Its point of attachment is the elevator, which permits three-dimensional access among offices, whose most important locational factor is accessibility to other offices rather than to the city as a whole. Government buildings also are commonly near but not in the center of the retail district. In most cities a separate "automobile row" has arisen on the edge of the central business district, in cheaper rent areas along one or more major highways; its attachment is to the highway itself.

The wholesale and light-manufacturing district. — This district is conveniently within the city but near the focus of extra city transportation facilities. Wholesale houses, while deriving some support from the city itself, serve principally a tributary region reached by railroad and motor truck. They are, therefore, concentrated along railroad lines, usually adjacent to (but not surrounding) the central business district. Many types of light manufacturing which do not require specialized buildings are attracted by the facilities of this district or similar districts: good rail and road transportation, available loft buildings, and proximity to the markets and labor of the city itself.

The heavy industrial district. — This is near the present or former outer edge of the city. Heavy industries require large tracts of space, often beyond any available in sections already subdivided into blocks and streets. They also require good transporta-

tion, either rail or water. With the development of belt lines and switching yards, sites on the edge of the city may have better transportation service than those near the center. In Chicago about a hundred industries are in a belt three miles long, adjacent to the Clearing freight yards on the southwestern edge of the city. Furthermore, the noise of boiler works, the odors of stockyards, the waste disposal problems of smelters and iron and steel mills, the fire hazards of petroleum refineries, and the space and transportation needs which interrupt streets and accessibility — all these favor the growth of heavy industry away from the main center of the large city. The Calumet District of Chicago, the New Jersey marshes near New York City, the Lea marshes near London, and the St. Denis district of Paris are examples of such districts. The stockyards of Chicago, in spite of their odors and size, have been engulfed by urban growth and are now far from the edge of the city. They form a nucleus of heavy industry within the city but not near the center, which has blighted the adjacent residential area, the "back-of-the-yards" district.

The residential district. — In general, high-class districts are likely to be on well-drained, high land and away from nuisances such as noise, odors, smoke, and railroad lines. Low-class districts are likely to arise near factories and railroad districts, wherever located in the city. Because of the obsolescence of structures, the older inner margins of residential districts are fertile fields for invasion by groups unable to pay high rents. Residential neighborhoods have some measure of cohesiveness. Extreme cases are the ethnically segregated groups, which cluster together although including members in many economic groups; Harlem is an example.

Minor nuclei. — These include cultural

centers, parks, outlying business districts, and small industrial centers. A university may form a nucleus for a quasi-independent community; examples are the University of Chicago, the University of California, and Harvard University. Parks and recreation areas occupying former wasteland too rugged or wet for housing may form nuclei for high-class residential areas; examples are Rock Creek Park in Washington and Hyde Park in London. Outlying business districts may in time become major centers. Many small institutions and individual light manufacturing plants, such as bakeries, dispersed throughout the city may never become nuclei of differentiated districts.

Suburb and Satellite. — Suburbs, either residential or industrial, are characteristic of most of the larger American cities.[6] The rise of the automobile and the improvement of certain suburban commuter rail lines in a few of the largest cities have stimulated suburbanization. Satellites differ from suburbs in that they are separated from the central city by many miles and in general have little daily commuting to or from the central city, although economic activities of the satellite are closely geared to those of the central city. Thus Gary may be considered a suburb but Elgin and Joliet are satellites of Chicago.

Appraisal of land-use patterns

Most cities exhibit not only a combination of the three types of urban support, but also aspects of the three generalizations of the land-use pattern. An understanding of both is useful in appraising the future prospects of the whole city and the arrangement of its parts.

As a general picture subject to modifica-

6 Chauncy D. Harris, "Suburbs," *American Journal of Sociology,* Vol. 49, no. 1 (July, 1943), p. 6.

tion because of topography, transportation, and previous land use, the concentric-zone aspect has merit. It is not a rigid pattern, inasmuch as growth or arrangement often reflects expansion within sectors or development around separate nuclei.

The sector aspect has been applied particularly to the outward movement of residential districts. Both the concentric-zone theory and the sector theory emphasize the general tendency of central residential areas to decline in value as new construction takes place on the outer edges; the sector theory is, however, more discriminating in its analysis of that movement.

Both the concentric zone, as a general pattern, and the sector aspect, as applied primarily to residential patterns, assume (although not explicitly) that there is but a single urban core around which land use is arranged symmetrically in either concentric or radial patterns. In broad theoretical terms such an assumption may be valid, inasmuch as the handicap of distance alone would favor as much concentration as possible in a small central core. Because of the actual physical impossibility of such concentration and the existence of separating factors, however, separate nuclei arise. The specific separating factors are not only high rent in the core, which can be afforded by few activities, but also the natural attachment of certain activities to extra-urban transport, space, or other facilities, and the advantages of the separation of unlike activities and the concentration of like functions.

The constantly changing pattern of land use poses many problems. Near the core, land is kept vacant or retained in antisocial slum structures in anticipation of expansion of higher-rent activities. The hidden costs of slums to the city in poor environment for future citizens and excessive police, fire, and sanitary protection underlie the argument for a subsidy to remove the blight. The transition zone is not everywhere a zone of deterioration with slums, however, as witness the rise of high-class apartment development near the urban core in the Gold Coast of Chicago or Park Avenue in New York City.

On the fringe of the city, overambitious subdividing results in unused land to be crossed by urban services such as sewers and transportation. Separate political status of many suburbs results in a lack of civic responsibility for the problems and expenses of the city in which the suburbanites work.

The Form and Structure of Cities: Urban Growth Patterns

11

Howard J. Nelson

A modern visitor strolling down Duke of Gloucester Street, the main street of Colonial Williamsburg, passes mainly private dwellings — single family detached houses large and small. But interspersed among then in an apparently random pattern are various retail shops, service centers, and small manufacturers, several taverns and inns, an apothecary shop, a printing office, a milliner, a clockmaker, a bootmaker, a wigmaker, and so on. At one end of the tree shaded street, not more than three quarters of a mile long, is

Reprinted from *Journal of Geography* (April, 1969), pp. 198-207 by permission.

the old capital of Virginia, and at the other, the college of William and Mary. Although today's buildings are merely restoration copies of the originals, many are built on the old foundations, and attention to authenticity is apparent. In all likelihood this mixture of residence, commerce, craftsmen, and public activity accurately portrays the undifferentiated structure of early American cities.

But the structure of cities in this country has changed markedly through the years. Today, even small towns with a population of 1,500 or so (the approximate colonial population of Williamsburg) show definite internal differentiation. Typically commercial establishments form a closely spaced cluster along a section of the main street, a lumber yard or other bulk handling facility is located next to a railroad or highway, and a small factory or two are attached to the same transportation lines near the edge of the town. The residential areas form their own districts, adjacent to, but apart from, the rest. And in larger cities an immensely complicated urban structure has developed, a constantly changing but delicately balanced areal organization composed of many highly specialized districts with complex linkages, the product of a variety of forces operating through several centuries.

The casual observer, in today's era of extensive travel, is perhaps first struck by the unique features of individual American cities. These characteristics that give each city a personality are often attributable to the physical qualities of the site or a distinctive historic past: the compact, hilly, water-encircled site of San Francisco, the level lake plain of Chicago, the charming Vieux Carre section of New Orleans, or the open squares in the street pattern of Savannah. But the more perceptive traveler soon begins to notice a repetitive pattern in the form and structure of our cities, and becomes almost instinctively aware of a kind of "normal" location of specialized districts, and of associations of activities within them. For, in fact, American cities have developed a highly stylized arrangement and characteristic, repetitive interrelations among the specialized areas that constitute their urban anatomy.

FACTORS IN THE GROWTH PATTERNS OF AMERICAN CITIES

The form and structure of the modern American city is the result of numerous economic, social, and cultural factors operating through the many decades since the evolution of the simple forms like Williamsburg. The forces contributing to the contemporary urban structure are many, some are obvious and strong, others are more subtle, but all add an important dynamic quality to urban development. Some of the most significant of these factors include rapid and massive growth, a heterogeneous population, the persistent desire of Americans for a single family detached house, and the changing forms of urban transportation. The amazing affluence of Americans in recent years has accelerated change.

American cities are the product of rapid and almost continuous growth. In 1790 about 200,000 people lived in urban places (over 2,500 population), by 1890 the figure was 22,000,000, in 1960 it was 125,000,000. The population increase of our cities in the 1950-1960 decade exceeded the total population of all urban places in 1900. Between 1930 and 1969 the urban population has about doubled. As a result, there has been an almost frantically rapid building and rebuilding of the structures that form our urban plant. With increasing populations cities have not only expanded areally in all directions, but urban lands in general, and favored locations in particular, have increased enormously in value, making rebuilding for a "higher use" profitable. Rapid growth has resulted in uncommonly dynamic cities, with constant change, sorting out, and filtering down in every section of the city.

The American urban population has not only been growing but it also has been unusually heterogeneous, resulting in many distinctive neighborhoods and much internal migration. In the past, much of the population variety was the result of a series of waves of migration. There was, for example, a heavy immigration from Ireland after 1847, another wave from Germany after 1852, and a tide of immigrants from other European countries beginning in the 1880's and continuing until about 1920. The ethnic neighborhood was common. Often the newer immigrants replaced the older groups in the oldest sections in the inner city as the earlier arrivals prospered and moved further out to newer homes. During and since World War II urban growth came mainly from migration from rural areas and included both whites and blacks, but with the blacks in many cases moving in typical fashion into the older homes in central locations in neighborhoods being abandoned by slightly more affluent residents. This succession of peoples results not only in shifts in living quarters, but also in changes in shops, schools, and churches. But even where assimilation has taken place, American cities remain heterogeneous, with segregation by income replacing that of ethnic group or race.

The deeply ingrained desire of Americans to own a single family house on a large open lot is a further factor influencing the structure of our cities. Regardless of the psychological origin of this drive — the difficulty

European immigrants experienced in owning such a structure in Europe, the pioneer tradition of a cabin in a clearing, the dispersed farmhouse familiar to the rural migrant, or notions about privacy, play space, and the nature and meaning of the family — the detached house has persisted for two hundred years in American cities. Whenever he can afford it, the American urban dweller appears to prefer ample space and a private yard over a short journey to work. Encouraged by governmental mortgage policy, perhaps as many as 15,000,000 single family homes have been built since World War II, mostly in suburban areas. These low density residential neighborhoods, covering vast amounts of space, and affecting patterns of commerce and industry, are a prominent and unique item in the American urban structure.

Urban transport not only laces the urban structure together, but it also profoundly affects the arrangement and function of elements in the structure of the city. In America, the horse-drawn omnibus was important from 1830 to 1860, the suburban railroad from 1850 on in the largest cities, cable cars from 1860 to 1890, and elevated rail lines and subways from around the turn of the century. The most universal transport medium from 1890 to about 1945 in all but the largest cities was the electric "street car." But the revolutionary transportation development of the twentieth century has been the spectacular rise of the automobile. There were only about 8,000 automobiles in America in 1900, less than 500,000 in 1910, about 8 million in 1920, but the number has risen spectacularly from about 25 million in 1945 to more than 70 million cars and 13 million trucks and busses today. And each automobile, on the average, is driven more miles every year. The effect on urban structure of this new private form of transportation, not confined to fixed routes, but with the vehicle requiring storage space near the driver, has been immense.

Impressed with the dynamic nature of the American city even before some of the factors just mentioned were operating at maximum strength, one geographer, Charles C. Colby, felt that two opposing forces could be identified. They were centrifugal forces that impelled functions to migrate from the central areas of the city to the periphery, and centripital forces that tend to hold certain functions in the central zone and attract others to it.[1]

Centripetal forces, Colby said, are the result of a number of attractive qualities of the central portion of the city. One of these is *site attraction*, often the quality of the natural landscape that invited the original occupance, such as a river crossing or deep water landing. *Functional convenience,* a second force, results from the possession of the central zone of maximum accessibility, not only to the metropolitan area, but often to the entire surrounding region. The concentration of one function in the central zone operates as a powerful magnet attracting other functions. This is called *functional magnetism.* Thus a large department store may attract a swarm of ladies apparel and accessory shops. *Functional prestige* stems from a developed reputation. One street may become famous for its restaurants, another for its fashionable shops, and doctors often cluster for reasons of functional prestige.

[1] Charles C. Colby, "Centrifugal and Centripetal Forces in Urban Geography," *Annals of the Association of American Geographers,* Vol. XXIII, no. 1 (March, 1933), pp. 1-21. The article has been reprinted in what may be a more accessible source: Harold M. Mayer and Clyde F. Kohn, *eds., Readings in Urban Geography* (Chicago, The University of Chicago Press, 1959), pp. 287-98.

Centrifugal forces on the other hand are not only opposite forces, but are made up of a merging of influences — a desire to leave one part of the city and the urge to go to another. Five forces are recognized. One is the *spatial force,* when congestion in the central zone uproots and the empty spaces of the other zones attract. The second is the *site force,* which involves the disadvantages of the intensively used central zone in contrast to the relatively little used natural landscape of the periphery. Another, the *situational force,* results from the unsatisfactory functional spacing and alignments in the central zone and the promise of more satisfactory alignments in the periphery. Then there is the *force of social evolution* in response to which high land values, high taxes, and inhibitions growing out of the past create a desire to move and the opposite conditions in the newly developing periphery provide an invitation to come. Finally, the *status and organization of occupance* creates a force for change, in which such things as the obsolete functional forms, the crystallized patterns, the traffic congestion, and the unsatisfactory transportation facilities of the central zone stand in opposition to the modern forms, the dynamic patterns, the freedom from traffic congestion, and the highly satisfactory transportation facilities of the outer zone.

Well aware of the importance of human choice, Colby added another factor which he called the *human equation* that could work either as a centripetal or a centrifugal force. Although today other forces may also be at work, these concepts are still useful in analyzing the dynamics of cities. In addition, more formal models of city structure have been constructed by other students of cities, sociologists, economists, and geographers.

Three of the most famous of these constructs follow.

CLASSIC MODELS OF CITY STRUCTURE

The earliest (1923) and best known of the classic models is the concentric circle or zonal hypothesis of Ernest W. Burgess.[2] The essence of this model is that as a city grows it expands radially from its center to form a series of concentric zones. Using Chicago as an example, Burgess identified five of these. In the center of the city was Zone I, the *central business district* or CBD. The heart of the CBD contained department stores, style shops, office buildings, clubs, banks, hotels, theaters, and civic buildings. Encircling it was a wholesale district. Zone II, the *zone in transition,* surrounded the CBD, and comprised an area of residential deterioration as the result of encroachments from the CBD. It consisted of a factory district as an inner belt, and an outer belt of declining neighborhoods, rooming house districts, and generally blighted residences. In many American cities of the 1920's, this area was the home of numerous first generation immigrants. Zone III, the zone of *independent workingman's homes* was the next broad ring, at the time largely inhabited by second generation immigrants, and characterized in Chicago by the "two-flat" dwelling. Beyond this ring was located Zone IV, the *zone of better residences.* Here lived the great middle-class of native born Americans in single family residences or apartments. Within this area, at strategic places, were local business centers, which Burgess implied might be likened to satellite CBDs. Zone V, the *commuter's zone* lay beyond the area of better residences, and consisted of a ring of encircling small cities, towns, and hamlets. These were, in the main, dormitory suburbs, with the men commuting to jobs in the CBD.

The operating mechanism of the concentric circle model was the growth and radial expansion of the city, with each zone having a tendency to expand outward into the next. Burgess assumed a city with a single center, a heterogeneous population, a mixed commercial and industrial base, as well as economic competition for the highly-valued, severely-limited central space. He explicitly recognized "distorting factors," such as site, situation, natural and artifical barriers, the survival of the earlier use of the district, and so on. But he argued that to the extent to which the spatial structure of a city is determined by radial expansion, the concentric zones of his model will appear. Given the limited data available, the Burgess model was a remarkably astute description of the American city of the time.

A second model of the growth and spatial structure of American cities was formulated by Homer Hoyt in 1939 and is known as the wedge or sector theory.[3] Hoyt analyzed the distribution of residential neighborhoods of

[2] First presented as a paper in 1923, Burgess restated his hypothesis at somewhat greater length five years later. Ernest W. Burgess, "Urban Areas," T. V. Smith and L. D. White, *eds., Chicago: An Experiment in Social Science Research* (Chicago, University of Chicago Press, 1929), pp. 114-23. An excellent contemporary review of the Burgess model is Leo F. Schnore, "On the Spatial Structure of Cities in the Two Americas," Philip M. Hauser and Leo F. Schnore, *eds., The Study of Urbanization* (New York, John Wiley and Sons, Inc., 1965), pp. 347-98.

[3] Homer Hoyt, *The Structure and Growth of Residential Neighborhoods in American Cities* (Washington, D.C., Federal Housing Administration, 1939). A suggestive fragment of this classic is reprinted in Mayer and Kohn, *op. cit.,* pp. 499-510.

various qualities, as defined by rent levels, and found that they were neither distributed randomly nor in the form of concentric circles. High rental areas, for example, tended to be located in one or more pie-shaped sectors, and did not form a complete circle around the city. Intermediate rental areas normally were sectors adjacent to a high rent area. Further, different types of residential areas usually grew outward along distinct radii, and new growth on the arc of a given sector tended to take on the character of the initial growth in that sector. In summary, Hoyt argued that "if one sector of the city first develops as a high, medium, or low rental residential area, it will tend to retain that character for long distances as the sector is extended outward through the process of the city's growth."

Although no geometric pattern can be superimposed upon a city to determine the position of high and low rent sectors, some generalizations can be made about their location. The area occupied by the highest income families tends to be on high ground, or on a lake, river, or ocean shore, along the fastest existing transportation lines, and close to the country clubs or parks on the periphery. The low income families tend to live in sectors situated farthest from the high rent areas, and are normally located on the least desirable land alongside railroad, industrial, or commercial areas. Rental areas, are not static. Occupants of houses in the low rent categories tend to move out in bands from the center of the city, mainly by filtering into the houses left behind by the higher income groups, or in newly constructed shacks on the fringe of the city, usually in the extension of the low rent section. It is felt by some that because Hoyt's model takes into account both distance and direction from the center of the city, it is an improvement on the earlier Burgess effort.

A third model, the multiple nuclei, was formulated by Chauncy Harris and Edward Ullman in 1945 as a modification of the two previous models.[4] They argue that the land use pattern of a city does not grow from a single center, but around several distinct nuclei. In some cases these nuclei, elements around which growth takes place, have existed from the origin of the city, but others may develop during the growth of the city. Their numbers vary from city to city, but the larger the city the more numerous and specialized are the nuclei.

Urban nuclei attracting growth might include the original retail district, a port, a railroad station, a factory area, a beach, or, in today's city, an airport. The authors identify a number of districts that have developed around individual nuclei in most large American cities. The *central business district* usually includes, or is adjacent to the original retail area. The *wholesale and light manufacturing* district is normally located along railroad lines, adjacent to, but not surrounding the CBD. The *heavy industrial district* is near the present or former edge of the city, where large tracts of land and rail or water transportation are available. *Residential* districts of several classes are identified with high-class districts on desirable sites, on well drained, high land, and away from nuisances, such as noise, odors, smoke, and railroad lines, the low-class districts near factories and railroad districts. Finally, *suburbs* and *satellites,* either residential or industrial, are char-

4 Chauncy D. Harris and Edward L. Ullman, "The Nature of Cities," *Annals of the American Academy of Political and Social Science,* Vol. CCXLII (November, 1945), pp. 7-17. Reprinted in Mayer and Kohn, *op. cit.,* pp. 277-86.

acteristic of American cities. Suburbs are defined as lying adjacent to the city, with satellites farther away with little daily commuting to the central city.

The rise of separate nuclei and differentiated districts is thought to result from a combination of four factors. 1. Certain activities require specialized facilities, i.e., a retail district needs intracity accessibility, a port requires a harbor. 2. Certain like activities group together because they profit from linkages. For example, retail activities may cluster to facilitate comparison shopping and financial institutions may locate in close clusters to make easy face to face communication by decision makers. 3. Certain unlike activities are detrimental to each other. Thus extensive users of land, such as bulk storage yards, are not compatable with retail functions, requiring dense pedestrian traffic. 4. Certain activities are unable to afford the high rents of the most desirable sites — low class housing is seldom built on view lots.

Models such as these which emerge from the process of analysis and generalization do not conform to the reality of any city. But anyone familiar with large or medium sized American cities will recognize many elements of each model in the vast majority of our urban areas. Obviously, too, they are not mutually exclusive, for the latter two models are both modifications of the concentric circle theory. Even in Hoyt's concept, residential areas expand outward concentrically. There has been extensive statistical testing of these models in recent years with no conclusive results. They remain as valuable conceptual tools for analyzing the modern city, and provide a basis for cross-cultural urban comparisons.

It is obvious, too, that the American city of the twenties and thirties, which provided the data upon which these models were built, is undergoing important structural changes. The traumatic effect of the automobile was not really apparent in the city studies that furnished the inspiration for these classic models. Other factors forming the basis for the urban form have been discussed previously, and some of their effects will be analyzed in the following section on the elements in the urban structure.

MAJOR ELEMENTS IN THE URBAN STRUCTURE

Central Business District

The most obvious and easy to recognize of the components in the spatial structure of American cities described by the classic models is the Central Business District. Generally located on or near the original site of the city, it became the focus of the city's mass transportation arteries, and was thus the point of most convenient access from all parts of the city. Here, in stylized juxtaposition, were found the largest department stores, women's dress shops, men's clothing stores, shoe stores, "five and ten cent" stores, jewelry stores, drug stores, and similar retail outlets. A visitor to an unfamilar city could anticipate this arrangement, and when he found it he could also be confident that he had located the heart of the CBD as well as the area of highest land values and the place of heaviest pedestrian traffic.[5]

Other groupings of activities into specialized junctional areas have also been traditional in the CBD's of large cities. These

[5] A more extensive discussion of the CBD is found in Raymond E. Murphy, *The American City, An Urban Geography* (New York, McGraw-Hill Book Company, 1966), pp. 283-316.

may include financial districts, with banks, savings and loan associations, stock and commodity exchanges, brokerage offices, trust companies, and so on. The civic center with its city and county buildings often attracts lawyers' offices and bail bond agencies. Occasionally a theater district may be present, associated with restaurants and perhaps candy shops. Hotels and office buildings are usually found several blocks from the center of the CBD. Occasionally an office building may specialize in particular services, perhaps housing doctors, dentists, and medical laboratories exclusively, or in the height of specialization, it may house the officials of a single company. The extent of an office building area, though, depends upon the headquarters quality of the city and may cover a large area or be almost nonexistent.

Although absolute areal growth of the CBD may have essentially come to an end with the invention of the elevator and the skyscraper, this area, like the others in the city, is constantly changing. Shifts in its boundaries have been recognized by Murphy, Vance, and Epstein, identifying a "zone of discard" and a "zone of assimilation" associated with this movement.[6] The area from which the CBD is migrating, the "zone of discard" often is characterized by pawn shops, family clothing stores, bars, low grade restaurants, bus stations, cheap movies, credit jewelry, clothing, and furniture stores. The CBD tends to migrate in the direction of the best residences, and in the area into which it seems to be moving, the "zone of assimilation," are found speciality shops, automobile showrooms, drive-in banks, head-

quarters offices, professional offices, and the newer hotels.

Not only are the boundaries of the CBD changing, but due to the reduction of dependence on mass transit and the rise of the more flexible automobile, the last several decades have seen the movement away from the CBD of some of its traditional functions. Department stores, once the exclusive possession of the CBD, have been built in large numbers in outlying areas. Other retail activities have followed their lead. The proportion of retail sales of the city credited to the CBD have gone steadily downward, and few new retail stores have been built here. A number of small and medium sized cities have attempted to reverse the declining retail importance of their CBDs by converting the main shopping street into a pedestrian mall. The success of this expedient is as yet unclear.

Many students of cities feel the CBD of the future will change considerably and perhaps will consist of two centers separated by a band of parking. The financial and office section in many large cities remains healthy, attracted to the focus of metropolitan transportation and the advantages of "linkages" with other office functions. As the traditional retail functions of the CBD decline, perhaps what remains will evolve into a separate center of dual services, comprising specialty shops serving the metropolitan area and mass selling stores supplying the needs of the inner part of the city.[7]

Outlying Commercial Centers

All cities, in addition to a CBD, have a

[6] Raymond E. Murphy, J. E. Vance, Jr., and Bart J. Epstein, "Internal Structure of the CBD," *Economic Geography*, Vol. XXXI (January, 1955), pp. 21-46.

[7] James E. Vance, Jr., "Emerging Patterns of Commercial Structures in American Cities," Proceedings of the IGU Symposium in Urban Geography Lund 1960, *Lund Studies in Geography*, Human Geography, ser. B., no. 24 (Lund, 1962), pp. 485-518.

variety of other commercial areas, and the larger the city the more complex the pattern and the more specialized some of the elements become. The largest of the outlying shopping centers, usually referred to as *regional centers*, are built around one or more department stores, with variety, apparel, and local convenience stores, and repeat in a planned or unplanned way, the retail types found in the very heart of the CBD. Usually these stores are smaller than the downtown counterparts and deal mainly in the staple and most profitable lines of merchandise. Early centers of this class grew at intersections of public transportation lines, but most have been built up recently at points of easy automobile access. Next in order of size are *community centers* with a large variety or junior department store, some apparel shops, plus a supermarket, drug store, bank, and similar establishments. The *neighborhood center*, built around a supermarket and with some associated stores, is an almost ubiquitious feature. Finally, *convenience centers,* perhaps consisting of a "pop and mom" grocery, a launderomat, and a service station, lie at the bottom end of the commercial hierarchy. Recently this hierarchy of commercial centers within cities has been compared to the centers of various orders in central place theory.[8]

Wholesaling and Light Manufacturing

Located in the concentric-circle model as a ring at the border of the CBD, the wholesale and light manufacturing activities have shifted considerably in response to newer forces. As the automobile has given mobility

[8] A discussion of the hierarchy of commercial centers within cities is found in Brian J. L. Berry, *Geography of Market Centers and Retail Distribution* (Englewood Cliffs, N.J., Prentice-Hall, Inc., 1967), pp. 42-58.

to the worker, many firms engaged in light manufacturing have moved away from the center of the city to the suburbs where land is inexpensive and large tracts facilitate one story plants, storage areas, and parking lots. Sites near belt highways are particularly desirable. Many wholesalers, too, have been attracted to similar locations.

On the other hand, certain types of wholesalers characteristic of large cities are affected by forces that make clustering advantageous, often in or near the CBD. Clustering of wholesaling establishments normally persists when the buyers gather in person at the market, where the goods are nonstandardized, when comparison of quality or style is important, and when the establishment of the price is an important function of the market. Wholesalers of jewelry, apparel, fruit and vegetables, or cut flowers are characteristic examples.

Similarly, although most manufacturers have moved out of the central part of the city, a few characteristically remain. For example, large segments of the garment industry are found at the edge of the CBD in cities where it is an important manufacturing activity. One factor involved in this location is the close linkages of the manufacturing and wholesaling aspects of apparel production. But, in addition, clustering in the garment industry results in "external economies" (economies external to the firm). For example, the presence of ancillary firms, such as textile dealers, sponging (shrinking) facilities, factors (textile bankers), trucking firms, repairmen, and suppliers of everything from pretty models to thread, provides external economies to the apparel firms.

Heavy Manufacturing

Heavy industry has almost entirely moved out of the inner ring as postulated by Burgess, much of it into the specialized sites as implied by Harris and Ullman. Early located adjacent to water transport, the development of railroads and trucks permitted industries to leave the central areas. Seeking extensive sites for sprawling factories, parking lots, and storage facilities, large manufacturing complexes are now characteristically found in outlying locations. Some newer industries, such as the aircraft industry, are linked to facilities found only in non-central areas, airports in this instance.

Residential Districts

Much has been said already about residential districts in American cities. Our heterogeneous urban population has shown a tendency to sort itself out one way or another into relatively homogeneous neighborhoods. As differences in language and ethnic character have become less important, segregation of residence has been mainly by economic status, with little mixing of the homes of the rich and the poor, as in some cultures. Race remains, however, as a segregating force, seemingly more powerful than economic status.

Another striking characteristic has been the propensity of the American urban dweller for the space consuming, expensive, single family dwelling. There is some indication that isolation and privacy are qualities of increasing importance. The front porch oriented to the street from which the family viewed the passing scene has disappeared from the post World War II house. Too, the room arrangement has been reversed: now the living room often faces the rear yard which has been designed as an addition to the living space. And in southern California, where life-styles often seem to originate, the backyard is now enclosed with a solid wooden fence or block wall, making the family's privacy complete. Continued spread of the traditional house in the middle of a lot (the now non-functional front yard remains, required by zoning ordinances reflecting an earlier era) forecasts continued suburban sprawl.

In contrast to this long term trend toward dispersal, in recent years, there has been a striking increase in the proportion of multiple housing in many cities. Perhaps this is simply a temporary phenomenon reflecting the changing age composition of the population due to the low birth rate of the 1930's; the young and old often choose apartments, those in their thirties choose single family homes. To the extent, however, that this changing construction mix reflects a movement of those who can afford to live anywhere into more central, accessible locations, as urban distances become greater, it may foretell a weakening, at long last, of the American's traditional willingness to trade commuting time for space.

The Pattern and Distribution of Manufacturing in the Chicago Area

12

Martin W. Reinemann

The Chicago Standard Metropolitan Area (Figure 1) is the second-ranking manufacturing area in the United States. Its national prominence is best indicated by the fact that in 1954 it contributed more than 10½ per cent of the nation's "value added by manufacture." Some recent studies, as well as data from the *Census of Manufacturers*, reveal several interesting relationships and trends within this important industrial area with regard to manufacturing activities in the central city as compared with the remainder of the metropolitan area.

CITY OF CHICAGO COMPARED WITH REMAINDER OF STANDARD METROPOLITAN AREA

Although the City of Chicago comprises less than 6 per cent of the Chicago Standard Metropolitan Area it contains two-thirds of the population and approximately the same percentage, or more, of the major economic activities associated with the American metropolis.

Table I shows that the suburbanization movement between 1940 and 1950 resulted

in a population loss of only 4½ per cent for the central city and that almost 66 per cent of the population still lived in the City of

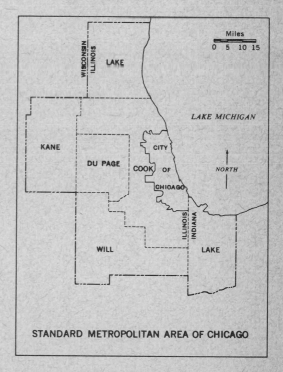

Figure 1.

Reprinted from *Economic Geography*, Vol. 36, no. 2 (April, 1960), pp. 139-44 by permission.

TABLE I

Percentage of Selected Economic Activities in the City of Chicago Compared With
Their Location in the Remainder of the Standard Metropolitan Area,
1947 and 1954

Activity	Percentage in City of Chicago		Change in percentage	
	1947	1954	1939—1947-48	1947-48—1954
Population	65.9 (1950)	—	−4.5 (1940-1950)	—
Manufacturing (value added)	69.2	62.7	2.2	−6.5
(establishments)	83.4	76.3	2.6	−7.1
(production workers)	70.4	65.4	−1.5	−5.0
Retail Trade (sales)	72.6	66.6	−3.3	−6.0
Wholesale Trade (sales)	94.8	90.5	−1.5	−4.3
Service Industries (receipts)	85.0	84.6	−2.1	−0.4

Chicago in 1950. While there has been additional suburbanization since 1950, it is significant that the primary labor market of the metropolitan area is in the City of Chicago and that this continues as a major factor attracting additional manufacturing establishments to the central city.

The high degree of centralization of manufacturing in the City of Chicago is also revealed in Table I.[1] Manufacturing expanded very rapidly in the Chicago Standard Metropolitan Area between 1939 and 1947 in both suburban and central areas. Industrial activity was actually slightly more concentrated inside the central city in 1947 than in 1939. This was not true for any of the other

economic functions. Neither was it true for population, which had suburbanized most

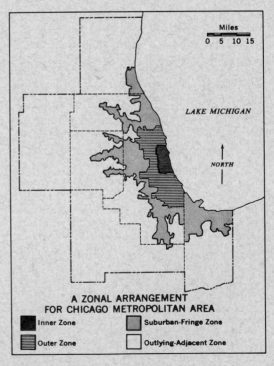

A ZONAL ARRANGEMENT
FOR CHICAGO METROPOLITAN AREA

◼ Inner Zone   ▨ Suburban-Fringe Zone
▤ Outer Zone   ☐ Outlying-Adjacent Zone

Figure 2.

[1] For a comprehensive study of suburbanization of manufacturing in all of the Metropolitan areas in the United States see Evelyn M. Kitagawa and Donald J. Bogue, "Suburbanization of Manufacturing Activity Within Standard Metropolitan Areas," *Studies in Population Distribution*, no. 9, 1955 (Scripps Foundation, Miami University, Oxford, Ohio or Population Research and Training Center, University of Chicago, Chicago, Illinois).

rapidly. Furthermore, the manufacturing labor force, as represented by production workers, drifted to the suburbs more slowly than the general population prior to 1948.

The strongest drift of industry to the suburbs occurred after 1947, according to 1954 Census data, with the greatest change being in number of establishments (see Table I). Production workers continued to decentralize less rapidly than did establishments or production, as measured by value added by manufacture.

A more detailed analysis of the industrial suburbanization trend is afforded by outlining zones for the Chicago Standard Metropolitan Area and by using information obtained from the records of the Territorial Information Department of the Commonwealth Edison Company of Chicago.

RECENT INDUSTRIAL MOVEMENTS BASED ON A ZONAL ARRANGEMENT FOR THE CHICAGO STANDARD METROPOLITAN AREA

A number of persons and organizations have ascribed zones to the structure of the Chicago Standard Metropolitan Area for a variety of purposes.[2] For purposes of de-

[2] E. W. Burgess, "The Growth of the City," Chapter II, in *The City*, by R. E. Park, F. W. Burgess, and R. D. McKenzie, originally published as an article in *Proceedings of the Amer. Sociol. Soc.*, Vol. XVIII (1923). Another system was originated by the Chicago Census Advisory Committee and members of the Department of Sociology at the University of Chicago about 1940. See Martin W. Reinemann, *The Localization and the Relocation of Manufacturing within the Chicago Urban Area* (Unpublished Ph.D. dissertation, Department of Geography, North-western University, 1955).
Based on 1940 and 1950 *Census of Population,* 1939, 1947, and 1954 *Census of Manufactures,* and 1948 and 1954 *Census of Business.*

scribing the pattern and distribution of manufacturing, four zones, shown in Figure 2, are suggested as follows:

Zone I, The Inner Zone

This zone has an area of about 40 square miles extending from Diversey Parkway on the north to 51st Street and Garfield Boulevard on the south, and from the lake shore on the east to Western Avenue on the west. The "Loop" of Chicago is considered a sector within this zone. In general, the zone is characterized by numerous, diverse, small, and older manufacturing concerns primarily occupying multi-storied buildings. Some very large establishments are also present.

Zone II, The Outer Zone

This area surrounds the Inner Zone and includes the remainder of the City of Chicago. Manufacturing is scattered, although many of the plants are grouped in clusters. The zone contains many very large concerns, several of them in multi-storied buildings. A few new single-storied structures have appeared in scattered locations.

Zone III, The Suburban-Fringe Zone

This zone, lying adjacent to but outside of the City of Chicago, contains a number of independent suburban municipalities that form a nearly continuous urban ring about the city. Manufacturing is characterized by both large and small concerns, either newly established or relocated, and for the most part occupying modern one-storied buildings.

Zone IV, The Outlying-Adjacent Zone

This is an area of widely dispersed, satellitic settlements that extends to the outer edge of the Chicago Standard Metropolitan Area. Manufacturing, with few exceptions, is located in the municipalities of Joliet, Aurora, Geneva, St. Charles, Elgin, and Waukegan.

The boundary between the Inner and Outer Zones is probably less significant for differentiating local site characteristics for manufacturing than it might be for analyzing other urban characteristics. Although the Inner Zone has many advantages for manufacturers, such as nearness to market, supply houses, and good transportation, the availability of a large labor market, and the general advantage of the high density of manufacturing establishments in closely related lines, it also has many conditions that push industrial development toward the periphery. Some of the relative disadvantages of the Inner Zone are the following: scarcity of land available for industrial use; the generally unattractive and obsolete condition of buildings; and the congested, noisy, and dirty streets with attendant parking and loading problems.

The city limits as the outer boundary of the Outer Zone is important because of the differences in the costs of a variety of community services, including taxes, on the two sides of the line, and the desire to avoid the excessive frequency and undesirable nature of factory inspections, solicitations, and other related political pressures so apparent in the City of Chicago. The boundary between Zones III and IV sets apart those suburbs that are contiguous or immediately adjacent to the city from the detached satellite cities surrounded by rural countryside. This boundary, with few minor exceptions, coincides with that drawn by the Bureau of the Census to mark the outer limits of the "urbanized area." Differences in labor market, availability of public transportation, time and cost

of shipping and receiving materials, supplies, and products, and differences in the availability of land and the quality of certain community services distinguish the two zones.

Three publications especially pertinent to this study, all based on the same source, have revealed the industrial expansion and suburbanization in the Chicago area since 1945.[3] From these three reports, and selected information relative to the first three zones described above, one can discern the general trend of recent industrial relocation in the Chicago Standard Metropolitan Area.

GENERAL TRENDS

Industrial expansion within the Chicago Standard Metropolitan Area demonstrated considerable areal differentiation during the period 1941-1950. There was a net loss of 120 industries in the Inner Zone during this period (Table II), whereas the Outer Zone of the city had a net gain of 88 plants. The Suburban-Fringe Zone, however, showed its attractive nature by a gain of 743 new and relocated industries during this interim. These data emphasize a reversal in the centralizing trend indicated by the 1947 *Census of Manufactures.* For the period 1941-1950 the City of Chicago (the Inner and Outer

[3] Chicago Plan Commission, *Chicago Industrial Study, Summary Report,* Chicago Plan Commission (Chicago, 1952); Leo G. Reeder, *Industrial Location in the Chicago Metropolitan Area, With Special Reference to Population* (Unpublished Ph.D. dissertation, Department of Sociology, University of Chicago, 1952); Norman E. Brown, "Location of Industries in Chicago and Northern Illinois," *Midwest Engineer,* Vol. V, no. 2 (July, 1952), pp. 2-18. Each of these studies used information from the records of the Territorial Information Department of the Commonwealth Edison Company of Chicago.

TABLE II

Movements of Manufacturing Establishments
in the Chicago Urban Area and Initial
Locations of New Industries for 1941-1950*

Section A. Firms leaving Chicago and moving
to Suburban-Fringe Zone

Years	Inner Zone	Outer Zone
1941-1945	18	37
1946-1950	126	117
Total	144	154

Section B. New industries moving into the
three zones**

Years	Inner Zone	Outer Zone	Suburban-Fringe Zone
1941-1945	46	67	113
1946-1950	75	78	332
Total	121	145	445

Section C. Inter-Chicago moves

Years	Inner Zone to Outer Zone	Outer Zone to Inner Zone
1941-1950	109	12

Section D. Net gain or loss over the decade
1941-1950

Years	Inner Zone	Outer Zone	Suburban-Fringe Zone
	Net loss	Net gain	Gain
1941-1950	120	88	743***

   * Includes only industries with ten or more employees.
  ** Includes only those industries new to the metropolitan area.
 *** Statistics for outmovement from suburbs not available for time period used but for the period 1945-1950 eleven plants moved from the suburbs to Chicago and there were six recorded moves from one suburban community to another.

Zones combined) had a net loss of 32 manufacturing plants.

The latest data available from the Territorial Information Department of the Commonwealth Edison Company of Chicago at the time of this study, show that the industrial suburbanization trend was maintained after 1950 and that it has continued unabated to the present. Between 1950 and 1953, for instance, 201 firms quit Chicago, sustaining the average of about 50 relocations per year first established during the period 1946-1949.

These data also indicate the destinations to which Chicago factories have shifted and afford a basis for showing direction and pattern of the industrial relocation. Of the 446 industries that moved out of the city during the period 1946 through May, 1954, 312 (70 per cent) moved to the Suburban-Fringe Zone, 71 (16 per cent) moved to the Outlying-Adjacent Zone, and 63 (14 per cent) moved to Illinois cities or areas outside the Chicago Standard Metropolitan Area.[4] Figure 3 shows relocations to the Suburban-Fringe Zone, where their concentration in a few suburbs is striking. Five suburbs — Franklin Park, Skokie, Cicero, Melrose Park, and Evanston — received about 53 per cent of the 312 relocated plants.[5] The general pattern of relocation has been to those suburbs adjacent to the City of Chicago, predominantly toward the north and northwest.

[4] No statistics are available concerning moves from Chicago to other states.
[5] The 1954 Census lists 127 establishments for Franklin Park, 115 for Skokie, 170 for Cicero, 75 for Melrose Park, and 130 for Evanston. Obtaining a percentage increase for the period 1947-1954 for the first two cities listed above is not possible because information on their 1947 status is not available. Percentage increases for the latter three were 27, 168, and 55, respectively.

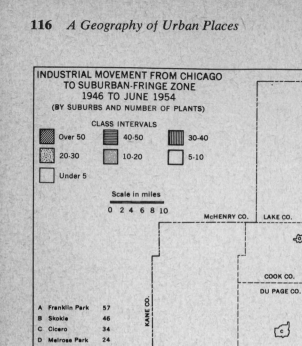

INDUSTRIAL MOVEMENT FROM CHICAGO
TO SUBURBAN-FRINGE ZONE
1946 TO JUNE 1954
(BY SUBURBS AND NUMBER OF PLANTS)

CLASS INTERVALS

Over 50	40-50	30-40
20-30	10-20	5-10
Under 5		

Scale in miles

0 2 4 6 8 10

A	Franklin Park	57
B	Skokie	46
C	Cicero	34
D	Melrose Park	24
E	Evanston	14
F	Bellwood	13
G	Shiller Park	10
H	Lincolnwood	10
I	Blue Island	9
J	Morton Grove	8

K	Niles	7	a	Hillside	2
L	Elmwood Park	7	b	Highland Park	2
M	Forest Park	6	c	Wheaton	2
N	Des Plaines	6	d	Deerfield	2
O	Stickney	5	e	Glenview	1
P	Lyons	5	f	Homewood	1
Q	Bedford Park	4	g	Northbrook	1
R	Maywood	4	h	LaGrange Park	1
S	River Grove	4	i	Northfield	1
T	Addison	4	j	River Forest	1
U	Chicago Heights	3	k	Westchester	1
V	Broadview	3	l	Oak Lawn	1
W	Arlington Heights	3	m	Melrose	1
X	Riverdale	2	n	Villa Park	1
Y	Wheeling	2	o	Palatine	1
Z	Bensenville	2	p	Westmount	1

Figure 3.

CONCLUSION

Manufacturing in the Chicago Standard Metropolitan Area remains highly concentrated in the City of Chicago despite rapid suburbanization since about 1945. Although there has been considerable relocation of manufacturing plants from the Inner Zone of the city to the Suburban-Fringe Zone, the primary increase in the Suburban Zone represents new industrial establishments. A net gain of industrial establishments in the Outer Zone of the city from 1941 to 1950 suggests that sufficient space and desirable factory sites were still available there during that period. The major direction of both industrial relocation and new industrial development has been toward the northern and northwestern suburbs immediately adjacent to the City of Chicago.

The Distribution of the Ethnic Groups in Chicago, 1960

13

Ying-Cheng Kiang

The purpose of this paper is to identify and explain the distribution of the major ethnic groups in Chicago since 1960. To a large extent, it is a follow-up of two previous studies dealing with the population succession in Chicago — one by Paul F. Cressey and the other by Richard G. Ford.[1] Cressey's paper covers the years 1898-1930; Ford's paper concerns 1940. Both papers include Negroes and seven groups of foreign-born whites — Polish, German (including Austrian), Italian, Russian, Irish, Swedish, and Czechoslovakian. This paper includes all these groups in addition to Mexican and Puerto Rican.

Following Ford's procedure, I have divided the city of Chicago into eighteen mile-wide concentric circle zones from the intersection of State and Madison Streets. The numbers of the ethnic groups in the different census tracts are recorded from the U.S. Census for 1960. Any census tract with 50 per cent or more of its area lying within a

[1] Paul F. Cressey, "Population Succession in Chicago: 1898-1930," *American Journal of Sociology*, Vol. XLIV (July, 1938), pp. 59-69; Richard G. Ford, "Population Succession in Chicago," *American Journal of Sociology*, Vol. LVI (September, 1950), pp. 156-60.

mile zone is listed as belonging to that zone. For purposes of comparison, I have grouped the tenth to eighteenth mile zones together, as Cressey and Ford did.

During 1940-60 the total population decreased from 15 per cent to 11 per cent of the total city residences for the first three mile zones, and increased from 7 per cent to 22 per cent for the tenth mile zone and beyond (Tables I and II). This indicates an outward movement of people from the Loop to the city's outskirts. The same trend is seen for all ethnic groups, except that there are no statistics showing the distribution of Mexicans and Puerto Ricans for the period of 1898-1940 in Cressey's or Ford's study. In 1940 up to 20 per cent of all the leading ethnic groups except Mexican and Puerto Rican were found in the inner zone (the first three mile zones). This reduced to 13 per cent or less in 1960. In 1940 from 2-11 per cent of all the leading ethnic groups except Mexicans, Puerto Ricans, and Negroes were found in the outer zone (the ten-mile zone and beyond). This increased to 13-47 per cent in 1960. The figures for Negroes were 1 per cent in 1940 and 9 per cent in 1960 in the outer zone. Generally speaking, the Irish moved

Reprinted from *American Journal of Sociology*, Vol. 74 (November, 1968), pp. 292-95 by permission.

TABLE I

The Distribution of the Ethnic Groups in Chicago, 1960*
(Percentage)

Mile Zone	Population										
	Total	German	Irish	Swedish	Polish	Italian	Russian	Czecho-slova-kian	Mexican	Puerto Rican	Negro
1	1	0	0	0	0	0	1	0	2	2	0
2	3	2	0	1	1	5	1	0	16	20	5
3	7	4	0	0	7	8	4	0	23	28	8
4	9	11	1	0	14	11	9	0	11	22	13
5	12	11	4	7	10	10	9	22	11	11	20
6	13	12	7	6	12	11	6	30	10	5	14
7	12	13	14	40	9	12	9	35	4	3	13
8	12	11	17	18	11	9	19	0	2	6	13
9	9	11	10	2	10	8	22	0	3	1	5
10	7	9	22	8	9	8	13	0	1	0	3
11	6	6	15	5	8	5	4	13	6	0	2
12	3	4	4	0	4	3	2	0	7	1	1
13	2	3	1	6	2	3	1	0	2	1	1
14	2	2	4	7	1	3	0	0	1	0	1
15	1	1	1	0	2	3	0	0	1	0	0
16	1	0	0	0	0	1	0	0	0	0	1
17	0	0	0	0	0	0	0	0	0	0	0
18	0	0	0	0	0	0	0	0	0	0	0
Total	100	100	100	100	100	100	100	100	100	100	100

* The city of Chicago is divided into eighteen mile zones from the intersection of Madison and State streets. The population figure in each mile zone is based on the U.S. Census. All census tracts with 50 per cent or more of their areas lying within a mile zone are listed as belonging to that zone.

farther than other foreign-born whites, who moved farther than the Negroes.

The 1940-60 trend was a continuation of the outward movement since 1898 except that the earlier movements were mainly from the inner zone to the middle zone located within 4-9 miles of the intersection of State and Madison Streets, rather than to the outer zone. As a result, the middle zone (proportionately) increased population before 1940. It declined afterward except that its Czechoslovakian population increased during 1940-60.

In 1960 the distribution of the leading ethnic groups in Chicago was partially due to a time factor in that those of the earliest group, such as the Irish and Swedish, were found farther from the Loop than the newcomers — the Mexicans and Puerto Ricans, and the Negroes. For example, in 1960 half of the city's Puerto Ricans were found in the inner zone and only about 1 per cent in the outer zone. The corresponding figures for the Irish were almost zero or less than 1 per cent, and 47 per cent, respectively.

Other factors related to the population

TABLE II

Percentage of Distribution of Ethnic Groups in Chicago*

Mile Zone	Population			
	1898	1920	1940	1960
Total:				
1-3	25	23	15	11
4-9	70	70	78	67
10 or more	5	7	7	22
Total	100	100	100	100
German:				
1-3	44	19	12	6
4-9	51	74	80	69
10 or more	5	7	8	25
Total	100	100	100	100
Irish:				
1-3	46	19	10	0
4-9	50	76	81	53
10 or more	4	5	9	47
Total	100	100	100	100
Swedish:				
1-3	38	10	8	1
4-9	52	78	81	73
10 or more	10	12	11	26
Total	100	100	100	100
Polish:				
1-3	60	38	20	8
4-9	29	48	69	66
10 or more	11	14	11	26
Total	100	100	100	100
Italian:				
1-3	85	25	15	13
4-9	12	73	83	61
10 or more	3	2	2	26
Total	100	100	100	100
Russian:				
1-3	72	30	8	6
4-9	25	66	88	74
10 or more	3	4	4	20
Total	100	100	100	100

TABLE II—*Continued*

Mile Zone	Population			
	1898	1920	1940	1960
Czechoslo-vakian:				
1-3	65	27	17	0
4-9	33	70	80	87
10 or more	2	3	3	13
Total	100	100	100	100
Mexican:				
1-3	—	—	—	40
4-9	—	—	—	42
10 or more	—	—	—	18
Total	—	—	—	100
Puerto Rican:				
1-3	—	—	—	50
4-9	—	—	—	49
10 or more	—	—	—	1
Total	—	—	—	100
Negro:				
1-3	66	24	15	13
4-9	33	75	84	78
10 or more	1	1	1	9
Total	100	100	100	100

* The figures for 1898, 1920, and 1940 are based on the diagrams in Richard G. Ford, "Population Succession in Chicago," *American Journal of Sociology*, Vol. LVI (September, 1950), pp. 156-60, except that there are no available data for Puerto Ricans and Mexicans during these years.

succession were the shape of the city, the reference point, and the direction of movement for each ethnic group. The city is longer from north to south than from east to west. Also, the intersection of Madison and State Streets is closer to the northern than to the southern city limits. As a result, within the city itself, the southward movement can go farther than the northern or western movement. A case to illustrate the point is that both Irish and German belong to the earliest immigrant group, but in 1960 there was a higher percentage of Germans in the inner or middle zone and more Irish in the outer zone. Actually, the Germans were dispersed as well as the Irish, but the latter moved toward the southern or the southwestern outskirts while the former were concentrated in the northern half of the city.

As a matter of fact, the whole city of Chicago contains seventy-six communities; each can be classified according to its ethnic composition in 1960 or afterward, as indicated in Table I. Two Negro districts and eight other ethnic districts can also be identified (Table II). The two Negro areas are the west (including the near west side, North Lawndale, East Garfield Park, and West Garfield Park) and the near south (including the near south side, Douglas, Oakland, Kenwood, Washington Park, Chatham, Armour Square, Fuller Park, Grand Boulevard, Englewood, Greater Grand Crossing, and Woodlawn), where the majorities have been Negroes since 1966. The other eight ethnic areas are the central, near north, far north, near northwest, far northwest, near southwest, far southwest, and far south. In 1960 the leading foreign ethnic group was German in the central and near north; Russian in the far north; Polish-German in the far northwest; Polish-German-Italian in the near northwest; the Polish in the near southwest (except German in Chicago Lawn); and the Irish in the far southwest. The far south was heterogeneous where Hungarians led in Burnside; Russians, in South Shore and South Deering; Polish, in South Chicago, East Side, Hegewisch, Calumet Heights, and West Pullman; Italians, in Roseland and Pullman; and Irish in Avalon Park; here Riverdale has been a Negro community. While the two Negro areas may remain unchanged ethnically, the other eight ethnic areas are subject to modifications because of recent developments.

Making a Living in Cities

Making A Living In Cities

Harold M. Mayer, in the opening paper of this section, overviews the characteristics of the types of economic activity common to urban places, and then deals in detail with examples of well established theories and methods of urban economic function analysis. References are made to many fundamental concepts of urban geography, primary, secondary, tertiary activities and their interrelationships; hierarchy and primate city; scale economies; trade areas; place utility. Special emphasis is given to transportation.

. . . the location of economic activities, and hence of urban places within which these activities are performed, depends upon transportation, and transportation geography and urban geography are practically inseparable.

The bulk of the paper examines the method of functional analysis available to the geographer interested in studying the urban economic base. Again, well established theory is discussed, the basic-nonbasic approach, the input-output approach, the minimum or average requirement approach, and factor analysis. Considerable space is devoted to outlining the basis of each and the problems related to their use. All of the approaches

. . . are concerned with the flows into and out of cities and regions and all of them develop the concept that the basic economic support of an area lies in the specialized functions which it performs for people and establishments outside of the area.

Mayer early establishes that urban socio-economic advantages

. . . depend upon the individual making a living.

The economic base, therefore, constitutes the reason for the development and growth of most cities.

Hans Blumenfeld in *The Economic Base of the Metropolis* argues vehemently and somewhat convincingly against the "basic-nonbasic" theory of urban economy for large cities. He also attempts to show how, in his opinion, the theory has been abused. Blumenfeld maintains that

It is thus the "secondary", "non basic" industries, both business and personal services, as well as "ancillary" manufacturing, that constitute the real and lasting strength of the metropolitan economy. As long as they continue to function efficiently, the metropolis will always be able to substitute new "export" industries for any that may be destroyed by the vicissitudes of economic life.

The paper provides for the student an example of argument and an example of how to substantiate argument. Blumenfeld makes his paper quite readable by using many examples from his own experience and a liberal selection of quotations from related work.

The Functional Bases of Small Towns, by Stafford, provides an easily read and understood application of simple statistics to geographic research. The economic function of small urban places is particularly well covered in the study of towns as central places. While this paper does provide insight into making a living in small urban places, it is the use of coefficient of correlation and regression that distinguishes it. Stafford relates his work to that of several other researchers, indicating how a seemingly isolated piece of research can be integrated with, and contribute to, the larger area of study.

The Function Of Cities

The following papers are selected as examples of studies in specific economic functions of urban places.

Two developments of human culture have been outstanding during the past century: The rapid advance of technology and the growth and spread of cities. Neither would have been possible without the other. Together they have made a revolution in the organization and pattern of land use. Transportation is the basis of both.

With this, Mayer introduces his paper on transportation and the city. In it he summarizes the development of the transportation methods, and shows how each has affected the city, morphologically and functionally. Mayer leaves little doubt about his feelings on the city-making characteristics and potentialities of the dominant urban modes of transport.

Voorhees, in *Transportation Planning and Urban Development* concentrates on the automobile. Congestion of cars produces traffic. Traffic is discussed from the point of view of factors causing congestion and the results. In conclusion some generalities are made on transportation solutions.

In *Retail Structure of Urban Economy* and *Emerging Patterns of Commercial Structure in American Cities,* the commercial function of urban places is discussed. The first paper, by Kelley, focuses attention largely on the 'regional shopping centre'. In so doing, however, comparisons are made with other types of retail organization and structure. The development and characteristics of the 're-gional shopping centre,' the factors of location and the relations of the centre to the CBD are discussed at length in the paper. The scope of the Vance paper is considerably wider. Here

the author provides the student with a well organized model of subject research and presentation. After an introduction, he deals in the theory of commercial location based upon recent developments and the historical growth of the retail function in America. The last half of the paper is an application of the principles established to the San Francisco Bay Area. In this section the method of research is outlined and much of the data plotted on maps.

William Goodwin in *The Management Center in the United States* raises the question of considering functions not easily classified by writers on the economic base of cities. After establishing the importance of the management function, he develops an easily understood spatial and functional analysis making excellent use of graphics in distribution maps, scatter diagrams, tables, and graphs.

Reference to the central business district is made in several of the above papers. It is a spacial entity which has received considerable attention because of critical changes that have taken place and because it is the focus of major renewal activity in almost all major cities. In *Public Policy and the Central Business District* and *The Core of the City: Emerging Concepts* the functions and problems of this zone are discussed and projections are made for its future. Boyce raises the question of whether the CBD will or should continue to exist.

City and Region

Certainly one of the most critical areas of concern for urban geographers and planners alike has been the area into which present day cities are expanding, and the much larger sphere of influence beyond. Each city is surrounded by its hinterland, umland, suburbia, exurbia, slurbs. These, and other terms coined by researchers, relate to some aspect of the region served by and serving the city at the centre.

Spelt, in *Towns and Umlands,* defines umland — its functions, and the relationships and feelings that have developed between the city and this area. Considerable space is devoted to the problem of fixing boundaries. Many examples of devices used for boundary definition are cited. Bonn, Germany is used to introduce some thoughts on regional planning.

External Relations of Cities: City — Hinterland, by Epstein, compares the functions of city and of hinterland. The distribution of functions is dynamic. Many shifts that have taken place relate to increased individual mobility. Residence and economic functions, once tied to the city proper, have relocated outside the corporate limits. Epstein examines the centrifugal and centripetal forces operative today causing shifts in the pattern of land use in city and region.

Gaffney in *Urban Expansion — Will it Ever Stop?* and Clawson in *Urban Sprawl and Land Speculation* attack a universal problem of North American cities, sprawl. The concern is for space — the amount of space consumed and the wasteful character of its consumption. The cause is seen to be economic. Gaffney's

. . . thesis . . . is that urban land prices are uneconomically high — that the scarcity of urban land is an artificial one, maintained by the holdout of vastly underestimated supplies in anticipation of vastly overestimated future demands.

The authors describe, document and explain the problem in detail.

Some solutions are offered. Neither author is particularly hopeful or very realistic when one considers the record of the individuals or institutions responsible.

Making a Living in Cities: The Urban Economic Base

14

Harold M. Mayer

People live in or near cities in order to secure advantages which would not be possible under non-urban conditions. Among these advantages are the satisfaction of many desires: social, religious, recreational, and economic, but most of them depend upon the individuals making a living. The economic base, therefore, constitutes the reason for the development and growth of most cities. Even essentially non-economic functions, such as defense, recreation, and pilgrimages to historic and religious shrines, constitute important income-producing activities for the cities and regions within which they occur. Knowledge of the economic base of cities, therefore, is an indispensable prerequisite to an understanding of urban geography.

Characteristics Of Urban Functions

Jean Bruhnes, two generations ago, called urban land uses such as houses and streets "unproductive occupation of the soil."[1] He was referring, of course, to the classical concept of the economist that the significant inputs into an economic system are land, labor,

[1] Jean Bruhnes, *Human Geography* (Chicago, Rand McNally & Co., 1920), pp. 74-229.

and capital, and that the natural resources of the site, including its agricultural, mineral, or silvicultural productivity, are the only productive forms of land use. More recently, Chauncy Harris pointed out that cities are efficient instruments for utilizing resources productively, including labor, which must concentrate in and near cities in order to perform its increasingly specialized roles, and that, in proportion to the amount of land used, urban land is thus extremely productive, in the sense that it creates utility by the processing, transfer, and distribution of goods and services.[2]

Economists and geographers find it useful to divide income-producing activities into several categories, which they designate as primary, secondary, and tertiary.[3] Primary activities are those which produce utility, and

[2] Chauncy D. Harris, "The Pressure of Residential-Industrial Land Use," *Man's Role In Changing the Face of the Earth*, by William L. Thomas, Jr., *ed.* (Chicago, the University of Chicago Press, 1956), pp. 881-95.

[3] Most standard textbooks in economic geography have adopted this terminology, for example: John W. Alexander, *Economic Geography* (Englewood Cliffs, N.J., Prentice-Hall, Inc., 1963), pp. 5-6.

Reprinted from *Journal of Geography* (February, 1969), pp. 70-87 by permission.

hence income, by extraction of the resources on the site, whether the resources are renewable, such as agricultural produce or waterpower, or are non-renewable, such as minerals and petroleum. Secondary activities are those in which goods are handled; included in that category of economic activities are manufacturing and transportation: any activity which involves the changing of the form or location of commodities. Tertiary activities involve either the performance of services or change in ownership of goods, as in wholesale and retail trade. With increasing complexity of society and its economic activities, there is an ever-increasing amount of record-keeping and "paper work"; some authors prefer to categorize these activities as quaternary, rather than tertiary.[4]

Few cities have as their most important functions the primary activities. Even though many urban places are directly dependent upon such activities, they actually function as manufacturing or service centers, utilizing the resources produced nearby or performing services for the organizations and people who, in turn, are directly involved in the primary activities. If the resource is non-replaceable, the urban center which serves the extractive operations may have a precarious economic base, and may decline or disappear when the resource is exhausted or becomes non-

competitive in the market with other sources or substitute resources. Such places may become "ghost towns" unless other activities can be introduced to replace the declining ones.

Urban land is valuable, then, not for its inherent productivity of natural resources, but, rather, because of its location with relation to the secondary, tertiary, and quaternary activities: the handling of goods and the performance of services.[5] Since land is valuable only for its present and prospective uses, and all urban functions, most of which are economic in character, take place on land, it follows that studies of the economic base must constitute essential parts of the field of urban geography as well as major components of the research which is an integral part of the process of city and regional planning. Because urban functions are highly localized and concentrated, the spatial aspects of the urban economy are the foci of the geographer's interest in economic base studies.

Communities which depend mainly on primary economic activities — the extraction of resources — directly or indirectly for their support, are, of course, resource-oriented with respect to their locations: they are located close to the resources. Those urban places which depend mainly upon secondary activities — manufacturing, assembling, and packaging of goods — may be resource-oriented in location, or market-oriented, depending upon many variables, such as the

---

[4] For an interesting account of the significance of these functions in metropolitan New York, see: Sidney M. Robbins and Nestor E. Terleckyi, *Money Metropolis* (Cambridge, Harvard University Press, 1960). Administrative functions may also be regarded as quaternary, as, for example, in Jean Gottmann, *Megalopolis* (New York, The Twentieth Century Fund, 1961), pp. 565-630. A discussion of business management as an urban function is: William Goodwin, "The Management Center in the United States," *Geographical Review*, Vol. LX, no. 1 (January, 1965), pp. 1-16.

[5] Location as related to urban land values is emphasized in all treatises on urban land economics and real estate. See, for example: Richard U. Ratcliff, *Urban Land Economics* (New York, McGraw-Hill Book Co., Inc., 1949); Ernest M. Fisher and Robert M. Fisher, *Urban Real Estate* (New York, Henry Holt & Co., 1954); and Arthur M. Weimer and Homer Hoyt, *Principles of Real Estate* (New York, The Ronald Press Company, 1954), 3rd. ed.

relations of weight, bulk, and value of the goods, and hence their ability to stand transportation costs as raw materials, semi-finished goods or components, or manufactured products, or they may be "footloose" and free to locate anywhere between the source of their resource inputs and the final markets.[6] As transportation costs are reduced relative to other costs, there is a noteworthy tendency for an increasing proportion of the manufacturing industries to become footloose or market-oriented.[7] This tends to accentuate the population and economic growth of the larger urban agglomerations, and to augment their attractiveness for still more activities and population; there is thus a "multiplier effect."

Wholesale trade may be regarded as a form of secondary economic activity in the sense that goods are handled and stored; orders are assembled for distribution, and warehouse buildings represent forms of industrial structures. Wholesale facilities, therefore, are subject to the same effects as are manufacturing establishments. They may be located in proximity to the manufacturing establishments, but more commonly they are located close to the major markets — the larger urban centers. On the other hand, competition for centrally-located urban land by other uses generally forces wholesale establishments having warehousing requirements to the peripheries of the larger cities, while the wholesale office establishments and display rooms may remain in more central locations. In general, improvements in transportation and changes in the methods of marketing, including the rise of chain stores, standard brands, and emphasis upon reduced inventories requiring storage, has reduced the relative importance of warehousing as an element in the urban pattern. The current trend is to consider wholesaling and warehousing as an "interface" or intermediate stage in a transportation route which, in turn, is part of a total distribution system.[8] With a trend toward separation of warehouses from offices and sales rooms of wholesalers, the latter may more properly be regarded as tertiary, rather than secondary, functions. On the whole, there have been far fewer studies of the locational patterns, both theoretical and empirical, than of location of either manufacturing or of retailing establishments.

The final stage in the chain of movement of resources, whether or not they undergo change enroute, is the distribution of goods and services to the ultimate consumer. Tertiary activities thus tend to be less concentrated in location than do the primary and

[6] There is vast literature on location theory relative to secondary activities. Some of the more important items include such classical studies as: Alfred Weber, *Theory of the Location of Industries* (Chicago, University of Chicago Press, 1928); August Lösch, *The Economics of Location* (New Haven, Yale University Press, 1954); and Edgar M. Hoover, *The Location of Economic Activity* (New York, McGraw-Hill Book Co., Inc., 1948). A brief summary of location theory relative to secondary functions is: William Alonso, "Location Theory," *Regional Development and Planning* by John Friedmann and William Alonso (Cambridge, The M.I.T. Press, 1964), pp. 78-106. For a comprehensive bibliography on the subject, see: Benjamin H. Stevens and Carolyn A. Brackett, *Industrial Location, A Review and Annotated Bibliography of Theoretical, Empirical and Case Studies* (Philadelphia, Regional Science Research Institute, 1967).

[7] Chauncy D. Harris, "The Market as a Factor in the Location of Industry in the United States," *Annals of the Association of American Geographers*, Vol. XLIV, no. 4 (December, 1954), pp. 315-48.

[8] Charles A. Taff, *Management of Traffic and Physical Distribution* (Homewood, Ill., Richard D. Irwin, Inc., 1968).

secondary activities. Some, such as food retailing, tend to locate in patterns closely resembling those of the consuming population, for everyone eats. Goods and services which are more specialized tend to be less ubiquitous, and to concentrate in larger urban centers, for they require a larger population base, or disposable income, for their support. Thus there tends to be a hierarchy of retail and service establishments, with the more specialized ones in fewer but larger urban centers, and there also tends to be a hierarchy of the urban centers which supply consumer goods and services, the larger centers, requiring a larger "threshold" of support, having larger and more specialized establishments. The "trade areas" or "hinterlands" of the larger and more specialized establishments, and consequently of the larger urban centers containing them, tend to be larger than those of the less specialized urban places. At the same time, the larger centers also have "lower order" functions within them, duplicating the functions of the smaller centers, and serving smaller trade areas than those of the more specialized functions within the same center.

The location and characteristics of the tertiary functions of urban places, and their respective service areas have been intensively studied over several decades by geographers and others, and a theoretical framework has been developed, generally known as "central place theory," following the terminology of Walter Christaller, who formalized the theoretical statement in 1933.[9] There is probably a larger volume of theoretical and empirical studies of central places than of any

other topic within the entire field of urban geography.[10]

In satisfying the economic demands of people everywhere, except in the few remaining isolated regions which are self-sufficient, goods and services are made available at the locations of the consumers, who constitute the market, regardless of where the resources are originally located. In terms used by economists, resources must be given "place utility": they must be transported. Goods must be delivered and services must be performed either at the residential location of the consumer or at an establishment so located as to involve a minimum of travel by the consumer. In any event, the complex of establishments providing goods and services (including consumption) involves clusters of inter-related complementary or competitive establishments, or central places. These places, in turn, must be accessible, and thus they are served by networks of transportation and communication routes. They are nodes or vertices, in an inter-connected network of lines or routes over which people and goods move in order to satisfy demands for goods and services. Central place theory relates tertiary functions and establishments to the transportation network. Location theory, which describes and interprets the patterns of

[9] Walter Christaller, *Central Places in Southern Germany*, trans. by Carlisle W. Buskin (Englewood Cliffs, N.J., Prentice-Hall, Inc., 1966).

[10] A comprehensive bibliography, listing hundreds of studies of central places is Brian J. L. Berry and Allen Pred, *Central Place Studies, A Bibliography of Theory and Applications, Including Supplement Through 1964* (Philadelphia, Regional Science Research Institute, 1965). A recent concise statement on the subject is Brian J. L. Berry, *Geography of Market Centers and Retail Distribution* (Englewood Cliffs, N.J., Prentice-Hall, Inc., 1967). The subject will be developed further by Bart J. Epstein in a subsequent article in this *Journal of Geography* series.

location of secondary functions and establishments, likewise depends upon the existence of a transportation network[11] for assembly of inputs — raw materials, fuels, components, and labor — and the distribution of outputs from the establishment to successive establishments for later stages in the transformation of resources from their original state and location into forms and locations to meet the consumer demands. Thus, the location of economic activities, and hence of urban places within which these activities are performed, depends upon transportation, and transportation geography and urban geography are practically inseparable.[12]

Accessibility is fundamental to the performance of any economic function. Since all inter-acting establishments and functions cannot be located in mutual proximity, transportation must be used to overcome distance.

[11] Some geographers have applied "graph theory" to the description and interpretation of transportation networks, with urban centers as the nodes or vertices. See, for example: Peter Haggett, *Locational Analysis in Human Geography* (New York, St. Martin's Press, 1966), pp. 61-86; W. L. Garrison, "Connectivity of the Interstate Highway System," *Regional Science Association, Papers and Proceedings*, Vol. VI (1960), pp. 121-37; and K. J. Kansky, *Structure of Transportation Networks: Relationships between Network Geometry and Regional Characteristics*, Research Paper No. 84 (Chicago, University of Chicago, Department of Geography, 1963).

[12] It is not within the scope of this series to review transportation geography. However, see Edward L. Ullman and Harold M. Mayer, "Transportation· Geography," *American Geography, Inventory and Prospect*, Preston E. James and Clarence F. Jones, *eds.* (Syracuse, Syracuse University Press, 1954), pp. 311-32; also Harold M. Mayer, "Urban Geography and Urban Transportation Planning," *Traffic Quarterly*, Vol. XVII, no. 4 (October, 1963), pp. 610-31.

In movement of resources between origin and place of utilization, and in providing goods and services at and from central places, movement along transportation routes must take place. Movement represents a cost, and the cost may be substituted for lineal mileage in the measurement of distance in determining the effectiveness and strength of the bonds which inter-relate places with one another. The boundaries of the areas within which resources may effectively compete with alternative sources, and the boundaries of trade and service areas around central places can be ascertained, in general, by application of the concept of "distance decay," which simply means that the farther apart two places are, the less traffic is likely to be generated between them, and there is a point in every direction from a place, where some other place is equally attractive; such a place is a "traffic-divide" or a hinterland boundary. The "distance decay" tends to be a negative exponential curve; the strength of the attraction to a particular place falls off at a decreasing rate with distance. Also, the larger and more diversified a place is, the stronger the attraction it exerts. This is analogous to the physical law of gravitation, and the gravity analog or model has been very useful in predicting the traffic generation to be exerted by cities, shopping centers, and other nodes, as well as to anticipate the volume of traffic to be moved on new links in the transportation networks. Similarly, the total gravitative attraction exerted by a central place or establishment represents the total attraction of that place relative to all other places with which it has interaction. The latter represents what is called "potential." If all of the places in the United States have their relative potentials represented by an imaginary surface, such as can be shown by contours, it can readily be seen that the places and areas with highest density of population and purchasing power — namely, the cities and urbanized regions — represent peaks and ridges of maximum potential.[13] These areas are especially attractive for new market-oriented establishments and activities.[14] In other words, the larger and more accessible urban places and regions tend to attract economic activity, and hence population, to a greater extent than do smaller places and less densely populated regions. The additional concentration of people, establishments, and activities, in turn, further reinforces the market, and gives rise to still further growth, specialization, and diversity, and thereby creates still additional attractive force. With larger markets, more goods and services can be, and are, provided, and the unit costs of production, spread over more units, can be reduced, making the large urban concentrations still more attractive; this is

what economists call "agglomeration economies" or "scale economies." Furthermore, the larger cities and metropolitan areas can support increased specialization; a wider variety of goods and services is available from an increasing number of specialized establishments, thereby reducing or eliminating the necessity for many auxiliary activities from being related to specific plants; the specialized establishment can be called upon to supply items or services which otherwise each plant would have to supply for itself. This increases overall efficiency and makes establishments in larger and more diversified urban areas better able to compete, with lower costs, in more distant markets, thereby overcoming to a major extent the transportation cost disadvantages in reaching distant markets. This phenomenon is called "external economies," and it is a major force in attracting many activities to the larger cities.[15] Its effects constitute an essential base for central place theory, and Mark Jefferson recognized it in his "Law of the Primate City," when he pointed out that the largest city in a region or nation tends to enhance its primacy by exerting the strongest attractions for the greatest variety of activities.[16] In one sense, the primate city may be regarded as a special case: it represents the top of the hierarchy of central places. In many countries and regions, the numbers of urban places of various population sizes seem to follow a rank-size relationship in which all places bear a definite size relationship to the largest place, in regular

[13] Gerald A. P. Carruthers, "An Historical Review of the Gravity and Potential Concepts of Human Interaction," *Journal of the American Institute of Planners*, Vol. XXII, no. 2 (Spring, 1956), pp. 94-102; Walter Isard, "Gravity, Potential and Spatial Interaction Models," *Methods of Regional Analysis* (New York, Technology Press and John Wiley & Sons, 1960), chap. 11; F. Luckermann and P. W. Porter, "Gravity and Potential Models in Economic Geography," *Annals of the Association of American Geographers*, Vol. L, no. 4 (December, 1960), pp. 493-504; Gunnar Olson, *Distance and Human Interaction, A Review and Bibliography* (Philadelphia, Regional Science Research Institute, 1965), pp. 43-70.

[14] John Q. Stewart, "Empirical Mathematical Rules Concerning the Distribution and Equilibrium of Population," *Geographical Review*, Vol. XXXVII, no. 3 (July, 1947), pp. 461-62 and 471-85; William Warntz, "A New Map of the Surface of Population Potentials for the United States 1960," *Geographical Review*, Vol. LIV, no. 2 (April, 1964), pp. 170-84.

[15] Robert M. Lichtenberg, *One Tenth of a Nation: National Forces in the Economic Growth of the New York Region* (Cambridge, Harvard University Press, 1960), especially pp. 56-70.

[16] Mark Jefferson, "The Law of the Primate City," *Geographical Review*, Vol. XXIX, no. 2 (April, 1939), pp. 226-32.

descending order of rank: thus the second-ranking place would tend to be half the size of the largest place, the third ranking place one-third the size, and so forth. Cities and metropolitan areas of the United States tend to have such a rank-size relationship.[17] Here, the primate city is, of course, the top-ranking one, and all others tend to be related in population size inversely to their rank; New York is the primate city, Chicago and Los Angeles metropolitan areas, respectively, are the next-ranking ones, but New York also contains regional functions for the eastern third of the United States, corresponding to the regional functions of Chicago for the Midwest and Los Angeles for the Far West. Below these regional primate cities, in each instance, there is a regular procession of metropolitan areas (SMSA's), having a rank-size relationship.

Traffic Flows And The Urban Economic Base

We have seen that cities constitute foci or nodes in networks of transportation and communication, making possible the inter-actions with other cities and with the service areas or hinterlands. The urban functions depend upon accessibility, which conditions specialization of land uses,[18] and give rise to interchange, or movement of people, goods, and ideas between and among cities, and between cities and their respective hinterlands.[19] These flows, constituting what Edward Ullman calls "spatial interaction,"[20] produce traffic, the volume of which, along transportation and communication routes, is the measurable result of the gravitative "pulls" exerted by the various urban centers or subcenters: the "traffic generators."

Since cities are essentially areas of specialized land uses, facilities, and establishments, which depend upon spatial interactions with each other and with external areas, it follows that an effective method of analysis of the economic base of a city or metropolitan area would be to study the volumes and composition of the traffic flows — of people, goods, and information — between the city and each area or region outside. These flows, of course, are two directional, and they reflect the nature of the urban functions which give rise to them.

Unfortunately, however, there are several major difficulties. One set of difficulties is the general lack of usable data on traffic flows for areas which are geographically significant.[21] There are several reasons for lack of useful data: among them are the high cost of gathering information, commercial competition in the United States where common and contract carriers are mainly private enterprises,

[17] For a further description of rank-size distributions, see Walter Isard, *Location and Space-Economy* (Cambridge, Technology Press, and New York, John Wiley & Sons, Inc., 1956), pp. 55-64; F. W. Boal and D. B. Johnson, "The Rank-Size Curve, A Diagnostic Tool?" *The Professional Geographer*, Vol. XVII, no. 5 (September, 1965), pp. 21-23.

[18] Walter G. Hansen, "How Accessibility Shapes Land Use," *Journal of the American Institute of Planners*, Vol. XXV, no. 2 (May, 1959), pp. 73-76.

[19] Harold M. Mayer, "Urban Nodality and the Economic Base," *Journal of the American Institute of Planners*, Vol. XX, no. 3 (Summer, 1954), pp. 117-21.

[20] Edward L. Ullman, "The Role of Transportation and the Bases for Interaction," *Man's Role in Changing the Face of the Earth*, William L. Thomas, Jr. (Chicago, University of Chicago Press, 1956), pp. 862-80.

[21] Problems of delimitation of urban areas were discussed in the preceding article: Harold M. Mayer, "Cities and Urban Geography," *Journal of Geography*, Vol. LXVIII, no. 1 (January, 1969), pp. 6-19.

the high proportion of the traffic which is carried in private vehicles, military security, and lack of agreement on area boundaries for statistical purposes.

Geographic studies of ports are numerous, nevertheless, and it was largely as a result of the concepts of hinterlands developed in port studies that the city-region relationships have been emphasized by urban geographers.[22] Port statistics are more readily available than are statistics for other transportation movements, and especially available are international movement statistics, for people and goods involved in transit through ports enroute to or from foreign countries are subject to regulation by immigration, customs, and public health authorities, all of whom maintain statistics, and many of whom publish aggregated figures on such movements in more or less usable form.

Ports, furthermore, are of special interest to geographers, because they are generally gateways to and between complementary regions, the interactions of which, in the form of traffic flows, may be indicative of the character of development of the respective regions. Extensive statistics are available, for many nations, on the volume, direction, and composition of flows of goods and people through their respective ports, although commonly the landward points of origin and destination are difficult or impossible to determine without elaborate supplementary studies.

Detailed point-to-point statistics are available for domestic and international movements of air passengers and cargo at airports of the United States and some other countries, though here, too, the actual landward origins and destinations, beyond the respective airports, may be difficult to determine. Nevertheless, the air traffic flows among urban areas are indicative of the character, extent, and volume of interaction among major cities, and several studies by geographers have been useful in determining the air traffic hinterlands of cities.[23]

Railway traffic flows are generally unavailable, or are not available for geographically meaningful areas, and it is difficult, and usually impossible, to determine the volume and nature of freight movements into, out of, and through, urban areas.[24] Similarly, movements by motor truck are not generally available, although a few special studies have been made to determine the motor truck hinterlands of cities; these, however, do not include information by commodities.[25] In some parts of the world, inter-city bus services carry significant proportions of the passenger

[22] Among the hundreds of port studies stressing hinterland relationships, the following represent a few of the more significant ones: Guido G. Weigand, "Some Elements in the Study of Port Geography," *The Geographical Review*, Vol. XLVIII, no. 2 (April, 1958), pp. 185-200; Donald J. Patton, "General Cargo Hinterlands of New York, Philadelphia, Baltimore, and New Orleans," *Annals of the Association of American Geographers*, Vol. XLVIII, no. 4 (December, 1958), pp. 436-55; Edwin H. Draine, *Import Traffic of Chicago and Its Hinterland*, Research Paper No. 81 (Chicago, University of Chicago, Department of Geography, 1963).

[23] For example: Edward J. Taaffe, *The Air Passenger Hinterland of Chicago*, Research Paper No. 24 (Chicago, University of Chicago, Department of Geography, 1952).

[24] State-to-state data, by commodities, have been available for the past two decades from one per cent waybill samples; see Edward L. Ullman, *American Commodity Flow* (Seattle, University of Washington Press, 1957).

[25] Magne Helvig, *Chicago's External Truck Movements*, Research Paper No. 90 (Chicago, University of Chicago, Department of Geography, 1964).

movement. In such instances the pattern of bus routes is indicative of the urban hinterlands, and may be used to indicate, also, the position of towns in the central-place hierarchy.[26] In the United States, however, only a small portion, less than 2.5 percent, of the inter-city personal movement is by bus, while private automobiles are responsible for over 90 percent of the passenger movement to, from, and between urban places. Knowledge of the volumes, directions, purposes, and other characteristics of automobile trips is indispensable, therefore, not only for the planning of street and highway systems, but also as an integral part of the process of city and metropolitan planning generally, in which the reciprocal relations between transportation systems on the one hand and the locations, functional characteristics, and densities of land uses on the other are studied in considerable detail, and projections are made of possible alternative arrangements of transportation routes and land uses in the future. Indeed, such studies, integrating the functional patterns of urban areas and the present and proposed locations of streets, highways, and other transportation facilities have been made mandatory by the federal government since 1965 as prerequisite for federal funding of many public improvements, including highways, mass transit, urban renewal, open space land acquisition, sewer and water supply systems, and many others. Such studies are required to extend beyond city boundaries and to include all metropolitan areas. They are generally conducted by designated metropolitan or regional planning agencies, which subsequently must indicate conformance with regional comprehensive plans if any local governmental unit is to receive financial aid from the federal government for each of a wide variety of public improvement programs. In these studies, urban and transportation geographers are playing increasingly important roles. Particularly significant is the fact that studies of origins and destinations of present and prospective trips are always major portions of such comprehensive planning operations, and economic base studies form the framework for population projections which, in turn, are highly useful in the preparation of comprehensive regional, metropolitan, and city plans.[27] The potentialities for utilization of the increasing number of such transportation-land use studies in determining the nature and extent of the economic base and hinterland connections of cities are very promising. As such studies are produced for more and more areas, intercity comparative analyses may yield significant generalizations and understandings relative to urban growth and

[26] S. Godlund, "The Function and Growth of Bus Traffic within the Sphere of Urban Influence," *Lund Studies in Geography, Series B, Human Geography*, Vol. 18 (1956); F. H. W. Green, "Motor Bus Centers in S.W. England Considered in Relation to Population and Shopping Facilities," *Transactions and Papers, Institute of British Geographers* (1948), pp. 57-68; "Bus Services as an Index to Changing Urban Hinterlands," *Town Planning Review*, Vol. XXII (1951), pp. 345-56.

[27] Examples of such comprehensive metropolitan planning studies include: *Report on the Detroit Metropolitan Area Traffic Study* (Lansing, Speaker, Hines and Thomas, Inc., 1955 and 1956), 2 vols.; *Chicago Area Transportation Study Final Report* (Chicago, 1959-1962), 3 vols.; *Pittsburgh Area Transportation Study* (Pittsburgh, 1961 and 1963), 2 vols. For a concise general description of the nature and findings of such studies, see John F. Kain, "Urban Travel Behavior," *Urban Research and Policy Planning*, Leo F. Schnore and Henry Fagin, *eds.* (Beverly Hills, Calif., Sage Publications, Inc., 1967), pp. 161-92.

development, leading to predictive models of great theoretical and practical importance. Furthermore, as subsequent studies are made, in future years, for the same areas as those subjected to earlier studies, detailed knowledge may be gained of changes and trends in the economic base, population distribution and characteristics, and travel patterns of such urban areas.

Such comprehensive metropolitan transportation studies confirm the fact that only a very small proportion of the trips originating or terminating within a metropolitan area cross the boundary of the area, as would be expected from the nature of the definition of such areas. Flows crossing the boundary, however — "external" trips — are significant to understanding the nature of city-hinterland relations. Flows of goods are less readily available statistically, but the proportion of total goods movements which are external undoubtedly far exceeds the proportion of internal trips, for urban areas consume tremendous quantities of goods and fuels, and must ship out vast amounts of products and wastes. If more detailed information relative to these movements were available, we could much better understand the nature and extent of the urban economic base.

For purposes of economic base analysis, however, the most significant classification of flows of both people and goods is the dichotomy between external movements, originating or terminating beyond the area boundaries, on the one hand, and internal movements not crossing the area boundaries, on the other hand.

Cities and regions, engaged in production of specialized goods and services, provide economic support for their populations by exchanging such production, to the extent that they do not consume it themselves, for the specialized goods and services produced by other cities and regions. Thus there are "inputs" and "outputs," the total representing the external trade of the given city or region. However, there are two additional considerations. One is that not all of the production can be "exported," because the needs of the people and establishments within the given area must also be satisfied, and a portion of the goods and services which the area produces are for local consumption. A second consideration is that the value of the inputs and outputs of an area may not be equal in value; therefore if the value of inputs exceeds that of outputs, the balance must be restored by outflows of money and credit, and, conversely, if the area exports are of higher value than the imports or inputs, money and credit must flow into the area. This, of course, has been extensively studied for nations, for which the balance of payments may be critical. National balance of payments accounts are relatively easy to determine, for records are kept and are available for flows of goods, services, people, money, and credit across national boundaries. For local or sub-national areas, however, such as cities and metropolitan areas, few usable records are available, and geographers cannot directly study the economic base of such areas in the same way as the national and international balance of payments can be investigated.[28] Furthermore, although income and its distribution is important, geographers are also interested in the numbers and char-

---

[28] For further discussion of the "balance of payments approach," see Wilbur R. Thompson, *A Preface to Urban Economics* (Baltimore, The Johns Hopkins Press, 1965), especially pp. 61-104, or the chapter by the same author in *The Study of Urbanization*, Philip M. Hauser and Leo F. Schnore, *eds.* (New York, John Wiley & Sons, Inc., 1965), pp. 431-90.

acteristics of the people supported by a city's income, the physical flows of goods and services, and the facilities for effectuating such flows; income flows alone tell only a part of the story.

Three approaches to the study of the economic base of cities have been extensively used by geographers. All are based upon the concepts of flows and the dichotomy of external and internal components of economic support. These approaches may be termed: (1) the basic-nonbasic approach, (2) the input-output approach, and (3) the minimum or average requirements approach. All of them are concerned with the flows into and out of cities and regions, and all of them develop the concept that the basic economic support of an area lies in the specialized functions which it performs for people and establishments outside of the area. The cliché that people do not live by taking in each other's washing is crude, but apt.

The Basic-Nonbasic Approach

The basic-nonbasic approach has particular appeal for geographic study because it provides a tool by which may be determined the extent of specialization within a city or region, as contrasted with larger regions of which it is a part, or of other cities and regions. Furthermore, it can furnish an indication, though crude, of the number of people, as well as their incomes, supported by each "export" activity, and it furnishes a measure of the extent to which the city or region is dependent upon other cities and regions. Such determinations are extremely useful in determining which activities are vital, and which serve the population within the city or region which is, in turn, dependent upon the "basic" or "export" activities. In planning and development programs, it follows that stimulation

of and provision for the "export" or "basic" activities would result in more leverage for growth than would the further development of the remaining functions or activities which are dependent upon the basic ones.[29] Since the population engaged in supplying goods and services for consumption outside the given region, such as a metropolitan area, must, in turn, be supplied with goods and services, the employment and income involved in such secondary or supporting activities represents a "multiplier effect." The population — to which must be added family dependents — and the income involved in the "export" activities are considered "basic" and the people and incomes involved in supplying the needs of the basic population is termed "nonbasic" or "secondary." This population, in turn, must also be supplied, so there is a succession of rounds of employment and income created, resulting in further population increases.

There are several ways in which the extent to which a given urban function is basic may be measured, and in which determination may be made of the extent to which any combination of functions contributes to the economic base of a community or region.[30] Thus, if a given activity, say steel production,

[29] A useful and concise statement of the history, assumptions, methods, and applications of the basic-nonbasic approach is John W. Alexander, "The Basic-Nonbasic Concept of Urban Economic Functions," *Economic Geography*, Vol. XXX, no. 3 (July, 1954), pp. 246-61, reprinted in *Readings in Urban Geography*, Harold M. Mayer and Clyde F. Kohn, *eds.* (Chicago, University of Chicago Press, 1959), pp. 87-104.

[30] Detailed discussion of economic base methodology is contained in a series of articles by Richard B. Andrews in *Land Economics*, 1953-1956, most of which were reprinted in *The Techniques of Urban Economic Analysis*, Ralph W. Pfouts, *ed.* (West Trenton, N.J., Chandler-Davis Publ. Co., 1960).

results in employment (or income, if the figures were available) within a metropolitan area to the extent that such employment represents twice the proportion of steel-production employment as steel-production employment percentage is of the employment in the same category of industry in a larger area, such as the nation as a whole, it is assumed that the difference, or surplus employment, represents that proportion of the workers engaged in producing steel for shipment outside the area. This is "basic" or "city forming"[31] employment, while the remaining employment in the steel plants of the metropolitan area is "nonbasic" or "city serving" employment, producing for local consumption. The ratio between basic and nonbasic employment — the "B/N" ratio — indicates the relative importance of each category of economic activity in producing employment and hence contributing to the economic support of the city or region.

There are many difficulties in applying this rather simple concept. One set of problems involves the difficulties of obtaining data. It is not always possible to ascertain the extent to which a given category of activity actually serves patrons or customers outside the region, particularly where, in large and complex areas such as metropolitan areas, there is a sufficiently large number of establishments so that individual questionnaires become prohibitively expensive and time-consuming; furthermore, because of commercial competition, a significant proportion of the business establishments would

withhold such data.[32] In most such studies, aggregated statistics, such as census reports, are used.[33]

Another problem is the selection of the appropriate measures. This is determined largely by the use to be made of the results, i.e.: whether it is desired to obtain the B/N ratio with respect to employment, income, present and prospective land use by categories of activity, or other types of findings. If employment figures are to be used, allowances must be made for part-time, seasonal, and other irregular employment, for the elasticity of demand for marginal workers, such as married women and young people who may or may not be on the labor market depending upon the level of economic activity and wages at a given time, commuting labor force from outside the defined area, absentee population such as members of the armed forces, remittances from people and establishments outside which may create a market and hence employment within the area, and many other variables.

The delimitation of the area boundaries may constitute another set of problems. Ad-

---

[31] Gunnar Alexandersson, *The Industrial Structure of American Cities* (Lincoln, University of Nebraska Press, 1956), pp. 14-20, reprinted in Mayer & Kohn, *op. cit.*, pp. 110-15.

[32] Nevertheless, in small cities it may be possible to obtain such information, where a limited number of large establishments may be questioned individually, together with a carefully selected sample of smaller establishments; for example, John W. Alexander, *Oshkosh, Wisconsin, An Economic Base Study and An Economic Base Study of Madison, Wisconsin* (Madison, University of Wisconsin Bureau of Business Research, 1951 and 1953).

[33] Since such sources are insufficiently detailed, the resulting economic base studies are necessarily crude; for example, Homer Hoyt, *The Economic Status of the New York Metropolitan Region in 1944* (New York, The Regional Plan Association, Inc., 1944).

ministrative boundaries — cities, counties, and states — rarely represent functionally meaningful boundaries, except for special purposes, such as public administration and fiscal purposes. City limits do not bound the geographically functional cities. People commute across such boundaries, and retail and service establishments on both sides of the line compete for their expenditures. If, however, a planner is concerned with the financial base, the allocation of land among potential uses, or administrative policy for such a jurisdictional unit, the boundary is determined. Metropolitan areas (SMSA's) are generally more appropriate functional units, but they, too, by no means have closed economies, so that people and money, as well as goods and services, are free to cross metropolitan area boundaries. Other things being equal, the larger and more complex an area, the more apt it is to furnish a high proportion of its needs for goods and services; thus it would have a higher proportion of nonbasic activities and employment.[34] However, urban areas generally do not produce significant quantities of the foodstuffs and fuels that they require, and they do not have adequate facilities for disposal of wastes within their boundaries, so that an "import-export" or "basic" component is always present. Thus, the location of an area's or region's boundaries has an important bearing upon the B/N ratio, both in total and for individual components of the economy. The economic base of a metropoli-

tan area is not the same as the economic base of its central city.

The basic-nonbasic approach has many limitations, and has been frequently criticized. One type of criticism is that the approach places too much emphasis upon the basic components. With increasing specialization, the growth of leisure, and growing affluence, the variety of demands for goods and services is increasing, and service functions are increasing more rapidly than is the supplying of goods. Most of the services are supplied internally, especially within the larger cities and metropolitan areas. Thus the internal or nonbasic portion of the economy is increasingly important. Hans Blumenfeld points out that much of the attractiveness of the large metropolis is not in the industrial jobs which it provides, in which the basic component is high, but rather in the attractions, including services, which the urban area itself can furnish. Such services are "non-basic" in the sense in which the term is here used.[35]

Economists and planners tend to emphasize the crude nature of the basic-nonbasic approach.[36] This, of course, is inherent in the paucity of the data which would be essential for more sophisticated methods. Other criticisms are based upon the limitations of the basic-nonbasic approach in not being able to allow for major changes in tech-

[34] This theme is developed by Victor Roterus and Wesley Calef, "Notes on the Basic-Non-basic Employment Ratio," *Economic Geography*, Vol. XXXI, no. 1 (January, 1955), pp. 17-20, reprinted in Mayer and Kohn, *op. cit.*, pp. 101-104.

[35] Hans Blumenfeld, "The Economic Base of the Metropolis," *Journal of the American Institute of Planners*, Vol. XXI, no. 4 (November, 1959), pp. 327-36.

[36] For example, Charles T. Stewart, Jr., "Economic Base Dynamics," *Land Economics*, Vol. XXXV, no. 4 (November, 1959), pp. 327-36.

nology or general social, economic, and political conditions in the future. However, these criticisms are .equally applicable to more sophisticated and refined methods of study which involve projection from past trends and present conditions.[37] How, for example, could one have accurately predicted the economic base of the central-east coast of Florida — including Cape Kennedy — as recently as a decade ago, or of any region subjected to the introduction of "random variables," such as the location of major new technological developments?

The "Input-Output" Approach

A second approach to study of the urban economic base which has been developed, largely by economists and "regional scientists," is known as the "input-output" approach. Inputs are those items: physical goods, including raw materials and components as well as fuels, labor, capital investment, and credit, which make possible an economic activity within a region or an individual establishment. The sum of the inputs to all establishments, including households, the ultimate consuming unit, is the total set of inputs into a region. Similarly, outputs are the products of the region or of individual establishments. In the case of a region, such as a city or metropolitan area, inputs and outputs may, in many instances, be entirely among the establishments within the area, but

some inputs and outputs will involve interactions with external areas — other cities and regions. In this respect, the "input-output" approach resembles the "basic-nonbasic" approach. It evolved from the work of Wassily Leontief, an economist, who developed the method in studies of national economies.[38] As has been pointed out, statistics on inputs and outputs for nations are far easier to obtain than for regions smaller than nations. Therefore, the method has not been widely used in studies of the economic base of cities and metropolitan areas. However, a few such studies have been produced, notably by Walter Isard and his colleagues, who applied the method to determine the economic base of Puerto Rico — an island, which is an unusually readily identifiable economic unit — and to an evaluation of the probable multiplier effects resulting from the establishment of a new steel plant in the eastern United States.[39]

Application of the input-output approach involves the gathering, assembling, and processing of great masses of statistics, and elaborately detailed matrices showing the

[37] An interesting attempt to project and predict from past trends is: Herman Kahn and Anthony J. Wiener, *The Year 2000, A Framework for Speculation on the Next Thirty-three Years* (New York, The Macmillan Company, 1967). City, metropolitan, and regional planners must consider probabilities relative to conditions fifty years ahead, which is the amortization period for many major public works projects.

[38] Wassily W. Leontief, "Input-Output Economics," *Scientific American* (October, 1951); "The Structure of Development," *Scientific American* (September, 1963); *Input-Output Economics* (New York, Oxford University Press, 1966).

[39] For a detailed description of the input-output approach, see Walter Isard, *Methods of Regional Analysis* (Cambridge, Technology Press and New York, John Wiley & Sons, Inc., 1960), and Walter Isard and Robert Kavesh, "Economic Structural Interrelations of Metropolitan Regions," *American Journal of Sociology*, Vol. LX (September, 1954), pp. 152-62, reprinted in Mayer and Kohn, *op. cit.*, pp. 116-26. Also, Walter Isard and R. Kuenne, "The Impact of Steel Upon the Greater New York-Philadelphia Urban-Industrial Region," *Review of Economics and Statistics*, Vol. XXXV (November, 1953), pp. 289-301.

input-output interrelations of each of many categories of economic activity both within and outside the region. The availability of modern electronic computers has made possible the processing of these masses of statistics, but the problems of availability and collection remain to inhibit the widespread use of the method.

Briefly, the method consists of studying the effect of a given volume of inputs of capital, labor, components, and other elements of production into each of the many categories of activity which are present in a region upon the inputs and outputs of every other category, both inside and outside the region. Each category is represented in a matrix, or table, by a row and a column, and each cell — the intersection of a row and a column — represents the effects of the inputs and outputs in one category of activity upon the inputs and outputs of another one. Thus, if there are five hundred kinds of economic activities, the number of cells will be the square of five hundred, or 250,000. Actually, the numbers of activities of different types, classified in sufficient detail to be meaningful, may be several times as great. In operating an input-output matrix, information is obtained on the input requirements proportional to the outputs, for each item such as labor, materials, etc., in each kind of establishment required from each other kind of establishment. Thus, a ton of finished steel, with present technology, requires a certain amount of input of iron ore, scrap, limestone, coke, water, labor, and so forth. The iron ore, in turn, must be mined, concentrated, transported, and stockpiled; so must the limestone, while the coke production requires coal which, in turn, must undergo these processes. At each stage in production, transportation, and distribution of goods, and in the performance of services, there are input requirements, which, in theory, can be quantified, and there are outputs produced, which can also be quantified. A change in input or output at any point in the change with respect to any item will be reflected in changes in inputs and outputs at many points in the chain of production. The steel workers must be fed, clothed, housed, entertained, educated, governed, and so forth, and each of these processes sets in motion other sequences of inputs and outputs, through many successive rounds, until, finally, the effects are "damped out," or subsumed in the total economy many stages removed from the original impetus. Thus, a change in labor input requirements in producing steel at Pittsburgh or Gary, because of changed market demands or improvements in technology within the steel plants will change the number of workers in the plant. This, in turn, will produce changes in the total requirements in those communities for goods and services of great variety, and each kind of changed demand will set in motion chains of input-output effects. These effects will by no means be confined to the local community. A change in demand for steel, for example, in Pittsburgh or Gary will change the amount of iron ore required from the mines in Minnesota or Quebec. This will, in turn, change the effective demand for goods and services supplying the miners in those distant areas. Furthermore, if the changes persist over a long period, it will affect the demand for transportation of ores, coal, stone, and other items constituting inputs to the steel plants, and this will, in turn, affect the number of workers required in the transportation industries and the demand for inputs into the multitudinous kinds of businesses and establishments serving them. If such changes persist, later there will be changes in the requirements for new railroad hopper cars and ore boats, and this will change the input-output relations in railroad car manufacturing plants, shipyards, and other establishments, including the demand for steel inputs into such plants, so that some of the relationships run full cycle. The magnitude of the work required for a detailed and meaningful input-output analysis then becomes obvious, and the practicality of such a method is thereby seriously limited.

Insofar as the inputs and outputs are confined to within the area of concern, such as a city or SMSA, even though they may involve a vast and complex series of interchanges among the commercial, industrial, residential, and other establishments within the area, they are internal with respect to the area, and thus "nonbasic" or "city serving," but insofar as they involve transfers of people, goods money, or credit across the regional boundary, they are "basic" or "city forming." Thus the "input-output" approach may, in one sense, be regarded as an elaboration and refinement of the "basic-nonbasic" approach.

Minimum Or Average Requirements Approach

Another method of economic base analysis which is finding increasing popularity is the minimum or average requirements method. This is essentially comparing the city or region of concern with other cities or regions which resemble it with respect to significant attributes, such as size, age, and location. Thus, if it is desired to determine, on the average, how much land will be required for certain uses, such as industrial plants of various types, or how much employment can be anticipated, or income generated, by various types of activity, it may be useful to determine the average amounts actually utilized by comparable cities or regions.[40] Similarly, cities and regions may be compared, in various categories, with respect to the minimum requirements for each of the items, by finding the city or region in analogous sets of cities and regions which has the least amount of the item, whether employment, land, income, or other. All of the standard statistical measures of concentration and dispersion, such as deciles, quartiles, standard deviations and others, may be applied further to refine the analysis.

Population size appears to be the most significant variable relative to the minimum requirements of cities and metropolitan areas; there appears to be a more-or-less regular progression, some requirements decreasing with size, partly, at least, the result of scale economies, while others, such as service employment, tend to increase with size. Population size, therefore, is generally used as the determinant for classifying cities into groups within which the cities are sufficiently alike with respect to their requirements for comparative purposes.

The minimum and average requirements approach has been used to study a number of

[40] Edward L. Ullman and Michael F. Dacey, "The Minimum Requirements Approach to the Urban Economic Base," *Proceedings of the IGU Symposium in Urban Geography Lund 1960* (Lund Studies in Geography, series B, Human Geography No. 24, 1962), pp. 121-43; also in *Papers and Proceedings, The Regional Science Association*, Vol. VI (1960), pp. 175-94. Recent evaluations of the technique include Richard T. Pratt, "An Appraisal of the Minimum-Requirements Technique," *Economic Geography*, Vol. XLIV, no. 2 (April, 1968), pp. 117-24, and Edward L. Ullman, "Minimum Requirements after a Decade: A Critique and an Appraisal," *Economic Geography*, Vol. XLIV, no. 4 (October, 1968), pp. 364-69.

cities, ranging from Utica, New York, a depressed area on the verge of rapid change in the composition of its industrial base,[41] to Canberra, Australia, a national capital seeking greater diversity with respect to its economic "mix" and attempting to determine, in the preparation of a comprehensive plan, how much employment to expect and how much land to reserve, for industries and other functions, by comparison with other Australian cities of similar size.[42]

In spite of its utility, the average and minimum requirements method has certain serious drawbacks. How can we be sure that the cities or regions selected for comparison are truly analogous? Is it not possible that there may be independent variables which were not taken into consideration, such as, for example, the introduction of technological change since the last statistics became available, or the prospects of major changes in technology and economic or social conditions affecting requirements in the future?

Classification Of Cities By Economic Function

In order to reduce the possibilities of error in comparing cities or regions with one another, it is desirable to take into consideration as large a number as possible of independent variables, for any one or combination of them may be significant in affecting the validity of the comparison. Fortunately, the means are now at hand for processing vast quantities of data, and for determining which variables are

related to each other. We can classify cities and regions by their economic functions, or by any other sets of variables for which statistics may be obtained. Modern computers have made possible the application of methods that would not have been feasible only a few years ago.

Functional classifications of cities by the distribution of employment in various categories of economic activity have been made by a number of geographers.[43] Such classifications, as well as later ones using employment distribution by kind of establishment, occupation, or activity,[44] are univariate classifications, in that they use only one variable: employment.

A new technique for comparison of cities and regions with respect to many, rather than one, attributes is available, in the form of what is known as factor analysis or principal components analysis.[45] A large number of variables, obtained from many sources, can be grouped, by a standard computer program, into a small number of groups of related variables, and then comparing the groups in accordance with the extent to which they are

[41] *Industrial Renewal: Determining the Potential and Accelerating the Economy of the Utica Urban Area* (New York, State of New York Division of Housing and Community Renewal, 1963).

[42] G. J. R. Linge, *The Future Work Force of Canberra*, a Report for the National Capital Development Commission (Canberra, 1960).

[43] For example: Chauncy D. Harris, "A Functional Classification of Cities in the United States," *Geographical Review*, Vol. XXXIII, no. 1 (January, 1943), pp. 86-99, and Howard J. Nelson, "A Service Classification of American Cities," *Economic Geography*, Vol. XXXI, no. 3 (July, 1955), pp. 189-210, both reprinted in Mayer and Kohn, *op. cit.*, pp. 129-162.

[44] Otis Dudley Duncan *et al.*, *Metropolis and Region* (Baltimore, The Johns Hopkins Press, 1960), especially pp. 279 ff.; Richard L. Forstall, "Economic Classification of Places Over 10,000, 1960-1963," *The Municipal Year Book 1967* (Chicago, The International City Managers' Association, 1967), pp. 30-65.

[45] H. H. Harman, *Modern Factor Analysis* (Chicago, University of Chicago Press, 1961); M. G. Kendall, *A Course in Multivariate Analysis* (London, Charles Griffin, 1957).

inter-related. It is also possible to measure cities or metropolitan areas with respect to the nature and extent of their similarities and differences. The groups of related cities then constitute classes with respect to all of the sets of variables used. Thus, many measures of economic functions can be combined, and groups or classes of cities determined with respect to each of the sets of variables, or, on the other hand, a number of different measures of economic functions alone may be used to classify cities. British towns have been classified in this manner with respect to 57 different social and economic characteristics,[46] and American cities have similarly been classified by social and demographic characteristics.[47] Functional classifications, using the techniques of factor or principal components analysis, have been published for cities in several countries, including Canada, Australia, and India, among others.[48] Generally it has been found that the characteristics tend to group in from four to six related clusters, and these can be used to determine the extent to which cities in the country or region resemble each other with respect to any or all of these characteristics. Thus it is possible to group the cities in any number of groups from one up to the total

number of cities involved, and to present cities classified into any intermediate number of groups based upon communalities, or resemblances. Thus, it is reasonable to transfer the experience in solving problems in one city, if successful, to other cities which closely resemble it, rather than to cities in which the similarities are less. Factor analysis thus becomes a tool of great potential.

Conclusion

In spite of the difficulties of analyzing the economic base of cities and metropolitan areas, such analyses are of great importance. Planners, and all who are interested in the solution of urban problems, realize that cities exist primarily in order to enable people to make a living, and that the employment opportunities, the income and other satisfactions resulting from employment, are the fundamental forces behind urban growth or decline. It is not possible to determine how many, or what types of houses and other facilities need to be provided, until one has some idea of the present and prospective opportunities for employment. These depend, in turn, upon the nature of the economic activities upon which the city or region is based. Availability of resources, of course, is fundamental, and the geographer can furnish insights different from, but no less important than, those of the economist in assessing the prospects for economic growth and development. Economic base studies clearly lead to the conclusion that no form of human occupance can replace cities, and that, in spite of the trend toward lower densities concommitant with improvements in transportation and communication, modern civilization cannot exist without cities. An understanding of the functions which they perform, a major proportion of which are economic functions, is therefore indispensable.

[46] C. A. Moser and Wolf Scott, *British Towns, A Statistical Study of their Social and Economic Differences* (Edinburgh and London, Oliver and Boyd, 1961).

[47] J. K. Hadden and E. F. Borgatta, *American Cities: Their Social Characteristics* (Chicago, Rand McNally & Co., 1965).

[48] Leslie J. King, "Cross-Sectional Analysis of Canadian Urban Dimensions, 1951 and 1961," *Canadian Geographer*, Vol. X (1966), pp. 205-24; Robert H. T. Smith, "The Functions of Australian Towns," *Tijdschrift voor Economische en Sociale Geografie*, Vol. LVI, no. 3 (May-June, 1965), pp. 81-92; Qazi Ahmad, *Indian Cities: Characteristics and Correlates*, Research Paper, No. 102 (Chicago, University of Chicago, Department of Geography, 1965).

The Economic Base
of the Metropolis

15

Hans Blumenfeld

1. THE CONCEPT OF THE ECONOMIC BASE

The terms "economic base" and "basic" industry or employment are being increasingly used and discussed in planning and related fields.

Sometimes the term "economic base" simply stands for "economy," considered as the base of the life and growth of an area[1]; or, the term "basic" is simply used as a synonym for "important."[2]

Geographers frequently denote the region which serves as market and as source of supply for a given city as its "economic base." So Harold M. Mayer: "the area which appropriately may be considered as constituting the economic base of a large metropolitan city."[3] Similarly John W. Alexander defines the "Bases for the Oshkosh Economy" as "I. The Market Base. II. The Supply Bases."[4]

However, both Mayer and Alexander[5] also make use of the term "basic" in the sense in which it has become increasingly accepted, as opposed to "nonbasic." This concept claims that all economic activities of an area can and should be divided into two fundamentally different and mutually exclusive categories.

Apparently the first American planner to formulate the concept was Frederick Law Olmstead, who said in a letter of February 21, 1921: "productive occupations may be roughly divided into those which can be called primary, such as carrying on the marine shipping business of the port and manufacturing goods for general use (i.e., not confined to use within the community itself), and those occupations which may be called ancillary, such as are devoted directly

[1] See, f.i., Economic Base Study of the Philadelphia Area, Philadelphia City Planning Commission (August, 1949).

[2] f.i., Grace K. Ohlson in Municipal Yearbook, ". . . that furnishes the major volume of employment." Quoted by Richard B. Andrews, "The Urban Economic Base," in *Land Economics* (1953), p. 265.

[3] Harold M. Mayer, "Urban Nodality and the Economic Base Study," *Journal of the A.I.P.* (Summer, 1954).

[4] John W. Alexander, *Oshkosh, Wisconsin, An Economic Base Study* (Madison, Wisconsin, 1951).

[5] John W. Alexander, "The Basic-Nonbasic Concept of Urban Economic Functions," *Economic Geography* (Worcester, Massachusetts, July, 1954).

Reprinted from *Journal of the American Institute of Planners,* Vol. 21, no. 4 (1955) pp. 114-32 by permission.

or indirectly to the service and convenience of the people engaged in the primary occupations.[6]

Haig and McCrea, in conformance with this concept, state: "It has been urged that a distinction should be drawn between 'primary' and 'ancillary' activities: that primary activities be given precedence in the city plan."[7]

In the same year M. Aurousseau wrote: "The primary occupations are those concerned with the functions of the town. The secondary occupations are those concerned with the maintenance of the well-being of the people engaged in those of primary nature. The more primary citizens there are, the more secondary, in a relation something like compound interest."[8]

Here we find the two ideas which have determined the further application of the "basic-nonbasic" concept.

1. Planning and promotion, with preference to be given to "basic" activities.
2. Prediction, with total future population being derived from "basic" employment by application of a "multiplier."

The bias in favor of the "basic" activities, implicit in such terms as "basic," "primary," "town-building," "town-growth," versus "nonbasic," "ancillary," "service," "secondary," etc,[9] is made explicit in such statements

as: "the first task of . . . Letchworth and Welwyn . . . was to secure that 'basic' industries would be attracted; the inhabitants . . . could not . . . live by taking in each other's washing."[10]

We will return to the question, if, when, and why people can or can not "live by taking in each other's washing." For the development of the concept the second application — for population prediction — has been even more important. It was broadly used by Homer Hoyt in his work for the F.H.A. The method, as developed by Hoyt, includes five steps.[11]

1. Calculate employment in each basic industry
2. Estimate ratio of basic to service employment
3. Estimate ratio of population to employment
4. Estimate future trend of basic employment
5. Derive future total employment and population from future basic employment.

This has become the accepted formula; frequently steps 2 and 3 are omitted in favor of a rule-of-thumb formula of "population to basic employment equals seven to one."
Hoyt defines his criteria for a "basic" activity in manufacturing was "basic," that all other employment was "service," and that their ratio was roughly one to one. For the purposes for which Hoyt developed his formula — a quick, rough-and-ready housing market estimate — it was serviceable. However, he soon discovered, first, the difficulties of identifying "basic" activities, and second, the

[6] Quoted in R. M. Haig and R. C. McCrea, *Regional Survey of New York and its Environs*, Vol. I, p. 43, footnote.

[7] Haig & McCrea, *op. cit.*, p. 42.

[8] M. Aurousseau, "The distribution of population," *Geographical Review*, Vol. XI (1921), pp. 567 ff. Quoted by Robert E. Dickinson, City, Region, and Regionalism (London, 1947).

[9] An exception is the use of the terms "surplus" and "domestic" in the sophisticated study by John M. Mattila and Wilbur R. Thompson, "Measurement of the Economic Base of the Metropolitan Area," *Land Economics* (August, 1955), pp. 215-28.

[10] J. H. Jones, "Industry and Planning," in E. A. Gutkind, *Creative Demobilisation*, Vol. II (London, 1944).

[11] See A. M. Weimer and Homer Hoyt, *Principles of Urban Real Estate* (New York, 1939).

existence of wide local variations in the "basic-nonbasic" ratio.

2. IDENTIFICATION OF "BASIC" WITH "EXPORT" ACTIVITIES

Hoyt defines his criteria for a "basic" activity as follows: "those industries and services which produce goods for people living outside the urban region being studied, and which bring in *money* (my emphasis, H.B.) to pay for the food and raw materials which the city does not produce itself."[12] Similarly, Richard U. Ratcliff defines "primary or city-building activities" as those "which bring into the community purchasing power from outside."[13] A Swedish geographer differentiates between "exchange (bytes)" production, which is regarded as "primary" and "own (egen)" production which is considered "secondary,"[14] and a Swedish planner has used this distinction to develop his method of population prediction.[15] Perhaps the most straightforward explanation of the concept of "basic" workers was given by Andrews who calls them "the wage earners of the community family."[16]

The concept sounds simple and convincing enough: In order to live a community, like a family, has to earn money. The number of families is determined by the number of breadwinners; the number of "housewives"

who "service" the breadwinners, and of dependents, can be derived from the number of the former.

There are certainly cases where the concept is fully applicable. Take, for instance, a copper mining village with 1,000 miners. There will be, say, 600 people employed locally in retail trade and consumer services; if the family coefficient is 2.5, the population will be 4,000. If the company hires another 1,000 miners, it is safe to predict that they will be followed shortly by about 600 more "secondary" employed persons and that the population will increase to 8,000. Inversely, if the company lays off 500 miners, the population will in due course shrink to 2,000. It is also safe to say that no attempt to promote development of any or all branches of "secondary" activity will make a noticeable impact on the economic life or the population size of the community.

Now, let us define the specific conditions of this experimental case:

1. There is no possibility of substitution of another "basic" activity for copper mining.

2. There is no source of income from outside other than wage payments.

3. Earnings of all "basic" employed are roughly equal (or at least average earnings for any group which may be added or subtracted are equal).

4. The family coefficient of all groups in basic employment is the same.

5. None of the product of any "basic" industry can be sold locally; or, looking at the same phenomenon from the other side, all goods and services (other than those which because of their physical characteristics can be supplied only locally) are being supplied from the outside.

[12] Homer Hoyt Associates, *The Economic Base of the Brockton, Massachusetts Area* (January, 1949), p. 4.

[13] Richard U. Ratcliff, *Urban Land Economics* (New York, McGraw-Hill, 1949), p. 42.

[14] W. William-Olsson, *Stockholms framtida utveckling* (Stockholm's future development) (Stockholm, 1941).

[15] Fred Forbat, "Prognos for Näringsliv och befolkning (forecast of industrial activity and population), *Plan*, No. 9 (Stockholm, 1948).

[16] Richard B. Andrews, *op. cit.* in *Land Economics* (1953), p. 161.

It is evident that every one of these five conditions is the exact opposite of conditions characteristic of a metropolitan area. A metropolis is not simply a sum of villages, and it can not be analyzed by adding up studies of its parts.

3. LIMITATIONS OF THE "BASIC-NONBASIC" CONCEPT IN TIME AND SPACE

As has already been pointed out, the literature on the subject is pervaded by a conviction that the "basic" activities are more important than the "nonbasic" ones. Emphatic statements abound. "Basic employment is the same as . . . destiny."[17] Harold McCarthy goes so far as to call "the base . . . that group of occupations whose presence . . . is not predicated on the existence of other types of production."[18]

This is evidently untrue. No "basic" industry in a modern city could function without such services as water, transportation, and communication. Some students of the subject are aware of this. "Urban-Growth and Urban-Serving Employment . . . are both equally essential," says Victor Roterus;[19] and the U.S. Chamber of Commerce speaks of "a chicken-and-egg relationship," adding: "industrial growth stimulates the remainder of the local economy and the existence of the community makes possible industrial growth."[20]

Here a new and important point is being made: the community with its services is the basis of industry, as well as vice versa; and it is startling to find that this point is being made by a promotional pamphlet of the Chamber of Commerce rather than by planners. It is the more startling as — alongside with the goal of "strengthening" or "broadening" the "economic base" — the American planning profession also proclaims the goal of the "self-contained community." The Greeks had a word for it: autarchy.

Evidently, the two goals are mutually exclusive. In a completely self-contained, or autarchic, community, nothing has to be bought from outside and consequently nobody works to earn money for outside payments. There is no "basic" employment; all people live by "taking in each other's washing."

On the other hand, the higher the percentage of the labor force in "basic" employment, the greater the dependence of the community on outside markets and on outside supplies, the less "self-contained."

It may help to clarify our concepts to look at extreme cases. The copper mining village comes as close to maximizing "basic" employment as any community is likely to come. An employed bachelor, who does not make his own breakfast nor sew on his own buttons, would be the perfect example of 100 percent "basic" and no "service" activity.

At the other extreme, a subsistence farm — or a truly "self-contained" community like

---

[17] *Working Denver, An Economic Analysis by the Denver Planning Office (1953)* (Department of Planning, City & County Bldg., Denver 2, Colo., 1953), p. 27. We will frequently exemplify our critique of the "basic–nonbasic" concept by reference to this excellent study, because it has developed the concept more completely than most others.

[18] Quoted by John W. Alexander, *The Basic-Nonbasic Concept, op. cit.*

[19] Cincinnati City Planning Commission, *The Economy of the Area*, (Cincinnati, December, 1946), p. 22.

[20] Chamber of Commerce of the U.S., Washington, 1954, "What new industrial jobs mean to the community".

the ancient Indian village — has no "basic" employment. All occupations are "concerned with the maintenance of the well-being of the people" which, according to the above-quoted definition by Aurousseau, is the criterion of "secondary" occupations.

Also, and perhaps more significantly, the global community of mankind is engaged exclusively in "secondary" or "service" activities. A large nation is not far from this extreme; the "basic-nonbasic" ratio for the U.S. is probably about 1:20. The generally accepted applications of the "basic-nonbasic" method — preferential promotion of "basic" (i.e. export) activities and prediction of future population by applying a "multiplier" to expected future employment in export activities — would be as patently absurd for the U.S. as they are sensible for a copper mining village.

We may tentatively derive from the juxtaposition of these extreme cases a first statement: the applicability of the "basic-nonbasic" concept decreases with increasing size of the community.

Size, however, is not the only factor to be considered. Let us return to the case of the subsistence farm. By any acceptable usage farming is its "basic" or "primary" activity. If the farmer or his wife engage, during the slack season, in some cottage industry, selling the product for cash, such activity is to them strictly "secondary" or "ancillary." Here the concepts appear reversed: production for own use — "taking in each other's washing" — is basic, and production for sale is ancillary. This is characteristic of a "natural" economy, while the reverse holds true for a "money" or "exchange" economy, which is dependent on division of labor. Hence our second statement: applicability of the "basic-nonbasic" concept increases with increasing specialisation and division of labor between communities.

Still another aspect may be illustrated by the ancient Indian village community, or, for that matter, by a village in medieval feudal Europe. Here a good deal of the economic activity was for "export," for the Lord of the Manor, the Church, or the King. But far from being basic in the sense of being indispensable for the economy of the village, this activity is the only one which contributes nothing to it. The reverse of this picture is the town which receives these payments without having to compensate by any "export" activity or employment. Richard U. Ratcliff quotes H. Pirenne as saying that the early medieval fortress town "produced nothing of itself, lived by revenue from the surrounding country, and had no other economic role than that of a simple consumer." Another historian characterizes the "economic base" of such cities as follows: "The principal, constituent elements of the town were those who are able by *power and wealth* (my emphasis, H.B.) to command a means of subsistence from elsewhere, a king who can tax, a landlord to whom dues are paid, a merchant who makes profits outside the town, a student who is supported by his parents. These are "town builders. . . ."[21]

Here the "basis" for the economy of the town is not "persons employed in producing goods and services for export," as the "basic-nonbasic" method assumes, but "power and wealth." It may here be recalled that in the "tableau économique," which Quesnay, founder of the "physiocratic" school of economics, developed in the 18th century, the

[21] F. L. Nussbaum, *A History of the Economic Institutions of Modern Europe* (New York, 1933) quoted by Richard B. Andrews, *op. cit.*, (1953), p. 161.

urban middle class was called "classe stérile," as serving the ruling class rather than working for the "producing" class, the farmers. Thomas Jefferson shared this physiocratic view.

In our context it is important to keep in mind that "nonbasic" activities are supported by money gained from the outside regardless of its source, which may be "power and wealth" rather than any "basic" employment. To the extent that this is the case, the "basic-nonbasic" ratio loses its meaning.

We may therefore formulate a third statement: the greater the amount of "unearned" income (i.e. income derived from sources other than payment for work performed) flowing into or out of a community, the less applicable is the "basic-nonbasic" concept.

We will later deal with attempts to assimilate "unearned" income to the concept of "basic" activities. Leaving aside this aspect, for the time being, and concentrating our attention on the relation of "basic" and "nonbasic" employment, we may accept as valid the existence of two opposite historical trends noted by Forbat in the above-mentioned article:

1. Replacement of local crafts by large-scale industry working for a national and international market; hence greater share of "basic" employment.
2. Increase in services; hence greater share of "nonbasic" employment.

Both trends result from increasing division and specialisation of labor, the first between communities and the second within the community. It should also be noted that the increase in services refers not only to services to consumers, which are generally the result of commercialisation of functions formerly performed by the household, but also to services to business, which were previously performed as auxiliary services within other businesses, but have now become so specialised and complicated as to require special establishments.

This specialisation of business activities reaches its highest development in large and mature communities. As mentioned before, the same communities also are nearest to "autarchy," because they contain the greatest number of branches of production.

We may therefore summarize:

The "basic-nonbasic" ratio is highest in small, new communities, lowest in large and mature ones.

4. MERCANTILISTIC AND PHYSIOCRATIC OVERTONES OF THE "BASIC-NONBASIC" CONCEPT

The difference between "basic" and "nonbasic" activities is the difference in their role in the balance of payments with the world outside the community. Strangely, and rather inconsistently, the "economic base" studies dominated by this concept pay practically no attention to the other side of the ledger: no attempt is being made in these studies to differentiate between those locally consumed goods and services which are produced locally and those for which payments have to be made to the outside world. Yet, rationally, the money earned by "basic" activities is merely the means to make these payments, not an end in itself.

The idea, underlying the "basic-nonbasic" method, that the acquisition of money from the outside world is the "basic" purpose of the urban or metropolitan economy has its historical precedent in the mercantilistic school of economics which regarded only gold and silver as true wealth. While in a study of the U.S. economy it is today taken for granted that increased production of goods and services for the home market is the goal, in the "economic base" studies of American cities these activities are regarded merely as supporting the "basic" ones working for export.

This is, of course, explainable by the role played by size which has been discussed above. If the slogan "export or die" is true for sizable countries like Great Britain or Germany, it is even truer for a single city or region which evidently can not produce everything which it consumes. In particular many base studies stress the need of earning money in order to pay for imports of food and raw materials. "Basic Employment . . . goods or services in exchange for food and raw materials . . . (is) the critical or crucial employment . . . ; without it the city ceases to exist."[22]

Here, as in many similar statements, there is the implication that the export activities are "basic" because without them the city could not buy food, which is a "basic" necessity, while New Yorkers would not "cease to exist" without such locally supplied goods and services as millinery or theatre performances. But they would cease to exist very rapidly without water supply, which is also a "service" or "nonbasic" activity.

The belief that there is something particularly "basic" in the production of food and raw materials also has its historical precedent; the antagonists and successors of the mercantilists, the physiocrats, believed in the superiority of farming and mining over other branches of production.

Incidentally, when we deal not with 19th century cities, but with the emerging, much larger and qualitatively different form of

human settlement defined by the U.S. Census as a "Metropolitan Area," a sizable part of the food may be supplied by "nonbasic" activities; that is, supplied by residents to residents of the area. The Philadelphia Metropolitan Area, f.i., containing 2.45 percent of the U.S. population in 1950, produced 1.03 percent of all dairy products sold in the U.S., 1.17 percent of all poultry, 2.28 percent of all vegetables, and 4.68 percent of all nursery and greenhouse products. Thus, dairy and poultry production equaled almost half, and vegetable production equaled almost the entire normal consumption of the area. Altogether about 14 percent of the area's proportionate (to population) share of all agricultural products were produced locally.

If the classification of economic activities attempted by the "basic-nonbasic" concept is to acquire scientific validity and practical usefulness, it will have to discard all explicit or implicit notions that earning money or buying food is specifically "basic." It should be clearly understood that we are dealing exclusively with a difference in the market; and the appropriate terms would be "export" and "home market" activities.

There is reason to pay attention to this difference. A product or service which has to compete in the national and international market is more vulnerable than one which, like local transportation or a corner drug store, by its physical nature is protected against outside competition; it is, for the same reason, also more capable of expansion by invading outside markets. But, by and large, the share of the national product which is sold locally is just as vulnerable to competition as is the part which is sold outside.

From the piont of view of vulnerability by outside competition as well as of ability to

[22] New York Regional Plan Association, *The Economic Status of the New York Metropolitan Region in 1944*, p. 3.

expand into outside markets, both of which we may identify as "criticality," the only meaningful distinction is between activities which, *by the nature of their product* have to and can compete with outside producers, *regardless of the location of their actual sales,* and those which do not compete; and it is just as important to measure the imported and the locally produced share of total local consumption as it is to measure the exported and the locally consumed shares of total local production.

5. DEVELOPMENT OF TECHNIQUES OF MEASUREMENT

a. Manufacturing versus services

The first studies, those made in the twenties for the New York Regional Plan and in the thirties by Homer Hoyt for the F.H.A., assigned entire activities to the one òr the other category according to their predominant market; as Frederic Law Olmsted put it in the letter quoted earlier, "primary"[23] are goods for general use (i.e., *not confined to* [my emphasis, H.B.] use within the community itself). Consciously, they were satisfied with a rough approximation; subconsciously, they were guided by the criterion of competitive character rather than by that of actual markets of an industry.

Such a rough approximation by allotment of broad categories to the two classes of activities was also used — but only as a first step — by the 1944 study of the New York Regional Plan Association. As "basic —

producing *in whole or in part* (my emphasis, H.B.) for persons living outside of the Region . . ." are specifically enumerated: manufacturing, wholesale trade, banking and insurance, transportation, administrative offices, hotels and amusements, federal and state employment. As "service — producing *entirely* (my emphasis, H.B.) for persons living within the Region" are enumerated: retail trade, professions, personal services, local transportation and utilities, construction, local government, business and repair services, real estate and local banking.

Parenthetically it may be noted that many of these last-named activities do not produce entirely for the local population, but also serve many persons living outside the Region.

There is reason to believe that the motive for concern with "basic" activities was their competitive and therefore critical character. Had the authors of the New York Regional Plan study accepted this criterion, they would have sought further refinements along lines which will be indicated later. However, they, like all others using the "basic" concept, interpreted it as meaning "export" and consequently sought to refine it by measuring the portion of each particular product or service which was sold outside the Region.

The measurement of this "exported" portion is easy in dealing with a national economy where exports and imports are counted at custom lines. In dealing with areas within a nation, however, no comparable data are available and other methods have to be developed.

b. Proportional apportionment

The method used by the N. Y. Regional Plan study and most others is to assume that the community consumes a share of the total national production of each category of goods

[23] The concepts of "primary" and "secondary" used in this type of studies should not be confused with the concept of "primary," "secondary," and "tertiary," meaning "extractive," "processing," and "service" activities, as defined by Colin Clark and other economists.

and services which is proportional to its share of the national population (in some cases purchasing power or other yardsticks are substituted for population). The surplus in excess of this proportional share is assumed to be exported or "basic". Frequently the relation between actual and proportional share of a given category of production is expressed as a "location — or localization — quotient." The "location quotient" is the percentage of employment in a given local industry of total local employment, expressed as a ratio to the percentage of national employment in the same industry of total national employment; or $\frac{ei}{et} \cdot \frac{Ei}{Et}$; e = local employment; E = national employment; i = employment in industry; t = total employment. "By means of the localization quotient . . . the extent to which an activity is basic . . . can be determined."[24]

The same method was applied by Victor Roterus in the Cincinnati study. "Urban-serving employment (was) calculated by assuming that the population will consume its proportionate share of the national production."

We have used this method in defining the "service" share of various branches of agricultural production in the Philadelphia Area. However, it would be quite erroneous to conclude from the fact that the location quotient of vegetable production for the Philadelphia Area is roughly equal to one, that Philadelphians eat no vegetables grown outside their area. They do, of course, and other vegetables are exported from the area.

To choose another illustration: the Philadelphia Area's share in the production of weekly periodicals may about equal its share of national population and (or) purchasing power. But it does not follow that all copies of the Saturday Evening Post are consumed in the Philadelphia Area and that Philadelphians never buy copies of the Reader's Digest. They do (unfortunately).

The method of proportional apportionment is based on the completely fallacious assumption that categories of goods and services — however fine the breakdown — can ever be uniform. International trade statistics show that most countries are both importers and exporters of the same categories of goods. The same certainly holds true to an even greater extent for the exchange of goods and services between areas within the nation.

Of course, if the location quotient is very high, it stands to reason that most of the product is exported. However, in such extreme cases the importance of that particular industry will be a matter of general knowledge. No location quotient has to be calculated in order to find out that Detroit exports automobiles or that Brockton exports shoes. On the other hand, if an area produces its "normal" share of, say, electrical machinery, it would be completely erroneous to assume that this is a "nonbasic" industry working exclusively for the local market. It is entirely possible, and indeed quite probable, that most locally produced electrical machinery is exported, while at the same time most locally consumed electrical machinery is imported. Mattila and Thompson unwittingly demonstrate the fallacy of the method by presenting a completely absurd result: the "proportion of surplus ("basic," H.B.) to service ("nonbasic," H.B.) workers," calculated by means of the "location quotient," is given as 1:1.99 for Chicago and as 1:4.47 for Philadelphia![25] Are we to believe that

[24] Harold M. Mayer, *op. cit.*

[25] *Op. cit.*, p. 226, Table III.

one "basic" worker supports 2 "nonbasic" workers in Chicago and 4½ in Philadelphia?

This is not to say that the location quotient does not deserve careful study. By analyzing it, much can be learned about market areas and about competitive advantages and disadvantages. But as a measurement of the share of "basic" activities or employment it is completely misleading.

c. Breakdown of markets by survey

The obvious inadequacy of this method has led several researchers to embark on the difficult and time-consuming attempt to follow up the actual sales of each establishment in the area under investigation. This was apparently first done in 1943 by Fred Forbut in his study of the small Swedish town of Skörde.

In Alexander's Study of Oshkosh, f.i., establishments employing 75 percent of the labor force were asked for the percentage of their sales that was local; the same percentage of their employment was then allocated to the category of "secondary" employment. The same approach was taken by Maxine Kurtz in the Denver study.

In addition to its high cost this method obviously encounters two obstacles: first, unwillingness to disclose one's market, and second, ignorance of the location of one's customers. The first obstacle appears to have been overcome fairly successfully both in Oshkosh and in Denver. Interviewing of cash customers of retail stores and other techniques have been used to narrow the gap of ignorance. The result of the studies may be regarded as a reasonably accurate measurement of local and outside sales.

However, this is still far from finding the answer to the question: how does the community earn the money to pay for the imports it needs? Leaving aside, for the time being, the question of modifying the needs for imports as well as the possibility of paying for them by money derived from sources other than export, the main shortcoming is this: we know the *gross value of the exported goods and services.* What we want to know is the *"value added" by the community.* A flour mill may export 10 millions worth of flour; but if it has to import 8 millions worth of grain, it earns no more than 2 millions for the community. Employment probably has been adopted as the only available, though extremely rough, approximation to "value added." However, those using the method are apparently unaware of this relation and of its implications.

If "value added" is sought, other difficulties arise. Assume that the grain has been grown locally. It is sold in the local market, to the local mill, by definition its production is a "nonbasic" activity. Yet the payment received for its sale (in the form of flour) is a net earning of the community, a "basic" support of its economy. Or, to take another example: a community exports a million tons of steel. If this steel is produced in an integrated metallurgical plant, the "value added" is the difference between the cost of ore, coal, etc., and the value of the steel; and all employment in the plant is considered "basic". But if the same steel is produced in a steel plant which buys its pig iron from an independent local blast furnace, then only the value added by the steel plant is considered "basic," and the value added by the blast furnace is, by definition, "nonbasic," because it is sold to a local customer. Thus the distinction between "basic" and "nonbasic" is a function of the inner organization of the industry: the higher the degree of specialization and differentiation, the breakdown of a process into parts performed by several independent establishments, the higher is the "nonbasic" share. This, incidentally, is one of the reasons why "nonbasic" activities appear to loom so large in metropolitan areas, where the process of differentiation reaches its apex.

This difficulty has given birth to the concept of "indirect primary" activities and employment. "Indirect primary" are all goods or services sold to a local establishment which in turn exports its products. But the steel mill does not only buy locally produced pig iron; it equally buys locally produced power, water, trucking services, banking services, local police and fire protection. Moreover, it buys locally produced labor power which in turn buys locally produced bread and movie shows. Once "indirect primary" activities are admitted as "basic," where can the line be drawn? The economy of an area is an integrated whole of mutually interdependent activities; the distinction between "basic" and "nonbasic" seems to dissolve into thin air.

d. "Criticality" or "Balance of Payments"?

Confusion worse confounded. The more we attempt to refine the "basic-nonbasic" concept, the deeper we get involved in contradictions. Whenever that happens, there is reason to assume that there is something wrong with the formulation of the question.

Let us return to the origin of the quest. It may be fairly illustrated as follows. If General Motors closes shop at Flint, no efforts to promote the development of department stores will save the town. On the other hand, if a Flint department store closes down, but the General Motors plant continues to operate as before, it will soon be replaced by other stores. Therefore, the thing to worry about,

the "base" of the Flint economy, is the automobile industry; once that works, the "services" will take care of themselves. Also, once we know how many people G.M. is going to employ, we know pretty well how many people there will be in Flint.

Unquestionably true. But why is the situation of the G.M. plant so much more critical than that of the department store? Leaving aside the difference in size which is extraneous to our problem, it is because the G.M. plant has to compete with all other automobile plants in the U.S. and in the world, while the department store has to compete, in the main, only with other stores in Flint (though its customers might purchase some goods in Detroit, or from a mail order house in Chicago).

The difference in "criticality" is determined by the extent of the area of potential competition. In actual practice this is, of course, a range of areas from the locality through ever-widening regions to the national and international markets. A development and refinement of the "criticality" approach would have to go in two directions. First, as much attention should be paid to the *actual and potential* source of locally consumed goods and services, as to the markets for local products; second, the potential area of competition should be broken down into areas of varying size.

Actually, both steps have been undertaken by many "economic base" studies. Most studies pay particular attention to industries with a location quotient smaller than one, assuming that here may be opportunities for new local industries to compete with outside suppliers. And most go into detailed analysis of their market areas; the Denver study, f.i., found that 54 percent of the sales outside the Metropolitan Area were made within the "region," defined as Colorado, Wyoming, and New Mexico.

This is contrary to the "basic-nonbasic" theory, which demands concentration of attention on the "basic" industries, those with a location quotient larger than one, and which regards all export activities as equally "basic," regardless of the size or location of the export market. Thus, the practice of the economic base studies has been generally more sensible than the theory which they claim to follow. This is, fortunately, not an uncommon occurrence in human affairs (vide the practice of American foreign policy versus the theory of "massive retaliation").

In our case the theoretical weakness lies in the confusion of the question of "criticality," that is the question concerning *potential competition* with the question of *"balance of payments,"* which is concerned with *actual sales*. Both questions are valid and important; but either can be clearly answered only if they are clearly separated.

The concept of the "balance of payments" is well understood; but the assembly of the relevant data is exceedingly difficult. Apparently the only attempt ever made was the famous "Oskaloosa versus the U.S." study undertaken by Fortune magazine in April 1938. In this study "a city of 10,000 people has been treated as if it were a little nation."

A "balance of payments" study evidently must use dollars as units of measurement, not persons. The widespread use of the categories of "basic" and "nonbasic" *employment* — a consequence of the attempt to use the concept for population prediction by means of the "multiplier" — has no place in a study of this type. What matters, is not how many persons work at supplying the outside world, but how much money they receive from it. For this reason some studies have used payrolls (and net earnings of self-employed persons) rather than number of persons employed. But payments for goods and services go only partly into payrolls, partly into profits, interest, taxes, etc. The appropriate measurement would be the one applied in international trade statistics: gross value of goods and services exported and imported. To these would have to be added taxes and disbursements of larger governmental units, as well as interest and dividend payments in both directions. However, the latter are "practically unobtainable," according to Charles L. Leven of the Federal Reserve Bank of Chicago.[26]

Nevertheless, the New York Regional Plan study of 1944 did make an estimate that "nearly one-third of the region's basic income was derived from dividends, rents, interests, and profits." It would seem that with the amount of labor and ingenuity that went into the Denver study, f.i., it might be possible to arrive at estimates realistic enough to construst a model of "Denver versus the U.S.A." As Victor Roterus wisely remarks, no economic base study can achieve more than a rough approximation.

The attempts to "refine" the "basic-nonbasic" concept have destroyed its usefulness for the identification of "critical" industries, while making no more than a very partial and dubious contribution to an identification of the balance of payments.

To repeat:

There is a need for two types of studies, related, and using much of the same material,

[26] Charles L. Leven, "An appropriate unit for measuring the urban economic base," *Land Economics* (November, 1954). This is the most concise study of the subject known to this writer.

but different in their conceptual framework:

1. A "criticality" or "variability" study, analyzing all actual and potential branches of production in the area from the point of view of the size and character of the area in which they compete and their consequent vulnerability to outside competition and potentiality to expand into outside markets.
2. A "balance of payments" study, including *all* types of payments, and giving equal weight to both sides of the ledger.

6. SPECIFIC PROBLEMS

a. Replacement of imports by local production

One of the purposes of the distinction of "basic" and "nonbasic" activities "consists in concentrating investigation on those industries and services which . . . bring in money to pay for the food and raw materials which the city does not produce itself," to repeat Homer Hoyt's formulation. But if the city would itself produce the goods which it now imports, the effect would be the same. Why should not investigation be concentrated on those industries and services, which do *not* produce a surplus for export, but, on the contrary, show a deficit in supplying the home market? Evidently, if Brockton, rather than increasing its capacity to produce shoes worth a million dollars annually, would build a clothing plant to supply its inhabitants with a million dollars' worth of clothing which they now have to import, the improvement of the town's balance of payments would be the same. It may here be noted that this might not be possible in Brockton, because, the local market may not be large enough to support an efficient plant. But it would certainly be possible in a large metropolis. The larger the

community, the greater the possibility of substitution for declining industries, hence the less significant the identification of "basic" activities.

Actually even the Brockton study does examine the possibility of substituting new industries for the "critical" shoe industry. Similarly the New York Regional Plan study concentrates its attention on "industries in which New York's share of employment is far below its proportion of population and income," stating: "these industries might be explored to ascertain why they have not expanded to a greater degree in the Region,"[27] and the Cincinnati study considers specifically "local industries not meeting local demands." Charles L. Leven, in the aforementioned article, agrees that "efforts might be more profitably directed at establishment of local industries (supplying) local exporters."

The important point, in our context, is that the "basic-nonbasic" method is of no help whatsoever in identifying such industries. It rather tends to deflect attention from them and to confuse the picture. Half a loaf is certainly better than no loaf; but half a balance of payments study may well be worse than none.

The reverse substitution is no less important: the replacement of local production by imports. As Fred Forbat has pointed out, this is one of the long-term trends of industrial society, a corollary of increasing specialization and division of labor between regions. However, it still remains possible to substitute local production for imports; especially where the growth of the community creates a previously nonexistent large market, imports may be replaced by locally produced

[27] *Op. cit.*, p. 19, 20.

goods and services. In this way growth induces further growth. "He who has, to him shall be given" is a basic law of economics.

b. An extreme case of the effect of the establishment of a new "basic" industry on the balance of payments

It is generally assumed that the opening of an establishment which exports part of its products will always improve the balance of payments of an area. However, if such an establishment is a branch plant of an outside firm and works mainly with imported material, and if the part of its products which is sold locally displaces the products of a local industry working largely with local materials, then the net effect may be the opposite.

In the hypothetical case presented here, "A" represents a group of local establishments producing $1,000,000 worth of goods for the local market. "B" represents the new branch plant which produces $2,000,000; of these $1,000,000 are exported and $1,000,000 are sold in the local market, displacing the local establishments.

In case "A" the community has to pay $310,000 to the outside world in order to procure the $1,000,000 worth of goods which it consumes. In case "B" it has to pay $410,000 ($1,410,000 minus $1,000,000 earned from export sales). Thus the establishment of the new "basic" industry has resulted in a deterioration of its balance of payments by $100,000.

Let us assume an average wage of $3,000 and an average per capita income of $1,500. Let us further assume that one-third, or $500, of this per capita income has to be spent to import goods and services from the outside. Then the loss of $100,000 in means of payment to the outside has the result that the community can support 200 persons less than before.

According to the standard formula one-half of the 100 workers in the new establishment, or 50 workers, would represent "basic"

Case	Item	Spent, Total	Spent Locally	Spent Outside	Net Payment to Outside
"A"	wages	220,000	220,000		
	materials	500,000	250,000	250,000	
	amortization	50,000	50,000		
	overhead	60,000	60,000		
	taxes	70,000	10,000	60,000	
	profit	100,000	100,000		
"A"	total	1,000,000	690,000	310,000	310,000
"B"	wages	300,000	300,000		
	materials	1,000,000	200,000	800,000	
	amortization	200,000	50,000	150,000	
	overhead	100,000	20,000	80,000	
	taxes	200,000	20,000	180,000	
	profit	200,000		200,000	
"B"	total	2,000,000	590,000	1,410,000	410,000

(It has been assumed that plant "B" uses more ordinary [more amortization] and fewer workers [less wages].)

employment. According to the rule-of-thumb "multiplier" of 7 persons for every one person in "basic" employment, there should be a population increase of 350 persons. But actually there would be a decrease of 200 persons.

This may be an extreme and unlikely case. It has been developed to point up the problematical character of the "basic employment" method.

Parenthetically, while this case is not likely to occur in the U.S.A. in 1955, it may be fairly typical of the impact of the establishment of branch plants of modern international concerns in under-developed countries; here the result is frequently aggravated by related effects on income distribution. The resistance of these countries to such apparently beneficial improvements by foreign investors may not be entirely due to short-sighted nationalistic prejudices.

c. Indirect primary activity

The problem of "indirect primary" activity has attracted the attention of many students of our subject. Fred Forbat[28] refers to a study of a new oil refinery in Aarhus, Denmark, undertaken by the economist B. Barford.[29] Barfod found that "the company's purchases of goods and services from local suppliers gave livelihood" to 70 persons for every 100 persons employed in the refinery. He classes these as "indirect primary" and derives the expected number of "secondary" employment by assuming that there will be 80 additional "secondary" workers for every 100 new workers in *all* "primary" employment, "direct" and "indirect" combined.

Andrews, in his series of articles in LAND ECONOMICS, repeatedly returns to this question. He recognizes that "linked activity . . . the chain of production . . . makes *all* activities basic" and calls this a "very serious blindspot . . . unless the anachronisms (?H.B.) of this situation can be reconciled."[30] When dealing with a concrete example, however, he says: "rigidly, we would classify the automobile-starter factory as a service activity . . . realistic(ally it) should be considered basic in that there exists only an organizational line between the starter and automobile manufacturer."[31]

Andrews seems to be unaware that "crossing an organizational line" is only a synonym for "sale" and that any method which — like the "basic-nonbasic" method — counts sales, consists in counting line crossings. He adds, however, the very pertinent remark: "the number of links involved may very well be in direct ratio to community size." But he again fails to draw the conclusion: that the applicability of the "basic-nonbasic" concept is in inverse ratio to community size.

Ullman also wrestles with the problem. He says: "a city with large basic plants might appear to produce many basic workers whereas . . . many small plants each feeding the other . . . appear to have many service workers." He then tries to compromise by stating that "some intermediate producers are classed as basic if they contribute directly to an export industry," but concludes finally that "in this light all activities appear indivisible."

Alexander is also troubled by the problem: "since these castings (made in a local foun-

[28] Fred Forbat, "Synpunkter pa Lokaliserings-multiplikatorn," *Plan* (Stockholm, 1948), No. 9.
[29] B. Barford, Local economic effects of a large-scale industrial undertaking (in Danish); E. Munksgaard, (Copenhagen, 1938. This writer has not been able to locate this study.)
[30] Andrews, *op. cit., Land Economics* (1954), p. 260 ff.
[31] Andrews, *op. cit., Land Economics*, (1953), p. 347.

dry, H.B.) are fabricated into axles which are exported, it could be said that this . . . production is for the primary market. However, this leads to complications, and the arbitrary decision has been made to classify each activity on the basis of its own direct sales."[32]

We have already shown that the complications are implicit in the ambiguity of the question. If the question is, instead, clearly directed to the balance of payments, the decision to count only direct sales is by no means arbitrary, but a matter of course. Nobody thinks of including the steel industry in the export statistics of American automobiles, because the "value added" by the steel and all other "indirect primary" industries is, by definition, included in the gross value of the automobiles. Dollars, not persons employed, are the correct yardstick.

If, on the other hand, the question is directed to the "criticality" of each establishment, i.e., to the range of its potential market and its potential competitors, the "indirect primary" activities fall into place alongside all others.

d. Inter-urban transportation

Practically all studies, while treating local transportation as "nonbasic," regard all other transportation as "basic." However, actually only those transportation activities which serve movements between two outside points earn money from the outside. A tanker, bringing oil from Venezuela to a refinery in the Philadelphia Area, exclusively serves and is paid by the Philadelphia plant. Its work might be called "indirect primary," but, as we have seen, that does not remove it from the "nonbasic" class under any consistent definition.

Normally, of the total exchange of goods

[32] John W. Alexander, *Oshkosh, op. cit.*, p. 12.

between two points about half will be paid at each end; thus 50 percent of it should certainly be classified as "nonbasic." The point might well be made that the entire interurban transportation system performs a service for, and at the expense of, the local import and export trade and should be classified as such.

From the point of view of competitiveness, or "criticality," interurban transportation (except for the portion serving movements between two outside points) is strictly noncompetitive; nobody but some form of transportation can move goods and passengers into and out of the city. It is true, of course, that if transportation is very poor, other branches of production may move to other areas that are better served by transportation, it thus may profoundly affect the competitive position of the area as a whole. It was probably this thought that caused people to classify it as "basic." Yet in this respect it is not principally different from supply of water, power, housing, or any other local service.

e. Public employees, students, etc.

A field in which the confusion of the "criticality" and the "balance of payments" approach has led to particularly glaring contradictions concerns those persons whose income, while clearly contributing to the economy of the community, is derived neither from sales to the local community nor from sales to the outside world. Andrews, Maxine Kurtz, Forbat, and others allocate employment in government institutions according to the population served (local or outside population); and allocate the staff of universities proportional to the number of local and "foreign" students.

From the "balance-of-payments" point of view, which these researchers are trying to apply, this does not make sense. From this point of view the only thing that matters is the source of the income, not who is benefited by the work performed. The income of *all* federal employees is a net gain to the community, whether they deliver letters to local residents or work on projects to deliver milk — or atom bombs — to the Hottentots; just as all taxes paid to the Federal Government are a net loss to the community. Similarly, if the university professor is paid by state contributions, by the G.I. Bill of Rights, by an outside foundation, or by outside parents of his students, his income is a gain to the community. But it is not if he is paid out of city funds, out of contributions of local alumni, or out of money earned by his students in the community. The home residence of his students has nothing to do with it.

Evidently these researchers were led astray because in the back of their minds, but not formulated, was the "criticality" approach. In a city of a certain size, post offices, local courts, elementary and high schools can indeed be taken for granted; while the city has to compete with other cities for a state university or for a regional office of the National Government, and also has to compete with them for students at its university.

f. Discrepancy between "basic" employment and outside earnings

If a given community with a given level of of living depends for 50 percent of the goods and services which it consumes on outside sources, its size is evidently limited by the amount of money which it can pay to the outside. It is the standard assumption of the "basic-nonbasic" method that in this case 50 percent of its employment would have to be "basic." The contribution to the "economic base" is assumed to be proportional to the number of persons employed in each branch of "basic employment." "Wholesale trade accounted for . . . 12 percent of its total basic employment . . . *therefore* (my emphasis, H.B.) . . . about one-eighth of the economic base.[33]

This comfortable "therefore" contains — and conceals — a number of unspoken assumptions, which should be spelled out:

1. average wages are roughly the same in all branches of production (the Denver study does touch on this question).
2. the ratio of "value added" to payrolls is roughly the same in all branches.
3. the proportion of the "non-payroll" section of "value added" going to local owners is roughly the same in all branches.
4. moneys paid or received by the community other than payments for goods and services balance out.

It is improbable that any of these assumptions correspond to the facts of life in a metropolitan area.

From the Denver study, f.i., can be seen that average annual wages in wholesale trade varied from $3,100 in "petroleum bulk stations" to $4,300 in "manufacturer's branches without stock."[34]

Sales per employee varied far more than average wages: in retail trade from $8,150 in "eating and drinking places" to $35,800 in "automotive"; and in wholesale trade from $28,000 in "auto & equipment" to $610,000 in "farm products (raw)."[35] These differences reflect largely, but hardly entirely, differences in mark-up. If we assume, f.i., that the mark-up was 20 percent in "auto & equipment" and 2 percent in "farm products," the

[33] *Working Denver, op. cit.,* p. 4.
[34] *Working Denver, op. cit.,* p. 68.
[35] *Working Denver, op. cit.,* p. 74.

mark-up, or "value added," per employee would still vary from $4,700 to $12,000.

Evidently the greater part of these $12,000 represents return on capital, and how much it will contribute to the purchasing power (the "economic base") of Denver versus the outside world will depend entirely on the share of the capital owned by Denverites.

Andrews, f.i., recognizes the importance of this factor of "absentee ownership" of capital, saying: "if a dollar-flow measurement device were employed, the loss would be clear . . . (and) the community receiving the profits would count them."

Andrews, not employing such a "device," does *not count* these losses. But he *does count* the gains in the receiving community where he classifies the income derived from investments in other communities as "capital export."

This is indeed a classical example of the confusion resulting from the attempt to achieve greater precision by refining a basically confused concept. The *export of capital* puts the community in the red; it is the *return on the capital* — and return of the capital — which produces income. Nor is this return contingent on previous "export" of capital by the community; the wealthy residents of Palm Beach derive their income from capital which was not exported by Palm Beach, but either was exported from New York and other places, or was not "exported" at all, but accumulated out of the returns of "outside" investments. Andrews' concept of unifying all sources of income of the community under the term "export of goods, services, and capital" in an unfortunate attempt to force strange bedfellows into the procrustean bed of the "basic-nonbasic" concept.

Other important factors affecting the balance of payments of a community are the ratio of payments to disbursements of state and federal taxes and the "terms of trade," i.e., the price relations between imported and exported goods. Assume, for example, that the work of 10,000 persons employed in export industries is required to pay for the food imported by a community of 150,000 persons. If food prices were cut in half, these 10,000 workers could pay for the food of 300,000 people.

Because of these many factors, "basic employment" is a very inadequate yardstick for the measurement of the economic base of the community.

g. The "basic-nonbasic" ratio

As has been noted before, the attempt to distinguish "basic" and "nonbasic" employment has been made primarily in order to find the ratio of the second to the first.

Jones had made the rather naive assumption that "the majority of the town . . . are employed in providing goods and services . . . for other communities. It could not be otherwise."[36] In fact, it is otherwise. In most cases the ratio is considerably greater than unity, but it differs widely.

Roterus and Calef, in the aforementioned article, succinctly state the reason for the difference: "the basic-nonbasic ratio is a measure of the degree of economic interdependence."

In new communities the ratio may be very low because they depend for most services on established neighboring communities. However, one "service" industry, construction, is usually over-represented in such areas. In Lower Bucks County, f.i., in March 1952, there were for every 100 persons employed in manufacturing only 35.7 employed in serv-

---

[36] J. H. Jones, *op. cit.*, p. 125.

ice industries other than construction, compared to a ratio of 90.4 in the Philadelphia Metropolitan Area in 1950. On the other hand, the ratio of employment in construction to manufacturing was 71.5 to 100 in Lower Bucks County as against 9.6 to 100 in the Metropolitan Area.[37]

It has been noted that the ratio is generally higher the larger the community. The reasons may be summarized as follows:

1. a greater completeness of all branches of production; the community is more nearly "self-contained" than a small one.
2. greater "round-about-ness" of production; the productive process is divided into a greater number of organizationally independent, though economically interdependent, units.

In addition, in most metropolitan areas there is:

3. higher average income, commanding more consumer services.
4. a concentration of "power and wealth," drawing unearned income from the outside and spending it for local services.

The New York Regional Plan study of 1944 found the abnormally high ratio of 2.2 "nonbasic" for every one "basic" employed. However, the study also states that nearly one-third of the region's "basic" income is derived from sources other than the export of goods and services. If it is assumed that a proportional number of service workers was supported by this source of income and only the remainder is related to the "basic" workers, the ratio is about 1.5, practically the

the same as the one found in Denver, which was 1.53.

The ratio also changes over time; nor can these changes be easily explained. In Cincinnati, f.i., between 1929 and 1933, the decrease in the number of factory workers was 29 percent above the national average, but the decrease in retail sales was 6 percent below the average for the nation.

A slightly different and rather interesting approach to the question of "service" employment has been taken by Swedish planners and geographers who have attempted to find the number of service workers required to serve a given population in communities of various types. Here the distinction of "basic" and "nonbasic" is used as a tool for identifying those industries which have to be studied directly and individually, while a global average figure is used for the prognosis of all "nonbasic" employment. Forbat found that in the three towns of Kristinehamn, Skövde, and Landskrona secondary employment varied only from 20.92 percent to 22.39 percent of the total population. Even this slight variation was due entirely to variations in agriculture, construction, and domestic service; after elimination of these three categories the range was 16.37 percent to 16.49 percent.

These are three towns with a population between 15,000 and 24,000. For villages of about 2000 population, Forbat found a percentage of service workers of 15 percent, and for Stockholm of 27 percent. This correlation of percentage of service workers with size is in accord with American experience.

Sven Godlund contributed to the discussion the concept of an "index of centralization" which is defined by the percentage of the total population employed in retail trade and consumer services. He found this to vary with size from 6.5 percent in regional centers down to 3.5 percent in villages, with even

[37] Economic Development, Lower Bucks County, Bucks County Planning Commission (February, 1954), p. 12 and table E8.

lower percentages in "special urban settlements," mainly industrial satellite towns.[38]

h. The "multiplier"

Investigation of the "basic-nonbasic" ratio is used to find the "multiplier," the ratio of total population to "basic" employment. The multiplier is determined not only by the "basic-nonbasic" ratio, but by three additional factors which are not always clearly recognized:

1. family coefficient of basic employed.
2. family coefficient of nonbasic employed.
3. percentage of nonemployed (incl. dependents) population.

Frequently a global ratio of population to employment is used. However, this ratio may vary considerably if any of these three factors change, or if their relative weights change.

In Denver, f.i., the ratio of population to "basic" employment — the "multiplier" — was 7.8 in 1940. Between 1940 and 1950, however, there were only 4.6 persons added to the population for every one person added to "basic" employment. It is evident that a population prediction based on the number of additional "basic" employed and using the "multiplier" found in 1940 would have overstated the decennial population increase by 70 percent.

Variations in the family coefficient between various "basic" industries are very significant. In the anthracite mining regions of Pennsylvania, f.i., the addition of a mining job would usually mean the addition of a family. The addition of a hosiery job generally means employment of a female former dependent of a miner's family.

Generally the family coefficient is low in industries with high female employment and in communities with a high rate of employment and with low percentages of the population in the extreme age groups, i.e., children and old people.

Forbat[39] found that the family coefficient in the Swedish countryside varied from 1.54 for textile workers to 2.49 for construction workers; for Stockholm both figures were considerably lower, 1.30 and 2.06 respectively. He also found that the family coefficient in trade and service employment averaged 1.7 to 1.8.

Forbat has developed a formula which takes into account the differences in the family coefficient for different types of employment. The formula is:

$$P = \frac{Ep \cdot Cp}{1 - Rs \cdot Cs}$$

P = population
Ep = employed, primary
Cp = family coefficient of primary employed
Cs = family coefficient of secondary employed
Rs = secondary employment as percent of population

If Ep equals 1, the "multiplier" becomes:

$$M = \frac{Cp}{1 - Rs \cdot Cs}$$

By applying this formula, Forbat found the following multipliers:

villages:	2.1 to 3.2
towns:	2.5 to 3.7
Stockholm:	2.3 to 3.3

These are large variations. They would be even larger except for the fact that high serv-

[38] Sven Godlund, "Studies in Rural-Urban Interaction," *Lund Studies in Geography* (Lund, 1951).

[39] Fred Forbat, "Untersuchungen über den Lokalisierungsmultiplikator" (investigations on the localisation-multiplier) *Raumforschung & Raumordnung*, no. 2 (1953), pp. 97-101.

ice employment and low family coefficient are generally associated, because both are correlated with high female employment, and that their influences tend to cancel each other. Thus, the multiplier is low in villages, despite a high family coefficient, because the villages depend for services largely on neighboring towns; it is low in Stockholm, despite high service employment, because the family coefficient is low.

A further difficulty in deriving the "multiplier" stems from the fact that there is a sizeable and highly variable group in most communities which is neither in "basic" nor in "nonbasic" employment nor part of the families of either group. These are the "independent nonworkers," who may derive their income from a great many sources: investments, pensions, social insurance, relief payments, etc. Forbat classifies these as "primary" ("basic"), because their number is not dependent on the number of those in other "basic" groups. In the little town of Skövde their number was equal to one quarter of all other "basic" groups. In many American cities it may be even higher. On the other hand, in new or rapidly growing communities their number is low; in some cases practically zero. Also, their number may vary widely and abruptly with changes in the labor market.

Swedish statistical data make it possible to derive a separate family coefficient for this group which is, of course, lower than that for employed persons. In Stockholm, f.i., it was 1.30 versus 1.63 for employed persons; in the Swedish countryside 1.43 versus 2.14.[40]

American statistics lump "independents" and "dependents" in the categories "unemployed" and "not in the Labor Force." They

also present no data from which family coefficients for specific industries in specific localities could be derived. This writer, in attempting to apply the Forbat formula to American cities, has therefore substituted for both C_p and C_s (family coefficient for "basic" and "nonbasic" employed) what might be called a "community-wide family coefficient"; that is, the ratio of total population to total employed. The resultant multipliers are 5.5 for Philadelphia and 6.46 for Denver; the latter being practically identical with the 6.6 found by Maxine Kurtz.

The fact that these figures are about twice as large as those found in Swedish towns is only partly due to the different classification of the "independent nonworkers." In a letter to this writer, of September 26, 1955, Forbat has recalculated the "multiplier" for five Swedish towns on the basis of the "community-wide family coefficient." The resulting figures are between 3.5 and 4.1. The difference between these multipliers and those found for Philadelphia and Denver are due first, to the fact that in Swedish cities employed persons average 49 percent of total population against about 40 percent in American cities; and second, to an unusually high percentage of "basic" employment which in the five Swedish towns was 53.3 percent to 60.0 percent of all employment. This, in turn, is partly due to actual differences in economic structure, and partly to differences in classification. Forbat classifies *all* "big" industry (as distinct from handicraft industry) as "basic." This appears quite permissible in small towns, but would lead to very serious distortions if applied, f.i., to the New York garment industry.

Barfod, in the above-mentioned study of the impact of a new oil refinery on the population of Aarhus, apparently ignored all these problems. He found a "multiplier" of 8.8 for

[40] F. Forbat, *Untersuchungen* . . . , *op. cit.*, p. 100, Table 2.

every person in "direct basic" employment and of 5.5 for every person in all (including "indirect") "basic" employment.

The enormous range in multipliers — from 2.1 to 8.8 — found by various methods shows that the multiplier is not the simple, unequivocal device for population prediction as which it appears at first sight.

7. APPLICATION OF THE "BASIC-NONBASIC" METHOD TO THE METROPOLIS

a. The "multiplier"

One of the main purposes of developing the "basic-nonbasic" method was its alleged usefulness for population prediction. Future population was to be found by multiplying future "basic" employment with a figure which could supposedly be derived from past experience.

We have seen that past experience does not and can not yield any figure applicable to future experience unless a great number of variables are known, in addition to the future number of persons in "basic" employment. The most important variables are:

1. average level of living of the community
2. percentage, in terms of value, of the goods and services constituting this level which have to be purchased from outside
3. net gain or loss to the community from money flow due to causes other than payments for goods and services
4. family coefficient of persons in "basic" employment
5. family coefficient of persons in "non-basic" employment
6. percentage of total population who are not employed, nor dependents of employed persons

These variables make it difficult to determine the multiplier for any community. But in metropolitan areas it is even more difficult to predict the figure which is to be multiplied: the future number of persons in "basic" employment.

The illusion that "basic" employment is better predictable than many other variables stems from the fact that future employment of individual enterprises is, indeed, frequently known with reasonable certainty. If a new steel work requiring 5000 workers is being built, it is highly probable that after its completion there will be 5000 steel workers living in the community. If the community is and will remain a company town, it is indeed possible to find its population by adding to the steel workers and their dependents those persons (and their dependents) who service the steel workers.

But in a metropolitan area there are many plants, big and small, which open up or shut down, expand or contract their employment. We have seen that "basic" employment, by definition, is critical, competitive employment. It is the part of the economy which is most vulnerable, most likely to disappear or contract as a result of outside competition, and also most dynamic, most likely to spring up or grow as a result of invasion of outside markets. As the most vulnerable and most dynamic part of the metropolitan economy, "basic" activities are its most variable, least predictable element.

In addition, there is the practical impossibility of measuring "indirect primary" employment. Moreover, as Walter Isard and others have emphasized, a new "basic" industry attracts not only those which supply it, but also those which it supplies; not only "indirect primary," but what we might call "primary indirect" activities. Here another complication arises. Assume that a new steel plant, producing a million tons of steel, attracts, over the years, steel fabricating plants which buy half of its production. Then one half of its workers must, by definition, be transferred from the "basic" to the "nonbasic" category, because they now work for the local market. In other words, the more the steel plant contributes to the community's economic base — in the commonsense meaning of that term — the less "basic" does it become according to the standard formula.

Some, like Isard, believe that, while application of the multiplier formula for prediction of the entire metropolitan population may not be practicable, it can be used to estimate the population to be added as a result of the impact of a specific known development, such as the new steel plant at Morrisville, Pa., for instance.

Isard's study of the impact of the Morrisville plant clearly shows two difficulties inherent in this method:

1. within what area will the added population live?
2. to which figure is the "new" population to be added?

The first difficulty is relatively minor: the region of impact comprises several metropolitan areas.

The second difficulty is fundamental. Obviously it makes no sense to add the "new" population simply to the present one, or to what the present one would be, as the result of natural increase, at the end of the impact period. The addition must be made to a figure predicted on the basis of past trends. But these trends reflect the dynamic nature of the metropolitan economy, the never-ceasing shrinkage of old industries and expansion of new ones. In the Philadelphia Area, f.i., they reflect the coming and growth of the oil refining industry, an event closely comparable to the coming of the steel industry, and even

due to the attraction of the same locational factors. Thus the figure derived from the trend already anticipated the coming of new industries, and if their impact is added separately, it will be counted twice. It is impossible thus to isolate the impact of single factors in and on the metropolitan complex.

It is worth noting that even the Denver study which had lavished so much care and ingenuity on the identification of "basic" employment, finally bases its prediction of the future growth of the economy and population of the area not on these figures, but on long-term trends and on estimates of the importance of locational factors.

We may conclude:

> As a tool for predicting the population of metropolitan areas the "basic-nonbasic" method is useless.[41]

b. Promotion of "basic" industries

The other main purpose for developing the "basic-nonbasic" method is its alleged usefulness in concentrating attention on those industries whose promotion will do the most good for the well-being of the community, which is supposed to depend primarily on improvement of its balance of payments.

We have already pointed out that the method, strictly applied, tends to divert attention from many industries which might contribute most to an improvement of the balance of payments, namely those whose products the community now imports, but might produce itself. We also noted that most

---

[41] Forbat, who has probably developed the "multiplier" method of population prediction more successfully than any other planner, informs this writer that he recently advised against applying it to a big city, because "in the economy of the big cities there evidently exists a different hierarchy."

authors of "economic base" studies have had the good sense to forget their theory and to give a good deal of attention to just these industries.

But suppose communities did succeed in advertising their locational advantages for all those industries which are not by their physical nature restricted to a local market and who therefore have a choice. What would be the effect on the national distribution of industry? Would it be more efficient than it is now?

There are two possibilities. If *all* communities do an equally effective job of industrial promotion, their efforts will cancel each other out and the net effect will be zero. If some communities only do a good job, industries will learn of and be attracted by their locational advantages. By the same token they will ignore and neglect equal or greater locational advantages in communities which do less or nothing for promotion. The net result can only be a less efficient national distribution than would result from the functioning of the market without benefit of local planning.

Location of industries working for the national and international market is a legitimate and most important function of national planning. Local planning organizations could make valuable, indeed indispensable, contributions to such national planning by discovering the potentialities and limitations of their areas.

Without such a national plan the value of their promotional efforts is highly dubious. Most likely they will be ineffective; if effective, they are more likely to do harm than good to the nation.

We can conclude:

As a guide for the concentration of local promotional efforts the "basic-nonbasic" method is not a useful tool.

This is not to say that all results of the work done in the framework of this method are to be discarded as worthless. They can be of great value, first, for the development of "balance of payments" studies, and second, for the exploration of the "criticality" of various industries.

c. The real economic base of the metropolis

What, finally, is the relative importance of "basic" and "nonbasic" activities in a metropolitan area?

We have seen that the percentage of persons employed in "basic" activities decreases as a community becomes more "metropolitan" quantitatively and qualitatively: that is the larger it is and the greater the variety and differentiation of its activities.

The more metropolitan the community, the more its inhabitants do "live by taking in each other's washing." Still, it remains dependent on the outside world for many goods and services and will have to pay for the major part of these by the products of its export industries. It is not legitimate to worry about these more than about the "nonbasic" ones?

Certainly, from the point of view of sales there is nothing to worry about the "local service" industries, because they cannot be replaced from the outside. For the same reason there is everything to worry about them from the point of view of the welfare of the consumer. If the Philadelphia subway system goes out of business, it can not be replaced by the New York subways. Inversely, from the point of view of sales there is everything to worry about the "competitive" industries; but from the point of view of the consumer's welfare there is nothing to worry about them. Their goods and services can be replaced by purchasing them from the outside; and the money they earn from the outside may be earned by other competitive industries which may be substituted for those which are lost.

The *ability to substitute* one activity for another is the crucial point. Most economic base studies touch on it in one form or another.

"Gold mining created service jobs, but when it 'petered out,' catastrophe was averted by local enterprise substituting for the erstwhile gold mine . . . ghost towns are evidence, however, that the substitution did not always occur," says the Denver study.[42] However, it does not inquire under which conditions substitution does or does not occur.

Part of the answer is given by Alexander who explains that Oshkosh owed its origin to sawmills which later disappeared, but only after having attracted the millwork industry. "The reservoir of labor persisted and became the dominant factor in the survival of the woodworking industry."[43]

Homer Hoyt adds other factors: "What does Brockton have to offer as attractions to existing and new industries? . . . Adequate power and transportation; decentralization; skilled machine operators; a location within the world's greatest concentration of buying power; and proximity to a great pool of technical knowledge.[44]

These advantages can be summarized under three headings:

1. Labor force of various skills; its presence is dependent on *local consumer services:* housing, schools, stores, local transportation.
2. *Business services,* including transportation with its terminals.
3. *Markets,* local and regional.

The more developed these three factors are, the more favorable are the conditions for substitution; and it is easy to see that all three are strongest in metropolitan areas, and the stronger, the more metropolitan the area, that is, the larger and more diversified it is.

The competitive advantage of a large home market is too well known from the field of international trade to require further elaboration.

The importance of a large and diversified labor force also needs little comment. Only some special aspects may be mentioned here. Edgar M. Hoover, Jr., says: "the more abnormal the sex and age requirements or the more pronounced the fluctuations, the more (such industries must be) located near others with complementary labor demands or in a large diversified labor market,"[45] that is, in metropolitan area. Hoover also shows that the big city is the natural habitat of the small plant which is most strongly dependent on the services of other plants. The average number of wage earners per manufacturing establishment in industrial areas in 1937 was 43 in central cities, 61 in major satellite towns, and 95 in the remainder of industrial areas.

The reason for this concentration of small plants in big cities is "external economies." Hoover says: "Many of these 'external economies' are based on the availability of more and more specialized auxiliary and service enterprises, with increased concentration of the main industry . . . the availability of service enterprises makes possible a very narrow specialization of function in relatively small plants."[46]

---

[42] *Working Denver, op. cit.,* p. 27.
[43] John W. Alexander, *Oshkosh, op. cit.,* p. 34.
[44] *The Economic Base of Brockton, op. cit.,* p. 6.

[45] Edgar M. Hoover, Jr., "Size of Plant, Concern, and Production Center", *National Resources Planning Board, Industrial Location and National Resources* (Washington, 1943), p. 251.
[46] Edgar M. Hoover, Jr., *op. cit.,* p. 245.

This development soon reaches a point where the "primary" industry is as dependent on the "auxiliary" ones as these are on it. "Often the number and variety of ancillary establishments clustered around some primary industry is such that the locational dependence of the primary industry on the ancillaries, though small in respect to each one, is great in respect to the total."[47]

It is this high development of "business services" and other "secondary" industries which, together with the availability of labor of all kinds, enables the metropolis to sustain, expand, and replace its "primary" industries.

It is thus the "secondary," "nonbasic" industries, both business and personal services, as well as "ancillary" manufacturing, which constitute the real and lasting strength of the metropolitan economy. As long as they continue to function efficiently, the metropolis will always be able to substitute new "export" industries for any which may be destroyed by the vicissitudes of economic life.

We have seen that such substitutions may occur even in small towns such as Oshkosh. In metropolitan areas they are the rule rather than the exception. The history of the past 40 years in Europe has given eloquent proof of the ability of metropolitan communities to survive not only physical destruction, but also the disappearance of those functions on which their existence had been based in the past. They developed new functions and survived. Vienna and Leningrad are only two particularly striking examples.

It is worth noting that this is a new phenomenon. The capitals of oriental empires soon turned into dust, once a new ruler transferred his court to a different location. Even Rome was little more than a village after the Western Empire had been destroyed. These cities were mainly centers of consumption, based on the concentration of "power and wealth." The modern metropolitan area is primarily a center of production, based on a concentration of productive forces. It is qualitatively different from the city as it has been known throughout history. It is a genuinely new form of human settlement, and, contrary to predictions of its approaching transformation into "necropolis," it is showing a greater vitality than any previous form of settlement. As far as this writer is aware, no community that during the last century has passed the half-million mark — a truer border line for the metropolis than the 50,000 adopted by the U.S. Census — has fallen below that population level.

The basis of this amazing stability are the business and consumer services and other industries supplying the local market. They are the permanent and constant element, while the "export" industries are variable, subject to incessant change and replacement. While the existence of a sufficient number of such industries is indispensable for the continued existence of the metropolis, each individual "export" industry is expendable and replaceable.

In any commonsense use of the term, it is the "service" industries of the metropolis that are "basic" and "primary," while the "export" industries are "secondary" and "ancillary." The economic base of the metropolis consists in the activities by which its inhabitants supply each other.

SUMMARY

1. The concept divides all employment in a community into "basic" or "primary" employment, working for export, and "nonbasic" or "secondary" employment, working for local consumption.

[47] Edgar M. Hoover, Jr., *op. cit.*, p. 276.

2. This method purports to serve two goals:
   a. Concentration of attention on the most important industries.
   b. Prediction of future total employment and population, which are to be derived from future "basic" employment by means of a "basic-nonbasic ratio" and of a "multiplier."
3. The method seeks the answer to two different questions, which it fails to distinguish:
   a. What is the balance of payments of the community?
   b. What are the most "critical" industries, i.e., those most vulnerable to outside competition and most capable of expansion into outside markets?
4. The confusion is increased by a widespread dual bias:
   a. A "mercantilistic" bias in favor of money-earning versus consumption-satisfying activities.
   b. A "physiocratic" bias in favor of food and raw materials versus manufactured goods and services.
5. The attempt to identify "basic" activities by the widely accepted method of proportional apportionment is misleading. The attempt to do it by actual market survey is costly and ends up by revealing the inherent contradictions of the method.
6. The method neglects the import side of the ledger which is equally important with the export side, both from the "balance of payments" and from the "criticality" point of view.
7. As a result of its confusion of these two points of view, the method is unable to solve the problem of "indirect primary" activities. If a consistent "balance of payments" approach were used, the problem would cease to exist; if a consistent

"criticality" approach were used, these activities would fall in line with all other activities.
8. The method fails to integrate into its conceptual scheme any payments received or made other than those for work performed.
9. Employment is not a usable unit of measurement for a "balance of payments" approach, which must use "value of product" and other value terms.
10. The proportion of "basic" activities increases with increasing division of labor between communities and decreases with increasing size of community and with increasing division of labor within the community.
11. The "basic-nonbasic ratio" is meaningful only in small and simply structured communities; the larger and more complex, that is the more "metropolitan" the community, the less applicable is the ratio and the entire method.
12. The "multiplier" varies not only with the "ratio," but also with the "family coefficient" of both the "basic" and the "nonbasic" employed, and with the percentage of the population which is not employed.
13. Because of these complexities the "multiplier" is not a useful tool for population prediction in a metropolitan area.
14. The identification of the "export" activities of each locality could be an important tool for a national agency planning industrial location. However, if local planning agencies use it as a guide to promotion, it will either be ineffective, or, if effective, result in a harmful distortion of the national locational pattern.
15. A large metropolitan area exists, survives, and grows because its business and consumer services enable it to sub-

stitute new "export" industries for any that decline as a result of the incessant vicissitudes of economic life.

These services are the constant and permanent, hence the truly "basic" and "primary"

elements of the metropolitan economy; while the ever changing export industries are the "ancillary" and "secondary" elements. The relation assumed by the method is, in fact, reversed.

16

The Functional Bases
of Small Towns

Howard A. Stafford, Jr.

The small town, small urban place, or small city, as designated in this study, is essentially equivalent to what Brush has included in his threefold classification of hamlets, villages, and towns.[1] The small town is of academic

interest because it represents the lower end of the central-place continuum. Any generalizations, theories, or laws developed for central places should hold not only for large urban places but also for all the gradations to the smallest. Thomas well stated the theoretical importance of the small city when he wrote, "First, logically, these small places provide

[1] John Brush, "The Hierarchy of Central Places in Southwestern Wisconsin," *Geogr. Rev.*, Vol. 43 (1953), pp. 380-402.

Reprinted from *Economic Geography*, Vol. 38 (April, 1963), pp. 165-75 by permission.

basic connection between the dispersed agricultural populations and the agglomerated urban population. For the most part, such direct connections as do exist are through the goods and services which are provided in these small towns for the agricultural population surrounding them. Second, even if small towns do not fulfill their logical role of providing goods and services for a dispersed farm population, the fact remains that these small places exist and that economic activities are performed in them just as they are in the larger places."[2] The motivation for this study is a desire to examine the functional bases for small southern Illinois towns and to compare the results with those of similar studies in other areas.

Recent geographic literature contains some fine studies of small urban places. Notable among these have been Berry and Garrison's Snohomish County, Washington, studies,[3] King's comparative study of the Canterbury Provincial District, New Zealand,[4] and Thomas' study of the functional bases for small Iowa towns.[5] The present study is an attempt to duplicate Thomas' Iowa study for selected southern Illinois towns; less rigorously, it also compares the southern Illinois study with those for Snohomish County and Canterbury Provincial District.

[2] Edwin N. Thomas, "Some Comments on the Functional Bases for Small Iowa Towns," *Iowa Business Digest* (1960), p. 10.

[3] Brian J. L. Berry and William L. Garrison, "The Functional Bases of the Central Place Hierarchy," *Econ. Geog.*, Vol. 34 (1958), pp. 145-54.

[4] Leslie J. King, "The Functional Role of Small Towns in Canterbury," forthcoming in *Procs. Third N.Z. Geogr. Conf.*, Palmerston North (1962).

[5] Edwin N. Thomas, *op. cit.*

SELECTION OF TOWNS

Thirty-one small towns were selected as a sample of small urban places. The selection was restricted to the southern 22 counties of Illinois, random choices being made from the listing of urban places provided by the Illinois State Department of Revenue report of October, 1960, on the collection of the Retailer's Occupation Tax (Sales Tax). The spatial distribution of the 31 sample towns is shown in Figure 1. Only towns with a 1960 population of 5000 or less were eligible for selection. The 1960 population of the 31 towns ranges from 40 for Welge to 3739 for Waterloo, with an average of 552. It should be noted that the criteria used in this study differ somewhat from those used by Thomas, in that he chose only incorporated municipalities with populations of less than 2500. The 42 cities used by Thomas had 1950 populations ranging from 42 to 2333, with an average of 462 persons.

DEFINITION OF TERMS

In order that a coherent analysis can be made of the functional bases of small southern Illinois towns, the mass of data collected by field work has been summarized for each urban place in terms of establishments, functions, and functional units; the concepts are borrowed directly from Thomas' Iowa study. "An establishment is essentially the physical manifestation of an activity and is generally the unit in which an activity is performed, e.g., the building in which the office for a filling station is located or the office of a physician are examples of establishments. In contrast, the term 'function' refers to activities which are performed in the establishments. According to these definitions, it is possible for more than one function to be associated

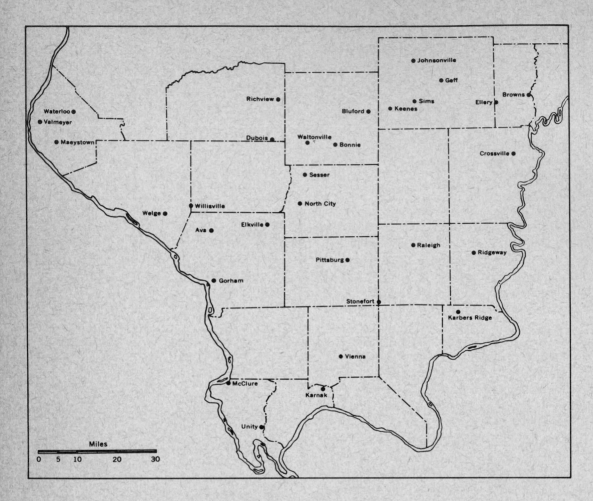

Figure 1. Distribution of sample towns in southern Illinois.

with a particular establishment. Each occurrence of a function constitutes one *functional unit*.

"Specific interest is focused on three indices by which the magnitude of the activities within an urban place may be measured. Each of these indices illuminates a somewhat different aspect of the overall distribution of activities. The three summary values which are provided for each place are (1) total number of establishments, (2) total number of functions, and (3) total number of functional units. Differences between these values may be illustrated as follows. Let us assume that there is a place with three establishments, A, B, C. Three functions are performed in establishment A; it is a gasoline filling station, bulk oil distribution station, and used-car lot. Two functions are associated with establishment B; it is a combination food store and filling station. Two functions are associated with establishment C; it is a combination food store and livestock feed store. There are in this case, three establishments, five functions, and seven functional units."[6]

THE OCCURENCE OF FUNCTIONS WITHIN THE SAMPLE CITIES

Data on the central-place functions performed in each of the 31 towns were obtained through field work, rather than from secondary sources. At the outset, a list was prepared of all functions that might be expected to occur at least once in the sample cities. This basic listing was altered as experience was gained. The final list includes 60 functions, ranging from gasoline-filling stations and churches, each of which occurs 96 times, to a candy store, veterinarian, photographer, tire store, chiropractor, and taxi service, each of which occurs only once in the entire group of 31 towns. The list of functions used in this study, while essentially the same, is not so exhaustive as Thomas' listing of 121 functions. Actually, data were collected for many more than the 60 functions finally used in the analysis, but these data were not included in the final tally because classification difficulties led to considerable distrust of their accuracy. The most frequently occurring functions included in the Iowa study but not in the southern Illinois study are meeting halls and insurance agencies.

At this point, a degree of similarity between the frequency of occurrence of functions in small southern Illinois towns and small Iowa towns can be noted. As indicated in Table I, the tally of the ten most frequently occurring functions in the two areas is strikingly similar.

Of the ten functions on the Iowa list, eight occur on the southern Illinois list and their rankings are not very different. That the ani-

TABLE I

Rank Order of Most Frequently Occurring Functions

Iowa	Southern Illinois
1. Gasoline filling station	1. Gasoline filling station
2. Church	2. Church
3. Animal feed store	3. Food store
4. Auto-repair shop	4. Tavern
5. Insurance agency	5. Restaurant
6. Food store	6. Beauty shop
7. Tavern	7. Insurance agency*
8. Restaurant	8. General store
9. Bulk oil distributor	9. Auto-repair garage
10. Meeting hall	10. Meeting hall*

* Data pertaining to insurance agencies and meeting halls were not included in the subsequent analysis due to the difficulty of accurate classification in some of the towns; however, the summations appear to be reasonably accurate.

mal feed store is not on the southern Illinois list may be a reflection of the greater importance of meat animals in the agricultural economy of Iowa. The high degree of occurrence of bulk oil distributors in Iowa may be a consequence either of the harsher winter climate or of the relatively small use of local coal or of both. That churches occur as frequently as gasoline filling stations in southern Illinois, whereas they definitely have second rank in the small towns studied in Iowa, may be an indication that church bodies in southern Illinois tend to be more fractionalized[7] and inde-

[7] Small independent churches are often thought of as being characteristic of denominations, such as the Baptist, which have large rural memberships. For an indication of the relative strength of the Baptist Church in Southern Illinois, see Wilbur Zelinsky, "An Approach to the Religious Geography of the United States: Patterns of Church Membership in 1952," *Annals Assoc. Amer. Geogrs.*, Vol. 51 (1961), pp. 139-93.

pendent, thus giving rise to a larger number of small congregations. Another interesting difference between the two listings is the relative importance of the general store in southern Illinois. It is possible that this is related to the diversified rural economy in southern Illinois and also to the less prosperous nature of the economy, the latter resulting in lower buying power and therefore relatively less opportunity for retailers to specialize.

The interesting deviations notwithstanding, the overall impression gained from a comparison of the two lists is that, assuming that the functions which occur most frequently are the activities which provide the economic bases for most of these towns, small Iowa towns and small southern Illinois towns exist for essentially the same reasons. As expected, considering population size, the goods and services provided by the small towns are frequently used and relatively standardized (convenience goods and services). In the present era, it appears that the economic bases for most of these small towns center on two general demands. The first demand is created by the insatiable appetite of the ubiquitous American automobile, giving rise to the frequent occurrence of gasoline filling stations and auto-repair garages. The more specialized demands created by the automobile, such as new-car dealerships, are not often found in the small town. As Thomas points out, it is ironic that one of the reasons for the decline of the small town, namely improved transportation, provides it, at the same time with a substantial portion of its present *raison d'etre*. The second general function performed by the small town appears to be the provision of facilities for religious, social, or purely recreational gatherings. Since people seem to pre-

fer to have contact with groups consisting of close friends and acquaintances the small town is in reality performing a convenience service in providing for meetings of neighbors. In the lists of the ten most frequently occurring functions, both churches and meeting halls are certainly catering to the tendency to congregate. It also appears that one of the major functions of the restaurant and the tavern in the small town is to help to satisfy this same demand.

RELATIONSHIPS BETWEEN THE THREE INDICES AND POPULATION

It is obvious, even to the most casual observer, that large urban centers perform more functions than do small urban places and that they also have more establishments and functional units. That a positive relationship exists between functions performed and population size is generally assumed. However, three questions might be raised. First, are changes in the indices directly proportional to changes in the population size from town to town, or are there changing rates of increase over the population range? Second, to what extent might there be disruption of the normal relationships in areas of general population decline, owing to the survival of certain functions as a result of inertia? Third, is it possible that the rate of population increase relative to the increase in functions from town to town is greater in some areas than in others? This section is concerned with examining the relationships in southern Illinois between population size and (1) number of establishments, (2) number of functions, and (3) number of functional units; the results are compared with those for similar analyses in Iowa.

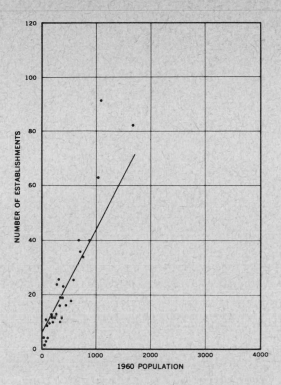

Figure 2. Relationship between town populations and number of establishments.

Relationship between number of establishments and population

The relationship between the number of establishments and population size in the small towns of southern Illinois is very close. The high degree of direct variation is indicated on the scatter diagram (Figure 2), the co-efficient of simple correlation being $+0.929$. Thus, the wide variations in population size are matched by a wide range of establishments per town (from 1 for Welge to 129 for Waterloo).

The close positive correlation indicates that, even in areas where towns are generally declining, the number of establishments is quite responsive to population change. That inertia will seriously disrupt the expected population-establishment relationship appears at this point to be an unsupported hypothesis, *unless* the degree of inertia is quite similar for *all* the towns. That this latter possibility is of consequence seems unlikely. Rather, it appears that population changes over time are quickly reflected by changes in the number of establishments.

Both in southern Illinois and in Iowa, the small towns exhibit a high degree of correlation between population use and number of establishments. Is it possible that, whereas the degree of association is quite similar, the nature of the relationship is significantly different in the two areas? A comparison of regression equations is interesting in this regard:

Southern Illinois: $y' = 5.49 + 3.8x$
Iowa: $y' = 9.60 + 6.6x$

In both cases, the relationship is linear. However, the Iowa line has not only a greater y-intercept, but also a steeper slope, indicating an establishment increment from town to town of 6.6 for each increase of 100 persons; this compares with an increment of 3.8 establishments for southern Illinois. Since *twice* as many classes of functions were tallied for the Iowa study as for the southern Illinois study (121 to 60), both constants in the southern Illinois regression equation should be doubled for purposes of comparison. When this is done, the resultant equation is very similar to that for Iowa. The conclusions, then must be that (1) the number of establishments is directly proportional to the number of people per town, and (2) that there is no significant difference in the relationship between population size and number of establishments for small towns in southern Illinois and Iowa.

Relationship between number of functions and population

The number of functions per town in southern Illinois ranges from 1 for Welge to 51 for Waterloo. In 27 of the 31 towns, the number of functions is less than the number of establishments. This is due to the tendency for a number of establishments to perform the same function in a given town, e.g., three or four filling stations. On the other hand, in the very small towns (less than 200 or 300 persons) the number of establishments is usually nearly equal to the number of functions; this is because of the small town's inability to support more than one establishment of a given type, and the fact that some duplication of establishments is offset by multi-functional establishments.

The relationship between population size and the number of functions in southern Illinois is shown in Figure 3. As expected, the degree of association is positive and quite high ($r = +0.892$). An examination of the best fit regression equation ($y' = 24.52 \log x -46.43$) reveals a curvilinear relationship, which is positive over the entire range. The curve increases at a decreasing rate. Thus, variations in town size in the very small centers (in this case, below approximately 500 persons) are associated with disproportionately large variations in the number of functions performed. Conversely, in the larger towns comparatively fewer functions are added. One suggested explanation for the curvilinear relationship between functions and population is that "there may be a definite limit to the functional complexity of urban places. As cities become larger, greater numbers of establishments and functions are

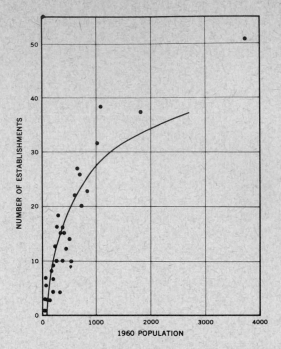

Figure 3. Relationship between town populations and number of functions.

formed within them. Once a certain level is reached, however, establishments are added much more rapidly than functions. This suggests that to a considerable extent greater numbers of people found in larger places do not desire different kinds of functions, but merely convenient access to the same ones."[8]

The regression equation between number of functions and population for Iowa is $y' = 39.91 \log x -66.31$. The nature of the association is very similar to that for southern Illinois. Again, the differences in constant values are probably explained by the difference in the number of functions eligible for inclusion. There appears to be little evidence, in this regard at least, that small southern

[8] Thomas, *op. cit.*, p. 15.

Illinois towns are significantly different from small Iowa towns.

Relationship Between Numbers of Functional Units and Population

The number of functional units in each of the southern Illinois towns surveyed ranged from 1 for Welge to 141 for Waterloo. This compares with a range of from 4 to 201 for the Iowa towns. Generally, there are, per town, more functional units than functions or establishments. By means of the same reasoning used in dealing with establishments and population, it can be hypothesized that there is a close, positive relationship between numbers of functional units and population per city. Figure 4 and a correlation coefficient of $r = +0.934$ substantiate the hypothesis. The regression equation ($y' = 6.18 + 4.2x$) indicates that, on the average, a change in town size of 100 persons will call for a change of slightly more than four functional units.

The association for small Iowa towns is also positive and very close, and the regression equation ($y' = 15.03 + 8.0x$) exhibits the same linearity as does the southern Illinois equation. Again, the differences in y-intercept and slope values are tentatively explained by variations in the data collection procedures rather than by any fundamental difference in the functional bases of small towns in the two areas.

Relationship Between the Functional Unit-Establishment Ratio and the Number of Establishments

Thomas computed for each of the Iowa towns a functional unit-establishment ratio which "indicates the number of functional units that are associated with each establishment located in the city and provides an approxi-

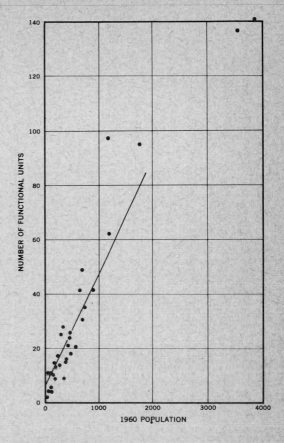

Figure 4. Relationship between town populations and number of functional units.

mate index of the degree of specialization of those establishments."[9] He found the association between this ratio and population size (Figure 5) to be significant, negative, and curvilinear ($y' = 1.75 - 0.266 \log x$), so providing evidence "that the establishments which are located in cities with fewer establishments are less specialized than the establishments which are located in cities with greater numbers of establishments."[10]

[9] *Ibid.*
[10] *Ibid.*

The nature of the relationship between the functional unit-establishment ratio and the number of establishments for southern Illinois (Figure 5) is very similar to that for Iowa. The degree of association, $r = -0.414$, is not high; but it is significant. The best-fit regression line ($y' = 1.39 - 0.19 \log x$) is curvilinear and negative over the entire range. This relationship suggests that in southern Illinois, as in Iowa, there is a tendency in the smaller towns as compared to the somewhat larger towns, for the establishments to be less specialized and their functions less segregated.

COMPARISONS WITH DATA FROM SNOHOMISH COUNTY, WASHINGTON, AND CANTERBURY PROVINCIAL DISTRICT, NEW ZEALAND

An examination of the data provided by Berry and Garrison for Snohomish County, Washington, reveals that the type and frequency of functions found in the urban places surveyed are very similar to the functions found in places of similar size in southern Illinois and Iowa. The coefficient of correlation between population and number of functions for Snohomish County is high and positive; the correlation is similar for the Canterbury Provincial District of New Zealand.[11] These compare to high positive coefficients between population and number of functions for southern Illinois and Iowa. Furthermore, the nature of the relationship is very similar (curvilinear) in the four areas.

King, in his New Zealand study, states that "the high correlation obtained between

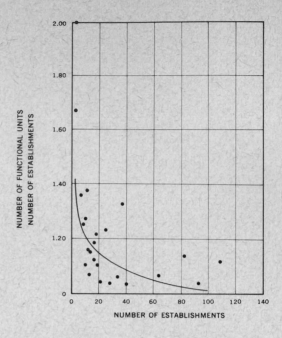

Figure 5. Relationship between number of establishments and the ratio of number of functional units to number of establishments.

population size and number of functional units confirms the belief that the majority of the small towns in Canterbury act as service centers."[12] The coefficient of $r = +0.930$ is almost identical to $r = +0.934$ for southern Illinois. These are both similar to the high positive association found by Thomas in Iowa and an $r = +0.789$ computed from the Snohomish County data.[13]

Table III presents the ten functions that appear most frequently in the towns studied

---

[11] The coefficient of correlation for Snohomish County is $r = +0.751$, compared to $r = +0.892$ for southern Illinois and $r = +0.823$ for the Canterbury Provincial District.

[12] King, *op. cit.*

[13] The correlation coefficients between population size and number of functions are $r = +0.93$ and $r = +0.77$ for the Canterbury District and Snohomish County respectively. However, these used only data on "variates," whereas those correlations computed for this study use data pertaining to "attributes" as well.

TABLE II

The Functional Bases of Selected Central Places in Southern Illinois

Town	1960 population*	Number of establishments	Number of functions	Number of functional Units	Functional unit establishment ratio
Waterloo	3739	129	51	141	1.09
Sesser	1764	83	38	94	1.14
Vienna	1094	91	39	97	1.03
Ridgway	1055	64	32	67	1.05
Crossville	874	40	23	41	1.03
Elkville	743	33	20	35	1.06
Valmeyer	709	36	26	48	1.33
Karnak	667	40	22	41	1.03
Ava	665	26	27	32	1.23
Willisville	532	17	14	20	1.18
Pittsburg	485	16	10	18	1.12
McClure	400	23	15	24	1.04
Waltonville	394	19	15	23	1.21
Bluford	388	19	16	21	1.10
Graham	378	16	12	16	1.00
Sims	376	12	10	15	1.25
Coello	362	10	5	10	1.00
Stonefort	349	26	18	27	1.04
Geff	330	24	16	24	1.00
Richview	255	12	10	14	1.16
Browns	251	13	13	18	1.38
DuBois	229	12	5	13	1.08
Raleigh	225	10	7	10	1.00
Bonnie	215	13	9	15	1.15
Macystown	158	9	8	11	1.23
Keenes	114	8	6	11	1.37
Unity	110	3	3	5	1.67
Johnsonville	96	10	7	11	1.10
Ellery	80	2	3	4	2.00
Karbers Ridge	50	4	3	4	1.00
Welge	40	1	1	1	1.00

* Population figures are from the U.S. Census of Population, 1960, except in the case of unincorporated towns for which estimates were made.

in the Snohomish County and Canterbury District areas. A comparison of its lists with those in Table I reveals a number of similarities as well as a number of differences.[14] The most striking similarities are in the food store category and in that for the services catering to the demands created by the automobile.

[14] A large measure of the dissimilarities between the Canterbury rank order and the others is due to the fact that King, in this section, relied on secondary data whereas the Iowa, Snohomish and southern Illinois data were collected in the field. King points out that his source (*The Canterbury Business and Trade Directory*, Auckland, N.Z.) does not consistently list all functions, notably halls and churches, and that, therefore, many functions were omitted.

TABLE III

Rank Order of Most Frequently Occurring
Functions

Snohomish County	Canterbury Provincial District
1. Filling stations	1. Insurance agency
2. Food stores	2. Motor service station
3. Churches	
4. Restaurant	3. Grocery
5. Taverns	4. Garage and motor engineer
6. Elementary schools	5. Library-lending
7. Physicians	6. Builder
8. Real estate agencies	7. Hotel
9. Appliance stores	8. Carrier and cartage
10. Barber shops	9. Restaurant-milkbar
	10. Engineer-general

There are two types of deviation from the general trends which should be mentioned. The first is that there are deviant towns *within* each of the study areas. Thomas offers two simultaneously-operating factors, nearness to a much larger town and an unusual amount of activity, to explain his outstanding deviate case, the town of Buffalo.[15] Berry and Garrison cite the towns of Beverly Park, Lowell, Lake Stevens, and Edmonds as exceptions, and point out that they are becoming dormitories for the Seattle area.[16] King indicates Kaiapoi as one of his deviant cases and concludes that "this undoubtedly reflects the importance of a large manufacturing component in the town's economic base."[17] He also indicates that the towns of Lincoln and Pareora are exceptions which "would seem to support Berry's contention that 'well defined popula-

tion: function ratios characterize a system of central places only where the major economic base of these centres consists of central place functions.' "[18] In southern Illinois, the town of Vienna has, for example, more establishments, functions and functional units than expected on the basis of population. This might be explained by the relative isolation of this county seat town from towns of comparable size.

The second kind of deviation is exemplified by the differences among the four areas in the type and importance of various functions found in the small towns. These differences are tentatively explained by (1) variations in the data collection techniques, and (2) by regional economic variations between the four areas — areal variations in the basic economic activities which these towns serve. That this second hypothesis is plausible is suggested by the fact that the areas which are most similar in terms of the functional bases of their central places, Iowa and southern Illinois, are the two which are closest together.

However, these deviations and differences do not negate the major conclusions of this study: (1) that the economic bases of small towns are highly predictable; and (2) that the economic structures of small towns in southern Illinois, Iowa, Snohomish County, Washington, and Canterbury Provincial District, New Zealand, are very similar.

SUMMARY

Data collected from 31 small, southern Illinois towns indicate that these towns are almost exclusively service centers. Practically all the employment opportunities in these

[15] Thomas, *op. cit.*, p. 12.
[16] Berry and Garrison, *op. cit.*, p. 154.
[17] King, *op. cit.*
[18] *Ibid.*

small urban places are in the service occupations such as those represented by store clerks, barbers, teachers, and insurance agents. The only type of manufacturing found with any degree of regularity is typified by the grain mill, an activity which has many of the attributes of a service function. Furthermore, the towns provide only standardized and frequently-used goods and services. As Berry and Garrison have indicated, this is to be expected, since the "threshold populations" of these towns and their trade areas are not sufficient to support the more specialized types of functions.[19]

A comparison of the types of goods and services offered in small towns in southern Illinois with those offered in the other areas referred to reveals that the types of function on each list are almost identical.[20] However, the frequency rankings of the functions differ from area to area; these differences appear to be reflections of differences in the economic bases of the areas. This observation leads to the hypothesis that small towns in "open country" areas such as Iowa and southern Illinois, are local service centers, the frequency and magnitude of the functions performed depending on the basic economic structure of the relevant regions.[21]

The correlations between population size and the three indices of functional size and complexity are, as was to be expected, high and positive. There appear to be no significant differences in the strength or the nature of the associations when the southern Illinois data are compared with the Iowa data. For both areas, changes in the number of establishments and the number of functional units are proportional to changes in population size from town to town. However, the number of functions added increases at a decreasing rate as towns become larger. An examination of the data indicates that essentially the same relationships exist in Snohomish and Canterbury.

Brush has stated that "an interesting field of comparative geographical research is open in the study of central places."[22] The present study, in conjunction with those that have preceded it, lends empirical support to Brush's statement that "small towns and villages in agricultural areas of Anglo-America exist mainly because of their function as central places for the exchange of goods and ser-

---

[19] Brian J. L. Berry and William L. Garrison, "A Note on Central Place Theory and the Range of a Good," *Econ. Geog.*, Vol. 34 (1958), p. 50.

[20] Brian J. L. Berry and Harold M. Mayer have recently (February, 1962) completed a report, "Comparative Study of Central Place Systems," for the Geography Branch, U.S. Office of Naval Research. In each of five study areas, southwestern Iowa, northeastern South Dakota, southwestern South Dakota, a portion of suburban Chicago, and a portion of central Chicago, attention has been focussed on the simple functions, and spatial patterns of central places. The sections of these studies concerned with the functioning of central places reveal results which compare quite favorably with the results of the present study. This is especially true when the data of the present study are compared with the data from the southwestern Iowa and the two South Dakota areas; Berry and Mayer appropriately point out that central place regularities are most pronounced in rural areas.

[21] An alternate, or additional, explanation of the variations from area to area in the frequency and magnitude of functions performed in the small towns is suggested by Berry and Mayer *op. cit.* It is probable that in areas of very low population density the small towns do not have a sufficient clientele in their effective trading areas to support certain functions which might be expected in such towns. In these cases, it is suggested that the affected functions will move to larger urban centers.

[22] Brush, *op. cit.*, p. 402.

vices, each for its local farm trade area."[23] By building one similar study upon another

[23] *Ibid.*, p. 380.

in different areas, progress is made toward valid generalizations concerning the economic functioning of central places, so making possible increasingly precise prediction.

17

Cities, Transportation, and Technology

Harold M. Mayer

Two developments of human culture have been outstanding during the past century: the rapid advance of technology and the growth and spread of cities. Neither would have been possible without the other. Together they have made a revolution in the organization and pattern of land use. Transportation is a basis of both.

About 4 percent of the United States popu-

lation was urban in 1790. Now about 70 percent of the population lives in metropolitan areas and other urban places, and the proportion is increasing rapidly. There also has been a substantial growth of rural nonfarm population, which depends on urban areas for employment or on the passing highway traffic from the cities.

The growth of cities has accounted for

Reprinted from *Land, The Yearbook of Agriculture* (1958) pp. 493-502 by permission of the author and the United States Department of Agriculture.

most of the increase in the population during the 20th century, while the farm population has declined.

Agricultural areas, because of improvements in farming, have furnished a substantial portion of the immigrant population, which, added to the high net reproduction rate in cities, has been responsible for much of the increase in urban population.

The largest metropolitan areas have been growing, in general, at a faster rate than smaller cities.

The location of the areas of most rapid population growth has shifted significantly since about 1920 with respect to their situations within the metropolitan areas. Until about four decades ago the cities were being subjected to increasing populations at ever higher densities, but since the end of the First World War the maximum rates of growth generally have been outside of the central cities of metropolitan areas. Suburban communities and unincorporated areas have grown much faster than the central municipalities in recent years. Metropolitan areas in many instances have had substantial increases in population but actually have shown declines in the populations of their principal or central cities.

Part of the reason is that municipal boundaries rarely coincide with the limits of the built-up urban area.

Cities once could rather easily annex nearby areas that became urbanized. Extensive areas could be annexed in advance of the spread of urban development. The formation of many small incorporated municipalities next to the central cities more recently has made annexation difficult or impossible. These small cities, towns, and villages have developed local governments and vested interests in their perpetuation. Many people move to the suburbs with the expectation of being able to have a more personal and intimate relation to their local affairs, and subsequent merger with the big city is therefore almost invariably resisted.

The average population density of most cities has dropped sharply in recent years. This reflects a demand for land that is increasing at a much faster rate than even the spectacular rate of increase of urban and metropolitan population. Ranchhouses or ramblers have become popular and 60- and 80-foot lots are replacing 30- and 40-foot lots. Single-story industrial plants, with extensive areas for parking and with substantial setbacks from the highways and access streets, are replacing the multiple-story industrial and loft buildings of the congested central parts of cities. The modern planned outlying shopping center includes at least three or four times as much area for automobile parking as it does floor area of selling space.

The increasing demand for land for urban uses has been met by an accelerating expansion of cities into the rural areas.

It has recently been estimated that urban areas in the United States occupy slightly more than 18 million acres — a little less than 5 percent as much as the total land area occupied by railroads and highways. The urban land area is about 1 percent of the total land area of the United States.

The outlook is for a faster rate of conversion of agricultural land into nonfarming use, particularly for urban expansion. Many of the metropolitan areas may be expected to double the amount of area they will occupy within the next two or three decades.

Much of the land they will occupy is cropland that is used for intensive production of specialty crops and has a higher value per acre than the average value of all agricultural land. These croplands, being devoted to intensive cultivation of specialized crops, are characterized by small farms. Thus they have a population much denser than the average for all agricultural areas.

Certain important areas of specialty crops, such as the truck-farming areas of New Jersey, the citrus areas of southern California, and perhaps the fruit belt of southwestern Michigan, may be expected to be invaded by the urbanization from nearby large cities.

While the total loss of cropland may not represent an actual net loss of agricultural production nationally, the loss of specialty crops, involving conversion to nonagricultural use of some of the best land for such crops, could well become significant.

Most cities exist primarily to satisfy economic needs. Growth of population occurs in response to economic opportunities. People live where they can earn a living. Since economic opportunities are greatest in number and variety in the larger metropolitan areas, it is those areas which have been experiencing the fastest growth. Great concentrations of economic opportunity depend on concentrations of labor force, which in turn produces additional incentive for population growth. Thus the metropolis expands.

Urban and metropolitan concentrations could not exist were it not for transportation facilities. Many of the outstanding technological advances have been in transportation, which affects the size, functions, structure, and growth of cities and metropolitan areas.

Functional specialization of areas — the differentiation of one land use from another — is made possible by the availability of facilities for the movement of goods and people between those areas.

Cities produce manufactured goods and perform certain services which are "exported" to other areas, in return for the goods and payments that are brought into the urban areas from other urban areas and from the countrysides.

The interconnections between cities and between individual cities and their respective service areas or hinterlands — as well as the interconnections among the various functionally specialized parts of city and metropolitan area — depend on efficient systems of transportation.

Streets alone in most cities account for 25 to 35 percent of the total built-up urban area. The building and maintenance of facilities for internal circulation, including streets, constitute a sizable part of the budgets of all cities.

Most urban street patterns have been inherited from the past and are inadequate for the needs of modern traffic. The obsolete patterns have been extended to newly developed areas on the outskirts of cities.

While street traffic faces delays because of insufficient numbers and capacities of arterial routes, an excessive proportion of the areas of most cities paradoxically is devoted to local access streets.

The largest parcels of land devoted to a single urban use and under single control in most cities are the airports, which may cover several square miles and influence land uses far beyond their own boundaries.

The construction, maintenance, and operation of transportation facilities and equipment directly contribute substantially to the employment base of urban areas. More than 20 million Americans are employed in public and private transportation. Automobiles and trucks account for a large proportion of this employment — nearly one-third of the total employment in the Nation.

A study by the Port of New York Authority indicated that about one in every four jobs in Greater New York is attributable directly or indirectly to the port function, which represents only a part of the multiplicity of basic transportation functions performed by the New York metropolitan area.

The effects of the transportation industries are felt through the entire economy, because transportation uses vast amounts of materials and equipment, the manufacturing and supplying of which create other millions of jobs.

The automobile industry used 22 percent and the railroads 11 percent of the steel produced in the United States in 1957, a typical year. Large tonnages of steel also were used in building highways and ships. Most of the oil and rubber and a major share of the coal used in this country are used in transportation.

The rapid changes in transportation are reflected in the changes in the growth and structure of cities: each major innovation in intercity and local transportation has been followed by significant changes in urban areas.

The uses of urban land are related closely to their "circulatory" systems. The relationship is reciprocal. Land uses — other than such uses as agriculture, forestry, and mining, which depend on primary production on the site — are where they are largely because of differences in the availability of transportation from place to place. On the other hand, land uses (individually and in combination) generate varying amounts of movement of goods and people that in turn make it necessary to provide varying amounts and kinds of transportation.

Each type of nonagricultural use of land has a different set of requirements as to location. For some — as, for example, the bulk-receiving industries that use raw materials in shipload amounts and therefore need loca-

tions along navigable waterways — the choice of location is narrow and rather inflexible. A much greater variety of locations is suitable for other uses, such as one-family homes.

Transportation in one sense is a substitute for nearness. Other things being equal, the best locations for interrelated activities are close together in order to reduce the amount, and hence the cost, of the transportation of goods and people.

Transportation costs — whether measured in money, or distance — are incurred because it is physically impossible and sometimes undesirable to place the activities and uses of land in the best locations for each because other activities and uses that require similar sites bring competitive pressures.

The increasing size and complexity of cities widens even more the separation of the urban functions and increases the amount of transportation that is needed. Separation of places of work from places of residence gives rise to the daily journeys to work, which are responsible for half of the total number of trips made in metropolitan areas.

The competition among all urban functions and land uses that could operate most effectively near each other engenders a high demand for centrally located sites. The demand drives up the values of such sites. Not all urban land uses or functions can afford central sites. Indeed, some functions can better be carried on at some distance from the urban centers if adequate transportation is available. Thus, in the normal operation of the real-estate market, urban land uses are sorted out in accordance with their relative ability to pay high costs for sites that are most desirable because of proximity to other uses or because of the accessibility provided by the convergence of local transportation in the central parts of cities.

For any given type of use, a balance exists

between the costs of competitive sites and the costs of overcoming the friction of distance. The uses that depend on maximum accessibility can afford the high costs of central locations. The other select locations at varying distances from the points of maximum accessibility in accordance with their ability to pay site costs. Transportation in most instances is the factor that makes possible the concentrations of land values, because it converges and produces maximum accessibility at the urban core.

The forces that affect the patterns of land uses in urban areas may be described as centrifugal, or outward, and centripetal, or inward. The resultant of these forces is reflected in the degree of decentralization or deconcentration of any individual land use or groups of land uses in urban areas.

When the centripetal forces are stronger, the city develops with heavier concentrations at higher densities.

When centrifugal forces are stronger, the average densities are lower. The relative importance of the forces varies for each type of urban land use and for each establishment, whether industrial, commercial, residential, or institutional.

The development of improved transportation generally has strengthened the centrifugal forces by making greater and more extensive areas around cities accessible for urban expansion. On the other hand, however, transportation has increased the numbers and the strength of "linkages" among establishments and so has created a demand for increasing concentrations of business activity in the larger cities, especially in the central parts, where face-to-face contacts are maximized.

The concentration of people in cities, the rapidly increasing number and complexity of urban functions, and the resulting competition for space have brought about an ever-increasing separation between places of employment and places of residence.

In the medieval city, manufacturing, commerce, and residence were usually on the same parcel of land or in the same structure. The craftsman produced and sold his goods and lived with his family in one building. With the Industrial Revolution, these functions had to separate because of the development of the factories, which formed nodes or nuclei in the urban pattern, and of markets, which later became the central business districts.

Thus the modern city has many nuclei: the central business district, which generally has the heaviest concentration of employment, industrial areas, and outlying commercial developments, which have other concentrations of basic economic activities.

The increasing complexity of the land use and functional patterns of cities has attracted the attention of many economists and sociologists, who have tried to make generalized descriptions that would fit most cities.

Ernest W. Burgess developed the concentric zonal hypothesis, based upon the work of J. H. von Thünen, a German economist, in the early 19th century.

Burgess described the city as consisting roughly of concentric zones. The central business district is the nucleus. The land uses in each successive zone outward from the core are sorted out in order of their relative ability to benefit from (and pay the costs of) proximity to the center. As a city grows, land uses and people successively "invade" each zone outward from the center. This creates a succession of land uses in each zone, and each succeeding group of uses is developed at higher density as a result of increasing competition for centrally located land.

Homer Hoyt, then of the Federal Housing

Administration, later propounded the wedge, or sector, theory.

It describes the process of urban growth and expansion in terms of differentiation of land uses and functions along wedges radiating out from the central core. The general character of the uses along each radial or wedge is similar in nature from the core to periphery.

Chauncy D. Harris, of the University of Chicago, and Edward L. Ullman, of the University of Washington, described the city as a series of nuclei — generally concentrations of employment. The various urban land uses are located with relation to relative proximity to each of the multiple nuclei.

None of these generalized descriptions fits all cities. All are based upon the concept of the balance of proximity to the core and other urban nuclei and the availability of transportation to overcome the lack of proximity resulting from the impossibility of locating all land uses with maximum mutual proximity.

Whatever the specific patterns of urban land uses and internal functional organization of cities may be, the specialization of areas and their separation from one another are made possible by the availability of transportation.

Each successive form of urban transportation has had significant effects in accelerating both the expansion of cities, on the one hand, and concentrating industrial and commercial activities in the nodal portions of cities, on the other.

Before urban transportation was mechanized, the extent of a city was limited by horse-drawn transportation, at an average speed of 3 to 4 miles an hour. Cities had to be small and compact so that all parts could be reached in a reasonable time. Factories were relatively small, and little need existed for wide separations of places of work and of residence.

The horse-drawn street railway car was the dominant form of urban transportation from the period immediately before the Civil War until nearly the end of the 19th century. Although placing the vehicles on rails reduced friction in comparison with the free-wheeled vehicle, speeds were limited, and cities, though expanding, remained crowded and compact.

The steam railway, with commuter schedules, offered opportunities for urban expansion during the latter part of the 19th century in the vicinities of some of the larger cities. Beyond the main urban mass, with its radius of 3 or 4 miles from the commercial core, the steam railroad, with its higher speeds, made possible the development of nodes of suburban growth.

The result was a moderately densely developed series of outlying settlements, clustered about each suburban railroad station, the railroad forming an axis. The pattern that developed resembled beads on a string, with nonurban land lying along the railroads between the stations.

Since the railroads radiated from the urban core, the resulting pattern consisted of radial strings of suburbs, each radial separated from the next by open country, and each suburb along a rail line separated from its neighbors by open country between the railroad stations. Beyond each railroad station, urbanization was limited by the range of horse-drawn transportation. Since the practicable commuting time in each direction to and from the core of the city was about 1 hour, the distance from each outlying station at which urbanization took place was limited by the combined time of rail trip and connecting trip by horse-drawn vehicle, or, in a few instances, by local electric car.

The development of electrified railway transportation in the early years of the 20th century expanded the areas available for urban development. The electric street railway lines were extended beyond the limits that were possible for the horse-drawn streetcar, because of the higher speed. The speed was still limited by urban congestion, however. Along the street railway lines, land values (and hence density of development) were concentrated.

The street railway made it possible for the main urban mass to expand along the routes that were in operation. The resulting pattern of the expanded urban development was roughly in the shape of a star, whose points developed along streetcar lines. Within the urban mass, the densest development was also along streetcar lines.

The main lines in most cities were radial, focusing on the central business district, where most of the employment was located. In some of the larger cities, circumferential or crosstown routes were in operation to provide service to factories and offices not directly associated with the commercial core. At the intersections of the radial and circumferential routes, major outlying shopping centers tended to develop at the transfer corners. Some of them became almost small-scale reproductions of the central business districts and created problems of traffic congestion and competition of commercial land uses to get nearest to the major intersection.

The application of electric power to suburban transportation beyond the main urban mass took two forms. One was extension of the street railway into suburban areas. The first two decades of the present century marked the heyday of the interurban electric railway. Because a car or train could stop at any place along the line, suburban devel-opment was freed from dependence on proximity to outlying railroad stations.

The electric suburban or interurban railway represented a considerable advance in opening up new areas for urban expansion. Rapid acceleration and deceleration permitted more frequent stops. The operation of several cars in a train related its power and speed to the fluctuations of traffic from day to day and hour by hour more readily than could the steam railway train. The result was that on the fringes of many cities electric railways were built parallel to the earlier steam railways in order to secure initial traffic from preexisting suburbs. These lines permitted a filling in of the areas between the steam railroad stations. The radial tentacles of suburban development filled in and became more or less continuous. Farmland was subdivided and converted into suburban residential land more rapidly than in the previous period.

The second form of application of electric power to suburban and urban passenger transportation was by the electrification of steam railroads near some of the larger cities. The advantages of the railroad as a heavy mass carrier of passengers on high-density routes was combined with the advantages of multiple-unit operation.

The electrified steam railroad, however, did not approach the flexibility of the interurban electric railway, which usually represented less investment and could be extended more easily into newly developing suburban areas.

Five large cities — New York, Chicago, Philadelphia, Boston, and Cleveland — developed rapid transit elevated and subway railways for internal transportation when the concentrations of traffic exceeded the capacities of the streets.

The rapid transit line, unlike other forms

of urban transportation, is separated from all other traffic. It is on a reserved right-of-way and has no conflicts with street traffic. Most rapid transit lines are operated with multiple-unit trains at relatively high speeds and with distances of one-third mile to several miles between stops. A busline operating on a right-of-way or lane reserved for its own use would also be a rapid transit line. The capacity of a rapid transit line exceeds that of any other form of local transportation in terms of the number of passengers that could be moved in a certain period.

Electric surface transportation has almost gone full cycle. The electric interurban railway has nearly disappeared in the United States being largely replaced by the automobile. The local street railway survives in only a few places, having been replaced by the motor bus. Only in the rapid transit line and the electrified suburban steam railway does the application of the electric power survive in rail passenger transport of daily home-to-work movements.

The development of the automobile and motortruck has produced the most rapid and far-reaching changes of any technological innovation in transportation in the rate, direction, and scale of urban expansion. No longer need urban development be tied to the limited number of routes feasible for rail transportation. The flexibility of the individual privately owned vehicle opens up vast areas beyond the former limits of cities and suburbs for urban development.

Our cities have been building up around the automobile. Many newly developed areas depend entirely on automobile transportation, for they are beyond the range of public carriers. The areas between the older radial prongs of suburban growth are filling in, be-cause the automobile can go anywhere where passable roads exist.

The areas of countryside available for urbanization are several times as extensive as the areas that could be developed when people had to depend on public carriers for the journey to work. Many industries no longer need to locate near the convergence of public transportation in order to assemble workers, who increasingly come by automobile.

The truck makes possible the assembly of raw materials and semifinished products from many sources and the delivery of manufactured goods—for which sometimes railroads now are not used at all. Many industries do not need railroad sidings, for they can truck their shipments to the nearest rail freight station. Piggyback — the transportation of motortruck trailers on railroad flatcars — combines flexibility of motortruck transportation and the economy of the railroad as a large-scale hauler.

Factories more and more are tending therefore to locate away from congested industrial districts, which were built when railroads provided the only intercity freight transportation.

Highways and motor vehicles also are opening up opportunities for lower urban densities. Thus residential areas can develop free from some of the disadvantages and limitations imposed by the need to be near mass transportation.

The effect of the new flexibility is generally to reduce the emphasis on relatively few focal or nodal areas and to spread the demand for land over larger areas.

Lower densities — if there is proper planning — provide opportunities for more open space and for many amenities that are lacking in the older sections of many cities. Parks, playgrounds, ample backyards, and larger sites for schools can be provided.

The amount of service provided by the mass carriers is less in most urban areas than ever before. Local transit systems face prospects of further cutbacks in service as their costs rise and patronage declines.

Some form of public transportation is essential in most cities, however. Central business districts still are the major foci of employment and shopping in nearly all cities, where parking has become the biggest problem of all. The larger the city, the more dependent is it on mass transportation, even though the relative dependence is declining.

The result is that mass transportation, instead of being the basic general intracity and suburban form of transportation as in the past, is increasingly specialized in function. It is best adapted to the transportation of heavy volumes of passenger traffic along high-density routes and during the peak hours of the day. Since the highest densities exist in the older sections of cities and the peak volumes are to and from the central business districts, mass transportation is most used for the journey to work in the central business districts of residents in the older and more densely developed sections of cities.

In outlying areas of sparser population, combining the flexibility of the automobile and the economy of the mass carrier sometimes is feasible by providing outlying parking facilities along the transit lines and at suburban railroad stations.

The expressway is a new element of increasing significance in the evolution of future urban land use.

An expressway — or freeway or thru-way — a specialized traffic artery for the high-speed movement of vehicles, is free of the delays and hazards of conflicting cross traffic. It is separated from other traffic routes. The ordinary arterial street combines through movement, local movement, parking, and loading and unloading of vehicles. The expressway has only one function — to speed up through movement.

Several hundred miles of expressways have been completed in cities and metropolitan areas. A number of cross-country expressways, some of them turnpikes, connect major cities. The program of Federal interregional highways, authorized by the Congress in 1956, provides for 41 thousand miles of modern highways. A substantial part of their mileage will be in metropolitan areas.

The effects of the expressways will be tremendous. The new routes will be basic elements in the entire structure of urban and metropolitan uses of land. Because the rights-of-way are 250 to 300 feet wide, each expressway in an urban area removes from other uses of a strip at least a city block wide for the entire length of the route. At the interchanges between expressways and between expressways and other arteries, vast areas of land must be taken and hence made unavailable for other development.

In the areas that must be taken for the rights-of-way are thousands of business establishments and hundreds of thousands of residences, which must be relocated. The selection of the relocation sites will strongly influence the future patterns of the cities. Relating the major transportation routes to comprehensive city and regional plans becomes more important than ever.

The expressways are being located primarily with reference to their ability to move vehicular traffic. That is their function. But too little thought is given to the relationships of the routes to the present and future patterns of commercial, industrial, and residential areas they serve.

Several vital questions need answers.

Will the new traffic facilities cause additional concentration and congestion in already congested areas?

What additional parking facilities will be needed to accommodate the vehicles after they arrive in the congested areas?

What effects will their routes have on the residential communities through which they will pass?

Will they increase neighborhood and community cohesion by forming barriers at the boundaries of the neighborhood and community areas — or will they disrupt existing communities by causing the removal of substantial populations and by creating barriers between the residences and such community foci as the schools, churches, parks, and shopping centers?

Time will provide answers of sorts to some of the questions. Right now we need to study objectively and thoroughly the existing physical and social patterns of cities that the expressways will affect.

We can foresee some of the effects of the expressways. By providing high-speed transportation for both the private automobile and the motortruck, they will increase further the difficulty of providing mass transportation facilities for peak loads to and from the central business districts. At the same time they themselves will not provide complete solutions to the problems of transportation to and from such districts.

Integration of planning of expressways and mass transportation — in other words, thinking about the movement of people and goods rather than just the movement of vehicles, and thinking about cities rather than about transportation alone — is essential.

Thus the new forms of urban growth, like the new technological inventions, produce new problems and accentuate the urgency of solving old problems.

They also produce new challenges. Among the most urgent challenges is the one represented by the lag of our social and political institutions behind the increasingly urgent problems which they are being called upon to solve. Our metropolitan areas, for example, are fragmented into dozens or hundreds of small political units — cities, towns, villages, school districts, park districts — each concerned with its own functions or its own limited area of jurisdiction.

Cities expand — but without equal expansion of the horizons of social and political organization. Some groups of the population, attracted to cities by the greater employment opportunities, meet resistance in some cities. Schools in most newly developed suburban areas are not planned and built sufficiently in advance of the population growth, and their problems are complicated by the small size and financial inability of many of the political jurisdictions.

Few metropolitan areas have adequate machinery to plan for the new conditions systematically and comprehensively.

Technological advances therefore must be paralleled by social, political, and economic advances if their full potentialities for the benefit of man are to be realized.

18 Transportation Planning and Urban Development

Alan M. Voorhees

There are, of course, many ways that we can look at traffic. Certainly we should consider it from the individual's point of view. We should get right down to his basic needs for travel. If we do this, we find that the average person makes about two trips a day. However, this will vary depending upon his status in life — whether or not he is a breadwinner, or a student, or just how old or young he may be. His economic position will also have an impact upon this average. Of course, there are other factors involved in trip frequency which are not solely related to the individual; for example, the geographical position, climate, adequacy of the transportation system, and the patterns of urban development.

TRANSPORTATION REQUIREMENTS

Trip Production

Although this approach is the best way to look at transportation needs, we have found it easier to analyze them in other terms. For example, how many trips are made by an auto in a given day? As you might expect, we have found that this is highly correlated with auto ownership. In fact, a great deal of research has been undertaken recently to explore the other elements that are involved in "auto trip production." Although these explorations have not been as revealing as we had hoped, they certainly indicate that many other factors are involved — family size, the number of retired persons in the family, the number of school age children, etc. However, it is very clear that car ownership is an excellent indicator of the trips that are made by a family and the mode of transportation that is used. Generally we know that about four daily trips per car are made in the larger cities — 200,000 or more with more trips being made in smaller cities. We also know that once the level of one car per family is reached, transit usage becomes very low. Therefore, it is very important to understand what influences car ownership.

Figure 1 shows what we feel are the key factors influencing car ownership; namely, type of residential area and income. It shows that with a rise in income there is a rise in car

Reprinted from *Plan Canada,* Vol. 4, no. 3 (1963), pp. 100-110 by permission of the Town Planning Institute of Canada.

ownership. This seems to "ceiling out" at about $8,000 to $10,000 income per family. Car ownership is particularly sensitive as families rise in the $3,000 to $5,000 income bracket. At this range there may be a 10 percent change in income and a 30-40 percent change in car ownership. Many European countries are moving through this range at the present time. We all went through this in the 30's and 40's. Right now, car ownership per person is going up quite slowly. By 1980 it should stop climbing. In fact, if we could keep the birth rate down, we might have the whole problem licked.

This curve also indicates that if we could keep everyone living in higher densities, we would be a lot better off. As shown by Figure 1, as the density increases the car ownership drops. Of course, this reflects many factors which influence transportation requirements. First of all, as the density increases there are generally errands that can be accomplished on foot, thereby eliminating the need of an automobile. But unfortunately, many of our new apartment house areas do not provide for this type of development — too often they are sterilized from commercial use and walking trips to the grocery store or laundry are almost impossible. So I am not too sure if these patterns will hold true for the new apartment areas. But certainly with higher densities we can gain a higher level of transit service, since there is a greater market.

Just how important the level of transit service is in this whole picture is still not clear. However, stepped-up transit service by itself cannot be assured usage. If parking is readily available people undoubtedly are going to have a car, and once they have a car they will tend to use it. The only time they will not use it is if the parking rates where they are going are exceedingly high, or if the transit service is much better than auto. Perhaps the zoning ordinances that we have which require sufficient off-street parking in apartment house areas have a greater impact than we realize upon the mode of travel. We have never adequately evaluated our zoning requirements, particularly in light of the impact they have upon the mode of travel that people use.

Trip Length

Another important element in transportation — probably more important even than the question of trip production is distribution and trip length. Surely we know that work trips must go to places where there are jobs and that shopping trips must go to shopping centers — but do they always go to the closest place of employment and the closest shopping center?

In reality we all know that they do not. People require and demand variety — not only in terms of where they shop, but where they work and where they spend their leisure. This desire is really the culprit behind our traffic problem. This can be made clear by a

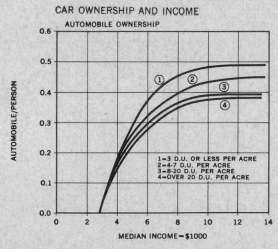

CAR OWNERSHIP AND INCOME

Figure 1.

simple example. If trip length could be cut in half, the traffic loads on all our streets could be reduced by half. If the trip length in Los Angeles were similar to that in Chicago, there would be one-third less traffic in Los Angeles. So trip length characteristics are of vital importance.

The next graph, Figure 2, shows the range of trip length for different purposes that have been found in various studies throughout the country. As might be expected, the work trip is the longest. In considering the various cities and localities in the country, it is quite evident that the communities that have had the greatest fluctuation in the job market and have the highest level of transportation service have the longest trip length. Los Angeles is a good example of this. However, areas like the New London Area in Connecticut have similar trip length mainly because of fluctuations in the economy. People are willing to travel great distances if necessary to get a satisfactory job. This has been the case in the New London region, since some of the basic industries have moved to the South. In other areas where social patterns and local traditions had made these areas more self-contained, the work trip may be very short, by comparison. This is true in some cities in Iowa where over the years people have lived and sought employment close to home.

Unfortunately, we have not been able to quantify all these things, but it does appear that an area that is subject to employment changes is likely to be subject to greater transportation problems than a stable community; therefore, a community that is expecting fluctuations in its economy should probably try to provide for greater flexibility in its transportation system than a more stable community.

Work Trips

The only solution I can see to shortening the work trip is by carefully planning and programming the development of our communities. As new industries or activities move into the area, their development must be tied in with housing programs. Adequate housing for their employees must be nearby. This must be available at the time industrial development occurs, and it must be at a price the worker can afford. Some of our faster growing metropolitan areas are plagued with this problem. For example, while industries were expanding in the Los Angeles Basin, a great deal of the housing was being provided in the San Fernando Valley twenty miles away. This naturally generated a long work trip. I feel that with proper coordination of public and private interests we can do much better in this direction than we have in the past. Certainly we should give more consideration to the work trip in our urban renewal programs and try to reduce the work trip wherever possible.

The other types of trips, such as those related to shopping, are going to be influenced by dispersion of our retailing activi-

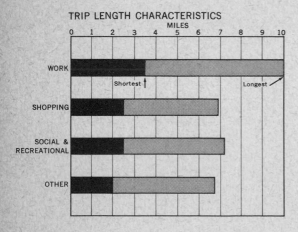

Figure 2.

ties and the transportation services to them. Although in many ways we should attempt to reduce them as much as possible, they do not have as great an impact on traffic since the majority of these trips do not occur at the peak hour. From a planning point of view, it is probably much more important to have strong commercial centers that have a depth of variety in merchandise than to have them close to everyone, which really doesn't benefit anyone.

As for the social and recreational trip, I feel that with our increased standard of living, we can expect nothing but additional increase. If our transportation facilities of the future permit it, we will undoubtedly see longer and longer trips — they may even exceed the work trips in length. This undoubtedly will put greater strain on our transportation facilities, particularly those that are serving the key recreational areas. I wish there were ways that we could reduce these trip lengths, but on the other hand a good plan for an urban area certainly would call for many types of social and recreational diversion and they should be accessible to all. This is undoubtedly what the people will want, and it is something that we will have to plan for.

We undoubtedly should be doing more transportation planning for our recreational needs than we have done in the past. Along this line, several recent transportation studies are developing a special analysis of recreational travel and plan to take recreational needs into consideration in designing for all future highways.

The City

Whenever we talk about transportation needs, I think we cannot gloss over the city itself. After all, transportation needs are related to the city, and the exact form that the city takes in the future will have a terrific impact upon transportation requirements. Thus, we are justified in emphasizing a few things that are occurring in urban growth, which provide a full perspective on our transportation problems.

The first one that I should like to stress is the flexibility that has been brought about by the automobile. As we all know, the automobile has provided a fantastic flexibility not only to the businessman but to the individual. The flexibility has permitted the individual to live almost any place that he chooses in the metropolitan area, and it has permitted the industrialist and businessman to move about freely and locate wherever they desire.

By providing this flexibility we have given people the opportunity to consider many other factors in making the decision as to where to live or work or locate their business. The individual is given the opportunity to consider the quality of the schools, residential amenities where the area has prestige, housing costs and many other factors in choosing his home.

This means that in making a decision as to where to live transportation is not having the influence that it once had when our cities were built around a rapid transit system. The individual under those conditions had little choice, but now with our extensive highway systems in urban areas and with the automobile he is given a great deal of freedom.

Furthermore, as he rises on the income scale, he seems to put more emphasis on larger lots and the amenities associated with such lots — as illustrated in Figure 3. This, of course, is somewhat related to the fact that people's values would change with a rise in income, and it also shows up in various other aspects about urban living. A curious fact that we have observed in connection with some of the attitude surveys we have been conducting is that as income goes up the proximity of commercial development become less and less important. The reasons involved are not established, but it appears that as income rises people would prefer to have "pure" residential areas, and hence travel several miles farther to a store rather than to have commercial areas mixed in with their residential neighborhoods.

This may be due to not having any example of how commercial areas have been effectively woven into residential development. But it is probably related to the fact that once people accept the fact that they have to use a car for an errand, they are not too concerned whether the trip is four miles or two miles. This is illustrated by Figure 4 which shows the satisfaction of people with various public services located at different distances from their home.

This was obtained simply by asking people if they were satisfied with the distance to their schools or shopping centers, and then determining the actual distance and rating the proportion of people who were satisfied at a particular distance from these various facilities. With the exception of mass transit, most people are not too concerned about having some of these facilities close at hand. It was found that they really would like to have mass transit close by in order that they could walk to this facility. For the other activities they more or less expect that they will have to go by auto and are not too concerned about additional distance. They are more concerned, in my opinion, at what they get at the end of their trip — is it the right doctor; is it the right store; is it their favorite hairdresser? So, in effect, their desire for variety in choice has magnified our transportation problem.

I don't think it is correct to say that "the spread city" is caused by the automobile, although it has made this possible. After all, some of the fast-growing downtown areas like Toronto or Montreal, and Houston, Texas,

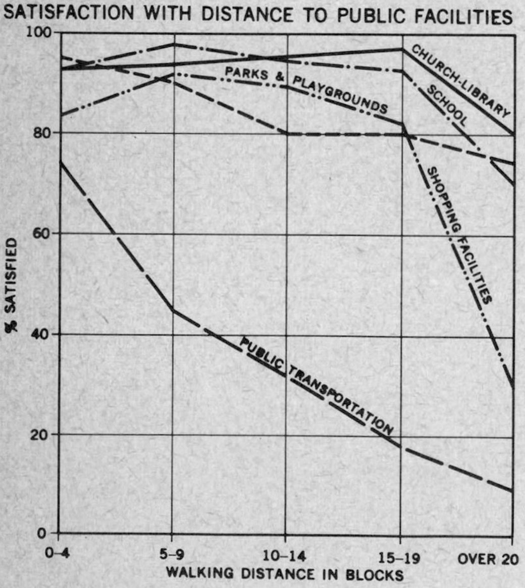

SATISFACTION WITH DISTANCE TO PUBLIC FACILITIES

Figure 3.

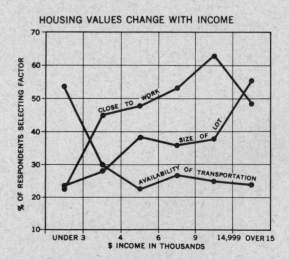

Figure 4.

are auto-oriented cities. The fact that Los Angeles has a relatively small downtown area is primarily related to the nature of the Los Angeles area — that it developed as an industrial complex of many downtown areas — Pasadena, Hollywood, Long Beach, etc. The long trip that is familiar to most Los Angeles residents is due to the way the city grew — the development of a large number of small, independent cities that have grown into one large metropolitan area. I cite these cities only to point out my basic thesis that there is much more involved in urban growth than transportation facilities, and that as planners we have too often over-emphasized the role of transportation in urban growth, while under-playing some of the key issues, such as social and technological change. Until we understand these latter factors better, we will not be able to truly plan for the future.

The technological change that has been occuring in urban areas is very remarkable. I think that one of the best indicators of this change is that with all the growth that we are getting in the United States we have had no increase in manufacturing jobs since 1955. An industrial city like Baltimore has less manufacturing jobs today than it did in 1948. During this period, the population has grown by 45,000. All this can mean is that service jobs have been growing at a fantastic rate to off-set the lack of industrial growth in employment. This undoubtedly will continue — meaning that more job opportunities will be created in our commercial centers in contrast to our industrial parks.

In attempting to look at the social changes that have been occurring, we have been studying leisure activities. Figure 5 represents a summary of these findings. This shows that with change in income we get change in leisure activities. Television becomes less important. Even in the higher income groups it

consumes 40 percent of their time, and in the lowest income groups it consumes about 70 percent of their time. I think that the startling thing from a planning point of view is that 80-90 percent of the time is spent around the house. The gay life just doesn't exist in the typical family. This, I think, influences the values that people have about their community. It certainly places a high degree of emphasis on the home and the areas immediately around it. It certainly indicates that as planners the way to make the greatest impact is to concentrate on the immediate neighborhood surroundings. We need to know more about these and other social changes. This will call not only for the kinds of studies that have been made but for more studies in depth than ever have been done before. We certainly have to watch changing technological development so that we can more adequately anticipate the needs of the future.

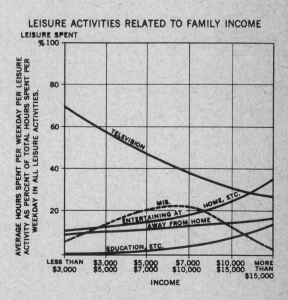

Figure 5.

TRANSPORTATION SOLUTIONS

These are some of the conclusions that can be derived from studies that have been made on urban transportation and urban growth. These points are seldom brought out in the report, but I think they are the key factors behind our planning problems. Unfortunately, we are not really using them as effectively as we could in our planning for the future.

Metrotowns

Here are a few areas where some of this knowledge is being applied. One of the most commendable is the work being done in the Baltimore Region where they have developed a concept of "metrotowns" which take into consideration the way people live in metropolitan areas today. This concept is aimed at reducing transportation requirements and obtaining greater amenity and personal identity. It attempts to eliminate the suburban sprawl by intelligently arranging the land so that it takes into consideration social as well as economic goals.

At the heart of these metrotowns is a commercial core which will house between 10,000 and 20,000 jobs. This core will be fed by freeways, and, it is hoped, by mass transit. The advertising values provided by freeways is almost essential if you are to provide strong commercial development in any particular section. The development of transit stations to this area will further strengthen this pattern.

A large portion of the high density development in these towns will be located nearest these centers. The density will decrease to the edge of the metrotowns where open space will be provided. This open space will help define these metrotowns and force commercial development to the center, for one of the best ways to prevent commercial spread is to create open spaces which automatically define market areas.

The type of metrotown center required is being planned for a community outside of Washington. It contains a subway station tied in with an improved arterial street system that tends to strengthen the whole core. Direct highway access is provided through the retail area; transit service is highly coordinated with the high density employment areas. It is felt that by this general pattern of development transit usage will be maximized and that the center will attain its greatest strength.

We hope that these metrotowns can be built through a cooperative relationship which will tend to assure that the right type of residential development is built for the jobs that are created in the towns. This will make it easier to find work within the town in which you live. However, it is well recognized that people are going to find jobs beyond the metrotown in which they live. It is believed by the intelligent planning of these towns and the programming of their development that perhaps 40 percent of the people within a town might work in it. This is in contrast to the 10 percent to 20 percent that is found in existing suburban complexes of similar size.

The one thing different about the concept of these "new towns" is that they are really part of the metropolitan area. The wide range of choice found in a large metropolitan area is still available. Our attitude studies in cities of less than a million indicate that people are generally quite unhappy with job opportunities in such areas.

The size of these metrotowns should be between 100,000 and 200,000, which is adequate to serve most of their daily and weekly needs. Current studies indicate that as a unit like a metrotown grows in size in a metropolitan area it becomes more and more dependent upon itself until it reaches 100,000 or more. This, of course, reflects the fact that we need 100,000 people to support the variety of activities that we desire — enough hairdressers, dentists and doctors to give your wife a choice.

Street Patterns

For those of you who do not live or work in a large metropolitan area you may be interested in knowing some of the thoughts we have been developing on street patterns for smaller cities. In such cities we have, for some time, recognized that streets should perform various functions and that the design characteristics should reflect these functions. We have talked about expressways, arterials, collector streets and local streets. In our smaller cities the expressway, or freeway, serves a unique function. It may bypass the community or it may provide important access to the downtown area or other key industrial areas, but the bulk of the traffic will have to be carried by the arterial streets. The spacing of these arterial streets will vary depending upon the density of development and the location of the streets in relation to other major traffic generators. In lower density areas — those with 3-5 families per acre — a street spacing of about one mile apart has been found satisfactory, but if the density gets higher these streets must be closer together. Often we find that it is desirable to have these streets spaced at one-half or one-quarter mile intervals in the more congested areas.

With regard to collector streets, we are beginning to recognize that streets which serve over 100 homes (100 homes generate 1,000 auto trips a day) have to be wider than the 30 feet generally recommended for residential areas. In such cases a 36 to 40 foot street of higher design standards is required.

If you accept that collector streets in residential areas should not have commercial development along them, every attempt should be made to keep the traffic below 10,000 trips a day. It should be less than 5,000 per day, because as soon as you get volumes of this magnitude commercial developers will think about developing along them — then your only hope is zoning.

The Neighborhood

As we all know, the classical neighborhood building around the elementary school does not tie in with the social patterns of the teenager or the adult today. In fact, the only thing that you can say about the neighborhood is that it is the sphere of interest of the elementary school child. For example, our studies have shown that 90 percent of the socializing people do beyond their home is done more than one mile from their home and only about 2 percent of the socializing is done on foot. Therefore, it would appear that the kind of neighborhood that made sense is one at a walking distance scale, which is probably less than 1,000 feet. And, instead of 1,000 or 2,000 families the only type of neighborhood unit that makes sense today is one of 100 to 200 homes which are tied together by unique topography, an original design concept, a common recreational area such as a swimming pool and tennis courts, or just a wooded area left untouched.

In considering this neighborhood concept — of 100 to 200 homes — we should attempt to keep through-traffic from piercing it wherever possible.

This certainly is a lot easier to do than laying out a classical neighborhood. It may be necessary to have a collector street in them, but often this can be avoided by keeping collectors on the boundaries of such neighborhoods. However, sometimes it has been found that collector streets in such neighborhoods can help knit the area together, particularly if the volumes do not exceed a couple of thousand trips a day.

If this type of neighborhood concept makes sense, then all that one needs to do is set up standards as to what type of activities should be located on various streets. For example, "collectors" might only serve

Elementary Schools

Minor Recreational Facilities

while "arterials" should serve

Commercial Areas

Industrial Areas

Major Public Facilities.

There are many other concepts that we could discuss which would show how to interrelate transportation and city planning, but I hope that these examples have given you some insight into how this can be done. We must analyze our traffic patterns more thoroughly and evaluate people's values. Until we understand the nature of our problems more clearly it is going to be difficult to develop the type of planning principles that we need to plan adequately for the future.

Retail Structure of

Urban Economy

19

Eugene J. Kelley

The spatial structure of American retailing is being changed by three forces familiar to those concerned with traffic and highway matters. These forces are the suburban population movement, the increasing dependence of the consumer on the private automobile for shopping, and the growing number of high speed roads enabling consumers to travel miles from home even for convenience goods purchases.

The response to these forces has produced substantial changes in consumer behavior and merchandising practices. It has been estimated that 50 percent of the automobile driving public will travel thirty minutes to reach a shopping center when assured of satisfactory merchandise assortments and parking conditions. But so slowly does our thinking adapt to change and so slowly do adjustments develop, that the full impact of these forces on the metropolitan economy may not yet be fully appreciated.

The average American city is still twenty or twenty-five years behind adjustment to the automobile. So when it is remembered that the three forces mentioned have gained momentum only since the end of World War II, it is understandable that some have not grasped fully the extent of the marketing revolution currently underway. As recently as 1950, only a handful of business men and economists visualized the change in spending-patterns that would be brought about by the suburban population movement and other forces. A statistical overview of some retailing results of this "painless" revolution was given by McMillan. These numbers in parentheses (1) refer to notes at end of article.

This article presents a conceptual scheme for analyzing the retail structure of the metropolitan economy and offers some guides to the placement of regional shopping centers in the structure. Regional centers are one of the most spectacular recent evidences of the dynamism of the retail structure and of the American economy. The use of space as a business resource is commented upon here prior to discussion of the retail structure and placement of controlled shopping centers in the structure.

Reprinted from *Traffic Quarterly*, Vol. 9 (1955), pp. 411-30 by permission of the Eno Foundation for Transportation Inc.

SPATIAL POSITIONING IN MARKETING

Sellers of goods have generally been preoccupied with the task of creating demand for their products. Certainly, the greatest amount of marketing managerial time, energy, and imagination has been focused on the product and its promotion.[1] The spatial and temporal conditions influencing the sales of the product typically have received less study than creating demand. Yet sellers are concerned with the creation of time and place as well as possession utilities. Creation of space utility is an area in which traffic engineers, architects, and planners have much to contribute to business. All of these specialists are interested in the intelligent use of space in the metropolitan economy.

A seller has four decisions to make about the ideal spatial relations or positioning of his product in the market.[2]

1. He must first select the area or areas in which he will offer his goods. These areas are his markets.

2. He must make a choice among the types of distributive agencies selling space in the market. Will space be preferred in drug or hardware stores, mail order catalogs or department stores? This is selecting the channel of distribution.

Institutions to supply the chosen retail outlets must be selected. Will a service wholesaler offering full decentralized spatial services be used or will a limited function middleman such as a manufacturer's agent represent the better channel?

3. He must select within competing retail and wholesale institutions of the same type. Will a policy of exclusive, selective, or intensive distribution be followed? Will Chain A or Chain B or both be used? Are urban, suburban, or rural positions preferred?

4. Finally, there are questions of the desired internal positioning of the goods within the outlets. This involves questions of layout and display.

This article is concerned with an aspect of the third level of spatial decision. Specifically, the nature of controlled shopping centers is examined and some impacts of these centers on the retail structure are suggested.

IMPACTS OF LOCATIONS ON RETAILING

Business men are generally quite aware of the importance of the right location to market oriented plants and stores. Some study has been given to the effect of different locations on the volume of goods sold. But many of the other relationships between locations and the creation of possession utilities have not been explored.

Location is important not only as it affects the volume of goods sold, but as it influences other variables of marketing transactions. For instance, what are the effects of different locations on: the quality and type of goods offered and sold, the degree of sales service required, and the amount of promotion and information needed to complete marketing transactions? What effects do different locations have on the time people buy, the frequency with which they purchase, the prices

[1] The art of marketing is the manipulation of temporal, spatial, and possessory forces to achieve an objective in management. As a discipline, marketing is the study of the temporal, spatial, and possessory forces influencing economic transactions, and of the interacting efforts and responses of traders (buyers and sellers) in the market.

[2] The writer is indebted to Dr. Lincoln Clark for this concept and for other guidance given during the preparation of a Ph.D. dissertation at the Graduate School of Business Administration of New York University.

they pay, and the cost of sales? What are the impacts of a new location on business done at other locations?

In terms of regional centers, how will the establishment of regional centers affect marketing transactions in other elements of the metropolitan retail structure? These questions concerning the effect of position in space on consumer behavior seem relevant whether one is concerned with increasing the profits of a particular enterprise or advancing science in business.

Merchants have recognized some differences between customers shopping downtown and in regional center stores. The two groups of customers are from different sections of the metropolitan area, from different income groups, have different tastes and attitudes, and even may be of different sizes. Specifically, shopping center customers buy more sports clothing, casual wear and children's clothing than do patrons of downtown stores.

It is probable that retailers experimenting with suburban locations will continue to find that merchandising problems vary between locations, even though basically the same lines may be carried. But what will the nature and extent of the difference be? How will the home-owning child-raising, casual living, do-it-yourself families of suburbia differ from their central city cousins shopping exclusively in downtown stores?

These questions are important since suburbanites represent the most important single market in the country. Forty million people comprise the suburban market today, but this figure alone does not tell the whole story. The suburban market contains more than its share of middle income consumers in the 25–45 year-old age bracket. *Fortune* reported that the average family unit income of the suburban population in 1953 was $6,500 or 70 percent higher than the rest of the nation.(2)

As a starting point for analyzing the above questions the elements comprising the retail structure are identified along with certain characteristics which may aid in formulating hypotheses about the questions raised. The shift of retail sales from the cores of the larger cities to other elements in the structure makes it more important than ever to consider as a market unit the entire metropolitan area rather than just the central city or any political sub-division.

In main outline the retail structure of the 168 standard metropolitan areas follows the pattern suggested in this article. In 1950 the areas had a population of 84,500,680 — more than half the people enumerated in the continental United States.

There is a wide variety in the distribution of the approximately 1,748,000 retail outlets in this country. Yet classification into groups for locational analysis is possible. Duncan and Phillips (3) maintain that in their main outlines the retail structure of cities and their surrounding areas is generally similar. These authors identify a central shopping district, secondary or outlying shopping centers, neighborhood business streets, and scattered individual stores or small clusters of stores.

ELEMENTS OF THE RETAIL STRUCTURE

Brown and Davidson (4) offer a five-fold classification of store locations found in most metropolitan areas; central shopping district, secondary shopping districts, string street locations, neighborhood clusters, and isolated locations. Weimer and Hoyt classify the retail structure into business districts, outlying business centers, and isolated outlets and clusters. (5) Other analyses in the literature of marketing and real estate follow a similar pattern.

A new classification of elements is suggested here, integrating controlled shopping centers into the retail structure of metropolitan areas. Some of the key relationships between elements are summarized in Table I.

THE RETAIL STRUCTURE

1. Central business district
   A. Inner core
   B. Inner belt
   C. Outer belt
2. Main business thoroughfares (string streets)
3. Secondary commercial sub-districts (unplanned)
   A. Neighborhood
   B. Community or district
   C. Suburban or outer
3a. Controlled secondary commercial sub-centers
   A'. Neighborhood
   B'. Community or district
   C'. Suburban or outer
4. Neighborhood business streets
5. Small store clusters and scattered individual stores
6. Controlled regional shopping centers.

1. Central business district

A Commerce Department study in 1935 used terminology that can be helpful in considering the structure of central business districts. The terms are "inner core," "inner belt," and "outer belt." Figure 2.

The inner core of the central business district is typically the point at which all intra-city traffic converges, the center of shopping and specialty goods activity and the home of the large department stores. (6) In the inner belt are found communication agencies, banks, law offices, the administrative offices of political, recreational, religious, and other services. The inner core and belt comprise the heart of the retail structure and also of these other activities as well. Through these offices the "manifold activities of the community are directed and integrated. The special function of the principal center is that of dominance or control . . ." (7)

The first two elements of the central business district are typically the home of the largest stores, both in floor space and volume. Some convenience-goods retailers are located in the central business district, but the shopping and specialty goods stores are the magnets which draw customers from the entire metropolitan area to shop downtown. The inner core of the central business district has the highest concentration of pedestrian traffic in its relatively small area. Because of these factors land values are highest here so that only high volume retailers can ordinarily compete for premium locations in this area.

In the inner belt immediately surrounding the core, land values are lower and pedestrian traffic much less concentrated than in the inner core. The separate but related functions of government, finance, professional services, cultural, entertainment, and wholesale activities are found here.

The third element of the central district is the outer belt. This generally includes less desirable commercial structures and dwellings, and some residential areas that have run down and are on the verge of becoming slums.

2. Main business thoroughfares

Leading out of the central business district are streets lined with all kinds of retail outlets and services. These thoroughfares are described as "string streets." Such streets are heavily traveled by automotive and pedestrian traffic. Retailers on these streets do not depend on the residents of their immediate area for patronage but are favored mostly by people using the street as a thoroughfare.

Some of these streets developed when streetcar routes from the central business district were laid out on fixed rails, and various types of commercial enterprises lined up along both sides of the streetcar system. Automobile dealers, furniture stores, and nearly every other type of consumer goods merchandiser can be found along the main business thoroughfares of most American cities.

3. Secondary commercial sub-districts

Commercial sub-districts develop as the population of the central city increases. It then becomes more convenient for people in neighborhoods away from the downtown area to shop closer to home more often, instead of journeying downtown to the central business district. Merchandise sold in secondary commercial sub-districts is similar to that sold downtown. However, the breadth and depth of lines carried is more limited, the stores smaller, and customers are drawn from a smaller area. A larger proportion of convenience-goods stores is located in these areas than in the downtown districts.

Typically secondary commercial sub-districts are located on heavily trafficked routes between residential areas and the central city. On the basis of parking facilities, two types of secondary shopping areas can be distinguished. The first is situated on or off the main business thoroughfares. In these sub-districts only curb parking is available for the automotive customer. Newer and modernized secondary shopping areas attempt to provide off-street parking for customers. All properly controlled neighborhood, commun-

ity, or district centers offer this service. The great majority of commercial sub-centers are uncontrolled.

3a. Controlled secondary sub-centers

Structurally each type of controlled center is placed in relation to the trading area it is designed to serve. Controlled neighborhood shopping centers are built near the areas occupied by neighborhood business districts. Community or district centers of the controlled variety are located in appropriate secondary shopping areas. Controlled suburban shopping centers are situated farther out near suburban cities. Controlled regional

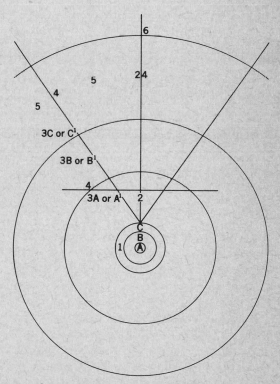

Figure 1. Schematic Presentation of the Retail Structure of Metropolitan Areas.

shopping centers are planned either in a suburban location or at a point beyond the typically suburban. In this matrix the next significant retail element is the neighborhood
business street.

4. Neighborhood business streets and areas

Neighborhood business streets contain convenience-goods stores with primarily a neighborhood appeal. These streets typically include a small cluster of several kinds of retail
establishments on heavily traveled streets or
at an intersection of two or more main
thoroughfares. The principal trade comes
from neighborhood residents.

5. Small clusters and scattered individual stores

Clusters and scattered individual stores also
deal basically in convenience goods. The clusters are made up of two or more complementary, rather than competitive convenience-
goods stores. Individual stores and small
clusters are scattered throughout the residential areas of cities and towns surrounding the
central city wherever population density in-
vites more convenient shopping facilities than
provided by neighborhood centers.

6. Controlled regional centers

Controlled regional shopping centers have
nearly all been built in suburban areas. But
the centers are intended not only to attract
patrons from immediately surrounding areas,
but from the entire region or quadrant of the
metropolitan area in which they are located.
A region may include all customers within a
given driving-time distance, usually thirty or
forty minutes from the site. Regional centers
are situated far enough out in suburbia for

the land to be relatively inexpensive. Tracts
can be used without the expense of demolish-
ing too many existing structures.

A basic reason for preferring the suburban
location is the large amount of non-selling
space needed for a regional center. The center's layout is designed to provide ample
parking facilities even for peak periods. Parking space may occupy from three to nine
times as much area as the floor space devoted
to the sale of merchandise. (8)

CHARACTERISTICS OF CONTROLLED CENTERS

Controlled shopping centers are considered
to have the following characteristics:

1. The land on which the center is situated
is owned by a single agency. Typically the
buildings are also owned by the developer,
but concessions in this respect might be made
to department store tenants. The factor of
single ownership makes possible an unusual
measure of control of architectural, parking,
service, and other features of the center by
the developers.

2. An assortment of different types of retail outlets offering a balanced representation
of goods and services is featured. The stores
are on one integrated site designed for one-
stop shopping at the level of trade area being
serviced, i.e., neighborhood, community, suburban area, or region.

3. Planning is done in advance of construction. The completed shopping center is
designed as an integrated, harmonious unit,
as an efficient merchandising machine. The
controlled center is developed according to
specifications by architects, market analysts,
and other types of consulting specialists.

On the basis of the trading area served,
four types of controlled centers have been
distinguished. These are the neighborhood,

community or district, suburban or outlying central city, and regional centers.

a. A neighborhood shopping center is one comprising seven to fifteen retail outlets selling primarily convenience goods. A supermarket is the core of this type of center. Neighborhood centers serve a minimum of 750 families or about 3,000 people. Larger neighborhood centers may serve as many as 15,000 people. Store groups of six or less are ordinarily better described as small store clusters than as shopping centers.

b. Community or district centers draw greater numbers of customers from wider areas than do neighborhood centers. The trading area usually includes several neighborhoods within one to three miles of the site. A population of between 15,000 and 30,000 is typical of the community center's trading area. The community center includes, in addition to the service stores found in neighborhood centers, a complete range of convenience-goods outlets, shopping and specialty goods stores emphasizing apparel and home furnishings in the middle price ranges, professional offices, and usually a branch bank.

It is characterized by a greater depth of merchandise than the neighborhood center. Automotive traffic is more important than in the neighborhood center and off-street parking facilities generally have to be provided. From sixteen to thirty-five stores are found in the usual community center.

c. Suburban or outlying central city centers normally serve a population of 30,000 to 100,000 people and are commonly built around a department store branch or two and several large supermarkets. Generally, except for unusual specialty items, an assortment of merchandise adequate to serve all needs of the trading area is offered. The centers serve a large suburban area consisting of many communities and neighborhoods. From twenty-five to fifty or more different retail outlets typically comprise the suburban center.

When the uncontrolled suburban or outlying central city center serves over 100,000 people, it begins to assume in miniature the retail structure of larger cities. It tends to develop its own "downtown" district and the resultant parking and traffic problems. When this occurs, the suburban center loses some of its attraction as a site for additional expansion, particularly by department stores.

d. The regional center services a trading area of from 100,000 to 1,000,000 or more people. In addition to convenience and specialty goods stores, it contains at least one department store branch. Usually the branch has between 100,000 and 300,000 square feet of selling space. A full line of shopping and specialty goods is featured in the center. Regional centers are in effect decentralized substitutes for the downtown center featuring forty to one hundred or more stores on a site of at least fifty acres.

CENTERS ARE POSTWAR OUTGROWTH

The controlled center is largely a post World War II development, though isolated controlled neighborhood and community centers were in operation as early as the 1920's. Various estimates place the number of controlled centers at probably between 2,000 and 3,000 controlled shopping centers of all four types, completed or in advanced planning or construction stages. Only six regional centers were in operation as of January, 1955.

The reasons for the emergence of large controlled centers have been discussed by Duncan and Phillips (3), Brown and Davidson (4), and others. There is agreement that the centers evolved to meet the needs gen-

TABLE I

The Retail Structure of the Metropolitan Economy

Retail Element	General Character	Source of Customers	Store Types	Parking	Traffic	Goods Sold
1. Central Business District A. Inner core B. Inner belt C. Outer belt	Inner core and belt solidly commercial. The business and recreational heart of metropolitan economy. Residents fill in back streets. Typically, residential areas are blighted.	Come from all parts of city and tributary area. Sites are most accessible to most consumers. Intracity transportation converges in this element.	Largest in floor space and volume. Multi-story department store is symbolic. Home of specialty shops. Outer belt activity less intense. These stores do smaller volume per unit.	Totally inadequate in inner core and belt. Trend to provide public lots and commercial parking lots to supplement limited curb parking in inner belt and outer belt.	Extremely heavy. Congested during peak periods.	Shopping and specialty goods emphasis. Area is center of apparel, home furnishings, other department store lines. Service and other commercial activities found in belts.
2. Main Business Thoroughfares (String streets)	Mixed zone of retail and light industrial enterprises and working class homes. Featured by long series of miscellaneous stores.	Basically trade is transient, consisting of commuters, suburbanites, and inter-city automotive traffic. Some patronage from neighborhood residents.	Concentration of larger food stores, automobile dealers, and supply houses, service and convenience-goods stores.	Usually dependent on curb parking. Inadequate during most periods.	Streets are main traffic arteries. Usually heavy, but particularly so during commuting peaks.	Essentially business streets. Stores are widely spaced over length of artery.
3. Secondary Commercial Subdistricts (unplanned) A. Neighborhood B. Community or district C. Suburban or outer	More residential than first two elements. Owner-occupied residences increase with distance from central business district. The subdistricts tend to appear, island-like along string streets.	Come basically from A, B, or C trade areas. The districts developed as city grew at focal points of intra-city transportation. Dependent on traffic brought by public carriers.	Unplanned competition featuring convenience and shopping goods. B and C tend to be miniatures of central business districts.	Mostly curb, plus some off-street parking provided by individual merchants.	Since stores are typically clustered at key intersections and transfer points of public carriers, the traffic is heavy.	Convenience-goods featured in A. Increasing shopping goods emphasis in B and C.

Type	Character / Setting	Customer Source	Store Composition	Parking	Traffic	Merchandise / Notes
3a. Controlled Secondary Commercial Sub-centers A'. Neighborhood B'. Community or district C'. Suburban or outer	Waste area and marginal stores at a minimum. Found near more prosperous residential areas. Unified architecturally. Most built after World War II. New, fresh appearance compared to 3.	Greater dependence on automotive traffic. Parking provided so customers are drawn from greater distances than in case of unplanned centers. Generally found in suburban district.	Balanced collection of supplementary stores possessing aesthetic appeal. Centers stress convenience and service, not price appeals.	Provided on a co-operative basis within the center. Parking and other facilities related in size to surrounding trade area.	Parking for private automobiles key consideration. Even so, automotive traffic heavy.	Attempt made to present an integrated retail organism to customers coming from A', B', or C' distances. A' stresses convenience goods. B' and C' feature shopping and specialty merchandise.
4. Neighborhood Business Streets	Residential with commercial use distinctly secondary.	Neighborhood is primary source. Most customers come from within walking or 5 minutes driving distance.	Usually rows of convenience-goods outlets found in center of neighborhood community.	Mostly curb. Due to convenience-goods nature of most items sold, parking turnover is rapid.	Heavy during peak hours. Otherwise not a handicap to trade.	Emphasis on food and drugs. Grocery store-drugs combination frequent. Service stores common.
5. Small Clusters and Scattered Individual Stores	More thinly populated residential areas. Neighborhoods tend to be middle class.	Come from homes not within easy reach of larger elements in structure. Many walk to stores.	Smallest outlets in structure. Many are marginal. This classification dominated by food and general.	Curb and small lot parking usually adequate.	Usually not a problem. The lack of traffic congestion, plus the availability of parking, represents an appeal of this element to customers beyond neighborhood range.	Usually supplementary and not directly competitive.
6. Controlled Regional Shopping Centers	Overall unity obvious at a glance. Landscaped frequently. Off-street parking. Harmonious effect is objective. May be equipped to serve as area's civic and cultural center.	Drawn from families within 30-minute driving range. Customers typically come from a number of suburban communities. Pull varies with effectiveness of central business district retailers and competing centers.	Attempt made to duplicate shopping facilities of central business district with minimum of overlapping. "One-Stop Shopping in the Suburbs."	Usually best facilities in metropolitan area. Adequate for all but occasional peak periods.	Problem usually under control as a result of coordinated planning.	One or two department store branches and satellite stores offer widest range of merchandise and services outside central business district.

erated by changing environmental factors in the economy. These factors include increasing urban population decentralization, increased use of the automobile, increased congestion in central business districts, the lack of economical and convenient parking facilities in downtown areas, and changing consumer buying habits. The important point is that these forces and others favoring retail recentralization seem to be increasing rather than diminishing.

A population of 221,000,000 by 1975 has been predicted. The increase in population alone will be enough to support dozens of large new shopping facilities. In addition, higher living standards brought about by automation and rising productivity, increased leisure time, and a rising educational level, all seem to favor further population decentralization and retail recentralization in large shopping centers.

Other forces, such as an increasing national income, are also likely to result in a response by entrepreneurs of more and better decentralized shopping facilities. It may well be the controlled shopping center movement is in its infancy. Of course, a saturation point for shopping centers can be reached. And merchants in shopping centers can fail. For location is still only one ingredient of a successful retailing operation. Many other questions of planning, financing, and operation must be answered before a center is assured of success.

LOCATING REGIONAL CENTERS

The ideal regional center site is the one from which the largest number of automotive customers in a trade area can be served at the minimum of transfer costs. Consumers' transfer costs include not only money costs but the expenditure of time and physical

and nervous energy that must be made to purchase goods. The reason controlled regional shopping center sites are preferred close to the center of the suburban population areas is that consumers' transfer costs are usually minimized at such sites.[3] In locating market-oriented facilities, the ideal is to choose a site as close as possible to the scarcest factor and the one having limited mobility — the customer.

It is believed the choice of a site at which transfer costs will be minimized for the largest number of automotive customers will be facilitated by using the following factors as criteria of site selection.[4] The factors are classified as either regional or site factors. Regional factors are those of population, purchasing power, growth, and competition. The site factors are access, traffic, size, expansion, parking, cost, terrain, and utilities.

REGIONAL FACTORS

Population

Regional centers are best located in concentrated residential populations in outlying sections of large metropolitan areas. Ordinarily a minimum of 500,000 people should reside within thirty minutes' driving time distance of the site.

---

[3] In economic theory the reason why sites at the center of urban activity are considered most desirable is found in the labor savings involved in a central location. This valuation is reflected in the form of higher rents.

[4] The criteria were prepared during a study of the processes used in locating the following regional centers: Shoppers' World, Framingham, Massachusetts; Cross County, Yonkers, New York; Roosevelt Field, Hempstead, New York; Garden State Plaza, Paramus, New Jersey; Bergen Mall, Parmus, New Jersey; and Northland, Detroit, Michigan. The writer is grateful for the cooperation of the developers and managers of these centers.

Purchasing power

Regional centers should be located in an area only after an analysis of the purchasing power and stability of income and expenditures of residents indicates the trade area is sufficient to support a regional center of the size contemplated.

Growth

The section of most rapid population growth and probable future expansion within the metropolitan area is normally the most promising sectional choice for a suitable regional center site.

Competition

The location of competition as it affects potential sites should be investigated both quantitatively and qualitatively. A regional center should be located in an area only when proof exists that operating and planned retail facilities are inadequate.

SITE FACTORS

Access

A regional center site should be easily accessible to automotive traffic. The site should be in a prominent location and be served by a system of primary and secondary roads, offering convenient, safe, and free flowing means of access and egress.

Traffic

Sufficient road capacity should be available to handle existing traffic around the site, traffic likely to be produced by future expansion in the area, and traffic created by the additional vehicular activity the center will generate.

Size

The site should be large enough to provide the desired amount of store and service facilities, and parking at a parking-space to floor-space ratio of at least three to one and preferably, four to one. Sufficient land should be acquired to serve as a buffer and possible expansion area. With regional centers these specifications usually require a minimum site of fifty acres.

Expansion

Provision should be made in the earliest planning stages for expansion after the center is established. The developers should attempt to build with expansion provisions for five and ten year periods ahead. Excess space can be used for landscaping and recreational purposes until needed for commercial use.

Provision for expansion may be necessary to hold a planned position in the event of an increase in population and trade after the center opens. If the center can not expand as needed, other shopping facilities will develop in the area pioneered by the first center.

Parking

The tract should be of a size and shape to provide parking in at least a three-to-one ratio of parking to store space. Shoppers should not have to walk more than four hundred feet from their automobiles to the nearest store. The ideal ratio of parking to store space increases with the size of the center.

Site cost

The cost of acquiring the site, preparing it for construction, and any extraordinary maintenance costs must be carefully measured and considered. In general, land costs are not to be economized upon at the expense of losing a premium site.

Terrain

The terrain should be thoroughly examined by architects and engineers in advance of purchase to ascertain conditions which might affect the locational decision. In general, level ground and solid earth represent the preferred terrain conditions.

Utilities

Utilities should be available to the site at the time of acquisition or at completion of the center. Regional centers will ordinarily maintain some of their own utility services, but power, water, and sewage facilities should be available to the property line.

These factors have been incorporated in the following site-ranking chart. The ranking chart assumes the availability of the rated site, together with its possibility of rezoning. The ideal site might be unavailable. In such a case, the next most promising site on the market should be rated. Similarly, rated sites should be zoned or rezonable for shopping center development. It is self-evident that a developer should not go too far in his planning about a particular site unless he has reason to believe the site is available commercially and legally.

The site-ranking chart is designed to serve only as a general guide in deciding on the site selection. It is recognized that an entrepreneur choosing sites might find it difficult, if not impossible, to focus on a particular site all of the information that might be relevant. Yet, the use of a site-ranking chart should produce more valid site ratings. Table II.

CONTROLLED CENTERS AND CENTRAL BUSINESS DISTRICTS

It appears probable that population and transportational forces responsible for the increase in regional centers after World War II will continue unabated for at least the next few years. But the central business district will continue to dominate retail trade in most metropolitan areas, although the proportion of business done by suburban centers will increase. Suburban volume will increase because of suburban residents' dissatisfaction with existing retail facilities in the major central business districts.

The chief complaint is transportational. It is a wearisome chore for suburban shoppers to overcome the friction of space and reach most central business districts through congested traffic and crowded streets. On reaching the central business district, finding a convenient parking space is typically a problem. Public transportation is available, but it can do only part of the job in a culture wedded to the private automobile.

Some evidence exists that central business district retailers are becoming concerned enough about suburban competition to take action to increase downtown trade. In some instances merchants are cooperating to obtain improved transportational and parking facilities for central business districts. Their cause is hopeful. There is no reason why central business districts served by efficient highways bringing suburbanites to the city and to the downtown areas, perhaps on expressways, and to adequate parking facilities, should not be able to compete successfully with regional centers.

But even with the adoption of every type of palliative advanced, it appears the factor of population increase and migration alone is

TABLE II

Controlled Regional Shopping Center Site Ranking Chart

Description of Site Being Rated..

....

Factor being rated	Ranking of site (in order of relative preference)				
REGIONAL FACTORS	1	2	3	4	5
Population					
within 15 minutes					
16-30 minutes					
Purchasing power					
amount and stability					
distribution					
Growth of population					
amount					
degree					
Competition					
amount					
quality					
SITE FACTORS					
Size of tract					
minimum size					
undivided					
buffer area					
Access and egress					
primary roads					
secondary roads					
Traffic					
present pattern					
future pattern					
Parking					
amount					
nearness to stores					
Cost					
acquisition					
maintenance					
Terrain conditions					
grading					
subsoil conditions					
Utilities					
proximity					
Expansion-Environment					
expansion					
environment					

enough to favor the creation of more recentralized retail facilities in the hinterland.

In both theory and fact central business districts have attractions that will insure their continued importance as centers for commercial and recreational life of metropolitan areas. But they will encounter more competition from other elements in the retail structure. However, the central district has a natural locational advantage of being the point which the greatest number of people in the metropolitan area can reach most economically. This advantage ordinarily should suffice to assure its dominant position.

Notes

(1) Samuel C. McMillan, "Decentralization of Retail Trade," *Traffic Quarterly* (April 1954).

(2) "The Lush New Suburban Market," *Fortune* (November, 1953), p. 128.

(3) Delbert J. Duncan and Charles F. Phillips, *Retailing Principles and Methods*, 4th ed. (Chicago, Richard D. Irwin, Inc., 1955), pp. 79, 82.

(4) P. L. Brown and W. P. Davidson, *Retailing Principles and Practices* (New York, Ronald Press, 1953), p. 75.

(5) Arthur M. Weimer and Homer Hoyt, *Principles of Urban Real Estate* (New York, Ronald Press, 1948), p. 138.

(6) U.S. Department of Commerce, *Intra-City Business Census Statistics of Philadelphia, Pennsylvania* (Washington, Bureau of the Census, 1937), p. 25.

(7) Amos H. Hawley, *Human Ecology* (New York, Ronald Press, 1950), p. 270. The influence of metropolitan centers was also examined by Donald J. Bogue, *The Structure of the Metropolitan Community: A Study of Dominance and Subdominance* (Ann Arbor, University of Michigan Press, 1949).

(8) Ernest M. Fisher and Robert M. Fisher, *Urban Real Estate* (New York, Henry Holt and Company, 1954), p. 317.

Emerging Patterns of Commercial Structure in American Cities

20

James E. Vance, Jr.

The traditional view of the retail trade pattern of cities needs reexamination in light of our growing awareness of the dynamic nature of urban structure. Particularly in the United States, the geography of urban commercial activity has ceased to be the study of the central business district with only minor attention given to small outlying business centers. In the post-war period virtually all growth in the commercial structure has taken place outside the city core. Concentration on that area alone would, at best, give us a picture of the realities of the pre-war world. Development outside the central business district is frequently cited as evidence of the decay and disintegration of the core region. Rather more accurate, it would seem, would be to view the newer growth as coming from a change in urban dynamic features, which calls for a reassignment of function between central and outlying districts. In truth the core is changing rather than decaying but until we understand that metamorphosis it is easily mistaken for decline.

The purpose of this paper is to attempt to establish the location factors in commercial land use. First the aspects of urbanism which lead to change are considered. The main currents in commercial structure over the years are briefly described and analyzed in order to discover trends in location. All these trends when carefully assessed provide us with an insight into the dynamics of urban commercial structure and allow us to formulate a body of simple location factors at work within that structure. To test commercial location factors a brief sample study of the San Francisco Bay Area is presented based on field investigation carried out during the last eighteen months. In conclusion, the changes that may be anticipated in urban retail structure in the near future resulting from current dynamics are suggested.

Dynamic Factors Affecting Commercial Structure

Without question the most important dynamic factor affecting commercial structure has been the changing means of personal transportation. Cities came into existence at a time of mass transport and the office and commercial

1962

Reprinted from *Lund Studies in Geography* (1958) by permission of the author and the Department of Geography, University of Lund, Sweden.

functions at the core are the creation of these fixed lines of movement. So long as individual transportation was not available there was little locational choice in the establishment of shops selling to a mass market. The focus of set routes necessary for the creation of office districts was equally as necessary for the formation of a major shopping district. But the functional linkages among diverse offices are stronger and more ramified than the linkages among diverse shops. When the automobile came into wide ownership it had far less effect on the convergence in the office quarter than it had on the focussing on the retail quarter. The stronger linkages in the former were not easily broken. In retail districts the tie between stores was largely one of similar location requirements rather than functional ties one with another, so that changed conditions of access could bring quite different location requirements.

A second dynamic factor is found in the matter of changing purchasing power and tastes. In the United States personal consumption expenditures, on a per capita basis, have gone up from 880 "constant dollars" in 1929 to 1,295 "constant dollars" in 1955. This 47 per cent increase has meant that the average individual's purchases have risen from $1,012 in 1929 to $1,527 in 1955, with the figures adjusted to 1955 prices. Any discussion of commercial structure must take into consideration this 50 per cent increase in per capita expenditures during the past thirty years. Also during this period there has been great change in consumer preferences among goods. This is not the place to investigate the matter of tastes other than to remark that a more mobile population with a greater influence of mass media of news and entertainment has shown an increasingly standardized taste in goods bought.

New patterns of housing have influenced commercial structure. Although these patterns of housing are dependent upon the wide ownership of automobiles, which has been proposed as the most important dynamic factor, it is best to emphasize that a virtual revolution has taken place in the housing of recent additions to American urban population. Perhaps this should be called a "counter-revolution" as it has done much to turn away from the course of urban physical development introduced with the modern industrial city. A romantic desire to abjure the city has seized a large part of American urban dwellers. The desire for single family housing and disassociation from the heart of the city has led to a vast urban sprawling. Particularly since the end of the Second World War additions to the total of urban housing have been (1) characteristically related to our automobile "civilization" in being mass produced, homogeneous over large areas, and characterized by price-class orientation; (2) typically found in areas where the initial land costs will permit medium density housing; and (3) usually given to a checkerboard or salient pattern of expansion which results in a greater extension of distance from the core of the city than is required by the absolute need for building land or the craving for the bucolic life. The considerably increased distance of this housing from the city core when tied in with the homogeneity of the areas has created a fertile ground in which to plant the new mass selling integrated shopping center. And these centers rather than supplementing the central business district, as did the older outlying shopping districts, have tended to assume part of the previous commercial function of the core.

A factor of great importance in the creation of new patterns of commercial land use has been the imposition of land use planning through zoning. Today virtually all areas which may be considered urban are covered with zone ordinances so we may assume that newer commercial locations reflect planning goals as well as the operation of location economics. These planning goals have sought to do away with the isolated shop and have reinforced the economic trend toward integration of shopping facilities.

A final dynamic factor affecting commercial structure is found in changes in merchandizing. The deification of size among American retailers and their craze for high volume of sales has, within a restricted local market, led to a fuzzing of the lines of demarcation among types of shops. The American drug store is the classic and incredible example. Here the expansion of sales volume in a local market with a relatively inelastic demand for goods has necessitated the combination of many "lines" of merchandise and the creation of the modern equivalent of the "general store". We have had to borrow the British term apothecary for the rare pharmacy which sells neither toys nor hiking equipment. Along with this commodity-combining which has greatly recast the form of commercial districts we should note the rapid rate of reconstruction of commercial buildings. On the average American commercial buildings are demolished and replaced at the end of two generations. This combined with the fluid boundaries among establishment types has led to a continual transforming of commercial districts.

The Elements in the Commercial Geography of American Cities

The geography of commerce in American metropolitan areas seems at first view appallingly complex. Without denying the absence of obvious organization in this land use, it is possible to establish a typology of commercial districts through a study of the history and function of these areas. Malcolm Proudfoot (1937, p. 425) distinguished five types of "retail structure": (1) the central business district; (2) the outlying business center; (3) the principal business thoroughfare; (4) the neighborhood business street; and (5) the isolated store cluster. His classification was concerned primarily with the morphology of these districts. To understand how the physical form is changing requires that we look into its origins.

The mercantilist basis of several of the British North American colonies brought trade and commerce at an early date. By the time of the American Revolution there was sufficient demand in the few major port cities to support a considerable artisan class which provided for a number of limited-appeal wants. The Boston silversmith Paul Revere is best known but he was certainly not alone in this realm. The mass-appeal goods were supplied in the leading towns of the new republic by merchants' establishments selling notably imported foodstuffs, cloth, and crockery. Naturally, so long as the rural areas of the country were tied to subsistence agriculture, little trade existed outside the port cities. With the rapid growth of industry and the equally rapid expansion of commercial farming in the early nineteenth century trading was carried out of the town to the agricultural village and the mill town. The vast scale and freehold nature of farming in America when commercialization was introduced brought about the creation of the first and most widespread of the commodity-combining store types. These "general stores" were for more than a century the center of rural commerce and held sway until the early part of this century when mail order merchandising and the building of farm-to-market roads introduced larger scale competition. Even as late as 1929 (Table I) the general store was basic to retailing, though by 1954 the competition of more diversified commercial districts which could be reached along the improved rural roads had destroyed the general store as a type.

By the mid-point of the nineteenth century the older port cities such as Boston, New York, and Philadelphia had grown greatly in size and become dominantly proletarian. Diversity of goods was desired by shoppers of much greater number than the small well-to-do group of merchants who had supported the artisan's shop. To meet this demand a second type of commodity-combining shop, the department store, was developed. By locating these stores in the heart of the city where the largest possible market for any specialized good would have its center and by combining all the specialties in a single establishment in order to maximize the total profit rather than the profit from each line of merchandise it was possible to offer a more diverse group of goods at a lower unit profit. Demand was greatly increased thereby, and the urban mass market came into existence for goods beyond the most staple sort. These department stores ultimately assumed such dominance in volume of sales, and attraction of customers, that they became the anchor of the central business district and, until the last fifteen years, were unique to that area.

Even the department store could not care for the most proletarian of demands and in 1879 F. W. Woolworth opened his first store in Lancaster, Pa., to sell variety merchandise at the lowest possible price by developing the mass market. The fact that the mass market was international is amply demonstrated by the rapid spread of the department store and "5 and 10" variety store to western Europe and Japan, in fact, anywhere that industrial society had introduced a money economy.

The American Civil War added still another mass-appeal shop to cities where it joined with the "5 and 10" and the department store to form the first and dominant nexus within the central business district. The demand for uniforms within the Union Army brought the first mass production of ready-made clothing. In the years after 1865 the producers of uniforms for the first modern conscription army sought to continue production by shifting their operations to mass-sale clothing for men. Only much later, after the turn of the century, was the women's ready-made clothing industry well developed, but in the case of both men's and women's clothing the introduction came in the mass market before the specialty market, so that the central business district location was essential. It remained for the mail order firms to demonstrate in the 1890's that clothing along with other mass produced and demanded items could be sold outside the core of the city. The American drug store came into existence soon after the "5 and 10" to carry standardization of product and combination of merchandise lines into those realms untapped by its predecessors. Although the four mass-selling establishment types, department stores, variety stores (5 and 10), ready-made clothing, and drug stores, have been in the van of development outside the core, they still account for 60 per cent of the sales in the central business district. As they brought the downtown commercial area into being it is not surprising that they also initiated the outlying shopping center.

Proudfoot writes that in the outlying business centers which grew up around interchange points on mass transit lines with the introduction of the street railway in the 1890's "are found shopping goods outlets such as men's and women's clothing stores, furniture stores, shoe stores, jewelry stores, one or more large (branch or junior) department stores, and an admixture of convenience-goods stores". This catalogue reads like an inventory of the core area except for the matter of specialty shops. With the passage of time, and increasing competition from outlying centers, the central business district became distinguished for price and commodity variety. The mass-appeal goods which had brought the downtown shopping area into existence could, like the earlier projection of trading into rural areas through the general store, be carried out closer to the consuming public. What could not be decentralized was trading in specialties, which continued to need the uniqueness of location to tap the entire metropolitan market that the core provided.

With the introduction of automobile travel the street railway interchange point lost much of its locational advantage because cars were first of greater use in the journey-to-shop than in the urban journey-to-work. As women had automobiles for shopping the principal business thoroughfare grew up in the form of strips of commercial land use along major arterial roads. There the universally needed food store combined with the mass-appealing stores selling clothing, furniture, and other staples. The blaze of neon signs along these strips of commerce attests to the fact that uniqueness of offering is far less common than strong competition for the mass market. The neighborhood business street and isolated store cluster were a logical elaboration of the city's commercial structure stemming from increasing city size and prosperity. The minimum tributary area for a store selling goods of universal appeal is very small. The recent replacement of many of these business streets by a single supermarket tells us mainly that

in American retailing there is constant pressure to expand the unit size of shops, which can only be done within a minimum tributary area by reducing what specialization may have existed in the past.

"In the decade following World War II the universal use of the automobile in the United States and Canada has superimposed a new retail structure upon the retail pattern developed in the previous decades [under mass transit] . . ." (Hoyt, 1958). The first large automobile-oriented stores were those built by Sears Roebuck and Co., when that mail order house entered the retail store field in the early 1930's. At first these stores were thought of by the owners as places for men to shop so that central location seemed unnecessary and the range of choice implied by the designation "style goods" was avoided. Emmet and Jeuck (1950, p. 490) in their authoritative study conclude "that Sears does, at best, a mediocre job in style merchandise but an outstanding job in staples". In addition it seems that Sears also understood, well before most retailers, that the outlying market can only be developed as a mass market as there unique location is impossible and there must be a sharing of the limited-appeal market among a number of competing sites. Although the Sears' stores were almost the only outlying department stores before the Second World War, since the close of the war the major part of store construction and virtually all the increase in sales has taken place in outlying areas. In the 48 larger Standard Metropolitan Areas of the United States, between 1948 and 1954 retail sales increased 32.3 per cent but the central business district rise was only 1.6 percent or a loss in relative terms.

The core of all the larger integrated outlying shopping centers has been the branch department store usually having at least 100,000 square feet of sales area. Like the Sears' stores built in the 1930's these branches have dealt almost exclusively with staples. Hoyt (1958) remarks that, "The largest regional shopping centers do offer a complete selection of both fashion and convenience goods, but in these new centers, built at today's high costs, the most profitable lines are selected, leaving for the older (downtown) stores, built at lower costs, the types of merchandise that have a less rent-paying capacity." By 1957 there were 36 centers with 100,000 square foot department store branches and since then the number has probably doubled. In the San Francisco Bay Area, where the type is well represented, the increase in three years has been from six to eleven. The largest of these regional shopping centers may have one million square feet and probably require a minimum tributary area of 200,000 people.

In addition to the regional centers there are smaller types. The community center usually has at its core a large variety (5 and 10) or "junior department store", that is a store dominated by the selling of readymade clothing and household linens, that ranges in size from 25,000 to 90,000 square feet. The center would normally total 100,000 to 400,-000 square feet. The community center is largely competitive with the older outlying business districts at interchange points on the street railways or suburban railroads. The tributary area normally would have at least 100,000 people.

Finally, there is the integrated equivalent of the older business street or isolated store cluster, usually called the neighborhood center. At the core is a supermarket with up to 50,000 square feet and the tributary area may be as small as 10,000 people due to the dependence upon the universal need for food shopping.

The planned shopping center differs from the older outlying shopping center in several important aspects. The most significant of these is the continuing ownership of the land, and often of the buildings, by the developer of the center, a fact which usually leads to a considerable control over the types of business conducted. This situation creates a carefully determined assorting of store types and makes possible a rigid application of the test of maximized profit in the selection of occupants as the land owner normally receives a share of the profits of the renting firm. In Proudfoot's classification the outlying shopping center was an area of individual ownership and chance assortment of shops, often with quite varying profits.

The planned centers also normally have a control on size because of the fact that the original site is usually restricted and cannot be enlarged because of zoning provisions. These centers, which depend on automobile access, are tied to highway junctions rather than to the older town centers and for this reason, along with the maximization of rent, seldom have any other appreciable use element than commerce. Being planned the centers are normally located in a section of the suburbs which is without competing centers, though up to the present the necessary tributary area population and distance over which customers could be induced to travel to shop there have been open to differences of thought. Because of the fact that these centers must depend upon the full exploitation of the immediately adjacent market there has been little interest on the part of developers for Hoyt's "low rent-paying merchandise lines". Thus, if these centers have a single dominant characteristic it is striking uniformity. The mass market in its very nature is uniform and the integrated shopping center fully reflects this. Obviously, uniformity leads to complete competition among centers and the restriction of their tributary areas largely on the basis of distance.

Location Factors in the Geography of Commerce

It has been traditional in discussing the location of commercial activity to distinguish between "convenience goods" and "shopping goods" on the assumption that certain goods are purchased so frequently that their sale must take place on the local level while other goods are infrequent purchases for which the customers engage in planned "shopping". On closer consideration, however, it must be noted that locationally the simple distinction is meaningless. What appears to have been overlooked is the fact that any aggregation of people requires convenience goods sales, even within the central business district, and that the class usually called shopping goods is so broad as to obscure the difference between goods of mass appeal and those of limited appeal.

In terms of location a much more analytical distinction is provided by visualizing two continua of specialization. It is possible to rank classes of establishments along lines of *locational specialization* and *commodity specialization* and thereby establish the geographically important relationship between trade center and tributary area as well as an hierarchy of trade centers on a local level. Locational specialization is a simple concept seeking to quantify the distinction among shops as to the economically minimal tributary area. It follows that a shop with a small minimum support area, measured more in terms of population than geographical area, has little locational specialization. A grocery store may prosper on the patronage of the inhabitants of a few city blocks but a rare book dealer may require the support of an entire nation. The point might be made that the rare book dealer would be classed as a shopping goods store in any event and we need not think about locational specialization. But it is obvious that locational specialization is a much more refined measure. In such a convenience good as food there are certain luxury or ethnically associated items which may be secured only in the largest metropolitan center and there only in a single locale.

The general conditions of locational specialization may be inferred from the data in Table I which shows the national totals of establishments for the 41 types of retail shops in the Censuses of Business carried out in 1929 and 1954. At the time of writing the data for the 1958 were unavailable. Between 1929 and 1954 the total number of shops decreased by one-sixth while the total of sales, in "constant dollars", increased three times as much. Of the 41 categories more than half, 23, declined in their percentage contribution to the total. These types displaying a *concentration of sales* into a smaller relative number of outlets were all types of food stores, all but one of the clothing types (women's ready-to-wear), all but one of the general merchandise types (variety stores), and approximately half the remaining types. Integration of several lines of merchandise in a single type, such as the supermarket, has gone on at the same time that the size of individuals has increased, as also in supermarkets. This results in a reduction in the number of specialty food shops and of food shops in general.

In the group of shops exhibiting an expansion of relative numbers the growth, with

TABLE I.

Rank of Retail Trade Establishments, by Total Numbers, for the United States 1929—1954

1929		1954		
Type of Establishment	*Number*	*Type of Establishment*	*Number*	
Grocery, without meat	191,876	Food stores	279,440 —	1
Gasoline stations	121,513	Gasoline stations	181,747 —	2
Grocery, with meat	115,549	Motor vehicle dealers	61,666 —	3
General stores	104,089	Drug stores	56,009 —	4
Candy, nut, confections	63,265	Hardware stores	34,858 —	5
Drug stores	58,258	Dry goods, gen. merchand.	34,113 —	6
Motor vehicle dealers	45,301	Liquor stores	31,240 —	7
Meat markets	43,788	Lumber, bldg. material	30,177 —	8
Dry goods stores	38,305	Women's clothing	26,893 —	9
Cigar stores and stands	33,248	Furniture stores	25,475 —	10
Men's and boys' clothing	28,197	Jewelry stores	24,266 —	11
Lumber, bldg. material	26,377	Shoe stores	23,847 —	12
Furniture stores	25,854	Meat markets	22,896 —	13
Hardware stores	25,330	Household appliance	21,974 —	14
Shoe stores	24,259	Variety stores	20,917 —	15
Fruit and vegetable stores	22,904	Candy, nut, confections	20,507 —	16
Tire, battery, auto acc.	22,313	Men's and boys' clothing	19,247 —	17
Jewelry stores	19,998	Tire, battery, auto acc.	18,845 —	18
Women's ready-to-wear cl.	18,253	Farm equipment	18,689 —	19
Radio stores	16,037	Florist shops	16,279 —	20
Second-hand stores	15,065	Second-hand stores	14,364 —	21
Millinery shops	12,433	Fruit and vegetable stores	13,136 —	22
Farm equipment	12,242	Gift and souvenir shops	12,149 —	23
Variety stores	12,110	Family clothing stores	11,056 —	24
Delicatessen shops	11,166	Paint, glass, wallpaper	9,249 —	25
Family clothing stores	10,551	Sporting goods stores	8,396 —	26
Newspaper dealers	10,285	Delicatessen shops	8,132 —	27
Household appliance	9,329	Farm-garden supply stores	7,262 —	28
Florist shops	9,328	Newspaper dealers	7,178 —	29
Paint, glass, wallpaper	8,870	Children's clothing stores	7,024 —	30
Fish markets	6,077	Cigar stores and stands	6,859 —	31
Farm-garden supply stores	5,740	Music stores	5,810 —	32
Gift and souvenir shops	5,186	Radio and TV stores	5,800 —	33
Department stores	4,221	Stationery stores	5,473 —	34
Stationery stores	4,047	Millinery shops	5,473 —	35
Office-store machine equip.	3,498	Fish markets	4,458 —	36
Book stores	2,809	Floor covering stores	4,335 —	37
Music stores	2,232	Camera and photography shops	2,896 —	38
Sporting goods stores	1,930	Department stores	2,761 —	39
Floor covering stores	1,503	Book stores	2,642 —	40
Children's clothing stores	1,309	Office-store mach.-equip.	2,216 —	41
Camera and photography shops	710		—	42
Totals	1,342,072		1,115,014	

Sources: U.S. Bureau of the Census 1929—1954.

minor exceptions, has occurred in newly intro-duced lines of merchandise or in the selling of luxury items where mass selling and low unit profit are not characteristic. This contrast between staple and luxury goods leads us to the conclusion that an increased scale of establishment size, to enhance the total rather than the unit profit, has led to an enlargement of the economically minimal tributary area.

Commodity specialization is distinct in form and operation and concerns the mini-mum range of merchandise types necessary to support a shop. Thus, we may progress from the single commodity shop, such as the Steuben Glass Shop in New York, to the local Woolworth store which also sells glass but of a very different sort and then only as part of a vast array of goods. Admittedly, the Wool-worth company has stores in several thousand towns in North America and Europe and Steuben a single shop in New York, so that locational specialization also enters the pic-ture. But it is important to note that outside of New York Steuben glass can be sold only as an adjunct to the selling of a diversity of other items.

The relationship between locational special-ization and commodity specialization is essen-tially direct. *As commodity specialization increases so must locational specialization.* Here, however, we must introduce the con-cept of mass-appeal and limited-appeal goods. Locational specialization is a simple con-tinuum from the least to the most restricted but commodity specialization has two series, one for mass-appeal goods and another for limited-appeal goods. It is this fact which makes it necessary for us to consider both types of specialization even though they oper-ate in somewhat the same manner. Without the distinction between mass- and limited-appeal goods we could not logically explain the different location factors shaping the several types of commercial districts.

Prior to the Second World War American suburbs tended to fall into two classes rather distinct from each other. There were strictly residential areas of generally high income housing and there were industrial satellites of the central city with worker's housing. It may be seen that the two classes of suburban hous-ing worked against the creation of a mass market with its need for standardization. The ties of each segment were with the central city rather than with each other so that the jour-ney-to-shop was either on a very local scale, with some small specialization in limited-appeal goods based on a restricted but soci-ally and economically homogeneous market focussed on an outlying shopping center, or a metropolitan scale which brought all journeys together in the central business district. Only there was mass selling possible. After 1945 the conditions in suburban areas were radi-cally changed. Vast areas of post-war housing grew up at the urban fringe and even though economic and social homogeneity held within individual development tracts these new resi-dential areas were joined together in being independent of pre-war patterns of shopping trips. The distance to the older outlying shop-ping centers was sufficient to impede the tying of the newer housing tracts to these places. As will be shown subsequently, local journey-to-shop movements are highly limited in dis-tance. For this reason new residential areas meant new shopping districts and the con-siderable mixing of tracts of contrasting socio-economic nature ruled out the creation of new shopping facilities on any but a mass base. The individual mobility provided by shopping by car and the increased size of tributary areas stemming from the joining of all classes of housing made the major regional center practicable when it had been imprac-ticable under mass transport and an economic segregation by area. A test of the contrast between the mass-appeal and limited-appeal shopping is provided by the fact that in the San Francisco Bay Area only three limited-appeal types of shops have grown greater growth in sales in the central business district than in the suburbs (San Francisco CBD Bulletin, 1954).

In general terms, we may say that the lower the position of a shopping district in the hierarchy of commercial centers the smaller will be its tributary area and the greater its domination by mass-appeal goods. Even though the central business district is the largest seller of standardized merchandise, it is less dominated by uniformity of goods than are the outlying centers. And it seems certain, though impossible to quantify at this time, that the central business district is changing from mass-selling to specialization to the extent that its importance today for the metropolis as a whole is that of a specialty shopping area. Just as the mass selling of food was removed from the core in the 1930's the mass selling of clothing is departing today, at least in terms of relative sales totals. Because of the broad nature of census classifications it is impossible from published statistics to test the trends in central business district sales between mass and specialty lines without an independent study. This should be undertaken but until it is, it may be conjectured that the bare maintenance of absolute sales volumes in the downtown area is the result of increasing specialty sales which counteract the decrease in mass sales. As specialty sales can never equal mass sales, the central business district has been unable to maintain its relative sales position.

William J. Reilly (1929) writing about the boundaries of trading areas concluded that retain centers attract customers in direct proportion to their relative population and in inverse proportion to the distance to each center. His "retail gravitation" is a charac-

teristic of any commercial district so we must ask whether these conclusions are valid for outlying centers as well as the central business districts he considered? The substantive part of this paper corroborates his findings with respect to the effect of distance but leads us to doubt that Reilly's formulation concerning population is applicable. Regional shopping centers in particular do require a minimum population but also appear to have a maximum supporting population due to the fact that an overly large trading area is quite susceptible to sub-division through the construction of a second, competing center. No doubt the density of population within the tributary area will affect the profitability of a center but any attempt to tie an unduly large area to a single center would probably be unsuccessful in the long run. Within the metropolitan area with dispersed selling of mass-appeal goods the concept of gravitation has been replaced by one of dismembering the market among equal and competing centers. Still unanswered is the degree of dissection possible, in other words, how small may the tributary area be?

If we accept that Reilly's concept of retail gravitation has been modified by the growth of the suburban integrated center, we are led to ask if the concept of equilibrium of location put forward by Lösch is also limited? Anticipating the answer, it should be noted that the generality of Lösch's ideas makes them fit the situation much more closely. His first condition of locational equilibrium notes that "The location for an individual must be as advantageous as possible" (Lösch, 1954, pp. 92-100). In retail location this has taken the form of dividing retail establishments into the two groups noted, the specialty shop in the core area necessarily dependent upon the entire metropolitan market, and the mass goods store, often combining several standardized merchandise lines, in outlying centers where proximity to the customers assures the maximum patronage from any given residential area. Locational advantage is quite a different thing for mass and specialty selling so that locations differ. The second condition of equilibrium that "The locations must be so numerous that the entire space is occupied" is borne out by the very proliferation of regional and other shopping centers. In the case of the highly specialized store at the core the limitation of profitability in condition 1 restricts location to a single central site. Lösch's third and fourth conditions are intimately interrelated in commercial location. In saying that "abnormal profits must disappear" (Condition 3) we imply in the case of tributary areas dominated by a single shopping center, usually with single establishments of a retail type, that "the areas . . . of sales must be as small as possible (Condition 4)". Otherwise, we would be hard put to explain why central department stores build branches as a single super-department-store at the core could yield a higher profit than a string of branches, where the fixed costs must be a greater part of the cost of selling. The situation is different in the case of specialty shops as a single central location does not produce an "abnormal profit." Any other location would most probably produce no profit. Lösch's fifth and final condition for locational equilibrium that "At the boundary of economic (tributary) areas it must be a matter of indifference to which of two neighboring locations they belong" requires that tributary areas be clearly defined. The study of San Francisco which follows suggests that in broad measure this condition is met in the case of outlying mass shopping centers by a segmentation of the suburban areas and in the case of specialty shopping in the central business district by the uniqueness of this area

within the metropolitan region. Thus, it appears that the present situation in a region highly developed with integrated shopping centers in outlying areas, such as the San Francisco Bay Area, is one of locational equilibrium under the current conditions of (1) residential distribution, (2) transportation, and (3) mass demand for goods.

The Commercial Structure of the San Francisco Bay Area

It is unfortunately impossible in the limited time available to dicuss the origin of the commercial structure of the Bay Area in any detail. This story is one affording interesting insights into the transformation of a primitive to an urban landscape in the course of one century. During this metamorphosis there was much rivalry among germinal cities for the commercial domination of the area but San Francisco was never seriously threatened in its leadership. One other city from the Mexican period, San Jose, and a latter day rival, Oakland, did manage a sufficient development by the time of the First World War to have their own central business districts. At that time these three foci of street railways were distinguished one from another mainly in terms of their degree of specialization, with San Francisco serving as the site of most of the limited-appeal goods shops and Oakland and San Jose as the site of mass selling alone. Each was tied to the surrounding area of residential towns by a well articulated street railway system and no adjacent commercial area could hope to compete in tapping the mass market. The five-mile-wide Bay, crossed at that time only by ferries, provided some protection to downtown Oakland's shopping area in relation to San Francisco, and San Jose was separated from San Francisco and Oakland by 45 miles of scattered residential and farm land. The Bay Area at the time of the First World War was an economic unit but not a morphological one (Figure 1).

A number of local shopping districts came into existence as residential land use spread onto the Berkeley Hills from the initial core in Oakland. At the place where the local street car lines in Berkeley came together at Shattuck Square shops were opened where those returning from work in Oakland and San Francisco could purchase perishable food daily. Here also the more commonly available dry goods and stock clothing items were on sale in a place which could easily be reached from all parts of the residential community. This pattern was reproduced in a number of places in the Bay Area where local street car routes came together and were connected to express routes to San Fran-

cisco. These major suburban business centers formed without any predetermined plan in Berkeley, on Alameda Island, and in East Oakland in the East Bay and at the more important stations on the suburban railroad south of San Francisco on The Peninsula. No one of them could assume a dominant position as the street car lines fed in only from the immediate vicinity. Each suburban center reflected the character of that vicinity so that there were book stores and young people's clothing stores adjacent to the University of California in Berkeley and Stanford University in Palo Alto, shopping areas for working class people in South San Francisco and Redwood City, and more expensive but not very specialized districts in Burlingame and San Mateo. This class orientation of outlying commercial districts reinforced the isolation imposed by a transit system joining all limbs together only at the city core. Under these conditions mass selling was possible only in the core.

There were many types of stores in the outlying business districts before the First World War because the unit size was small. But the diversity was actually within a narrow range controlled by a test of restricted local support. The supermarket of the present combines the goods of at least six independent shops at the turn of the century. The "specialization" found within the 1900 business district was primarily a function of minute division of a few staple lines among a number of family operated shops, not of a then smaller minimum for tributary areas. The assembling of formerly separate food and staple clothing lines into larger stores has been mainly to maximize profits rather than to carry the selling into smaller markets. Today the specialty food shop or narrowly stocked clothing store can exist only in central business districts or the largest shop-

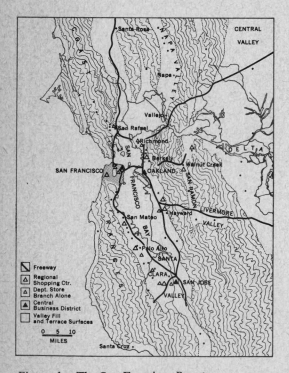

Figure 1. The San Francisco Bay Area.

ping centers where a volume of sales sufficient for profitable operation within a single type of sales can be secured.

Outside the major outlying business centers isolated store clusters and individual stores were widespread. These morphological forms were given over mainly to the selling of food as the absence of mechanical refrigeration made daily food shopping more necessary and the absence of individual transportation made easy access more important. The imposition of land use zoning ordinances since 1916 along with the introduction of refrigeration and automobiles has spelled the doom of many of these small commercial districts and has prevented their reproduction in new housing areas. Today there are fewer but larger business districts.

Throughout the years after the First World War the number of automobiles increased rapidly, particularly so in California which early became and still remains the site of the world's highest per capita automobile ownership. Today there is one car for more than every second Californian. For some time after automobile ownership became common in the 1920's there seems to have been little change in the commercial pattern. The lag between the gaining of individual transportation and its impact on shopping resulted from the inherited residential patterns. As long as people lived where the street car had put them, the pattern of commerce inherited from that era continued. But with the rapid growth of residential areas in what had formerly been open land, which took place to a small degree before the Second World War and to a much larger degree after the war, new commercial areas had to be developed. Only then could the revised location factors operate. To understand the revision we must appreciate that (1) population densities in the center of the Bay Area, and

of cities in general, have tended to decrease, (2) the newer housing here as elsewhere was built in areas without preexisting commercial districts as the typical pattern of post-war housing developments was one of massive tracts of residence placed in formerly farming land rather than concentric additions to older towns, (3) the distance from the newer residences to the central business district was very much greater than for the housing they replaced, and (4) particularly in California there was no attempt to locate housing tracts so that mass transit could be used, which enforced an automobile journey-to-shop. Under these conditions there was a loosening of the ties of the growth element of the population with the central business district. The people left in the heart of the city were mostly the young childless or the elderly. This fact in itself helps to explain the exchange of functions between central and outlying business districts as the mass market tends to fall between these two age extremes. In California, and in other sections of the United States where suburban development has been on a large scale in recent years, the developers of residential tracts commonly included in their plans what we have called neighborhood business centers even during the initial phase of suburbanization but in the beginning there was little realization that more was needed. The neighborhood center was essentially an updated version of the staple goods business centers which had been in pre-war towns. What was needed in addition was the projection of the mass selling component of central business district activities to this new mass market now far removed from the core. For the five years between 1945 and 1950 a situation of locational "disequilibrium" existed. A very rough measure of this is the fact that between 1945 and 1950 all retail sales increased by 96 per cent whereas for department stores alone, which were then largely in downtown areas, the increase was only 36 per cent. Between 1951 and 1955 total retail sales and department stores sales showed a closer correspondence in their increase, 17 and 11 per cent respectively. During this period the disequilibrium of concentrating department stores in the downtown area was considerably overcome by the building of branches in the regional shopping centers.

In this context we may view the building of regional shopping centers as a restoration of equilibrium, which between 1939 and 1950 was lacking because of changed settlement and transportation patterns but unchanged commercial patterns. For an answer to what sort of commercial pattern has emerged in the decade of the 'fifties we may turn to the San Francisco Bay Area where evidence is strong that adjustment has been restored.

Due to the absence of separate data on retail trade within the central business district before 1948 it is impossible to trace earlier changes in the relative position of the district and outlying shopping centers. In the period 1948 - 1954, while the San Francisco-Oakland Standard Metropolitan Area was experiencing the most rapid growth of any large city (over 500,000 population) metropolitan region, an increase of 53.3 per cent, the central business district of San Francisco remained completely stable in its retail sales (1948=$408 million and 1954 =$410 million). The relative loss is apparent, resulting in a decrease for the central business district from 18 to 14 per cent of the metropolitan total of sales. Oakland's central business district differs only in having suffered an absolute loss during this six year period from $187 million to $182 million. Only San Jose, in the burgeoning Santa Clara Valley, experienced a rise in central sales,

from $96 million in 1948 to $115 million in 1954. Thus, out of a total of $2,579 million sales in the two SMA's (San Francisco-Oakland and San Jose) in 1948 the three central business districts accounted for $691 million or 27 per cent. In 1954 the total sales of the two SMA's were $3,418 million with $707 milion or 21 per cent in the three central business districts.

It is apparent from the diminution of sales, both absolutely, in terms of constant dollars, and relatively, in terms of percentage contribution, that the post-war commercial development in the Bay Area has been peripheral. This has been particularly true with respect to department stores. San Jose's central business district has no true department store and those in Oakland cannot be assessed because of the Census "disclosure rule" but in downtown San Francisco the department stores dropped in sales, measured in constant dollars, from $98 million to $94 million in the period 1948 - 1954.

Prior to the end of the Second World War there were no integrated regional shopping centers in the Bay Area. The only department stores outside the central business districts were a single "A type" Sears Roebuck store in each of the two core cities and a much larger Montgomery Ward store in their branch mail order plant in Oakland. Each of these was a product of the initial stages of the mail order companies' expansion into retail operation after 1927. The three were outside the central business district but sufficiently close to it so their position was not truly outlying. Only the Montgomery Ward store was above the minimum of 100,000 square feet established in the late 'forties as the size for outlying stores. At the time of construction the fact that these stores were built by mail order houses caused most observers to conclude that their construction represented no strong trend away from the central business district in mass selling operations.

When the pent up demand for housing engendered by the rapid growth of the Bay Area metropolis during the Second World War could be met after 1945 there was a five year lag in commercial construction, thus, the figures for retail trade in 1948 may be thought fairly typical of the summit of central business district trading. Between 1948 and 1954 the San Francisco and Oakland central shopping areas had a ten per cent drop in sales measured in constant dollars. At the same time the retail trade of the whole metropolis increased 15 per cent in constant dollars.

The increase in the mass selling of goods other than food has obviously tended to concentrate in the regional shopping centers and the larger community centers. Of the regional shopping centers the first to be completed was the Stonestown center in the southwestern section of the city of San Francisco. This location within the central city is unusual and resulted largely from the construction in the area of two large "high-rise" apartment developments, both oriented toward middle and upper income groups. In addition, this area, though served by a long street car tunnel connecting to the San Francisco central business district, was rather isolated by the high range of hills forming the spine of the San Francisco Peninsula all the way to its culmination at the Golden Gate. At the present time this center receives a surprising part of its patronage from pedestrians and street car riders, quite in contrast to the conditions in other outlying shopping centers. In many ways Stonestown Center represents a rather tentative initial experiment in the decentralization of mass selling, to a point outside the core but not outside the central city. This

center has been set up to care for the needs of a prosperous area in the central city and its patronage is largely restricted to city dwellers as is shown by the map of tributary areas. Stonestown has succeeded in the eight years it has been open in developing a total of sales approximately one-tenth as large as the San Francisco central business district.

Before continuing, the origin of the data used to evaluate the tributary areas of outlying centers should be discussed. In undertaking the analysis of the relative functions of regional and central business districts it is of critical importance to discover the form and size of areas tributary to each type and to individual regional centers. The transitional nature of a center such as Stonestown makes it necessary for us to determine whether it is functionally in the group with integrated regional centers or more precisely an adjunct of the city's central business district. In the case of the central business district numerous studies of San Francisco and other large cities have shown that patronage is metropolitan-wide in origin, though demonstrating a concentration of staple goods customers within the closer residential areas. Thus, we may generalize to the extent of saying that the metropolitan core has the entire metropolis as its tributary area. In the case of the regional center data have been lacking for any comparison among centers.

To overcome the absence of reliable data with which to compare regional centers a sample of the registration number plates of cars parked in the customer parking spaces of the eleven regional centers of the Bay Area was carried out between December, 1958, and August, 1959. In addition, similar samples were secured from two community shopping centers, two independent branch department stores, and six of the older outlying shopping districts which were established before the period of integrated development. In preliminary tests a sample was taken five or six times during the last three days of the shopping week to determine any differences in residence pattern among shoppers visiting centers at different times. But careful analysis suggested that there is no appreciable divergence among the patterns on the basis of time. Thus, for nine of the regional centers and the majority of the other classes of commercial districts the data stem from a single sample time. The size of the sample varied between 100 and 500 registrations depending upon the size of the commercial district. The total sample contained approximately 5,000 registrations for which the owner's address was secured on IBM punch cards from the Registry of Motor Vehicles of the State of California. This was necessitated by the fact that there is no areal assignment of registrations in California and the total number of automobile registrations currently exceeds seven million. When the punch cards were sorted by the commercial district where the registered automobile was found parked and by political sub-division of the owner's residence the location of the residence was plotted by street address on large scale maps, one for each center. The tributary areas for the places derived from this plotting of residence of shoppers are presented in somewhat generalized form on the figures 2 - 4. Before discussing the findings it should be noted that although care was taken to avoid "sampling" cars parked by employees or salesmen visiting the center their exclusion was not completely successful. The inability to exclude also implies the inability to measure the inclusion. With some knowledge based on the multiple-time samples, however, it seems probable that the area of labor-shed is coterminous with the normal tributary area and the number of em-

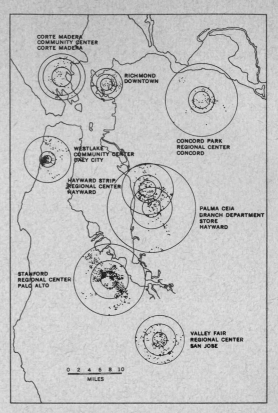

Figure 2. The trading area for shopping centers in the San Francisco Bay Area. The spacing of concentric circles is established so that each successive circle encloses one quarter of the total shoppers using the center. Data derived from parking surveys, 1958-1959.

ployee cars should not exceed three per cent of the total. It also seems that the degree of refinement afforded by larger samples is not worth the labor and considerable expense. A sample of 300 cars for a regional shopping center appeared adequate to apportion by residence location the shoppers at the center.

If the assumption is made, as here, that the dynamics of urban commercial structure is comprised of differing degrees of locational and commodity specialization, then it follows that to test this hypothesis we must consider

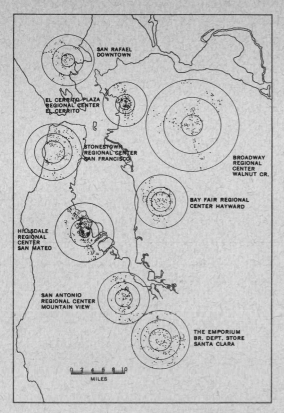

Figure 3. The trading area for shopping centers in the San Francisco Bay Area. The spacing of concentric circles is established so that each successive circle encloses one quarter of the total of shoppers using the center. Data derived from parking surveys, 1958-1959.

(1) the nature, size, and hierarchical relations of areas tributary to the several types of commercial center, and (2) the number and diversity of commercial establishments within these same types of commercial district.

A tool for establishing the characteristics of tributary areas has been developed through the registration sample method described. Table II summarizes the information secured from this sample. The most notable result of this investigation is quantification of the radial extent of the tributary area. Within the

21 places investigated, regional shopping centers, community shopping centers, "free-standing" stores, and older business districts, there are 16 department store branches (all but two with 100,000 square feet or more) whose aggregate sales are approximately $130 million, a total which is essentially equivalent to the total sales in department stores in the central business districts of San Francisco and Oakland. Thus, in the fifteen years since 1945 there has been a doubling of the sales of department stores but the entire increase has come in outlying branches. Sharply contrasting with the great increase in sales at the periphery is the narrowing of the tributary base there. Most certainly San Francisco, and to a lesser degree Oakland, in the pre-war years tapped the whole metropolis. In the regional centers and free-standing department stores two-thirds of the customers come from within a tributary area which extends no farther than 4.5 to 5.5 miles from the commercial place. As might be anticipated, an even greater concentration of

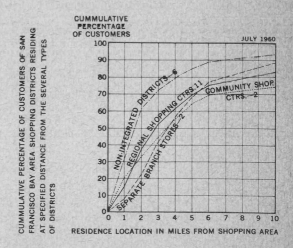

Figure 4. Cumulative percentage of customers of San Francisco Bay Area shopping districts residing at specified distance from the several types of districts.

TABLE II

Distribution of Customer's Residences by Distance Zones from Various Commercial Areas

Type of Commercial Area	Estimated Annual Sales	Per Cent of Total Number of Customers Residing Within Band (in miles)							
		0.00—0.99	1.00—1.99	2.00—2.99	3.00—3.99	4.00—4.99	5.00—5.99	6.00—9.99	10.00—
Regional Centres (11)									
"Stonestown" (1952) San Francisco	$42,000,000	15.64	16.94	14.98	9.78	10.42	7.82	3.57	20.85
"Hillsdale" (1955) San Mateo	60,000,000	21.60	19.40	12.10	8.60	8.40	6.20	13.70	10.00
"Broadway" (1955) Walnut Creek	25,000,000	7.98	15.54	10.08	10.08	2.52	5.46	13.86	34.45
"Stanford" (1956) Palo Alto	40,000,000	14.00	27.60	18.40	8.60	11.20	7.00	9.90	2.90
"Valley Fair" (1956) San Jose	15,000,000	14.22	17.99	18.83	10.04	7.95	5.44	9.63	15.90
"Bay Fair" (1956) San Leandro	20,000,000	11.56	21.33	16.45	11.12	8.00	6.22	7.56	17.78
"San Antonio" (1957) Mountain View	17,000,000	15.60	31.90	10.60	20.50	6.30	6.30	6.30	2.10
"Hayward Strip" (1957) Hayward	30,000,000	14.54	23.79	16.74	7.44	7.04	7.05	4.40	19.38
"Concord Park" (1957) Concord	22,000,000	6.92	34.62	13.08	3.85	5.39	3.85	6.93	25.38
"El Cerrito Plaza" (1959) El Cerrito	25,000,000	26.06	23.51	11.54	5.56	7.69	7.26	5.32	13.25
"Palma Ceia" (1958) Hayward	unknown	10.82	17.75	14.28	9.52	6.49	4.76	11.26	25.11

Separate Branches (2)

"Emporium" (1958) Santa Clara	6,500,000	8.29	12.90	16.59	17.51	9.67	9.67	9.21	16.13
"Sears Roebuck" San Jose	14,000,000	7.90	15.80	23.30	12.00	14.20	9.30	13.50	5.60

Community Centers (2)

"Westlake" (Daly City)	—	27.51	15.34	10.59	11.11	6.87	4.24	8.99	15.34
"Corte Madera" (Corte Madera)	—	13.23	10.29	12.50	12.50	8.83	6.62	0.00	36.03

Non-Intgr. Older Ctrs. (6)

Burlingame		45.70	35.50	8.40	5.00	1.70	3.40	1.70	0.00
San Mateo		38.00	22.00	13.00	3.00	4.00	8.00	8.00	4.00
Redwood City		32.70	36.00	8.20	6.50	3.20	4.80	6.40	1.60
Palo Alto		32.30	41.50	7.70	3.00	12.30	3.00	0.00	0.00
Richmond		21.97	28.03	16.67	6.07	6.82	2.27	3.79	14.39
San Rafael		19.72	18.30	11.27	17.60	4.93	2.11	4.93	21.13

Average Percentage Values by Class of Commercial Area

Regional Centers		15.21	22.76	14.28	9.55	7.40	6.12	8.40	17.01
Separate Branches		8.10	14.35	19.94	13.76	11.94	9.49	11.36	10.87
Community Centers		20.37	12.82	11.55	11.81	7.85	5.43	4.49	25.69
Non-Intgr. Older Ctrs.		31.73	30.22	10.87	6.86	5.49	3.93	4.14	6.85
All Types of Areas		18.85	20.04	14.16	10.50	8.17	6.24	7.10	15.11

customers is found for the older noninte-grated outlying business areas. The restriction of suburban tributary areas is highly signifi-cant in relation to Lösch's conditions of equilibrium of location, particularly the condition that sales areas will be reduced to the minimum (constantly sub-divided by new sales places) and the condition of indiffer-ence at the boundaries. The mean spacing of centers one from another, within the Bay Area, is 8 miles and the median spacing is 9 miles. The correspondence between the radial extent of tributary areas and one-half the mean and median spacing is worthy of em-phasis. Also this relationship supports the belief that the boundaries do represent re-markable "indifference lines" as positted by Lösch in a condition of locational equili-brium. The fact that half the customers, on the average, come from within three miles of the center supports the contention that the socio-economic character of this immediately adjacent area must be directly reflected in the composition of the establishments in the center, and even more significantly, that with-in such a limited trading area all possible patronage must be secured. Mass selling alone would make this possible. With so small a base a partial market would be uneconomic. This is the most significant contrast between the central business district and the outlying center. The core draws widely but selectively whereas the shopping center draws narrowly but necessarily as completely as possible. The outlying center does not, in any meaningful way, replace the core *as a unit* despite the fact that it may nearly completely replace it *with respect to individual establishments or individual lines of selling*.

It should be noted that the areal extent of tributary areas differs with the spacing of the centers. In the case of centers more removed than average from competition

(Walnut Creek) the percentage contribution from the inner ring of customer residence is less. This condition supports the belief that the parcelling of the metropolitan market among centers is effectively one of mutual exclusion. If we consider the number of dis-crete locations where department stores or their branches exist within the Bay Area, 20 places, in relation to the total population of the whole region, we discover that an equal sharing of the population would result in an exclusive tributary area for each department store of 180,000. The average population within five miles of the 11 regional shopping centers is 237,000 but the range among in-dividuals is great. Stonestown within San Francisco itself has 640,000 people within five miles while the shopping center at Con-cord at the very edge of the metropolis has no more than 82,000 people within five miles. Despite this great difference in population, the two centers have 69 and 64 per cent of their patronage from within five miles. In general terms the volume of sales at a region-al center increases as the density of popula-tion in its vicinity increases but its attraction at a distance does not appear to be greatly enhanced. All regional centers are primarily of local importance.

Turning to the establishment content of regional centers, which provides the obverse view to the size of tributary area in evaluating commercial location theory, it is possible to analyze a recent inventory of outlying shop-ping centers issued in 1959 by the *San Fran-cisco Examiner* (1959). Table III contains the totals of establishments, by type, found in the 150 integrated centers of all sorts within the Bay Area. Of these, 11 are regional cen-ters, 15 community centers, and 124 neigh-borhood centers. Recasting this simple in-ventory to correspond with the classification of commercial establishments used by

TABLE III

Number of Integrated Centers in the San Francisco Bay Area with Specified Types of Establishments

Type of Establishment	No. of Centers	Type of Establishment	No. of Centers
Supermarket	147	Furniture store	18
Cleaning and laundry shop	120	Confectionery store	17
Barber or beauty shop	119	Music store	17
Drug store	113	Post office	15
Variety store	96	Sporting goods and hobby shop	15
Restaurant or bar	95	Stationery store	14
Hardware or paint store	77	Weight reducing shop	13
Bakery or doughnut shop	66	Auto accessory store	12
Liquor store	66	Department store branch	12
Women's apparel store	64	Junior department store	12
Service station	54	Pet shop	10
Insurance or real estate off.	54	Family clothing store	8
Shoe store	52	Bowling or amusement	7
Jewelry store	41	Sewing machine sales store	7
Bank branch	41	Book store	5
Children's clothing store	40	Public Library branch	4
Yardage, yarn, rugs	39	Stockbroker's office	4
Shoe repair shop	36	Movie theatre	2
Men's apparel store	33	Employment agency office	2
Appliance or TV store	33	Automobile sales establishment	2
Gift shop	31	Automobile washing establishment	2
Medical or dental office	29	Trailer rental agency	1
Offices not otherwise counted	25	Office equipment store	1
Toy shop	24	Newspaper publication office	1
Camera and photography shop	23	Lawn mower repair shop	1
Loan or finance office	20	Church	1
Nursery or florist shop	20		
Optician office	19	*The total number of centers of all*	
Food specialty shop	19	*types was*	*150*

Murphy and Vance (1955. Appendix B) in the study of American central business districts we may compare the overall content of outlying and core shopping districts. Important contrasts show up in the percentage of the total space used for retail and service trades in the two types of commercial district and in the nature of the retail and service components. In the nine central business districts only 40 per cent of the total floor space was given over to retail and service space whereas in the 145 outlying centers over 95 per cent of the space was in retail and service uses. The office, transient residence, public and organizational, and manufacturing and industrial components of the central districts are little represented, with transient residence unrepresented in outlying centers and the other non-retail and service elements virtually absent. In the retail group food stores take up nearly three times as much space in the outlying centers as in the core even though restaurants fall within this class in both places. Household goods sales space is nearly twice as large in the downtown districts as in the outlying business areas mainly because of the large number and large size of downtown furniture stores. This class of establishment is unusual in integrated centers because of its low "rent-paying" character. The fact that automotive districts are part of the core area and usually separate in the suburbs accounts for the contrast between downtown and exterior with six times as much space used at the center. Miscellaneous sales, the group that includes most of the non-clothing specialty shops, is three times as large proportionally in the central business district as in shopping centers. Variety store space is 60 per cent larger in proportion to total retail and service space in the outlying areas mainly because of the great dominance

of department store branches in the larger integrated centers.

Within the eleven regional centers the department store branch is notably dominant, accounting for 45 per cent of all space. Apparel and shoe stores rank next with 15 per cent of regional center space. Other types of commodity-combining stores, mainly variety and drug stores, account for 13 per cent of the regional center space so that nearly three-quarters of all the floor space in these large planned facilities is taken up with mass-selling stores merchandising fashion but not "high-style" clothing, non-durable household goods, and small durable household items. Food stores are much less important in regional as opposed to all outlying centers comprising only 11 per cent of the space in the

TABLE IV

Average Size of Establishments, by Type, for 150 Centers in the San Francisco Bay Area

Establishment Types	Aver. Size	Establishment Types	Aver. Size
Department store	155,133	Liquor store	1,787
Junior department store	29,774	Stationery store	1,684
Bowling or amusement pl.	23,913	Yardage, rug, or yarn	1,621
Supermarket	13,905	Music store	1,554
Furniture store	11,542	Gift shop	1,438
Automobile washing estab.	9,368	Camera or photography shop	1,269
Variety store	8,664	Appliance or TV store	1,265
Bank branch	4,900	Food specialty store	1,184
Drug store	4,476	Bakery or doughnut shop	1,137
Women's apparel store	3,652	Loan or finance offices	1,134
Men's apparel store	2,910	Insurance or real estate	1,129
Shoe Store	2,861	Confectionery store	1,122
Hardware or paint store	2,819	Jewellery store	1,115
Auto accessory store	2,600	Cleaning or laundry store	1,098
Post Office	2,454	Book store	1,045
Toy shop	2,268	Family clothing store	969
Sporting goods or hobby	2,180	Pet shop	820
Restaurant or bar	2,162	Barber or beauty shop	738
Children's clothing store	2,044	Shoe repair shop	596

Average size is given in square feet of rented building space
Source: *San Francisco Examiner* (1959).

larger centers. In number of establishments rather than size apparel stores are dominant with a quarter of all shops. Food stores make up 15 per cent, shoe stores 12 per cent, and

APPORTIONMENT OF SPACE BY MAJOR LAND USE TYPES IN NINE CENTRAL BUSINESS DISTRICTS IN THE UNITED STATES AND ELEVEN OUTLYING INTEGRATED SHOPPING CENTRES IN THE SAN FRANCISCO BAY AREA OF CALIFORNIA

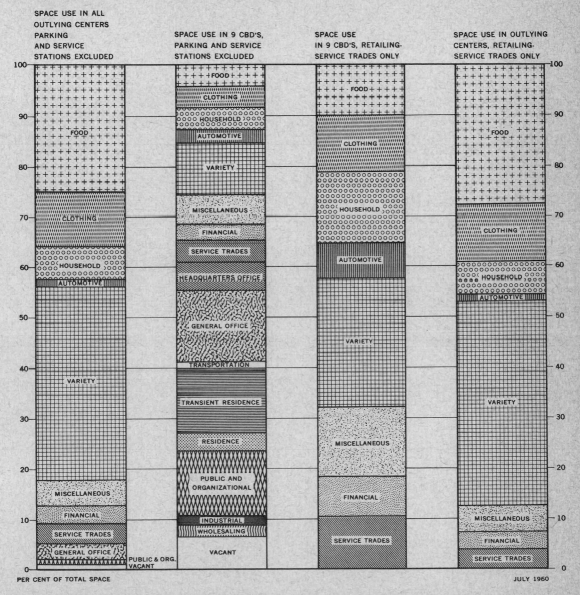

Figure 5. Apportionment of space by major land use types in nine central business districts in the United States and eleven outlying integrated shoppng centers in the San Francisco Bay Area.

service trades shops such as barber and beauty shops, shoe repair, and laundry-dry cleaning stores are numerous. Only medical and dental professional offices are at all numerous and there are very few general offices. Each center has but a single department store, much as it usually accounts for half the floor space in the center.

The outlying center, even in the case of regional centers, is a place for selling highly standardized and rapidly disposed of goods to a local market. Within the service trades only most commonly sought personal and clothing services are found and there is no appreciable amount of business or office service. Financial services are restricted to personal loan companies, small branch banks, and a few stock broker's branch offices, along with a great number of real estate and insurance offices aimed at the youthful and home-buying inhabitants.

Conclusions

The purpose of this paper has been three-fold: (1) to consider briefly what factors have in the past influenced the location and nature of American commercial districts, (2) to undertake to formulate the general location factors affecting commercial development today, and (3) to test this formulation against actual conditions in the highly diversified commercial structure of the Bay Area.

Throughout the history of commercial development in the United States there has been a constant effort to develop economically viable units of selling as close to the residence of customers as possible. If we relate this effort to Lösch's five conditions of equilibrium, we may say that there has been a continuing reduction in the size of trading areas to the point that we seem to have reached the minimum size economic area in the case of

mass selling with the regional shopping center. It seems probable under the conditions of automotive transportation that much reduction in the size of tributary areas from that presently encountered in a region such as the Bay Area would result in unprofitable operations.

The consequence of this progressive contraction of trading areas, or dispersion of selling, has been that only mass demands for goods can be met within the basic (suburban) trading areas. This is fully demonstrated by the absence of specialty selling on this local level. The emerging pattern of commercial geography in the United States is the separation of mass selling from specialty selling with the removal of the former from the central business district save for that part which serves the local population within the central city. The result is that the expansion of sales, and the consequent morphological growth which we would anticipate from expanding population, has occurred at the periphery where the condition of minimum tributary area for each sales place would dictate the siting of increments to the commercial structure.

The central business district will continue to exist but shorn of much of its former purpose. A growing body of urbanists in the United States views the core as a place of office rather than of large stores. The focus of metropolitan arteries along with the functional convenience of geographical integration for offices tend to maintain the financial sub-district at the core. This focus is in some places being reinforced by the introduction of rapid transit which meets the needs of the office district. But in the case of the retail sub-district mass transit appears to hold much less promise. Shoppers at most visit the downtown infrequently and prefer the flexibility of driving to shop. The result is that the "best location" for the specialty shops which remain in the core is away from the focus of the journey-to-work in offices with its congestion and preëmpted parking. Although this is not the place, much study should be given to the contrast between the two downtown functions, a contrast which appears to introduce two rather divergent trends within the core to the extent that today the two parts may be "pulling apart" in location to be separated by a band of parking facilities severing the two. If this trend continues, the single focus which has in the past characterized the core will be lost and we may find ourselves a generation from now restricting the term central business district to the office area and coining a new name, perhaps metropolitan specialty district, for what we still by tradition consider the downtown business district.

In sum it seems that the central business district has become the mass seller to the inner part of the metropolis, the specialty seller to the geographical city, and the office area for the region. In turn, the regional integrated center has become the mass seller to the individual suburb alone, with no other important function, And through this change

it seems that there has been an adjustment to the urban dynamics of transportation and settlement which has restored locational equilibrium in commercial structure after two decades of instability and doubt.

References

[1] Emmet and Jeuck, *Catalogues and Counters* (Chicago, 1950).

[2] Hoyt, H., "Classification and Significant Characteristics of Shopping Centers," *Appraisal Journal* (April, 1958).

[3] Lösch, A., *The Economics of Location*, trans. by W. H. Woglom (New Haven, 1954).

[4] Murphy, R. E. and Vance, J. E. Jr., *Central Business District Studies* (Worcester, 1955).

[5] Proudfoot, M., "City Retail Structure," *Economic Geography*, Vol. XIII (1937).

[6] Reilly, W. J., "Methods for the Study of Retail Relationships," University of Texas, *Bureau of Business Research*, Research Monograph No. 4 (1929).

[7] San Francisco CBD Bulletin, *Census of Business* (1954).

[8] *San Francisco Examiner*. Unified Shopping Centers, San Francisco Bay Market Area, 1959 (San Francisco, 1959).

[9] U.S. Bureau of the Census, *Retail Trade Bulletins* (1929, 1954).

21

The Management Center in the United States

William Goodwin

In the literature on the classification of cities little or no attention has been given to management per se or to management centers. A recent bibliography of central-place studies,[1] which lists the significant studies of tertiary activities, does not contain among its more than five hundred entries a single reference explicitly to management centers; and neither this work nor the extensive bibliographies in Isard's "Methods of Regional Analysis"[2] make any mention of management functions.

Among the better-known functional classifications of cities, none appears to regard management as a separate function. Harris[3] states that his classification "is based on the

activity of greatest importance in each city." Functional importance, in the Harris classification, is measured mainly by the number of people employed in each industry. Harris recognizes nine classes of cities but does not include management among their activities.

More recently, Nelson has also presented a functional classification of American cities,[4] based, like Harris's, on United States census categories. Although Nelson includes a wider range of activities than Harris, he makes no mention of management as a separate category. Alexandersson,[5] in his comprehensive analysis of the functional role of American cities, which utilizes the concepts of "city forming" and "city serving," evidently does not regard management as either and therefore does not include it in the classification. Hart's study of the cities of the American

[1] Brian J. L. Berry and Allan Pred, "Central Place Studies: A Bibliography of Theory and Applications," *Bibliography Ser. No. 1*, (Philadelphia, Regional Science Research Institute, 1961).

[2] Walter Isard, *Methods of Regional Analysis* (Cambridge, Mass., New York and London, 1960).

[3] Chauncy D. Harris, "A Functional Classification of Cities in the United States," *Geogr. Rev.*, Vol. XXXIII (1943), pp. 86-99; reference on p. 86.

[4] Howard J. Nelson, "A Service Classification of American Cities," *Econ. Geogr.*, Vol. XXXI (1955), pp. 189-210.

[5] Gunnar Alexandersson, *The Industrial Structure of American Cities* (Lincoln, Nebr., and Stockholm, 1956).

Adapted from *Geographical Review*, Vol. LV, no. 1 (1965), pp. 1-16. Copyrighted by the America Geographical Society of New York. Reprinted by permission.

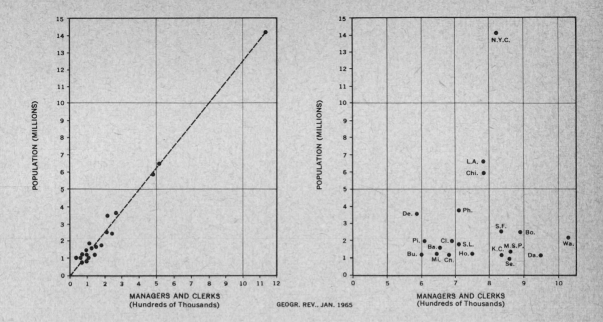

GEOGR. REV., JAN. 1965

Figure 1. Managers (except farm managers) and clerks in relation to total population for the twenty largest urbanized areas in the United States. Source: 1960 Census of Population and 1958 Census of Manufactures.

South[6] follows the general pattern set by Harris; it likewise makes no mention of the importance of management and fails to identify any city as a management center.

In "Metropolis and Region" Duncan and his associates classify standard metropolitan areas with 300,000 inhabitants or more in 1950 into seven categories according to "metropolitan functions and regional relationships."[7] Although these investigators did

---

[6] John Fraser Hart, "Functions and Occupational Structures of Cities of the American South," *Annals Assn. of Amer. Geogrs.*, Vol. XLV (1955), pp. 269-86.

[7] Otis Dudley Duncan and others, *Metropolis and Region* (Baltimore, 1960), pp. 259-75. The seven categories are as follows: National Metropolis (N); Regional Metropolis (R); Regional Capital, Submetropolitan (C); Manufacturing, three classes (D, D-, and M); and

Figure 2. Managers (except farm managers) and clerks per 100,000 workers in relation to population for the twenty largest urbanized areas in the United States. Key: N.Y.C., New York City; L.A., Los Angeles; Chi., Chicago; De., Detroit; Ph., Philadelphia; Pi., Pittsburgh; Bu., Buffalo; Mi., Milwaukee; Ba., Baltimore; Cn., Cincinnati; Cl., Cleveland; S.L., St. Louis; Ho., Houston; K.C., Kansas City; Se., Seattle; M.-St.P., Minneapolis-St. Paul; S.F., San Francisco; Bo., Boston; Da., Dallas; W., Washington, D.C. The horizontal scale has been expanded to permit clarity in reading the graph. Source: 1960 Census of Population; 1958 Census of Manufactures.

not consider management as such, their grouping of the SMA's appears to correspond closely with the grouping resulting from the work presented in this paper.

The omission of management in the classifications reviewed above is readily explained

---

Special Cases (S). These are based on a scattergram that plots per capita value added by manufacture against per capita wholesale sales; the third dimension of population is indicated by the size of the circle (pp. 264 and 271).

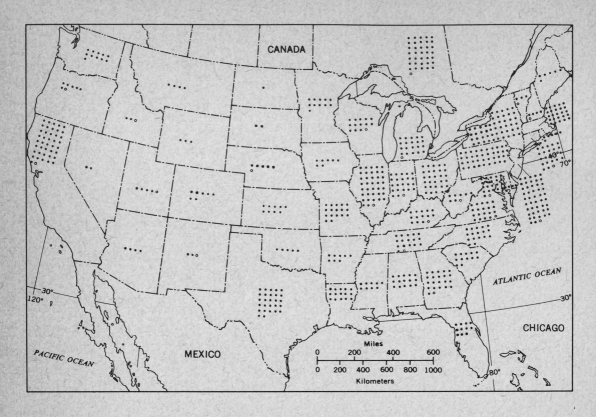

Figure 3. The number of companies, by states, whose headquarters offices are located in New York. A solid dot represents two plants; a circle, one plant. Source: *Moody's Industrials,* 1962; *Thomas' Register of American Manufacturers,* 1961.

by the fact that their basis was the most important "function" as measured by employment. By this criterion the number of people engaged in management is not large enough to be of significance. Moreover, although it is possible to extract "managers" from the census data, the category is too inclusive to be satisfactory. In any case, it is questionable whether or not employment is a proper measure of management activities.

It is hoped that the present paper may contribute toward filling the gap in the literature by identifying the cities in which management is important. Admittedly, the methods used are not wholly satisfactory, but it is believed that they are a step in the right direction.

Management and Management Centers

Management is an idea-handling, not a materials-handling, function, and as such it is somewhat intangible. Vernon[8] points out that "whereas manufacturing, transportation, retail trade, and wholesale trade are economic activities whose existence is easily

[8] Raymond Vernon, "The Changing Economic Function of the Central City," *Supplementary Paper No. 1,* Area Development Committee of CED; Committee for Economic Development (New York, 1959), p. 55.

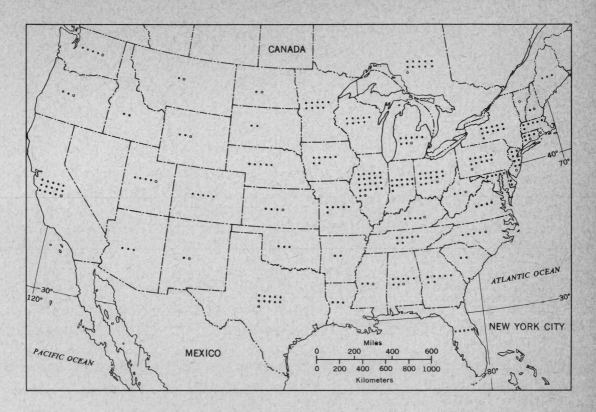

Figure 4. The number of companies, by states, whose headquarters offices are located in Chicago. A solid dot represents two plants; a circle, one plant. Source: *Moody's Industrials,* 1962; *Thomas' Register of American Manufacturers,* 1961.

recognized and catalogued, many aspects of office activity are more difficult to classify." Managerial operations are office activities if nothing else. As part of the national and local urban scene, managers, the offices they occupy, and the distribution of these offices invite investigation.

Vernon also observes:[9] "To the extent that the office function grows, therefore, the growth may well occur to a disproportionate extent in the office districts of the *larger central cities,* at the expense of the regional

[9] Vernon, *op. cit.,* p. 60. Italics are the present writer's.

centers. The possibility [is] that only the largest cities may be the principal benefici- aries of continued office growth — indeed, . . . they may be the only beneficiaries." If, as it appears, office functions and, particularly, the headquarters offices of nationally impor- tant companies are to continue to gravitate to the already existing office centers, it is per- tinent to establish which are the presently important cities.

In the past twenty years the electronic com- puter has grown from a curiosity to a much- used tool of management. Many routine decisions are programmed for electronic com- puters; many data are processed by punch

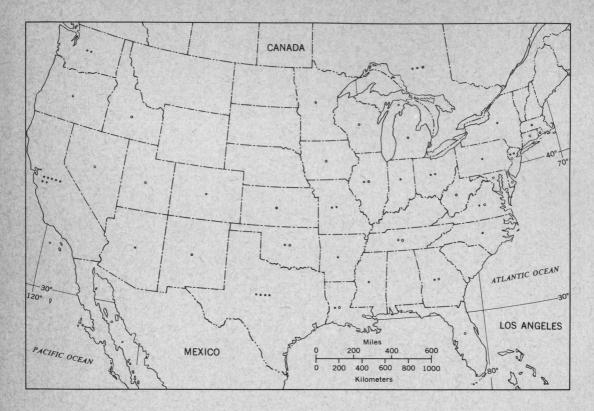

Figure 5.   The number of companies, by states, whose headquarters offices are located in Los Angeles. A solid dot represents two plants; a circle, one plant. Source: *Moody's Industrials,* 1962; *Thomas' Register of American Manufacturers,* 1961.

cards rather than by pencil, paper, and desk calculators. This "revolution" has reduced the number of clerks needed to prepare the raw materials for decision making. The change now taking place in the mechanics of decision making may have either of two opposite results with respect to the location of management centers. On the one hand, the reduction in the number of employees needed to staff a headquarters office may hasten the concentration of decision making in a few locations; on the other hand, it may well mean dispersion of headquarters because of the flexibility of data flows through a computer. At the moment it is not clear just what effect the rapid introduction of electronic data

processing will have on the concentration of office functions, but one must be aware of its great potential for changing the pattern of "office" cities.

Although the making of decisions is the function of only a very small part of the American labor force, the influence of the decision makers on the social and economic welfare of the nation is enormous. The day-to-day decisions of the executives of the largest businesses, together with the decisions made in Washington, D.C., determine the course of economic events in the country — and, to no small degree, in the rest of the world as well.

A management center may therefore be

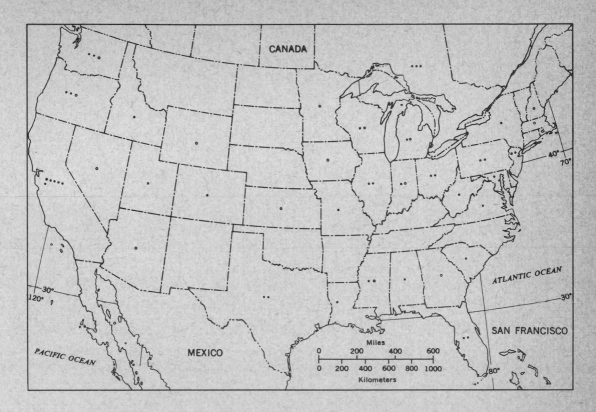

Figure 6. The number of companies, by states, whose headquarters offices are located in San Francisco. A solid dot represents two plants; a circle, one plant. Source: *Moody's Industrials,* 1962; *Thomas' Register of American Manufacturers,* 1961.

defined as a city in which there is a *concentration of headquarters offices of nationally important companies*. It is a place apart from the production centers. The people identified as "managers" are those who sell their managerial talents irrespective of the nature of the company that employs them. A management center is a reservoir of managerial talent available for hire.

Management and Population

New York City would unquestionably be accorded the position of prime management center of the United States, but which other cities exhibit the same general characteristics as New York?

Intuitively, and probably by common assumption, the relative importance of a city as a business-management center is considered to have a more or less positive linear relation to the size of its population. The most readily available measure of management would be the count of managers and clerks made by the census. Figure 1 plots the total number of managers and clerks for the twenty largest (according to population) urbanized areas of the United States against the populations. Clearly a straight-line relationship exists.

However, when the relation of managers and clerks to all other workers is calculated and the result plotted against the population (Figure 2), no such straight-line relationship

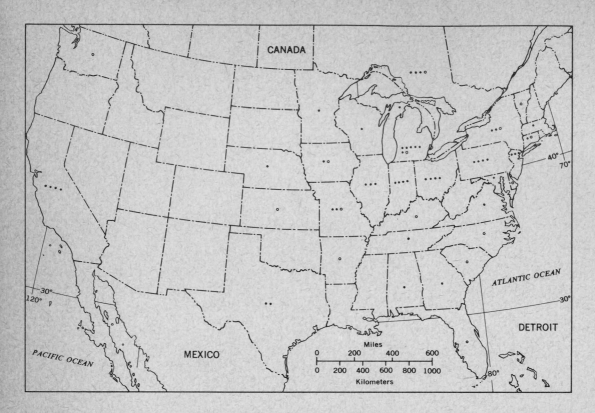

Figure 7. The number of companies, by states, whose headquarters offices are located in Detroit. A solid dot represents two plants; a circle, one plant. Source: *Moody's Industrials,* 1962; *Thomas' Register of American Manufacturers,* 1961.

emerges. Rather, a distribution of cities can be observed from left to right across the graph, from the industrial centers of Detroit, Pittsburgh, and Buffalo to the purely administrative center of Washington, D.C. Thus it would seem that the intuitive view is both confirmed and questioned, and one is led to further consideration of the question.

Sources of Data

It can be assumed that large companies require a large managerial personnel, and therefore the concentration of large companies in a city is indicative of managerial concentra-

tion also. Relevant information about individual companies was assembled and summarized, city by city. Publicly owned companies are required to publish annual reports of their financial status, and these reports carry a wealth of additional information. The business publications, such as *Moody's,*[10] and the *Standard and Poor* investors reference manuals[11] publish annually the information available about companies. *Fortune* has made a

[10] Published by Moody's Investors Service, New York.
[11] Published by Standard and Poor's Corporation, New York.

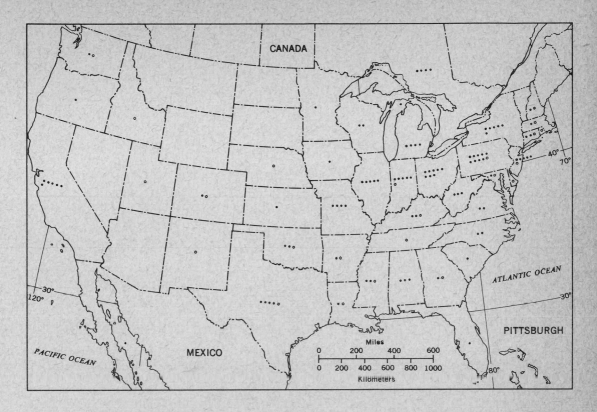

Figure 8. The number of companies, by states, whose headquarters offices are located in Pittsburgh. A solid dot represents two plants; a circle, one plant. Source: *Moody's Industrials*, 1962; *Thomas' Register of American Manufacturers*, 1961.

survey of America's largest companies, both industrial and nonindustrial, and for the past nine years has published annually (July and August) a list of America's five hundred largest industrial companies, and for the last five years a list of the fifty largest commercial banks, insurance, transportation, utility, and merchandising companies respectively.

Since it is presumed that only companies of national importance can collectively create a management center of national importance, the 750 companies listed in the *Fortune* survey served as a base. Each company was checked against one or both of the standard investors manuals and also against *Thomas'*

Register of American Manufacturers,[12] 1961 edition, for accuracy and to determine the location of the production facilities of the company. The data used in this study refer to the 1962 status of the companies. This list, published in 1963, was first compared with the lists published in earlier years[13] to determine whether there had been significant shifts

[12] Published annually by the Thomas Publishing Company, New York.

[13] A careful company-by-company comparison was made with the annual surveys for 1955, 1957, 1959, 1961, and 1963. It was disappointing that no significant trends in concentration were discernible.

in the composition. Only the companies in the lower ranks appear to have changed completely, though naturally there has been some shifting of relative importance over the years. It was felt, however, that changes over the last ten years had not been sufficient to warrant taking earlier years into account, because the appearance or disappearance of companies from the list did not modify substantially the relative importance of a city as a management center. Also, comparison of the two years 1954 and 1963 did not reveal any substantial geographical shift in management centers.

Results of the Analysis

The results of this investigation are most easily presented in a series of tables. Because of the limited scope of the data, these results are certainly neither final nor conclusive, and undoubtedly other means of attacking the problem need exploration.

Table I presents data concerning the 500 leading industrial companies of America aggregated according to the locations of their headquarters cities. Three reasonable, if arbitrarily chosen, criteria served to determine the cities that seemed to meet the test of national importance as management centers: (1) at least ten headquarters offices, (2) at least two billion dollars in assets or sales in 1962 (about 1 percent of the total assets and sales of the 500 companies), and (3) at least 100,000 employees (about 1 percent of the total employment of the 500 companies). Centers included in the original compilation but eliminated from the table are Akron, Minneapolis-St. Paul, Wilmington, Bethlehem-Allentown, Seattle, Cincinnati, Dallas, Toledo, Milwaukee, and Bartlesville (Oklahoma). Although these cities had one or both of the other qualifications, each failed to have more than ten offices.

It is not enough that a city has a large concentration of offices; these offices should represent widespread control, both spatially and industrially, and separation from production facilities. To determine the extent of the "empire" controlled from each city, a tabulation was made of the states in which each company with headquarters in that city had located one or more plants, and the totals were summed. For example, 83 companies with headquarters in New York City had one or more plants in California. However, for determining the extent of geographical control of a city the total number of plants was not considered necessary, merely the number of companies with branch plants in the various states. A city whose control did not extend to at least twenty-four states and Canada was not regarded as a management center. Only New York City and Chicago companies are represented in all forty-eight states of the conterminous United States and in Canada; the most poorly represented is Cleveland, with twenty-nine states and Canada. Table II summarizes this information.

A more satisfactory view of the extent of the control of a city can be gained from a map on which have been plotted the basic data from which Table II was constructed. Six such maps are presented, for New York, Chicago, Los Angeles, San Francisco, Detroit, and Pittsburgh (Figures 3-8). The importance of New York and Chicago as headquarters cities emerges clearly from these maps and contrasts strongly with that of the West Coast centers of Los Angeles and San Francisco. Detroit and Pittsburgh, notable manufacturing centers, appear to have their control principally in the industrial sections of the country.

Although a city need not necessarily have a diversity of industries to qualify as a management center, undoubtedly a larger pool of broader managerial talents would be available

TABLE I

Concentration of Industrial Headquarters Offices

City	Number of Offices	Sales (In thousands of dollars)	Assets	Number of Employees
New York	163	84,355,806	124,477,751	3,650,089
Detroit	13	28,801,564	19,319,678	1,594,487
Chicago	51	19,798,326	14,300,775	717,541
Pittsburgh	21	10,760,815	12,031,841	439,313
Los Angeles	16	8,361,378	5,698,259	307,056
San Francisco	14	5,690,201	6,973,327	206,227
Philadelphia	16	4,423,190	4,372,831	171,613
St. Louis	12	4,229,250	3,177,712	185,734
Cleveland	15	4,172,215	3,512,877	188,902
Boston	12	2,140,787	1,503,882	118,358

Compiled from *Fortune*, July, 1963 and *Moody's Industrials*, 1962 edition.

TABLE II

Extent of "Empire" by City of Control, Conterminous United States and Canada*

Headquarters City	No. of States with Branch Plants	Total No. of Plants	Headquarters City	No. of States with Branch Plants	Total No. of Plants
New York City	48	1,455	San Francisco	34	97
Chicago	48	528	Wilmington[a]	34	51
Minneapolis-St. Paul[a]	43	128	Detroit	30	112
Pittsburgh	40	212	Philadelphia	30	82
St. Louis	38	125	Cleveland	29	99
Los Angeles	38	98	Boston[b]	21	48

Source: *Moody's Industrial*, 1962 edition; *Thomas' Register of American Manufacturers*, 1961.

* All cities listed have a plant or plants in Canada.

[a] Not included in Table I because of failure to meet requirements, but included here for completeness and the fact that it is industrially significant.

[b] The small extent of its industrial empire eliminates Boston as an industrial management center, in accordance with the criterion.

in a city with many different industries than in a one-industry city. Other things being equal, a city with a wide range of nationally important companies is better qualified to claim a position of rank among managerial centers. An attempt was made to classify all companies studied according to the United States Standard Industrial Classification (Table III), but only at the two-digit level.[14]

[14] In the Standard Industrial Classification (SIC) all industries are divided into 9 major groups at the one-digit level, into 99 groups at the two-digit level, and into 999 groups at the three-digit level.

TABLE III

Number of Companies According to United States Standard Industrial Classification

Management Center	Sic Number																				
	20	21	22	23	24	25	26	27	28	29	30	31	32	33	34	35	36	37	38	39	Ua
New York	19	5	9	2	1	1	10	5	30	6	4	0	2	13	12	11	12	7	5	0	9
Chicago	14	0	0	1	0	0	2	0	4	1	1	0	1	2	5	4	9	3	1	0	3
Pittsburgh	1	0	0	0	0	0	0	0	1	2	0	0	1	6	2	3	2	0	0	0	3
Los Angeles	2	0	0	0	0	0	0	1	2	4	0	0	0	0	0	1	0	4	0	0	2
Philadelphia	0	0	1	0	0	0	2	0	2	2	0	0	1	0	0	1	2	2	0	0	3
Cleveland	0	0	0	0	0	0	0	0	4	1	0	0	0	4	1	4	0	1	0	0	0
San Francisco	3	0	0	0	2	0	1	0	1	0	0	0	0	1	1	1	2	0	0	0	2
Detroit	1	0	0	0	0	0	0	0	1	0	0	0	0	2	1	2	1	5	0	0	0
St. Louis	4	0	0	0	0	0	0	0	3	0	0	2	0	0	0	0	2	1	0	0	0
Boston	1	0	1	0	0	0	0	0	2	0	1	0	1	0	1	1	1	0	2	0	1
Minneapolis-St. Paul	3	0	0	0	0	0	1	0	0	0	0	0	0	0	1	1	1	0	0	1	0

aUnknown.
Code: 20, Food; 21, Tobacco; 22, Textiles; 23, Apparel; 24, Lumber and wood products; 25, Furniture and fixtures; 26, Paper and allied products; 27, Printing and publishing; 28, Chemicals; 29, Petroleum and coal; 30, Rubber and plastics; 31, Leather; 32, Stone, clay and glass; 33, Primary metals; 34, Fabricated metals; 35, Machinery (except electrical); 36, Electrical machinery; 37, Transportation equipment; 38, Instruments; 39, Miscellaneous manufacturing.

The internal diversity of many companies makes it impossible to use a more detailed category, and for a few it was not possible to use even the two-digit categories; these companies are listed as unknown. Where possible, the company was assigned to a class according to its principal product. A summary appears in Table III. Clearly, certain cities that rank high in Tables I and II have little diversity in production, and consequently little diversity in management talent.

Ranking of Industrial Management Centers

If it can be assumed that the four criteria of Table I have equal value as measures of management concentration and that the extent of areal control and diversity are also of about the same value, the cities can be tentatively ranked (Table IV) by a simple averaging of the total rankings of each city. Akron, Wilm-ington, and Bethlehem-Allentown, with small "empires" and little diversity but important for particular products, are not general management centers, even industrially.

Nonindustrial Position

The importance of a city as a management center has so far been confined to its importance as a center of industrial management, but this is inadequate, for it does not take into account other business activities. For example, the large commercial banks and the insurance companies exercise an all-pervasive influence as major sources of funds that recognize no visible bounds. Legal restrictions and banking and insurance laws place limits on the tangible evidence of control, but the size of assets alone is indicative of relative importance. Few transportation companies are national in scope, but the larger airlines

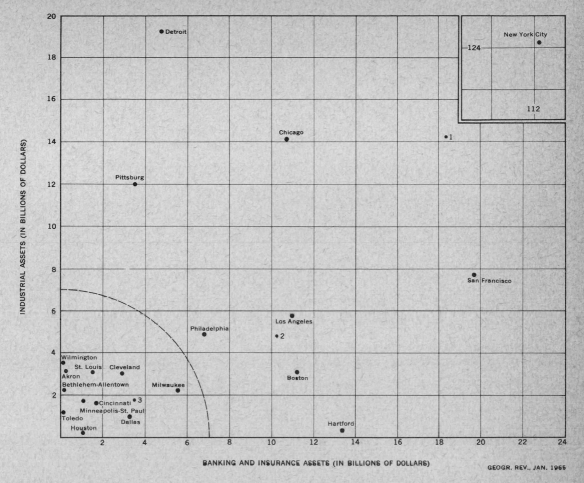

Figure 9. Industrial assets plotted against banking and insurance assets. The numerals 1, 2, and 3 represent the positions that Chicago, Philadelphia, and Minneapolis-St. Paul respectively would have had if the assets of transportation companies had been included in the nonindustrial assets. The arc in the lower left corner roughly delimits the nationally important centers from the centers whose influence is more restricted.

and railroads serve large sections of the country and may therefore be considered of national importance. Utility companies, with the exception of American Telephone and Telegraph and Western Union, are commonly local, both in service area and in outlook; therefore only the national service utilities were included in the computations. Inasmuch as the sole common denominator among the various kinds of business activity is assets, this criterion was used, though "policies in force" or "policyholders" might have provided a better measure for insurance companies. Table V presents a compilation of the nonindustrial assets of the cities in the same fashion that the industrial data were summarized.

Many of the important industrial cities are

also important nonindustrial centers, but Hartford, Milwaukee, Houston, and Dallas, as measured by assets, are obviously more important as financial centers than as indus-

trial centers. Thus a second criterion of rank is suggested, namely the total of nonindustrial assets. In addition to repeated proof of the importance of New York City and Chicago as

TABLE IV

Ranking of Cities as Industrial Management Centers

City	Rank						
	No. of Offices	Sales	Assets	No. of Employees	No. of Plants	Diversity	Average Rank
New York	1	1	1	1	1	1	1
Chicago	2	3	3	3	2	2	2
Pittsburgh	3	4	4	4	3	4	3
Detroit	8	2	2	2	5	6	4
San Francisco	7	6	5	6	8	4	5
Los Angeles	4½	5	6	5	7	9	6
Philadelphia	4½	7	7	9	9	4	7
Cleveland	6	9	8	7	6	7	8
St. Louis	9	8	9	8	4	9	9

TABLE V

Nonindustrial Assets, Fifteen Largest Centers
(In billions of dollars)

City	Assets				
	Bank	Insurance	Transport	Utility	Total
New York	49.0	63.6	4.9	36.0	153.5
San Francisco	19.9	—	2.8	—	22.7
Chicago	9.9	0.9	6.0	0.7	17.5
Hartford	—	13.5	—	—	13.5
Boston	2.0	9.2	—	—	11.2
Los Angeles	8.8	1.6	0.1	—	10.5
Philadelphia	3.6	3.3	3.2	—	10.1
Cleveland	3.5	—	2.2	—	5.7
Milwaukee	0.9	4.5	—	—	5.4
Houston	0.9	—	—	3.9	4.8
Detroit	4.6	—	—	—	4.6
Pittsburgh	3.6	—	—	—	3.6
Dallas	2.5	0.9	0.1	—	3.5
Minneapolis-St. Paul	0.7	0.4	2.4	—	3.5
St. Louis	1.5	—	1.9	—	3.4

Source: *Fortune*, August, 1963; *Moody's Financials*, 1962 edition.

control centers, the great banking wealth of San Francisco is pointed up, together with the insurance centers noted above.

With the two rankings of importance before us, it is now necessary to attempt to combine them into a single measure. The one set of data common to all economic activities and to all cities is assets. Assets, whether of a business firm or of a bank, are commonly recognized as a measure of importance. Table VI combines all assets, industrial and nonindustrial, for each city with assets of more

than one billion dollars and ranks the cities accordingly.

The relation between the industrial and nonindustrial assets can be analyzed both arithmetically and graphically. The simple ratio of nonindustrial to industrial assets was computed (Table VII), and the relative importance of the cities was graphed (Figure 9). The graph serves as a basis for qualifying the cities as balanced in management control or more important industrially or financially. If the graph is read clockwise from the vertical

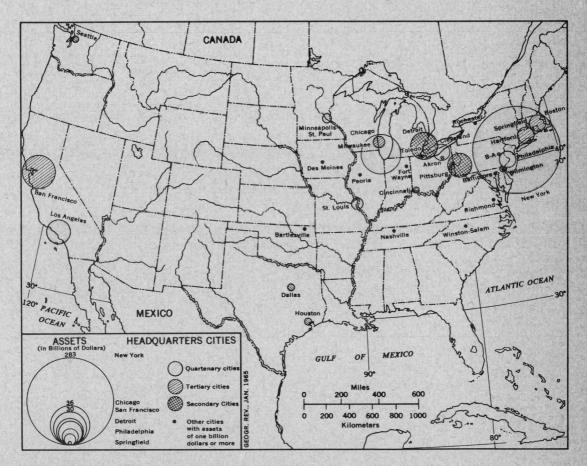

Figure 10. Headquarters cities. This map is based on the total assets held by major companies in the 31 cities shown. The cities have been differentiated into three major categories according to the source of their power.

TABLE VI

Total Assets Controlled by Companies in
Management Centers*
(In billions of dollars)

Rank	City	Assets
1	New York	283.3
2	Chicago	36.5
3	San Francisco	30.2
4	Detroit	24.7
5	Los Angeles	16.4
6	Pittsburgh	15.7
7	Philadelphia	14.4
8	Hartford	13.5
9	Boston	13.0
10	Cleveland	9.2
11	St. Louis	7.0
12	Houston	6.7
13	Milwaukee	6.6
14	Minneapolis-St. Paul	5.4
15	Dallas	4.5
16	Seattle	3.8
17	Wilmington	3.5
18	Cincinnati	3.3
19	Akron	3.1
20	Springfield (Mass.)	2.7
21	Bethlehem-Allentown	2.4
22	Winston-Salem	2.0
23	Des Moines	1.9
24	Bartlesville	1.7
25	Fort Wayne	1.6
26	Richmond	1.5
27	Toledo	1.2
28	Rochester	1.2
29	Peoria	1.14
30	Baltimore	1.12
31	Nashville	1.0

Compiled from *Fortune, Moody's, Standard and Poor.*

* Includes assets held by national merchandising companies but not used in previous calculations. Their inclusion here is to indicate full economic power and thus the magnitude of management control centred in each city.

TABLE VII

Ratio of Nonindustrial to Industrial Assets

City	Ratio
Akron	0.16[a]
Toledo	0.16[a]
Bethlehem-Allentown	0.21[a]
Detroit	0.26
Pittsburgh	0.31
St. Louis	1.06
Cleveland	1.48
Cincinnati	1.54
Chicago	1.58
New York	1.82
Los Angeles	1.89
Minneapolis-St. Paul	1.98
Philadelphia	2.35
Houston	3.00
San Francisco	3.34
Milwaukee	3.86
Dallas	4.00
Boston	7.35
Hartford	13.50

[a]Estimate based on assignment of nonindustrial assets as determined by summing the assets of banks and the like within these as recorded in *Moody's.* Nonindustrial assets include assets of nationally important merchandising companies.

axis, the cities are seen to be arrayed in order from those dominated by industry to those which are primarily financial centers. In addition, the graph shows the relative importance of each city, at least with regard to assets held by its major companies, and thus, if assets of large companies are a reliable measure of management, their importance as management centers. A similarity is apparent between Figures 2 and 9. It would seem that the relation of managers and clerks to all workers is indicative of a management center — an assumption confirmed by the analysis in this paper.

Types of Management Centers

Three distinct groups of cities emerge: (1) general management centers of two sizes, regional and national, called by Gottmann[15] *quaternary centers;* (2) financial cities of regional and national importance, here labeled *tertiary centers;* and (3) industrial cities, in which the bulk of the wealth and control is in industry, here called *secondary centers.*

Figure 10 identifies all cities with assets of one billion dollars or more held by nationally important companies (Table VI). The twenty-one largest are identified according to their relative importance as quaternary, tertiary, or secondary. It is clear that few cities can be called national management centers. The dominance of New York is overwhelming; its total assets are nearly eight times those of its nearest rival, Chicago. No other

[15] Jean Gottmann, *Megalopolis* (New York, 1961), p. 576.

city can approach the diversity of operations performed, and it must be remembered that using only the five hundred largest industrial companies and the fifty largest of each kind of major nonindustrial company has not revealed the full importance of the city. In the quaternary group, New York, Chicago, Los Angeles, and Philadelphia can be considered national management centers (though the case for Los Angeles is weakened by its heavy dependence on the aircraft industry for the bulk of its industrial assets), and Cleveland, St. Louis, Minneapolis-St. Paul, and Cincinnati regional management centers. In the tertiary group, San Francisco, Hartford, and Boston must be classed as nationally important; Milwaukee, Dallas, and Springfield (Massachusetts), all with important insurance companies dominating the pattern, are of lower rank, as is Seattle. The secondary centers are Detroit, Pittsburgh, Akron, Bethlehem-Allentown, and Wilmington.

22 Public Policy and the Central Business District

Ronald R. Boyce

The nature, future place, and importance of the *central business district*, or CBD as it is commonly called, is a subject of extreme controversy. Some say it is no longer necessary — indeed, is an anachronism. For example, the geographer Edward Ullman said, "If we were to apply private enterprise depreciation principles to the inner portions of cities we would write them off, just as machinery is scrapped, and throw them away. But where would we throw them?"

Others claim that the CBD is so vital an organism in the metropolitan anatomy that any city without a healthy CBD is dead or in danger of dying. They argue that the CBD should be restored to its former and rightful place as the heart of the metropolis — indeed, should surpass anything it was in the past. Charles Abrams, a planner, recently claimed that "without the CBD the suburbs cannot exist" because they are not viable without it. In this light the CBD is looked upon as an opportunity to build a truly representative symbol of our urban civilization.

These two different conclusions result largely from two very diverse perceptions as to what the city is. The social scientist, on the one hand, views the city as a laboratory for analysis, as a phenomenon which primarily serves and reflects man's needs and technology. He sees the city as population clustered tightly together in order to serve better the assembly, production, service, and distribution needs of its inhabitants; he sees it as a tightly knit web of spatial, economic, and social interconnections. Melvin Webber, former president of the American Institute of Planners, recently stated that "the history of city growth, in essence, is the story of man's eager search for ease of human interaction." Viewed in this light cities, and the CBD, are expected to change and to adjust to man's changing technology and needs.

This perspective of the city is vastly different from that of those who view the city as an artifact, or as an ideal expression of our civilization. Thus, the architect-designer is ever proposing utopian, or ideal, urban designs. In this context the city must have order, beauty, harmony, and symbolic meaning as an entity. Each structure should complement all others in a vast symphony of con-

Reprinted from *Journal of Geography* (May, 1969), pp. 227-32 by permission.

crete and pattern. The city is viewed as a single expression with finite boundaries and discernible internal sub-units. Urban sprawl is therefore treated as a disease. This philosophy was perhaps best expressed by the late architect-city planner Eliel Saarinen, who said, "Just as any living organism can be healthy only when that organism is a product of nature's art in accordance with the basic principles of nature's architecture, exactly for the same reason town or city can be healthy — physically, spiritually, and culturally — only when it is developed into a product of man's art in accordance with the basic principles of man's architecture."

Almost all concerned are in complete agreement that the CBD is unsuited to present needs and, furthermore, has been rapidly losing its monopolistic and dominant position in the metropolis. This is demonstrated by the rapid and continuing decline in CBD retail sales, by the dilapidated and dis-functional condition of many downtowns, and by the continual erosion and decentralization of activities to outlying locations.

This article attempts to do three things: to look objectively at the major assets and deficits of the CBD in terms of the two stated perspectives, to attempt to pose some reasons for the many problems and trends which are affecting the CBD, and to present conclusions as to the public policy which I think should be adopted for the American central business district.

Assets Of The CBD

The central business district is an outstanding asset for at least two reasons: first, it contains a concentration of activities and employment, and it exerts control over the urban fabric. Second, it has symbolic, cultural, and historical value. The first asset is one perhaps most appreciated by the geographer; the sec-

ond one is most appreciated by the architect-designer.

The concentration of activities and employment is demonstrated by the fact that well over one-half of all employment in most central cities occurs, in, or very near, the central business district. About 80 percent of all department store sales, and about 90 percent of all banking occurs in the CBD of even the largest metropolises. The small sub-CBD nodes of Wall Street, LaSalle Street, and Market Street undoubtedly control the finances of much of the nation. The daytime population in downtown Chicago, for example, amounts to almost 300,000 persons — more than the total population of Greater Des Moines, Iowa. Such concentration is reflected in the value of land and buildings in the CBD, which often amounts to upwards of 15 to 25 percent of the physical value of the entire city. Over one million dollars an acre was recently paid merely for air rights in downtown Chicago; $10,000 a front foot is not an unusually high price for CBD land in our largest cities.

The cultural and historical value of downtown is equally impressive. It contains the great hotels, restaurants, night clubs, movie houses, and theaters. In addition, it represents the initial beginnings of the city and contains the historical buildings and places. It is the area which most people associate with any given city. In short, it is the distinctive attribute of the metropolis. The subdivisions and industrial parks look much the same from city to city, but the downtown is different. It is most representative of the character and nature of any given city. Because of this and other reasons, a business location in the CBD carries with it great prestige. By the same token, the vitality of the downtown is often taken as the bellwether of a city's growth by the casual visitor.

Deficits And Problems

If the assets of downtowns are impressive, the deficits are even more so and are surely the reason for paying so much attention to the CBD. The major difficulties or problems of the CBD are primarily related to its inability to adjust to new needs. This inability is most clearly reflected in the problems of obsolescence. The buildings of most downtowns date back a half century — before the motor car — as do their streets and general physical layout. As a consequence such structures and blocks are not suitable for many of today's space needs.

One has only to observe the space now being used by outlying business and industry to note the disparity. Many industries occupy the equivalent of 10 or 20 downtown blocks. The new Prudential office building in Houston alone occupies some 28 acres. Yet many of our largest CBD's contain only about 50 acres. It is not unusual for a new regional shopping center to cover 100 acres.

The general appearance of downtowns is also a severe handicap. The dilapidated and unesthetic appearances are partly the result of the age or the structures. In addition, there is a great lack of landscaping and general architectural style as well as a void in the physical coordination of structures. Most buildings have been placed with little regard as to how they would fit into the general scheme of things. Finally, many downtowns are characterized by a great deal of broken frontage where buildings have been torn down and used for parking lots, thus making great gaps in the business pattern. There has been little thought as to the best arrangement of functions inside of the central business district, and consequently many institutions such as banks, insurance companies, and the like are so located that a shopper must walk farther to get between stores than would be necessary if conscious thought had been given to the order and arrangement of functions, as in modern shopping centers.

The most talked about problem in the central business district is, of course, traffic and parking. Congestion has reached huge proportions in many downtown areas. There is a great lack of parking space, and many people visiting the downtowns have to walk considerable distances or pay very high parking fees. Although high-rise parking ramps are being built, they are still inadequate to serve the needs in most cities. Mass transit has been continually deteriorating in both service and quality, while the price has been increasing, and it is no longer nearly as convenient as formerly. Moreover, transit does not truly serve many of the outlying residential territories adequately.

Many of the problems in the central business districts are the result of the extreme governmental fragmentation in our metropolises. Central city municipalities, which often contain only about half the total metropolitan population, are greatly concerned about their central business districts and do, in fact, undertake various renewal and redevelopment schemes which would not ordinarily be undertaken if the metropolis were under one municipal government. This, of course, creates a tax burden on the population within the city limits. It also causes the central city government to become gravely concerned about the decentralization and new placement of functions and activities which would otherwise be welcomed. The decentralization of retailing to outlying locations is in many regards a real asset and benefit to the consumer. The problem of the central city government is that such relocation generally occurs outside of its particular municipal boundaries.

A lack of progressiveness is also evident in most central business districts. This is reflected in decor and general appearances, as outlined previously, as well as the parking problems, which have been referred to. Although many downtowns have now developed various "save downtown" associations, few of these are of significant value. Most are concerned with promotional and superficial schemes rather than with obtaining a solid base on which to make decisions.

Reasons For CBD Change

But what are the major reasons for such central business district problems? Let's examine some of the changes which have been occurring in the central city — the municipality which contains the central business district. A metropolitan area includes the central city, the county in which it is located, and other surrounding counties which are significantly associated with the central city. Metropolitan areas increased in population 26 percent between 1950 and 1960, whereas the central city has barely held its own, populations averaging an increase of only one and one-half percent during this time. Many central cities of large metropolises have actually lost population in the last fifteen years. Such population decline has had a major impact on the downtown area.

Moreover, such population decline has not been offset by increases in nonresidential activities, as was formerly the case. In fact, the population remaining has become far less affluent than that which preceded it. The zone immediately surrounding many downtowns is often characterized by slum conditions.

The factors which have caused central business district decline are reflections of the new mobility of the population as represented by the automobile, the increased leisure time,

and the general technological advancements made in construction since World War II. Such changes are reflected most clearly in what is commonly termed suburbanization. Subdivisions, planned industrial parks, and planned shopping centers have augmented the population decentralization. The great increase in the importance of and territory occupied by municipal airports during the past decade have, in turn, sparked outlying residential, industrial, and commercial development. Development of freeways is exerting tremendous decentralization pressures by providing outer circumferential highways and encouraging people to live even further from their places of work.

As monopolistic effects have been broken, the end result is that the central business district has continued to become more off-center. Until the past decade, most cities occupied very small territories. Today, however, with large subdivisions and the generally more generous use of land, the location of the central business district has become problematical. Although it is still the focus of the major transit routes and even the interstate freeway system, distance has become a major factor in determining whether people will patronize or work in this center. Generally, as a city grows the central business district tends to become more off-center inside of the metropolitan complex. As cities continue to expand into new rural territories, the location problem with regard to CBD's will surely become of even greater significance.

Developing A Public Policy For The CBD

Given these few facts, what should one conclude about the CBD? All signs point to a continuation of the rapid decline in the CBD and a continuation of rapid growth in most other parts of the urban complex. If current trends continue, the CBD will become but one of the many nodes of commercial activity in the metropolis; and perhaps not even the dominant node. It is also clear that the architectural thesis that the city is dead without a healthy CBD is unjustified. In fact, Los Angeles, the city in search of a CBD, is one of the most rapidly growing in the nation and now is the second largest metropolis in the United States and the sixth largest in the world.

This kind of argument perhaps obscures the real policy questions, however. The first question is not really whether the metropolis *can* effectively operate without a CBD, but whether it should or must. It clearly can. The second question is whether deliberate intervention is necessary in order for the city to operate effectively. The CBD is truly tied to other urban components, and, if not operating effectively, can have a deleterious effect on the entire urban system.

My conclusion with regard to the first question is that, given existing conditions and investments in the CBD, almost every metropolis should probably continue to have one, but not to the present extent for any given sized city, and surely not an augmented and symbol-laden CBD as envisaged by many architect-designers. Although presently there are many functions exclusively limited to the CBD, I can think of no single function, or activity, which must of necessity be located here in the future. While the CBD might be the best location, given the location of complementary activities for many functions, especially in smaller cities, there is no compelling reason why such functions should be encouraged and promoted here. The variety, pedestrian contacts, and other generally desirable urban features can be created in outlying locations in perhaps better form than is

possible in remodeling our central business districts.

My conclusion with regard to the second question is that the CBD has indeed become a drag on the urban system, inasmuch as it is overbuilt, and requires a catalyst for change which will diminish its prominence. It seems abundantly clear that without major governmental intervention the CBD will never again regain its former high position of value, prestige, and general importance in the metropolis.

But if one accepts these premises, what specifically should the CBD be like in the future? What specific catalytic actions and public policies are necessary in order to achieve this?

Lest the reader think that I am going to untie the Gordian Knot, let me hastily assure you that I really do not know the answer. I can partly describe the role of the future CBD by describing what I think should *not* be the nature of things in the future. First, I do not think that the city should be looked upon as an artifact of mankind for the simple reason that I think the city is far too important to be used as a monument or a museum. Neither do I think the future CBD should be the captive promotional device of special interest territories or groups such as the central city municipality or various "save downtown" groups. It is necessary that goods and services be distributed throughout the metropolis in a way which best serves the total metropolitan citizenry, not just a selected few. Many downtown functions might best be decentralized as soon as possible so as to be within closer range of the consumers. Finally, I do not think plans for downtown or the central city should be made independent of the entire urban complex, and perhaps even the composite urban interests of the nation. This, in simple terms, means that most city planning departments which serve merely central city governments are obsolete.

This, in turn, leads to a major public policy statement: planning should be done on a super-metropolitan basis. This necessitates metropolitan government or some such alternative. Despite the many pitfalls and bitter experiences connected with attempts at metropolitan government, this policy must be continued with renewed energy. Indeed, one might argue that the metropolitan unit is already far too restrictive a concept for today's and especially tomorrow's urban residential patterns.

Second, the U.S. Government should establish a more comprehensive department of urban affairs than that currently envisaged, so that major and comparative research on the city complex can be undertaken. It is a national disgrace that there is probably as much information available on the swamp-lands of Florida as is available on the cities of the United States. For example, it is not even known within thousands of acres how much land is now occupied by urban residents in the United States. Almost nothing specifically is known on a comparative basis about the location and extent of many major components of the metropolis. Until more information is available, and more comprehensive studies are made, we must continue to operate partly in a vacuum.

References

1 Gruen, Victor, *The Heart of Our Cities: The Urban Crisis, Diagnosis and Cure* (New York, Simon and Schuster, 1964).

2 Horwood, Edgar M. and Boyce, R. R., *Studies of the Central Business District and Urban Freeway Development* (Seattle, University of Washington Press, 1959).

3 Vernon, Raymond, The Changing Economic Function of the Central City (New York, Committee for the Economic Development, 1959).

23

The Core of the City: Emerging Concepts

Edgar M. Horwood

Malcolm D. MacNair

For the past five years there has been increasing interest among urban researchers and planners concerning the core of the city. A large body of literature on the subject has been developed[1] and this topic has been on the agenda of nearly every recent major city planning conference.

Amid this sea of literature it becomes very difficult to grasp central issues both in regard to research constructs and the development of planning policy. Most articles and books deal with only certain segments of CBD (Central Business District) study or planning. In fact, we are at the point where only a summary article in the *Reader's Digest* can save us from being devoured by our own words. This article will attempt to present such a summary and at the same time touch upon a few ideas which the authors believe will absorb attention in the near future.

One could classify literature on the CBD into the following broad groups:

1. *Studies based on defining and describing the CBD*. This group tends to define what we mean by the CBD, how to measure it, and in general how to define it in certain universal terms that will be applicable from city to city.[2] These studies are done mostly outside of city planning agencies. They are usually made by university scholars from one of a number of disciplines relating to urban analysis and financed by some agency or foundation with broad research objectives. The importance of studies in this group is that they paint a very broad picture of the nature of the CBD to serve as a framework for the conceptualization of local agency studies. Their disadvantage, from a local agency point of view, is that they do not answer specific questions for CBD planning in specific cities.

---

[1] See bibliography in Shirley F. Weiss, *The Central Business District in Transition, Methodological Approaches to CBD Analysis and Forecasting Future Space Needs* (City and Regional Planning, University of North Carolina, 1957).

[2] Perhaps the most noteworthy of these are the studies by Raymond E. Murphy and J. E. Vance, Jr. in *Economic Geography*, Vol. XXX (July, 1954), and Vol. XXXI (January, 1955).

Reprinted from *Plan Canada,* Vol. 8, no. 3 (1961), pp. 108-14 by permission of the Town Planning Institute of Canada.

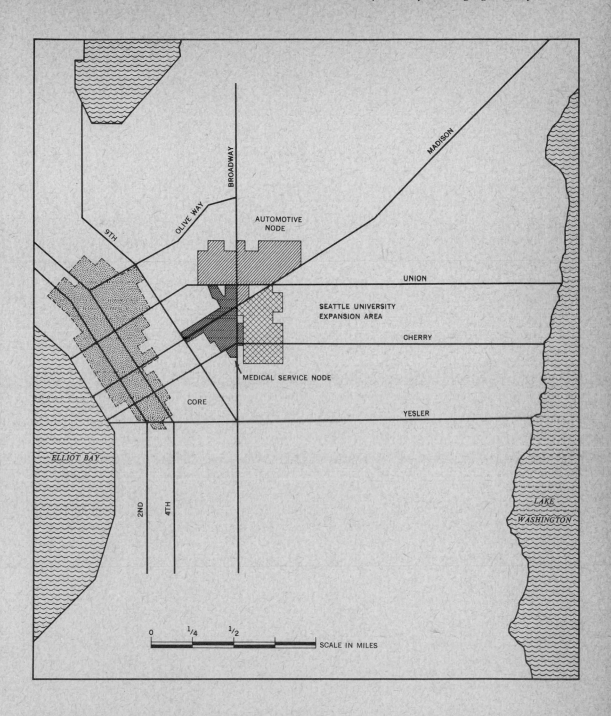

Seattle Central Business District, Functional Centres, 1959.

2. *Planning agency studies dealing with the CBD of specific cities.* These studies are typically the counterparts of those just mentioned. They tend to present specific inventories of what the CBD contains in different space uses, they project trends into the future, and they generally throw in a little graphic art depicting an anticipated future condition such as a pedestrian mall, open plaza, or other manifestation of esthetic improvement.[3] The strength of these studies is that they are oriented to a specific problem and geographic locale, and their weakness tends to lie in their lack of being based on a sound conceptual framework. Also, there is rarely enough across the board information presented upon which local forecasts can be tempered, such as the general parameters of certain types of uses in cities of varying sizes.

3. *Market analyses relating to central land use.* This type of study deals with central land use marketability and other factors relating the economic base to the demand for central land. They are usually carried on by public agencies or consultants in regard to specific urban renewal programs, and arise out of the demand for reuse appraisals of land coming under the clearance axe.[4] The strength of these studies is that they are generally realistically founded in terms of a local real estate market. Their weakness, on the other hand, arises out of the fact that they are typically oriented to coming up with predetermined answers to support a renewal program, or they bring facts together only regarding the marketability of land apart from the planning for an improved urban form.

There are, of course, many specialized studies not mentioned in the above categories, such as analyses of daytime population, transportation and goods movement in the core of the city, and studies of the core of a city in terms of its regional market, to mention only a few. In the latter instance, many specific questions can be answered by studying the entire region, in regard to CBD planning, which cannot be answered from studying the internal characteristics of a particular CBD itself. For example, the central place importance of a city has much to do with the capacity of its CBD to cater to particular specialized functions.

Work by the authors in CBD analysis has been mainly in regard to the first of the three groups mentioned, namely, those dealing with problems of definition, measurement and description which are common to all cities. At this time the authors desire to present some emerging ideas on the organization of the core of the city which have not generally been dealt with in the city planning literature. It will be necessary to recapitulate for only a moment on some general universals recognized by all students of the CBD.

Almost all observers of CBD phenomena have recognized that the central region of the city is not one of uniform intensity, but contains an exceptionally limited area of very high land value upon which most of the downtown retail and office uses exist. This area is generally referred to as the core area of

---

[3] This group includes the large number of reports published by local planning agencies on the subject of plans and studies for specific CBDs. The best reference on these studies is the annual index pages of the *ASPO Newsletter*, American Society of Planning Officials, 1313 East 60th Street, Chicago, Illinois.

[4] Larry Smith, Real Estate Consultant of Seattle, and Homer Hoyt, Land Economic Consultant of Chicago, have contributed materially to Studies of this classification over several decades. Most of these studies, however, are private consulting reports for specific client agencies and not generally available for public circulation. See a compilation of some of Larry Smith's findings in "Space for the CBD's Functions," *Journal of the American Institute of Planners,* Vol. XXVII, no. 1 (February, 1961), pp. 35-42.

the city, and often as the CBD itself. Further, it has been recognized that this core area is not directly a function of city size, but is related more to the human scale of convenient walking distance between establishments. For example, cities of quite disparate size, one perhaps ten or twenty times the other, have essentially the same size of pedestrian core measured in ground area.

It is this intensively used core area which has been the focus of most of the recent interest in the resurgence of the city center as a dynamic force in the urban scene. Good, bad or indifferent, the fact remains that business interests in this portion of the city in most areas of western culture have adopted a deterministic attitude as to the value of a strong CBD, and are supporting their attitudes by both private actions and co-operative group effort through their downtown associations. As a matter of fact, it is no longer a perplexing question as to whether or not the central core will survive in this age of apparent decentralization. Recent events in most of the regional capitols of North America give testimony to the fact that the core of the city is not withering away and dying. Although retail sales in the core are diminishing as a percentage of citywide sales, as they have been doing for the past 50 years, central office space is growing sufficiently to more than counterbalance the outward flow of retail activity.[5]

One might conceive of the structure of the center of the city as being composed of a quite laterally restricted core given over to the retail sales and office functions (people, paperwork, and parcels), with a relatively large frame surrounding this core given over to a variety of business and commercial functions as well as institutional and high density residential uses, all of which are a little bit less apparent in their organization than the spectacular core area itself with its tall buildings. This observation has come to be accepted as the Core-frame theory of the CBD region, and it is with the frame that the authors have now become quite concerned in terms of analysis and planning.[6]

The main proposition to be presented here is that the CBD is substantially more than a highly intensive core where face-to-face contacts make possible the social, economic and political leadership of the urban region. We have come to equate the CBD to this very apparent core. The core is vocal. It is urbane. It is what we have come to recognize as the character of the city, more than any other part of the city. And yet in relation to the entire central area the core is something like the seventh part of the iceberg, which is the only apparent part as far as the surface observer is concerned.

The CBD frame, on the other hand, constitutes landwise the six-sevenths of the central area, including many vital organs of the city, and generally either neglected or casually dealt with in CBD studies. This area has hitherto been identified in the sociological literature as the area of transition of the city center. At one time it was thought that core functions would reach out and occupy the surrounding space. History has proved otherwise. The core area grows vertically rather than horizontally. Although there are many transitional uses in the frame, certain strongly identifiable functions have been growing in these areas in most western cities for the last half-century at least. The frame is the neg-

[5] Edgar M. Horwood and Ronald R. Boyce, *Studies of the Central Business District and Urban Freeway Development* (Seattle, University of Washington Press, 1959), Chapters 3 and 4.

[6] *Ibid.*, Chapter 3.

DISTRIBUTION OF MEDICAL PHYSICIANS, SEATTLE, CENTRAL BUSINESS DISTRICT

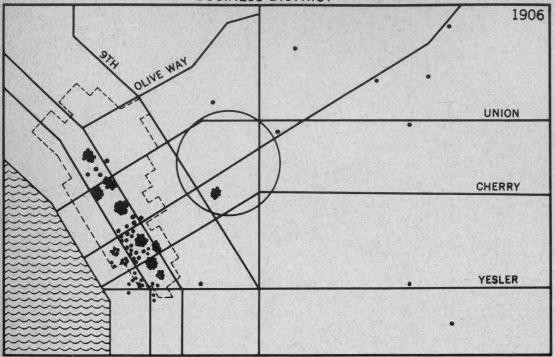

One dot represents one physician.

lected area of urban analysis and planning. It is more difficult to classify than other areas of the city. Many parts of it, such as the warehousing and wholesaling portions, lack esthetic interest. It invariably contains slums. It does not fit into the planners' neighbourhood configuration. Its telephone poles and wires are not buried, as in the core, and its pedestrian amenity is lacking. We tend to sweep this piece of urban real estate under the carpet in city planning effort. It has taken a decided second place to the more spectacular core as well as the more apparent neighborhood units on its outbound side.

From preliminary or windshield observation the frame is difficult to classify. In fact, its true identity may never become known if conventional land use classifications are used. It must be studied first in a functional sense through an establishment survey. From this beginning its functional nodes may be identified and subsequent work may be done to clarify the different component parts of the frame, to measure them, and to test their dynamic changes over a time span.

There are invariably about a half-dozen distinct functional sub-regions within the CBD frame areas of our North American metropolises, and in fact including European cities as well. One typically finds within this region such activities as wholesaling with stocks, transportation terminals, medical

DISTRIBUTION OF MEDICAL PHYSICIANS, SEATTLE, CENTRAL BUSINESS DISTRICT

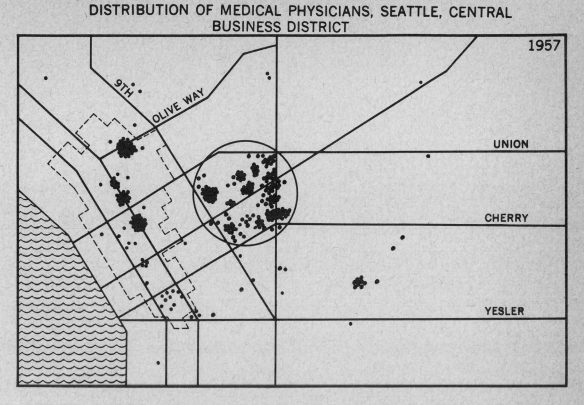

Within a 50-year period the medical service cluster had virtually deserted the core area of the CBD and moved to the frame. This change in both scale and location reflects not only changes in the technology of medical practice, but improved regional transportation as well. The completion of the emerging urban regional freeway system will further accelerate the trends in the medical service area by vastly expanding the geographical limits of the service. That is to say, the *commuter shed* for medical services will be doubled in size by the new transportation facility. Although many more interesting facts were ascertained about this particular part of the Seattle frame, one of the most revealing findings was the complete lack of realization of the cluster and its needs in public policy.

service centers, automobile services and often some manufacturing or assembly of goods. These uses are all interspersed with both old and new housing and many non residential uses which are related to the functional nodes in a symbiotic way. The latter tend to obscure the basic function of the establishment cluster under study, much as trees obscure some of the geologic features of the earth's surface.

In spite of certain observable trends toward decentralization, there are a great many activities which, by virtue of the need for transport economies must have locations within the frame area.[7] For example, one rarely finds truck terminals outside the CBD frame because of the need for these concerns to minimize short haul pickup and delivery costs which are extremely high in relationship to the relatively low cost of moving goods via consolidated shipments in intercity transport.

[7] *Ibid.*, Chapters 5, 6 and 7.

A verification of the observations regarding the CBD frame as discussed above obtains from a series of studies under way at the University of Washington concerning the frame of the three largest cities in the state, Seattle, Tacoma and Spokane. An effort is being made in this program to analyze systematically the major functional nodes of the CBD frames of these cities with a view toward sharpening the theory and advancing techniques for its analysis. Space here permits only a limited description of these studies, and rather than becoming overextended in the presentation, an example will be presented instead. The example deals with the medical service node of the Seattle CBD frame, as one of several functional areas examined within that frame.[8]

The methodology of this study was a detailed examination of all establishments of a medical service nature within a general area recognized to be accommodating growth of these activities. Linkages were then studied between the establishments to determine the scale of exchange of goods, persons and communications. These linkages gave an interaction concept of the concentration. Another important examination was changes over time. By means of old medical directories and phone books the development of the node was reconstructed for a time span of 50 years. Finally, ancillary and competing uses were examined, as well as the constraints imposed by city zoning policy. In the process of these studies indices were developed to delimit the node, which should be applicable to other cities. The entire procedure required many interviews, as well as the examination of both

internal records of the establishments themselves and documents of the type customarily not used in land use studies. An important distinction was made between arriving at conclusions from what could be seen by visual observation and what could be comprehended from the examination of the establishment activity itself.

Among the important findings of this study was the amazing growth of the concentration of specialized medical services. Well over half of the specialized medical practitioners in Seattle have offices in this area. Within a 50-year period the medical service cluster had virtually deserted the core area of the CBD and moved to the frame. This change in both scale and location reflects not only changes in the technology of medical practice, but improved regional transportation as well. The completion of the emerging urban regional freeway system will further accelerate the trends in the medical service area by vastly expanding the geographical limits of the service. That is to say, the *commuter shed* for medical services will be doubled in size by the new transportation facility.

Although many more interesting facts were ascertained about this particular part of the Seattle frame, one of the most revealing findings was the complete lack of realization of the cluster and its needs in public policy. On Seattle's comprehensive plan the area shows up as a high density residential area, with a ribbon of commerce along one of the principal streets cutting through it. No studies have ever been made by the planning agency to ascertain growth trends of medical service space. In fact, twelve-storey apartment buildings are permitted in the node, whereas clinics are restricted to two storeys. Further, wholesaling establishments specializing in medical supplies are prohibited by zoning code from locating either in this area or its en-

[8] Malcolm D. MacNair, "The Medical Service Area, Seattle: A Functional, Spatial and Linkage Analysis," Unpublished Master's Thesis, University of Washington (1959).

virons. In the face of these restrictions the need for medical service and hospital space in the Seattle frame is expected to double by 1980, and is doubling every two decades.

Similar techniques of study were also applied to other activity clusters in the Seattle frame and findings of similar scale made. The City of Tacoma studies, conducted by the city planning agency staff using the general format of the Seattle studies mentioned above, also corroborated the same findings.[9] The

[9] Tacoma City Planning Commission. *The Central Core*, Central Business District Studies (June, 1959).

Spokane studies are not yet complete, but will be materially enhanced by the use of both electronic data processing techniques as well as the electronic mapping of land use data. It is hoped that by the completion of this group of studies there will arise new theories of central urban organization or the corroboration of old. Findings to date lead the authors to believe that the Core-frame construct is a valid one, and worthy of attention in all local agency planning studies.

24

Towns and Umlands

Jacob Spelt

If modern town planning wants to measure up to its task, it will have to plan for both city and umland as one unit. Town planning can no longer permit itself to be limited in scope by municipal boundaries, as was the case in the past, when the field was mainly concerned with architectural forms and artistic points of view. Town and umland are, so emphasizes Hans Carol, only two different aspects of one and the same coherent whole.

THE TOTALITY OF TOWN AND UMLAND

Much of the discussion in this category has been familiar to geographers for a long time. On the other hand, it is gratifying to see it appear in a planning journal and even more so to see it used as a basis for planning.

At one time town and country each had its distinctive forms of production and people lived where they worked. Now a daily and in part a weekly migration between place of work and place of residence has become typical. The 1950 census of West Germany revealed that one out of every seven gainfully employed persons leaves his municipality every day to work elsewhere. In total, more than 3,000,000 commuters were counted on the enumeration day. Sixty-seven per cent originated in places with fewer than 5,000 inhabitants; in other words, they came from the umlands of the larger cities and towns, which now have become the greatest concentrations of employment opportunities.

The central city depends on its umland not only for labor supply but also for a steady influx of people to maintain a steady population growth. In his article "Das Stadt-Umland-Verhältnis in seiner planerischen Problematik" Dittrich points out that migrants came from the umland, but that now a large city draws many of its people from a much wider area, sometimes covering the entire nation. On the other hand, the newcomers no longer settle exclusively in the central city, but also in the suburbs and towns in the umland. As such, umland and city have a combined drawing power and the absorptive capacity of the umland is of vital significance to the city. A city, therefore, may have national or world-wide connections, but this does not mean that its roots in the umland could be severed.

Reprinted from *Economic Geography*, Vol. 34, no. 4 (1958), pp. 362-69 by permission.

One of the most important functions of the umland is to provide and maintain open space for the benefit of the population in the central city. There the city population can find opportunity for recreation and relief from crowded and congested conditions.

On the other hand, the city performs many other services for the umland besides employment opportunities. At one time, weekly town markets played a vital part in the provision of goods and supplies for the population. Now, stores in varying degrees of specialization offer a great diversity of goods and have replaced the old markets. Dittrich points to the importance of the fact that these stores are located in the city, and that modern means of transportation make it possible to serve the population of both umland and city on a day to day basis. In addition, the city is the focal point for the umland in matters of finance, education, health, administration, entertainment, and others. In many ways the city is the exclusive provider of such services.

The relationships between city and umland are so intimate that the one puts its imprint on the other. Dittrich reaffirms that the cities and towns of Europe are not standardized and uniform. Each of them is unique, an individuality forged not by the city alone but also by its umland. The natural conditions of the umland, the character of its people, and their ways of life contribute greatly to the fashioning of the city.

Unfortunately, however, city and umland have generally not been aware of the significance of this interdependence. On the contrary, often tensions have developed and accusations have been flung back and forth, sometimes justified, sometimes not.

The city became a powerful economic concentration and in part acquired this position in collaboration with its umland which provided it with workers, maintained its population growth, and provided open space for suburban expansion. At the same time its population patronized the city stores.

The central city accumulated considerable wealth and big financial differences arose between it and the predominantly residential municipalities in the umland. The umland considered itself exploited and impoverished. Many of the services and functions of its villages and towns were usurped by competitors in the central city. In Germany, as in other European countries, a system of tax equalization has helped the umland municipalities whose citizens are employed in the central city to pay for their educational, social, and other services. By means of this equalization the communities in the umland share in the industrial and commercial tax yields of the central city.

The city is inclined to cite the expenditures it makes to maintain facilities which are also used by the inhabitants of the umland, but which are not supported by them financially. In Germany this applies in particular to hospitals, certain forms of education, museums, and theaters. Klüber in his article "Kommunalwirtschaftliche Verflechtungen zwischen Stadt- und Landkreis" calculates that the Landkreis Offenbach[2] is saving over 320,000 DM annually on its educational expenditures, because pupils in the Kreis attend schools in Offenbach a.M. The same is true for hospital costs. The city of Offenbach (104,800 population) has three private and one municipal hospital with 794 beds. Only the latter is supported financially by the city. The Landkreis (154,200 population) maintains only two small hospitals with a total of 225 beds. Over 25 per cent of the patients in the Offenbach municipal hospital come from the Landkreis, constituting an extra annual expenditure of about 380,000 DM for the city. The insurance authorities object to higher fees for out-of-town patients and the Landkreis refuses to pay subsidies towards the care of its population in the city hospital. On the other hand, hydroelectricity, gas, and water for the Kreis population are supplied by companies in the city which operate on a profit basis. For them the inhabitants of the Kreis are important customers. The Landkreis took 5.3 per cent of the water, 28 per cent of the gas, and 55 per cent of the hydroelectricity sold by the companies in Offenbach.

However, only in certain cases is it possible to calculate a numerical value for the degree of dependence of umland on city and vice versa. There are many other services and expenditures for which values cannot be calculated. The inhabitants of the umland come to the city for a great variety of reasons and invariably spend money, thereby stimulating the economy of the town. On the other hand, city people frequently spend money in the umland, while seeking recreation there.

Klüber emphasizes the vital significance of the umland as a source of labor for the central city. But then he also points out that the umland municipalities are able to compete with the central city for new industries. They can offer lower wage rates and lower taxes. In towns close to the central city these advantages are not offset by poorer transportation facilities, and consequently the central city may experience serious competition. It is especially painful for the urban tax payer, when the children of those competitors come to attend city schools and their employees are admitted to city hospitals.

Both Dittrich and Klüber consider it unlikely that it will be possible to draw up a balance sheet of the relationships between towns and umland, but this does not reduce the significance of the fact that umland and town constitute economically, culturally, and socially a closely integrated entity. Existence of one without the other is virtually impossible. Furthermore, action taken in one may have far-reaching repercussions in the other.

Recognition of the umland-town entity by planners has resulted in a new approach to planning problems in Germany. In certain instances this has crystallized in the form of planning satellite towns in order to organize the umland in a functional relationship with the city. Roads may be built into the umland to open up new areas for recreation or to bring fruit and vegetable growers closer to the city market. The first steps toward modern land use planning in Germany were measures to preserve open space in the Rhine-Westphalian industrial district. Specific attempts may be made to counteract undue "bleeding" of the umland by the city. Tax equalization is a step in this direction, but Dittrich suggests the possibility of moving certain establishments from the city to the umland. Careful analysis of the city-umland relationships may reveal that a city does not utilize the potentialities of its umland to the fullest extent and plans can be formulated accordingly (Klöpper). In brief, planning in both city and umland must be founded on the premise of the fundamental unity of town and umland.

DRAWING THE BOUNDARIES

The matter of boundaries cannot be neglected. This involves the boundary of the city complex and also the umland boundary.

The City Complex

So far it has not been possible to develop in Germany a concept similar to the Urbanized Areas in the United States, the Conurbations in Britain, or the Tätorter in Sweden. Horst Fehre in his paper "Zur Abgrenzung der Stadtregion" emphasizes that a clear definition is urgently needed in view of the 1960 census. Attempts before 1945 display a great deal of unanimity in the selection of criteria such as settlement forms, population data (density, rate of growth), transportation, economic relationships, and the movement of commuters. Geographers especially emphasized the trend and mode of settlement without attempting, however, to apply an objective system of measurement. In general no agreement was reached on the relative significance of the criteria or which of these should be combined. However, the more the problem was studied, the clearer it became that no sharp boundary could be drawn between city and countryside. The outcome of these earlier attempts was a twofold approach. One group, mainly geographers, searched for a solution in the form of transitional belts or zones between city core and countryside. The other, the statisticians, preferred one single line, which could only be drawn after much generalization. Some advocated simply the drawing of a circle with a certain radius. In both cases it was a disadvantage that the method evolved lacked a theoretical structure, and could be applied only to the city studied.

More recently Voigt and Boustedt have used only economic data as criteria for boundary definition. Voigt took the proportion of the total population engaged in farming (20 per cent) and Boustedt the proportion of the total gainfully occupied population engaged in farming (35 per cent) as a criterion to draw the boundary of the city area. The boundaries, as arrived at by Voigt and Boustedt, of course do not coincide, but if the umland is divided into an inner and an outer zone, then the 35 per cent line of Voigt coincides with the 50 per cent line of Boustedt.

Voigt and Boustedt considered also the number of commuters working in the central city, although again in a slightly different manner. Voigt took the proportion of the gainfully occupied population of the umland community which commutes to the central city (40 per cent) and Boustedt took the proportion of commuters in the gainfully occupied population in non-agricultural employment, which corresponds to 20 per cent in the Voigt system. Boustedt supplements the two aforementioned criteria by those of population density and house types. A municipality has to have at least 500 people per square kilometer and not more than 33 per cent farm houses before it can be considered as an extension of the central city area.

Sirp tried to apply the Voigt-Boustedt method to the Cologne area, but found it unworkable, partly due to short-comings in the method and partly because of special conditions in the Cologne district. To the southwest of Cologne lies the Erft lignite district which complicates considerably the pattern of commuter flow. There are some very extensive municipalities for which the census does not supply data on the basis of the various residential quarters within them. This was the main reason for the failure of the method in this area. Large numbers of commuters go to the central city but also to other neighboring centers. The problems in the Cologne district are, first, to draw a boundary between the central city complex and a district with a non-agrarian economy and, second, to decide whether this district should be added to the central city. Sirp found that the number of dwelling units per residential structure could be used to distinguish between truly urbanized municipalities and those with only a non-agricultural economy. Districts with 1.8 or more dwelling units per structure may be considered as truly urban. Sirp has come forward with a fresh idea, but according to Fehre he did not succeed in finding a real solution.

Other workers such as L. Fisher, K. Hook, and Eicher resumed the earlier attempts of others to define the boundary by drawing concentric circles around the center of the city. The difficulty of this method lies in determination of the length of the radius. There are three possibilities: a) one radius for all cities; b) radii in proportion to the size category of the town; and c) a separate radius for each city. Fehre suggests that the third approach probably would offer the most satisfactory solution. There are, however, some serious shortcomings in the circle method. Most cities are star-shaped and thus entirely contrasting areas may be included in one particular ring. Then there is the problem of overlapping circles between neighboring towns. Fisher suggests that the common chord could be taken as the boundary. However, a boundary arrived at in this manner would probably not depict reality and might easily separate what really belongs together. According to Fehre the method remains at best a temporary solution.

According to Rudolf Klöpper, the problem of whether a city has an umland and how far it extends can only be determined after a survey in the field.

THE HIERARCHY OF CENTRAL PLACES

In Germany the study of the city as a central place was initiated by Bobek with his examination of Innsbruck, Austria, in 1928. A whole series of similar studies, entitled "The City X and its Lebensraum," followed. A few years later, this type of research was given new stimulus by Christaller's theory on the location of central places (1933).

Of special interest in this field is the con-temporary contribution of Hans Carol (Sozialräumliche Gliederung und planerische Gestaltung des Groszstadtbereiches — Dargestellt am Beispiel Zürich). Carol made studies in Switzerland and South Africa during the late forties and early fifties and from these he recognized central places of upper, middle, and lower order, distinguished on the basis of services provided. The central places of lower order are characterized by 12 services such as certain professions, banks, shops, cinemas, newspapers, farmers' markets, railway connections, and postal deliveries. Cartographically, the quantity of each of these indicator services is shown by means of radials in clockwise arrangement around the symbol of the central place. In order to avoid an impractical length of the radials, the latter are composed of three types of dot symbols, each the equivalent of a certain number of units. Depending on the number of indicator services present, the central places of lower order are further classified as fully central, semi-central, and sub-central. Carol intends to develop a more valuable quantitative classification by making use of the average number of persons required to support a certain central service. This should provide a unit to summarize such varied criteria as physicians, clothing stores, and cinemas.

Central places of middle order have as main indicator secondary schools, supplemented with eleven other services, such as book shops, automobile dealers, banks, wholesalers, technical schools, and daily newspapers. Depending on the number of services available there is again a classification into fully central, semi-central, and sub-central places.

The main criterion for the central places of upper order is a university. To the remaining eleven criteria belong such services as foreign legations and consulates, inter-canton organizations, large daily papers, medical centers, etc. There is a similar breakdown in the three categories. Switzerland has five fully central and several semi-central and sub-central places of upper order.

Carol considers it the task of planning to improve the existing distribution pattern of service centers. He is an advocate of decentralization and a controlled growth of Zürich, which he visualizes as gaining a stronger metropolitan function as the umland experiences greater economic development. In particular he calls for better conveniences for the rural population, thus slowing down the migration to the cities. Carol proposes to select only a few well established market centers at one time for development into well equipped towns (5,000-20,000 pop.) with central services of lower order. In areas where such small centers do not exist, new ones should be created. Carol also suggests that the desired goal may be reached by improving the transportation facilities between the places to be developed and the metropolitan city, in this case Zürich. Other steps suggested are advice for industries on matters of location, the creation of conditions which would appeal to new and expanding industries, and greater financial help for the centers to be developed.

PLANNING FOR TOWN AND UMLAND

Planning in different cities gives an excellent illustration of the foundations upon which modern town planning in Germany is founded. The new federal capital of Bonn may be taken as an example.

Bonn, situated in the apex of the Gulf of Cologne, has always tended to expand upstream along the Rhine River instead of seeking the open spaces of the widening low-land in the opposite direction. The expansion of the city complex followed generally the transportation routes and extends at present over a distance of about 15 miles along the Rhine River. After the selection of Bonn as the federal capital, the building density increased considerably and the population of the city proper grew from 101,000 before the war to 142,000 at present. Suburban Bad Godesberg almost doubled its population and has now over 58,000 inhabitants. Not much land remains for further building. The great building density already there does not leave enough open space for recreation, a problem which will become more pressing with the gradual shortening of the work week. These and other problems can only be solved by drawing the umland within the framework of local planning.

The umland still offers many possibilities for recreation. However, roads built to open up areas for this purpose are often considered by municipalities as means to promote industrial, commercial, and residential developments. This attitude of the municipalities in the umland counteracts the aims of the planners in the city.

In addition to space for recreation, Bonn needs land for residential expansion, not only on account of Bonn's new administrative function, but also because of its importance as a university center and cultural center (Beethoven), its tourist industry, the settlement of refugees and last but not least its residential function (Bonn is a pleasant place in which to live, attracting persons as far away as Cologne).

The local planners do not look favorably upon satellite towns as a solution. This would reduce the freedom of the individual to change his place of work if he so desires, since such a move would probably involve a change of residence. If the aim is to promote pride in home ownership and neighborhood, and if one wishes to avoid a home becoming a commodity lightly to be disposed of, then the largest number of employment opportunities must be easily accessible. The planners, therefore, intend to guide the new expansions to sites attractive as places of residence and with easy access to the main transportation arteries. They hope to avoid as much as possible restrictions on the freedom of movement for the individual.

Such considerations led to the decision to locate the new extensions on the northern boundary of the city. This decision was also influenced by the results of climatological studies in the Bonn area. The new suburbs will house 20,000 to 15,000 people, and will consist of two parts separated by a greenbelt. The greenbelt extends right into the center of the city proper and constitutes an attempt to improve the climate of the city. The belt or wedge is oriented in the direction of the prevailing winds and should serve as a huge breezeway. With these expansions, the rebuilding projects, and the filling in of still available open spaces, Bonn will be able to accommodate 200,000 inhabitants.

Of vital importance is a wise planning of new transportation routes. Not only will the success of the new suburbs depend on a judicious layout of a new network of roads, street car lines, and bus lines, but there are also other implications which reach far beyond the municipal boundaries of Bonn. The new routes can be used to stimulate the economic prosperity of both city and umland.

A new east-west connection is needed to relieve traffic congestion in the central part of Bonn. The best location of the new Rhine bridge would be to the north of Bonn. This would make the large airport which serves both Bonn and Cologne much more accessible to the capital. At the same time industrial towns across the river would fall within easy commuting distance of the new suburbs in north Bonn, thus enlarging the employment opportunities for the residential population in these suburbs. A measure of stability would be achieved, especially significant if the capital were to return to Berlin. The new bridge would also provide greatly improved market opportunities for the fruit-growers to the north of Bonn, on the other side of the Rhine River. Finally a bridge at this point would open up the Sieg Valley as one of the new recreation areas for Bonn's population. Water sport is rather difficult on the Rhine River with its heavy traffic and pollution. The Sieg River opens entirely new vistas.

Thus there are many possibilities for the creation of a harmonious development of the area, but this can only be realized if city and umland are taken as an integrated unit. It is only on this basis that Bonn and its umland could create the most desirable milieu for their inhabitants.

External Relations of Cities: City—Hinterland

25

Bart J. Epstein

As Harold Mayer has demonstrated in the first article of this series,[1] consideration of urban problems and relationships necessitates a definition of major terms. This is no less necessary in considering the external relations of cities.

Since the "real city"[2] extends to the limits of an urban density of settlement, a focus on what is beyond in relation to what is within leaves little other than agricultural production, extractive industry, and specialized points of manufacturing or recreation. These are important functions and are often vital to the existence of the city, but are hardly as vital and interesting as a more introspective view.

The urban population of the U.S. and of many parts of the world[3] is increasing at a spectacular rate. Since most of our cities in the U.S. (the major focus of the article) are past the days of great annexation possibilities,[4] growth has continued outside the corporate city limits, giving rise to the phenomenon we describe as urban sprawl.[5] Sprawl is hardly a new phenomenon; it is only recently that its problem value has been recognized and attempts made to control it. To some degree external relationships of cities are expressed in the process of sprawl and its physical and socio-economic characteristics. Our focus in this discussion will be on the corporate rather than the real city.

HINTERLANDS

A city's hinterland[6] is a vast physical area

[1] Harold M. Mayer, "Cities and Urban Geography," *Journal of Geography*, Vol. LXVIII, no. 1 (January, 1969), pp. 6-19.

[2] For a brief discussion of the "Real City" or "Geographic City," see Raymond E. Murphy, *The American City* (New York, McGraw-Hill Book Company, 1966), pp. 13-14.

[3] Statistics are available in United Nations Publications. Note also Gerald Breese, *Urbanization in Newly Developing Countries* (Englewood Cliffs, N.J., Prentice-Hall, Inc., 1966), pp. 1-32.

[4] Major exception is Jacksonville, Florida, which on October 1, 1968, spread its corporate boundaries to the Duval County Line, making it the largest areal city in the United States.

[5] Planning literature on sprawl is abundant, for a geographer's viewpoint see Jean Gottman and Robert A. Harper, eds., *Metropolis on the Move: Geographers Look at Urban Sprawl* (New York, John Wiley & Sons, Inc., 1967).

[6] For a brief discussion of hinterland concepts see Raymond E. Murphy, *The American City* (New York, McGraw-Hill Book Company, 1966), pp. 52-71.

Reprinted from *Journal of Geography* (March, 1969), pp. 134-67 by permission.

compared to the city proper, and it performs a variety of functions.[6] Its major development is governed by the economics of space.

The size and complexity of the city will govern the size and complexity of its hinterland and the relationships between them.

Perhaps the simplest example of external city relationships to be found today involves settlements in agricultural areas. In the string of communities that dot the Rio Grande Valley in Texas, communities such as McAllen and Weslaco perform urban functions for extensive areas devoted to farming. These areas abut the urban settlements themselves.

The fact that there may be dominant cities which may extend their influence to lesser developed cities,[7] in no way detracts from the individual hinterland relationship.

At the other extreme is *the* megalopolitan city, New York, whose hinterland may well include not only Gottman's *Megalopolis*,[8] but possibly the U.S., North America, and, perhaps, the world.

HINTERLANDS AND URBAN FUNCTIONS

Somewhere between the two extremes used for illustration lies "the city" that will permit consideration of function and process at a useful and manageable scale. Omitted from consideration will be agriculture and extractive activities. Therefore, major concern will be with

(1) Residence
(2) Manufacturing
(3) Distribution
    (a) Wholesale
    (b) Retail
(4) Recreation
(5) Personal and professional service (including government)
(6) Communication and transportation.

Throughout each discussion, either stated or implied, will be the effects of the major catalysts for growth and functional differentiation — communication and transportation.

RESIDENCE

Commencing at the corporate boundary line of our "city," residential development describes the most obvious land use. This residential function was the earliest expression of extension of the city into its hinterland. Pressure on the land to accept greater numbers of urbanites is present to day and shows no sign of diminishing. On the simplest of terms — the hinterland is the catch-basin for the growing city as well as for its suburbs (both old and new).

This residential push, a centrifugal force,[9] is the result of many pressures. Our cities today are growing from both natural increase and immigration from rural areas and, to a minor extent, from abroad. Where the natural increase and immigration have increased Negro or Latin population, there has been an additional racial force which may ultimately

[7] A useful source for central place studies is Brian J. L. Berry and Allen Pred, *Central Place Studies, A Bibliography of Theory and Applications, Including Supplement Through 1964* (Philadelphia, Regional Science Research Institute, 1965). For a review of central place systems, see Brian J. L. Berry, *Geography of Market Centers and Retail Distribution* (Englewood Cliffs, N.J., Prentice-Hall, Inc., 1967), pp. 1-25. Note also that this latter publication points to a lack of theory development within the metropolitan complex.

[8] Jean Gottman, *Megalopolis: The Urbanized Northeastern Seaboard of the United States* (New York, The Twentieth Century Fund, 1961).

[9] Charles C. Colby, "Centrifugal and Centripetal Forces in Urban Geography," *Annals of the Association of American Geographers*, Vol. XXIII (1933), pp .1-20.

effect substantial changes in city-hinterland relationships.

In addition to biological and racial pressures, there are also physical, socio-economic, and governmental pressures assuring a continued bedroom function for the city's hinterland.

Atmospheric conditions such as smog in the Los Angeles metropolitan area, the fouled air of New York City, the acrid odors of the chemical plants near Niagara Falls provide a physical incentive to escape the city and the affected parts of the metropolitan areas. Lack of enforcement of zoning and building codes may also produce urban building deterioration.[10] Temporarily, the slum may house a greater density than ever before, but ultimately there must be a physical spillover, which is combined with the desire to escape to the hinterland. An additional social force considers association with the periphery of the slum undesirable, and thereby adds to the outward movement.

Another centrifugal residential force is socio-psychological — the search for the "good life." In middle class American terms this is the struggle to have one's own single family home on a green plot of ground, away from the "city" (nevertheless, seeking the creature comforts and services of the city). This outward movement, in which man attempts to upgrade housing and improve his environment, is also evident in the movement from suburb to exurb.

Regardless of motivation or of physical or social impetus, residence in the hinterland is closely tied to the city; very often the tie is literal, even physical; i.e., via utilities. Population pressure develops in the city and the close-in hinterland, and the outer hinterland supplies the escape area. No doubt there are residents of the hinterland with only loose ties to the central city, but a trip on the Bayshore Freeway (San Francisco) or the West Side Drive (New York City) or the Southeast Expressway (Boston) any weekday morning will vividly demonstrate the tie to the central city. A lesser flow of traffic in early evening hours is also obvious, indicating yet another functional association. (See section on Recreation.)

The dynamics of residence in a metropolitan area is not a one directional phenomenon. It is not only rural immigrants who settle in the central city, but also the affluent and the aged. Housing for the aged is commonly placed within the corporate city limits, very often near the central business district. Akron, Ohio, has just completed one group of apartments for the elderly within walking distance of 100 percent point;[11] St. Joseph, Michigan, has also completed an "old age" high rise apartment at the very edge of the central business district. Further, such housing developments as the West End project in Boston and Society Hill in Philadelphia have displaced low and moderate income families in substandard housing with higher income families in luxury apartments and town houses. A river setting and proximity to both the central business district and financial districts, and to all other central city amenities have made these developments a counteractant to the usual outward flow of population, albeit they constitute a relatively tiny force.

Nevertheless, the net effect of all forces is outward, thereby making residence the single

---

[10] In addition to urban renewal, planners are seeking to rehabilitate the city by enforcing building codes. Proper code enforcement might have initially acted as a great deterrent to slum development.

[11] The 100 per cent point is usually regarded as the point of highest land value in the city. It is most often at the key traffic intersection of the central business district.

most outstanding, most important urban function performed by the hinterland for the city. This may be an oversimplification of a complex relationship, but until we can exercise complete control over our environment and over urban development, we may look forward to more manifestations of the same phenomenon.[12]

MANUFACTURING

Historically, manufacturing has been a centralizing force (centripetal). From the early days of handicrafts and the Guilds through the Industrial Revolution, there was a banding together for purposes of production of goods. This phenomenon was common to agricultural production as well. Strong forces operating in the distant past through recent times kept a large share of manufacturing a captive of the inner city.

Development of ports and the spread of railroads permitted and encouraged a degree of decentralization, but did not develop the freedom of modern times. The automobile, the truck, and improved highways have indeed permitted and encouraged the diffusion of the manufacturing function beyond the corporate city and beyond the dominant influence of navigable water and railroad lines. There has been a liberation from restrictive locational factors.

It should not be inferred that there is only one set of forces at work. Surely, the development of Bethlehem Steel at Sparrows Point, in Baltimore's hinterland, was but slightly influenced by existing overland transportation facilities. The deep water port and the economy of water transportation in addition to

proximity to substantial markets were prime location factors. Nonetheless, Baltimore's proximity was the ultimate key, since this was the home base of the labor force, (despite the construction of a company town). The recent development of the aluminum industry, oriented to power, provides a somewhat similar situation.

These hinterland phenomena are being overshadowed today by the shifts taking place within the urban metropolitan areas. There are a variety of forces at work in decentralizing industry. Some of these follow.

Modern Design

There is a stress in most manufacturing production lines on single story operations (breweries are a major exception). This creates a need for extensive acreage for buildings alone. In Everett, Washington, Boeing has recently built a plant to produce the 747 jet; it is the largest building in the world, containing 160 million cubic feet.[13] Added to the land used by the structure is a substantial additional area for employee parking, trucking, and storage. This type of land need could not be satisfied in Seattle; consequently, the move was made to the hinterland (even within Everett the move was westward, peripheral to the built-up part of the city).

Modern Technology

At least two striking phenomena have been evident in recent years. Industrial engineers have been successfully diminishing air and water pollution and have also abated noise. This has made previously noxious industries into acceptable neighbors.

---

[12] It may be fair to ask if much of present day zoning is not in effect producing controlled sprawl!

[13] Seattle-First National Bank, Annual Review, *Summary of Pacific Northwest Industries* (May, 1967).

There has also developed a new type industry including cybernetics and electronics which can be housed in aesthetically pleasing structures which produce no smoke and no noise — only traffic and payrolls. There are also the research parks which resemble campuses rather than industrial complexes.

These developments have made it easier to decentralize production jobs, and have made production facilities more welcome in the hinterland.

Government Policy and Land Economics

Zoning is an instrument of public policy. By means of restrictive codes, manufacturing has been forced to areas within the city that are least desirable for any other use.[14] Combining this restriction with relatively small land holdings in the city and the relatively high prices for land acquisition, there results a great incentive to escape the city and to seek friendlier, more available opportunities outside — both outside the city and outside of its hinterland.

Taxation is inescapable, but its impact is manageable. Manufacturing is so desirable from the point of view of the community tax duplicate, that there will often be incentives to move it to a particular place. At least part of the motivation for the desertion of New England by the textile industry was a favorable taxation climate in the South. In any case, the hinterland often escapes the problems and the "costs of doing business" of the city, thereby permitting a friendly tax en-

vironment, enriching the hinterland and possibly adding to the financial problems of the city.

Labor

There is one other major force at work between the locus of manufacturing and a city hinterland spatial arrangement — labor. The simple act of increasing population in the hinterland, as described in a previous section, provides a varied labor force for wandering industry. For example, what better attraction might there be for needle trades to leave the city than a large potential female labor force in the suburbs? Skilled workers today earn enough to break the city bond. It is no longer necessary to locate manufacturing facilities in the midst of densely built-up urban areas. The labor force is dispersed and perhaps most important is mobile.

In many cities there is a reverse commuter rush with the hinterland supplying the jobs for the city dweller. Metropolitan areas in the extreme east and west provide vivid examples: Route 128 in the Boston Standard Metropolitan Statistical Area is not only a Boston circumferential by-pass, but is a new industrial belt complete with industrial parks and more independent types of facilities; e.g., Polaroid. Most of the major arteries originally aimed at Boston can now be considered as spokes in the 128 wheel and carry the heavy flow of outward bound traffic that eventually feeds into the circumferential. Equally striking has been the development of automotive industry in Fremont, California, in the southern part of the Bay Area. The Bayshore together with the Nimitz and the more local San Jose roads feed large numbers of commuters to these plants. These workers are in addition to the local inhabitants who have recently moved to be close to work and

---

[14] Manufacturing has rated very low on the scale of land use quality. In old zoning codes it was possible to build higher rated uses on lower rated land. It is more common today to find exclusive manufacturing zones which may be used for nothing else. Nevertheless, manufacturing is still delegated to lands undesirable for residence or commerce.

to the general developmental excitement in this new area.

DISTRIBUTION

The distribution of goods is a function shared by the city and its hinterland. In the recent past, the city had a virtual stranglehold on wholesaling and an even stronger hold on sales of general merchandise to the consumer (especially department store sales). The post-World War II era has witnessed noticeable changes in both re-distribution (wholesaling) and direct distribution to the consumer (retailing).

Wholesaling[15]

In many respects wholesaling's history resembles that of manufacturing; perhaps it was responsive to physical and transportation centrality to an even greater extent. So long as urban relationships remained simple, wholesaling was keyed to primary transportation networks. Goods arriving by sea or rail were assembled at or near the central place and then organized for re-distribution. (Witness the old wholesaling areas associated with a port, railroad yards, or the central business district itself.)

Additional pressures due to increased population that was more dispersed than ever, a cost price squeeze experienced by all business, an accent on truck transportation within metropolitan areas, congestion within the city, taxation problems (real property and inventory) — all of these forces were at work and decentralization has taken place.

Just as there is reverse commuter traffic, there is a reverse wholesale traffic. Modernization and automation of goods handling facilities have created the need for "assembly line" type efficiency. Indeed, the modern wholesaling or distribution center today resembles the modern manufacturing plant. Sprawling single story buildings with substantial service area acreage is the rule today, and land (and other) pressures have brought this redistributive function to the hinterlands. The city has not abdicated its redistributive role completely. Defensive action such as the South Philadelphia Distribution Center and the new Boston Market attempt to reverse the new tide. There are, indeed, advantages to a central city position, but the "lock" is broken and the hinterland now shares this vital function.

Retailing

Perhaps no other phenomenon of the post-World War II era is as striking as the retail revolution. Its basic element has been described in the previous section on residence, and since most people with their greater disposable incomes to spend have been caught up in its wake, they have experienced the changes and played an important part in it.[16]

The central business district is, and has been, the epitome of commercial development in our cities.[17] Its dominance in an area can be appreciated by shopping there or by

[16] For a discussion of the relationship between retailing, population and sprawl, see Bart J. Epstein, "The Trading Function," Jean Gottman and Robert A. Harper *eds., Metropolis on the Move: Geographers Look at Urban Sprawl* (New York, John Wiley & Sons, 1967), pp. 93-101.

[17] A landmark study of the central business district by American geographers is Raymond E. Murphy, James E. Vance, Jr., and Bart J. Epstein, *Central Business District Studies* (Worcester, Massachusetts, Economic Geography, 1955).

[15] For a definition of wholesaling, see Bureau of the Budget, *Standard Industrial Classification Manual* (Washington, D.C., United States Government Printing Office, 1957), Code 51.

making a simple map analysis. In almost all cases the central business district can be located by inspection of the transportation network. Certainly, most main roads lead there and often a railroad confluence is also nearby. This commercial hub was most easily accessible to the city's population and to its hinterland as well — as long as the hinterland was relatively close-in. Here we find the super stores — department stores — with the widest range of goods and services offered in the total market place. These stores are almost always the highest sales producers in a metropolitan area. They are the "unreproduceables," at least on a store-to-store basis. Here, too, is found the widest range of speciality stores, the greatest concentration of furniture stores (at the periphery), and the greatest concentration of services. The city and its hinterland have provided the market upon which these developments depend. Most of the goods purveyed here are commonly called "shopper's goods."[18]

Together with the spread of population (sprawl) has come substantial retail development. Early retail development outside the central business district (described by Proudfoot)[19] has been accompanied by a phenomenon of the forties and more recent days — the planned shopping center. Historically, business has developed in conjunction with its markets. (Witness the proliferation of stores along old street car lines such as Lake St. in Minneapolis and the present day extension along major roads.) Most of the devel-

opment centered on "convenience goods"[20] with an occasional shopping goods concentration at points where major transportation lines met and crossed (Coolidge Corner, Boston). This built-in hinterland potential has been met in a variety of ways, among them the planned neighborhood shopping center and the planned community shopping center. These developments are little more than a response to meet a mobile, mechanized market potential as close as possible to where it resides. The city dweller rarely crosses into the hinterland for this type of shopping trip, with one possible exception — the discount department store with its discount supermarket associate.

The discount store is a "child of the city." It originated in the deserted mill buildings of the central cities of New England, attracting its business in much the same fashion as a small central business district.[21] The rapid acceptance of the "new" type of merchandising (surely influenced by the super-market) encouraged discount store entrepreneurs to leave for the hinterlands, where they could get cheap land and escape restrictive building codes (and perhaps the union as well), and started a helter-skelter pattern of store facilities in the hinterland. It did not take long for competition to weed out the poorly financed and the poorly located.[22] After greater and

---

[18] Shopper's goods satisfy long term needs and are bought relatively infrequently — as shoes and apparel, furniture and household appliances.

[19] Malcom J. Proudfoot, "The Outlying Business Centers of Chicago," *Journal of Land and Public Utilities Economics*, Vol. XIII (1937), pp. 57-70.

[20] Convenience goods are necessities which are bought frequently as food, kitchen supplies, liquor, and notions.

[21] The discount store has evolved into the self-service department store, and has been accounting for an increasing share of the general merchandise sales dollar.

[22] *Discount Store News*, a weekly newspaper, chronicles the events of this new retailing industry. In recent years there has been a great deal of news on corporate mergers. Previously, equal space was concentrated on business failures (for a variety of reasons).

greater acceptance, the discount store became respectable and sought better locations, even within the city itself (e.g., Alexander's and E. J. Korvette in downtown New York). These latter moves are restoring an equilibrium, keeping city business potential within the city (away from the hinterland) and even attempting to capture some hinterland sales potential when the suburban dweller "comes to town."

Bureau of Census data[23] and Urban Land Institute[24] studies have described the most revolutionary retail force of the sixties and its effect on the city — the planned regional shopping center. Although the central business district is still the single largest, highest sales volume shopping centrality in the standard metropolitan statistical area, it has not kept its share of market and is being overshadowed by the regional centers. Some of the loss in position is no doubt due to lack of central city growth, especially compared to the hinterland. (But rising incomes have at least balanced the loss, and the total effect is still a loss of position.) Whereas the neighborhood and most community centers are self supporting within the hinterland, the regional

center taps both city and hinterland market potential.

Most regional shopping centers are situated at key access points and provide free (and adequate) parking for all customers. For many shopping trips this ease of access draws trade from a wide variety of areas.

Further, the location of department stores within a short walking distance, combined with attractive walkways where frontage is occupied by specialty stores makes shopping more efficient than in the central business district where distance, traffic, vacancy, and the elements provide deterrents to shopping ease.

Regional centers which started by featuring one department store (e.g., Shoppers World — Framingham, Massachusetts, originally Jordan Marsh) have now worked their way up to as many as four (naturally passing through the 2- and 3-store stage) department stores (e.g., Yorktown Mall, Lombard, Illinois: Montgomery Ward, J. C. Penney, Wieboldt's, and Carson, Pirie, Scott) occupying centers with over one million square feet of space.[25] Further enhancing the regional center is its most recent innovation: the enclosed, air-conditioned mall. This single development may provide the most serious impact on the central business district. Cities such as Rochester, New York, and Green Bay, Wisconsin are already geared to meet this attack, but most central cities will not be as fortunate.[26] The enclosed, air-conditioned

[23] Bureau of the Census, *Major Retail Centers, 1963 Census of Business* (Washington, D.C., United States Government Printing Office, 1965). This is a series of reports on SMSA's, CBD's, and MRC's for selected areas.

[24] The Urban Land Institute has published a series of reports on shopping centers, some of which are:

    1) Technical Bulletin No. 33, Homer Hoyt, *A Re-examination of the Shopping Center Market.*

    2) *The Dollars and Cents of Shopping Centers* — Parts I and II.

    3) *The Dollars and Cents of Shopping Centers* — 1963 and again 1966.

Note also that Saul B. Cohen prepared an annotated bibliography on shopping centers for the Kroger Company which was published for limited distribution in the mid-1950's. These may still be available on a limited basis.

[25] Yorktown Mall will not have a great impact on Chicago proper, for it will attract only the occasional shopper who may be drawn to the shopping center by curiosity.

[26] Rochester, New York has already built a downtown, enclosed mall on a small scale. Green Bay, Wisconsin's downtown urban renewal plan calls for creation of an extensive downtown, enclosed mall with a special circumferential traffic pattern including tunnels for north-south through traffic (under the mall).

mall provides a controlled environment both winter and summer, as well as a wide range of goods and services. With strategic location and vigorous sales promotion, these centers will keep more business out of the central business district and will also attract present CBD business into the hinterland. This does not suggest the death of the central business district (it is still virtually impossible to duplicate), but may yet force a new function upon it. In any case, the regional shopping center has, in its way, reversed the traditional flow of retail dollars.

RECREATION

A consideration of recreation within the urban complex once again illustrates centrifugal and centripetal forces. As in retailing, the forces are powerful, but perhaps not as competitive (except for the competition for the total recreational expenditure in the market).

Centripetal

A major portion of nighttime activity in the central business district is associated with recreation — entertainment. New York's "Broadway" may be too over-powering an example to cite, but surely it is no less typical than San Francisco (with its North Beach complex as an additional lure) or Toronto (with its recent addition of the O'Keefe Center to an already highly developed night-life complex including Bay-Bloor and the central business district), or "any city" with its concentration of movie theaters, night clubs, restaurants, and hotels. (Las Vegas is perhaps the gaudiest example of this phenomenon.) As in shopping and in personal services, the central business district is also the bright light mecca for the standard metropolitan statistical area. Indeed, the trading area for entertainment centers may even be national in extent — Broadway and Bourbon

Street certainly serve broader areas than the New York and New Orleans standard metropolitan statistical areas.

Centrifugal

Just as the city provides a concentration of recreation facilities unmatched elsewhere in the Standard Metropolitan Statistical Area, so does the hinterland have its peculiar characteristics. Whereas there is rarely a concentration of facilities, there is a great variety dispersed through the hinterlands, parts of which cannot be matched by the city.

Recreational opportunities and facilities will often occur in a considerably larger hinterland than has been used to this point. Home recreational facilities such as those that lawn and garden may provide are important, but highly localized, and not comparable to the commercial aspect of recreation found in the city.

Perhaps the *cash* factor provides an initial point from which to progress. Open land, except for occasional green strips within the city, is the most important and striking feature offered by the hinterland. Most often it is here that the city dweller can find camping, boating, swimming, and other outdoor activity. It is here that scenic views can be found. Here "nature" is displayed for the citizen accustomed to a manmade environment. Some of this may be free, but there is a commercialized segment of this phenomenon that attracts sales as well as participants.[27] This pull outward generates sales as well as traffic, and also supplies a service virtually impossible to obtain in the city.

The city's hinterland should not be inferred to be barren of "city functions." The

[27] Usually, sight seeing traffic is carried by "old type" roads which have had limited control of roadside development. The souvenir shop, gas station, restaurant, and produce stands all capture city dollars.

differentiation is one of concentration. We can all find examples of the fine restaurant nestled in a rural setting or even associated with a new shopping center. We are familiar with the summer theater and the outdoor performing centers such as the Blossom Center between Cleveland and Akron, Ohio. Although dispersed spatially, they nevertheless draw "trade" from the city, where these facilities are not available (despite the seasonal nature of some of these recreational activities).

Today there is a rebirth of the motion picture industry and the movie theater. The TV doldrums which resulted in the abandonment of many downtown movie houses have finally been passed. Where Hollywood and others are supplying film matter impossible (at least temporarily) to present on the TV screen, the cinema entrepreneurs are providing new, "slick" theaters for the viewing public, but mostly outside the central city. We may even find twin theaters, very often within shopping centers which once discouraged their association.[28] This, of course, is a variation of an older phenomenon which has been the property of the hinterland — the drive-in theater. These developments have had their greatest effect where the central business district did not have a well-developed or modern entertainment center.

There is two-way traffic in recreation. The stream of cars coming into the city at night is partially balanced by the Sunday exodus, each area performing the services that it can do best, but there is an overlap despite specialization.

SERVICES (PERSONAL, PROFESSIONAL, AND GOVERNMENTAL)

The dominance of the central city has been challenged on many fronts. Medical specialists, lawyers, and craftsmen are leaving their traditional locations in order to be closer to (or more convenient to) their growing markets. It is no longer unusual to see large office buildings under construction in even the most distant parts of the suburbs.

Again, it is the residential sprawl from the city which creates concentrations of sufficient size to warrant establishment of hospitals and their associated medical facility concentrations outside the central city area. It is the increased efficiency in communication that permits attorneys to leave the central business district and also permits insurance companies to erect large complexes in the hinterland (American Mutual Insurance Co. — Wakefield, Massachusetts). Despite the outward move, the central business district and the central city still have the greatest concentration of office space and the greatest concentration of all types of service specialists. The ambulance with an emergency case most often is inbound, as is the man with business problems. Even those specialists who leave the central area often do not cut their ties completely, for they operate dual office facilities. Regardless of proliferation of facilities outside the city, there is still a basic centripetal power which is exercised on the whole metropolitan complex.

Just as the concentration of hospitals in the inner city draws the medical profession, so does the concentration of government draw the attorney, the accountant, the realtor, the

[28] Theaters were once on the undesirable tenant list in shopping centers, especially where parking was a problem. Long term parking during peak shopping periods was the chief problem created by the theater. Today, shopping centers are attempting to perform more community functions and encourage establishment of theaters in order to foster additional trips to the center. The General Cinema Corporation of Boston has been a leader in this recent theater surge, in many cases, establishing twin theaters within the planned shopping complex.

title company, and the architects, engineers, and other business service professions. Even without metropolitan government, the seat of power is most often in the city. Where else can one find the legislative, judicial, and executive functionaries of government together with the economic giants such as banking and finance? Whether the smaller communities in a metropolitan complex admit it or not, they are dependent on the city. The hinterland dwellers may believe they escape physical contact with city problems, but it is an illusion. This has been recognized by the federal government and the metropolitan areas in the establishment of planning areas for transportation studies underway in almost every metropolitan complex. Toronto has established a form of metropolitan government, as has Dade County, Florida (Miami). In many other areas metropolitan commissions are concerned with a variety of problems such as transportation, law enforcement, and supplying public utilities.

City planners have been most sensitive to the needs for supra-government in our metropolitan areas. Suburbanites guard their governing rights most zealously, but they are still affected by the actions of the city and one day must yield to its dominance. Perhaps a first step is the income tax (variant of a head tax) now levied on "outsiders." Lest the residents of the hinterland think there is escape, they may well read a short article in *Atlanta Magazine,* an organ of the Atlanta Chamber of Commerce, by Opie Shelton entitled "The Day That Atlanta Disappeared."[29]

[29] The historians later called it the greatest unexplained phenomenon in the history of the world. No one disputed their claim.

Imagine one day there sat Atlanta, dynamic and bustling, one of the nation's greatest cities. The next morning it was gone, having disappeared during the night without leaving the slightest smidgen of a clue behind.

Gone were the towering office buildings, the banks, the stores, the public utilities, the factories, the hospitals, the schools, the colleges and universities, the centers of culture, the stadium, the homes, the people, the churches, everything.

The suburbs were left untouched. But when early risers attempted to turn on the water, nothing happened. Neither would the electric lights turn on. Their battery-powered radios offered a hint of things to come. Only a handful of the radio stations were on the air, but there was nothing on their news tickers about what had happened during the night.

It was only when these suburbanites headed to their downtown jobs that they actually became a part of the nightmare. As they reached the city limits they suddenly were jolted by the scrub trees and weeds which stood where only yesterday had been a majestic city.

Panic followed.

By word of mouth, the news spread. ATLANTA HAS DISAPPEARED!

Some of the less enchanted chorused, "Good Riddance!" A few said, "Well, we finally got rid of all the niggers."

But the masses didn't join in the chorus.

Those who went to their jobs in the suburbs found the doors of most establishments locked. Lockheed had posted a notice, saying that all of their skilled engineers and scientists had resigned en masse, leaving to accept their choice of dozens of other jobs in other areas. The same was true of the automobile plants and of most of the other job producers of the suburbs.

It took a few days for the original shock to wear off. Then came the mass exodus.

The young and talented pulled up roots and headed for other cities to seek their fortune. The displaced college students began knocking on other college doors, seeking admittance. Doctors and dentists packed up their tools and left. Anyone who could joined the exodus. Soon all that was left were the very old, the feeble, the untrained and the unskilled.

Within one year's time from The Day That Atlanta Disappeared the once prosperous suburbs lay prostrate. Homes were boarded up and abandoned. The automobile had become the only means of transportation available. No longer was there the sound of jetliners or trains. The few stores that were left did little business. No one was moving in, only out.

In short, these once flourishing suburbs had taken on the same desolate look which marks so many of the decaying and dying towns over the nation.

There has always been a dispersion of service activity concomitant with a dispersion of population (the market). Despite the growth (relative and actual) of medical, legal, and personal services in the hinterland, the basic thrust and orientation is inward. The central business district and the central city have strong attractive forces, and overshadow the equivalent activities in the hinterland.

COMMUNICATION AND TRANSPORTATION

Communication

Communication is the unifying influence on the metropolitan or even megalopolitan area. Its role in permitting functional differentiation both within and without the city has been demonstrated amply. Nevertheless, there are special points to be made regarding this extremely complex phenomenon.

Communications are possibly the most centralized urban function. Recognizing that NBC in the Los Angeles area operates from "beautiful downtown Burbank,"[30] it is more

---

There were acrimonious afterthoughts.

"Perhaps we had more stake in the well being of the core city of Atlanta than we were willing to admit," some said.

But, alas, it was too late to turn back.

On The Day That Atlanta Disappeared the suburbs became doomed to a slow but sure death. The umbilical cord which had fed them had been severed.

Oh, if only those people had understood that the fortunes of their city and their suburbs were inextricably tied together. Opie L. Shelton, "The Day That Atlanta Disappeared," Reprinted from *Atlanta Magazine*, April 1966.

[30] The recent NBC comedy show, "Laugh In," has made this facility one of the best known in the nation.

---

common to find radio and television studios centralized in the city.

The centralizing power of airborne communications should be recognized by all of us who live outside the corporate city limits, or for that matter, outside the urbanized area.[31] New York's radio and television signals invade Connecticut and New Jersey; Los Angeles stations can be heard in Redlands; cable television brings in signals from even greater distances. City news and city phenomena are distributed outward. In many areas the big city stations, both radio and television, even present the farm news! It would be difficult to measure the effect of these media in establishing a metropolitan identity, but surely they must create at least a metropolitan awareness and character.

Newspapers function the same way in their preparation and publication. Although there may be a proliferation of daily and weekly newspapers throughout a metropolitan area, the major media are central city citizens. Within the past 10 years this writer has witnessed the movement of two large newspapers, the Boston *Globe* and the Boston *Times Herald,* from the central business district to other close-in central city locations. Employment in this medium is drawn from all parts of the metropolitan area. The product originates centrally and is dispersed through wide areas.[32]

Newspapers, radio, and television are all

---

[31] For a definition of urbanized area, see Bureau of the Census, *United States Census of Population: 1960* (Washington, D.C., United States Government Printing Office, 1961). Definitions are in the introduction.

[32] The Audit Bureau of Circulation publishes circulation data — numbers and places — for newspapers subscribing to the service. These data may be obtained at the newspaper general office.

unifying phenomena. They provide a vital link between city and hinterland, one that operates in both directions but which is centered on the city.

Certainly, telephone communication, regardless of the location of equipment or offices, has fostered urban growth. It is possibly the most important factor permitting decentralization of population, business, industry, and virtually all major urban activities.[33]

Transportation

The most visible and critical communications medium is transportation. Our homes are surrounded by streets which, in turn, lead to highways and terminal type facilities. Indeed, it is this means of circulation associated with the automobile that has formed our cities and metropolitan areas.[34] These surface phenomena are most obvious to us, and the recent creation of a Department of Transportation and the recent federal requirements for transportation studies underline their importance in understanding and planning the city (real city).

Rail and rapid transit — the important pre-automobile surface lines — have played relatively minor roles in recent years. However, as the need for parking facilities increases, as congestion becomes more severe, and as air pollution becomes a greater problem, we find renewed interest in this mode of travel. Although the Japanese have led the way recently, the American cities are now

awakening. In the Boston area the Massachusetts Bay Transit Authority has begun functioning during this decade and has returned rail commuter service to the South Shore and added it to the western suburbs. The Bay Area Rapid Transit System has been having difficulties, but is proceeding with development of a new system for the San Francisco-Oakland Metropolitan area. Los Angeles held a referendum on November 5, 1968 regarding a beginning on a rapid transit system. That these lines operate both in and out of the city needs no elaboration, but the major function is to get the hinterland dwellers into the central city for work and play, and then return them home. This type of development, together with the development of the Northeast Corridor rail commuter service will make the hinterlands even more attractive to the city escaper.[35]

Intercity, transcontinental, and intercontinental travel have created problems that the hinterland must solve for the city (and the metropolitan area as well). Air travel and the development of bigger and better planes has created traffic jams as dramatic as the "freeway rush." New York's commercial air traffic must be handled by three airports — two in the city proper and the other in Newark, New Jersey. The need for a fourth facility already exists. Surely, if political considerations can be sublimated, it will be planned in a hinterland location. Whether the airport represents a city exclave or not, new facilities must be placed farther from its center.

Although Chicago is now considering construction of a new air terminal in Lake Michigan, it long ago replaced Midway with

[33] Note that telephone call data are considered by the Bureau of the Census in its definition of standard metropolitan statistical areas.

[34] For a recent discussion of Ekistics, see C. A. Doxiadis, "Man's Movement and His City," *Science*, Vol. CLXII, No. 3851 (October 18, 1968), pp. 326-34.

[35] The Department of Transportation has taken the lead in developing high speed rail transportation between Boston, New York, and Washington, D.C.

O'Hare.[36] Dallas and Fort Worth have finally decided to cooperate in operating a joint airport between them. Kansas City is in the process of replacing a small "downtown" airport with a modern supersonic-capability airport in the northern part of the standard metropolitan statistical area. Dulles Airport, 50 miles from Washington, D.C., is finally receiving some of the traffic for which it was designed. Surely it will replace National as the major airport for Washington, D.C. Here, too, there was experiment which was perhaps too early. Friendship Airport between Washington and Baltimore has not become for D.C. what might have been expected; rather, it is Baltimore's airport.

Airports and airport problems are not restricted to any part of the country or the world. It appears that we may look forward to a decentralization of the large jet ports which, in turn, may be connected to the central city by smaller local airports serviced by

[36] After virtually abandoning Midway for commercial flights to Chicago, a number of airlines have recently re-established service there. This change has been due to the traffic problems at O'Hare, and has been fostered by the development of jet aircraft that can safely use Midway's shorter landing strips.

helicopters or STOL craft.[37] The hinterland is already performing a "break of bulk" function for the city and is likely to increase that particular function.

CONCLUSION

City-hinterland relationships cover the whole range of economic and social functions within the metropolitan complex. Whether or where a line is drawn creates the initial and major problem in delineating inside vs. outside functions and relationships. The major focus in this chapter has been on the administrative boundary line. This focus is on intra-metropolitan phenomena. Had the line been drawn at the extreme of the urbanized area, a new set of problems would arise, but they would still fit the major categories discussed here.

There are no self-sufficient cities or metropolitan areas. Neither are there completely static situations. Cities are in a dynamic equilibrium with their hinterlands and their total environments. Analysts may stop the action momentarily to view relationships, but they must recognize that such relationships are ever changing. These are entities whose-limits are indeterminate.

[37] Great emphasis has been placed on development of Short Take Off and Landing aircraft, both conventional and vertical. These craft have been very busy on commuter runs to and from Los Angeles International Airport, supplementing and possibly supplanting helicopter service at some Los Angeles metropolitan area airports.

Urban Expansion— Will it Ever Stop?

26

Mason Gaffney

When you walk down Main Street in any large city, each step takes you past several thousand dollars' worth of frontage. Frontage is a common measure of city land, and it goes by the foot, like a precious commodity. A front foot is a foot along the sidewalk with a strip behind it 100-150 feet to the rear of the lot. A foot on the right street is worth whole farms.

Among the dearest is State Street in Chicago, where some frontage goes for 30 thousand dollars a foot. At that rate an acre would bring 13 million dollars. Market Street in San Francisco runs up to 10 thousand dollars a foot. A foot on Fayetteville Street in Raleigh, N.C., is worth about 4 thousand dollars.

Why do these strips of otherwise common dirt command such prices? The answer lies in the forces of urban centralization.

Urban land, which serves a region much as the farmstead serves a farm, is a central storage base for collecting and distributing outputs and inputs and for sorting, processing, and reassembling them.

It is a center that affords easy, reliable access to enough volume and variety of resources to supply complex, specialized, continuous, and large-scale operations, and enough markets to absorb their outputs and byproducts.

It is a reservoir of goods and labor whose abundance gives the slack to allow flexibility of operations, meet emergency needs, and afford the innovator endless possible combinations of skills and resources to experiment with.

The city is a convenient gathering place where buyers can rely on finding sellers, and sellers buyers — a place to inspect, compare, and exchange goods and render and receive services. Its large local market attracts a variety of specialized goods and services. Its compactness permits cheap distribution, which in turn facilitates savings from large-scale central operations.

It is a central store of information and ideas — a place to confer and arbitrate face to face, to plan and administer, to do research and educate. It is a place where many minds

Reprinted from *Land, The Yearbook of Agriculture* (1958), pp. 503-22 by permission of the author and the United States Department of Agriculture.

can associate freely to stimulate, evaluate, and diffuse new techniques and ideas: in all, the brain, control, and power center of society.

Urban land commands a premium, too, as a place to reside. For living, as for business, its advantage is access to a wide selection of opportunities and associations.

Although it need not be fertile, or flat, or even dry, good urban land is scarce. The value of land for urban functions depends on its location relative to transportation, resources, and markets. Large-scale producers attach a special premium to the best lands, as they require access to the widest markets for economical operations. Being large, they also require large areas, so that competition for the best land is extremely keen.

The entire network of location factors defies simple analysis. But the greatest cities develop at strategic central locations, where they assemble and process many resources for many markets. Junctions and hubs of transportation have obvious merits, as do heads of navigation and other load-breaking points.

Good location is not enough to fit land for urban functions. Access, the basic urban resource, is partly man-made. The city enhances its natural advantages by pushing out routes to tap wider territories, but that is only a start. To realize its full potential, the city develops a network of local transportation — a system of general access through which its lifeblood moves.

So vital is transportation that most cities devote more than half their developed land to it. In 53 central cities — "central" meaning the major downtown city of a metropolitan region, excluding suburbs and satellites — which were studied by Harland Bartholomew for his book, *Land Uses in American Cities,* streets and alleys alone occupied 28 percent of the developed area.

Autos are voracious off-street land consumers, too. One parking space, with access lanes and a little to spare to allow for human weakness, preempts more than 300 square feet. The driveway and garage on a residential lot occupy about as much surface as the house. Many factories occupy less space than their own parking lots and loading and delivery aprons. The modern, auto-oriented shopping center allows 4 or 5 square feet of parking for each square foot of floor area. Filling stations are almost entirely open space.

Other forms of transportation are less demanding, but still they take a good deal of land. Railroads took 5 percent of the cities studied by Mr. Bartholomew, including much very costly land near downtown. Considerable space is devoted also to docks, bus terminals, airports, and easements for pipes and wires to transport water, gas, and electricity. Halls, elevators, and stairs take space inside buildings.

Most of this spacious network of public and semipublic lands dedicated to free movement yields little direct income, but the city can ill afford not to devote generous spaces to these corridors, which allow full release of the enormous productive forces inherent in specialization and exchange and give the private lands their value.

The final essential for productive urban land is the improvement of adjoining land. One lonely storehouse no more makes a city than one smoldering stick makes a fire. Assembled buildings compete for customers, suppliers, and use of public spaces, but generally they also complement each other so as to enhance enormously their overall productive value.

For the essence of urban value is access,

and every resource the city adds increases the volume and variety of resources accessible to all. Each new seller is a magnet for more buyers.

Each buyer is a magnet for sellers, pulling trade from farther away, attracting more transportation routes and scheduled runs, and helping establish the city as the place to rely on finding what you want, selling your wares and services, and, in a dynamic, competitive world, keeping touch with the latest products, information, techniques, and ideas.

Each addition to the local market helps also to spread the overhead of more specialized and larger operations. Each new taxpayer shares the burden of large public works and improves the city's credit. Each new producer helps diversify the city's economic base and insure its stability. Each new seller tends either to bring in outside money or reduce leakages of money to outside sellers, and thus he creates new demand for local services.

A growing city therefore may enjoy a long stage of increasing returns, when growth begets more growth. Thus the one best location in a region has a decisive advantage over the second best, and the earliest development has a commanding lead over later comers. The largest urban nucleus tends to snowball, while others shrivel.

The European scholar Georges Widmer has provided an interesting demonstration of increasing returns in urban growth. Widmer worked with Swiss census data, and published his results in the Revue Economique for March 1953. He found a direct relationship between size of city and several measures of per capita economic activity, such as wages and tax revenues.

A limit to increasing returns is the cost of transportation. The larger the city grows, the farther it has to range for markets and ma-terials. And many cities are stopped short of this limit by the city fathers' fears of spoiling their markets, lowering rents, risking money on public works, raising wages and taxes, admitting outsiders, spoiling the fishing, or losing control of city hall.

But a number of metropolitan titans have burst these bonds to accumulate a large share of the population, capital, and the land value of the country. New York City (excluding suburbs and satellites) in 1955 had about 7.8 million people (4.8 percent of our population), and its annual real-estate taxes were 746 million dollars, 7 percent of the national levy.

The gravitational pull of a city does not stop at its fringes. The center of gravity, the downtown district of maximum access, draws the whole city in upon itself, story on story. In this focusing of demand, the city finds further increasing returns from large-scale building.

The most economical layout to interconnect given space users is in three dimensions, in which central heating and other utilities can be distributed over shorter conduits than in two dimensions and each room has quicker access to most of the others. One roof and one foundation serve many stories. Inner partitions need not be weatherproof; the outer surface of a cube increases in less proportion than the space it encloses. So a large, multistory building provides given space, services, and access more cheaply than several small buildings.

There are limits to the economical height of buildings and to the amount of crowding people will endure, of course, and everyone knows that a conspicuous centrifugal surge started some years ago. But nevertheless a city keeps its basic cohesive tendencies, which are its reason for being.

Just how large an area cities occupy no

one knows, for no one can say where a city ends. The United States Census defines "urbanized areas" roughly as those in and around cities of at least 50 thousand inhabitants. That was about 8 million acres in 1950, evenly divided between the central cities and their urbanized fringes. Eight million acres equals the area of Maryland and Delaware, 0.42 percent of the continental United States, and a little less than the 9 million acres in farmsteads. It seems a modest space requirement for its 70 million residents, particularly the 50 million in central cities.

The census has been conservative in its definition, for the area enclosed inside far-flung urban outposts would be much greater. Eight million acres is the area of a circle with a 63-mile radius, or two circles with 45-mile radii, and stray bits from any one of our metropolitan giants may be found that far from its center.

But even the census' limited area is urbanized only in a loose sense. Despite the advantages of compact land use, central cities themselves are surprisingly patchy. In Mr. Bartholomew's 53 central cities, the undeveloped portion was about 29 percent. Although his surveys are not all up to date, many local planning surveys show comparable figures after 1955.

His developed urban land was about 0.06 acre per capita, or 5 yards on a football gridiron. At that density, the 50 million inhabitants of central cities of more than 50 thousand use nearer 3 million acres than 4 million.

Even some of that 3 million acres they "use" only in a poetic sense. It is mostly open space. The area actually covered by buildings is probably less than 400 thousand acres, less than some western ranches and less than 15 percent of the developed area of the central cities.

No one expects that every building should occupy 100 percent of its site, but just how big a yard and grounds should be so as to be designated as developed by a building somewhere on it is a puzzle. Some urban buildings do occupy their entire sites, and by contrast such other sites as the 75 acres around Ford's new administration building in Dearborn seem nearer akin to undeveloped lands. No one can say exactly how we are to designate such lands, but some sort of allowance would certainly reduce the central cities' land "use" appreciably below 3 million acres.

If the central city is a little patchy, its outskirts are in shreds. Here, to be sure, are big users of land like golf courses, dumps, drive-ins, and airports, serving the central city. But it would be hard to define any segment of this nebulous territory that was not largely in weeds. Probably less than half the 4 million acres of urban fringe cited in the census deserves to be called "developed."

For cities under 50 thousand, our data are progressively less detailed.

Hugh H. Wooten and James R. Anderson, of the Department of Agriculture, estimated that all cities of more than a thousand inhabitants in 1954 occupied 18.6 million acres — about the area of South Carolina and 1 percent of the continental United States. Smaller communities may occupy another 10 million acres. But all these figures include empty spaces, which make up larger portions of the smaller cities.

As to urban values, they are prodigious. It is easy to underestimate them because of the comparatively modest space requirements of cities. There is nothing modest about the prices of urban land, however.

Residential lots in respectable established neighborhoods sell for 50 dollars to 250 dollars a foot and for more than 500 dollars a foot along a few gold coasts. Apartment sites average higher, going above 1 thousand dollars along Lake Shore Drive in Chicago. Slum sites are often held at fancy prices because of an expectation of future industrial, commercial, or public demand. Some subsidiary shopping districts sell for 1 thousand dollars a foot. The best industrial sites in large central cities command well over 100 thousand dollars an acre.

Prices of land out from the center are much lower, but still impressive, especially after the multifold increases since 1950. Undeveloped residential or industrial land along new superhighways was bringing several thousand dollars an acre in 1957, and more around New York City. Industrial acreage near Eastshore Freeway, Oakland, averaged 10,500 dollars as early as 1953. Potential sites of shopping centers brought 10 thousand to 50 thousand dollars an acre, as did motel sites near the better interchanges of the new turnpikes and thruways.

Airspace above the golden ground of the city also carries high price tags. An option on air over the Pennsylvania Railroad tracks in New York specified more than 3 million dollars an acre in 1955. A Times Square billboard brings 15 thousand a year.

At such prices, it does not take many cities to outvalue all the farms in whole States, and in most States one or a few of the largest cities do. New York City real estate in 1955 was worth some unknown but large amount over its assessed valuation of 20 billion dollars, which was the current market value of all the farm real estate in New York State and 19 other Eastern States. For the whole country, urban values exceed farm values several times over.

It may even be that urban values exceed farm values per capita. One cannot be certain. Land prices swing violently and rapidly, yet the only general source of data on urban values is from moss-covered tax assessments. Urban assessments are more obsolete than rural assessments — if that is possible.

But we do know how much taxes property pays. It may surprise some farmers to learn that farm property taxes are less per capita than nonfarm property taxes — roughly 54 dollars, compared to 72 dollars in 1956. Of some 11.7 billion dollars levied that year, farm property bore only 1.2 billion dollars.

The higher urban levies might reflect higher urban tax rates, rather than per capita values. The average rate on farm real estate, as reported in 1957 by the Agricultural Finance Review, was about 1 percent of market value. There is a general impression that urban real rates average higher — and some evidence to back it up. David Rowlands, of the University of Pennsylvania, in a report on the Property Tax in Atlanta and Other Large Cities, estimated effective tax rates in 20 large cities for 1956. Only 2 of them fall under 1 percent, and a few exceed 2 percent.

On the other hand, a study published in the Review of Economics and Statistics for February 1957 found otherwise. Scott Maynes and James Morgan, analyzing voluminous questionnaire data from the University of Michigan Survey of Consumer Finances and the United States Census Residential Financing Survey, found the real rate of property taxation on owner-occupied urban residences in 1953 to be nearly 1 percent.

They did not check the possibility that respondents may have tended to understate their taxes. Nor did they discover to what extent the low tax rates on owner-occupied residences resulted from homestead exemption, which would not apply to other classes of real estate. Still, it is other classes of real estate, especially rented slum and vacant land, that are most frequently found to be underassessed.

One might reason that city tax rates must be higher because city property pays city taxes on top of county taxes — although, of course, the most urbanized counties might have lower overall rates than predominantly rural counties. City people get more local governmental services, it is true, but they get them cheaper because they live closer together. They also have more non-property-tax sources of revenue.

Then, too, a census study under Allen Manvel found farm real estate overassessed — hence overtaxed by the counties — relative to urban real estate in 101 counties of downstate Illinois in 1946. Arthur Walrath found the same in several counties around Milwaukee in 1955. Remember, too, that an appreciable share of urban real estate is tax-exempt institutional ground.

None of these studies provides a solid basis for estimating urban real-estate values. The United States Census of Governments planned to release in 1958 what should be a definitive study of tax assessment ratios. Even that omits tax-exempt real estate from consideration, and also it omits suburban acreage, but still it may provide the first firm estimate of urban real-estate values in the United States.

Meanwhile, we have reasonable grounds for putting the real rate of urban property taxation between 1 and 2 percent, which means the aggregate value of urban real estate is of the order of seven or eight times greater than farm real estate. It is entirely possible that a 100-percent comprehensive reckoning, including tax-exempt holdings and suburban acreage, would reach as high as 10 times farm values, or 1 trillion dollars.

Other indirect evidences of real-estate values are the mortgages they carry. As of September 1957, the farm mortgage debt was 10 billion dollars, compared to 143 billion dollars on nonfarm residential and commercial real estate. Nonfarm real estate in 1957 probably carried a higher ratio of debt to value — it is impossible to say for certain because most real estate is unmortgaged. On the other hand, however, nonfarm mortgage figures do not include the debt on industrial, rail, or utility holdings, or on institutional and public real estate.

Several studies also indicate that urban families occupy dwellings valued at two to three times their annual incomes. This suggests that urban residences alone are worth more than 500 billion dollars.

These last two lines of reasoning yield no definite numerical estimates of urban values, but they do confirm the belief that they dwarf the value of farm real estate.

Real estate is more than land, of course, and conceivably urban real-estate values inhere largely in the buildings — we hear a good deal about the declining importance of land in an urban society. That may be a misconception, however.

Builders putting new single-family homes on cheap outlying land reckon the site at one-sixth or one-fifth of the total cost. But not many urbanites live in new homes on cheap outlying land. Even in 1957, after 12 years of record-smashing construction, 75 percent of all urban dwelling units were built before 1945 and most of them before 1929. There are almost no new residences in older central cities. A study by the Real Estate Board of New York in 1953 found that 80 percent of Manhattan's apartments were more than 50 years old.

In fringe areas, where new buildings do outvalue their own sites, a large share of the sites have no buildings. Around Cleveland, for example, 57 percent of the Cuyahoga

County Planning Commission's "suburban ring" and 84 percent of the "rural ring" were vacant in 1954. In commercial districts, with their majestic frontage prices, it takes a new and substantial structure to match the site value.

All in all, from the limited information available, there is no reason to dismiss land value as a minor part of urban real-estate value, especially if we include vacant lands at their current market prices. It may even be the larger share. And, interestingly enough, the ratio of land to building values tends to be highest in the centers of large, densely populated, and built-up cities, where economic life is supposed to have lost touch with the land most completely.

A striking aspect of today's cities is their rapid outward thrust. Urban values being what they are, cities gobble up farmland at will. There is no accurate survey of the wide and ragged urban frontier, but various estimates suggest it has been advancing recently about 400 thousand acres a year into the heart of America's farmlands.

Is this in the farmers' interest? Many thoughtful observers are raising voices in alarm for the future. The most vocal of them seem to think the city should be contained. There is another side to the question, though.

The city serves the farmer and buys his products. It is the farmer's interest that cities have ample land to serve him well. He would only suffer if he were to confine the city into a bottleneck between the barn and the table.

In fact, the city is all too likely to become a bottleneck, anyway, with no help from the farmer — but much to his detriment.

Because of increasing returns in urban growth, many cities in strategic spots have a measure of monopoly power over parts of their trade territories. Without the spur of competition, they are easily tempted to settle back comfortably and take their customers' money without the costs and bother of offering very adequate or modern service. Their strong position lets them do this simply by vegetating quietly without necessarily having any active monopoly motive. Because downtown sites are favorite investments for absentees and heiresses, too, a high proportion of them fall into ownerships that tend to resist progressive management and risky improvements.

There is competition within each city, of course, but the city fathers who are so inclined can minimize it by restrictive policies. They may lay out streets so as to limit the business frontage; maintain obsolete traffic patterns to protect vested investments; discourage new buildings by overassessing them relative to old — a practice that has become especially common since the war — and assessing undeveloped land at next to nothing; zoning out new developments; limiting the height of buildings; winking at tax-delinquent land speculators and selling off foreclosed properties only slowly; fostering obstructive building codes; endowing tax-free institutions with grounds vastly beyond their needs; neglecting essential public works and services; and refusing to act decisively against obsolescence and blight.

Whether by design, apathy, or sincere devotion to an obsolete tradition, probably most cities contrive to remain inadequately developed to serve fully the demands on them.

To protect themselves, the farmers' best assurance of adequate, modern, and competitive urban services may be to release lands for new development around stagnant central cities. With all its faults, such expansion does introduce new competition for farm trade.

The urban expansion bears critical watching, however.

Are efficient cities evolving — cities that distribute goods with minimum time, motion, and cost?

Are cities swallowing much more farmland than they need?

Above all, does the present pattern of urban expansion contain the same elements of instability that have brought most previous land booms to collapse?

To answer these questions, it is necessary to analyze the process of urban expansion more closely.

Like the eager suitor who leaped onto his horse and dashed madly off in all directions, the city moves out hither and yon with little apparent consistency or reason. Here is Washington, D.C., growing out from the back door of the Capitol, in defiance of its planner's best-laid schemes. There is the shopping district gravitating toward a high-income residential area, but radiating influences that create slums in its van and erode away the attracting force. Here are sewers without-houses, while out beyond arise new houses without sewers. There is hardly any predicting where the construction crews will turn up next.

What are the builders seeking?

More space? There is considerable unused space in the central city itself.

Lower taxes? Fringe residents, scattered broadcast with more school-children per capita and without the downtown commerce and industry to share tax burdens, in general must pay more taxes to finance given municipal services.

Surveys in 1955 by Amos H. Hawley and Basil G. Zimmer, of the University of Michigan, found fringe residents around Flint, Mich., actually more willing than residents of the central city to assume higher taxes. And it is evident that many people flee central cities in search of better schools and other costly public services that the city fathers are to parsimonious to finance.

Freedom from traffic? The farther one lives from jobs and markets the more traffic he must buck in between.

Freedom from restrictive policies? Often so — yet many suburban enclaves become more restrictive than the central city.

Of the many, many things that urban refugees are seeking, most are to be found in the central city. The refugees want municipal services, access to social and economic opportunities, and other urban advantages — but not at any price. To oversimplify a complex politico-socio-economic phenomenon, urban outmigrants, like the westward pioneers before them, are seeking cheap land. The very advantages of the city prove its major liability when they promote asking prices so high as to drive builders out of town.

The quest of cheap land leads the city not just to expand, but to disintegrate. The quest turns very much on the individual seller. Asking prices for comparable lands vary widely with the seller's finances, tax position, information, sentiments, or just plain cussedness. Jack Lessinger, of the University of California's Real Estate Research Program, has found tentatively that in the Santa Clara Valley, around San Jose, it is the smaller farmers who succumb earliest to the city, and larger landholders who hold out longest. The French geographers, M. Phlipponeau, J. Tricart, and C. Precheur, describe the same tendency around Nancy and Paris. Buyers find a bargain here, another yonder, and build accordingly, so that development proceeds in patches and freckles.

State highway builders can stretch funds much further where the right-of-way is cheap. Besides, holders of cheap land are less likely to band into militant "Property Owners'

Protective Leagues" and the like to block new thruways; and railroads are just as happy to see highway funds diverted to routes not paralleling their own. New highways, like railroads before them, often tend to bypass congested areas and develop earliest and most fully in less settled territory. They open wide new areas to hunt-and-peck development and establish new urban nuclei where they converge.

These outlying nuclei are bases from which even farther flung developments are launched. Especially along trunk routes, they coalesce into gangling, diffuse urban complexes that some writers, fancy running free, are describing as "polynucleated urbs," "conurbations," "cities as long as highways," "atomic megalopolises," and "scrambled eggs" and hailing, with enthusiasm or resignation, as forerunners of a new era.

Our first question was, "Are they efficient cities?" By any ideal standard they are not.

Transportation and utility lines to join the scattered pieces cost billions. The result at best is a poorly coordinated tangle. Commerce bypasses old bottlenecks but meets an obstacle course that consumes untold time and motion and can hardly avoid reflecting itself, among other ways, in a wider farm-market spread.

Such coherent patterns as do emerge are geometrically imperfect. Some variation on a linear theme, strung out miles along a railway, waterway, or highway, is commonest. But why go 20 miles west when there is open land 5 miles north? It takes three-dimensional development to afford maximum access at minimum cost among given users of space. Linear developments do not even use two dimensions, but force all traffic along one long, congested line. That, often as not, was built originally for through traffic.

One can probably understand how linear patterns develop. Cities fail to provide adequate two-dimensional street networks; and interurban trunk lines, financed by the State or National Government, offer ready-built, open-ended avenues of escape to cheap, accessible land. Landholders along existing routes can subdivide without dedicating 25 percent of their land for streets and without submitting to central controls over subdivision plans. But to explain is not to justify.

Our second question was: "Do cities need to swallow so much good farmland?"

We should probably concede the city first choice over the best land, even the most fertile, just as farmers concede corn first choice of the best wheatland. It may not make much sense to farm steep slopes in the Ozarks, but it would make less sense to put St. Louis there, to put Minneapolis in the north woods, and so on. But this hardly settles the question.

Cities, even central cities, are not using nearly the land they already contain. These undigested pieces are of negative value to the city itself. Cities exist to bring people together. Vacant and underdeveloped lands keep them apart and thus destroy part of the city's basic resources: cheap distribution and easy access. Even if land had no alternative use in farming, it would pay many a city to draw itself together.

Dispersion also forces heavier reliance on those hungry land gobblers, automobiles and trucks. Their demands for highway, turning, and parking space displace tens of thousands of dwelling units a year, scatter the city out farther, and consume more farmland. Dispersion requires that each plant, far from the storehouses and services of the central city, be more self-sufficient, which of course increases its space requirements.

It is especially out from the center, though, that cities preempt vast lands they do not use and may never use. Little urban fragments, prospering busily among fields and orchards, excite speculative hopes for land sales around and between them until urban price influence extends millions of acres beyond the city limits.

Urban prices have a baleful influence on farming. The dirt farmer has struggle enough financing title to lands priced by their anticipated income from agriculture alone. Urban prices push him out of the market completely. Landholders near cities must be speculators as well as farmers.

Often they are not farmers at all. High-priced lands in areas with urban possibilities tend to gravitate to those who have the financial power to wait.

Urban financial power is something few working farmers can match.

Federal income-tax laws tend to aggravate the dirt farmer's disadvantage, for they make speculative gains especially attractive to those in higher tax brackets. To begin, any interest and local taxes are fully deductible. Then the speculator may qualify for "capital gains" treatment — that is, for excluding 50 percent of any realized increment from taxable income, with a maximum tax rate of 25 percent on the increment. That is of great value to the man in an 80-percent tax bracket and tends to make him a high bidder in the market for appreciating suburban lands.

To qualify for capital gains treatment, the speculator must establish that he is not "in the real-estate business," but is a passive "investor," neither improving land for sale nor soliciting buyers. Or he may establish that he is "using the land in his trade or business" (other than real estate).

Should he lose on one sale he can offset the loss against other capital gains. Better yet, if he establishes that he is using the land in his trade or business, he can offset losses against ordinary income, even though any gains would not be taxed as such.

Still better, if it is his residence that he sells, and he puts the proceeds into a new residence within the year, the entire gain is tax free — and with a little effort a commuter may learn to "reside" over a considerable investment.

Best of all, one who buys land years ahead of his own needs never pays a tax on the rise of value so long as he does not sell — something many large corporations, with huge reserves "for expansion," have little expectation of doing. Wilbur Steger, writing in the National Tax Journal for September 1957, estimates that 90 percent of all capital gains were thus left tax free from 1901 to 1949.

The result of all this is a virtual scorched-earth policy for many lands around cities. Why risk any improvement or overt sales effort that might land you "in the real-estate business" and thus disqualify your increments from "capital gains" treatment? Why not hoard up vast industrial estates for "future expansion"? Should your alleged need actually eventuate and if the value of the land has gone up in the meantime, you will have achieved a kind of tax-free income. Should you sell, you can probably get capital-gains treatment for increments and ordinary offset for any losses.

For lands that do remain farmed, the influence of urban prices often means a wasting away of farm fertility and capital.

Dr. Lessinger has documented this phenomenon in his dissertation, *The Determination of Land Use in Rural Urban Transition Areas* (Berkeley, Calif., 1956). Around expanding San Jose, Calif., prune and apricot orchards are deteriorating as the city infiltrates the Santa Clara Valley. He analyzes the age distribution and bearing condition of orchards in different zones around the city and finds deterioration of orchards closely related to anticipations of urban demand, as reflected in land prices.

Thus the city takes land from the farm long before actually putting it to urban use. To a degree this is economical: farm improvements are wasted on lands marked for immediate urbanization. But Dr. Lessinger's studies indicate that urban prices, with their blighting influence on agriculture, already extend over an area of the Santa Clara Valley well beyond any likely urban demand. Is this a general condition throughout the United States?

Suppose we allow the entire nonfarm population of the United States the luxury space standards of Winnetka, a Chicago suburb. With a golf course, spacious parklands, playfields, beaches, wide, tree-lined streets, two railroad rights-of-way, large lots and yards, private driveways and two-car garages, estate districts, and almost no apartments, Winnetka has 0.16 acre of developed land per resident — far more than the 0.06 acre in the 53 central cities that Mr. Bartholomew surveyed.

At the Winnetka standard, an urban population of 150 million would require 24 million acres — about the area of Indiana — which we can safely take as beyond any foreseeable demand.

The "regional cities" that enthusiasts are envisioning and promoters are touting along the Atlantic, Pacific, and gulf coasts, the Great Lakes, dozens of State freeways and turnpikes, resurgent inland waterways, and anticipated Federal-program superhighways (along with a more conventional accretion around established cities) by the simplest count exceed that 24 million acres by a wide margin.

Twenty-four million acres would be contained in 6 circles with 45-mile radii; or 24

circles with 22-mile radii; or 120 circles with 10-mile radii. As small a city as Eugene, Oreg., extends its price influence more than 10 miles from the center (not around a full circle), but there are 340 cities in the country larger than Eugene and the price influence of some of them radiates more than 50 miles. If that were not enough, there are thousands of smaller towns. A careful survey would probably show at least 100 million acres — the area of California — under the influence of urban prices.

The answer to our second question, then, is that cities are taking and leaving undeveloped more farmland than they need.

This raises the third question: "Can urban expansion continue?" Or have the onrushing urban armies overextended their lines and lost themselves in agriculture's defense in depth?

Many writers since 1955 have been projecting trends of the past 10 years forward another 20 years or so and viewing with alarm the startling inroads on farmland. History warrants few things less than it does projecting land booms far into the future. Cities typically have expanded in waves.

May we expect the present wave to break and recede?

This also is a prospect to view with alarm. The enormous financial impact of urban expansion is a vital element of our prosperity. New construction, excluding farm and military construction, has been running around some 40 billion dollars annually. That is nearly 12 percent of the national income. It consists mainly of residential, commercial, industrial, highway, and public-utility building. Most of it is tied closely to urban expansion.

The role of construction in sustaining the flow of spending is greater than its volume alone would suggest. A good deal of purchasing power in most years leaks out of the circular flow of spending into savings and allowances for depreciation. The leakages must be offset each year by new investment to avoid a multiple decline in national income.

A decline of annual investment under most conditions will produce a multiple decline in national income because consumption spending, which declines when income declines, is also a creator of money income. Lower investment means lower income. Lower income means lower consumption. That in turn means still lower income — and so on through several stages.

Autonomous declines in consumption would have similar multiple effects, but consumption usually is a relatively passive factor, which economists are inclined to treat as primarily a function of income itself. Investment is more independent and temperamental a variable, and probably most economists would agree that maintaining national income is in large part a problem of maintaining investment spending.

Of the investment on which so much hinges, 40 billion dollars of construction spending is a large share. It is also the most independent share. Other private investment is mostly in less durable goods — machinery, equipment, and inventories. Replacement and turnover of these are passive functions of time and income to some extent. Other public spending is mostly relatively rigidly committed.

The importance of the third critical question is equaled by the difficulty of answering it.

On one hand, cities have rarely expanded rapidly without tragedy — neither, for that matter, has agriculture. We have experienced land development booms along wagon roads, canals, steamboat channels, plank roads, steam railways, horse railways, cable carlines, trolleys, subways, elevated railroads, and motor highways, with townsites and subdivisions proliferating on every hand. Most of the booms busted.

The disasters of 1819, 1836, 1857, 1873, 1893, and 1929 greet the tourist through history like bones bleaching by the trailside. Will future historians shake their heads sadly over the "second automobile bubble," as today they do over the first, and over the "canal fever," "plank-road delirium," and "railroad mania" of the past?

Perhaps — but, on the other hand, history is under no iron necessity to repeat itself. Optimists who seem to believe that collapse is unlikely today cite several reasons: increasing population; strengthened monetary and banking regulation and insurance; Federal willingness and ability to spend; longer term, fully amortizable mortgages; more prudent subdividing practices; large private holdings of liquid assets; and other reassuring phenomena.

These are not completely tranquilizing, however, in light of the cocksure optimism that has preceded and even accompanied — yes, even followed — great crashes of the past. It is worthwhile questioning more closely the stability of forces that lead cities to preempt lands beyond their needs.

The dynamic process of overexpansion seems to be a complex urban variation on a familiar problem of agricultural land settlement.

The process in simplest outline is this: new demand raises land prices; supply responds slowly but massively; high prices over the long period of response ultimately stimulate more new supply than the demand can absorb.

Supply responds very slowly to demand because the process of converting land to urban use involves many steps by several slowly moving, poorly coordinated, frequently reluctant and sometimes downright obstructive public and private agents and because it usually takes land speculators a long time to release or develop most of the sites for actual service.

Say a new State-financed freeway begins the process of bringing farmland into an urban market. Besides transportation, the land needs water, storm and sanitary sewers, telephone, gas, electric power, schools, fire and police protection, and sidewalks, to name some elementary items.

Not only are many services needed. Several steps must be taken to extend most of them from trunklines out through forks and branches to the ultimate distributive tracery that finally brings service to each parcel of land. Governments and utilities must decide to extend their lines and networks to individual parcels. Landholders must decide it is time to receive them — that usually means subdividing, dedicating lands for streets and easements for utilities, often paying for part of the utility extensions and street improvements, and perhaps being annexed and saddled with municipal taxes.

It would be nice for each party involved if all the others would commit themselves to development before he did — or at least when he does. Then he need only pluck the ripe fruit from the tree, instead of undergoing years of risk, interest, depreciation, and obsolescence while he waits for complementary investments to help his own pay out. The situation lends itself to a long impasse of "after-you-my-dear-Alphonse." At every stage, there is inertia, nostalgia, fear, and long bargaining and jockeying.

The final step — actual building on prepared lots — may be as slow as the others, for there are still the lot speculators to wait out. Even when all utilities are in, there is a further rise to speculate on as homes, stores, churches, and so on make a community.

We are also witnessing a sort of municipal land speculation on a grand scale. Many metropolitan suburbs have incorporated undeveloped land, which they proceed to overzone out of reach of the middle-class market. That is done in hopes that its exclusive tone will one day attract upper crust residents who will pay high taxes, handsomely support local merchants, and send their few children away to school. Many communities are ready to wait a long time for such profitable fellow citizens, even when chances of success are slim.

Ralph Barnes and George Raymond, New York planning consultants, warn in the Journal of the American Institute of Planners for spring 1955, that such municipal policies have become more restrictive than even the communities' parochial self-interests would dictate. New Canaan and Greenwich, Conn., New York suburbs, have actually increased the minimum size of building lot to 4 acres in some sections, in the most congested metropolitan area in the United States. Mountain Lakes, N.J., has gone so far as to buy up a large share of its land to forestall building.

Now scarcity breeds substitution, and while supply is thus developing so dilatorily in areas most logically destined for urban growth, the impatient demand probes outward. It finds a warm welcome in many outlying communities that have urban aspirations. Some of them even offer subsidies, tax favors, and sites to woo industries.

Moreover, a large share of building is outside any incorporated area. The Sacramento housing market is an extreme instance. An unpublished report of the Federal Housing Administration, dated April 1957, states that 80 percent of all private dwelling units authorized there from 1954 through 1956 were outside incorporated areas.

These latter-day pioneers demand utilities, which often are willing to come if the customers are there first, especially if rival sellers are within striking distance and if regulatory commissions let them balance any losses with higher rates charged to all their customers. The newcomers also demand public services, which usually come where there are votes and a tax base.

Thus the scattering of urban settlement leads the basic urbanizing distributive net-[1] works and services to proliferate over wider territories than the ultimate demand can absorb.

Just how wide and how empty these territories are is startling to discover. The New York engineering firm of Parsons, Brincker-hoff, Hall & MacDonald surveyed land uses and potentialities in connection with its 1953-1955 report to the San Francisco Bay Area Rapid Transit Council. It found ample suitable acreage in the Bay area for the entire projected 1990 population of the whole State of California: 22 million to 31 million people — 7 to 10 times the Bay area's population of 3 million in 1953-1955. This is allowing ample areas for recreation and industry.

The California State Water Resources Board surveyed the area independently in 1955, using aerial photographs, and published the findings in its Bulletin No. 2. For the 10-county Bay area metropolitan region, only 15 percent of the suitable urban land, or 10 percent of the gross land area, was actually developed for urban use in 1955.

In the crowded city of San Francisco itself, the Water Resources Board survey showed 23 percent of the usable land was undeveloped in 1955. Along the Bay side of San Mateo County (the "Peninsula"), which is often hastily described as having become "a solid mass of suburbs," 75 percent was undeveloped. On the Bay side of Alameda County, which includes Oakland and Berkeley, the survey reported 62 percent was undeveloped.

In the Santa Clara Valley (around San Jose), whose "total urbanization" is often forecast as imminent, 86 percent of the suitable land was undeveloped for urban use in 1955. The total suitable urban land in this valley, 155 thousand acres net of streets, exceeds the area used in 1955 in the entire Bay area (129 thousand acres, also net of streets). The developed portions, however, are scattered over the valley floor. By one estimate, 7 square miles of postwar subdivisions in 1954 were scattered over 200 square miles of Santa Clara County, with at least one subdivision in each square mile. Transportation and utility networks are or must someday be extended to most of these urban islets, and thereby to the lands among them.

The California Water Resources Board bulletin said that 65 percent of the suitable land was undeveloped for urban use in the Los Angeles hydrographic unit — that is, in the city of Los Angeles, the immediately surrounding cities, and the more or less urbanized unincorporated lands.

Another 1955 survey, Bulletin 87 of the Regional Planning Association of New Jersey, New York, and Connecticut, reported the following percentages of suitable land undeveloped in some of the counties of metropolitan New York: Bronx, 9 percent; Kings (Brooklyn), 44 percent; Richmond, 32 percent; Hudson, 21 percent; Bergen, 54 percent; Westchester, 63 percent; Fairfield, 81 percent. (They counted estates of 2 acres and more as "undeveloped.") For the entire 22-county, tristate metropolitan region, dotted from end to end with fragments of New York City and laced with transportation and utility lines, only 21 percent of the suitable land, or 16 percent of the gross land area, was developed for urban use.

To occupy these vast territories calls not only for transportation and utility networks, but also for enormous private investments in autos, trucks, service stations, and the whole complex of individualized transportation equipment. This mobilizes consumers to bring their demand to every nook and cranny of undeveloped territory. Scattered stores, schools, factories, churches, and other basic creators of urban land value also shed their influence on the included undeveloped lands.

The unfilled demand pushes upward, too. The high price of land stimulates more intensive vertical building (and generally closer economy of land) on a few sites than demand can begin to absorb over the entire area subject to urban influence.

Here are the makings of a cycle of over-expansion that should come to light when speculators holding the better lands try to find markets. But a great deal remains unclear.

Perhaps some land developers do plunge ahead under the sole stimulus of current prices, but it seems doubtful whether most investors would commit themselves for long terms without an eye to the future.

How shall we explain the tenacity of the speculators who confidently hold for a rise and the dauntless optimism of developers, builders, home buyers, utilities, municipalities, and still more speculators who invest in growing areas in contempt of mounting hoards of half-urbanized land within the market sphere?

One reason for surplus development is that rival districts and cities race for position. Racing differs from economic competition, as usually conceived, in that races end. Where new population and transportation are opening and promising to open new urban potentialities, the fixed layout of routes becomes temporarily fluid. During the developmental period of uncertainty, several contestants vie enthusiastically for prized positions in the new pattern before it freezes.

Because of increasing returns in urban development, these positions, once established, are quite secure and should appreciate in value as outsiders flock to them. So it makes sense for each contestant to risk great resources in a race which most of them must lose.

Cities and districts race by improving themselves to attract trade, routes, and investments. They push out their own routes to capture undeveloped trade territory from rivals, just as some cities push out aqueducts to stake out scarce waters well ahead of need. Because the motive is to secure territory and position quickly before it is too late, extension of trunklines may proceed when the fever is high without much thought for immediately foreseeable demands.

Trade racing also helps explain the behavior of land speculators. Should a district win its race, it is primarily the land that would appreciate, buildings being duplicable. But should it lose, any buildings, being immobile and fairly specialized, would stand a good chance of finding themselves obsolete. The rational gambler therefore may often prefer to bet on the race from the sidelines by holding unimproved land, postponing building until the uncertainties of racing have been resolved.

He thus lessens his district's chances of victory by retarding its development, of course, but one individual is not likely to think his influence is great.

The irrational gambler also is a factor — a major one — to consider. With several contestants running for the same prize, the average chances of success obviously are not good. Yet land prices in each contending district often seem to run higher than the statistical probability of success would warrant, and the sum of the prices over entire developing areas seem to exceed considerably what would reasonably be justified by income from the land.

Just why this should happen is a mystery social scientists are only beginning to probe. Milton Friedman, of the University of Chicago, and G. L. S. Shackle, of Cambridge, England, have developed some interesting hypotheses about it. The fact that it does happen is well established, however. Economists of several generations have observed, with Alfred Marshall, a renowned Victorian economist, that ". . . if an occupation offers a few extremely high prizes, its attractiveness is increased out of all proportion to their aggregate value." Certainly the urban land market is of that description — frontage prices in some areas increase 100 times within a few blocks.

Just as gamblers who love gambling for its own sake will bet against a wheel they know is fixed, land gamblers bid up land prices higher and over more area than the possibilities of urban income can justify.

Perhaps the most powerful stimulant to demand for land is the emergence of a Malthusian climate of opinion. Opinion is a powerful agent in the land market because land prices are based on opinions of the future and because there is so little factual information to go on.

Try to find a simple statistic, like the number of lots subdivided annually in the United States or, indeed, in any region. Few jurisdictions compile even this information, and few of those include entire metropolitan areas.

Urban outskirts especially are beyond the ken of established centers of information — and it is in these far reaches that the greatest excesses have occurred in the past. There might be enough land prepared and preparing for urban use to swamp a metropolitan market for 20 years, and it is doubtful if more than a few real-estate men, who are not given to broadcasting such gloom, would be aware. Not until June 1957 has there been any semblance of an inventory for the Nation. That, compiled as part of the study of urban tax assessments by the Census of Governments, does not purport to tell anything about the lots other than that they are "of record."

We have no systematic data at all on more difficult but equally important questions, such as the trend of land prices, the number of unrecorded and illegally subdivided urban sites, the areas in various stages of partial urbanization, plans for impending redevelopment, and so on.

Land developers must grope to decisions primarily by the present feel of the market, without factual basis for the longer sighted analysis that is so essential to an activity whose product is as nearly permanent as anything produced by man.

And so, lacking information, the market relies on opinions, which always are in long supply. Some of these are based on careful inference. Others are sheer folklore or glib platitudes circulated by professionally optimistic salesfolk.

Many students of past booms have commented on the propensity of contemporary opinion, unsoundly based, to underestimate the emerging supply of urbanized land and overestimate the demand for it. It is possible to trace out several primrose paths by which opinion falls into these errors.

One is the plausible presumption that construction tends to exhaust the supply of urban land. The sight of childhood haunts covered with fresh masonry seems especially to stir deep Malthusian anxieties that find their way into poignant articles, indignant editorials, goading investment counsel, and finally urgent land hoarding that transcends prosaic computations of supply and demand.

Yet construction urbanizes as much land

as it consumes, or more. Even if a city grew in a compact circle, the ring around its widening circumference would grow ever larger, roughly with the square of its radius. And because cities scatter out all over the landscape, building (especially of roads and utility networks) brings wide supplies of new land into the urban market.

Another primrose path is the equally plausible presumption that skyrocketing land prices reflect an acute scarcity of urban land. But this is to reckon without the vast supplies held in cold storage by speculators and holdouts of one kind and another. The economist's nightmare of inflation without full employment of resources has characterized land markets toward the close of every boom period.

There also seems to be a tendency to underestimate the regenerative power and absorptive capacity of downtown.

There is no denying that autos and trucks, unbound by central terminals and fixed routes, have made it more feasible to bypass downtown and thus have drastically weakened its central position. The big swing has been toward expansive, cheap-land, single-storey development. But many persons in their enthusiasm tend to write off downtown land as though it had become as obsolete as the buildings on it, without due account of human factors like inertia, monopolistic thinking, absentee ownership, speculative land pricing, and restrictive policies.

Others seem to have accepted too uncritically part of the thesis of the late Harvard economist, Joseph A. Schumpeter, and others, that capitalists require security from competition before they will risk funds in large investments like buildings.

But the sleeping giant downtown once aroused by the sting of effective competition and running scared is still no mean competitor itself. Decentralization has tended to deflate speculative anticipations that buoy up downtown land prices and thus has made the most expensive land in the world a bargain relative to outlying sites whose asking prices have multiplied since 1950. Downtown can rebuild and finally has begun to do so.

When downtown rebuilds, it still has the primary advantage of location that made it downtown in the first place — why run around end when you can step through center? And a few skyscraping hotels, office buildings, department stores, and apartments — as only downtown has the focused demand to support — can do the work of square miles of sprawl outside the city limits. 3-D development can work wonders with very little surface. In Philadelphia, for example, just one building, No. 3 Penn Center, increased by 4 percent the city's rental office space when it opened in 1955.

There has been a widespread idea that downtown building space is saturated. Yet the editors of Architectural Forum noted in March 1957 that the architect, Victor Gruen, retained to replan downtown Fort Worth, found that "the underused or derelict reservoir was large enough to provide space for a belt highway, parking garages for 60,000 cars, greenbelts, a 300 percent increase in office space, 80 percent in hotel space, and new civic, cultural, and convention centers. . . . Fort Worth is not a special case. . . ."

The urban economic geographers, R. E. Murphy, J. E. Vance, and B. J. Epstein, discovered from a close study of eight central business districts that six of them were so decayed at the core that building heights in the zone of peak land values averaged much less than in the central business district as a whole. Large parts of the districts were taken up with what they considered "noncentral business district" uses, especially in the older eastern cities. Central business districts occupied well under 1 percent of the areas of their cities and thus had ample room to expand. The authors published their work in Economic Geography, January 1955.

In the downtown of downtowns, Manhattan's accelerating office boom accounts for much more than half of the postwar office space in the country. The postwar increase alone exceeds the total space in any other city in the United States. It is augmenting Manhattan's office space by 40 percent over 1946, yet — far from exhausting the land supply of that tiny island — it is contained in a mere 84 new buildings. And these are focused on two narrow districts, the financial and commercial centers, which are already most congested.

Homer Hoyt, an urban planning consultant, in his monumental *100 Years of Land Values in Chicago*, has shown how the percentage of Chicago land values contained in the Loop has risen and fallen many times in the short span of Chicago's lifetime from 1833 to 1933. Decentralization has not been a continuing process. In the development of American cities, both centralizing and decentralizing forces have worked. Now one dominates; tomorrow it may be the other.

Opinion often seems to stray, too, in interpreting the effect of a few skyscrapers and other intensive developments on future land values. Their advent convinces many landholders that high land prices can be met.

But multistorey buildings are substitutes— enormously effective ones — for land. A few of them can pay high land prices, but to do it they drain demand from blocks around. To be sure, they are also magnets pulling trade to the city from miles away. But when cities all over the country are racing to the sky, outside competition tends to offset this benefit.

High buildings are symptoms of high land prices. But to let a symptom be a cause is to run a danger of circular reasoning.

If land prices are prematurely high to begin — higher than long-run supply-demand balance warrants — intensive vertical development must ultimately deflate the price balloon. The longer this deflation is delayed, the more the error compounds, and the more violent must be the reaction.

The same general lines of reasoning apply to horizontal urban expansion. This is land substitution, too, destined ultimately to cheapen urban land. Yet the psychological impact may be to create a feeling of central position that leads to higher asking prices, more horizontal extension, and a rude awakening some day.

Along with those underestimates of supply there are overestimates of demand.

A prominent cause is exaggerated reliance on population forecasts. These have been notoriously unreliable in the past. Techniques have improved, but there is little warrant for the utter confidence with which forecasts are often repeated. But this is not the main point.

Population forecasts, if accurate, tell us something about the volume of "need," but not so much about effective demand, which is another animal, and the one whose power makes the economic world go round.

Some half of the postwar building boom has been to produce more space per person —that is, greater spending per capita has been as much a factor as greater population. Undoubling of families, which was one element in this trend, has now virtually halted — the average number of persons per household has leveled off at about 3.3 since 1954. The recent and immediately forecast swelling of population is in the relatively unproductive age groups under 18 and over 65. But neither babies nor aged dependents increase one's income or borrowing power.

Supporting them does tend to reduce breadwinners' savings. Many analysts translate this into increased effective demand. It may increase demand for toys and TV, but no factor that increases the urgency of present over future needs is likely to increase the investment demand for a long-term, deferred-income asset like title to land, especially undeveloped land. Reduced saving, higher interest rates, and lower land prices follow in logical sequence. More schoolchildren also mean higher real-estate taxes, which tend to reduce the investment demand for land.

Then there are two sources of demand that almost by necessity are only temporary but that operators on the field of action may be unable to distinguish from more permanent sources of demand.

One is demand premised on anticipations of rising land prices. High prices themselves, once realized, tend to depress demand, of course, but expectations of rising prices have the opposite effect. They increase demand not only from avowed speculators but to some extent from all land buyers, including builders and owner-occupants, who are as glad as anyone to board the price elevator on the ground floor.

This demand is inherently very unstable. On the way up, it helps fulfill its own expectations, in the familiar pattern of speculative markets wherein expectations of rising prices make prices rise. Eventually, however, even if higher prices fail to dampen expectations of further rises, they certainly increase carrying costs and dampen the basic demands of ultimate consumers.

Once prices stop rising, this unreliable element of demand is likely to collapse. If it is a large share of the total demand, its desertion will then let prices sink. Stability is next to impossible in such a market. Prices either continue up or turn down.

A second unstable element of demand is that generated by investment in construction.

Construction is largely a migratory industry, which creates temporary demands on local facilities in areas of growth. This poses no difficult forecasting question around fly-by-night construction camps. But elsewhere it is all too easy to confuse temporary demand from construction spending with demand from more permanent sources. They are hard to distinguish in a complex, interdependent, growing urban economy.

A small confusion of this sort may be multiplied into a large error because of the leverage effect of outside money on the development of a region.

Because growth areas are capital-hungry as a rule, construction usually is financed largely from outside. Outside money flowing into an area serves as part of its economic "base" — that is, it sets up demand for local services and sustains it by offsetting the inevitable cash outflows.

Because local services account for roughly half of the incomes of most cities, each dollar of income financed from outside serves as "base" for another dollar or so of income from services sold locally. Then there are many market-oriented or camp-following industries, which move to an area largely because consumers are there ahead of them. When we consider them, a dollar of outside money may exert several dollars' leverage on local income, depending on the locale.

Because these local sellers also require buildings and urbanized land with utilities for working and living, they set up demands for more construction, which means more outside money — and so on. Such a sequence, once started wrong, can send development veering off course like a sliced golf ball. We have seen this happen in the midst of our postwar prosperity around the atomic boomtowns of Portsmouth, Ohio, Paducah, Ky., and Aiken, S.C. with full foreknowledge that construction payrolls were temporary, these three communities contrived to overbuild anyway, and each suffered its depression-in-a-teapot when the crews left town.

Expansion of local banking often adds to the possibility of error. Outside money flowing in increases the reserves of local banks and encourages them to lend. Under our banking system, they can expand their loans by more than the increase of reserves. This expansion would generally lead to drains on reserves that would stop it short. But it need not happen immediately, especially in a booming district, where much of the banking system's new loans come back to it in new deposits. The expanding loans of local banks meanwhile, serve like outside money, as part of the economic "base."

The situation may be complicated once more where outside money flows in, not simply to finance construction or buy land, but to speculate in the extreme sense of the word — to buy and sell and buy again. It is well known that New York banks have large deposits held to speculate in Wall Street. When a city or district catches the imagination of the more colorful part of the investment community, funds pour into its banks for similar purposes. Homer Vanderblue, then of Harvard University, found that bank deposits tripled in14 months of 1924 and 1925 in the Florida land boom, only to flow out rapidly with the crash.

The wisdom of investors, or at least their conservatism, might seem proof against this sort of folly. But investors in boom times have been notoriously susceptible to fads and stampedes.

Homer Hoyt laid down as a general rule: "In each successive land boom there is a speculative exaggeration of the trend of the period. . . ."

And as long as outsiders are ready to finance it, there is nothing to stop a new district or town from prospering while the residents, exporting little but mortgages, deposit slips, and land titles, simply build the place and take in each other's washing.

Outside investors are not going to do this knowingly. Jacob Stockfisch, economist at the University of Wisconsin, maintains that individuals can foresee tolerably well the complex interactions of their investments with those of others and trim their sails so as to achieve an orderly integrated economic development. But history leaves little doubt that this ideal behavior presupposes a foresight and exchange of information which fallible, suspicious man seldom achieves.

We return to our third critical question: can urban expansion be a stable process?

A pattern of expansion that stimulates vast oversupplies of urbanized land to meet a demand that is partly collapsible obviously presents some danger of instability. The United States Census of Governments, in its Advance Release No. 3 for 1957, reported the number of vacant lots of record in the United States at nearly 13 million (not counting parking lots). That is 21 percent of all city lots, and about 13 times the annual consumption in new construction.

The census figure does not purport to be more than an aggregation of local records, and some of the "lots" recorded are no doubt that in name only. On the other hand, some actual lots never find their way into local records. And the figure is especially striking in light of the universal observation that subdividing land for sale of lots to avowed speculators has been at a minimum during the postwar building boom, with its emphasis on mass-produced suburban developments from which lots are sold only underneath houses.

The larger part of the land hanging over urban markets is acreage not yet subdivided into lots, but with ready access to farflung urban transportation and utility networks.

A study of Greensboro, N.C., in 1956 by George Esser, Jr., of the Institute of Government of the University of North Carolina, found 125,000 persons scattered over a quasi-urbanized area big enough for all the needs of 600,000. We have no reason to believe that that is anything but typical of American cities.

Will private and public developers add indefinitely to so swollen an inventory?

Will speculators and holdouts want to continue meeting the rising carrying costs on just the present supply?

Will lenders continue to extend credit on such hazardous collateral? With 143 billion dollars in nonfarm residential and commercial mortgages (in September 1957), could the credit system stand a real-estate collapse?

No one knows for certain. History puts the burden of proof on the affirmative. Cities have rarely expanded other than in crashing waves, and today one sees several portents reminiscent of previous crests.

Some of these portents are:

The rapid, manyfold rise of land prices around growing cities since 1950;

the sharp rise of construction costs;

the wildfire spread of municipal zoning and regulations very hostile to mass-market building;

the decline of residential construction since early 1955, coupled with an increase of land-substitutive construction in extensions of roads and utilities, and multistorey buildings;

the disproportionate increase of transportation costs and utility rates since 1950;

the disproportionate increase and high level of residential and commercial debt. (Its average annual increase has been 9.5 billion dollars from 1945-1956, and its annual percentage growth rate 14.4 percent over the 1946 base. That compares to 2.2 billions, and 9.4 percent, for the period 1920-1930. In September 1957, it reached 143 billions, 48 percent of disposable personal income. That compares to 37 billions, and 45 percent, in 1929.) ;

the general deterioration in the quality of credit, as noted by Geoffrey Moore, of the National Bureau of Economic Research, and others, and as exemplified by the growth of second-mortgage financing;

the high level of interest rates;

the almost universal confidence that growing population and living standards are pressing on the land supply and insure a continual rise of land prices.

The result of these combined causes will depend largely on human response, private and public, which few would be so bold as to forecast.

Past mistakes, if that is what they are, have not trapped us in any dilemma beyond the power of informed, intelligent action to resolve.

It is heartening to see so much concern quickening today over problems of urban expansion. There is hope that today's more literate and prudent American public can avert the disasters that beset the past.

But whatever the immediate outcome, the public and its representatives, including farm-dominated State legislatures, would probably serve themselves well to attend closely to the compelling problems of harnessing urban land. This resource holds economic forces of titanic power for welfare or destruction. Harnessed, these forces could serve the public commensurately with their unrivaled market values. Untamed, unpredictable, and irresponsible, they could figure in a national calamity.

Indeed, they have already done so in a measure. The disintegration of our cities could be described conservatively as a national calamity of some proportions, whose mischievous consequences only wait to be recognized. To forestall more of the same, the reasoning of this chapter suggests that policymakers might do well to take steps to lower the prices asked for urban lands.

The thesis of this chapter is that urban land prices are uneconomically high — that the "scarcity" of urban land is an artificial one, maintained by the holdout of vastly underestimated supplies in anticipation of vastly overestimated future demands. I think this uneconomical price level imposes a correspondingly uneconomical growth pattern on expanding cities. High land prices discourage building on vacant lands best situated for new development and divert resources to building highways, utility networks, and whole new complexes of urban amenities so as to provide and serve substitute urban lands further out — substitutes for something that is already in long supply. Not only is this pattern wasteful of time, steel, cement, gasoline, and good farmland; it founds national prosperity on the film of a land bubble.

And so it would seem wise for policymakers to set about lowering asking prices for urban land. But here they meet a dilemma. What stimulates building is not falling prices, but the end result of the fall — low prices. Falling prices themselves tend to depress building. Few there are who want to invest money on the foundation of a sinking land market.

Policymakers are tempted to put off the day of reckoning, to tolerate and, in fact, actively support high land prices. But the irony of such policies is that they stimulate development of still more substitute urban lands, and set the stage for more drastic ultimate collapse.

There seems one obvious escape from this dilemma. As it must be done, do it quickly. Bring land prices down fast, and get it over with.

If this is a desirable policy, however, history offers little comfort that it will be enacted without painful changes in established attitudes. Squeezing the water from speculative land prices has usually been a slow process of attrition, with public agencies often bending their efforts toward delaying the inevitable as long as possible, while building stagnated.

But whatever policies are desirable, I believe there certainly is urgent need for public-minded citizens to agree on what those are now, before an emergency strikes. For the suburban land boom shows many evidences of evolving along the same lines as its notorious predecessors, which have confronted us with several of the most trying crises in American history. We can ill afford to meet one today as indecisively and ineffectively as in the past.

Urban Sprawl and Speculation in Urban Land

27

Marion Clawson

The rapid spread of suburbs across the previously rural landscape is a common phenomenon in the United States today. Even the most casual observer cannot but be impressed with the magnitude of the changes. There has been much criticism, on aesthetic and other grounds, as to the kind of suburbs being built; they have also had their defenders, or at least those who say the results cannot be hopelessly bad because people still move in great numbers to the new suburbs. This article will not attempt a general critique or appraisal of modern suburbanization but rather will consider only one phase of it.

One feature of postwar suburbanization has been its tendency to discontinuity — large closely settled areas intermingled haphazardly with unused areas. This intermixture of open and developed areas is largely independent of the density of the settlement within the developed areas; the question of the ideal density of settled suburban areas is another issue, which we shall not explore. The lack of continuity in expansion has been given the descriptive designation of "sprawl," which well connotes its hit-or-miss character.

"Sprawl" has been widely criticized as leading to unnecessarily high costs of social services and of private transportation, as well as for the frequent lack of publicly available open areas. It is also responsible for, or associated with, much wastage of land, since the intervening unused areas are mostly not used at all. Others have tended to minimize these deficiencies, arguing that they are but part of a growth process, not too serious in nature. Whatever may be the verdict on sprawl, it is clear that suburbanization has been the result of a relatively aimless process. It seems highly doubtful if any participant in suburban growth, or any observer, actually chose the pattern which has resulted. Possibly no one objects violently enough to exert the force required to change it but neither will anyone defend it as ideal. One aspect of this picture has been large-scale speculation in land, with consequent high costs to the actual settler and with large areas priced out of any market except urban usage, but the latter not yet taken over. Although nearly everyone seems aware of this process, and although most are critical of the results, yet it appears there is a serious

Reprinted from *Land Economics* by permission of the Regents of the University of Wisconsin.

lack of understanding as to just what is going on.

The purpose of this article is to explore the economic process in suburbanization — why some areas are developed, why intermingled ones are not, why land speculation invariably accompanies the process, and the like. The economic forces will be described, as far as possible, and some judgment offered as to which are manipulatable and which are not, and how. A basic premise is that no significant progress can be made in developing better suburbanization until the present processes are better understood.

Role of Agriculture

Perhaps the place to start is by eliminating one possible major causative factor of suburban sprawl — agriculture. Urban growth and urban demand have a major effect upon agricultural land use as a whole; in fact, as one surveys the history of agricultural development in the United States, one concludes that urban demand has been the main causative factor in agricultural development.[1] But the differential or locational effect of agriculture upon suburban land values has been very small. For one thing, some of the physical qualities which make land valuable for agriculture also make it suitable for urban use.

Locational theory as applied to agriculture, from von Thünen downward to the present, has emphasized the effect of the urban market on agricultural land use and land value but has also stressed the effect of transportation costs, as well as such differential factors as land fertility.[2] Under conditions of primi-

tive transportation methods and high transport costs, agricultural production may be highly stratified, with bulky, low value, perishable products near the market, and those with higher value in relation to weight and with less perishability produced farther away. The width of the zones in any model depends upon transportation costs to a large extent; and the sharpness of the boundaries between zones depends largely upon natural production conditions and upon intra-farm economies, such as the need to grow feed for draft animals.

Today, the chief agricultural commodity with a clear orientation to the nearby urban market is fluid milk and it is held there largely by "health" regulations which make its importation from more distant areas impossible. Although there are some advantages in producing fruits and vegetables near the market, yet as a matter of fact the great bulk of urban supplies of these commodities comes from a considerable distance — from across the continent in many cases. Today this nation has a combination of good, relatively cheap transport, and technology — such as refrigeration which makes long distance transport of perishable commodities possible. Even the fluid milk zone is more than 50 miles in radius for our larger cities, and within this zone there is almost no local advantage to agriculture. The widest arc of the suburban spread is far less than the nearest edge of the zone within which agriculture might have any differential effect upon local land values.

Some farm or rural land near cities will indeed come to have relatively high values as country estates or as a certain type of gentleman farming. But in this case the value of the land arises from the urban settlement not from agricultural production. Although such estates may lie outside of the usually defined suburban area, yet in fact the same value-

[1] Marion Clawson, R. Burnell Held and C. H. Stoddard, *Land for the Future* (Baltimore, Johns Hopkins Press, 1960), see esp. p. 247.

[2] For a clear recent statement of locational theory as applied to agriculture, see Raleigh Barlowe, *Land Resource Economics: the Political Economy of Rural and Urban Land Resources Use* (New York, Prentice-Hall, 1958).

making processes are at work. It is the city as a place of residence and of work which gives value to such estates, not their agricultural output.

Farmers in some areas, notably in California, have tried to protect their farm districts from encroachment. In general, such efforts have not been conspicuously successful, in part because such farmers are ambivalent: they want their land left in farms but they also want a chance to sell at the best possible price. It seems highly doubtful that agriculture can perfect an institutional barrier against urban expansion; at the most, it may help guide the direction and nature of the suburbs which develop. If we are to explain the suburban growth and land speculation processes, we must therefore look to forces other than agricultural land use and output.

Characteristics of the Market for Raw Suburban Land

The market for raw, undeveloped suburban land has several peculiar characteristics. First of all, land for suburban development is not a homogenous commodity, any more than is land for any other possible use. While differences in soil texture and fertility may be less important, as compared to these same qualities for agriculture, they are not neglible. Slope of land may be highly important, as affecting building costs. The risks of flood damage differ greatly from area to area. In these and in other ways, the native or natural qualities of potential suburban land may differ greatly.

The history of land ownership usually results in a present ownership pattern of variable size tracts of land owned by different owners. Some pieces are large, others small. Some owners have one objective, others another. A potential new owner must deal with what he finds, buying as he can. He will find

it impossible to buy exactly as he wishes but must deal with discrete tracts in different ownerships. Subdivision of large tracts often creates a "plottage" value, which is at its peak when the size of tract coincides with the tract best suited to the use for which the land is intended. Tracts either larger or smaller than the optimum have lower value. The passage of time may change the use of land and hence the optimum size of tract. It is significant, we think, that since the war the major railroads of the country have purchased potential industrial sites along or near their tracks when they could, largely to prevent subdivision which would spoil the larger tracts for industrial development.

The owner of a discrete tract often must sell it all, or a major part, if he wishes to sell any. Suburban land, equally with or perhaps more than other land is not, perhaps cannot be, sold in incremental pieces, but rather in relatively large chunks — chunks not necessarily adjusted to the needs of the buyer or seller.

Society, acting through government at some level, has given suburban land further special characteristics. Location with respect to transportation, to water supply, to sewerage, and to other services vitally affects potentiality of land for suburban development. These qualities were given the land without action by the landowner, except as far as he was able to influence the public action which resulted in these services. Individuals may buy and sell land to take advantage of the services provided by group action but they are not responsible for the services.

Society has affected the value of suburban land in other ways — by taxes, by zoning and building codes, and the like. If master plans, zoning, and building codes were explicit, firm, enforceable, and enforced, and if there were confidence they would remain so, they would greatly limit if not completely determine land values in many areas. In fact, zoning in particular and others to some degree can be changed under political and other pressures. Even the courts do not always accept values consistent with zoning regulations, when private land is condemned for public use. Public action through zoning and other related measures affects land values; but the major effect may be through the uncertainty created. While some of these services or action by society affect land over large areas more or less equally, yet some have a highly local effect.

Suburban land also differs greatly in accessibility, especially to major highways and sometimes to rail lines. The quality of accessibility may affect its price and its saleability greatly. Accessibility is generally not provided by the individual landowner but rather through the public, as in the case of highways, or by large private undertakings, as in the case of rail lines.

The market for suburban land is a derived one, dependent upon the market for the dwellings, shopping centers, or industrial plants erected on it. As such, it is subject to the uncertainties of market for the final product, compounded by the uncertainties of the conversion process. The market for suburban housing is a fragmented and not wholly consistent one, often variable in short distances or over brief times. Differences in price for houses are often reflected back into differences in price for undeveloped land, but in varying degree.

Lastly, the market for suburban land is usually very thin. There are very few buyers and very few sellers at any one time. Annual turnover in relation to total area is small. For almost any commodity there is a liquidation value at forced sale; a normal value between willing seller and willing buyer; and a forced purchase price when for some reason the buyer must buy almost regardless of price. For suburban land these prices might well stand in the ratio of 50 or less, to 100, to 200 or more, respectively. The time required to make a sale of land may be considerable, and directly related to the price obtainable. Part of these variations may be due to lack of information on the part of buyers and sellers but much is probably due to the character of the commodity itself. One need only contrast these characteristics of the market for suburban land with the market for wheat or even for autos. For these latter and for many other commodities there are many buyers and sellers; and forced sale, normal sale, and forced purchase prices stand in much closer relationship to one another. Some of these characteristics we have described for urban land do apply to all kinds of land for any purpose. Although empirical studies are lacking we hazard the judgment that these factors are more serious for urban than for other land.

Value-Making Process for Undeveloped Suburban Land

Undeveloped suburban land, not yet in use for urban purposes but already taken out of other land uses, obviously must derive its value from the expectation of its later development as urban land. As we have noted, agriculture does not contribute in any important way to the value of potential suburban land, especially when the land is no longer actually used for agriculture. Most land has a value based on its agricultural productivity of less than $400 per acre, although of course there are exceptions; much suburban building land at the time of development sells by the lot at prices equivalent to $4,000 per acre or more, with modest subdivision improvements, or at least $2,000 per acre as completely raw potential suburban building sites, and often at much higher figures. The potential subdivision value depends on many factors not the least of which is the popular estimate of the kind of suburban district it will ultimately be, which in turn depends somewhat upon neighboring districts but also somewhat upon the prices the subdivider puts on his lots: that is, to a degree, to put a high price on suburban lots gives them a high value. The conversion value of the raw potential suburban land into actual developed suburban land is somewhat uncertain at any date, depending in part upon the action of the community as a whole, and in part upon the skill of the subdivider and developer himself.

The date at which there will be an active demand for the raw suburban land for actual development is to a large extent uncertain. In some instances a piece of land may lie close to areas developed within the past few years and toward which the tide of development is flowing. Under such circumstances its present value is moderately forecastable on the basis of estimated probable future conversion date and value. In other cases, land may lie at greater distance or in directions where future development is less certain; then both its conversion date and its conversion value are more uncertain. The timing of development of a particular piece of suburban land is partly outside of his control. He may obviously withhold it for later development, if he thinks a greater net income can be obtained thereby — he is less able to speed up its development. The large, well-financed, skillful developer can bring about the development of a particular tract more nearly on his terms than can a smaller developer; but each operates within the general market structure.

An expected future income or value can be discounted back to a present worth or value. An interest or discount rate is required to do so. The discount rate may be thought of as having two parts; a more or less normal interest rate based upon alternative sources of investment or alternative sources of funds in competitive money markets; plus an uncertainty factor. The latter relates not only to the date of future conversion from raw to developed status for the land — and even as to "whether" as well as "when" — and the value at that date, but probably should include a large allowance for illiquidity as well. As we have noted, suburban land can be sold quickly or at forced sale only at prices substantially below its normal value when ample time is available to negotiate a sale. In practice a single discounting figure will be used, large enough to include all these and perhaps other factors as well.

The appropriate interest rate in land speculation depends to a large extent upon the situation of the particular individual.[3] A man with ample investment funds, perhaps faced with a high marginal income tax rate and hence eager to secure capital gains on which a lower rate is paid, could afford to speculate on land at interest rates perhaps no higher than 2%. A farmer, short of capital and hence forced to ration his scarce capital among various potentially profitable farm enterprises, or forced to borrow at 6% or more, would necessarily use a much higher rate — perhaps 6, 8, or even 10%. A real estate developer, perhaps short of capital and eager to use his available capital in enterprises where the turnover was rapid, would be in a position similar to that of the farmer. These differences among individuals would logically lead to greatly different positions in land

[3] For a very stimulating discussion of this point, see Mason Gaffney, "The Unwieldy Time-Dimension of Space," *Am. Jour. of Economics and Sociology* (October, 1961).

speculation, but we shall not explore them in more detail here.

In addition to delays and uncertainties as to time and value of suburban land for conversion to development, there are some holding costs to be taken into account. Taxes over a period of years may be considerable even at low assessments and low rates. Occasionally charges other than taxes must be met annually. One cost of holding is interest on the value of the land if sold, but of course the discounting formula includes this factor.

One could easily construct or adopt formulae to show these relationships, or give illustrative tables of different time periods, different final conversion values, different discount rates, and different holding charges. The best guess as to land values 10 years from now will justify present values well under half of that level; and the best guess as to values 20 years from now will justify present values much less than a fourth as high. It is altogether possible that normal or free market values may be higher than this because of widespread optimism over ultimate values, time of conversion, costs of holding, uncertainties, and the like.

The ownership of any suburban land for a rise in value is a speculative undertaking. Profits, when all factors are taken into account, are by no means assured nor large on the average. Everyone knows, or at least has heard, of others who have made substantial gains from holding suburban land for a rise in price. This type of common knowledge nearly always is ignorant of or ignores the cases, perhaps more numerous, when increases in value were much less or even negative. The chance for profit in holding suburban land for development arises entirely out of error in consensus or out of individual judgments more astute than the consensus. If there was complete knowledge as to the time

of future conversion, as to value at that time, as to holding costs and as to discount rate, then obviously everyone would be in complete accord as to present worth. There would be no opportunity for speculative gain, because all future value would have been fully and accurately discounted into present value. It is altogether possible that at times the consensus on these matters is in error — everyone is sure of something which later history proves not to be true. Under such circumstances, a sounder judge with a minority view may reap a profit. At other times a consensus may be lacking but one view may prove in time to have been closer to the fact than any other; if the person who held it acted upon his convictions, he may have profited.

As long as the price of land ripe for conversion from undeveloped to developed status is relatively high, then the price of land less ripe for development will be somewhat lower until at the margin the prospects for conversion into developed status are so uncertain or so remote that even the most optimistic will not bid up the value of this land. As long as we have free markets in suburban land and as long as the total effect of the various factors in the formula promise some present value above alternative use value, and given imperfections of knowledge and incomplete consensus, then we can reasonably expect speculative bidding up of suburban land values. Viewed in this way, land speculation in and beyond the suburbs is not only normal but inevitable. The possibilities of its control will be explored later.

Forces Leading to Development of Particular Suburban Tracts

Given the nature of the market for raw suburban land and given the value-making process for such land, what are the forces leading to the development of particular tracts of such land? How can we account for the fact that a relatively few of the many possible suburban tracts are developed in a particular year and how can we predict which ones will be developed and which left for a later future?

One basic factor is the over-all market demand for urban land for the whole urban area concerned. Some cities or metropolitan areas are growing rapidly, others at a more modest pace, and some are essentially stagnant. The amount of new land needed for urban purposes annually will obviously vary greatly among cities, depending upon this factor. At some times the real estate and building market is much more active than at others, depending in large part upon credit availability as well as upon general economic demand. When the demand for new urban land is high, not only is more land needed but the profitability of conversion is probably greater. This means not only greater profits to landowners, on the average, but also that some tracts or types of development which would be marginal in other circumstances will now be promoted — it is the time for the long chance, for the unusual deal.

The extension of essential public services to particular areas or districts will bring land within such areas or districts closer to the point of actual development or building. Provision of new roads, schools, water supply, sewerage, and other services, or marked improvement in them, add greatly to the impetus for development. The possibility of alternative devices, such as septic tanks instead of trunk sewer lines, may have the same effect. Viewing the subdivision developments which actually take place, one can hardly say that these public services, which he is tempted to call essential, are in fact either essential or necessary to building development on specific

sites — one sees too many areas that get built up, at least to a degree, without them, or at least without satisfactory services. Yet the provision of new services undoubtedly gives a fillip toward development. On the other hand, it is unlikely, of itself alone, to be sufficient. That is, mere extension of one public service, or even of a group, to an area previously lacking them, may not lead to much actual building. Other factors — above all, over-all demand — must be present.

Though empirical data are lacking, at least to this author, yet one cannot but suspect that the personal desires, projections, and preferences of present landowners must be a major factor responsible for some tracts developing while other intermingled ones do not. Institutional factors, such as estate holdings, trusts, defective titles, covenants, and others, may affect marketability of particular tracts, especially in the shortrun. Some present landholders may be optimistic about future increases in value of their land, others more cautious; some may have ample capital for which they seek investment outlets, others may have pressing need of any capital they can raise by sale of their land; and in other ways landowners may differ considerably. It seems wholly probable that owners of identical land (if one can imagine such a thing) might react quite differently to exactly the same offers for their land. Moreover, the differences between individual landowners may well be so great that a small increase in offered price, such as another year or two might bring, will be insufficient to move the man who wants to hold for later profit. Anyone familiar with urban real estate knows of many tracts remaining vacant for many years while all around them development proceeds apace. Surely one major factor must be the characteristics of the landowner himself.

As we have noted above, raw suburban

land differs greatly in physical suitability for development and also in size of parcel which each owner possesses. A residential builder may wish a moderate size tract; some will appear too small for his needs, others larger than he needs, but not available in part. An industrial development is likely to need a relatively large tract, as well as one of specific locational and other qualities and thus many smaller tracts are practically unavailable or nonexistent to him.

When all of these factors are combined one should expect a rather hit-or-miss type of suburban development as normal; it will not normally be incremental, even regular. Instead, some tracts will be developed, other nearby ones remain vacant for long periods, relatively more distant ones developed sooner than some nearby ones, and so on. One should, in fact, anticipate exactly what we have experienced: sprawl! The frontier of urban land use or building will not move slowly and regularly, taking in all land as it goes; instead, development will leap ahead to more distant tracts, passing over nearby ones, taking in some large and some small tracts, and leaving others of assorted sizes. While there has been much criticism of sprawl, and even a little wonder at why it looks as it does, in fact, given the institutional and economic forces we have described, one should have expected exactly the same kind of sprawl we have experienced in such a large way since the war. Those who are surprised at it have even ignored history for this is exactly the way the farm frontier passed across the nation a century or so ago. Canada has succeeded in some provinces in requiring a more uniform filling-up of the frontier areas before additional areas are opened for settlement but this has been difficult to enforce even there.

Effect of Speculative Land Prices and of Suburban Sprawl on Use of Intermingled Land

It is a matter of fairly common knowledge that the land within the suburban zone of sprawl for the most part is not used for any economic output until it is actually developed for urban usage. Vacant lots, larger vacant leap-frogged areas, and surrounding vacant lands characterize the suburban scene. Why should there be so much idle land, hopefully "ripening" for later transfer to urban use?

The processes we have described bid up the price of this land far beyond its value for agriculture, forestry, or other rural land use. This alone need not render the land idle for these purposes. It is true that the farmer who formerly farmed it is likely to prefer to take his gain, go elsewhere, and buy a bigger and/or better farm with his enhanced capital. It is also true that the new buyer, particularly the land speculator, may not know how to farm, or perhaps care to try. Yet it is possible that he might lease the land to an actual farmer; the gains, while small, perhaps would nevertheless meet the annual cash holding costs of the land and possibly more, thus facilitating in some degree the holding of this land speculatively.

When land comes within the zone of suburban influence, or possible later development, its taxes often rise. Until new public services are extended to the area, the increases in taxes may be small, often less than the rise in land values. Land speculators and the "Court House gang" are sometimes the same people, or at least not unknown to each other. But special services in the form of more roads, better or bigger schools, water lines, sewer lines, and the like often are extended to the potential urban area; and this is almost sure to lead to higher taxes on the land. The taxes may indeed rise so high that they exceed any possible return from land used for farming. But this alone would not necessarily take such land out of farming. High as the taxes might be, some net income from farming would seem to be preferable to none at all from idle land. High taxes mean high annual carrying costs to the land speculator and thus either depress present values (future values discounted back to the present) or provide an incentive for early sale, especially by the landowner who either cannot meet these costs or is pessimistic about future increases in value. Thus, a farmer might be even more willing to take a rise in land prices and transfer his capital elsewhere where farming was more profitable. But again, presumably the land could be rented for farming and at least some income obtained. Taxes in excess of income attributable to land make continued land use of any type impossible but not necessarily short-term use of this type.

A more serious fact is that in the suburban zone the planning horizon has shortened drastically and uncertainty greatly increased for any land user. The farmer now does not know when he may one day receive an offer for his land so high he simply cannot resist it; the speculative landholder is faced with a similar situation. Each knows that such generous offers come at most irregular intervals and to forego this one does not mean that another equally good one will come along soon. A tenant farmer under these circumstances will have no assurance of continued operation. A generation ago, agricultural economists pointed to the depressing effect on good farming of the uncertainty in the typical Southern share crop farm. The cropper never knew from year to year where he

would be the following year; hence he made no investment nor plan for more than the current year. Under that circumstance, however, the landlord knew that the farm would be operated by someone in successive years and at least some expectation of continuity existed on his part. The farmer, whether owner or tenant, in suburban zones has no such expectation of continuity. If he has high fixed investment in land improvements such as an orchard it will pay him to operate it as long as he can and recover as much of the sunk investment as he can. If he has high movable investment that might be jeopardized by loss of the land, such as a herd of high-producing dairy cows, his move will be accelerated. Not only is the actual farm operator affected by this shortened planning horizon and increased uncertainty but so also are the innumerable marketing and supply services which are indispensable to modern agriculture. As farming declines, some of these move out also, further hampering successful farming within the zone.

At any rate, land within the suburban zone, not actually used for urban purposes, typically is not used at all. Our best estimate is that there is about as much idled land in and around cities as there is land used (in any meaningful sense) for urban purposes. In the suburbs, the idled land is an even larger proportion. While this is a waste, we think it is inevitable, given the economic and institutional structure we have described. That is, land speculation, sprawl, and intermingled idle land are all natural outgrowths of economic and institutional forces, not perversions of them. Instead of surprise and shock that these situations exist, we should expect them. Perhaps we regard the result as socially undesirable; if so, we should examine wherein the economic and institutional base might be modified. We should look for causes, not moan over or try to treat results.

Possibilities of Controlling Sprawl and Suburban Land Speculation

The following criticisms have frequently been levied at sprawl. Others denied them or at least argued that in practice the situation is not as bad as pictured. Our personal conviction is that sprawl deserves many of these criticisms. But, regardless of the reasons, society (acting through government at some level) might decide to reduce or eliminate suburban sprawl and speculation in raw suburban land. The common criticisms of sprawl are: (1) A sprawled or discontinuous suburban development is more costly and less efficient than a more compact one, each of the same density within settled areas. Many costs depend on maximum distance or maximum area; if these were reduced, costs would be lower per capita or per family served. (2) Sprawl is unaesthetic and unattractive. (3) Sprawl is wasteful of land since the intervening lands are typically not used for any purpose. (4) Land speculation is unproductive, absorbing capital, manpower, and entrepreneurial skill without commensurate public gains. It destroys or impairs economic calculations that ideally lead to maximum general welfare. (5) It is inequitable to allow a system in which the new land occupier is required to shoulder such a heavy burden of capital charges or debt merely for site costs — costs which in large part are unnecessary and avoidable.

That is, we may accept urban sprawl and speculation in raw suburban land as the natural consequences of the economic and social processes we have described and at the same time we may seek to change one or more stages or bases of those processes because

we dislike their final outcome if unchecked. Where might society intervene, and how? A number of possibilities seems to exist. The following suggestions are largely complementary; most would be effective alone but jointly they would be more so.

First of all, effective market reporting of transactions in suburban land would be helpful. If numbers of parcels, total area, location of parcels, prices paid, and other terms of sale were widely reported and generally publicized, this would provide a solid factual basis now lacking or at least not generally known. Such market reporting for unimproved urban and suburban land should be supplemented by similar reporting for suburban developed real estate. We have in mind something like the market news reporting for agricultural produce markets for other primary materials such as metals and lumber, or even stock market reports. With the low turnover in the real estate market perhaps monthly reports would be frequent enough. Obviously, such reports must be city by city to be really useful. But broad regional and national totals and averages would be helpful, also. Such reports might well be limited to information of public record such as recorded deeds or transfer tax receipts unless buyers and sellers could be induced voluntarily to report unrecorded sales. If limited to public information some may doubt the advantage of such reports. However, even if everything in them was known to the alert land speculator, such reports, if widely distributed, would bring useful information to many who otherwise would be uninformed. This type of market information might be provided by federal, state, or municipal government or conceivably by real estate boards.

Secondly, this type of reporting on transactions made could be supplemented by demand and outlook studies of the type long established in agriculture. Given the best possible forecasts of population growth in a city or metropolitan area, how much land will be needed annually, and over the next 10 years? How does the amount required compare with the area presently available? Several past studies have shown platted and subdivided land adequate to accommodate 20 or more years anticipated growth in a city.[4] The ratio of land available to average area developed has varied greatly from time to time though perhaps nearly always far in excess of a rationally optimum area. Under these circumstances a few astute speculators may make substantial profits; but all speculators as a group will lose unless present prices are lower than one-fourth to one-tenth of sale price when actual development occurs. Information of this type would at least help actual developers and builders to avoid some speculative traps and excesses and should exert some stabilizing effect on speculation.

Thirdly, urban planning and the subdivision controls and zoning which make it effective might be made into a stabilizing force rather than the unsettling one we have suggested it now is. This assumes that some means could be found which would make the results of urban and suburban planning more generally known and more widely accepted so that the necessary public and political support would be forthcoming to secure adherence to the plans in the face of aggrieved group or sectional interest. As we have noted, zoning controls and similar regulations are simply not taken seriously in the land valuation process; it is assumed they can be changed upon a political or interest group demand.

If planning, zoning, and subdivision were firm — enforceable and enforced — then the

[4] For a summary of better known studies of this kind, see Clawson, Held and Stoddard, *op. cit.*, pp. 70-74.

area available at any one time for each kind of use could bear some reasonable relation to the need for land for this use. That is, area classified for different purposes could be consciously manipulated or determined in relation to market need. Sufficient area for each purpose, including enough area to provide some competition among sellers and some choice among buyers, should be zoned or classified for development; *but no more.* By careful choice of the areas concerned sprawl could be reduced, perhaps largely eliminated. Forcing relatively full development of each zone before opening up the next zone to settlement would put landowners in a very strong position to exploit buyers. This could be dealt with in a different way, discussed below.

Fourthly, local real estate taxes could be made into a conscious instrument to implement plans. This could be done by gearing taxes more closely to land values as the latter are affected or established by zoning and subdivision regulations. Taxes should be sharply raised in most suburbs on land zoned and classified for reasonably early development. They could be put high enough to bring severe pressure on landholders, forcing or inducing them to sell relatively soon. High taxes in the zones classed for early development would increase the cost of speculative holding of land and thus make early sale more attractive. At the same time, taxes might well be lowered on lands not classed as ready for early development. This would remove one incentive for early development. It would also lower costs of holding land and thus would encourage speculative holding and higher prices. This could be dealt with as explained below. Keeping taxes lower but at the same time putting the land in a class for deferred development might encourage use of intermingled and adjacent land for other purposes, at least for a few years more in each case.

The lands not classed for early development might have part of the tax deferred. The part payable annually could be adjusted to a reasonable level for other land use; the deferred part would reflect value for later development. The deferred part would accumulate from year to year and would be a lien on the land. The deferred part might come due when the owner sold for actual development or it might come due when the public planning body classified the area as ready for development. The former would encourage longer holding for speculative gain and hence probably more urban sprawl. Many more owners would prefer to gamble on higher future land prices. Making deferred taxes due when the planning body classified the areas as ready for development would have the opposite effect: now pressure would be exerted for early sale and hence more nearly solid development encouraged.

Assessment and taxation have not generally been used deliberately to modify land use but they have nevertheless exerted great influence in this direction. Some may question the wisdom or the legality of taxes based on land use plans or the conscious use of taxes to implement plans. But, to the extent the plans are backed up by vigorous land zoning and subdivision controls, they do in fact vitally affect if not determine land values.

Fifth, the public, acting through government at some level, should acquire as much of the vacant lands as it needs for public purposes. By-passed or leap-frogged areas are often suitable for parks or other public purposes. Owners of such areas are often willing to sell. Others will prefer to hold for later possible gain. The area actually required for public use is often small compared to the total vacant area. But its early public action

would have two effects: (1) the parks, schools, and other public uses would considerably affect private land use; and (2) offers by public agencies, or asking prices by such landowners, establish the market price of such land. If local tax assessments for such land could quickly be adjusted to the customary ratio of assessed to market price, then the profitability of continued speculative holding would be sharply decreased and urban sprawl correspondingly lessened. Close cooperation between school, park, and other bodies interested in acquiring land for public purposes on the one hand, and tax assessment bodies on the other, could be most effective.

Sixth, a more purposeful and coordinated use of public services such as roads, water lines, and trunk sewers could greatly affect urban sprawl. By refusing to extend any of these or other services to more distant areas until most of the intervening area was filled up, urban sprawl could be substantially reduced. The wisdom to plan public improvements in this way and the courage to enforce such plans would require a substantially higher level of performance than urban and metropolitan public service agencies typically now have. Such a program by public agencies should be accompanied by an educational program so that the general public would understand how and why such services were used for this purpose. Unless accompanied by some of the measures previously described for bringing pressure on closer-in landholders to sell, this too would give them monopoly power and large gains in land prices.

Underlying all these suggestions is the idea that government at some level possesses great powers for influencing, if not controlling, the future form of the city and metropolis. To achieve positive goals, suburban sprawl and speculation in raw suburban land must be greatly reduced or eliminated. The net effect of these various measures would be to greatly change general expectations of future land prices and dates of maximum net gains. Some reduction in land prices at time of development might be achieved; timing of development and hence of gain in land prices based on it would be more predictable. Hence, some of the basis for land speculation would be gone. Users of land for other purposes would have a longer and more certain planning horizon.

These suggestions assume that these varied powers of government can be marshalled to such a coordinated program. This may be unrealistic. Most of these programs are for local government. Local government is notoriously fragmented and uncoordinated — much more so, really, than federal government about whose deficiencies we hear so much. If a really coordinated and effective attack is to be made on urban sprawl and speculation in raw suburban land then perhaps we shall have to use the Suburban Development District which I have proposed elsewhere.[5] Under that proposal, various local governmental and private interests, subject to some regulation by the state, would be empowered to form special districts, with very wide powers over all aspects of the suburbanization process. Such powers would have a limited time duration and the districts would pass out of existence once an area were reasonably well settled.

[5] Marion Clawson, "Suburban Development Districts: A Proposal for Better Urban Growth," *Journal of the Am. Institute of Planners* (May, 1960).

The ultimate in public control over land settlement and land speculation is achieved only when a public agency first acquires all the land from present owners and then sells it to new owners. Experience in the United States and abroad with forced land reform, land colonization, or other land use arrangements where the public objective diverges significantly from private objectives has shown rather clearly that anything less can somehow be evaded in some way. However, it seems to this author most unrealistic to think of wholesale public acquisition of land in potential suburbs with its subsequent sale to actual occupiers and developers. We have, it is true, gone about this with the seriously decadent slums in the older parts of our cities; one reason we were willing to do so there was that the process required a major infusion of public funds. Public acquisition, possibly public development, certainly sale to private users of land in new suburbs would, on the other hand, be highly profitable; for that reason, if none other, private interests will bitterly oppose it. On the governmental level we are not willing to take strong measures to prevent a possible or probable future disaster or difficulty; we wait until it is upon us. Thus, while for logical completeness one should include wholesale public acquisition and subdivision of suburban land as a means of achieving better cities, through reducing sprawl and speculation, as a practical matter it probably is not a real alternative.

The Effects of Urbanization

Scholarly critics seldom agree on the correct description of our urban society. Some argue that the achievements outweigh the defects, while others see only problems and the ultimate destruction of the total environment. Too often the detrimental effects of urban growth are the most publicized by our news media. But, if the picture of our cities depicts much that is wrong, why do they continue to grow and attract more people? Analysis of some aspects of the problem may lead to at least partial answers.

Jane Jacobs' *The Kind of Problem a City Is* presents an interesting concept of a city as a process. The dictionary defines process as 'a continuing development involving many changes'. If the process is the essence of a city, then man is the catalyst of that process and cities may contain the seeds of their own regeneration.

In his discussion of Riverside, the Olmsted designed suburb of Chicago, Eaton, in *The American Suburb: Dream and Nightmare*, criticizes the modern suburb as a monument to the greed of the developer. The parkways, spacious lawns and open spaces of Riverside have been forgotten in the search for wealth. *Why Planners Fail* by Stanford presents an explanation for the decline of the American suburb. He maintains that the fault lies with the planners themselves who do not see their work as an integral part of the administration and planning of a city but as something above all the red tape. Stanford suggests that planners should enter the lifeblood of a city. The failure of planners to adequately consider rurban lands is the main issue of Kinsel's *A Concept of Rural-Urban Regions*. He presents an argument for more study of those agricultural lands that have become enclosed or surrounded by an expanding urban region. Thorsell, *Open Space for the Urban Region*, gives us an alternate look at open areas. Not only agricultural lands but parks, green-belts and forested areas must be preserved and maintained in the city.

Spelt, in *The Development of the Toronto Conurbation*, opens to the student a discussion of the growth of a large portion of the Golden Horseshoe (Mississauga) with some thoughts to the future. Following a literal use of the title *A Tale of Two Cities*, Richardson discusses the development of two planned cities.

The average citizen is usually not aware of the political and administrative red tape needed to put urban renewal into effect. Tanner in *Who Does What in Urban Renewal?* and Fountain in *Zoning Administration in Vancouver* have clarified many aspects of this vexing problem. Tanner's explanation of the general manner in which renewal is achieved is backed by detailed steps in planning by zoning.

Urban areas have presented unique problems that are often contradictory in terms of development and solution. Stokes in *A Theory of Slums* presents a sociological explanation for the existence of slums in cities of a very wealthy nation. Rooney, *The Urban Snow Hazard in the United States*, attempts to explain why the northern cities, which are the best prepared, are often the worst disrupted by heavy snowfalls.

It is only fitting to terminate the book with a plea for better cities. Beecroft in *Let Us Make Our Cities Efficient* points out that better access routes might encourage more people to stay in the city rather than move out to the suburbs. Shopping plazas are popular because they are efficient. Wilson, *Cumbernauld New Town*, describes an efficient but pleasant urban development, suitable for man, now and in the future.

The Kind of Problem a City Is

28

Jane Jacobs

Thinking has its strategies and tactics too, much as other forms of action have. Merely to think about cities and get somewhere, one of the main things to know is what *kind* of problem cities pose, for all problems cannot be thought about in the same way. Which avenues of thinking are apt to be useful and to help yield the truth depends not on how we might prefer to think about a subject, but rather on the inherent nature of the subject itself.

Among the many revolutionary changes of this century, perhaps those that go deepest are the changes in the mental methods we can use for probing the world. I do not mean new mechanical brains, but methods of analysis and discovery that have gotten into human brains: new strategies for thinking. These have developed mainly as methods of science. But the mental awakenings and intellectual daring they represent are gradually beginning to affect other kinds of inquiry too. Puzzles that once appeared unanalyzable become more susceptible to attack. What is more, the

very nature of some puzzles are no longer what they once seemed.

To understand what these changes in strategies of thought have to do with cities, it is necessary to understand a little about the history of scientific thought. A splendid summary and interpretation of this history is included in an essay on science and complexity in the 1958 *Annual Report of the Rocke-feller Foundation*, written by Dr. Warren Weaver upon his retirement as the foundation's Vice-President for the Natural and Medical Sciences. I shall quote from this essay at some length, because what Dr. Weaver says has direct pertinence to thought about cities. His remarks sum up, in an oblique way, virtually the intellectual history of city planning.

Dr. Weaver lists three stages of development in the history of scientific thought: (1) ability to deal with problems of simplicity; (2) ability to deal with problems of disorganized complexity; and (3) ability to deal with problems of organized complexity.

Reprinted from *Death and Life of Great American Cities* (New York, Random House, 1963) pp. 428-48, by permission of the author and publishers.

Problems of simplicity are problems that contain two factors which are directly related to each other in their behavior — two variables — and these problems of simplicity, Dr. Weaver points out, where the first *kinds* of problems that science learned to attack:

Speaking roughly, one may say that the seventeenth, eighteenth and nineteenth centuries formed the period in which physical science learned how to analyze two-variable problems. During that three hundred years, science developed the experimental and analytical techniques for handling problems in which one quantity — say a gas pressure — depends primarily upon a second quantity — say, the volume of the gas. The essential character of these problems rests in the fact that . . . the behavior of the first quantity can be described with a useful degree of accuracy by taking into account only its dependence upon the second quantity and by neglecting the minor influence of other factors.

These two-variable problems are essentially simple in structure . . . and simplicity was a necessary condition for progress at that stage of development of science.

It turned out, moreover, that vast progress could be made in the physical sciences by theories and experiments of this essentially simple character. . . . It was this kind of two-variable science which laid, over the period up to 1900, the foundations for our theories of light, of sound, of heat, and of electricity . . . which brought us the telephone and the radio, the automobile and the airplane, the phonograph and the moving pictures, the turbine and the Diesel engine and the modern hydroelectric power plant . . .

It was not until after 1900 that a second method of analyzing problems was developed by the physical sciences.

Some imaginative minds [Dr. Weaver continues] rather than studying problems which involved two variables or at most three or four, went to the other extreme, and said, "Let us develop analytical methods which can deal with two billion variables." That is to say, the physical scientists (with the mathematicians often in the vanguard) developed powerful techniques of probability theory and of statistical mechanics which can deal with what we may call problems of *disorganized complexity* . . . .

Consider first a simple illustration in order to get the flavor of the idea. The classical dynamics of the nineteenth century were well suited for analyzing and predicting the motion of a single ivory ball as it moves about on a billiard table. . . . One can, but with surprising increase in difficulty, analyze the motion of two or even three balls on a billiard table. . . . But as soon as one tries to analyze the motion of ten or fifteen balls on the table at once, as in pool, the problem becomes unmanageable, not because there is any theoretical difficulty, but just because the actual labor of dealing in specific detail with so many variables turns out to be impractical.

Imagine, however, a large billiard table with millions of balls flying about on its surface. . . . The great surprise is that the problem now becomes easier: the methods of statistical mechanics are now applicable. One cannot trace the detailed history of one special ball, to be sure; but there can be answered with useful precision such important questions as: On the average how many balls per second hit a given stretch of rail? On the average how far does a ball move before it is hit by some other ball? . . .

. . . The word "disorganized" [applies] to the large billiard table with the many balls . . . because the balls are distributed, in their positions and motions, in a helter-skelter way. . . . But in spite of this helter-skelter or unknown behavior of all the individual variables, the system as a whole possesses certain orderly and analyzable average properties . . . .

A wide range of experience comes under this label of disorganized complexity . . . . It applies with entirely useful precision to the experience of a large telephone exchange, predicting the average frequency of calls, the probability of overlapping calls of the same number, etc. It makes possible the financial stability of a life insurance company . . . . The motions of the atoms which form all matter, as well as the motions of the stars which form the universe, all come under the range of these new techniques. The fundamental laws of heredity are analyzed by them. The laws of thermodynamics, which describe basic and inevitable tendencies of all physical systems, are derived from statistical considerations. The whole structure of modern physics . . . rests on these statistical concepts. Indeed, the whole question of evidence, and the way in which knowledge can be inferred from evidence, is now recognized to depend on these same ideas . . . . We have also come to realize that communication theory and information theory are similarly based upon statistical ideas. One is thus bound to say that probability notions are essential to any theory of knowledge itself.

However, by no means all problems could be probed by this method of analysis. The life sciences, such as biology and medicine, could not be, as Dr. Weaver points out. These sciences, too, had been making advances, but on the whole they were still concerned with what Dr. Weaver calls preliminary stages for application of analysis; they were concerned with collection, description, classification, and observation of apparently correlated effects. During this preparatory stage, among the many useful things that were learned was that the life sciences were

neither problems of simplicity nor problems of disorganized complexity; they inherently posed still a different kind of problem, a kind of problem for which methods of attack were still very backward as recently as 1932, says Dr. Weaver.

Describing this gap, he writes:

One is tempted to oversimplify and say that scientific methodology went from one extreme to the other . . . and left untouched a great middle region. The importance of this middle region, moreover, does not depend primarily on the fact that the number of variables involved is moderate — large compared to two, but small compared to the number of atoms in a pinch of salt . . . . Much more important than the mere number of variables is the fact that these variables are all interrelated . . . . These problems, as constrasted with the disorganized situations with which statistics can cope, *show the essential feature of organization*. We will therefore refer to this group of problems as those of *organized complexity*.

What makes an evening primrose open when it does? Why does salt water fail to satisfy thirst? . . . What is the description of aging in biochemical terms? . . . What is a gene, and how does the original genetic constitution of a living organism express itself in the developed characteristics of the adult? . . .

All these are certainly complex problems. But they are not problems of disorganized complexity, to which statistical methods hold the key. They are all problems which involve dealing simultaneously with a *sizable number of factors which are interrelated into an organic whole*.

In 1932, when the life sciences were just at the threshold of developing effective analytical methods for handling organized complexity, it was speculated, Dr. Weaver tells us, that if the life sciences could make significant progress in such problems, "then there might be opportunities to extend these new techniques, if only by helpful analogy, into vast areas of the behavioral and social sciences."

In the quarter-century since that time, the life sciences have indeed made immense and brilliant progress. They have accumulated, with extraordinary swiftness, an extraordinary quantity of hitherto hidden knowledge. They have also acquired vastly improved bodies of theory and procedure — enough to open up great new questions, and to show that only a start has been made on what there is to know.

But this progress has been possible only because the life sciences were recognized to be problems in organized complexity, and were thought of and attacked in ways suitable of understanding that *kind* of problem.

The recent progress of the life sciences tells us something tremendously important about other problems of organized complexity. It tells us that problems of this *kind* can be analyzed — that it is only sensible to regard them as capable of being understood, instead of considering them, as Dr. Weaver puts it, to be "in some dark and foreboding way, irrational."

Now let us see what this has to do with cities.

Cities happen to be problems in organized complexity, like the life sciences. They present "situations in which a half-dozen or even several dozen quantities are all varying simultaneously *and in subtly interconnected ways*." Cities, again like the life sciences, do not exhibit *one* problem in organized complexity, which if understood explains all. They can be analyzed into many such problems or segments which, as in the case of the life sciences, are also related with one an-

other. The variables are many, but they are not helter-skelter; they are "interrelated into an organic whole."

Consider again, as an illustration, the problem of a city neighborhood park. Any single factor about the park is slippery as an eel; it can potentially mean any number of things, depending on how it is acted upon by other factors and how it reacts to them. How much the park is used depends, in part, upon the park's own design. But even this partial influence of the park's design upon the park's use depends, in turn, on who is around to use the park, and when, and this in turn depends on uses of the city outside the park itself. Furthermore, the influence of these uses on the park is only partly a manner of how each affects the park independently of the others; it is also partly a matter of how they affect the park in combination with one another, for certain combinations stimulate the degree of influence from one another among their components. In turn, these city uses near the park and their combinations depend on still other factors, such as the mixture of age in buildings, the size of blocks in the vicinity, and so on, including the presence of the park itself as a common and unifying use in its context. Increase the park's size considerably, or else change its design in such a way that it severs and disperses users from the streets about it, instead of uniting and mixing them, and all bets are off. New sets of influence come into play, both in the park and in its surroundings. This is a far cry from the simple problem of ratios of open space to ratios for population; but there is no use wishing it were a simpler problem or trying to make it a simpler problem, because in real life it is not a simpler problem. No matter what you try to do to it, a city park *behaves* like a problem in organized complexity, and that is what it is. The same is true of all other parts or features of cities. Although the inter-relations of their many factors are complex, there is nothing accidental or irrational about the ways in which these factors affect each other.

Moreover, in parts of cities which are working well in some respects and badly in others (as is often the case), we cannot even analyze the virtues and the faults, diagnose the trouble or consider helpful changes, without going at them as problems of organized complexity. To take a few simplified illustrations, a street may be functioning excellently at the supervision of children and at producing a casual and trustful public life, but be doing miserably at solving all other problems because it has failed at knitting itself with an effective larger community, which in turn may or may not exist because of still other sets of factors. Or a street may have, in itself, excellent physical material for generating diversity and an admirable physical design for casual surveillance of public spaces, and yet because of its proximity to a dead border, it may be so empty of life as to be shunned and feared even by its own residents. Or a street may have little foundation for workability on its own merits, yet geographically tie in so admirably with a district that is workable and vital that this circumstance is enough to sustain its attraction and give it use and sufficient workability. We may wish for easier, all-purpose analyses, and for simpler, magical, all-purpose cures, but wishing cannot change these problems into simpler matters than organized complexity, no matter how much we try to evade the realities and to handle them as something different.

Why have cities not, long since, been identified, understood and treated as problems of organized complexity? If the people concerned with the life sciences were able to identify their difficult problems as problems of organized complexity, why have people professionally concerned with cities not identified the *kind* of problem they had?

The history of modern thought about cities is unfortunately very different from the history of modern thought about the life sciences. The theorists of conventional modern city planning have consistently mistaken cities as problems of simplicity and of disorganized complexity, and have tried to analyze and treat them thus. No doubt this imitation of the physical sciences was hardly conscious. It was probably derived, as the assumptions behind most thinking are, from the general floating fund of intellectual spores around at the time. However, I think these misapplications could hardly have occurred, and certainly would not have been perpetuated as they have been, without great disrespect for the subject matter itself — cities. These misapplications stand in our way; they have to be hauled out in the light, recognized as inapplicable strategies of thought, and discarded.

Garden City planning theory had its beginnings in the late nineteenth century, and Ebenezer Howard attacked the problem of town planning much as if he were a nineteenth-century physical scientist analyzing a two-variable problem of simplicity. The two major variables in the Garden City concept of planning were the quantity of housing (or population) and the number of jobs. These two were conceived of as simply and directly related to each other, in the form of relatively closed systems. In turn, the housing had its subsidiary variables, related to it in equally direct, simple, mutually independent form: playgrounds, open space, schools, community center, standardized supplies and services. The town as a whole was conceived of, again, as one of the two variables in a direct, simple, town-greenbelt relationship. As a system of order, that is about all there was to it. And on this· simple base of two-variable relationships were created an entire theory of self-contained towns as a means of redistributing the population of cities and (hopefully) achieving regional planning.

Whatever may be said of this scheme for isolated towns, any such simple systems of two-variable relationships cannot possibly be discerned in great cities — and never could be. Such systems cannot be discerned in a town either, the day after the town becomes encompassed in a metropolitan orbit with its multiplicity of choices and complexities of cross-use. But in spite of this fact, planning theory has persistently applied this two-variable *system of thinking and analyzing* to big cities; and to this day city planners and housers believe they hold a precious nugget of truth about the *kind* of problem to be dealt with when they attempt to shape or reshape big-city neighborhoods into versions of two-variable systems, with ratios of one thing (as open space) depending directly and simply upon an immediate ratio of something else (as population).

To be sure while planners were assuming that cities were properly problems of simplicity, planning theorists and planners could not avoid seeing that real cities were not so in fact. But they took care of this in the traditional way that the incurious (or the disrespectful) have always regarded problems of organized complexity: as if these puzzles were, in Dr. Weaver's words, "in some dark and foreboding way, irrational."*

Beginning in the late 1920's in Europe, and in the 1930's here, city planning theory began to assimilate the newer ideas on probability theory developed by physical science.

* *e.g.* "a chaotic accident," "solidified chaos," etc.

Planners began to imitate and apply these analyses precisely as if cities were problems in disorganized complexity, understandable purely by statistical analysis, predictable by the application of probability mathematics, manageable by conversion into groups of averages.

This conception of the city as a collection of separate file drawers, in effect, was suited very well by the Radiant City vision of Le Corbusier, that vertical and more centralized version of the two-variable Garden City. Although Le Corbusier himself made no more than a gesture toward statistical analysis, his scheme assumed the statistical reordering of a system of disorganized complexity, solvable mathematically; his towers in the park were a celebration, in art, of the potency of statistics and the triumph of the mathematical average.

The new probability techniques, and the assumptions about the kind of problem that underlay the way they have been used in city planning, did not supplant the base idea of the two-variable reformed city. Rather these new ideas were added. Simple, two-variable systems of order were still the aim. But these could be organized even more "rationally" now, from out of a supposed existing system of disorganized complexity. In short, the new probability and statistical methods gave more "accuracy," more scope, made possible a more Olympian view and treatment of the supposed problem of the city.

With the probability techniques, an old aim — stores "properly" related to immediate housing or to a preordained population — became seemingly feasible; there arose techniques for planning standardized shopping "scientifically"; although it was early realized by such planning theorists as Stein and Bauer that preplanned shopping centers within cities must also be monopolistic or semimonopolistic, or else the statistics would not predict, and the city would go on behaving with dark and foreboding irrationality.

With these techniques, it also became feasible to analyze statistically, by income groups and family sizes, a given quantity of people uprooted by acts of planning, to combine these with probability statistics on normal housing turnover, and to estimate accurately the gap. Thus arose the supposed feasibility of large-scale relocation of citizens. In the form of statistics, these citizens were no longer components of any unit except the family, and could be dealt with intellectually like grains of sand, or electrons or billiard balls. The larger the number of uprooted, the more easily they could be planned for on the basis of mathematical averages. On this basis it was actually intellectually easy and sane to contemplate clearance of all slums and resorting of people in ten years and not much harder to contemplate it as a twenty-year job.

By carrying to logical conclusions the thesis that the city, as it exists, is a problem in disorganized complexity, housers and planners reached — apparently with straight faces — the idea that almost any specific malfunctioning could be corrected by opening and filling a new file drawer. Thus we get such political party policy statements as this: "The Housing Act of 1959 . . . should be supplemented to include . . . a program of housing for moderate-income families whose incomes are too high for admission to public housing, but too low to enable them to obtain decent shelter in the private market."

With statistical and probability techniques, it also became possible to create formidable and impressive planning surveys for cities — surveys that come out with fanfare, are read by practically nobody, and then drop quietly into oblivion, as well they might, being

nothing more nor less than routine exercises in statistical mechanics for systems of disorganized complexity. It became possible also to map out master plans for the statistical city, and people take these more seriously, for we are all accustomed to believe that maps and reality are necessarily related, or that if they are not, we can make them so by altering reality.

With these techniques, it was possible not only to conceive of people, their incomes, their spending money and their housing as fundamentally problems in disorganized complexity, susceptible to conversion into problems of simplicity once ranges and averages were worked out, but also to conceive of city traffic, industry, parks, and even cultural facilities as components of disorganized complexity, convertible into problems of simplicity.

Furthermore, it was no intellectual disadvantage to contemplate "coordinated" schemes of city planning embracing ever greater territories. The greater the territory, as well as the larger the population, the more rationally and easily could both be dealt with as problems of disorganized complexity viewed from an Olympian vantage point. The wry remark that "A Region is an area safely larger than the last one to whose problems we found no solution" is not a wry remark in these terms. It is a simple statement of a basic fact about disorganized complexity; it is much like saying that a large insurance company is better equipped to average out risks than a small insurance company.

However, while city planning has thus mired itself in deep misunderstandings about the very nature of the problem with which it is dealing, the life sciences, unburdened with this mistake, and moving ahead very rapidly, have been providing some of the concepts that city planning needs: along with providing the basic strategy of recognizing problems of organized complexity, they have provided hints about analyzing and handling this *kind* of problem. These advances have, of course, filtered from the life sciences into general knowledge; they have become part of the intellectual fund of our times. And so a growing number of people have begun, gradually, to think of cities as problems in organized complexity — organisms that are replete with unexamined, but obviously intricately interconnected, and surely understandable, relationships.

This is a point of view which has little currency yet among planners themselves, among architectural city designers, or among the businessmen and legislators who learn their planning lessons, naturally, from what is established and long accepted by planning "experts". Nor is this a point of view that has much appreciable currency in schools of planning (perhaps there least of all).

City planning, as a field, has stagnated. It bustles but it does not advance. Today's plans show little if any perceptible progress in comparison with plans devised a generation ago. In transportation, either regional or local, nothing is offered which was not already offered and popularized in 1938 in the General Motors diorama at the New York World's Fair, and before that by Le Corbusier. In some respects, there is outright retrogression. None of today's pallid imitations of Rockefeller Center is as good as the original, which was built a quarter of a century ago. Even in conventional planning's *own given terms*, today's housing projects are no improvement, and usually a retrogression, in comparison with those of the 1930's.

As long as city planners, and the businessmen, lenders, and legislators who have learned from planners, cling to the unexamined assumptions that they are dealing with a problem in the physical sciences, city planning cannot possibly progress. Of course it stagnates. It lacks the first requisite for a body of practical and progressing thought: recognition of the kind of problem at issue. Lacking this, it has found the shortest distance to a dead end.

Because the life sciences and cities happen to pose the same *kinds* of problems does not mean they are the *same* problems. The organizations of living protoplasm and the organizations of living people and enterprises cannot go under the same microscopes.

However, the tactics for understanding both are similar in the sense that both depend on the microscopic or detailed view, so to speak, rather than on the less detailed, naked-eye view suitable for viewing problems of simplicity or the remote telescopic view suitable for viewing problems of disorganized complexity.

In the life sciences, organized complexity is handled by identifying a specific factor or quantity — say an enzyme — and then painstakingly learning its intricate relationships and interconnections with other factors or quantities. All this is observed in terms of the behavior (not mere presence) of other specific (not generalized) factors or quantities. To be sure, the techniques of two-variable and disorganized-complexity analysis are used too, but only as subsidiary tactics.

In principle, these are much the same tactics as those that have to be used to understand and to help cities. In the case of understanding cities, I think the most important habits of thought are these:

1. To think about processes;
2. To work inductively, reasoning from particulars to the general, rather than the reverse;
3. To seek for "unaverage" clues involving very small quantities, which reveal the way larger and more "average" quantities are operating.

If you have gotten this far you do not need much explanation of these tactics. However, I shall sum them up, to bring out points otherwise left only as implications.

Why think about processes? Objects in cities — whether they are buildings, streets, parks, districts, landmarks, or anything else — can have radically differing effects, depending upon the circumstances and contexts in which they exist. Thus, for instance, almost nothing useful can be understood or can be done about improving city dwellings if these are considered in the abstract as "housing." City dwellings — either existing or potential — are *specific* and particularized buildings *always involved in differing, specific processes* such as unslumming, slumming, generation of diversity, self-destruction of diversity.*

For cities, processes are of the essence. Furthermore, once one thinks about city processes, it follows that one *must* think of catalysts of these processes, and this too is of the essence.

The processes that occur in cities are not arcane, capable of being understood only by experts. They can be understood by almost anybody. Many ordinary people already understand them; they simply have not given these processes names, or considered that by understanding these ordinary arrangements of cause and effect, we can also direct them if we want to.

Why reason inductively? Because to reason, instead, from generalizations ultimately drives us into absurdities — as in the case of the Boston planner who knew (against all the real-life evidence he had) that the North End had to be a slum because the generalizations that make him as expert say it is.

* Because this is so, "housers," narrowly specializing in "housing" expertise, are a vocational absurdity. Such a profession makes sense only if it is assumed that "housing" *per se* has important generalized effects and qualities. It does not.

This is an obvious pitfall because the generalizations on which the planner was depending are themselves so nonsensical. However, inductive reasoning is just as important for identifying, understanding and constructively using the forces and processes that actually are relevant to cities, and therefore are not nonsensical. I have generalized about these forces and processes considerably, but let no one be misled into believing that these generalizations can be used routinely to declare what the particulars, in this or that place, *ought* to mean. City processes in real life are too complex to be routine, too particularized for application as abstractions. They are always made up of interactions among unique combinations of particulars, and there is no substitute for knowing the particulars.

Inductive reasoning of this kind is, again, something that can be engaged in by ordinary, interested citizens, and again they have the advantage over planners. Planners have been trained and disciplined in *deductive* thinking, like the Boston planner who learned his lessons only too well. Possibly because of this bad training, planners frequently seem to be less well equipped intellectually for respecting and understanding particulars than ordinary people, untrained in expertise, who are attached to a neighborhood, accustomed to using it, and so are not accustomed to thinking of it in generalized or abstract fashion.

Why seek "unaverage" clues, involving small quantities? Comprehensive statistical studies, to be sure, can *sometimes* be useful abstracted measurements of the sizes, ranges, averages and medians of this and that. Gathered from time to time, statistics can tell too what has been happening to these figures. However, they tell almost nothing about how the quantities are working in systems of organized complexity.

To learn how things are working, we need

pinpoint clues. For instance, all the statistical studies possible about the downtown of Brooklyn, N.Y., cannot tell us as much about the problem of that downtown and its cause as is told in five short lines of type in a single newspaper advertisement. This advertisement, which is for Marboro, a chain of bookstores, gives the business hours of the chain's five stores. Three of them (one near Carnegie Hall in Manhattan, one near the Public Library and not far from Times Square, one in Greenwich Village) stay open until midnight. A fourth, close to Fifth Avenue and Fifty-ninth Street, stays open until 10 P.M. The fifth, in downtown Brooklyn, stays open until 8 P.M. Here is a management which keeps its stores open late, if there is business to be had. The advertisement tells us that Brooklyn's downtown is too dead by 8 P.M., as indeed it is. No surveys (and certainly no mindless, mechanical predictions projected forward in time from statistical surveys, a boondoggle that today frequently passes for "planning") can tell us anything so relevant to the composition and to the need of Brooklyn's downtown as this small, but specific and precisely accurate, clue to the *workings* of that downtown.

It takes large quantities of the "average" to produce the "unaverage" in cities. But as was pointed out in Chapter Seven, in the discussion on the generators of diversity, the mere presence of large quantities — whether people, uses, structures, jobs, parks, streets or anything else — does not guarantee much generation of city diversity. These quantities can be working as factors in inert, low-energy systems, merely maintaining themselves, if that. Or they can make up interacting, high-energy systems, producing by-products of the "unaverage."

The "unaverage" can be physical, as in the case of eye-catchers which are small elements in much larger, more "average" visual scenes. They can be economic, as in the case of one-of-a-kind stores, or cultural, as in the case of an unusual school or out-of-the-ordinary theater. They can be social, as in the case of public characters, loitering places, or residents or users who are financially, vocationally, racially or culturally unaverage.

Quantities of the "unaverage," which are bound to be relatively small, are indispensable to vital cities. However, in the sense that I am speaking of them here, "unaverage" quantities are also important as analytical means — as clues. They are often the only announcers of the way various large quantities are behaving, or failing to behave, in combination with each other. As a rough analogy, we may think of quantitatively minute vitamins in protoplasmic systems, or trace elements in pasture plants. These things are necessary for proper functioning of the systems of which they are a part; however, their usefulness does not end there, because they can and do also serve as vital clues to *what* is happening in the systems of which they are a part.

This awareness of "unaverage" clues — or awareness of their lack — is, again, something any citizen can practice. City dwellers, indeed, are commonly great informal experts in precisely this subject. Ordinary people in cities have an awareness of "unaverage" quantities which is quite consonant with the importance of these relatively small quantities. And again, planners are the ones at the disadvantage. They have inevitably come to regard "unaverage" quantities as relatively inconsequential, because these are *statistically* inconsequential. They have been trained to dicount what is most vital.

Now we must dig a little deeper into the bog of intellectual misconceptions about cities in which orthodox reformers and planners have mired themselves (and the rest of us). Underlying the city planners' deep disrespect for their subject matter, underlying the jejune belief in the "dark and foreboding" irrationality or chaos of cities, lies a long-established misconception about the relationship of cities — and indeed of men — with the rest of nature.

Human beings are, of course, a part of nature, as much so as grizzly bears or bees or whales or sorghum cane. The cities of human beings are as natural, being a product of one form of nature, as are the colonies of prairie dogs or the beds of oysters. The botanist Edgar Anderson has written wittily and sensitively in *Landscape* magazine from time to time about cities as a form of nature. "Over much of the world," he comments, "man has been accepted as a city-loving creature." Nature watching, he points out, "is quite as easy in the city as in the country; all one has to do is accept Man as a part of Nature. Remember that as a specimen of *Homo sapiens* you are far and away most likely to find that species an effective guide to deeper understanding of natural history."

A curious but understandable thing happened in the eighteenth century. By then, the cities of Europeans had done well enough by them, mediating between them and many harsh aspects of nature, so that something became popularly possible which previously had been a rarity — sentimentalization of nature, or at any rate, sentimentalization of a rustic or a barbarian relationship with nature. Marie Antoinette playing milkmaid was an expression of this sentimentality on one plane. The romantic idea of the "noble savage" was an even sillier one, on another plane. So, in this country, was Jefferson's intellectual rejection of cities of free artisans and mechanics, and his dream of an ideal republic of self-reliant rural yeomen — a pathetic dream for a good and great man whose land was tilled by slaves.

In real life, barbarians (and peasants) are the least free of men — bound by tradition, ridden by caste, fettered by superstitions, riddled by suspicion and foreboding of whatever is strange. "City air makes free," was the medieval saying, when city air literally did make free the runaway serf. City air still makes free the runaways from company towns, from plantations, from factory-farms, from subsistence farms, from migrant picker routes, from mining villages, from one-class suburbs.

Owing to the mediation of cities, it became popularly possible to regard "nature" as benign, ennobling and pure, and by extension to regard "natural man" (take your pick of how "natural") as so too. Opposed to all this fictionalized purity, nobility and beneficence, cities, not being fictions, could be considered as seats of malignancy and — obviously — the enemies of nature. And once people begin looking at nature as if it were a nice big St. Bernard dog for children, what could be more natural than the desire to bring this sentimental pet into the city too, so the city might get some nobility, purity and beneficence by association?

There are dangers in sentimentalizing nature. Most sentimental ideas imply, at bottom, a deep if unacknowledged disrespect. It is no accident that we Americans, probably the world's champion sentimentalizers about nature, are at one and the same time probably the world's most voracious and disrespectful destroyers of wild and rural countryside.

It is neither love for nature nor respect for nature that leads to this schizophrenic attitude. Instead, it is a sentimental desire to toy, rather patronizingly, with some insipid, standardized, suburbanized shadow of nature —

apparently in sheer disbelief that we and our cities, just by virtue of being, are a legitimate part of nature too, and involved with it in much deeper and more inescapable ways than grass trimming, sunbathing, and contemplative uplift. And so, each day, several thousand more acres of our countryside are eaten by the bulldozers, covered by pavement, dotted with suburbanites who have killed the thing they thought they came to find. Our irreplaceable heritage of Grade I agricultural land (a rare treasure of nature on this earth) is sacrificed for highways or supermarket parking lots as ruthlessly and unthinkingly as the trees in the woodlands are uprooted, the streams and rivers polluted and the air itself filled with the gasoline exhausts (products of eons of nature's manufacturing) required in this great national effort to cozy up with a fictionalized nature and flee the "unnaturalness" of the city.

The semisuburbanized and suburbanized messes we create in this way become despised by their own inhabitants tomorrow. These thin dispersions lack any reasonable degree of innate vitality, staying power, or inherent usefulness as settlements. Few of them, and these only the most expensive as a rule, hold their attraction much longer than a generation; then they begin to decay in the pattern of city gray areas. Indeed, an immense amount of today's city gray belts was yesterday's dispersion closer to "nature." Of the buildings on the thirty thousand acres of already blighted or already fast-blighting residential areas in northern New Jersey, for example, half are less than forty years old. Thirty years from now, we shall have accumulated new problems of blight and decay over acreages so immense that in comparison the present problems of the great cities' gray belts will look piddling. Nor, however destructive, is this something which happens accidentally or without the use of will. This is exactly what we, as a society, have willed to happen.

Nature, sentimentalized and considered as the antithesis of cities, is apparently assumed to consist of grass, fresh air and little else, and this ludicrous disrespect results in the devastation of nature even formally and publicly preserved in the form of a pet.

For example, up the Hudson River, north of New York City, is a state park at Croton Point, a place for picnicking, ballplaying and looking at the lordly (polluted) Hudson. At the Point itself is — or was — a geological curiosity: a stretch of beach about fifteen yards long where the blue-grey clay, glacially deposited there, and the action of the river currents and the sun combined to manufacture clay dogs. These are natural sculptures, compacted almost to the density of stone, and baked, and they are of a most curious variety, from breathtakingly subtle and simple curving forms to fantastic concoctions of more than Oriental splendor. There are only a few places in the entire world where clay dogs may be found.

Generations of New York City geology students, along with picnickers, tired ballplayers and delighted children, treasure hunted among the clay dogs and carried their favorites home. And always, the clay, the river and the sun made more, and more, and more, inexhaustibly, no two alike.

Occasionally through the years, having been introduced to the clay dogs long ago by a geology teacher, I would go back to treasure hunt among them. A few summers ago, my husband and I took our children to the Point so they might find some and also so they might see how they are made.

But we were a season behind improvers on nature. The slope of muddy clay that formed the little stretch of unique beach had been demolished. In its place was a rustic retaining wall and an extension of the park's lawns. (The park had been augmented — statistically.) Digging beneath the new lawn here and there — for we can desecrate the next man's desecrations as well as anyone — we found broken bits of clay dogs, mashed by the bulldozers, the last evidence of a natural process that may well have been halted here forever.

Who would prefer this vapid suburbanization to timeless wonders? What kind of park supervisor would permit such vandalism of nature? An all too familiar kind of mind is obviously at work here: a mind seeing only disorder where a most intricate and unique order exists; the same kind of mind that sees only disorder in the life of city streets, and itches to erase it, standardize it, suburbanize it.

The two responses are connected: Cities, as created or used by city-loving creatures are unrespected by such simple minds because they are not bland shadows of cities suburbanized. Other aspects of nature are equally unrespected because they are not bland shadows of nature suburbanized. Sentimentality about nature denatures everything it touches.

Big cities and countrysides can get along well together. Big cities need real countryside close by. And countryside — from man's point of view — needs big cities, with all their diverse, opportunities and productivity, so human beings can be in a position to appreciate the rest of the natural world instead of to curse it.

Being human is itself difficult, and therefore all kinds of settlements (except dream cities) have problems. Big cities have difficulties in abundance, because they have people in abundance. But vital cities are not helpless to combat even the most difficult of problems. They are not passive victims of chains of circumstances, any more than they are the malignant opposite of nature.

Vital cities have marvelous innate abilities for understanding, communicating, contriving and inventing what is required to combat their difficulties. Perhaps the most striking example of this ability is the effect that big cities have had on disease. Cities were once the most helpless and devastated victims of disease, but they became great disease conquerors. All the apparatus of surgery, hygiene, microbiology, chemistry, telecommunications, public health measures, teaching and research hospitals, ambulances and the like, which people not only in cities but also outside them depend upon for the unending war against premature mortality, are fundamentally products of big cities and would be inconceivable without big cities. The surplus wealth, the productivity, the close-grained juxtaposition of talents that permit society to support advances such as these are themselves products of our organization into cities, and especially into big and dense cities.

It may be romantic to search for the salves of society's ills in slow-moving rustic surroundings, or among innocent, unspoiled provincials, if such exist, but it is a waste of time. Does anyone suppose that, in real life, answers to any of the great questions that worry us today are going to come out of homogeneous settlements?

Dull, inert cities, it is true, do contain the seeds of their own destruction and little else. But lively, diverse, intense cities contain the seeds of their own regeneration, with energy enough to carry over for problems and needs outside themselves.

29

The American Suburb: Dream and Nightmare

Leonard K. Eaton

With American cities expanding at an unprecedented rate, the time has arrived for a reconsideration of the traditional role of the suburb in the urban picture. While the history of the suburb goes back into medieval times, its most characteristic development in this country took place in the 19th Century. The typical suburb was an attempt to escape from the crowded conditions and ugly industrialism of the central city. Its virtues were openness and greenery. Invariably it was connected to the metropolis by railroad, and most of the male inhabitants were commuters. At the end of a hard session in the office or factory, the businessman could enjoy some of the advantages of country living, while his wife and children might have them during the entire day.

Among American practitioners of the difficult art of suburban design, the name of Frederick Law Olmsted, Sr. stands out most clearly. No less an authority than Lewis Mumford has commented extensively on Olmsted's achievement, laying particular emphasis on Riverside, a Chicago suburb, and Roland Park, just outside Baltimore. Because the plan has been so well preserved, the example of Riverside is particularly interesting. What is the story behind the planning of this remarkable community, which even today offers unusual amenities?

In 1868 a group of affluent Eastern businessmen formed a company to build what they hoped would be a necessary adjunct to the rapidly growing city of Chicago. They recognized the need for a suburb easily accessible to the city, a place affording home sites where the families of businessmen could enjoy some of the benefits traditionally associated with rural life. After a long search they settled on a sixteen-hundred-acre tract of land west of the city and bounded on two sides by dense woods and the Des Plaines River. The area already had some reputation as a resort center, since it possessed a good country hotel where fashionable Chicagoans were accustomed to take their families for Sunday dinner; moreover, it had been connected to the heart of the city by a railroad in 1862. In 1869 the company showed both good business judgment and esthetic sense by employing Olmsted, at that time the most

Reprinted from *Landscape,* Vol. 13, no. 2 (Winter, 1963-64), pp. 12-16 by permission.

eminent landscape architect in the United States, to lay out the plan.

Olmsted, at this time age 47, was something of a public figure. He had written what were universally admitted to be the best social and economic commentaries on the pre-war South; with Calvert Vaux had won the competition for Central Park in New York; and had, in fact, developed a national reputation as an expert in park design. At the same time Olmsted was planning Riverside, he was also doing Delaware Park in Buffalo and Prospect Park in Brooklyn, two of his finest efforts. It is interesting to note that although the General Grant era was characterized by widespread political corruption, it was also the period when American cities began to set aside substantial quantities of land for public recreation. While Chicago owes its magnificent lake front to events following the World's Fair of 1893, the land for its equally important West Park System was purchased as early as 1871. The park commissioners retained William LeBaron Jenney, the noted skyscraper architect, to do the first landscape work.

Olmsted's writings reveal that his object in the design of Riverside was a combination of urban convenience and rural charm. In common with many of his contemporaries, Olmsted had an extremely romantic attitude toward nature. He held contact with it was a positive good; while he did not share the pantheistic views of Emerson and Thoreau, he believed that experience of nature had a definite moral value. In studying the area he was therefore delighted to find that it was heavily wooded with elm, oak, hickory and walnut trees and that a river bounded one edge of the property. His design took full advantage of this favorable natural situation. With gently rolling land and a curving river as his major terrain features, he sought to avoid the harsh regularity of a rectangular plan. Instead of the squares and rectangles so common elsewhere in 19th Century planning, the pattern becomes a series of ovals and circles of various sizes. Where the ovals and circles meet, spaces for small parks and village greens are developed. It is not surprising to find Olmsted writing to his clients, "The ordinary directness of line in town streets, with its resultant regularity of plan would suggest eagerness to press forward without looking to the right hand or the left; we should recommend the general adoption, in the design of your roads, of gracefully curved lines, generous spaces and the absence of sharp corners, the idea being to suggest and imply leisure, contemplativeness and happy tranquility." Today the residents of Riverside sometimes boast that not one of their streets follows a straight line, and Olmsted's small parks are much used by children for ball games, tree climbing, or just sitting in the grass and talking.

Not neglecting the problem of access from Chicago, Olmsted observed that the railroad was not a sufficient means of transportation and that a road should be constructed from the center of the town. This approach road was another romantic scheme. The plan involved a separation of traffic by green strips planted with trees, watering places and benches at intervals for rest. The entire idea was to induce a feeling of serenity and restfulness as one traveled along the road. "We see no reason why," wrote Olmsted, "if this suggestion is carried out liberally, it should not provide, or at least begin to provide, another pressing desideratum of the city of Chicago, namely a general promenade ground." In other words, Olmsted proposed a formal parkway with naturalistic planting. His route today is heavily traveled and is called Long Common Road because of the large strip of grass and trees between the two directions of traffic. Here is one of the earliest and most effective American usages of the parkway idea, later employed with excellent affect in the Burnham plan of 1909.

Olmsted's thinking on the design of individual dwellings, while advanced for its time, did not contemplate strict architectural controls. "We cannot judiciously attempt to control the form of the houses which men shall build," he remarked, "we can only, at most, take care that if they build very ugly and inappropriate houses, they shall not be allowed to force them disagreeably upon our attention when we desire to pass along the road upon which they stand. We can require that no house shall be built within a certain number of feet of the highway, and we can insist that each householder shall maintain one or two living trees between his house and the highway." In truth, Riverside is not a community made up of architectural gems from the past, although it does possess distinction in Frank Lloyd Wright's Coonley House, one of the masterpieces of his early period, as well as several other structures of the same vintage. The town's other showplace was Louis Sullivan's Babson House (1909), now torn down to make way for a "development." Most of the dwellings are medium to large size clapboard houses, set back from 30 to 70 feet from the roadway. They are placed at various angles to the street, thus contributing to the planned irregularity of the town. Many of the older homes were designed by Olmsted and Jenney.

While Riverside's commercial district possesses little architectural quality, the town's center itself has a strongly defined form. This is partly a matter of scale and partly a matter of vertical accent. Borrowing a concept from Kevin Lynch, we may say that the water tower is the major landmark. Somewhat diffi-

cult to see in summer because of the heavy planting, it is easily viewed in winter when the leaves have fallen from the trees. Riverside is, in fact, a highly imageable community. The river is a strong, natural edge, and the small parks act as nodes. As might be expected, the entire area has a park-like quality. This impression is reinforced by one of Olmsted's master strokes, the suggestion that the river bank be reserved for a public playground. In winter it is heavily used for sliding, and the river itself becomes a skating rink. All year round, Riverside provides ample opportunity for both active and passive recreation.

For the visitor to Riverside the dominant impressions are the winding street pattern and the luxuriance of the landscaping. The constantly changing direction of vision while strolling or driving on these streets is a source of pure delight to pedestrian and motorist alike. In this respect the town has an almost medieval quality; it recalls the twisting streets of Siena and Perugia, though it lacks the changes in elevation so characteristic of those cities. Because of this unusual street pattern, there is very little through traffic and automobile accidents are few. The landscaping makes an overwhelming impression. Some of the trees which are today so stately were planted by Olmsted himself; others, such as the lilacs, are carefully tended replacements. The thinning out process is apparently held to a minimum. In fact, many of the residents seem quite conscious of their heritage and are intent on preserving it insofar as is possible. For example, they insist on retaining the charming (but antiquated) street lamps. A typical comment in an interview was, "My husband and I have lived here forty years and raised our children here. They live in California now, and we go there to visit them, but we always have a yen to get back to Riverside." One is reminded of the famous remark of D. H. Burnham ". . . a noble, logical diagram once recorded will never die, but long after we are gone will be a living thing, asserting itself with ever-growing consistency."

In short, Riverside exemplifies the virtues of the 19th Century upper middle class suburb. It has a strong and compact core, a fascinating street pattern and an ample allowance of light, air and greenery for everyone. Its landscaping, which differentiates it immediately from the surrounding communities, is unique.

By way of contrast, let us examine Allen Park, a 20th Century suburb of Detroit, named after the land speculator Lewis Allen. Incorporated as a village on April 4, 1927, with a population of 664, it has subsequently clung steadfastly to the gridiron pattern imposed at its founding. The name Allen Park is, of course, an ironical indication of the romantic landscape atmosphere which was sought. By 1927 Detroit was well developed industrially, and the town purported to offer the customary suburban luxuries of fresh air and green space to those who wished to escape from the industrial atmosphere of the central city. For a few years it must indeed have been a refuge. In 1940 the federal census counted 37,393 inhabitants; Riverside in contrast has remained small — slightly over nine thousand in 1960. The cause of the remarkable growth of Allen Park was the post-World War II boom in the Detroit automobile plants. The chief beneficiaries were the real estate speculators who had laid out the town in a completely mechanical pattern. Theoretically, it is a bedroom community, in concept much like Riverside. Every morning the male population arises an hour before job time to make the long, frustrating trip into Detroit over expressways which are continually more crowded.

The inhabitants are mostly middle class with an average income of about $8,000 per year. The average house costs anywhere from $15,000 to $25,000 and is provided with the customary city services such as paved roads, utilities, snow removal and fire and police protection. The city has numerous commercial establishments, one hundred acres of parks and playgrounds, six churches of various denominations, four hospitals, a public library and a community building. A close observer remarks that most of the citizens of Allen Park have moved there for one of three reasons: (1) It is "a better place to raise a family." (2) A house in Allen Park is a status symbol, and most of these people are upwardly mobile. (3) It is a retreat from the hustle and bustle of Detroit. This inventory of institutions and sociological analysis indicates nothing whatever about the visual quality of this environment. A photographic survey of Allen Park shows that the suburban dream has become a nightmare.

The center of the town has become a tawdry commercial area filled with small businesses, most of them struggling to meet the competition of neighboring shopping centers. Striking landmarks, such as the water tower in Riverside, are altogether lacking. Even more appalling is the carefully engineered monotony of the residential districts. For this hideous dullness the city building code is partly responsible. Even on Allen Road, which is the strategic backbone of the town, the setback is uniformly established at sixty feet from the center line, while on the three secondary roads it is seventeen feet. An attempt has been made at the suburban atmosphere of open greenness through the regulation of fences, which are restricted to side and back yards only and must be of non-solid construction with a maximum height of four feet. These regulations would tax the

ingenuity of a Leonardo Da Vinci and contrast dramatically with the lack of restrictions
in Riverside.

Equally important in the development of
Allen Park has been the avarice of the speculative builder. The residences are completely
standardized; almost all are brick veneer with
white trim. There is a maximum residential
building height of thirty-five feet or two and
one-half stories, but the majority are a storey
and a half. These dwellings are placed in a
minimum lot of 5,000 square feet, and the
structure must cover not more than 30 percent of the total lot area. Lots must be at least
fifty feet wide with a front yard minimum of
twenty feet, an interval of three feet on one
side and eight feet on the other, and a backyard depth of thirty-five feet. The land has
been developed as intensively as possible.
The result is a series of ludicrously small
spaces between the houses; even the bicycles
are crowded together. Population density is
relatively high and privacy is almost impossible to obtain.

Are there any elements of interest in this
community? Quite clearly, the most striking
buildings are the schools. The somewhat conventional but neatly detailed South Junior
High School is typical of the structures recently put up by a harassed school board,
which must struggle to educate an increasing
number of children on a decreasing tax base.
Such green space as the community possesses
tends to be concentrated around the schools.
Here little league baseball games go on, while
in the background the monotonous rows of
identical houses extend in straight lines far
into the distance.

The primacy of the school is symbolic.
Along with the church, the bridge club and
the family circle itself, the school is a major
center of social activity. As Lewis Mumford
has pointed out American suburbs are turning more and more away from metropolitan
centers for their social interests. Allen Park
is hardly conscious of the museums, theatres,
concerts and general intellectual stimulus
offered by Detroit. In contrast, Riverside,
precisely because it is bound closely to Chicago by the Burlington Railroad, has a much
more organic connection with its mother city.
One wonders about the children growing up
in Allen Park. Will they be forever oriented
to suburbia and ignorant of the potentialities
of the city? It is a terrifying possibility.

Like most other suburban communities in
the Detroit area, Allen Park has two severe
economic problems. They are: insufficient
parking area to accommodate the invasion of
the automobile, and a rising public demand
for city services accompanied by an unwillingness to pay for these services through personal taxation. The response to these problems will determine its future.

Because the housewife ordinarily insists on
using the automobile to go to the corner market, she has difficulty finding a parking place.
Consequently, she patronizes a shopping
center in a neighboring town, leaving the individual commercial establishment bereft of
customers. In order to save some of the business of the small merchant, the town is now
forced to cover large quantities of valuable
land with asphalt or concrete. Frequently
residences have had to be torn down, and
sometimes park area has had to be taken for
parking lots. This radical measure, of course,
removes valuable land from the tax rolls so
that Allen Park is truly caught in a vicious
circle. In small compass it has the same problem as downtown Los Angeles, where 60 percent of the total land area is now donated to
super highways, parking structures and parking lots.

At present Allen Park has an excellent
array of city services, but, because of the un-

willingness of its citizens to pay for them, it has been forced to allocate a portion of its land to industry. Since most of its area has already been built up, this allocation is rather limited in extent; nonetheless, five major industrial concerns have been attracted: The Ford Motor Company, B. F. Goodrich Co., a pattern works, Wolverine Tube division of Calumet and Hecla, Inc., and a Montgomery Ward regional office. The land zoned for industrial use is near a branch of the Detroit, Toledo and Ironton R.R. (an important freight carrier, not a commuter's railway), and in addition, super highways carry the products of Allen Park to midwestern markets such as Detroit, Chicago and Cleveland. All of this development scarcely squares with the classic picture of the 19th Century suburb, which we can still observe in Riverside. Olmsted's suburb offers the very real advantages of close contact with the city, less emphasis on commercial expansion and more places for informal sociability. Its townscape is a living monument to the wisdom of Olmsted and the foresight of its citizens. Allen Park, by way of contrast, is a monument to the greed of the real estate speculator, though it was supposedly founded to secure for its people most of the same benefits as Riverside. When there is such a great discrepancy between ideology and reality, it is usually wise to admit that a concept is outmoded and to begin thinking anew.

30

Why Planners

Fail

John H. Stanford

One need only sample the literature of planning to sense the pervasive underlying emotion among planners these days: frustration. In their more frankly written essays, particularly those aimed at enlisting sympathetic support, the cities are pretty clearly assessed as going from bad to worse. Then men-with-the-plans who are supposed to reverse what they generally see as distressing urban deterioration seem discouraged, and irritable. Despite more recognition, more planning offices, bigger budgets and a general sense of respectability that contrasts sharply with the pre-World-War-II attitude toward planning, the sum total of specific accomplishment seems disappointing, even to the planners themselves.

Let us recognize that some of the invective against "the city" is deliberately heightened for the purpose of influencing public attitudes and opinions, as, for example, to sell the need for more urban planning. The natural sales campaign of any specialist group which seeks increased status is to paint the blackest possible picture of the present and an even more ominous vision of what will happen if their particular prescriptions are not accepted.

Beyond all this, however remains a generous measure of frustration, of even self-doubt among planners. Looking at the grand scope of the mission which planning theory assigns to them, and at the impressive amounts of time, talent, money and hope invested, one may wonder why the return is so small. Why do so many plans remain unimplemented? Why do planners feel so remote from the centers of effective decision-making, so alienated almost from the city? Some planners in their frustration seem well along toward a hostile rejection of modern urban life itself.

My hypothesis is a modest one: I believe that a major cause of unproductivity in planning is the general failure of planners to understand how to do effective staff work. Moreover, most planners do not even sense the causes of this failure because they do not conceive of their work as an integral part of the administrative processes of government.

Concentrating on the physical description of the plan he would like to achieve, the tradi-

Reprinted from *Landscape,* Vol. 13, no. 2 (Winter, 1963-64), pp. 8-11 by permission.

tional planner is naïve in his concept of how to get things done. The traditional approach contains the causes of its own frustration.

Let us look at some of the traditional approaches of the planner and the assumptions behind them. Certainly not all planners use them all of the time, but they are very influential in planner behavior.

First is a belief that fact-finding, objectivity and application of planning principles will (or at least, should) lead to general acceptance of the resulting plans. The preparation of plans is considered essentially an intellectual process, consisting of the application by experts of generally accepted standards to the facts at hand and the drawing therefrom of conclusions and recommendations. Or (and this is really not quite the same thing) the planner thinks of himself as already knowing certain "right" answers, and the plans based on these should therefore be accepted. While there is considerable attention to "selling", the traditional planner does not seek much real participation by non-specialists until after the conclusions have been pretty clearly established. The dominant idea is that planning should be turned over to planners, who can then get on with it if not excessively interfered with by others.

Second in the list of traditional planning approaches is the faith in the "master plan." The future patterns of desired physical development are portrayed on a master plan diagram or in a model, and this is supposed to guide future development. Supplemental devices are used — zoning, descriptive reports and pamphlets, lists of future public works projects, statistical projections of basic data. But because the planner's approach tends to be basically architectural, the "master plan" blueprint remains central among his devices. Although it is customary to describe it as

flexible and subject to revision, the planner really would like it to be the civic commandment by which the right-thinking citizen and public official will pattern their own actions.

Third, the planner does not expect to have to be very articulate about the "how" of planning. How, for example, he derives a specific master plan from his basic data is seldom described in much detail. One does not hear much about the value judgments involved, the alternatives considered, or the whole complex process by which such a plan is evolved. Nor does the planner have much to say about how he intends people to live their daily lives in this future city. One sees the idealized physical layout, but hears little of the "program" for the occupants. Will life be better there? The planner tends to assume that physical environment controls all else, and into that physical design he tends to project his personal goals and values as universal.

Similarly, the "how" of implementing the master plan is fairly casually treated. The troublesome specifics of public law, finance, organization and administration and the complex issues of public and private ways and means are mostly left for future consideration. At worst, the planner seems to say, "I've told you what to do; now it's up to somebody else to figure out how to do it." Too often, of course, nobody does.

A fourth tenet comes into play when the planner *does* decide that virtue alone is not enough protection for his plans. At this point, he tries either to get power enough vested in the planner himself to force others to comply or attaches himself as closely as possible at the ear of top executive or legislative authority so that the voice of that authority will silence opposition. Such opposition or even questioning of plans is likely to be labeled as mere ignorance or sabotage. The possibility that resistance to plans reflects real shortcomings in the plans themselves is a possibility scarcely to be considered.

What are the defects of this approach to planning? It is easier to answer this question now than it was twenty years ago or even ten. Other staff specialists in the managerial system have relied on these same approaches, found them wanting and are evolving other, newer, more effective techniques. In recent years, the concepts and techniques of management have become somewhat more knowledgeable and sophisticated. New insights from the behavioral sciences make us much less cocksure about the scientific objectivity of our approaches and much more aware of the importance of the processes by which people work together to evolve and to achieve common goals. We still don't know a great deal but we do know more than we used to.

During these developments planners seem mostly not to have been listening. With fragmentation of knowledge and the increasing specialization of specialists this is not so unexpected, but still it is curious that planners in their frustration seem not to have recognized their kinship with others who try to bring the impact of special skills and values to bear upon public management. I do not doubt that individual on-the-job planners who have achieved results have learned new and non-traditional approaches, whether by pragmatic common sense, by bitter experience or by borrowing from other specialties. It still seems fair to say, however, that the central body of planning literature and of planners has remained remote from the behavioral approach and from the general field of public administration.

The defects of the traditional approach in planning or in any of the other staff specialties are (1) an assumed "right" to take over very broad and important areas of public policy as belonging only to one particular special discipline — an assumption which generates conflict and resistance from others whose interests extend to these same areas; (2) a tendency to repeat over and over the same litany of proposals, with little energetic self-criticism and great reluctance to go deeply enough into specific real situations to evolve specific and creative solutions; (3) an oversimplified view of the administrative process and of society and particularly a reluctance to accept and understand the processes of power, status, tradition, human feelings, communication and persuasion which are intensely "real" elements in that society; (4) an ivory-tower tendency to prefer the "big" picture and the "big" plans, and to scorn the drudgery (and the discipline) of carrying on down to detailed ways and means of implementing broad goals and of stimulating the processes of evolution along desired lines; (5) an implicit faith in centralized power in administration (since the peak of the pyramid of hierarchy is where the planner prefers to reside) and a reluctance to experiment with planning approaches where the planner himself might not be dominant; (6) a tendency to ignore or to depreciate all planning not done by planners.

This partial catalog also suggests why planners who use traditional approaches are frustrated by resistance and meager results. The experience of specialists using traditional approaches in other fields of administration is the same, whether one looks at organization analysts, systems specialists, management trainers, personnel experts, fiscal specialists or any of the other burgeoning fields of staff endeavor.

The traditional approach in any of these fields tends to be pseudo-scientific, authoritarian, stereotyped, and a largely closed system concentrating upon emphasizing limited values central to the specialty. Such approaches, however well-intentioned, generate resistance and opposition which limit effectiveness and frustrate achievement. Only in periods of crisis will large systems yield passively to drastic surgery by such traditional specialists; but unfortunately it is the business of planners to prevent crises, and the very nature of their work focuses on the long-range future rather than the immediate solution of today's problem.

If the traditional approach to planning is defective in this regard, what alternative is available? Again, planners might look over the fence to other staff specialties for an answer. The alternative is for planners to accept and to learn to perform a *consultive staff role* in the administrative processes of government.

The essential elements of this approach are implied in the criticisms which have been made of traditional methods. Most fundamentally, the staff role means accepting that this is a multi-valued world and an extremely complex one. It means giving up the drive for exclusive power or control by a specialist-oriented group, and undertaking instead the more complex task of gaining acceptance for ideas, of working with and through older people, and of evolving *specific* solutions to problems. It means seeking for solutions which integrate a broad spectrum of conflicting forces into new and mutually acceptable courses of action. It means emphasizing the planning process as much as the plan or more, and aiming not so much at a single static "master plan" solution as at a continuing evolutionary change. It means learning in depth the real community and its people in all its complex variations. It means a basic concept of obtaining results through others by stimulating, by communicating, by educating, by "making things happen." In short, the consultive role means that the planner gives up the effort to dictate the shape of the future by "divine right" and accepts instead the tasks of catalyst and counselor.

What, specifically, would such a planner do differently? He would work as part of the management processes of the government in which he is located, considering his work inseparable from other problems of public policy and administration.

He would seek to heighten the ability to plan effectively throughout the government, and to launch systems by which planning considerations will be more recognized and given weight in day-to-day operations. He would seek to accomplish his objectives through building planning into the entire activities of government, rather than through the activities of his own office alone. He would try to be a stimulant, an expediter, balancing his objectivity with an informed empathy toward those with whom he works.

He would seek to build confidence in planning and greater acceptance of its worth by seeking out first those problems which others have with which he could be helpful, and working hard on their solution.

He would accept decentralization and evolutionary change as normal parts of the administrative processes of large organizations and would seek a proper pace and balance in both.

He would try to develop throughout the government an enlightened understanding of planning values and a broad consensus on goals, so that gradually the whole activities of the governmental entity and the full exercise of its powers would be contributing toward the achievement of these goals.

He would try to remain free of bureaucratic routines and paper approvals which, however helpful in justifying staff increases and in calming bureaucratic feelings of insecurity, steal precious time from more basic activities. He would try to keep his staff small, highly trained and mobile — seeking always to place continuing operating work elsewhere so as to remain free to deal with emerging problems.

In relation to the broader urban environment in which he works, the planner would accept the fact that no absolute power can be found, no "owner" of the city to be client for his blueprints. He would accept the necessity of working within a framework of cooperation and complexity rather than seeking to achieve simplicity through power. He would approach his planning much more in terms of people and their relationships rather than in terms of architectural arrangement of urban spaces.

The same general techniques can be applied in the community at large as within the government itself, but the setting is much more complex. The planner must understand in detail how the city really works, in the full social economic and political sense, and how people live in it. He must accept the role of leadership without power on planning issues. He must evolve effective planning processes which work in that specific setting and with that particular combination of people and forces. And, he must have a willing enthusiasm for processes of citizen participation, education and communication that immerse the planner deeply in the realities of his community.

The planner as staff consultant to government and to community alike must earn the right to influence the future. This right is earned not merely by being a planner but by entering into the life of the city and seeking out every possible opportunity to influence and to assist the people and the processes which guide its development.

Perhaps all this seems too demanding a task. Is it reasonable to expect the planner to obtain results without power? There is no question that it is difficult; but who ever thought that planning could be simple? The fault, if fault there be, lies rather with oversimplified aproaches which have promised more than they can deliver and which have frustrated and disappointed the planners themselves.

A Concept of Rural-Urban Regions

31

John Kinsel

We are becoming urbanized in a hurry. Of the two million new noses counted in Canada's 1956 Census, 92 percent were in cities or towns of 1,000 population and up. Two-thirds of all Canadians now live in these urban communities.

By and large, this postwar move to the cities caught us unprepared. And now we're running to keep from slipping backward. Water supplies, sewage disposal systems, housing developments, recreation facilities, schools and many other services have had to be expanded enormously to accommodate new thousands each year. Many urban municipalities have solved one emergency only to find themselves faced with a new one. Costs have compounded faster than new resources could be uncovered, and capital borrowing has increased rapidly.

Many Problems are Rural-Urban

It is not surprising, then, that we have tended to regard the need for planning as something peculiarly associated with urban expansion. The obvious differences between rural and urban problems, the separation between rural and urban local government jurisdictions, and the urgency of extending urban facilities have succeeded in splitting our vision. Preoccupied with our special problems, we have lost sight of the many common interests which are shared by the residents of an urban centre and by those who live in its rural area of influence.

What are some of today's problems where this community of interest is evident?

First of all, consider the physical expansion of urban centres. Urban dispersal may take one or more of several forms: gradual encroachment on the surrounding rural land, encirclement of non-urban territory, radial penetration along main highways, or "leapfrogging". Industrial decentralization, which is becoming steadily more prominent, contributes to the dispersal of population and creates special problems of its own. In a few cases, urban dispersal may be systematically planned as a green belt development.

There can be little argument that cities and towns must have room to expand. But in our

Reprinted from *Community Planning Review* (September, 1957), by courtesy of *Community Planning Review*.

approach to the planning problem we have tended to overlook the fact that "rurban" transition involves rural as well as urban adjustments. For example, one technique which is extensively applied in "rurban" areas is agricultural zoning. But agricultural zoning has been used almost exclusively as a tool for urban land use — a means of controlling undesired urban development. A parcel so zoned may or may not be an economic farm unit. The zoning may or may not be permanent enough to justify certain kinds of intensive agricultural development. As pointed out by Ernest A. Engelbert, Land-Use Planning for 'Rurban' Areas, (Farm Policy Forum, Winter 1957), the role of agriculture in "rurban" land use deserves considerably more study than it has received thus far.

Countless problems encountered in urban expansion require joint rural-urban planning. The question of zoning outside urban limits is one such problem. The location of industries on rural land well outside the jurisdiction of the neighbouring town or city where workers live is another. "Leapfrogging" suburban communities create demands for access routes of high standard through non-urban territory — demands which rural jurisdictions are not prepared to meet. Nearly every aspect of the problem of "urban spread" affects rural as well as urban interests.

No urban centre can be self-contained. It must seek its water supply outside the city gates. Usually it must dispose of its waste products in the rural area. Certainly its people must be fed from farms, near or far. Many of its people earn their living as handlers or processors of farm products or as suppliers of farm production needs. Similarly, the farmer is directly dependent on the urban centre to market his produce, to provide and service his equipment and to supply his many needs as producer and consumer. In this sense,

urban and rural people are closely interdependent.

The need for joint rural-urban planning has not gone unrecognized. Nearly every expanding urban centre of any size has attempted to set up some kind of machinery in conjunction with the surrounding rural jurisdiction to deal with mutual planning problems. But such efforts have not been uniformly successful. In the first place, such arrangements are almost invariably and necessarily informal, with final action depending upon ratification by the separate jurisdictions. In the second place, the relationship is frequently one-sided, since very few units of rural local government have planning resources of their own. Finally, it frequently occurs that the urban centre must deal with not one but two or more rural jurisdictions to embrace the area necessary for planning purposes.

And, while the need for urban planning is receiving much attention, coordinated planning in our rural areas is no less urgent. City dwellers have no corner on problems. The same forces which are concentrating our people in urban areas are throwing life out of joint in farming communities.

Tendency Toward An Urban-Centred Life

For rural people (in the Canadian West at any rate) the past two decades have been years of continual social and economic adjustment. A rapidly advancing farm technology has meant substantial increases in the output per unit of farm labour. Farm size has increased rapidly. As a result, some farm families have higher incomes; many others are forced to leave farming and migrate to cities and towns. In many areas traditional rural neighbourhoods have disappeared entirely.

At the same time, farming is becoming less of a distinct way of life and assuming more of the attributes of other commercial enterprises. Greater commercialization means less self-sufficiency. The impact of higher incomes, mass communication, and the automobile has had a distinct urbanizing effect on farm values. The habits and attitudes of farm families are becoming less distinguishable from those of urban families. The social and economic focus of farm living is becoming centred on the nearby urban community.

Farm people are less content than they were to accept second class services: one room schools, impassable roads, inaccessible doctors and hospitals. At the same time, sparser population means higher per capita costs for nearly all rural services. A substantial number of farm families have sought individual solutions to these problems by taking up residence in urban centres near their farms. Where this has occurred, remaining farm residences are even more isolated. Even initially, the prairie farm settlement pattern was one of extreme dispersal. Depopulation has made that dispersal doubly extreme. The costs per farm of providing essential services such as roads and education have risen sharply because of this factor alone. Reinforcing this rise has been a steadily-growing demand for services of higher quality.

The need for intelligent rural planning is indeed urgent. Planning is needed to ease the transition of rural living to a new and larger urban-centred community. Planning is needed to improve and extend services to rural people — services comparable to those available in modern urban centres. Planning is needed on a coordinated rural-urban basis to contend with the growing list of mutual rural-urban problems.

Lack of Workable Planning Areas

If the province of Saskatchewan is typical, we are ill-prepared to meet these planning needs. The Royal Commission on Agriculture and Rural Life has recently completed a four-year study of a broad array of rural problems in that province. Its findings and recommendations, comprising over 3,000 pages in 14 volumes, cover subjects ranging from farm credit to the rural family. But throughout its investigation, the lack of facilities for rural planning, the lack of awareness of the need, and the lack of appropriate rural planning areas were matters of recurring concern. It devoted special attention to the problem of defining appropriate regions for rural planning and administration. And the regional concept which the Commission developed has important implications, not only for rural areas, but for urban centres as well.

The Commission's concern with defining rural-urban regions grew out of its appraisal of rural local government in Saskatchewan. It found a near-chaotic situation, characterized by:

(1) A basic local government unit in inadequate size. Although there is some variation, the typical rural municipal unit in Saskatchewan contains nine townships in an 18-mile square. This uniform small size creates some serious inefficiencies in planning and administering services. Small size means limited fiscal capacity, small population, and the absence of a meaningful planning area. In the provision of roads, for example, tax resources in most municipalities do not permit the purchase of modern efficient machinery; the small area precludes its economic use. Qualified supervisory personnel cannot be hired. Few local planning facilities exist and, in any case, road use is often oriented to points outside the municipality's jurisdiction.

(2) A multiplicity of units. In addition to almost 300 rural municipalities and some 500 incorporated urban centres, Saskatchewan has

literally thousands of special purpose districts and quasi-governmental jurisdictions. These include school districts, consolidated school districts, larger school units, union hospital districts, health regions, municipal doctor plans, agricultural representative districts, and many, many more which fulfil some kind of local government function. Including them all, there is one such unit for every 130 people in the province.

(3) Overlapping jurisdictions. Most of the special purpose districts, which have been superimposed on the small rural municipal units, are larger and fail to conform to the municipal boundary lines. The resulting welter of overlapping boundaries makes integrated planning and administration practically impossible.

The historical explanation for this confusing situation is simple enough. Initially, rural municipalities were logically designed to provide very limited services in a horse and buggy age: dirt roads, minimum health and welfare services, and some agricultural services. School districts needed to be large enough only to supply population for a one-room school with a single teacher. What happened? Population began to thin out and at the same time people began to demand more and better services. Each new or expanded service failed to fit into the established rural municipal pattern. Rather than reorganize the basic structure to fit changing conditions, succeeding governments added new jurisdictions to meet each new situation. The resulting unwieldy structure resembles a building in which each floor has been constructed according to a different design and unique specifications.

What is a Rational Planning Area

It was obvious to the Commission that the situation demanded rather drastic reorganiza-

tion. As a first step the Commission was faced with the fundamental task of dividing the province into regions of appropriate size with appropriate boundaries. Certain criteria in establishing size were readily apparent: fiscal capacity, population, administrative efficiency, and so on. But where to draw the boundary lines? The settled portion of Saskatchewan is a reasonably homogeneous farming area with few natural boundaries and with few impediments to transportation, other than the condition of roads. What was the common denominator whereby the interrelated services of local government could be coordinated? What constituted a rational planning area for Saskatchewan's sparse and scattered rural population?

No single set of boundaries, of course, would be suitable to define all local government services and regional administrative functions. Some involve the administration and use of natural resources; here, boundaries and size are determined largely by the occurrence and use of the resource. Water users' districts would be one example; forestry administration another. Then there is a group of services which are oriented to consumers with dispersed consumption — such things as rural power, telephones and police protection. The location of boundaries and administrative centres for this kind of service are largely matters of technical necessity and administrative convenience.

In the third category are those services which are supplied more or less universally and which require consumption at a central point. These include some of the more important services typically assigned to local government agencies — such things as health, education and recreation. Roads become a vital adjunct to this group of services because of the mobility required for central consumption — bus routes for schools, access to doctors and hospitals and to municipal offices for the payment of taxes, and so on. These were the services which most concerned the Commission. They were services vital to the general welfare of people and they also exhibited the clearest need for coordination and integration.

The Trading Area

The search for means to define an area of "natural association" which possessed a focal centre led the Commission to examine the urban centre and its trading area. The idea of a trading area is, of course, a familiar one. It has always been a preoccupation of retail merchants and is part of the stock-in-trade of market analysis. It defines a region, not in terms of geographic characteristics, cultural traits or typical economic activity, but rather in terms of economic interdependence. The trading area describes a pattern of association built on years of trial and error in the exchange of goods and services essential to our economic mode of life. If a farmer goes to Centre "X" to repair his equipment, buy his suits and play golf, why should he not go to the same centre to get hospital care, pay his taxes and educate his children?

The logic appeared inexorable. But to determine whether the trading area did in fact have the qualities necessary to define a meaningful region, the Commission conducted two field studies in widely separated areas of the province. In each of these field studies, farmers selected from a cross-section of location in the trading area of a medium-sized urban centre were interviewed. Detailed information was obtained on the economic and social relationship between the farm family and all the urban centres, large and small, which it visited. From these surveys, the Commission was able to construct the patterns of association

for each area. Moreover it was able to gauge the effectiveness of the trading area as an organizing principle; to measure its economic and social meaning to the rural residents of the area. The result of these surveys offered strong confirmation to the validity of the Commission's concept.

The Service Centre Principle

Although encouraged to proceed, the Commission soon faced a number of problems in attempting to apply the service centre principle:

(1) It was apparent that any given farm family was "attached" to several urban centres rather than one. Thus, the farmer markets his grain or buys his groceries in the hamlet closest to his farm. For other needs he travels farther to the village, the town or the city. The small centre performs certain functions within its small trading area. But the larger centre performs additional functions for residents of a wider area — including the residents of the smaller centres within its orbit. Out of well over a thousand centres of varying size in Saskatchewan, how was the Commission to determine which were the suitable centres and areas to define regions appropriate to the given public services?

(2) Regional boundaries must exhaust the area of the province. Did trading areas offer a reasonable basis for dividing the entire populated area?

(3) What about regional subdivisions? For some purposes sub-areas were necessary. Was there a basis in the organization of service centres for a rational subdivision of larger regional planning and administrative areas?

(4) The accepted method of defining an urban trading area — the market analysis technique — involved costly local surveys.

Was there any alternative practical method for delineating trading areas?

The Commission pursued its analysis of these questions in a report on Service Centres. The study set out to do three things: (1) establish a basis for classifying service centres according to function; (2) examine the principles governing the location of service centres in an agricultural economy; and (3) test the applicability of the trade-centred community to the definition of regions through an actual analysis of service centers in a portion of the province.

Without attempting to deal here with some of the more complex and theoretical aspects of the Service Centres report, it is useful to examine some of the Commission's conclusions and their practical application.

First of all, the Commission demonstrated that it is relatively easy and inexpensive to classify urban centres in the order of the functions they perform for the rural population. For its purposes, the Commission adopted a classification of six levels of centres, ranging from the crossroads hamlet to the provincial city. As a measure, the Commission counted the number of services — both commercial and public — which farmers and their families used in each centre. Centres with 2-10 services were designated Hamlets; those with 11-25 were called Villages; and so on. Additional classifications were Towns, Greater Towns, Cities and Provincial Cities. The range of services available was the key to the classification system.

In the course of this classification, it became apparent that each rank of centre was marked by certain characteristic services. Services for which the demand was universal and the required scale of operation small were found in centres of all sizes. In Saskatchewan's farming area, for example, every centre has at least a grain elevator and a general store. These are the minimum services characteristic of a hamlet, although most hamlets also have one or more of the following: post office, railway depot, one-room school, church.

The next higher rank of centre — the village — typically offers all the services available in hamlets. In addition, it has a new range of services such as lumber yard, fuel dealer, municipal office and telephone exchange. These services require a larger market

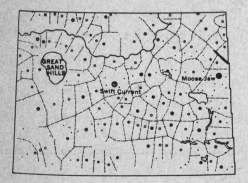

Figure 1.   First approximation of boundaries of Village-centred Service Areas in Southwestern Saskatchewan.

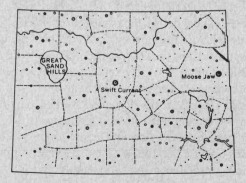

Figure 2.   First approximation of boundaries of Town-centred Service Areas in Southwestern Saskatchewan.

for economic operation than hamlet services. The trading area of the village, therefore, is correspondingly larger and includes not only the farm population but the population of the hamlets which surround it.

For each succeeding rank, the progression is similar. The number of centres in the higher rank is smaller and the trading areas are larger. And each rank has its characteristic range of services which are seldom found in centers of lower rank.

With respect to the location of centres, the Commission found evidence to indicate that centres are distributed with reasonable uniformity throughout any populated agricultural area.* In Saskatchewan, the adherence of centres to rail lines disturbs the uniformity of distribution to a degree. The populated area, however, has a relatively dense network of rail lines; as a result, the "gaps" between trading areas are not of serious proportions. Generally speaking, the trading areas for any particular class of centre pretty well blanket the populated area.

It was also found that, by utilizing the tributary areas of two ranks of service centers, sub-regions could be delineated, although some compromises in boundaries were necessary to keep subsidiary regions wholly within the major region. Because of certain characteristics in centre location, it proved best to select alternate ranks of centres to define major regions and their subdivisions. The trading area of a Greater Town, for example, is most satisfactorily subdivided by Village trading areas rather than those of the intermediate Town. The reason for this is that Towns tend to straddle the border separating the trading areas of Greater Towns, while Villages tend to mark the limits of Town influence, and so on.

This latter characteristic proved extremely useful in developing a method for preliminary mapping of trading areas without resorting to costly local surveys. Between two adjacent Towns, for example, one will usually find a Village; between two Cities, a Greater Town. The Commission found evidence to support the thesis that trading area boundaries between two centres of a given rank are marked by the occurrence of a single centre of the next lower rank. By locating all such boundary markers, the general outline of trading areas can be derived.

In general, the Commission found that the trading area concept fulfilled its initial hopes as a sound method of approach to defining meaningful regions. In a detailed analysis of centres in Southwest Saskatchewan, it was

---

* The concept of centre location adopted by the Commission depends largely on theories advanced by Walter Christaller in explaining the location of central places in southern Germany. (See Die Zentralen Orte in Suddeutschland, Jena, Gustav Fischer Verlag, 1933). The development and application of Christaller's theories in the Saskatchewan environment is the subject of a monograph: P. Woroby, Functional Relationships Between Service Centres and the Farm Population, unpublished thesis, University of Manitoba, 1957.

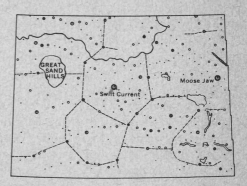

Figure 3. First approximation of boundaries of Greater Town-centred Service Areas in Southwestern Saskatchewan.

able to rough out the approximate boundaries of trading areas for various ranks of centres without recourse to actual field surveys (see maps).

At the same time, the Commission makes no claims that boundaries located in this fashion can be considered final in any respect. They are only first approximations. In the first place, boundary lines in the above figures were drawn without detailed knowledge of local factors which might cause residents in the boundary areas to gravitate to one center or the other. In any event, any final boundaries for administrative or planning purposes would need to be altered so as not to pass through smaller centres, and their local trading areas. In the second place, the Commission points out that other factors such as fiscal capacity, population, administrative loads, and problems of coordination must be considered in establishing boundaries. The trading area is proposed only as a rational starting point in defining regions.

Advantages of the Trading Area

So much for the method developed by the Commission. What are some of the advantages of the trading area as a planning unit?

(1) It defines an existing pattern of association of people for certain economic and social purposes. It therefore lends itself to efficient organization for some of the more important public services. It defines boundaries (albeit in general terms) and locates the logical administrative centre for greatest convenience to the population being served. It provides the only sound orientation for planning local roads and contains the proper area for planning a local road network.

(2) Because of the functional differences between ranks of service centres, trading areas

provide the basis for integral tiers of major and minor planning areas. Different levels of services and different levels of administration can be accommodated in an integrated system. Health services provide a good example here. General hospital care can be provided economically to a relatively small population, and minimum facilities need to be distributed widely to give adequate service. More specialized hospital and diagnostic services, however, require a much larger population unit for economic operation. A two-tier arrangement composed of smaller trading areas contained within the larger area tributary to a City, provides the logical base for integrating two levels of service.

(3) Because the trading area is oriented to its urban centre, it delineates the most suitable area for integrated rural-urban planning. In attacking the problems of urban expansion, the trading area is the natural unit. It defines and includes satellite communities which attract suburban movement. It includes all the access routes to the major centre. It includes the rural population dependent on the centre for commercial services, public services and recreational and social activities. At the same time, it includes those nearby rural areas which the urban population uses for recreational activities. While it certainly does not solve all rural-urban planning problems, a unit based on the trading area nonetheless provides a framework with a minimum of structural handicaps.

*Other Considerations Affecting
Regional Planning*

The Commission, of course, was primarily interested in defining regions appropriate to the requirements of rural local government. Its recommendations for the reorganization of local government in Saskatchewan embraced additional considerations, a number of which have implications for regional planning.

It was the Commission's conclusion that local government — in the sense of a single local authority with comprehensive responsibility — had practically ceased to exist in Saskatchewan. In its place was a series of separate and sometimes conflicting jurisdictions, each serving some segment of local needs. The rural municipal unit, once the mainstay of local government, was essentially left with two residual functions: construction and maintenance of roads and collection of taxes. Health services were administered by hospital districts and health regions. Schools were administered by larger school units and school districts. Agricultural services were administered in a variety of ways: a few through municipal councils, some through special districts and others through relatively informal local arrangements. Other functions, once locally administered, were now in provincial hands. Jurisdiction had become so segmented that to identify any given rural area with a single responsible unit of local government was impossible.

The implications of this situation were far-reaching, in the Commission's view. The inability of citizens to fix local responsibility was contributing to an obvious decline in political participation and to a growth of apathy in rural areas. The lack of any comprehensive budgetary control over local rural expenditures was making long-term plans in the allocation of resources virtually impossible. The accurate determination of local tax load and tax carrying capacity was also out of the question. This, plus the very number of taxing authorities, made debenture financing difficult and costly. In addition, the inefficiencies and added costs involved in providing related services through unrelated jurisdictions were obviously high.

Aims of the Royal Commission

The Commission's recommendations for a fundamental and sweeping reorganization of rural local government in Saskatchewan are directed towards the achievement of the following:

(1) Coterminous planning and administrative areas of adequate size for a maximum number of local government functions. First priority is given to the functions of education and public works (roads).

(2) Establishment of boundaries on the basis of trade-centered communities. This involves matching units of optimum size to trading areas of the appropriate rank of service centres.

(3) Integration of the maximum number of functions under a single authority within the reorganized areas. The Commission favours the county form of administration, with standing committees assigned to individual local government functions: education, public works, agriculture, social welfare, area planning, etc.

While the Commission made no firm recommendation in the matter, it also called attention to the need for integrated rural-urban jurisdiction over a greater number of functions. Particularly is this true in the case of Saskatchewan's small and middle-sized urban municipalities. The trend in education is toward integration of rural and urban school systems. Health services on an area basis often include both rural and urban residents. Certainly the joint rural-urban planning problems cited earlier would be immensely simplified if jurisdictional gaps were somehow bridged.

The Commission recognized that a number of difficulties stand in the way of achieving unified rural-urban jurisdiction. Land assessment as a tax base is not fully comparable in rural and urban areas. In the matter of political representation, rural residents hold some fears of urban dominance. And, despite the growing community of interest, certain aspects of local government are exclusively urban, others exclusively rural. Above all there are age-old prejudices and traditions to be broken down.

Nevertheless, the Commission proposed that careful study be made of incorporating villages and towns into the county system in Saskatchewan. The obstacles to this final step in integration may be more apparent than real.

In any event, the core of the Commission's approach to reorganizing and unifying local government in Saskatchewan is its concept of the rural-urban region — a region based on the patterns of association which people have built up to satisfy their day-to-day economic and social needs. How generally this concept may be applied remains to be seen. It appears to be particularly suited to Saskatchewan's problem: the definition of meaningful regions in an area characterized by relatively uniform agricultural development and by a system of service centres which evolved primarily to serve the rural population.

Open Space for the Urban Region

32

James W. Thorsell

Woe onto them that join house to house, that lay
field to field, till there be no place that they may
be placed alone in the midst of the earth.

Isaiah V, viii.

Woe unto Urban Man who in the twentieth
century is fast approximating the condition
prophesized by Isaiah 2200 years ago. Today
urbanization has become the way of life of a
majority of our population. Social factors such
as the need to "get out of the crowds into the
country" and the growing cultural sanction for
extensive travel made possible by improving
economic factors, are making leisure and recreation great problems and challenging opportunities in developing our "Great Society".

Herein lies an obvious paradox: outdoor
recreational resources are becoming more and
more remote from the urban dweller at a time
when improved social and economic conditions have increased his need to enjoy this
freedom. Perloff and Wingo sum up the present problem:

. . . suddenly we find ourselves face to face with
a major urban need unsatisfied and commanding
attention. For two generations we have accumulated a backlog of recreational needs; now wealth
and leisure have converted these needs into an
active economic demand and a pressing political
force (Perloff and Wingo, 1962, p. 83).

This need for open space stems from the
relatively recent massive urbanization and the
technological revolution which gave it birth.
Canada's urban population set at 62 per cent
in 1966 should rise to 80 per cent by 1980.
Reinforcing the effects of the pull of the cities
on the need for recreational open space is the
effect of a 50 per cent reduction in the work
week in the last hundred years. Three-
sevenths of the year will be available for
leisure time pursuits in 1980.

While the number of potential recreation
seekers is increasing as a result of these factors, the developing suburbs are ironically
making recreational escape from the city more
difficult. Haphazard fringe development has
spread a thin veneer of low-density dwellings

Reprinted from *Ontario Geography*, no. 7 (1967) by permission.

over large tracts of potential recreational open space that is needed by recreation-hungry residents of the central city. Moreover, only rarely have planners provided for sufficient public open space within the new communities.

What are the specific problems involved in the complex task of providing open space for urban man? The remainder of this paper will offer a brief survey of the literature on the subject and attempt to analyze some of the problems of demand for and supply of open space.

What is Open Space?

Tankel defines open space as ". . . all land and water in and around urban areas which is not covered by buildings . . . the space and light above as well" (Tankel, 1963, p. 57). More specifically, open space includes all non-asphalted private and public land that confronts the urban resident in the different spatial frameworks through which he moves from his backyard to a far distant wilderness preserve. In this manner a hierarchy of open space is conceptualized which proceeds from street to community to county to regional levels.

The form and function of open space can vary considerably. More than just parks and playgrounds, open space consists of all open "wanderable" land such as may be found on college campuses, institutional lands, or agricultural areas. Basically open space then exists to provide relief from the urban social, commercial and industrial jungle by offering free open land with greenery and flowers to replace the artificial frame of everyday city life.

In their stress on recognition of open space as a valid urban land use, Tunnard and Push-karev (1963) identify four functions of open space: protective, productive, ornamental,

and recreational. The first two can be grouped as open space for structure and the latter two as open space for service. Similarly Tankel distinguishes between open space that people can see and open space they are probably not aware of. Open space that can be seen is that which is *used* for recreation, *viewed* from vantage points or *felt* in that it offers landscape relief. That which is not necessarily perceived either does urban work or helps to shape the development pattern of the city (a water supply area or an airport buffer zone).

This latter use of open space as an urban form determinant is a major weapon in planning procedure recommended in the open space plan of the Chicago metropolitan area. One of the primary uses of open spaces there is:

. . . to give structure, shape and form to the city — separating clusters, preserving wedges, dividing and giving identity to urban communities and maintaining a balance between urban and rural land uses (North-eastern Illinois Metro Area Planning Commission, 1963, p. 1).

With the often haphazard character of metropolitan development underlying the need for this controlling and directing function, open space thus assumes a multi-purpose role. No longer is open space planning only concerned with what to do with the leftover areas and "sloips".* It has now become an integral part of the master plan as an urban land use, as important as other types of land use in the city.

Metropolitan Structure and Open Space Distribution

Much has been written on the per capita and per acre areas of open space that are needed

* A colloquial term meaning "space left over in planning".

for a city region. Reference standards, however, are only helpful guidelines. The land set aside for urban and suburban recreation space has been reported as low as 4 acres per 1,000 urban population (the present goal in London, England) and as high as 12.5 acres per 1,000 population (the present Chicago ratio). London, Ontario has 4.5 acres per 1,000 population, well below an arbitrary desirable standard of 19 acres per 1,000 population. As Chapin points out:

> . . . the amount of land required for open space is open ended for as yet we have no basis for quantifying the need for breathing space in cities (Chapin, 1964, p. 419).

However, the emphasis should perhaps not be on the amount but on the proper distribution of open space. The conspicuous need for open space occurs where the man-land conflict is most intense — in and near large cities. Even the most urbanized areas have some open spaces which are potential recreational sites, such as ravines, river-valleys, woods, and wetlands. Furthermore the acquisition costs for these marginal and commercially undevelopable sites are usually lower than for the surrounding land.

In examining the problems of urban open space it is helpful to view the region in three spatial contexts: the central city, the outer ring, and the urban region.

Central City Open Space

The residents of urban cores of large cities only rarely have adequate space. Along with the keen competition for, and intense use of land one of the reasons for this deprivation has been the obliteration of the remaining unprotected open space by the expansion from the city core to the urban fringe. Except

for some of the larger, more outstanding urban parks such as are found in the cities of Vancouver, New York and Auckland, the central core of cities is too often devoid of adequate areas of greenery, silence, and "stretching room". Even in the above exceptions the existing facilities are being taxed to their limits.

Different socioeconomic characteristics of the central city resident add further to the awkwardness of his open space situation. As the United States Outdoor Recreation Resources Review Commission pointed out, the average central city resident has below median income, lesser mobility (53 percent of New York City families have no car), and lives in an area with a much higher residential density than a resident of the suburbs. Moreover, it is here that the senior citizens and racial minority groups congregate in an environment with fewer possibilities to engage in outdoor recreation activities. Even the high income resident of the central city to some extent shares with the lower income groups the disadvantages of the crowded core. The Commission concludes:

> . . . the people on whom the environment of the city with its close-packed living, its constant pressure on the concrete, brick and asphalt environment, and its lack of pleasant surroundings which is most oppressive have less than average access to the out of doors (Outdoor Recreation Resources Review Commission, 1962, p. 10).

Outer Ring Open Space and the Greenbelt

Deficiencies in recreational amenities and blight in the central city were factors hastening the flight to the suburbs which began after World War II. Physical deterioration, appropriation for other uses of remaining open space in the core, as well as the desire to return to a form of life more akin to country living were reasons for this suburbanization. But the initial ready access of the older suburbs to recreation space declined as the city, in its outward growth, absorbed more and more of the surrounding countryside. The subdivisions of yesterday became the slums of today. Indeed, the suburban residents of large metropolitan areas found themselves crowded out of parks and off the highways that lead to them by the sheer weight of numbers of neighbours from the core. Thus, the urgent planning problem is to find methods to preserve suburban open space by controlling the gradual sprawl of the suburbs.

There is one technique which can be used in the outer ring that helps to alleviate this problem: encircle the urban perimeter by a greenbelt. This idea is not new. In 1898 Ebeneezer Howard provided Letchworth, England, his model garden city, with a greenbelt (Figure 1) to prevent the town from overspilling its natural boundaries, to act as a link between town and country, and to prevent less skillfully planned adjoining neighbourhoods from invading the Letchworth territory (Ho-

ward, 1898). But setting a fixed limit to the growth of the city often presents too many additional problems to the modern exploding metropolis. The original greenbelt concept has been adapted to present urban conditions by town planners and often takes more the form of green wedges, ribbons, or internal blocks of open land (Figure 1). These "fingers" are frequently scattered throughout the city thus allowing more flexibility and better access for central residents.

The Conservation Authorities of Ontario are unique in considering river valleys and ravines as elements in greenbelt formation. Anderson's work on the importance of day-use river valley recreation in the London, Ontario region is an outstanding example of open space research using this modern multipurpose greenbelt approach (Anderson, 1962).

Metropolitan Toronto offers an interesting example of the use of drainage corridors as the main structural elements in the provision of urban open space (Figure 2). Here, as in such other large cities as Winnipeg and Edmonton, extensive river flood plains and

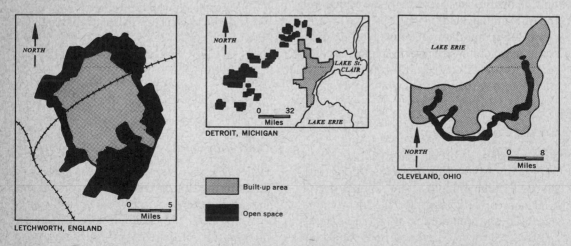

Figure 1. Open space pattern in Letchworth, England, Cleveland, Ohio and Detroit, Michigan.

wooded ravines are presently, or can readily be, developed as open space reserves. At the same time they can function as storage areas for flood waters and serve as open space buffers and wedges to relieve the monotony of urban development.

Regional Open Space

Less critical problems appear in the provision of large scale regional areas of accessible and continuous countryside. Perloff and Wingo call for a more urban-oriented open space policy where emphasis is on nearby, user-oriented space rather than on distant resource-based preserves:

The evolving need is not so much for more Yosemites, Grand Canyons, and Okefinokees as it is for millions of acres of just plain open space endowed in many cases with only per-haps modest landscape and topographical interest but richly and imaginatively developed — this is the basic shift in approach that is called for by the logic of the present day situation (1962, p. 62).

The critical shortage in this country is underlined by Brooks:

No large population centre in Canada can be said to have even a passable system of close-in regional parks to meet the day-to-day and week-end outdoor recreational demands . . . (Brooks, 1965, p. 6).

Even though provision of extensive stretches of national Resource-oriented space such as National Parks and Recreation Reserves are required for preservation of natural environments offering the ultimate in urban contrast, the problems of such provision are less immediate. An ecological, holistic view

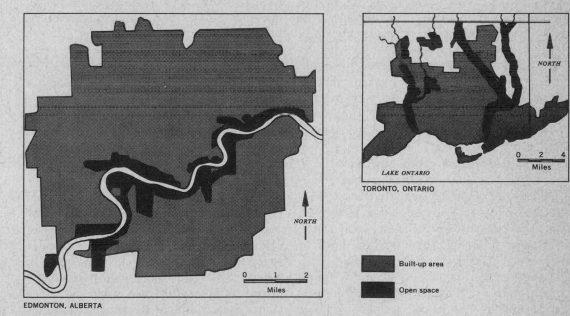

Figure 2. Open space pattern in Edmonton, Alberta and Toronto, Ontario.

does, however, demonstrate that these large regional tracts must be provided in order to achieve a viable "system". In fact, the problems of incompatible uses presently being forced into Canada's National Parks can be seen as a type of negative feedback·which originated in the deficient and over-crowded conditions that exist at lower open space levels.

Planning a Metropolitan Open Space System

It is evident that the provision of adequate urban open space involves an area greater than the local area. The very nature of providing adequate open space calls for the design of broad regional recreational systems which can best exploit and merge the available resources and human demands. For example, the city of Denver, Colorado has gone far beyond its urban boundaries in purchasing several mountain peaks for the use of its residents. Likewise the Lincoln County, Ontario lakeshore study requested co-operation as well as financial aid from surrounding municipalities in developing the public shoreline. Concluding that "the lakeshore does not and cannot exist independently of the active hinterland", the report stressed the need for a regional outlook to solve a regional problem (Niagara Regional Development Association, 1959, p. 9).

Because of present conditions, however, long range planning for recreation space is usually extraordinarily difficult. In transcending city boundaries there are seldom conventional government structures or analytical frameworks available to deal with the broad environment planning required. Striving for a new open space outlook, Perloff and Wingo suggest there is great merit and potential in using the systems approach to bring into better perspective the recreational behavior of the urban population. The systems technique would identify such key elements as population, activities and facilities and determine the interactions and casual relationships that exist among them. Invaluable and relevant tools available for analysis are the gravity model and linear programming. Dr. Clawson has vividly advocated the necessity of systems planning by sketching what happens if it is not used (Clawson, 1963). The birds-eye view of the "recreation shed" of the urban region appears to be a most fruitful method for planning and integrating open space into the environment framework of the region.

It is useful to look at an example of the methodology that could be used in planning for the provision of open space in an urban region. A suggested general procedural outline based on the North Eastern Illinois study is:

1. *Inventory* the existing regional open space and evaluate its adequacy.

2. *Estimate* the future open space requirements for recreation and other purposes.

3. *Examine* the possible use of open space as an urban form determinant.

4. *Survey* the open space resources to identify the areas of greatest adaptability for open space use.

5. *Review* the methods available for preserving and acquiring this space.

The Outlook

Action is needed as the hunger for more public open land becomes acute. One of the first major forward steps was the enactment of Ontario's Conservation Authority Act which suggested the provision of open space in watersheds as a major multi-purpose by-product of other conservation measures. The United States Outdoor Recreation Resources Review Commission, the ARDA Recreational

Land Inventory, and the recent formation of the National and Provincial Parks Association of Canada are some important federal and private examples of progress which has been made.

On the local level positive action has been taken in setting up regional planning commissions in large metropolitan areas. Prominent among these are the California State Outdoor Recreation Planning Committee, the North Eastern Illinois Metropolitan Area Planning Commission, and the Metropolitan Toronto and Regional Conservation Authority. In spite of the obvious value of these regional boards much work is needed in establishing them. In stressing the need for a comprehensive planning approach because of the interdependence of all open space uses, an Israeli architect concludes:

In looking for a solution to the recreational problem, our main concern must be with regional development and regional design. We cannot return to past conditions, and we are therefore compelled to turn our thoughts and energies to the comprehensively planned reconstruction of town and landscape as well as to the change of attitude towards environment (Glikson, 1965, p. 904).

Glikson, by broadening the scope of the open space and recreational land problem, included it as part of the general problem of natural resources conservation. It is also in this wider context of total environmental reconstruction that open space plays an important role in the evolution of the civilized landscape.

In this discussion of the need for open space, two themes have been apparent. First, open space for urban needs is a pluralistic concept. It involves, at the same time, recreation, conservation of natural resources and wildlife, flood control, aesthetic satisfaction, and control over the direction of urban development. Secondly, there is need for regional planning in systems terms to effectively meet and manage the myriad problems and opportunities of developing urban areas. As a prodigious user of land and water resources, the city challenges our ability to use our outdoor resources wisely. Urbanization leaves its indelible imprint on the natural landscape but, unfortunately, not always in a planned and efficient way. In addition to the effects of relentless metropolitan growth, the accumulated backlog of inadequate past solutions have tended to be "specific rather than general, limited rather than extensive, piecemeal rather than comprehensive, and finally . . . site rather than market oriented" (Outdoor Recreation Resources Review Commission, 1962, p. 40). In preventing future open space shortages, we must act now to allocate and reserve open spaces for all required purposes. The ultimatum issued by the United States Department of the Interior sums it up: "we must blend beauty with utility or sacrifice quality to chaos" (U.S. Department of the Interior, 1965, p. 6).

References

Anderson, D., *River valley recreation — London day-trip zone*, Unpublished M.A. Thesis, Department of Geography, University of Western Ontario (1962), 201 pp.

Brooks, L., *Perspectives on Canada's parklands*, Paper presented to the Parks and Leisure Seminar, University of British Columbia, Vancouver (1965), mimeo, 19 pp.

Chapin, Jr., F. S., *Urban land use planning* (Urbana, University of Illinois, 1964), 479 pp.

Clawson, M., "Planning and managing a system of parks for a nation," *Proceedings of the federal-provincial parks conference* (Ottawa, 1963), pp. 28-35.

Glikson, A., "Recreational land use," *Man's Role in Changing the Face of the Earth*,

Thomas, W., *ed.* (Chicago, University of Chicago Press, 1956), p. 1193.

Howard, F., *Garden Cities of Tomorrow* (London, Faber and Faber, 1898), 168 pp.

Niagara Regional Development Association, *Lincoln's lakefront problems* (Niagara Falls, Ontario, 1959), 30 pp. North Eastern Illinois Metro Area Planning Commission, *Open space in north-eastern Illinois* (Chicago, 1963), 107 pp.

Outdoor Recreation Resources Review Commission. *The future of outdoor recreation in metropolitan regions of the United States*, Study Report No. 21, Vol. I (Washington, D.C., 1962), 161 pp.

Perloff, H. and Wingo, L., "Urban growth and the planning of outdoor recreation," *Outdoor Recreation Resources Review Commission*, Study Report No. 22 (Washington, D.C., 1962), pp. 81-100.

Tankel, S. B., "The importance of open space in the urban pattern," *Outdoor Recreation Resources Review Commission*, Study Report No. 22 (Washington, D.C., 1962), pp. 57-71.

Tunnard, C. and Pushkarev, B., *Man-made America: chaos or control* (New Haven, Conn., Yale University Press, 1963), 479 pp.

United States Department of the Interior, *Quest for quality* (Washington, D.C., 1965), 45 pp.

The Development of the Toronto Conurbation

33

Jacob Spelt

Towards a New Municipality

The 19th century development had created some serious problems making a further efficient functioning of the urban complex exceeding uncertain. Thus the citizens and their government were forced to make a critical re-appraisal of their environment, a process which led to the gradual emergence of planning as a branch of government administration and this in turn helped to bring about the creation of a new administrative framework.

The first attempts at improvement, with the exception of the reconstruction of the water supply and sewage system, were almost entirely aimed at beautification of the city, in order to discard some of the more ugly aspects of the 19th century legacy. It was a phase which more or less would last until the end of the 1920's and which culminated in the University Avenue project. There were also attempts to find a solution for the traffic problems and the deficiencies of the street pattern. Suggestions for improvement included the building of an impressive system of boulevards, also the construction of a large viaduct in Bloor Street across the Don Valley, and the northward extension of Bay Street from Queen to beyond Bloor. To enhance the beauty of the City and to give personality to its heart, it was proposed in the years before the First World War to create a civic centre between the City Hall of 1899 and Osgoode Hall. It even was suggested to open a new, wide avenue through the middle of the long blocks between York and Bay Streets to connect the proposed centre with a new Union Station. The square was eventually acquired by 1947 and became the site for the new city hall.

The problems of street lay-out and traffic conditions remained major concerns until the 1930's, when attention also began to be focused on the deteriorating housing conditions. A subsequent report noted the inadequacies of city planning and recommended among others the immediate establishment of a city planning commission. This together with a concern about post war reconstruction and planning led to the appointment of the

This contribution is in essence a revised part of an article originally published in the Buffalo Law Review, Vol. 13, No. 3, Spring 1964.

Toronto City Planning Board in 1942. Although this board was only an advisory body, its work had far-reaching effects in the late forties and fifties. Its report, rather gingerly received by the City Council, was the first comprehensive plan for the city in that it dealt with all aspects of land use, from greenbelts to a civic square, from substandard housing to a flight of industries to the suburbs. In dealing with the greenbelt plans and policies for industrial land use the Board became increasingly aware of the need for co-ordination between the municipalities of the conurbation and the creation of a planning authority more regional in scope. The result was the formation in 1947 of the Toronto and York Planning Board, York being the county which contains the Toronto conurbation.

In 1947, of the 13 municipalities which later would enter into a federation, only three, North York, Etobicoke and the City had appointed planning boards. Three of the remaining municipalities had only planning committees and the remaining seven nothing. This illustrates clearly to what extent the Toronto built-up area, which contained a total population of more than 1.1 million in 1951, had grown under a system allowing a minimum of official planning. It is not surprising, therefore, that problems had arisen of such magnitude that they no longer could be solved within the existing administrative framework.

Through lack of funds, several municipalities were unable to make the necessary investment in public services. A 1947 planning report stated that the taxes obtainable from a six-room house could not hope to meet the financing of public services, including education, unless additional revenue could be obtained from commerce and industry.

This was especially true for East York, North York and Scarborough. The suburban municipalities therefore attempted to promote industrial development by laying out properly serviced industrial areas, but not all municipalities succeeded in balancing their assessment in this manner.

Most serious were the problems in connection with water supply and sewerage facilities. The city acted as a barrier between Lake Ontario and some of the inland municipalities, a condition reminiscent of Yorkville, many decades earlier. The lack of proper sewage facilities had become a menace to public health. Dwellings had been crowded on small lots with soils entirely unsuitable for septic tank disposal systems. To the extent that local municipalities did build sewage treatment plants, they tended to locate them on the Don and Humber Rivers so that the discharge of these soon overloaded installations created other problems farther downstream.

By the late forties, serious water shortages had developed and enforced curtailment of the use of water became a normal feature of suburban living. Especially in the Township of North York the situation became critical. However, through lack of foresight, Etobicoke Township although fronting on Lake Ontario suffered almost as badly.

The highway network and public transportation in the conurbation were poorly integrated. In 1949, fully 30 per cent of the population found itself outside the limits of the universal fare system; co-ordination of transportation services was most urgently needed. A plan for the preservation of open space could not be implemented, because of lack of co-operation among the municipalities concerned, each viewing the problem from a purely local point of view. Thus chaos was rapidly developing and in its 1949 report, the Toronto and York Planning Board was quite outspoken in pointing out the underlying causes: ". . . constructive progress is in every case barred by the difficulties of securing municipal co-operation in the development and extension of public services. . . ." One of the solutions suggested by the Board was a unification of groups of municipalities. The recommendations of the report were endorsed by the City Council and an application was made for amalgamation. Eventually this resulted in 1953 in the creation of a new municipality in the form of a federation of the city and the 12 suburbs; it was called Metropolitan Toronto. Soon the morphology of the area began to reveal the effects of the new administrative organization. Some of these, such as expressways, housing developments, park improvements, better water supply and sewage disposal facilities profoundly influenced the further development of the built-up area.

The further growth of the Toronto urban complex, however, also meant continued changes in population distribution and assessments patterns. In 1953 Toronto accounted for 59 per cent of the total metropolitan population. By 1966 this had declined to 37 per cent. Industrial expansion improved considerably the taxation base of the suburb. Then changed circumstances and also the inability of the city to solve urban renewal and housing problems led to a reorganization of the metropolitan administrative structure. The 13 original municipalities were reduced to six. The Metropolitan council was enlarged to 32 seats with a distribution more in accordance with the new population and assessment patterns. A slightly enlarged City of Toronto obtained 12 seats compared with 20 seats for the other five municipalities or boroughs as they are now called. The city, however, retained half of the seats on the Executive Committee. The newer organization became effective January 1968.

THE PRESENT-DAY LAND USE PATTERN

The most important factor in the area differentation within cities undoubtedly is the transportation system. After Los Angeles and Detroit, Metropolitan Toronto has the highest motor vehicle ratio on the continent in terms of registrations per 1,000 of population. Gradually it became impossible to handle the volume of traffic, especially in the downtown part of the city where the great majority of streets originally were 66 feet or less in width. Until quite recently, the only through highway in Toronto was the Lakeshore Boulevard which had emerged from a partial reorganization of the waterfront. It linked the Queen Elizabeth Way with Highway 2 on the east side of the city. Even so, access to the road was not controlled and its traverse of an amusement park in the west and the harbour zone in the downtown area reduced its capacity to handle through traffic.

At present, an extensive plan for expressways, proposed in broad outline as early as 1943, is being implemented. The broad scheme is to enclose Metropolitan Toronto within a triangle of expressways. Two of these, Highway 27 to the west and Highway 401 to the north are provincial roads, while the third side of the triangle, the F. G. Gardiner Expressway, mainly an elevated structure, has been completed from the West as far as the Don River and the Don Valley Parkway. The Province is engaged in widening Highway 401 over a distance of 17 miles to a minimum of 12 lanes.

Within this triangle, the crosstown arteries

will be supplemented by a system of widened streets and expressways, giving access to the centre of the city. The construction of one of these, the Don Valley Parkway, is completed, and a beginning has been made with the building of the Spadina Expressway which will run in a northwesterly direction. These two highways combined with the Gardiner Expressway and possibly another east-west expressway south of the Iroquois shoreline may eventually form a ring around the inner city. Nevertheless, the system of expressways, extensive though it may be, is not expected to be able to meet all transportation needs; in the field of public transportation it is being supplemented with a network of subways.

The traditional importance of Yonge Street to the central business district is reflected in the building of the first subway. Completed in 1954, the Yonge Street subway contributed greatly towards improving the connections between the centre of the city and the areas to the north. It reinforced certain functions of the central district, but paradoxically it also stimulated some decentralization from downtown and favoured the expansion of office buildings near the stations. This together with new apartment complexes, accounts in part for the new traffic generated by the Yonge subway. At present the line, which runs over a distance of 4.6 miles from Union Station to Eglinton Avenue, operates at capacity during rush hours. The original system was extended with a line along Bloor-Danforth and under University Avenue. The Yonge line is being extended into North York. The total system is at present (1970) 21 miles long.

The railway pattern in the metropolitan area was established in the 19th century and is focused for the most part on the downtown area, not far from the waterfront. Access from the city to the waterfront was improved with the completion of a new viaduct in 1930. Seven new underpasses between the Don River and Spadina Avenue replaced the time-consuming crossing of myriads of tracks. At the same time all the railway stations were eliminated by the new Union Station, opened in 1927.

The extensive marshalling yards and associated facilities in the downtown part of the city will be replaced by new establishments now under construction by the two railway companies outside the metropolitan area. Indeed, this may provide the city with a new opportunity to re-appraise its links with the waterfront, since the downtown yards no longer will be needed. It may be possible to fulfill the aspirations of the founders of the city and to create an organic link with the lake, giving new dimensions to a confined and crowded city core. Attempts along these lines are also made in the area of the central waterfront. The reduction of freight trains moving through the Union Station area has made the latter more accessible to commuter trains, the first of which has begun to serve the lakeshore communities between Hamilton and Pickering.

The pattern of residential districts in Metropolitan Toronto is similar to that of other large North American cities. Around an inner core with only a small number of permanent residents, extends a zone of housing largely built in the 19th century with densities varying from 101 to over 150 persons per net residential acre. Beyond this, the net residential densities decrease to 16 persons per acre along the fringes of the built-up area. About 60 per cent of the developed area of Metropolitan Toronto is in residential uses. The Metropolitan Toronto Plan aims at an increase in population densities by encouraging a mixture of varying house types, including apartment buildings in the low density districts. It is expected that the gross residential population density will be increased to between 20 and 29 persons per acre in most of Etobicoke, North York and Scarborough. A main advantage of increased densities would be the possibility of providing adequate public services, in particular public transportation.

In the last decade, suburban development occurs with more imagination and serious attempts are made to create attractive communities. This trend began with the building of Don Mills, a community with a variety of house types, including multiple dwelling structures; it is built on an irregular street pattern, protected against the inflow of outside traffic, and arranged around a modern mall-type shopping and service centre. It stands in sharp contrast with the earlier amorphous subdivision plans devoid of any personality or identity. Swedish concepts are being incorporated in other projects.

One of the most striking changes in the landscape of Metropolitan Toronto over the last decade has been the great increase in the number of apartment buildings. Until the late 1940's, Toronto was predominantly a city of detached and semi-detached homes. Even as late as 1953, there were fewer than 30,000 apartment units in Metropolitan Toronto, or about ten per cent of the total number of housing units. Apartment complexes have arisen in widely scattered areas, but especially in locations with easy access to subway stations. The widely assumed identification of apartment living with residence close to the centre of the city is not valid for Metropolitan Toronto. Indeed substantial complexes are found at the very edge of the built-up area. Apartment developments tend to arid areas suitable for redevelopment or urban renewal, but they prefer good residential areas, especially when these also have large lots.

A second significant change has taken place within the residential population itself. Throughout the 19th century and well into the 20th, Toronto was almost entirely a city with Anglo-Saxon population. The city was not only Anglo-Saxon in composition, but perhaps even more so in outlook — *plus royaliste que le roi*. Even as late as 1951, the British element accounted still for about 70 per cent of the population. Ten years later, however, 46 per cent of the city's population came from countries other than the British Isles. The largest non-British elements are the Italian, German, French (largely French Canadian), Polish and Ukranian groups. The newcomers are almost entirely concentrated in the city proper, especially in its 19th century parts. Here some districts have experienced tremendous changes in the ethnic composition of their population. Once solidly British in character, now the language spoken in the streets, the style of clothing, the stores with their signs, and their displays of strange merchandise, remind one of cities and towns in Europe. It is to the credit of the city, that these profound changes in the make-up of its population have taken place without ethnic strife.

As noted previously, the site was endowed with a rich potential for the development of park land. Yet over one-third of the inhabitants of Metropolitan Toronto live in areas which are deficient in parks. Since the early fifties, vigorous programs initiated by the city and after 1954 augmented by the Metropolitan Parks Commission have resurrected old parks and developed several new ones. The Island, just opposite the city's most crowded residential areas, is being transformed into a multifunctional park. It involves the removal of some 650 residential and commercial structures and eventually some 575 acres will become available for recreational purposes.

Approximately 10,000 acres, or 11.7 per cent of the developed land in Metropolitan Toronto has been appropriated for manufacturing, wholesale and warehouse complexes. The first industries and warehousing arose on the waterfront. There were no water power sites which could have attracted major industrial concentrations. Instead, manufacturing tended to move to open land just outside the built-up area at points of good access. The heavy dependence of manufacturers on railway transportation before World War II is reflected in most pre-war industrial districts — long tentacles of industry extending out from the centre of the city, mainly to the west and northwest, along the lines of the C.P.R. and the C.N.R. In recent years, the rise of the trucking industry has reduced the dependence of manufacturing on the railways and many of the industries in new suburban developments have no access to rail sidings. Nor are there any rail facilities in large parts of the inner city where industry also is based entirely on truck transport.

The modern metropolitan area therefore, contains several areas of conflux in the pattern of the daily journey to work. The city proper has some seven major concentrations of manufacturing and warehousing within its limits giving employment to a total of over 120,000 workers. Outside the city, ten additional concentrations are well distributed throughout the old and new suburbs, with a total employment of more than 85,000.

By 1950, industrial employment in the city had reached a peak of 160,000, after which time it has declined steadily mainly due to the migration of firms from old and overcrowded quarters to the suburbs. The newer suburbs showed remarkable increases in manufacturing employment. Etobicoke, North York, Scarborough, East York and York saw their industrial employment rise from 6,000 in 1950 to 66,700 in 1960. This has led to the formation of a much more solid assessment base and consequently a desire for greater influence in metropolitan matters. The city contributes 42 per cent of the total taxable assessments in Metropolitan Toronto.

Toronto's central business district offers employment to some 145,000 people, or about a fifth of the total employment in Metropolitan Toronto. Within its confines, it reveals a great deal of diversity both in form and activity. According to the 1951 census of retailing, 34 per cent of all sales in Metropolitan Toronto were concentrated in downtown. By 1961, however, the proportion had declined to 23.5 per cent, a loss the more striking when viewed against the background of population increase in the total metropolitan area. Nevertheless, downtown is still by far the leading retail concentration between Montreal to the east and Winnipeg to the northwest.

The retail centre migrated from its early location on the market along King Street westward to the intersection of King and Yonge Streets which by the end of the 1870's had become the city's leading shopping area. Eventually, however, Yonge Street was to assume the part played by King Street. This re-orientation of the retail trade began with the establishment of the department stores at the intersection of Yonge and Queen Streets around 1870. The success of these companies stimulated an expansion of retailing along Yonge Street which accelerated in the 20th century and at present by far the bulk of downtown retailing is concentrated in a strip along Yonge Street, to the north of King Street. The confinement of downtown retailing to a single street is a unique feature among the large North American cities, where retailing of this type generally encompasses several blocks.

The department stores hold complete sway over downtown retailing, leaving little room for competitors. A significant concentration of high-class stores which effectively could compete with them does not exist in downtown Toronto, but is located farther north, on Bloor Street between Yonge and Avenue Road. In spite of the improvements in transportation and the very substantial growth of the population in Metropolitan Toronto and surrounding areas, the downtown stores have not been able to expand accordingly. It is quite obvious that competition from other business centres, such as the Bloor area and the large suburban plazas, have contributed to the relative decline of downtown retailing. The department stores and other downtown shops have responded by opening branches in the major suburban plazas, such as Yorkdale.

In the late 1920's, the low buildings along Bay Street were demolished and tall office buildings arose in their place. By that time, the connotation of Bay Street as a leading financial street had been established. The building of the Toronto Stock Exchange gave it further definition. In recent years a remarkable expansion of office buildings has made University Avenue an integral part of the downtown office core. In contrast to retailing, the financial and general office concentration appears to be the expanding cell of the downtown business core.

Of some 32 million square feet of office space in Metropolitan Toronto, about 11.9 million square feet is found in the downtown area. Increasingly, office complexes are being erected outside the central business district. Some of the subway stations and major highway intersections have attracted office concentration.

A distinct part of the general office zone is the complex of municipal and other administrative buildings such as the city hall, the city registry office and Osgoode Hall, the seat for the administration of justice in the province. The completion of the new city hall and civic square have brought about the realization of plans formulated many years ago. The commanding style of the new structure seems a fitting symbol for the throbbing metropolis which has arisen since the Second World War and has at present a population of more than 2.3 million.

34

A Tale of
Two Cities

N. H. Richardson

Between the Pacific Ocean and the 4,000-foot crest of British Columbia's Coast Mountains, the westernmost mainland range of the Canadian Cordillera, is a rugged, forest-covered land of rivers and fiords. Among the mountains, away from the sea, its summers are cool and its winters bitterly cold; but on the lower levels, along the inlets and the coast, the climate is milder, with mean monthly temperatures between 55° and 65° in July and between 20° and 35° in January. Precipitation is high, reaching 160" or more annually in some areas, and rain or snow fall throughout the year; except on the sea-coast the land is blanketed by thick snow during the winter months.

Until the latter part of the nineteenth century the region was virtually unknown to the white man, though scattered along the fiords and the rivers were the villages of the Tsimshian, Bella Coola and Kwakiutl, dependent on fish for their livelihood as most of their descendants are today. The first systematic exploration was carried out in 1859 and 1860 by Major William Downie, who was impressed by the potentialities of the Skeena Valley as a transportation route. Five years later the "Collins Overland Telegraph", which was to link North America with Europe across the Bering Straits and Siberia, reached the Skeena, but in 1866 came the news that a cable had been successfully laid across the Atlantic, and the project was abandoned. But many of the workers stayed to look for gold, which in due course was found on the upper Skeena, and by the seventies the rush was on. The riches of the Skeena, however, did not compare with those of the Yukon and the Cariboo, and, as elsewhere, frustrated prospectors turned to less colourful occupations: logging, farming or fishing, for the most part. By the 1890's fish canneries were being established at several points along the coast and the rivers. White settlement was firmly established by the end of the century.

Surveys for a transcontinental railway were carried out as early as the 1870's, and it seems that serious consideration was given to the adoption of a northern route through the Yellowhead Pass and along the Skeena Valley. But the CPR chose the southern route instead, and Vancouver rapidly blos-

Reprinted from *Plan*, Vol. 4 no. 3 (1963), pp. 111-25 by permission.

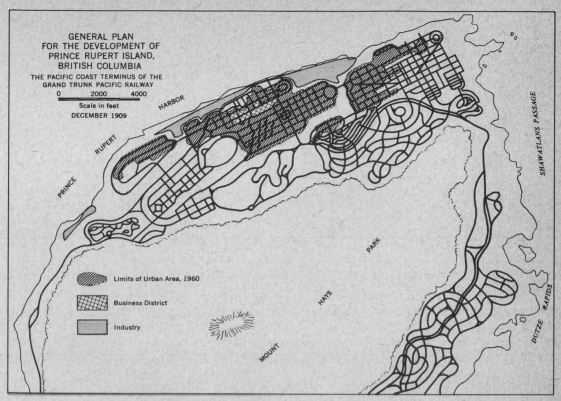

GENERAL PLAN
FOR THE DEVELOPMENT OF
PRINCE RUPERT ISLAND,
BRITISH COLUMBIA
THE PACIFIC COAST TERMINUS OF THE
GRAND TRUNK PACIFIC RAILWAY

0   2000   4000
Scale in feet
DECEMBER 1909

Limits of Urban Area, 1960

Business District

Industry

Prince Rupert: New Town, 1904

somed from a cluster of shacks along the shore to British Columbia's chief city. However, the possibilities of the northern route were not forgotten. In 1903, with the support of Sir Wilfrid Laurier, the Grand Trunk Pacific Railway Company was incorporated. The Grand Trunk Pacific was the brainchild of C. M. Hays, General Manager of the Grand Trunk Railway, a line beset by chronic financial difficulties, and it was Hays' scheme to build a second transcontinental railway to compete with the CPR and, in fact, by bringing the railhead five hundred miles closer to Oriental ports, to outstrip the CPR in the race to carry the rich trade that was expected to develop with the Far East. Construction of the line eastward from the coast was started in 1907; in 1914 the route was completed, from North Bay, Ontario, to the Pacific.

Meanwhile, even before any track was laid, a site had been chosen on Kaien Island, some ten miles north of the mouth of the Skeena, for the city that was to be the line's western terminus. The company bought 10,000 acres of land from the provincial government at $1 per acre, on condition that a quarter of the townsite and a quarter of the waterfront would be reserved for government use. It then took a step of considerable significance in the history of Canadian town planning by engaging a prominent U.S. firm of landscape architects, Messrs. Brett and Hall of Boston, to design a townsite layout for the new city of Prince Rupert.

The planners were faced with a twofold objective. First, they had to plan for a city of 100,000 people, which might before very long have a population considerably exceeding that figure. If that now seems a trifle ridiculous, one must recall that in 1904 Vancouver, which was barely a village at the time it was reached by the CPR, less than twenty years previously, already had a population nearing 50,000 and in fact destined to reach 100,000 only seven years later, and a spectacular rate of population increase was no more than consistent with the rosy prospects that were thought to lie before Vancouver's rival.

Second, Brett and Hall were expected to design a city of beauty and dignity, according to the formal civic aesthetics of the day, on a topographically difficult site consisting largely of rock and muskeg and covered by dense forest. Considering the circumstances, their layout was remarkably sucessful. A series of monumental thoroughfares, terminating in natural elevations or sites for public buildings, was skilfully adapted to the form of the land. The streets connecting them were laid out broadly on a grid, but where topography demanded it the planners were prepared to modify the grid or even depart from it altogether. In fact, the care and deftness with which a formal street layout is fitted to a rough and broken site commands great respect, particularly when the Prince Rupert plan is compared with the infinities of rectangles which were being imposed elsewhere upon the land of British Columbia with brutal disregard for hill, stream or coastline. The two main axes which dominate the plan, with their related systems of avenues, circles, crescents and public sites, were in fact intended as the commercial and institutional foci of a great city. The residential areas which were to house a hundred thousand people were to be more freely and informally laid out, their

streets curving along the sides of the hills that rise behind the city center.[1]

In anticipation of the tremendous boom that was to occur when the railway was opened to traffic and the docks of Prince Rupert were crowded with transoceanic shipping, and in an attempt to regain some of the money that it had spent, the Grand Trunk Pacific soon began to sell lots. And in the euphoric atmosphere of the time, and with the rosey image of a Canadian San Francisco before their eyes, many people bought them. Streets, sidewalks and utilities were laid in the forest. Within a couple of years of establishment of the town, Prince Rupert had a population of over four thousand, a Council, an apparently firm financial base, electricity, water supply and a telephone system.

Prince Rupert: Development After 1912

Then the bubble burst. In 1912 Hays went down in the *Titanic*: the new docks were almost unused; the real estate boom was over; the City was in serious financial difficulties. In Prince Rupert's hinterland there were riches of minerals and timber indeed, but the time was not yet ripe for them to be tapped. Farming was scattered and marginal. In 1914 Prince Rupert was stagnant, and the coming of war destroyed what hope there might have been that the opening of the railway would revive the golden prospects of a few years before. Eight yearst later the Grand Trunk Pacific was absorbed into the Canadian National Railways. In 1929 most of the land purchased by speculators twenty years be-

[1] For a contemporary account of the planning of Prince Rupert, see George D. Wall, "The Future Prince Rupert as conceived by Landscape Architects," *Architectural Record,* Vol. XXVI, no. 2 (August, 1909).

fore began to revert to the City for tax delinquency. In 1933 the City itself went bankrupt.

For a quarter of a century Prince Rupert's population remained almost unchanged at about 6,500 people engaged mainly in fishing and fish processing, but also in government and other services, logging and sawmilling. The Second World War brought a temporary boom (during which the population, including servicemen, rose to some 20,000), plus the more lasting benefits of enlarged docks, a seaplane base, and, most important of all, a road which for the first time linked Prince Rupert to the provincial highways system. A pulp mill was established near the City in 1951, a new airport has recently been built, and a ferry service to Alaskan ports will soon be started. The City's population, which dropped to 8,500 after the war, reached 12,000 by 1961.

Physically, the City's growth has taken place almost entirely within the area originally intended for commercial, institutional and governmental use. Ironically, however, the street which was intended as the principal boulevard of the City is now not even the main business street, chiefly because speculation raised lot prices so high that businessmen preferred to establish themselves on a parallel street a block away, which is now in effect Prince Rupert's "Main Street" — a lesson not without contemporary relevance. Prince Rupert is still not a wealthy place; shabby frame houses and weed-grown vacant lots adjoin the wooden sidewalks of streets built over gullies or blasted through rock, streets that were to have been lined with tall and stately buildings. Comparing the vision of 1905 and the plan which grew out of it with the reality of a half-century later, one is reminded of an impoverished family squatting

in the ballroom of a palace abandoned long before it was completed.

But from the viewpoint of physical development Prince Rupert has two great assets. Almost all its unused land is in public ownership, amounting in total to over half the City's land area; and, partly as a consequence of this, the built-up area is fairly well-defined and compact, with a minimum of "sprawl". There is, however, a housing shortage, and much existing housing is in poor condition.

Today, the future of Prince Rupert looks brighter, perhaps, than it has since 1912. The old dreams are unlikely ever to be realized, but new transportation links to the south and north, development of timber and other resources, and tourism, hold out hopes of better times to come. At the same time, the silver lining has a cloud in the form of indications of a decline in the City's staple industry, fishing. In the face of these prospects, the City Council recently engaged a Vancouver firm to carry out an economic survey and a study of housing conditions, and a report on planning.[2] These were completed early in 1963, and may provide a sounder basis for future development than the febrile optimism in which Prince Rupert was born.[3]

The Origin of Kitimat

From the beginning of the First World War to

[2] Associated Engineering Services Ltd., *Prince Rupert: Economic Prospects and Future Development* (Vancouver, B.C., January, 1963).

[3] For general accounts of the geographical background, early history, and planning of Prince Rupert, see A. D. Crerar, *Prince Rupert, B.C.: The Study of a Port and its Hinterland*, Unpublished M.A. Thesis, University of British Columbia (1951); and P. D. McGovern, "Prince Rupert, British Columbia," *Town and Country Planning*, Vol. XXVIII, nos. 4-5 (April-May, 1960).

the end of the Second, as mining was almost completely abandoned in the face of adverse economic conditions, the North Coast — Skeena region as a whole depended almost entirely on fish and lumber for its livelihood. By 1951 it had only 20,000 people, about a third of them Indian. 8,500 people lived in Prince Rupert and the remainder mainly in small towns strung along the railway — now part of the Canadian National Railways system — or in isolated logging communities scattered along the coast and in most cases accessible only by sea or air, still the only direct means of communication between the region and the main population centres of the province. But in addition to fish and forests the north coast had an almost untapped reserve of hydroelectric power from the drainage of the Nechako Plateau between the Coast Range and the Rockies, estimated at three million kilowatts. It was this potential supply of cheap power which in 1951 led the Aluminum Company of Canada ("Alcan") to decide on the establishment of a major aluminum smelting plant; for while the raw materials of aluminum reduction can be shipped cheaply in bulk by sea, the process requires enormous quantities of power — 20,000 kilowatt-hours for every ton of ingots produced. Smelters are thus tied to sites near sources of ample power and with deepwater docking facilities as well as road and rail transportation, requirements which were met at the head of the Kitimat Arm, some fifty miles inland and connected with the railway and the Prince Rupert-Prince George highway by a convenient valley.

To provide the power, Alcan undertook several major engineering projects, including the reversal of the drainage of an entire lake system. The physical and economic problems were thus overcome; but the human problem remained. The plant, located in almost virgin wilderness forty miles from the nearest town, needed a workforce of thousands, and to get and keep a stable and contented workforce meant providing living conditions that would compare favourably with those obtainable in the cities and towns to the south. Thus Kitimat was born, the region's second planned "new town", only eighty miles as the crow flies from its first, making them next-door neighbours in the terms of that vast country.[4]

The Plan for Kitimat

Alcan, like the north coast, had had previous experience with new towns, and in the Company's case, like the region's, the experience had not been entirely happy. It is likely that the problems created by Arvida, established under similar circumstances on the Saguenay in Quebec in 1926, had a good deal to do with the care devoted to the physical and administrative forms of the new venture. To shape the general conception and principles of the town plan for Kitimat, the Company engaged Clarence Stein, the author of the Radburn plan, working in collaboration with the New York firm of Mayer and Whittlesey; while a team of experts prepared proposals on the administrative, fiscal and social aspects of the scheme. The result was a remarkably comprehensive series of detailed studies and plans embracing every important consideration

4 For general accounts of the Kemano-Kitimat project, see: Aluminum Company of Canada Ltd., *Kitimat-Kemano: Five Years of Operation, 1954-1959*; Paul Clark, "Kitimat — A Saga of Canada," *Canadian Geographical Journal*, Vol. XLIX, no. 4 (October, 1954); L. G. Ecroyd, "Start-Up at Kitimat," *Western Business and Industry*, Vol. XXVIII, no. 7 (July, 1954); "The Nechako-Kemano-Kitimat Development," *The Engineering Journal* (April, 1953 and November, 1954); "Kitimat: A New City," *Architectural Forum* (July and August, 1954); Pixie Meldrum, *Kitimat — The First Five Years*, Corporation of the District of Kitimat (1958).

which could be expected to apply to the building and operation of a town of ten thousand or more people in a virgin wilderness, forty miles from its nearest neighbour and four hundred from a large city.[5]

Twelve years have now passed since the decision was made, and a decade since Kitimat was formally incorporated as a Municipal District by a special Act of the British Columbia Legislature. The town is today generally recognized as one of the most significant of contemporary North American contributions to planning principles and practice, and one of the few ventures on the continent to compare in scale and character with the British New Towns. A first assessment of the true extent of its achievement can now be attempted.

In doing so, however, one must bear in mind the physical circumstances and the handicaps which were imposed upon the planners thereby. When Alcan came, the country was largely unexplored and unsurveyed. Since it was covered by dense timber, mistakes were made even after aerial photography, mapping, ground surveys and test drillings. Ravines were discovered that had not been suspected, and the site of the City Centre was found, after construction had actually started, to consist in part of muskeg, and the intended arrangement of the Centre had to be drastically altered.

These were the circumstances under which Stein had to devise his plan. There were two courses which he could have adopted: to adapt to geography and climate or to adapt to people and culture. The former would have meant probably a tight design, a huddling together of people and buildings about a compact, perhaps multilevelled centre, a solution such as has been adopted in northern Sweden and has been proposed in other parts of Canada. Instead Stein chose the latter. He assumed that the people of Kitimat would be the same sort of people as those of Vancouver or Winnipeg or Toronto, living as far as possible in the same way; and he adapted to the rugged landscape the "Radburn idea", the principle of the loose-knit community based upon but not subjected to the use of the automobile. He designed a pattern of trafficways linking the City Centre to neighbourhood centres, and, connected to the trafficways, a series of loops and cul-de-sacs around which the houses are built. Among the buildings run pedestrian walks and park strips by means of which supermarket, drugstore, movie theatre, church and school can be reached on foot, in complete safety from vehicular traffic.

All this presupposed a car-owning society, and although the car is kept to its place, serving but not dominating the houses and excluded entirely from the inner ways which link homes to community facilities, the mobility which it gives and the demands which it makes have clearly been the chief determinants of the pattern of the town to the almost complete exclusion of any deferring to the exigencies of land and climate. Kitimat has as a result been described derisively as "Radburn revisited" and "A suburb without a city", and indeed it seems at first a little strange to find amid the forests and rugged hills of British Columbia a town which would seem quite at home in the suburban fringe of any North American city. But social values and habits are facts to be faced as much as are snow and muskeg, and less easily overcome; and this being so Stein's application in Kitimat of the principles which he had

[5] See Clarence S. Stein et al., *Kitimat Townsite Report*, edited and reissued by the Corporation of the District of Kitimat (December, 1960).

pioneered in Radburn to permit peaceful co-existence between man and machine was not only sensible but perhaps inevitable.

Kitimat Assessed

In fact, if any criticism can be levelled at Stein's general conception it is that he did not fully appreciate the extent of automobile domination; while he allowed in effect for two separate but equally complete systems of circulation, one for motor traffic and the other for bicycles and pedestrians, it has proved in practice that much of the latter has been neglected and has served little useful purpose. While the internal "greenway" or park belt is well used, the connecting footpaths running between the rows of houses have mainly degenerated into mud tracks littered with garbage cans and junk, and they are likely to be abandoned in the design of new neighbourhoods. It could be argued that for a town set in the midst of a wilderness of tremendous potential for hunting, fishing, skiing and other forms of outdoor recreation, with fifteen feet of snow in the winter and much rain the rest of the year, the whole system of parks and greenways is unrealistically generous; that for its real value the cost of landscaping and maintenance will be too high. The present municipal administration would not agree, but as time passes and the consciousness of and pride in being part of a new venture fades, future municipal councils may well look on all this open space flowing through the town with more jaundiced eyes.

While the quality of the two-dimensional plan of Kitimat can be considered worthy of the tremendous enterprise of which the town is a part, the same unfortunately cannot be said of its physical form. Once the decision was made to go ahead with the project, time was of the essence; production had to be started and houses for the workers had to be built as quickly as possible. For several years shortage of accommodation was a chronic condition, and quality of design and construction was hardly considered. Alcan in any case left the provision of housing to others as far as possible; where necessary it had houses and apartment buildings erected to rent to its workers, but for the most part it sold land to private developers, mainly from the Vancouver area, and left them to build as they saw fit. This meant in practice that the standards of construction were those imposed under the National Housing Act as a condition of N.H.A. financing, while the standards of design were, aesthetically speaking, nil. In terms of space, Kitimat houses and apartments are quite acceptable; in terms of solidity of construction they are no better than N.H.A. minimum, which is not high; in terms of appearance they are at best undistinguished and at worst quite bad. One looks in vain for any evidence of care for civic design. Among other things, the visitor to Kitimat quickly notices that the builder, accustomed to the standard Vancouver suburban grid, was clearly puzzled by the Stein concept of the inward-facing house turning its back upon the street, which is quite contrary to the North American convention. It is obvious that the same applies to many of the residents; the consequence is that some houses are oriented toward the street, in the usual manner, with the orderly, well trimmed "front yard" located accordingly and the washing hung out at the back; while others are reversed according to the Stein conception to face the pedestrian ways or greenways.[6] As a consequence, the vista whether

---

[6] After this was written the author was informed that this was in fact a deliberate attempt to introduce "variety". If so, it succeeded only in introducing visual chaos.

of the street or of the interior frontage is generally scruffy.

To such criticisms Alcan's reply would be that its business is to produce aluminum, not to build towns; and that its policy, based on its Arvida experience and pursued vigorously by means of second mortgages at N.H.A. rates, home-ownership bonuses and repurchase guarantees, is to encourage its employees to own their own homes, to avoid the "company town" stigma, and generally to encourage Kitimat to become in every possible way a "normal" Canadian community. These principles are sound enough, and have undoubtedly greatly helped the town to become, as it now is, a vigorous community largely free of company paternalism. Nevertheless, it is a matter for regret that Kitimat's physical manifestation is so far removed from the high aspirations of Stein's original conception; and it is particularly regrettable that no attempt has been made in the building of the town to take account of its geographical circumstances. The same buildings might equally well have been erected in Vancouver or Halifax or for that matter in Chicago or Boston; in conception they are as much mass-produced as cars or coffeepots. As a single example, the canopy which surrounds the main block of the City Centre — the commercial heart of the town — is perhaps six feet wide, a token shelter which is of little value in a place with heavy rain or snow during most of the year. This failure to respect, even to consider, the nature of the place is unfortunately completely characteristic of the building of Kitimat; no attempt whatever has been made to try out ideas and methods geared to the circumstances of the site rather than to custom and convention. Even apart from the lack of experimentation the general level of design is low. There is not one building in the town with any claim to

architectural distinction, though there are several examples of uninspired but respectable contemporary design. The only obvious examples, in fact, of imaginative design lie in a few such details as the street-name signs, which are colourful, legible and handsome (and made of aluminum).

There has in fact been a general lack of concern with the quality of execution, all the more striking and disappointing when contrasted with the care and skill devoted to the preparation of physical, administrative, fiscal and social plans. There has been a similar lack of concern, the job once having been done, with the success of these plans or with finding out how they have worked, despite the largely experimental nature of the project and the enormous potential value of such an experiment for the planning not only of future ventures of a comparable nature but of new communities generally. In particular, it is impossible to know how successful the conception and exception of the scheme has been for the people most closely concerned, those who live in the town, and it is impossible also to know what relationship exists between physical conditions, planned and unplanned, and their way of life and the degree of satisfaction which it provides.

This failure to consider Kitimat as anything but an expedient design, however competently, to meet the exigencies of an immediate practical problem has in fact been apparent from its very inception. Consider the circumstances; here was a town established in a region with a great and almost untouched store of natural resources, a town confidently expected to be the largest in hundreds of thousands of square miles, yet next door to another which had been founded only a few decades earlier amid even rosier hopes only to become a shabby fishing community. But almost no thought was given to its prospects as a regional centre, almost none, in fact to the eventual settlement pattern of the region or to the appropriateness of Kitimat's location from this point of view, or even from the point of view of the eventual development of resources other than hydroelectric power. Here was a site that met the requirements of the company for the production of aluminum; that was sufficient. Its suitability in terms of the future economic development or human settlement of the region was simply not a relevant consideration.

To sum up, Alcan must be given credit for the care which was taken in the planning, physical and otherwise, of Kitimat. The site plan is not beyond criticism but it is unquestionably distinguished. But a townsite had to be planned and from a purely businesslike point of view it made more sense to do the job well than to do it poorly. Good industrial and a stable labour force were important to Alcan, and anything necessary to aid in maintaining them made sense. This attitude was hardly novel. Alcan is in the direct line of descent in this respect from the New England mill-owners of the early nineteenth century, from Salt, Lever, Cadbury, Pullman and other industrialists who, over the last century and more, have provided their workers with better living conditions for the sake not only of social ideals but of hard cash. Alcan probably had its eyes fixed more firmly on the latter rather than the former than had some of its distinguished predecessors. As evidence, one may point to the three main areas of criticism which have been discussed: the lack of interest in the quality of building design, particularly from the aesthetic viewpoint; the failure to make any but the most tentative efforts to learn from so valuable an experiment in town planning, social organization and local administration; and the lack of regard for Kitimat's place in the economic,

geographical and social evolution of the region as a whole. Kitimat was, in short, seen in exactly the same light as was the Kenney Dam, the Kemano powerhouse, the plant itself, or any of the other components of a single tremendous industrial project: as a job to be designed by the best men available, to one end only — the production of aluminum.

The Lessons of Prince Rupert and Kitimat

A comparison of the histories of Prince Rupert and Kitimat produces some striking parallels. Both towns were created (almost exactly half a century apart) as integral parts of great commercial enterprises intended to tap the vast resources of the north. Both towns received generous allotments of land from the provincial government but both were developed entirely by private enterprise, with little or no government interference. Both towns were planned by American firms according to the most up-to-date principles of their time.

But the most significant similarity lies in the fact that neither town has achieved what was to be its appointed destiny. In the case of Prince Rupert, the economic base upon which a great city was to grow proved to be an illusion; the second Canadian transcontinental railway was a failure; and the new town, almost stillborn, had to struggle along on a single industry which had hardly, if at all, entered the calculations of its founders. The economic planning which produced Kitimat was more thorough and more realistic. The ingots flow from the Alcan plant and will probably continue to do so — but they are not flowing at the rate that was originally expected. In the face of unexpected adverse conditions in the world markets, production has levelled off and has even been cut back, instead of rising steadily as was anticipated when operations were started. Furthermore, the Company and the municipality have so far found little success in their search for new industries to broaden the community's economic base and lessen its dependence on Alcan. Consequently, the town's population seems to have stabilized at a figure between 8,000 and 8,500, having dropped from a peak of ten or eleven thousand accounted for by construction workers. This may be compared with the estimate of 35,000 to 50,000 used by Stein as the basis of his plan.

Today the attention of Canadians is turning more and more to the north — to the last land frontier, with what we are assured is its vast storehouse of riches. Where there are riches men will certainly go; new communities will come into being; thousands of people — eventually, perhaps, millions — will call the north their home. What lessons do the stories of Prince Rupert and Kitimat hold for us as we contemplate this prospect?

That depends on the answer to another question. When we talk about northern "development" (a word which, as every planner knows, covers a multitude of sins), do we mean *resource* development or do we mean *regional* development? Because, in practice, these are very different things involving very different philosophies. Resource "development" is too often mere exploitation of natural riches for financial gain, without regard to the long-run fate of the region which supplies them or of the communities to which the process gives birth. Canada can supply many examples; the fact that no consideration other than the requirements of aluminum production entered into the choice of Kitimat's site is only one illustration. It may well be that in this particular instance no other location would have served, but in view of earlier experience in other parts of Canada — experience in which

Alcan has been involved — it seems most regrettable that so little thought was given to future regional development. The case of the Saguenay-Lac St. Jean region may be cited: this part of Quebec offered a variety of natural resources, including, like British Columbia's north coast, minerals, timber and water-power; but each of these resources was exploited independently without reference to the development of the others or to the future of the region as a whole. The result today is a settlement pattern consisting of a scattering of small or medium-sized one-industry towns (including Alcan's Arvida) within a relatively small area, in some cases only a few miles apart, none of which can aspire to the size or functions of a genuine regional centre. The economic dangers, human deficiencies and general inefficiency of such an arrangement both for the individual community and for the region as a whole are obvious enough; yet the same pattern seems to be emerging around the Skeena Valley.

The best known example of the alternative approach, of course is TVA. Certainly TVA was concerned with making use of resources, but always as part of the process of developing, improving and helping a *region*. TVA's achievement lies not in the number of dams it has built or the number of kilowatt-hours of energy it produces, but in the fact that the Tennessee Valley is a better place, its economy stronger and more diversified, its communities more prosperous, the lives of its people fuller, healthier and more secure, than they were thirty years ago. This is regional development in the true sense of the words, and it is to be hoped that the future settlement of Canada's north and the utilization of its resources will be carried out in this spirit. On this assumption, let us return to the question: what lessons can be learned from the experiences of Prince Rupert and Kitimat?

First, a single industry is not a satisfactory basis for a permanent community. This is perhaps a truism; certainly after the experience of Elliot Lake, to name only the most famous recent example, the point is unlikely to be disputed. But even if an industry is soundly based, stable and prosperous, it is not a healthy thing for a community to be almost solely dependent upon it for employment, for tax revenue, sometimes even for welfare assistance, entertainment and social facilities. Sometimes it may be unavoidable; but when a new town is to be created, every effort should be made to find a site with the best possible chance of attracting industries other than the one which called it into being; and every effort should be made to encourage such diversification within the community and the concurrent development (in the true sense) and settlement of the area around it. In other words, the enterprise should not be seen as a matter of a single industry and a community serving and subordinate to it, but as the initial phase in a coherent regional development programme whose object will be not only the exploitation of the region's natural resources but also the establishment of a sound and broadly based local economy and of a full and secure way of life for the people of the region. Really successful new town planning, in short, is inextricably bound up with regional planning and economic planning, and regional planning and economic planning are but two sides of the same coin.

The second lesson to be drawn from the history of the Skeena-Coast region is that regional development planning of this coherent and comprehensive kind cannot be expected from private enterprise. This is no criticism of the Grand Trunk Pacific or of the Aluminum Company of Canada or of any other private firm. Their function is to run a railway or to produce aluminum or what-

ever the case may be, and to pay dividends to their shareholders, not to design towns or to develop regions. It is to the credit of both the GTPR and Alcan that, the nature of their commercial activities requiring the creation of new communities, they went to considerable pains and expense to create good ones, at least to the extent that enlightened self-interest dictated. They could not be expected to do more. It follows, therefore, that if future regional development based on the exploitation of the natural resources of the north is not to be the hit-or-miss process that it has been in the past; if the tapping of natural riches is to provide the basis for permanent and stable settlement providing the best possible way of life for the entire regional community, then public participation will be required in very considerable measure.

New Approaches to Building Frontier Regions

Let us consider briefly where models of such participation might be found.

Several Canadian provinces, notably, perhaps, Alberta and British Columbia, have legislation providing for the establishment of regional planning agencies. But these are clearly envisaged as essentially *intermunicipal* bodies operating in settled areas. Their function, broadly, is to prepare plans to regulate private development and to guide the works programmes of other public agencies. Several provinces also have statutes providing for special forms of administration for new communities.[7] But again, this legislation is in general terms designed to provide a special form of local government to apply

[7] e.g., Local Improvement Districts in Newfoundland and Manitoba; Mining Towns and Mining Villages in Quebec; Improvement Districts in Ontario; New Towns in Alberta; Local Administrative Districts in the North-West Territories.

during the life of a temporary settlement or pending the establishment of normal municipal administration. In neither case does it appear to be envisaged that the special agency, either regional or local, will play a very positive role in the development of the area under its jurisdiction. On the other hand, there is a number of agencies established by federal statute — the Prairie Farm Rehabilitation Administration, the Agricultural Rehabilitation and Development Administration and the Atlantic Provinces Development Council, for example — whose purpose is quite explicitly to play an active and constructive part in the development or revitalisation of the economy of some part of the country, including making changes in the accustomed manner of land use. None of these, however, is concerned primarily, if at all, with the opening up of largely undeveloped and uninhabited areas, but rather with improving the situation of regions where development has been unsoundly carried out or has not kept up with the more prosperous parts of the country. (One is tempted to suggest an analogy with urban growth, wherein the profitable building of new houses at the edge of the city is left to private firms while government assumes the cost of tearing down the old and decayed areas at the centre and replacing them with something better.)

Thus there exist in this country at least the seeds of three relevant ideas: regional planning, special administrative arrangements for new towns, and government action to aid and stimulate the economies of particular regions. But in pursuing possible avenues of approach to Canadian regional development it is also worthwhile to consider two cases outside Canada, neither of them new: the British New Towns Act of 1946 and the Tennessee Valley Authority itself, born in 1933. Both are too familiar to Canadian planners to warrant detailed description, but it is useful to recall briefly the features of the two schemes which are particularly relevant.

The New Towns Act, based upon the Scott and Barlow Reports and upon Abercrombie's Greater London Plan, had as its chief object the dispersal of population from Greater London. What is of interest here, however, is not the purposes of the New Towns but the manner in which they are established, financed and operated. A New Town, under the Act, is the responsibility of a Development Corporation appointed by the Government with the power to acquire land, to build, to construct utilities, to provide community facilities, and ". . . generally to do anything necessary or expedient for the purposes of the new town or for purposes incidental thereto." (the words of the Act). Apart from the fact that they are financed by Government loans and grants, the role of the Development Corporations in relation to the New Towns has in fact been very much the same as the role of the Grand Trunk Pacific or Alcan in relation to their respective offspring — with the very important exception that the former are instruments of national policy rather than private investment, and that consequently the first consideration has been the establishment of sound, viable and permanent communities, and each New Town (apart from special cases such as Corby) has been carefully sited and designed with a view to attracting a wide range of industries and not just to serve the needs of one.

The special relevance of TVA lies in the fact that the utilisation of a resource was regarded not as an end in itself but as a vehicle for the economic and social enrichment of an entire region, and that this enrichment took many forms and was effected in many ways — direct action by the federal government being the exception rather than the rule.

TVA's way was to educate, to demonstrate, to assist, to encourage, not to step in and do the job itself; beyond its immediate statutory task of harnessing the Tennessee River for power production, navigation and flood control; but it did these things to such good effect that a poor and primitive region achieved prosperity and vitality.

From all these — from present Canadian regional planning and special local administration legislation, from PFRA, ARDA and APDC, from the British New Towns and the American TVA there are valuable lessons to be learned, and it is to be hoped that they will be noted and applied. For the experience of Prince Rupert and Kitimat shows unmistakably that good town planning under the aegis of private firms is not enough. Each of the two towns is a fine example of the best *town* planning thought and skill of its day, and the differences in approach, planning and execution provide a fair measure of the progress that has been made in this field in half a century. But in origin and concept, in the kind of consideration that led to and conditioned the establishment of the two communities, there was no significant change at all. In each case the first consideration was economic exploitation, not the creation of a good environment for living or the future wellbeing of a region. It is here that progress in thinking is long overdue; it must be understood that the use of the resources of the north means the building of new human communities, urban and regional; that the creation of such communities demands an enlightened and comprehensive economic development and regional planning policy; and that this in turn requires a large measure of public participation, public iniative and public responsibility.

While the manner in which these responsibilities could best be exercised is obviously a matter for careful and expert study, the requirements of the job as well as experience both in Canada and elsewhere indicate the need for some special form of regional planning and development agency, adequately financed and with the authority and capacity to undertake a variety of functions, including resource surveys, provision of roads, harbours, airports and other elements of the economic "substructure", industrial promotion and investment, town planning and building, and perhaps also local administration. There is no exact model to be slavishly followed in meeting the special conditions of the Canadian north, but there are many examples to learn from, not only those already mentioned but others in many parts of the world. By such means, not only could the resources of the north be brought into use more rapidly and more efficiently, but settlement and urban development could take place in a stable and orderly fashion to the lasting benefit of the people who are, in the final analysis, what really matter.

Who Does What in Urban Renewal?

35

Ogden Tanner

All across the country, more and more people are waking up to the fact that their cities are in trouble, and that it is up to them to do something about it. But what? Here is what some hard-headed businessmen, professionals, and good citizens have done, each contributing his special talents and resources to the common problem.

By now most Americans know that their cities need help. More and more people realize that slums are dangerous cancers affecting everyone, and that a crowded, decaying downtown somehow must be reshaped on new and better principles. But few know how to go about it — what practical moves each individual in the community can make to get the vital process moving.

If there is a lesson that can be drawn from the hundreds of examples of redevelopment across the country, it is this: broad-scale renewal of real consequence can never get off the ground unless it 1) gets strong, working support from the city's business leaders, and 2) gains wide understanding and help through the city's communications network — its newspapers, associations, clubs, churches and neighborhood groups right down to the store-owner, the home-owner, the voter. A city planner, or a mayor, or a chamber of commerce can not get it done alone.

The great surge of interest in renewal in the U.S. is not just a sudden coincidence of civic virtue. It is growing out of the business facts of life in every lagging community: the mounting distribution costs of inefficient traffic patterns, the loss of trade to the suburbs and to newer cities, the headaches of manufacturers, the bad living conditions of employees. These were the reasons behind such classic transformations at Pittsburgh, where the Mellons and other bankers and businessmen formed the Allegheny Conference to pitch in and clean up and persuade business to stay. These were the reasons behind St. Louis' equally famous Civic Progress, Inc., a smaller spearhead of 21 leaders who joined with the mayor and patiently dramatized the issues of renewal for two years before letting $100 million in bonds be put to a vote.

What businessmen can do

The experience of Pittsburgh and of St. Louis

Reprinted from *Architectural Forum* (November, 1956), pp. 128-34 by permission.

and of Cleveland, Kansas City and other alert cities suggests some practical steps for any smart businessman interested in his own future and the future of his town, large or small:

• Get into the parts of government whose proper functioning depends on the part-time service of responsible citizens: the planning commission, the zoning board of appeals, the housing or redevelopment authority, the board of education, the board of health.

• Publicly support those local officials who are doing a good job for the community. These men are often under attack from special interest groups, and sometimes their worthwhile projects are politically unpopular. Unless community leaders back good officials, government becomes tired and timid; its projects become those which will bring the least amount of criticism.

• In particular, get acquainted with the people in the city planning office, find out what the city looks like from their trained, over-all point of view, where blight exists and where it will strike next, what movements are underway or expected. Eventually, this is where renewal must fit into a comprehensive plan.

• Work on Chamber of Commerce city planning committees, use the National Chamber of Commerce's growing fund of advice and literature on urban renewal.

• Help set up a citizen's urban renewal committee that can enlist and coordinate the myriad organizations and interests of the city through a representative cross-section of its leaders.

• Join with fellow businessmen in creating a revolving fund and a redevelopment corporation. Without these financial tools, renewal can never get started (see Cleveland, below).

• Pay top architects and planners to draw up rebuilding schemes that not only will work, but ones that are capable of firing the public imagination.

• Publicize to reach all elements of the community. Enlist the thinking and support of newspapers, and of those trained in advertising and promotion. *Do it in the beginning*, rather than coming in later with a "story" and expecting it to be worthy of printing. Donate advertising space, billboards, spot announcements on radio and TV. Make short, hard-hitting films on renewal and urge theaters and TV stations to show them as their contribution to the citizen effort.

• Focus first on one outstanding issue that can unite the whole community and create a climate in which the rest of the issues can be brought up and carried out. In Pittsburgh, this theme was soot; in St. Louis, soot and blight; in St. Louis and Chicago, rat-bitten children; in Cleveland, the slow and painful loss of standing among the first rank of U.S. cities. Things like Los Angeles' famed smog could become a useful banner for a broader battle.

• Get other citizens out to renewal exhibits and meetings. Some 90 cities are now focusing attention on big citizen gatherings to see a wide-screen slide and movie show made by LIFE magazine and now touring the country as a contribution to ACTION (the well-publicized American Council to Improve Our Neighborhoods, which is rapidly moving in its own thinking from "fix-up" to include over-all city planning redevelopment and rebuilding).

Some examples:

In Detroit, a "Detroit Tomorrow Committee" of 100 business and professional men is giving Mayor Cobo invaluable advice and support on slum clearance, civic center redevelopment, park programs. Businessmen have raised a $16 million Metropolitan Detroit Building Fund to finance capital improvements for 43 health, welfare and recreational agencies. The nonprofit Citizens Redevelopment Corp., conceived by Mortgage Banker Walter Gesell and other community leaders (including the UAW's Walter Reuther), raised an initial $400,000 from industry and labor, helped a big developer start on 53 acres of the long-delayed Gratiot-Orleans clearance and rebuilding project (AF, April '56).

Fort Worth's famed downtown plan by Architect Victor Gruen (AF, May '56) was commissioned by a utilities man, J. B. Thomas of Texas Electric Service Co., who was understandably concerned about the long-term growth of the whole area in which his power lines and lights were permanently built in.

In Indianapolis, a group of downtown businessmen have formed the Civic Progress Assn. aimed at rehabilitation and erection of new office buildings, a new civic auditorium, demolition of blighted areas, new walk-to-work apartments developed with private capital.

In Cleveland, the new Garden Valley planned community offers a close-up study of how renewal can get started and the roles that various business and professional men can play. Four years ago, a *Plain Dealer* writer assigned full time to cover urban renewal reported to his Editor Paul Bellamy that redevelopment would never get moving unless it had strong support from the City's industry and commerce. At his suggestion, Bellamy called a meeting of prominent citizens, including the mayor, the Chamber of Commerce president and Utilities President Elmer Lindseth of Cleveland Electric Illuminating Co. Lindseth proposed a development committee, suggested it be headed by John C. Virden, then a lighting fixtures manufacturer and board chairman of Cleveland's Federal Reserve Bank. When City Planning Director James Lister came up with 247 acres of industrial wasteland owned by Republic Steel as the only available site for a needed housing project, the "Virden Committee" turned itself into the Cleveland Development Foundation, a nonprofit group of industrialists who put up a $2 million revolving fund for this and other renewal projects. Working with the Chamber and with five company presidents, Virden campaigned to raise the money from some 100 companies. Republic Steel's Thomas Patton got his company to sell the land to the Foundation at cost and fill in a deep gully traversing it. (The Foundation in turn has sold the land to the city and will get its money back as it is purchased by private developers and the Metropolitan Housing Authority.) Construction company President A. M. Higley donated engineering studies and construction advice estimated at $25,000. Lawyer Seth Taft worked at cost as the Foundation's counsel, supported by Republic's Patton, also a lawyer. Through Lister the city planning department did the site planning. Board Chairman A. A. Stambaugh of Standard Oil of Ohio released his assistant, Upshur Evans, to become executive director of the Foundation. So concerned was Cleveland's business community about the need for redevelopment all over the city that Newspaper Editor Louis Selzer tried to get Planner Ernest Bohn to run for mayor on a renewal platform. (Bohn insisted he could serve the community better in his role as planning and housing expert.)

In Oakland, Calif., the Henry J. Kaiser Co. helped get renewal back on the track by heeding the call of an embryo citizens' committee, lending the full-time administrative help of its vice president in charge of community relations. Under Norris Nash, the committee has coordinated the city offices concerned with renewal, obtained a budget for its official coordinator, got Oakland designated as a pilot city by the federal government and is now making a sample survey of a 78-block slum area with the help of the University of California. Nash sees the work of his committee as "priming the pumps so that private enterprise can go ahead and do the job."

In neighboring Vallejo, Bank of America Branch Manager Leon Coleman picked up an earlier redevelopment survey, and working through Vallejo's downtown association got a redevelopment agency appointed, the first big step toward rebuilding downtown. In nearby San Leandro Coleman's opposite number, A. J. Oliveira, helped bring together 52 community leaders aimed at forming a redevelopment agency.

Across the bay in San Francisco, Paper Manufacturer J. D. Zellerbach got into the fray after looking downtown for an office building site and finding the foot of Market St. almost entirely blighted. After talking to Mayor George Christopher, Zellerbach and Investment Broker Charles Blyth formed a group of 11 businessmen which has advised on the problems of a product market and an Embarcadero Freeway, and helped persuade Architects Skidmore, Owings & Merrill to contribute a study of freeway costs to the city for a nominal fee.

In East Chicago, Ind., Inland Steel, Cities Service, du Pont, Socony Vacuum, Standard of Indiana and Youngstown Sheet and Tube joined Purdue University in a $1 million foundation for slum clearance, neighborhood rehabilitation and conservation.

What big companies can do

Companies with a nation-wide interest in healthy communities and their buying power are adopting urban renewal as a major policy.

Recently some 60 General Electric branch plant executives met in New York with ACTION executive vice president James Lash and his staff for a second workshop session to swap ideas on how GE could participate in the dozens of communities in which it is involved.

Some of the reports:

In Cicero, Ill., Hotpoint Executive R. H. Thomas heads a citizens' action committee which has torn down 65 shacks in various parts of town, turned a municipal dump into a drive-in theater, persuaded the railroad to demolish 30 railroad workers' shacks and find them decent housing elsewhere, organized high school students into block-by-block surveys to photograph substandard houses for later evidence, encouraged Boy Scouts to clean up vacant lots, cooperated with the Cicero *Light* on a series of renewal articles, made renewal films available to other local organizations. Next steps: a Cicero ACTION information center and staff, a professional planner for the city's staff, renewal films and lobby displays in local movie houses.

In Brockport, N.Y., a town of about 5,000, GE Appliance Executive Joseph Orbin has taken the lead in the new Chamber of Commerce, spoken on urban renewal to a handful of community organizations, helped the Chamber beat the drum for a new planning commission. Orbin faced the typical attitudes of old, tightly bound communities, had to work carefully and quickly, in part to divert the idea that it was all a conspiracy between big business and local realtors. He found his civic job easier after a blue-sky planner from out of town had aroused the citizens' ire by proposing that Main St. be turned into a huge pedestrian mall. The day after that appeared in the news, the paper was full of letters to the editor and the next Chamber of Commerce meeting was packed to the rafters with fearful and angry property owners. Brockport had started to think about its future. Says Orbin of his civic work: "We're trying to show a small town that we're not in here as a carpetbagger, but that industry and community need each other."

In Bloomington, Ill., GE Executive Richard Ehrman is chairman of the 50-member Citizens Advisory Committee and a member of the City Planning Commission. The CAC membership was made purposely large to get as many people as possible interested in studying the new city plan report by Planner Harland Bartholomew. Especially effective in stimulating public support and understanding was a series of 15 four-page special tabloids published by Bloomington *Daily Pantagraph* (whose publisher is also the chairman of the city planning commission). These profusely illustrated special editions, once a week, examined each aspect of Bloomington at close range. Sponsors of the tabloids, along with the *Pantagraph*, were 105 local businesses, ranging from the big GE plant down to the smallest local drug store. The CAC also raised $50,000 in subscriptions to remodel the YMCA, got local labor organizations to donate free labor, local suppliers to give free materials. Every major lumber company in town now has a free advisory service which includes plans for new houses or remodelings.

Sears, Roebuck, with 700-odd stores around the country, has its own Director of Urban Renewal, Harry N. Osgood, encourages its local representatives to take an active personal part in local programs. Sears, like GE, held an ACTION workshop to acquaint its field men with techniques, has provided them with such tools as urban renewal glossaries and legislation manuals. The effects are already being felt in such towns as Columbia, S.C., Greensboro, N.C., and near Sears' big Chicago plant, where the company has

backed the Greater Lawndale Conservation Commission by sponsoring a contest for home improvement. Says Osgood: "We can help arrest a million houses a year from sliding into slums. And in bringing about better communities, Sears will make money too."

What merchants can do

In any city, store owners obviously have a big stake in a healthy community, especially in its downtown business district. Some of the contributions merchants have made are mainly self-interested, such as the promotion of downtown expressways and parking. Others, showing a broader awareness of civic problems, have:

• Contacted their own national associations for renewal information. The National Retail Dry Goods Association, like its counterparts in the real estate and building fields, has accumulated considerable data, and the chain druggists and others are on the verge of their own programs.

• Stirred up whatever local bodies they belong to or can join.

• Campaigned for *peripheral* parking near downtown to keep traffic from snarling the very heart of the city.

• Put on a bright front by remodeling their stores and encouraging other owners to follow their example.

• Initiated area competitions among architects and planners, with the help of city planning departments and local AIA chapters.

• Given over display windows and inside store space to these and to other city planning and architectural exhibits.

• Donated some of their large budgets for newspaper advertising space to periodic backing of renewal projects.

• Encouraged editors to give editorial support to these projects.

In Chicago, Marshall Field, which has a special vice president in charge of civic affairs (Earl Kribben), backed the Ft. Dearborn renewal project. Carson, Pirie, Scott & Co. celebrated its 100th birthday by sponsoring a $32,500 competition to redesign the Loop area for the coming 100 years; the contest drew 106 professional entries and provided the city with invaluable data and ideas (AF, Nov. '54).

In Detroit, the J. L. Hudson Co., working with the citizens' committee and the city planning department, donated its display staff and auditorium to stage a big "Detroit Tomorrow" exhibit.

In Denver, renewal got started when Developer William Zeckendorf was prodded into making good his intentions of major development in Mile High Center and following projects. Another step forward came when Joseph Ross, president of Daniels & Fisher department store, became president of the city's new Urban Renewal Commission as well as director of the executive committee of the Downtown Denver Improvement Association. Ross, who had headed a big Dallas rehabilitation project while at Niemann-Marcus, is now looking to a ten-year program for Denver that includes three pilot projects in renewal, a downtown plan for blight elimination and a new expressway, two more major slum clearance projects. Says Ross: "The first important thing in urban renewal is a good housing code, enforced humanely, flexibly, and patiently. You must prepare neighborhoods for it by working with local ministers, school principals and other leaders and helping them form neighborhood councils to advise the central citizen group." Ross' citizens' commission is a good cross-section of community skills: a merchant, a banker, a private developer, an insurance man, a lawyer, a professional planner, a labor leader, a councilman and a newspaper publisher.

What bankers can do

As a financial expert a banker, mortgage banker or insurance executive can contribute valuable experience to a citizens' committee in setting up redevelopment corporations to deal with federal, state and city governments and with private developers. He can also set aside a portion of regular funds for low-cost home-improvement loans, always a desperate need in a tight money market. For example:

In Kansas City, Mo., Banker James Kemper helped form and head up the Downtown Redevelopment Corp., a group of 98 businessmen which bought part of the city's "skid row" prepared under Title I, turned it into the 1,850-car Northside Parking Project just inside Kansas City's ring-road redevelopment (AF, No. '55).

In Cleveland, five banks backed up "Operation Demonstrate" by extending home-improvement loans from three to eight years, offering to consolidate any old mortgages with new ones to reduce monthly payments.

In Memphis, Mortgage Banker William Galbreath, besides serving on the city planning commission, has worked to get other bankers interested in Title I loans for rehabilitation.

What realtors can do

Any citizens' group needs real estate men to point out where blight is coming, to advise on land values, trends, taxes, costs. When renewal gets underway, they can also set up a relocation bureau to help small businesses in the path of redevelopment find new space or building sites elsewhere in town. Other contributions:

In Norristown, Pa., a committee of the local real estate board surveyed every property in town, notified owners of unsightly conditions, got them to bring 500 units up to standard and demolish 50 others.

In Memphis, Realtor-Developer Russel Wilkinson helped his local real estate board establish a loan and advisory group to help home owners finance improvements.

In San Francisco, Realtor Lloyd Hanford spearheaded the formation of a Citizens' Participation Committee which has set off hot and healthy public debates over San Francisco's freeways, produce market and other redevelopment projects. Hanford's committee also circulates among property owners, showing them how things are financed, what it will cost them to do and what the committee thinks they must get to do eventually, sketching out for them how to work with city departments, architects, contractors.

In Atlanta, Real Estate Developer Frank M. Etheridge helped prod the Georgia legislature into urban renewal laws, pushed for a slum redevelopment program for a downtown area near the Capitol. The real estate board has agreed not to lease property designated as slums by the city building inspector, and insurance men have ceased to write slum fire insurance.

What architects can do

As the trained professionals most needed to shape actual redevelopment, too many architects are still busy deploring wrong solutions among themselves instead of getting out and starting right ones. On the lists of various groups sponsoring urban renewal — in big towns and small, at the state house and on Capitol Hill — the number of architects' names is distressingly small. Not enough of

them know their public officials, inform themselves on prospective redevelopment jobs or go out and find developers to promote and build their ideas. Few are able to present a clear, dramatic picture of urban design and renewal to the general public. Some notable exceptions:

• Nathaniel Owings of Chicago, former planning director for the city and now a participant in several large projects for its renewal.

• Oskar Stonorov of Philadelphia, who helped set up a remarkable city planning exhibit at Gimbel's store and has worked endlessly for rehabilitation projects sponsored by the Friends' society.

• Harry Weese, also of Chicago, who has helped on plans for both the north and south sides of town and has stimulated Chicago's vision of what it might do in the middle — create islands off the downtown lakefront.

• Edmund Bacon of Philadelphia, a planning director with a broad architectural background and an active liaison with the city's leaders.

• Kenneth C. Welch and Victor Gruen, two architects who trained themselves in planning and merchandising, have not only built outlying shopping centers but have developed challenging schemes for whole commercial districts downtown (Gruen at Fort Worth, Welch at Grand Rapids).

Other recent examples:

In San Francisco, Wayne Hertzka led the local AIA chapter in a successful attempt to get a coordinated plan for civic center expansion, something the chapter had been trying to achieve for seven years. Guided by the architects, the center will now enjoy a new exhibit hall, and underground garage topped by a park with properly laid out fountains and floral displays.

In Tulsa, members of the Architectural League went to the city with a proposal to design, at cost, a brand new civic center of public buildings linked by plazas and underground parking. Developed step by step with the practical advice of a mayor's committee of leading citizens and a six-man staff paid for by the city, the $28 million scheme has been well publicized and made part of the city's master plan (AF, Feb. '56).

In Springfield, Mass., Planner Reginald Isaacs used the town as a case study for his Harvard students, got the citizens aroused enough to consolidate groups and go to work on urban renewal problems (AF, July, '56).

In Elyria, Ohio, 31-year-old Architect Richard Miller came back from a Harvard conference on urban planning, wrote a dramatic series of ten sharply worded, well-illustrated articles showing how other cities were handling their problems and how Lorain County's new planning commission and citizens' groups could work together to get action at home. The windup: a full-page, four-color sketch plan, complete with ring roads and radials, parks and parking, for an Elyria of Tomorrow.

What newsmen can do

As Publisher Otto Schoepfle of the *Chronicle-Telegram* did with Miller's series in Elyria, other newspapermen have led their cities in the first steps toward urban renewal. In Washington, both the *Post* and the *Star* have not only given full-time coverage in news, features and editorials, but have in fact assembled so much valuable data that they are continually sought out for vital information — and for speakers. The famed St. Louis *Post-Dispatch* series "Progress — or Decay?" was invaluable in getting broad-gauge support. In addition to editorial support, the Detroit *News* actually sponsored a panel study of the city's problems by local leaders and an Urban Land Institute team of experts. In Cleveland, both the *Plain Dealer* and the *Press* got into renewal in the early, talking stages, have full-time reporters and occasionally help coordinate action. (Said one Cincinnati leader: "If we had the kind of newspaper support Cleveland is getting, we'd be twice as far along in our program.")

In Fresno, Calif., the *Bee* ran 18 articles under a "Community Crisis" headline, later compiled the pieces in a special tabloid edition that went like hot cakes. Since then a volunteer committee has drawn up a new building code, others are improving county zoning and studying metropolitan-area government. Says the author of the series, *Bee* reporter Gordon Nelson: "In political campaigns around here today, being for planning is as necessary as being for motherhood."

In Bloomington, Ill., the *Pantagraph* got local businessmen to support a series of special supplements. In St. Louis and other cities radio and TV stations have broadcast interviews with slum-fighters, renewal films and cartoons, round tables, spot commercials.

What the professions can do

• *Educators* are bringing the story of slums, renewal and planning to school children, through children to their parents, and to parents directly. Schoolbooks like Chicago's famed old *Wacker Manual*, a child's primer on community planning, have appeared in Atlanta and other cities. High school civics teachers are sitting in on briefing sessions with citizen committees, taking current programs back to class.

In Memphis, Dr. Laurence Kinney of Southwestern University turned adult-education studies into a highly successful series of nine television programs called "The City is You," with the help of a small grant from the Twentieth Century Fund. Timed with the presentation to the city of a new master plan report, the series showed how each citizen could get into the urban renewal act, ended with a picture of what Memphis could be in 1984.

In Sioux City, Iowa, John Schmitt of the local adult education center obtained a grant from the Fund for Adult Education, used TV and other media to mobilize citizens behind community improvement.

In Newark, N.J., the city's education department followed up a citizen's rehabilitation program with neighborhood studies by high school juniors and seniors, has included slum prevention in its adult education program as well.

On New York's west side, other schools are following the lead of Joan of Arc High School in teaching housing problems and slum prevention.

• *Doctors* and health departments have provided urban renewal groups with data on sanitary facilities, health figures and hospital needs and have given valuable appraisals of the group health and mental health aspects of urban programs.

• *Lawyers* have proved indispensable members of citizen groups in studying existing laws and codes at city, state and federal levels, recommending enabling legislation, revisions and new laws to implement urban renewal. Lawyer-volunteers representing the citizens can serve as a valuable check on the city attorney's office, can also help set up a speakers bureau to explain renewal, a pool of free or low-cost legal advice for property owners and tenants in the path of redevelopment projects.

• *Ministers* have been invaluable on the board of citizens' organizations, both as advisers and as spreaders of the word to their flocks. Not only do neighborhood people have more confidence in projects affecting them when ministers are involved, but the backing of church groups makes it difficult for special interests to attack real movements for civic progress. The church sometimes starts the movement itself:

In Cleveland, two Catholic priests have been the leaders in winning the city's interest in their area and getting officials to apply for a federal grant. Rev. William McMahon and Rev. Stephen Radecky repeatedly stressed neighborhood improvements from the pulpit, insisted that parishioners attend meetings of the West Side Civic Council to talk about them. They met with residents, street by street, to explain proposed zoning changes. Result: when public hearings on the zoning changes were held before the City Planning Commission, the people were prepared and the proposals moved along smoothly. McMahon also wrote to over 100 cities and agencies all over the country to collect available literature on urban renewal for distribution among West Side Civic Council members.

Another minister who has played a vital role in Cleveland's renewal is Rev. Robert L. Fuller, Negro pastor of Mt. Hermon Baptist Church. When Fuller learned that his church was to be demolished in clearing a central slum area, he came in to discuss the redevelopment plan with Cleveland's urban renewal chief, James Yeilding. He studied it and became convinced that it would work to the advantage of his church and his parish. Then he went about interpreting and selling the plan to his people, dispelling the fears that could have built up to solid resistance of the program.

Still another spark plug for renewal just getting underway in downtown Cleveland is

Reverend John Bruere, pastor of Calvary Presbyterian Church and leading member of the Hough Area Council. In this area, where fine old residences have been allowed to run down as absentee landlords cut them into suites and crowded them with low-income minority groups, Bruere has worked doggedly with street clubs comprising the Council to get members to do voluntary rehabilitation. After ten years of hounding city hall to enforce building codes and save the area, Bruere has finally been able to get the City Planning Dept. to make a comprehensive study of the area, concerned not only with which buildings should be rehabilitated and which demolished, but also with entire neigh-

borhood problems of overcrowding, traffic, parks, playgrounds and zoning. Volunteers are helping out by making house-to-house surveys to get planners valuable information on size of families, income, number of autos, etc.

Says Bruere, summing up the grass-roots problem and, in a sense, the whole nature of urban renewal: "Individually, people feel they are alone and nothing can be done about their problems. When they are brought together in a common cause, they find they had been thinking along the same lines after all. Things begin to happen. They take action — and city hall listens."

Zoning Administration

in Vancouver

36

G. F. Fountain

Many planners know zoning in its relation to the preparation of a zoning by-law but beyond that point administration of the rules laid down in the by-law is left largely to others, usually to the City's Building Inspector. Thus the close contact of the planner with the application of his zoning by-law is often missing.

There is a school of thought that asserts the planner should stick to planning and leave the implementation of his plans to others. In this way the planner can sit back and take a detached view and with half-closed eyes and feet up on the table can best produce that which is best for the City.

The other school of thought is that the planner should live with his plans after they are produced and by being in daily contact with the problems of land use and its development he will then more readily appreciate the problems that arise in making zoning a practical tool of Government.

The latter is the method adopted in the City of Vancouver. Land use administration is the responsibility of the Director of Planning who has under him a division of the Planning Department whose duty it is to deal with zoning

in all its aspects and with subdivision control, the other major factor in land use administration.

This paper will not deal with the theory of zoning, nor with other methods of zoning administration, but will describe the way in which the zoning problem is tackled in Vancouver.

Vancouver Planning Department Establishment

The Vancouver Planning Department under the Director and the Deputy Director, divides into three main divisions, Administration, Plan Production and Redevelopment.

The main activities of the Administration Division are Development Permit Control, Rezoning Procedure, Zoning Appeal staff work and Subdivision Approval. The Planning Department has close contact with three independent boards, the Technical Planning Board, the Town Planning Commission and the Zoning Board of Appeal.

The technical planning board consists of eleven senior officials, representing all those

Reprinted from *Plan*, Vol. 2, no. 3 (1961), pp. 115-24 by permission.

civic departments whose responsibilities include the execution of public projects contained in the unfolding development plan for
the City. This Board has broad planning
powers delegated to it by the City Council. It
acts as a co-ordinator in technical and administrative matters bearing on the development
of the City. It acts in an advisory capacity to
the Council on planning matters, and has
power to approve of development permit applications and to grant relaxation from specific
compliance with some phases of the zoning
regulations.

The Vancouver Town Planning Commission consisting of 15 members is now basically
an advisory body to the City Council on planning. Prior to the creation of the City Planning Department in 1952, the Commission
had a modest but efficient staff of its own
under the late Mr. J. Alex Walker, as its
Executive Secretary, and it carried out the
planning function of the City. The Commission has operated continuously for 35 years
under able leadership and is held in high
regard by the City Council. The early planning in Vancouver was done by the consulting
firm of Harland Bartholomew and Associates,
engaged by the Commission. Now the Commission confines itself to consideration and
advice on rezoning applications, to certain
land use applications such as churches, hospitals and community centres, to advice on
the unfolding Plan for Vancouver, and, by
special legislation, to approval of subdivisions
in a high-class residential area of the City
known as Shaughnessy Heights.

The Zoning Board of Appeal is a statutory
body of five members, two appointed by the
Provincial Government, two by the City
Council and the fifth, being the Chairman, by
the other four. The term of office is three
years, with the members receiving a modest
annual stipend for their services. The Board
meets every two weeks to hear appeals against
decisions on questions of zoning. Basically
the Board decides cases concerning the issue
or refusal of development permits or matters
concerning relaxation of the provisions of the
Zoning By-law. The work is onerous but important in ensuring equity in zoning administration.

Legislative Authority for Planning in Vancouver

Vancouver operates under its own Charter
from the B.C. Legislature, whereas all the
other municipalities in the Province operate
under the B.C. Municipal Act.

Insofar as Vancouver is concerned this
arrangement, though having its good and bad
features, is generally satisfactory. It allows
Vancouver to do things, if it can persuade the
Legislature to enact them, without first having
to persuade the other municipalities to co-
operate. Thus there are various ideas in the
Vancouver Charter, particularly related to
planning, which are not yet available to other
B.C. municipalities. For instance, we have
through our own Charter, secured the right
to control development by the development
permit procedure and to introduce conditional
uses and to delegate Council powers to a
Technical Planning Board and to relax the
provisions of a zoning by-law in certain
instances.

The Legislative authority granted the City
is then in turn translated by the City Council
into enabling by-laws, the most important of
these by-laws insofar as this discussion is concerned, are the Zoning and Development By-
law, the Zoning Board of Appeal By-law, and
the Subdivision Control By-law.

The Zoning and Development By-law

The present Zoning and Development By-law

came into force in 1956, superseding the former zoning by-law which originated back in 1928. The new by-law is more positive in character than its predecessor. It tells you what uses and regulations are allowable in the various zoning districts, rather than what may not be allowed. It adopts a uniform style of presentation in each zoning district, and for the first time it sets out full standards for parking and loading requirements applicable to the various types of land use irrespective of the particular district. It provides for both outright and conditional uses in each zoning district, and it brings into force a development permit procedure.

The number of zoning districts is steadily increasing in Vancouver. We seem to add one almost every year: so that at the present time we have 22 zoning districts. These include four One-Family Dwelling districts, two Two-Family, four Multiple Dwelling, seven Commercial, two Industrial districts and three others covering special categories.

In each zoning district the permitted uses are divided into two categories, namely, those which are allowed, as of right, provided the application meets all the specified regulations concerning height, yards, site area, floor space ratio, parking and loading, etc. These are known as outright uses. The other category lists the uses which are allowed subject to prior approval of the Technical Planning Board. These are known as conditional uses, being in the main, borderline cases which could be allowed provided they do not adversely affect the neighbourhood.

For instance, an automotive repair shop is an outright use in the industrial districts, but is a conditional use in (C-2) Suburban Commercial District, and is not allowed at all in the (C-1) Local Commercial District. Some of the conditional uses, such as a hospital in a One Family Dwelling District, also require

prior consultation with the Town Planning Commission, before the Technical Planning Board may act.

The Development Permit System

Probably the most interesting feature of our new Zoning and Development By-law is the introduction of the development permit system.

Most zoning by-laws couple administration and enforcement to the issuance of the building permit, and prescribe that the building permit shall not be issued until the applicable zoning provisions have been met. Under the development permit procedure the building permit (with minor exceptions) is not issued until the applicant first produces a development permit.

The development permit relates solely to zoning matters, leaving the building permit to take care of the structural features. There are a number of land uses where no building permit is involved, such as a storage yard or parking lot. These in a proper case would be issued a development permit. Conversely there are a number of situations arising where a building permit is necessary to ensure structural safety, but a development permit is unnecessary. For instance a development permit would not be required for internal structural alterations to a building where no change of use is involved.

For administrative purposes, and as a convenience to the public, all applications for a development permit are made to the Building Inspector's Department and not to the Planning Department. More often than not the applicant applies for both his development permit and his building permit at the same time. But he does not need to do so. If he wishes assurance that his proposed development will be acceptable in regard to zoning prior to spending time and effort on detailed drawings, he applies for his development permit first, on the basis of preliminary sketches. If then he secures his development permit he has 12 months in which to obtain his building permit.

When the development permit application is received by the Building Inspector it is identified in relation to its zoning district and to the use within the district. If the use happens to be an outright one, the application is processed by the Building Inspector. If it is a conditional use, it is forwarded to the Planning Department for processing and for presentation to the Technical Planning Board.

In both outright and conditional uses the application is referred to the City Engineer for a clearance on any public works matters such as street widening, lane opening, and availability of sewer and water services; also with regard to such matters as drainage, soil stability and air pollution.

In like manner all development permit applications are checked against a comprehensive Index Map (or series of maps on 100 ft. scale) kept up-to-date in the Planning Department. The Index Map shows all former development permit applications, all zoning appeals, all subdivision applications and similar matters affecting the site. In addition, by a series of transparent overlays all planning proposals which are under consideration or which have been approved are shown. Thus it is possible, on short order, to identify all the features of public knowledge which might have a bearing on the development permit application.

If perchance the proposed development is found to be in conflict with a public project, such as, for instance, the extension of a park site, issuance of the permit is deferred until the case can be reported to the City Council. The Technical Planning Board refers the application to Council, for instructions either to negotiate for the purchase of the site or to allow the application to proceed. Ordinarily no such complications arise and in the case of an outright use, which meets all the prescribed regulations, issue of the development permit is made by the Building Inspector in about 48 hours.

In the case of the conditional uses the time is considerably longer as the application has to be processed through the Technical Planning Board.

It will be appreciated that the members of the Technical Planning Board, who are the top officials of the City, cannot spend too much time away from their own departments discussing development permits. Instead the processing work is done in the Planning Department and the application is then sent to a Sub-Committee of the Board on which the Planning, Building, Health and Engineering Departments are represented. The Sub-Committee meets each Wednesday morning and makes a written report with recommendations on each case in the form of minutes of the meeting which go to the Board meeting the following Friday afternoon for approval. Any difficult or contentious cases or any involving new matters of policy or principle are specifically brought to the attention of the Board for decision and for future guidance of the Sub-Committee. Then the ratification of the minutes of the Sub-Committee, as amended, becomes the official approval of the Technical Planning Board to these conditional uses.

The Civic Design Panel

The Vancouver Zoning and Development By-law makes provision for control of the external appearance of new buildings by providing for the referral of any development permit application to a Design Panel for advice on the building design prior to issuance of the permit. This procedure has operated successfully now for four years and already the direct and indirect effect is quite evident in the improved appearance of the new buildings in the City. The Design Panel is composed of six members appointed by the City Council, consisting of the Director of Planning as Chairman, the City Building Inspector, three local architects nominated by the Vancouver Chapter of the Architectural Institute of B.C. and one professional engineer nominated by the Association of Professional Engineers of B.C. In addition four alternate members are appointed for the architectural and engineering representatives. The alternates are permitted to attend all meetings of the Panel and participate in the discussions, but they only have a vote when the regular member is absent.

The work of the Panel is purely advisory to the Technical Planning Board. All public buildings, all apartment buildings and all unusual buildings are submitted to the Panel for advice. Ordinarily single family dwellings and the like are not dealt with by the Panel. In order to expedite the processing of the design aspect of the buildings, the plans are first submitted to the Director of Planning. As Chairman of the Design Panel he has a good knowledge of the views of the Panel, and the Panel has agreed in general terms on what ordinarily it would be prepared to approve. Thus by agreed arrangement the Chairman is allowed to clear those designs which obviously would meet the Design Panel approval without waiting for a meeting. However, if there is any doubt the design is submitted to the Panel in the usual way.

The Design Panel does not seek to dictate the style of architecture. It is concerned only with quality. In the case of poor design, it encourages improvement, quite often by meeting with the architect and showing him where improvement can be made. However, the Panel is careful not to impose its ideas on the designer and does not undertake to give gratuitous architectural service for the improvement of defective work.

The Design Panel reports to the Technical Planning Board by submission of minutes of its meetings, giving a report with recommendations on each case that comes before it. The Technical Planning Board considers these minutes and, of course, endorses any approved designs. If the report from the Design Panel is unfavourable, the Board then decides whether in its opinion the design is sufficiently bad that it would adversely affect the amenity of the neighborhood. If it is that bad, the Board has the power to reject the development permit application.

The Bonus System For Improving Exterior Appearance

Zoning by-laws ordinarily contain provision for regulating the size, and location of new buildings. Inevitably such provisions tend to dictate the shape and external appearance of the building. The classic example of this is the "wedding cake" type of tall buildings produced in New York City under their original zoning by-law. Different setbacks were required at different heights for the purpose of allowing light and air to percolate through into the streets below. The basic intention of the by-law was good, but the resulting appearance of the buildings left much to be desired.

In 1956, Vancouver introduced a fairly new idea into our apartment zoning regulations whereby the windows of any habitable rooms had to command an unobstructed view through a horizontal arc of 50 degrees, for a radius of 80 ft. In addition, in the denser zoning districts there was a vertical light angle control which to some extent achieved a similar result to the New York pattern of setbacks. We also had the normal yard requirements. At the same time, a floor-space-ratio was introduced as a control of density. These various controls were intended to be mutually in harmony, so that no one of them was more restrictive than another. In other words, the maximum amount of building that could be produced under the setback, yard, vertical and horizontal angle and parking controls would just about meet the maximum size of building permitted by the floor-space-ratio. However, this has tended to produce a stereotyped building with little room for flexibility in the design.

This is one of the reasons which has led us to introduce a bonus system in our apartment regulations. We still provide for the normal type of setback and light angle controls, and the same old type of shoe box design can be produced but if an owner wishes to do better he is allowed to erect a larger and taller building through earning an increase in the floor-space-ratio. He is allowed to score an increase in the floor-space-ratio for any one or all of three basic improvement factors. These three, in order of merit, are:

(1) Encouragement of more open space around the buildings.
(2) Increase in the proportion of required off-street parking placed below ground or within the building.
(3) The development of larger sites.

An interesting problem has been to set the bonus factors in such a way that they will, in fact, be attractive to developers. In Vancouver, the Building Code permits a two-storey building with a basement and a penthouse to be constructed in wood frame, but anything bigger must be constructed in masonry. Masonry construction is more ex-pensive by 15 percent to 20 percent than wood frame. To achieve a bonus for the extra space it is necessary for developers to build higher. Consequently the bonus system encourages masonry buildings, but the bonus offered had to be sufficiently attractive to offset the extra 15 percent to 20 percent cost above that for wood-frame construction.

A different type of bonus system has just been proposed to the City Council for the Vancouver downtown area. The three factors to be bonused are:

(1) Open area at ground level.
(2) Open volume up to a height of 80 ft.
(3) Arcading.

The open volume factor gives the largest bonus, through the factors are adjusted to provide a different bonus for the three factors in different districts. For example, in the proposed retail shopping district the arcade bonus has a higher factor than in other districts. Again, in the center of the downtown area where we want to concentrate and stabilize the maximum shopping and office development, the bonus factors make it easier for a developer to achieve a maximum floor space ratio of 12.00 than in the fringe areas where it is necessary to develop a larger site to achieve the same F.S.R. We have eliminated height and setback controls in the downtown area thus giving designers more flexibility.

In both the apartment areas and in the downtown core we hope to secure a better type of building than in the past. Those architects who have tried the proposals report favourably on them, which leads us to believe that we have found a solution through the bonus system of encouraging better exterior appearance of buildings.

Illegal Suites

Most of our larger cities have a problem in seeking to preserve the integrity of their single family dwelling districts, and of the other residential districts as well, against the encroachment of illegal suites. Our problem in Vancouver started in the West End of the City in the early '30's with the migration of the original home owners to newer areas on the outskirts of the City. Many of these old homes were surreptitiously converted into multiple occupancies of various kinds without the necessary building, plumbing or electrical permits. Some were well done, but mostly the results were substandard accommodation barely meeting minimum health requirements.

Then during the War years the blight spread to other parts of the City. With the advent of P.C. Order No. 200 allowing the sharing of living accommodation as a War emergency measure, the problem got out of control and the City could do nothing about it. Rightly or wrongly Vancouver interpreted the Federal Order No. 200 to mean that structural alterations and increased plumbing could be allowed in dwelling houses to facilitate the sharing of accommodation. In consequence at the end of the War there were thousands of houses, both large and small, new and old, good and bad throughout the City which had been converted to other than single family use. The spread of illegal conversions continued after the War during the period of housing shortage with no real action being taken to control it, only within the last half-dozen years have firm steps been taken to deal with the problem.

We now have a program whereby any illegal suites found to have been created since 1956 are required to be removed forthwith, otherwise the owner or operator faces prosecution. Any illegal suites created prior to 1956 and continuously occupied since then can be allowed to remain for a limited period of time depending upon the quality of the accommodation and the character of the district. A large old dwelling can receive a permit to convert to other residential uses except in the best class of our One Family Dwelling districts. In our (RS-1) One Family Dwelling Districts no further conversions to multiple use are allowed and a program of progressive elimination of illegal suites is under way anticipating the complete restoration of such districts to one family dwelling use by December 31, 1970.

Originally we invited owners, by public notice, to seek validation of their illegal suites, with the promise that they would be allowed reasonable time to recoup their investment before restoration, but practically no one responded. We have to find the illegal suites through the various civic inspectional services.

The present policy then in other than the (RS-1) districts is to allow illegal suites to remain for a limited period of time, up to the life of the building, depending upon the quality of the accommodation, and the zoning district in which it is located. If the quality of the accommodation is rated very poor the owner is given up to three months to remove it. In all other cases the owner is encouraged to improved the accommodation and if it meets a rating of fair or good the owner can anticipate a renewal and continued renewals of his development permit during the ordinary life of the building.

In the (RS-1) One Family Dwelling districts a policy of concerted action to deal with illegal suites was put into operation at the beginning of January 1961. A systematic inspection of all houses in the district is being undertaken by a special housing inspection staff under the Building Inspector. When illegal accommodation is found the owner is told to restore the building to its lawful use or to apply for a development permit. If the owner elects to retain the accommodation, a further inspection is made to determine what work is required to bring the plumbing, gas and electrical installations up to by-law standard. The owner is told what is needed and the approximate cost. If the owner still wants to proceed and elects to bring the services up to standard he then applies for his development permit. Meanwhile the Building and Health Department staffs have rated the accommodation into one of three categories — good, fair or poor. Likewise the (RS-1) districts have been subdivided on a map, into three categories of good, fair or poor, depending upon the amenity of the neighbourhood. Now by matching the rating for the accommodation to the rating for the district the agreed expiry date approved by Council for that particular accommodation is readily ascertained. The poorest accommodation in the best district gets the shortest time, and the best accommodation in the poorest district the longest.

It is too early yet to make any predictions on this concerted effort to eradicate illegal accommodation in the better one family dwelling districts. To date about one house in ten seems to have some form of illegal accommodation and the owners appear to be willing to spend up to $12.00 for the privilege of retaining it for a few years longer.

In-law Suites

A related problem to that of illegal suites is that of in-law suites. Actually in-law suites are illegal suites being used for a special purpose.

The Vancouver City Council shows some sympathy towards those owners who wish to use or create additional accommodation in one-family dwellings for their parents. There is no problem in allowing relatives to live together as one family. The problem comes when one group of relatives wishes to establish separate living accommodation from the rest of the family in the same house. How do you distinguish relatives from non-relatives and how do you ensure that after the family use is discontinued that the premises can be restored to accommodate only one household? The problem which the City Council posed was made even more complicated by restricting the in-laws to parents or grand parents who through age and infirmity or financial dependency are arranging to live in the homes owned and occupied by their children.

Insofar as Vancouver is concerned there seems to be no straight-forward answer to this problem. Our Charter does not allow us in zoning to discriminate between one class of persons and another. Thus we are not able to allow additional separate accommodation to be provided in a home to be used by parents unless non-parents and non-relatives are also allowed the same privilege. Then there is the difficulty of administering the further restrictions whereby only aged parents of ill health or low income can occupy the in-law suites, and the added restriction that the home must be otherwise a one family dwelling owned and occupied by the children of the parents.

We are making some progress, but no real solution has been found short of introducing a modified occupancy certificate system. The most promising solution seems to be to seek a Charter amendment from the Legislature to allow the City to discriminate between parents and others in permitting more than one household to be established in a one family dwelling. Also for the City to seek Charter powers to compel the removal of additional sinks and cooking facilities once the in-law use has expired. In addition it may be necessary to secure authority to set up an independent Board of Referral composed of members outside of the civic service who would process applicants for in-law suites and in a proper case issue an occupancy certificate allowing designated persons to occupy designated premises within a home. Then if the occupancy, on subsequent inspection, reveals different people in residence than allowed under the occupancy certificate remedial measures could be undertaken.

The in-law suite problem serves to illustrate how complicated a seemingly simple social problem can become when it comes to the matter of its administration.

Zoning By-law Enforcement

Forty years ago there was no zoning, as we know it, in any of our Canadian cities. The earliest zoning by-laws were introduced about 1925. Since then the impact of zoning on our cities has been tremendous. Zoning is evident wherever you go. If you walk around the residential areas of Vancouver you can quickly spot those which were developed without zoning controls. If you look at the skyline of New York you can see the horrible examples of the effect on architecture of the early zoning setback regulations.

We tend to take it for granted that zoning is now an accepted way of municipal life, and perhaps it is. The early struggles to get City Councils to adopt the first zoning by-laws are a long way behind us. We tend to forget the shaky start when there were no precedents to guide us and the Courts were none too friendly to this new invasion of property rights. The reason zoning succeeded was that the pioneer administrators were content to progress slowly, but securely, being never too far ahead of public acceptance. Some of us may become impatient and expect our ideas to be accepted because they are designed to improve conditions. It comes as a distinct disappointment when City Councils do not

always follow along as fast as we want them to go. Sometimes we fail to appreciate that progress must be geared to public acceptance.

Another thought to remember is that the more complex our zoning laws become, the more difficult they are to administer. The calculation of floor-space-ratio, horizontal and vertical light angles and similar features of zoning control take time and skill to process, much beyond what was required in the earlier simpler zoning by-laws. Here again, unless there is general public acceptance of the more elaborate zoning controls, criticism and complaints of bureaucracy and of unreasonable delay in processing development applications can lead to difficulties for the zoning administrator.

It, therefore, behooves the planner in devising more and better ways for controlling our mode of municipal development to take heed that his ideas are reasonable and practicable when it comes to administration. In fact, at times, one wonders whether some of our zoning controls can be administered effectively and equitably, or whether we are just leaning upon our inherent national characteristic of obedience to the law. If we cannot enforce our zoning controls in those instances where enforcement becomes necessary, then zoning administration quickly falls apart and becomes a mockery.

We have had our enforcement problems in Vancouver, and still have them, but fortunately many of our former difficulties are being resolved. In the past enforcement suffered from divided authority, inadequate or unenforceable provisions in the by-law and a somewhat apathetic attitude of the Courts towards all by-law enforcement.

First we amended our Zoning By-law, under advice from the City Prosecutor, so as to make it an offence to disobey an order from a zoning enforcement officer. Previously we were taking offenders into Court for, say, having an illegal suite. But if it had been there longer than six months apparently it was protected under the Summary Convictions Act. Now the owner is prosecuted for failure to comply with an order to eliminate the illegal suite.

Another difficulty with us is that the Vancouver Planning Department has no inspectional staff of its own and has to rely on other departments for this service. Unless there is very close harmony between the several departments concerned enforcement can fall apart. We are arranging for all zoning enforcement to be handled through a branch of the Building Inspector's Department. The staff will work in close contact with the City Prosecutor and will become specialists in handling cases needing Court action. In this way we hope to solve some of our past shortcomings in dealing with enforcement.

It is not suggested that we are quick to turn zoning offenders over to the Courts for prosecution. Far from it. Court action is a last resort. It is costly in staff, time and resources and the fines collected do not reflect the cost of this service. Unfortunately, there are some people who do not want to co-operate and prefer to ignore zoning controls. These are the people who when all else fails must be brought into line by Court action. Otherwise, your influence over the more co-operative section of society is undermined.

This review of land use administration has concerned itself with some of the features of zoning control as practised in the City of Vancouver. I do not pretend that our Vancouver system is perfect or that it is the precise pattern for other cities to follow.

However, we have had zoning control in Vancouver for well over 30 years and the present procedures have emerged through a long period of trial and error. They seem to suit us fairly well; but we in the Vancouver Planning Department are well aware of imperfections in the system and are always on the alert for improvement, particularly if such improvement tends to simplify and to expedite the procedures.

Ony passing reference to the subject of subdivision control will be made at this time. Vancouver carried the torch for so many years, seeking to convince the B.C. Government of the importance of giving the municipalities full control over the subdivision of land. We may look with critical eye upon the stereotyped subdivision pattern common to many of our B.C. municipalities and we will probably fail to realize that it took 30 years of effort before the Legislature vested the right of full control in the municipalities. This was only achieved in 1954.

In conclusion, it may be worth recalling that the early pioneers in the field of planning — idealistic and visionary as they might at times have been — nevertheless, have given us in zoning a tool whereby the orderly development of land for the benefit of the people can be achieved. Zoning is one of the most progressive ideas to emerge in the Twentieth Century. Without it our cities, today, would be unimaginable areas of confusion. It is our responsibility as professional planners to jealously guard this heritage and to ensure that our cities develop and redevelop along sound rational lines in step with the advancement in knowledge and in techniques in other spheres of human activity.

A Theory

of Slums

37

Charles J. Stokes

The paradox of slums is that despite the wealth and the high level of economic development of the United States, they are as prevalent in our cities as in many an overseas urban area. Moreover, slums persist here despite attempts over the past three decades at least to eliminate them. Is there a justification or an explanation for slums in this country?

Many explanations of slums do in fact exist. They are used as a basis for the actions taken to eliminate slums. One is tempted, though he ought not yield to such a temptation, to suggest that a possible reason why the elimination of slums has failed is that the explanations are inadequate. It is, however, worthwhile to suggest that in view of the very large sums of money about to be spent on urban redevelopment more careful attention might well be paid to a complete theory of slums. That is what this article attempts.[1]

Assuming that slums do have a function in the development of the city, we intend in this paper to see how this function evolves and show its direct relation to the growth of the city. But theory of slums presented here will seem a bit odd to the reader familar with the literature because it is not concerned with buildings or neighborhoods except tangentially. Rather what emerges is a socio-economic analysis which is in fact a branch of the theory of the labor force.

We seek to find meaningful relations among the major variables assumed to be associated with slum situations and to derive a hypothesis about the rates of change of these variables in such a manner that predictions can be made about slum development. What follows arose out of a need to explain to Latin American audiences both the future of the slum problem so obvious in their large cities and the reasons why they persist in the United States. It evolved as the author wandered through the slums of Caracas, Lima, Buenos Aires, Guayaquil among other cities and made comparisons with what was fami-

[1] The research upon which this article is based was in part financed by the Faculty Research Fund of the University of Bridgeport which awarded a grant.

Reprinted from *Land Economics,* Vol. XXXVIII, no. 3 (August, 1962), pp. 187-97 by permission of the author and the Regents of the University of Wisconsin.

liar to him in American cities. The theory is outlined here in the hope that unemotional thinking about slum formation may provide an ultimate solution.

What is slum in the city landscape is of spontaneous origin. This very spontaneity makes the definition of slums difficult. Slums appear to be planless and even antiplan. Slums, it is argued, do not yield themselves readily to rearrangement. Indeed, are they not like cancer? Cancer has its own growth process distinct and ultimately inimical to the human body. Is the presence and continued growth of slums destructive of the city? Suppose the answer were affirmative. Then one possible definition follows. Slums, it may be asserted, are those areas of the city in which housing and resulting social arrangements develop by processes so different from those by which the general growth of the city proceeds that they will destroy the city. All we have now to do is to look for these areas.

Whatever other merits such a definition has, it does suffer from two difficulties. It does not tell us what to look for. And there is a doubt about the analogy. Slums may be a necessary and even helpful phase of the ecological processes by which city growth can be described.

A good descriptive definition must be capable of fitting a wide range of apparently analogous situations. We must in the definition account for the community housing standard, the community's evaluation of its housing requirements, as well as the community's techniques for handling and absorbing the poor and the stranger. Indeed, the slum is the home of the poor and the stranger, if nothing else. These are the classes not (as yet) integrated into the life of the city. The poor are not integrated because of an ability barrier which tends to separate the city populace into those who will be fully utilized

in the economic and social life of the city and those who will not be regarded as being of the required level of social development. The strangers are not integrated by reason of a "different" culture and the stage to which their own acculturation has come.

Slums differ from the districts in which the lowest stratum of the integrated classes live by failing to conform to the standards which this stratum has set for itself. The distinctive feature of slums is not appearance as such, then, but the relation between the slum and its inhabitants and that neighborhood and its inhabitants which the city regards as having met minimum livability standards. By this kind of definition what is slum in Lima may not be slum in Guayaquil. The function of the slum at any moment in city development is to house those classes which do not participate directly in the economic and social life of the city.

To illustrate the complexity of slum formation and to attempt a theory of slum growth which correlates with a theory of city growth, it will be useful to construct a simple model.[2] This is done in Figure 1.

The model sorts out from a welter of variables two which are thought to be determinants of slums.[3] One of these is the psychological attitude toward the possibility of success in moving up through the class structure by assimilation or acculturation to full

---

[2] The model which follows and which is elaborated in the appendix grew out of an attempt to explain the observations of Professor Robert Lampman. See his *The Low Income Population and Economic Growth*, Study Paper number 12, Joint Economic Committee, United States Congress, Washington, D.C., 1959. See also, *Making Ends Meet on Less Than $2,000 A Year*, Senate Document number 112, Washington, D.C., 1952.

[3] Lampman finds many more variables than these, *op. cit.*, p. 6.

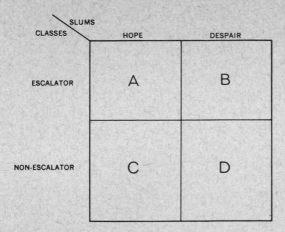

Figure 1.

participation in the economic and social life of the community. The other is a measure of socio-economic handicaps and barriers to such movement.

Horizontally, we distinguish slums of "hope" and slums of "despair," and vertically, escalator and non-escalator classes. The distinction between "hope" and "despair" is one which to some degree must be intuitive. By "hope" is meant that quality of psychological response by the inhabitant of the slum which indicates both his intention to "better" himself and his estimate of the probable outcome of such an effort. "Despair" by the same token denotes either a lack of such intention or a negative estimate of the probable outcome of any attempt to change status.

An escalator class is a group of people who can be expected, barring unusual circumstances, to move up through the class structure. A non-escalator class is one which is denied in some way the privilege of escalation.

The psychological distinction between "hope" and "despair" may readily be converted into a distinction between the employable and the non-employable. There may

be some fuzziness about the exact location of the boundary line but its nature is clear. What is involved is some social measure of "ability" seen objectively as well as subjectively. At any moment of time, the city will have determined a minimum set of "ability" standards. For each job, for example, there may be age limits preventing those who are too old or too young from gaining employment or it may prove difficult to find employment for breadwinners whose education does not go beyond the 8th grade of grammar school.

The distinction between escalator and non-escalator classes implies the concept of caste. There are thus two categories of jobs one of which permits escalation and another which does not.[4] It is important to make a careful difference between caste and ability in this model. Caste membership need not mean residence in a slum provided adequate opportunities for employment exist on this side of the caste line. This in no way denies that some form of racial or religious integration may be a more effective method than separate-but-equal job opportunities. Adequate job opportunities within the caste lines will, however, work to eliminate slums if permitted to do so.

The slums of "hope" have an additional characteristic of importance. They are the home of the stranger, the in-migrant, the recent arrival.[5] These strangers have been attracted to the city by the social or economic opportunities the city offers. Or they may

---

[4] It may be objected that a caste system implies inadequate as well as unequal job opportunities. Logically this need not follow. "Separate but equal" is a possible solution regardless of its desirability.

[5] In its *Primer About Slums* (1958), the New York State Division of Housing makes immigration the first reason for slum formation. However, this reason is overstressed.

have been driven from their homes in the countryside or in other nations by economic, political or social upheaval. In this model, it has seemed best to emphasize the demand side postulating that an economic differential, more than likely wage levels, between the city and its hinterland is the motivating force leading to in-migration.

The strangers come to the city seeking "improvement" but, if they lack the language abilities, educational attainments and other necessary social and economic resources, they may find escalation difficult even if it remains possible. This is all the more true if as is likely to be the case the number of in-migrants in the early waves may exceed the actual new job opportunities made available. The result is that the strangers will tend to fill up the poor housing facilities and spill over into shanty towns.

Note that the slums of "hope" are so characterized because, given normal conditions, it can be expected that many of the strangers who inhabit them will be absorbed into the general employable population. They will learn the language. They will become acclimated and they will acquire the cultural resources necessary. So much the history of migration has taught us. At any moment of time prior to complete integration there will, however, be slums of "hope."

Not all the strangers, though, will be successful in moving up through the social class structure. Some will lack "ability." A group that we have called the "C" group will be debarred from making the same rate of progress as the "A" group by reason of skin color or religion. More important, a proportion of both the "A" and "C" groups will end up in slums of "despair" because they have found it impossible to get over the "ability" hurdles the city erects. Slums of "hope" disappear as migration slows down. Slums of "despair" do not disappear. For in the slums of "despair" live the poor.

"Poor people" in an underdeveloped or developing nation may be taken to be those whose standards of living are below some cut-off point. We may say, for example, that, if we have made a careful study of necessary expenditures for normal subsistence, those who do not obtain this minimum amount are "poor". It is, of course, possible and even likely that in an underdeveloped society the per capita income may thus only permit a standard of living which must lie at or below the poverty level so defined. As society develops, in the sense that per capita income increases, there will be a widened gap between average incomes and the poverty level. But this is not the only observable change. Whereas, in underdeveloped countries it is very possible that the distribution of incomes will be positively skewed as contrasted with the distribution of abilities which is more than likely normal, with the growth in per capita income there is a tendency for the distribution of income to approximate more and more closely the distribution of abilities. What this means is that in advanced societies poverty and lack of ability become more and more correlative. Thus, in an advanced nation the "poor" — not only the poor in income terms but more significantly the poor in "ability" — will be found living in the slums of "despair." That is where those who cannot meet the society's minimum standards for full utilization and employability on any normal basis reside.

In short, we can say that slum formation depends on the rate of in-migration as well as on the rate of integration or absorption of the migrants. Obviously, too, slum formation depends on the existence of barriers to escalation as well as the distinction between income and "ability" classes.

Having set up the model, let us now see how it fits actual cases. In what follows, four distinct city slum neighborhoods are presented for analysis in terms of the model.

A

Guayaquil, Ecuador's largest city and situated near the mouth of the Guayas River, has grown since World War II to have more than 500,000 inhabitants. The fast rate of growth has been dependent upon in-migration, a good deal of such migration coming from the surrounding tropical countryside but perhaps an even larger proportion deriving from the temperate and occasionally cold valleys of the Sierra of the Andes. The "serranos" have rather more Indian blood than the "costeños."

From Calle Los Rios west and Bulevar 9 de Octubre south and especially along Avenida Gomez Rendon — the Boulevard of the Poor — a vast area of bamboo shacks stretches to the salt water estuaries. Much of this Barrio de los Pobres — city of the poor — is below the tide, especially in the rainy "winter." City planning engineers in Guayaquil estimate that at least half the city's population lives in such areas as this.

The Barrio de los Pobres is a Type A slum. It is inhabited by strangers who hope to rise and who see themselves held back by no insurmountable barriers. Unlike Quito, Ecuador's capital (where racial distinctions are made much of) in Guayaquil, mestizos and Indians who have been assimilated play important roles in the life of the city.

The institution of the "relleno" — the filling in of the marshes — is a key indicator of the nature of the slum process in Guayaquil. The slum dweller builds his bamboo shack as high as the possible level of the

"relleno," whenever he or the city can do the filling-in.

At the inner edges of this Barrio of the Poor and along its principal streets can be seen the active phase of the transition process. Each week finds the filled-in areas pushed farther out. With "relleno" completed, those who live in the marginal areas rapidly bring their neighborhood up to standard, particularly as the city paves the streets. Now more permanent buildings, largely of heavier wood than bamboo with facades of concrete, and in some cases of all concrete construction — the preferred building material — dot the reclaimed area. Out on the far edge of the slums the shack city extends itself farther west week by week as the squatters move in. Withal there is a sense of a victorious struggle against the elements.

For Guayaquil, slum formation is basic to the process of city growth.[6] The slum is a temporary home and a kind of a school house. If we classify the Barrio de los Pobres as a type A slum, we observe the paradox that the Type A slum is probably the least attractive of all slums because it is the most temporary. By the same token, it is the one most apt to "clean" itself up.

Admittedly this "cleaning up" process may not be apparent to the casual observer because it can take a number of forms depending upon the rate and nature of in- and out-migration. The slum families, for example, as they become adjusted to their new community and acquire the necessary social and

[6] Dr. Humberto Palacios, director of Economic Research Institute of the University of Guayaquil, argues that Guayaquil owes its growth entirely to this "pioneering" by the inmigrants. Not only is land for development provided but the process gives tone to the economic life of the city. Certainly Guayaquilenos are a very aggressive people.

economic resources may find it possible to leave their slum homes. If they do so and are followed in these same dwellings by other more recent arrivals with the same background, the dwellers have changed but the slums remain. On the other hand, if the growth of the city is rapid in a limited land area — as in the case of Guayaquil — the slum itself may disappear.

B

The first impression a casual visitor has of Boston's South End is one of rundown gentility. Along streets which often have parks down their center stand four- and five-storey brick houses with bowed fronts. There is a haunting charm to these elm-shaded streets. But the second impression is more lasting. Decay is everywhere. An air of hopelessness pervades the atmosphere.

This is a type B slum, an area in which the social residue live. While the South End does have Negro sections at its edges, it is largely a place for old, once well-to-do, poor, cast-off Bostonians. Here, too, live the shady characters, the prostitutes, the citizen at the margin of social respectability. Here and there occasional houses, churches and other public buildings indicate successful attempts to fight off the persistent down-grading. Except for the slum clearance project at Franklin Square, the cleaned out New York Streets area and the Hospital Zone, little if any new buildings have gone up in the South End for three generations.

The barriers to movement upward and outward for the South Ender are largely subjective. The poverty one sees in its streets appears to have some correlation with the large numbers of taverns. The South End does not expand physically. It slowly dies and with it

what was once one of the best areas in Boston.

The type B slum, the slum of "despair," is frequently found in United States cities. Like the South End, they are often genteel in background but are the present home of the cast-off plus those who have been unable to complete the process of acculturation. These are those for whom society has pity but has somehow been unable to help effectively. It is unlikely that the major part of the inhabitants of the slums of "despair" will ever leave them but there does appear to be a steady movement into them.

It is difficult, however, to guess at what rate these slums of despair increase or decrease. Notice that slums of type B are more "attractive" than those of type A. They are much less livable; psychologically less productive of progress.

C

Deceptively similar to Boston's South End is Chicago's South Side — Bronzeville. This area is a vast Negro slum which is continually pushing out from an area once bounded by Roosevelt Boulevard on the north, the railroad tracks at 63rd Street on the south, Wentworth Avenue on the west, and the all-white enclaves of Hyde Park and Kenwood on the east.

Social barriers against Negroes need no detailing here, but that these barriers can be overstressed is apparent in Bronzeville. Chicago Negroes have had a reputation for aggressiveness. They have established newspapers, magazines, insurance companies, factories and the like. In fact, "hope" is evident everywhere.

Unlike Guayaquil, however, there is no easy transition in Bronzeville into better neighborhoods. Bronzeville in its growth gives little clue to the life and growth of the gigantic city of which it is a part. Forced to develop their own subculture, Bronzeville's inhabitants are building their own city.

Type C slums, of which Bronzeville is an example, are like type A with an important difference. While they are, to be sure, the slum of "hope," homes of the stranger, their inhabitants have subjectively as well as objectively effective barriers to acculturation. They do not belong to an escalator class. Yet these slum dwellers are "strivers." Evidencing above average mental and social talents, as they acquire a permanent foothold in the city into which they have come, they are more likely to reclaim their neighborhoods, if they can (as in Baltimore) or if they can't they will push toward better neighborhoods. One characteristic needs stressing, since type C slum dwellers have substantial difficulties to overcome, they are likely to be militant along with their aggressiveness. Occasionally, this militance may manifest itself in a growth of economic crimes — gambling, prostitution, bootlegging, et cetera. Some of these activities are obviously wealth-producing and act as pressures toward invasion of better neighborhoods.

D

Lima, Peru is a city of magnificence. But far away from the charm of Avenida Arequipa, the impressive Miraflores and San Isidro districts as well the beauty of Plaza de Armas, is the infamous Ciudad de Dios, an Indian slum. Unlike Guayaquil where racial barriers are for all practical purposes nonexistent, Lima in a subtle as well as direct way bars the Indian from participation in its economic and social life. The Indian coming

down from the Altiplano finds his home beyond the city limits in shacks built of what he can find. Though Lima grows, its growth neither benefits him nor affects him. Immigrants from Asia and Europe as well as elsewhere in Latin America, provided only that they are not Indian in culture, find more ready acceptance into Lima's life than he does. Not wanted, unaggressive, he sits in despair at the city's gates. Physically near, he is actually as far from social integration as he was in his mountain village.

The type D slum, of which Lima's City of God is an example, is even more a slum of "despair" than type B, for in addition to all the subjective disabilities characteristic of the dwellers of the type B slum, those of type D suffer because of their different color, religion or race. For them society has little sympathy. The community has made no provision for housing these people and does not intend to absorb them. There is literally no other place to which they can go. In the words of the Negro spiritual, "there is no hiding place down here."

Can the theory of slums we are outlining here be of help in setting forth a policy for slum elimination? We think so.

In underdeveloped and developing countries, slums of type A are quite evident as indeed they were in pioneer America. However disturbing these slums may be to the sensibilities of the casual observer, they are serving a necessary purpose. To be sure, better organization might reduce the need for this type of slum but it is not likely that developing nations will have either the resources or the governmental techniques which will permit a less disturbing way of handling the movements of laborers into the cities.

The advisor on economic development should be cautious in recommending that same form of solution for growing nations and their slums which he has seen tried at home. Perhaps a good example of the best form of slum elimination and even avoidance in an underdeveloped nation is that tried in the Puerto Rican city of Ponce, where basic sewage and water facilities along with sidewalks and macadamized pavement have been provided in slum areas as a part of the slum dwellers' own efforts to upgrade their neighborhoods. This implies a program of education, community organization as well as slum clearance.

South Africa's racial areas program, whatever may be said against it by those who quite rightly oppose residential segregation, is an attempt to find a rational solution to the helter-skelter growth of slums at the edge of the city. In Durban, Port Elizabeth and Johannesburg, among other cities, native "locations" have been bulldozed and have been replaced by carefully planned native townships. One of the world's most famous slums, Cato Manor, is now gone from the center of Durban.

Slums of types A and C (the slums of "hope") are self eliminating if the society has the time to wait. How fast they disappear depands upon the rate at which society absorbs the stranger to it. In West Germany we have an example of planning for housing of East Germans and of absorption which has prevented slum growth. However, the experience of the United States, Argentina and Canada suggests that the rate of absorption also depends upon continuing economic growth. The higher the demand for labor continues to be — assuming that there is no great self-impelled migration — the more rapid the integration of the stranger. But even if the self-impelled migration were large, for integration to proceed it would only be necessary that economic growth and absorption be faster.

While the slums of "hope" may pass away with economic growth, the same cannot be said for types B and D. To the extent that poverty and lack of "ability" become socially synonymous, the problem of the elimination of the slum of "despair" becomes more and more like that of a disease requiring a therapy which we have not yet worked out. Clearly evident in the United States is the fact that in many of our slum clearance projects we have tended to segregate types B and D people. If in any one generation there are the seeds of improvement of the next, slum clearance — should it continue to produce the same sorts of results — may deter the elimination of slums. This is the paradox of today's efforts.

Conclusion

Some types of slums persist because they are an index of a paradox. Rising standards of living are accompanied by rising standards of ability and competence. In the United States poverty has become a term which describes the condition of a class more and more composed of the "incapable". These are the people who because of society's standards for entrance into job opportunities have not been integrated into full participation in the economic life of the community. How to provide for these unfortunates lest their presence yield a costly dividend of crime and disease remains the problem of highly developed society.

This slum problem is, however, distinct from the problem of earlier and less developed days and countries. In those distant days and lands, slums were and are an index of growth and of unabsorbed immigration to cities. Their presence is and was a sign of economic health though this need not mean that careful social organization might not make them largely unnecessary. Such a level of organization implies a stage of development not yet reached in most countries which are yet developing.

Clearly outlined in this theory of slums is the role of caste. That this caste membership need not imply slum residence should be evident but it is one of the factors which provides for a differential rate of absorption as between castes. These differential rates of absorption have led to lingering slums of "hope" among minority groups in the United States. These, however, are disappearing. Ultimately the problem of caste as a determinant of slums coalesces with that of "ability" and becomes part of the same force at work in slum persistence.

APPENDIX

I. Migration and the Rate of Absorption

Assume that at any moment of time the level of population of a city of substantial size is steady. It is not increasing either from natural growth or from in-migration from the city's hinterland. Assume, moreover, that employment is full. There is no excess demand for labor.

In the hinterland, assume that there are no factors at work which would induce out-migration other than an excess demand for labor in the city. To be sure, these assumptions make in-migration a demand phenomenon. However, there is no neglect of the supply side. Rather supply enters into the analysis rather oddly. For one thing, if as is part of our tradition, out-migration depends upon non-economic motivation, we can not produce a normal supply function. For another, since our concern is with the impact of migration upon the formation of slums, we need only to observe that migration will probably not be directed toward those cities where no economic opportunity exists.

An excess demand then for labor is the measure of existence of that economic opportunity and leads to in-migration. The excess demand leads at full employment to an increase in the city's going wage but, more important, given different rates of economic growth as between the city and its hinterland, to a widening of the differential between wages levels in the two market areas. It is in fact this growth in the differential which becomes the economic incentive directing migration toward the city.

Now we are ready to consider the nature of the migration. It is likely that, given the unsettled labor market in the hinterland plus the accumulation of non-economic motives, once the in-migration is induced to begin, it will exceed the actual initial demand. The city will be faced with absorbing the newcomers.

In addition, of course, to the excess supply of labor now created and the absorption problem thus inherent, there is the problem of the "quality" of the migration. It can be assumed that the migrants will be divided into those who can readily be absorbed into the labor force, provided such opportunity be available, and those who will not be readily absorbed because of the lack of "ability" of some of the migrants.

If there were no such division by reason of ability, then the rate of absorption would depend upon the rate of economic growth or what is the same thing, the rising level of average income. But if this rate of economic growth be slow — slow relative to the flow of in-migration — slums will appear. These will be slums of hope because in them will live a potentially utilizable labor force. These "temporary" slums will be an index of the rate of economic growth and the excess supply of labor.

The persistence of slums of hope will presumably depend upon the differential rates of growth of the cty and its hinterland as well as upon the internal rate of growth of the city alone. They will disappear as demand for labor moves toward equality with the supply. The slower the rate of absorption, the faster the rate of slum formation spreads blight across the city landscape. As growth in the hinterland — possibly a spillover from the city — proceeds, it will tend to counteract the non-economic motivation to out-migrate. The differential declines, in-migration slows down and absorption steps up. Internally, the city rate of growth insures that jobs are provided for the newcomers. Slums disappear.[7]

II. The Poor and Their Replacement

There are, however, ability hurdles which the in-migrants must surmount. A significant proportion of the newcomers will find or will react such a way as to indicate that they understand that little chance exists for full integration into the community. These are

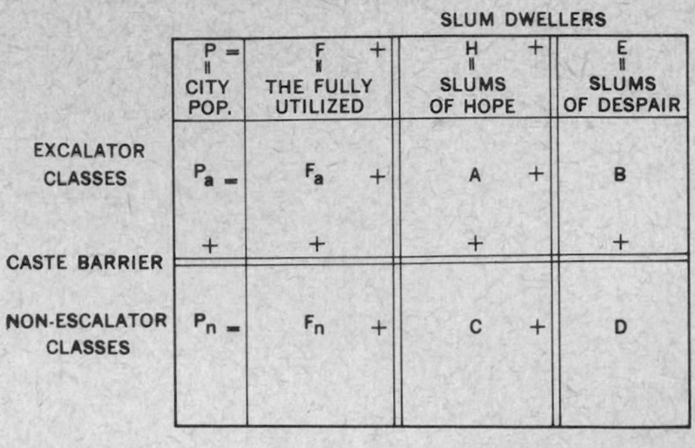

----

[7] In Figure 2 a diagram of the rate of absorption and its interaction with the formation of slums is presented. If we begin at OP_1 (equal to P_1F and to OF) where we have full utilization at a population equilibrium and observe what happens as population increases through migration from P_1 to P_2 to P_3 to P_4, we can trace out the genesis of slums. During period 2, in-migration occurs (equal to FA_2). B_2F is that proportion of the in-migration which is absorbed. The slope of $FB_2B_3B_4$ is the rate of absorption. By period 3 the rate of absorption has become parallel to the rate of full absorption indicating that a given absolute number of the in-migrants have found it impossible to get over the ability barrier. The gap A_2B_2, A_3B_3, A_4B_4 represents slums of despair which persist. The gap B_2F, B_3F represents slums of hope which finally disappear. This model assumes one "shot" of in-migration.

Figure 2.

the "incapable," the un-utilized or under-utilized.

To be sure, if the rate of growth is slow and if the proportion of "incapables" to the total flow of migration is low, then in the early period of in-migration, poverty arising from this source will be largely an economic phenomenon. But as absorption proceeds with ability barriers remaining at previous levels, a larger and larger proportion of slum dwellers (the "poor") will be characterized by a lack of "ability." In fact, if economic growth permits, absorption will finally have reached some maximum possible level and the "poor" and the "incapable" will be the same persons. Lacking any hope of integration, they inhabit the slums of despair.

It should be observed that some of the "incapable" may have come from the present population of the city. These are those who have "fallen" into poverty by reason of a lack of ability or who have been "cast off."

What can we say about the persistence of the slums of despair or about their possible rate of growth? In this case we can not rely upon the rate of economic growth, a rising level of income, or full employment to eliminate these slums.

To the extent that ability, however defined, is normally distributed — a likely hypothesis — it may be expected that with a fixed ability

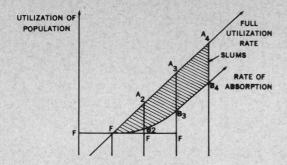

Figure 3.

hurdle, slums of despair will not only persist but will grow at about the rate of growth of the general population, assuming no further in-migration. If in-migration continues it is possible that slums of despair may grow faster than the general population. One of the reasons for this likelihood is that society will tend to impose a higher standard for entering than for remaining among the utilized. It is also likely that the very growth in the economy which makes possible absorption brings with it a rising standard of competence — a level of ability — making a larger proportion of the in-migrants "incapable."

III. Income as a Determinant of Slum Formation

It might be argued that income should have been introduced at an earlier stage in the analysis but its consideration has been postponed to now to permit a detailing of the role of "ability."

Assuming that ability is normally distributed is rather different from assuming that income is normally distributed. Certainly in the earlier stages of economic growth it is evident that income distribution is decidedly skewed to the right. But there is also evidence that suggests a tendency for income distribution to move toward normality as income levels increase.

Just as there is an ability cutoff or barrier, so society has an income cutoff or barrier below which we have poverty. In earlier stages of economic growth, mean ability levels will lie considerably above mean income levels, so that the poor in income terms include many whose ability levels are above the ability cutoff. But as the mean income level shifts upward the income and ability cutoffs tend to become synonymous. To the extent that this becomes true, poverty and lack of ability become one and the same thing. This is another way of saying that a low level of income does lead to poverty and slums but that a rising income is limited in its ability to remove slums if ability barriers exist.

IV. Escalator and Non-escalator Classes

Up to now we have assuming that migration, ability and income growth are the factors which affect the rate of slum formation. So they do but it needs also to be pointed out that there may be differing rates of absorption within the city's population due to the presence of caste lines.

What is implied by caste is that, even if ability, however defined, did not act as a barrier to integration and full utilization, there would still be a third barrier. What is true is that the city will have divided its job opportunities into two categories. The one category permits those who retain the jobs to move up the social scale — escalation. The other category includes those jobs whose retention does not necessarily permit such escalation. This third hurdle or cutoff differs from the first two — ability and income — in being horizontal. It cuts across income and ability groupings.

V. The Basic Matrix.

We are in a position, now that we have the variables defined, to consider the basic matrix which underlies our model of slum growth. In Figure 3 we can distinguish two vertical barriers — income and ability. The income barrier separates the fully utilized from the poor and depends for its position upon the level of economic growth. The ability barrier divides the poor into two groups, those who reside in slums of hope and whose absorption and ultimate utilization depend upon the rate of economic growth and those who reside in slums of despair and who will not be fully utilized regardless of the rate of economic growth at present ability standards.

The horizontal barrier — the caste barrier — separates each grouping into two categories each. For each escalator group there is a parallel non-escalator group. For the non-escalator groups a different rate of absorption applies, as well as a different level of utilization and perhaps even a different and higher cutoff for ability. Economic growth has a weaker effect below the caste barrier in bringing about the absorption of the capable. The result is that poverty and slums of despair remain a more serious set of problems than for the escalator class.

It is, of course, possible to conceive of a model in which the caste barrier is sufficiently high that economic growth has practically no effect on the non-escalator class. It is also possible to conceive of a caste barrier which is less effective at the upper end than at the lower. The one makes the model more nearly applicable to the Indian countries of South America, for example, and the other aids in understanding better the present picture in the United States.

The Urban Snow Hazard in the United States

38

John F. Rooney, Jr.

Traditionally the mid-latitude American city has coped with snow and ice in an organized but inefficient manner. Even in this age of galloping technological advance, most of our northern cities annually experience the crippling impact of at least one severe snowstorm. The brunt of the disruption, ironically, occurs in areas that are "well prepared" to handle any snow emergency. The continuing trend toward urban sprawl has been a major factor in accentuating the difficulties that stem from an occasional snowstorm. Distances separating urban dwellers from their everyday affairs and transactions have lengthened, and dependence on both private and mass transportation facilities has increased. By introducing snow or ice into an urban setting with hypersensitive movement patterns, any form of chaos may be precipitated.[1]

The present study is designed to assess the impact of snow in urban areas, using several lines of investigation. Snow's disruptive effects on man are analyzed, with an emphasis on the identification of the critical physical-environmental variables (amount and kind of snow, wind, temperature, terrain, and so on). Then the role of community adjustment and adaptation is examined, and, finally, attitudes concerning the snow hazard are probed, by means of interviews, to gain an understanding of the adaptations and adjustments that are characteristically made. The study focuses on seven selected cities, but the findings presumably have much wider application.

THE SNOW HAZARD

The snow hazard may be defined as comprising all the perils that snow and ice present, both in themselves and in association with other weather conditions. The hazard is also influenced by the nature of the terrain and the kinds of road-surfacing materials used in the area in question.

Most of man's activities are to some degree sensitive to weather. Certain of them are highly sensitive to cold (highway construction, outdoor painting), some to wind (struc-

[1] Quite apart from snow and ice, consider the effect of an accident on an expressway in Chicago, New York, or Los Angeles, especially during rush-hour periods.

Adapted from *Geographical Review* (October, 1967) pp. 538-59. Copyrighted by the American Geographical Society of New York. Reprinted by permission.

THE URBAN SNOW HAZARD
A CONCEPTUAL FRAMEWORK

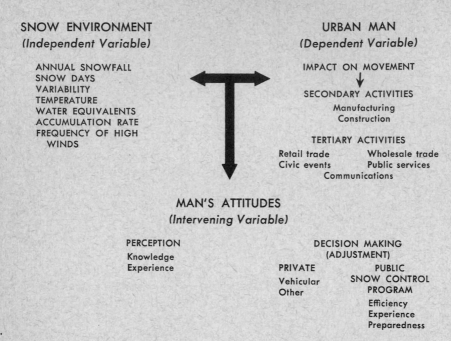

SNOW ENVIRONMENT
(Independent Variable)

ANNUAL SNOWFALL
SNOW DAYS
VARIABILITY
TEMPERATURE
WATER EQUIVALENTS
ACCUMULATION RATE
FREQUENCY OF HIGH
   WINDS

URBAN MAN
(Dependent Variable)

IMPACT ON MOVEMENT

SECONDARY ACTIVITIES
   Manufacturing
   Construction

TERTIARY ACTIVITIES
Retail trade   Wholesale trade
Civic events   Public services
   Communications

MAN'S ATTITUDES
(Intervening Variable)

PERCEPTION
Knowledge
Experience

DECISION MAKING
(ADJUSTMENT)

PRIVATE   PUBLIC
Vehicular   SNOW CONTROL
Other   PROGRAM
        Efficiency
        Experience
        Preparedness

Figure 1.

tural-steel erection, roofing installation, recreation), and many others to precipitation, especially snow.[2] Transportation is the activity most critically affected by snow, but a host of others also suffer, including construction, merchandising, manufacturing, agriculture, power supply, communications, recreation, and public-health and safety services. The catalogue of problems caused by weather provides ample evidence of the disruptive impact of snow. It is noteworthy that snow cover is cited as a hindrance to transportation more often than any other meteorological

phenomenon, and that surface icing and glaze are considered to be only slightly less severe.[3]

The snow hazard has a number of important implications for urban geography. Perhaps the most notable is the impediment it poses to spatial interaction, both within the city and between the city and its tributary area. Normal movement — for example. the journey to work, shopping trips, and travel to participate in recreational activities — is often changed or curtailed. As many individuals rearrange their plans and patterns of action, the density and direction of traffic flow are also altered. In the snow hazard's most extreme form it may sever tributary connec-

[2] See, for example, J. A. Russo, Jr., K. Thouern-Trend, R. H. Ellis, and others, *The Operational and Economic Impact of Weather on the Construction Industry of the United States* (Hartford, Conn., Travelers Research Center, Inc., 1965), pp. 11-17.

[3] R. R. Rapp and R. E. Huschke, *Weather Information: Its Uses, Actual and Potential* (Santa Monica, Calif., The Rand Corporation, 1964), p. 31.

tions for extended periods, cutting off supply and distribution lines and thereby resulting in emergency situations.

From an economic standpoint snow may induce heavy financial losses. The cost of combating snow and ice, fixed capital and overhead costs for schools, factories, and stores, and damage to property are some of the direct losses. A diversion of expenditures is also a common economic response; money that might have been spent on clothing or recreation may be reallocated to snow-control equipment for homes and cars, for instance.

Some of the myriad relationships that exist between "urban man" and his snow environment are depicted in Figure 1. This diagram attempts to portray the typical urban dweller confronted by his snow environment, which includes not only snow but the associated conditions (wind, air temperature, and other forms of precipitation) that often affect the degree of difficulty he experiences. Within this framework, man's accumulated contacts with snow hazards will influence the action he takes. His decisions will be affected by the kind of adjustments he has made to counter-act the hazard, both independently and as a part of the total urban population. These adjustments are influenced in turn by his attitudes concerning snow and ice, which have been shaped by his perception of these phenomena.

ASSESSMENT OF DISRUPTION

The investigation of the disruptions caused by snow covers a period of ten years, 1953-1963. This period is long enough to provide an adequate sample of conditions and recent enough so that a reasonable amount of information was available.

Seven cities served as the basic laboratory in which the effects of snow were examined.

Cheyenne and Casper, Wyoming, and Rapid City, South Dakota, were the pilot sites. After testing for relationships between disruption and the snow environment in these cities, four more sites — Green Bay and Milwaukee, Wisconsin; Muskegon, Michigan; and Winona, Minnesota — were selected for study (Figure 2).[4] In addition to being in another section of the country, they represent different types of snow environments and public adjustments. Man's attitudes concerning the snow hazard and his subsequent adjustments to it were investigated in each city, but extensive interviewing was confined to Cheyenne, Casper, Rapid City, and Winona.

Six of the cities studied are of medium size, ranging in population from 25,000 to 65,000. One larger place, Milwaukee (*ca.* 750,000), was included so that the measures developed could be tested at a locale of authentic urban stature. Medium-size cities were selected for several reasons. It was felt that cities of this size would provide a less complicated setting than larger cities, and, in fact, they proved to be excellent laboratories, though their problems do not approach those of huge metropolitan areas such as New York, Chicago, and Boston. The seven sites chosen for study were large enough to possess a nearly complete span of urban functions, yet small enough to permit a careful analysis of snow-caused disturbances. At the same time, distances between sections of the cities were long enough to augment disruption when snow and ice were present.

METHODS OF INVESTIGATION

Information concerning disruption was taken

---

[4] Figure 2 also shows the location of ten other sites that were investigated more generally to test the significance of the moisture content of snow.

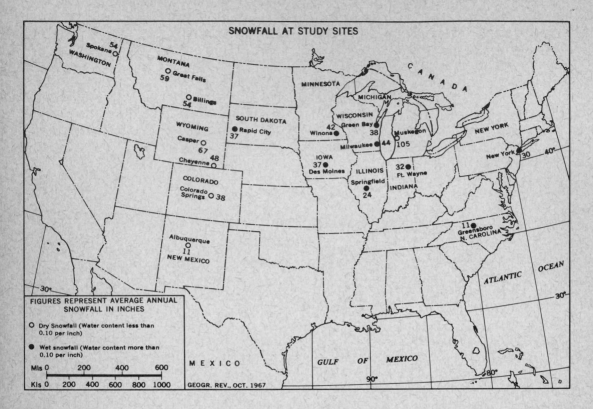

Figure 2.

chiefly from daily newspapers and public records.[5] From this material it was possible

[5] The major newspapers used were the *Wyoming Eagle* (Cheyenne), the *Casper Tribune-Herald*, the *Rapid City Daily Journal*, the *Winona Daily News*, the *Green Bay Press Gazette*, the *Milwaukee Journal*, and the *Muskegon Chronicle*. The public records that proved most helpful were police accident reports, parking-meter revenue summaries, and street maintenance reports. Telephone company files and information compiled by public utility firms were among the private sources consulted. The most dependable sources were newspapers, police and city records, and the data on power failures kept by public utility companies. School attendance records were too general for more than token use, and since the telephone company records were available only on out-of-city calls, they proved to be of limited value.

to classify the impact of all snow days[6] under consideration. Each snow day (event) was rated as to severity of impact within a hierarchy or scale of disruption.

Some measure of data reliability was thought desirable. The use of newspapers to identify trends and to form a basis for generalization falls under recognized research techniques of "content analysis" — that is, the categories of analysis used to classify the content are clearly and explicitly defined so that other individuals can apply them to the same content to verify the conclusions; the

[6] A "Snow day" is one on which one inch or more of snow is recorded. In the case of a storm that lasts more than one day, the entire snow period is considered as one snow day.

analyst is not free to select and report merely what strikes him as interesting, but must methodically classify all the relevant material in his sample. By using this technique to analyze communications media, much of the ambiguity is eliminated.

Interviews with private individuals and with proprietors of commercial establishments were used to probe attitudes and adjustments concerning the snow hazard.[7] The questions were designed to reveal the respondents' attitudes toward snow and ice and to determine their ability to cope with the hazard personally and as members of a group. Merchants were asked to comment about the effect of snow on their business, and to discuss the municipal snow-control program. Interviewing was done on an area-sampling basis. A total of 255 personal interviews were conducted, and 61 firms made up the commercial sample.

PATTERNS OF SNOWFALL

Before analyzing the disruption attributable to snow, it is necessary to examine the snow patterns of the seven cities. In terms of mean annual accumulation (ten-year averages),[8] Muskegon leads with 105 inches; Casper has 67; Cheyenne, 48; Milwaukee, 44; Winona, 42; Green Bay, 38; and Rapid City, 37. The Midwestern cities are characterized by a concentration of snowfall from December

[7] The questionnaires used for both types of interview appear in Appendix B of the writer's doctoral dissertation, "The Urban Snow Hazard: An Analysis of the Disruptive Impact of Snowfall in Ten Central and Western United States Cities" (Worcester, Mass., Clark University, 1966); also available from University Microfilms, Ann Arbor, Mich.

[8] The ten-year averages were within 2 inches of the long-term averages at all sites except Muskegon, which was 33 inches in excess of the long-term average of 72 inches.

through March, with January the peak month. In the Rocky Mountain area and adjacent plains, most of the fall comes later, and March and April are usually the snowiest months. In general, snow is wetter in the Midwest and in the East than it is in the Rocky Mountain region. The water equivalent of ten inches of snow at the Wisconsin, Minnesota, and South Dakota sites is approximately one inch, while at Casper and Cheyenne fifteen to sixteen inches of snow are required to produce one inch of water.

GENERAL IMPACT

Most of the difficulties caused by snow stem from disruption of transportation facilities. Even small accumulations may effectively curtail movement and contribute to accidents. Disruptions of retail trade, industrial production, school attendance, construction, civic events, and numerous other activities can be traced largely to the impairment of movement. In the disruption model developed here, highway transportation constituted the major link between the cities and their tributary areas. Although rail transportation is also vital, its functions are more important on a long-term basis; curtailment of rail facilities for a day or two does not generally produce the repercussions associated with disruption of highway transportation. The airlines that serve the study sites currently play only a minor role in the total transportation pattern.

To assess accurately the troublesome effects of snow in urban areas, some kind of categorization is desirable. The hierarchy of disruption presented in Table I rests on the assumption that snow unleashes its most damaging effects against transportation. The orders of disruption are ranked along a scale ranging from first order, the most severe, to fifth order, the minimal, which designates assumed but unvalidated inconvenience.

TABLE I

Hierarchy of Disruptions: Internal and External Criteria

Activity	1st Order (Paralyzing)	2nd Order (Crippling)	3rd Order (Inconvenience)
INTERNAL			
Transportation	Few vehicles moving on city streets City agencies on emergency alert, Police and Fire Departments available for transportation of emergency cases	Accidents at least 200% above average Decline in number of vehicles in CBD Stalled vehicles	Accidents at least 100% above average Traffic movement slowed
Retail trade	Extensive closure of retail establishments	Major drop in number of shoppers in CBD Mention of decreased sales	Minor impact
Postponements	Civic events, cultural and athletic	Major and minor events Outdoor activities forced inside	Minor events
Manufacturing	Factory shutdowns Major cutbacks in production	Moderate worker absenteeism	Any absenteeism attributable to snowfall
Construction	Major impact on indoor and outdoor operations	Major impact on outdoor activity Moderate indoor cutbacks	Minor effect on outdoor activity
Communication	Wire breakage	Overloads	Overloads
Power facilities	Widespread failure	Moderate difficulties	Minor difficulties
Schools	Official closure of city schools Closure of rural schools	Closure of rural schools Major attendance drops in city schools	Attendance drops in city schools
EXTERNAL[a]			
Highway	Roads officially closed Vehicles stalled	Extreme-driving-condition warning from Highway Patrol Accidents attributed to snow and ice conditions	Hazardous-driving-condition warning from Highway Patrol Accidents attributed to snow and ice conditions
Rail	Cancellation or postponement of runs for 12 hours or more Stalled trains	Trains running 4 hours or more behind schedule	Trains behind schedule but less than 4 hours
Air	Airport closure	Commercial cancellations	Light plane cancellations Aircraft behind schedule owing to snow and ice conditions

[a]Warnings are the key to this classification. They provide excellent indicators because they are widely publicized.

TABLE I (*Cont.*)

4th Order (Nuisance)	5th Order (Minimal)
Any mention	No press coverage
Traffic movement slowed	
	No press coverage
Occasional	No press coverage
	No press coverage
Any mention	No press coverage
Any mention	No press coverage
Any mention	No press coverage
	No press coverage
Any mention for example, "slippery in spots" warning	No press coverage
Any mention	No press coverage
Any mention	No press coverage

Urban snow disruption is of two kinds: internal, when interchange within the city itself is hampered; and external, when conditions affect the relationships between a city and its tributary area. First-order disruptions may occur in either or both of these situations. So far as internal activity is concerned, the complete restriction of mobility is normally the most serious problem that can be attributed to snowfall, since most functions characteristic of urban areas require movement from one section of the city to another (journey to work, shopping, appointments, and so on).

An inspection of the effects of snow situations on other forms of urban and tributary activity serves to confirm transportation curtailments. For example, if schools were dismissed and a number of business establishments closed, we have verification that traffic flow throughout the city was greatly impeded. In the same vein, the postponement of athletic contests between teams from the city schools and those from other institutions in or near the tributary area provides additional evidence. Another inconvenience associated with snow concerns electric power and communications. On rare occasions a wet clinging snow may result in widespread breakage of cables and wires. In some cases electricity and telephone service may have been disrupted for extended periods, in which event first-order categorization seems warranted.

The hierarchy of disruption is arranged largely on an economic basis. First-order disruptions generally, but not always, cost more than second-order ones, second-order more than third, and so on. However, cost is not always an ideal measure. Thirty accidents do not necessarily result in a greater monetary loss than twenty, and the infrequent fatality associated with a lower-order disruption may produce a more serious loss than might occur in some first-order situations, depending on the value placed on human life.

A combined internal-external first-order or "paralysis" disruption generally finds a community in a state that resembles suspended animation. Vehicular and pedestrian movement is at a standstill; most stores, schools, and offices are either empty or closed. Air, highway, and rail transport are severely hampered, and on occasion the city is completely cut off from its surrounding area.

Perhaps an example will best serve to illustrate both the conditions that may obtain in first-order disruptions and the operation of the classification system. In Cheyenne, snow began to accumulate at 7:00 p.m. on April 8, 1959, and continued throughout the following day, reaching a total of 8.4 inches.[9] Curtailment of internal and external movement was severe enough to merit a combined first-order disruption rating. The wet snow, accompanied by winds of 15 to 25 miles an hour, halted city bus service and brought private transportation to a standstill. Abandoned automobiles blocked streets throughout the city. Traffic in and out of Cheyenne was confined mainly to emergency vehicles, attempting to get aid to the more than three hundred motorists stranded on United States Highway 30 to the west of the city. All outbound air traffic was grounded, and no planes were able to land at the municipal airport. City and rural schools closed their doors, and retail trade was heavily curtailed. The ineptness of the Cheyenne snow-control program was all too evident on this occasion. Crews began the removal job the evening of the ninth, too late to combat effectively the impact of the storm. It was like beginning sandbag operations after the stream has crested.

[9] *Wyoming Eagle*, (April 9, 1959), pp. 1-3.

Classification as second- or third-order disruption is based mainly on city motor-vehicle-accident data and on reports on road conditions in the tributary area filed by the State Highway Patrol. Other criteria include the condition of rail and air transportation, activity in the Central Business District, traffic jams, postponements, and school-attendance patterns. Disruption of the fourth order occurs when the impact of snow is not sufficient to cause a breakdown of the activities affected. A fifth-order classification designates an inconvenience so trivial as not to merit mention in the press.

ANALYSIS OF DISRUPTION

Disruption in the seven cities is summarized graphically in Figure 3. In general, lower-order disturbances ("inconvenience," "nuisance," and "minimal") are the rule, and paralyzing disruptions occur only at intervals. However, certain differences among the cities are conspicuous. The Midwestern communities tend to have a higher percentage of paralyzing and crippling situations than Casper and Cheyenne do. Both Wyoming sites and Winona (for a different reason) demonstrate a greater clustering of disruptions at the lower end of the scale. The profiles of the two largest cities, Milwaukee and Muskegon, are quite similar, and show greater concentrations of first- and second-order situations. Rapid City is also characterized by a higher proportion of crippling storms, though not of the paralysis variety.

Basically, frequency of disruption increases with annual accumulation of snow (Table II). The relationship is not perfect, but it is nevertheless significant. Muskegon, which has recorded an annual average of 105 inches of snow, has experienced 206 higher-order disruptions, or an average of 20.6 a

DISRUPTIONS ATTRIBUTABLE TO SNOWFALL IN SEVEN SELECTED SITES, 1953-1963

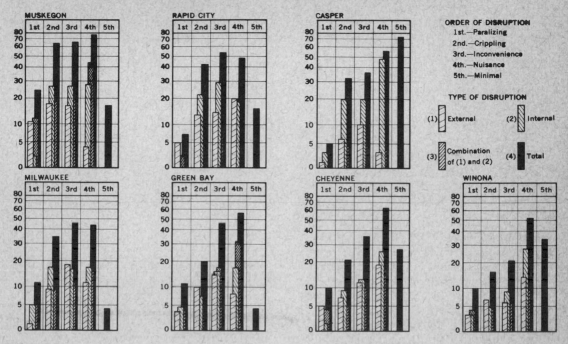

Figure 3.

year over the past ten years. Among the Midwestern sites with snowfall averages ranging from 37 to 44 inches, the pattern of snow-caused inconvenience is similar, with Winona the only exception.

The relationship between accumulation and disruption is less apparent when the Western sites are considered. Cheyenne (48 inches) averages 8.7 higher-order disruptions in the normal year and Casper (67 inches) experiences only 8.4. To search out the causes of this discrepancy, ten additional cities were investigated, on a ten-year sampling basis similar to that used for the original seven sites. Western sites in the sample were Spokane, Great Falls, Billings, Colorado Springs, and Albuquerque. To supplement the Midwestern sites, New York City, Fort Wayne, Des Moines, Springfield (Illinois), and Greensboro (North Carolina) were selected.

The graphic comparison of disruption and the snow environment suggests that basic differences exist between the Western disruption patterns and those characteristic of the areas east of the High Plains (Fig. 4). Most of the Western cities experience fewer snow problems. This generalization applies regardless of whether magnitude or intensity measurements are used.

Why do these differences exist? It appears that the most important factor is the lower water content associated with the majority of snowfalls in the West. The drier snows generally present a less formidable barrier to movement and hence on the average tend to

TABLE II

Relationship Between Snow Environment and Disruptions of the First, Second, and Third Order

Sites	Snow Environment		Disruptions in 10-year Period					
	Mean Annual Snowfall (in inches)	Snow Days per Year	No. of 1st, 2nd, and 3rd Order	Intensity per 10 Inches of Snow	No. of 1st and 2nd Order	Intensity per 10 Inches of Snow	No. of 1st Order	Intensity per 10 Inches of Snow
10-year averages								
Casper	67	18.5	84	1.25	36	.54	6	.09
Cheyenne	48	12.3	87	1.82	40	.83	14	.29
Spokane	54	13.5	129	2.39	70	1.30	25	.46
Great Falls	59	14.0	106	1.81	77	1.31	2	.03
Billings	54	13.2	99	1.83	55	1.02	15	.28
Albuquerque	11	3.3	34	3.27	19	1.83	5	.48
Colorado Springs	39	11.1	76	1.95	37	.95	11	.28
Muskegon	105	20.2	206	1.96	120	1.14	37	.35
Rapid City	37	11.2	119	3.21	56	1.51	9	.24
Milwaukee	44	10.2	118	2.68	55	1.25	16	.36
Green Bay	39	10.8	101	2.59	38	.97	15	.38
Winona	42	13.1	62	1.48	35	.83	14	.33
Springfield	24	9.1	76	3.18	44	1.83	16	.68
Des Moines	37	10.5	105	2.84	57	1.54	15	.41
Fort Wayne	32	9.4	119	3.72	72	2.25	16	.50
Greensboro	11	3.4	54	5.04	48	4.48	21	1.96
New York	30	7.2	96	3.20	71	2.36	42	1.39

cause less disruption.[10] However, this is not to say that in a given situation (for example, abundant snow buffeted by blizzard-force winds) dry snow is incapable of producing as much difficulty as the wetter variety.

A second factor that reduces disruption at the Western sites is the way in which the hazard is perceived. The view that regards snow as an element that must be coped with by the individual has produced a much more comprehensive range of personal adjustments

than are commonly found farther east.[11] Such adjustments are particularly effective at reducing disruption of the second and third orders. "Western perception," on the other hand, has contributed to the pathetic ineptitude of public adjustment in the region. This inability of the public sector to react has cre-

[10] Dry snow refers here to snow with a water content of less than one inch per ten inches of snow.

[11] A considerable percentage of those interviewed in the West carried emergency provisions such as canned food and blankets in their automobiles. Also, many more Westerners than Easterners equipped their cars with snow tires or chains, and made greater use of professional advice provided by the United States Weather Bureau and the State Highway Patrol.

TABLE III

Disruption in Relation to Physical Variables

Sites	Criteria (Averages)	Order of Disruption				
		1st	2nd	3rd	4th	5th
Muskegon	Depth (in.)	14.0	5.7	3.7	2.0	1.3
	Wind (mph)	15.2	12.1	11.2	11.7	13.8
	Water content[a]	16.1	16.2	16.2	12.1	15.2
	Number[b]	25	53	47	57	17
Rapid City	Depth	8.8	2.3	2.1	1.5	1.4
	Wind	24.8	15.5	11.7	13.3	15.8
	Water content	10	9.1	10.1	9.6	10.1
	Number	7	33	35	22	11
Milwaukee	Depth	12.0	4.2	2.7	1.6	1.4
	Wind	23.5	16.6	13.3	14.3	7.5
	Water content	11.3	10.9	11.7	12.1	12.2
	Number	11	26	34	29	4
Green Bay	Depth	6.9	2.9	2.7	1.8	1.4
	Wind	16.7	15.1	11.4	9.8	8.3
	Water content	10.5	11.7	10.6	10.3	10.2
	Number	11	14	33	42	4
Casper	Depth	7.7	4.2	3.1	3.1	1.7
	Wind	15.9	12.1	11.8	12.9	12.2
	Water content	13.7	14.9	16.8	13.6	14.8
	Number	5	27	29	57	69
Cheyenne	Depth	8.8	5.0	3.3	2.0	1.5
	Wind	25.6	15.6	14.3	13.7	13.6
	Water content	10.9	12.7	16.2	13.9	12.3
	Number	10	16	33	36	27
Winona	Depth	10.7	5.8	3.6	2.8	1.7
	Wind					
	Water content	11.6	11.2	10.2	12.9	12.6
	Number	10	11	19	44	34

[a]Amount of snow equivalent to one inch of water.

[b]Represents only the highest-order disruption for any snow day. For example, if a snow day is rated 1st order internal and 3rd order external, only the former is included in the sample. The fact that combination disruptions are not counted twice in these computations also decreases the number in the sample.

ated a greater vulnerability to severe snow conditions than exists in the East. As a result, the Western cities are no better than their Eastern counterparts in reducing first-order disruption, and under most circumstances their recovery period is considerably longer.

The graphs also suggest that disruption, though it increases with annual snowfall, does

AN ANALYSIS OF SNOW ENVIRONMENT—DISRUPTION RELATIONSHIPS

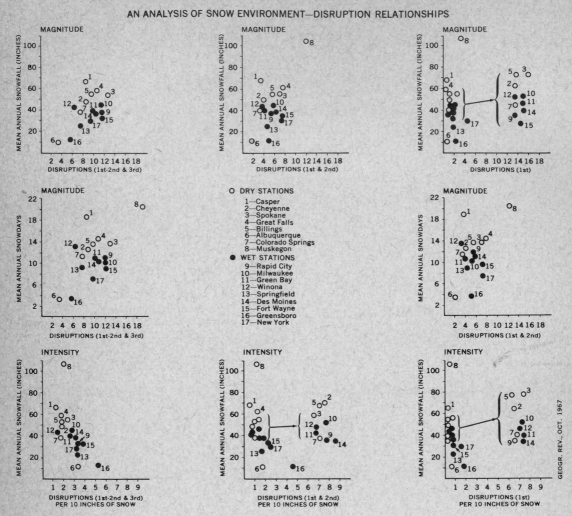

Figure 4.

so at a diminishing rate. Inversely, the intensity of disruption decreases with increasing annual accumulations. The matched pairs of Alburquerque-Greensboro and Cheyenne-Milwaukee are clearly demonstrative of such a pattern. A larger sample of north-south cities would probably further validate this relationship.

SPECIFIC CAUSES OF DISRUPTION

The relationship between disruption and snow depth, water content, and wind in individual storms at the seven original sites is presented in Table III. The data illustrate a strong correlation between depth of snow and curtailment of human activity. Storms that resulted in first-order situations almost invari-

TABLE IV

Effect of Wind in Promoting Disruption

Sites	Wind Velocity	Order of Disruption			
		1st	2nd and 3rd	4th and 5th	Total
Muskegon	Data incomplete				
Rapid City	≥ 15	9	48	20	77
	< 15	0	62	54	116
Milwaukee	≥ 15	13	58	21	92
	< 15	3	44	38	85
Green Bay	≥ 15	14	32	15	61
	< 15	1	54	75	130
Casper	≥ 15	4	26	43	73
	< 15	2	52	87	141
Cheyenne	≥ 15	13	35	39	87
	< 15	1	38	67	106
Winona	Data unavailable				

ably registered accumulations of five inches or more. Only on rare occasions — for instance, a sleet storm, drifting of snow on the ground from a previous fall, extremely high winds — did lesser accumulations produce widespread havoc.

Most of the snowfalls that caused first-order disruption accumulated during twenty-four-hour periods. Such rapid falls generally resulted in conditions that were extremely difficult to deal with. Only in Muskegon did a significant number of paralysis situations develop over a period of two or more days; on several occasions it snowed continuously for as long as nine days, creating conditions of severity unknown at any of the other sites. However, even during some of these prolonged falls, crews were able to prevent complete curtailment by maintaining operations around the clock.

Although deep snow and severe disruption are strongly correlated, deep snow by itself often tends to produce only moderate, and sometimes even minimal, disruption. Most accumulations exceeding five inches were accompanied by winds of more than fifteen miles per hour. However, on many occasions when winds were light and the snow was dry, the problems were substantially reduced.

Wind. A significant statistical difference exists between the impact of snow in association with winds of fifteen miles per hour or more, and that accompanied by winds of lesser velocity.[12] Nearly all first-order occurrences developed with wind velocities in excess of fifteen miles per hour (Table IV). On the other hand, lower-order disruptions char-

[12] For the purposes of this study a statistically significant association is one (measured by chi-square, representing the sum of the differences of the observed distribution and one that might be expected if there were no association between the given variables) that had only one chance in twenty or less of arising purely by sampling variability or by chance (.05 level of significance).

acteristically were associated with lower wind velocities.[13]

A reexamination of Table III reveals average wind velocities to be substantially higher in first-order situations than in lower-order disruptions. Winds of more than fifteen miles per hour are common in first-order disruptions at all sites, and exceed twenty-three miles per hour at Milwaukee, Rapid City, and Cheyenne. In addition, a precipitous drop in wind velocities is associated with second- and third-order cases at all sites, and particularly in these three cities.

Further evidence in support of the impact of high winds was obtained through personal interviews at four of the seven sites. Respondents were asked to select from a list of six types of snow conditions the two they felt presented the most serious hazard in their area. The responses are summarized in Table V. Snow in association with high winds was ranked as the most severe type of hazard in Cheyenne, Rapid City, and Casper, while deep snow in itself was given low priority. The respect afforded ground blizzards in those locations also demonstrates the role of wind. Such evidence, though not conclusive, does substantiate the data procured from newspapers and public records. It also indicates an awareness on the part of the respondents of what proved to be the most significant cause of disruption.

Water Content. Snow made heavier and stickier owing to relatively greater moisture content often tends to present a more formidable hazard, as we have seen. In Cheyenne it was found that wetter snow resulted in a considerably greater amount of disruption.[14] Although a statistically significant difference between the impact of "wet" and "dry" snow was not characteristic of the other sites, it appears, again, that moisture content of snow is responsible for areal differences in disruption. The Midwestern and Eastern cities, where higher-order disruptions are considerably more frequent, experience snowfall which on the average is about 50 percent wetter than that recorded at the Western sites.

Temperature. The role of air temperature is difficult to measure.[15] An analysis of high, low, and mean temperatures provides little evidence concerning the function of temperature in maximizing or minimizing disruption. Mean temperatures associated with all orders of disruption did not vary more than four degrees at any of the sites.

Temporal Variation. Another element that tends to complicate and obscure the relationship between disruption and the snow environment is the time of occurrence. Temporal variation as used here refers to the rate of fall and the time of day when it occurs. The rate of fall governs the ability of snow-control operations to keep pace; the time of fall often means the difference between a fourth-order and a second-order disruption. For example, three inches immediately preceding the morning rush hour can cause great difficulty, whereas the same amount accumulating during the late evening or early morning hours might result in minimal inconvenience. Week-

---

[13] Chi-square tests were significant at the .01 level of probability (that is, there is less than one chance in a hundred that the association is attributable to chance) at all sites except Casper and Muskegon.

[14] The chi-square test was significant at the .01 level of probability.

[15] At temperatures below 15°F salt has little effect on ice, and when the temperature approaches 0°F even calcium chloride is ineffective. A temperature hovering around the freezing mark is critical, for variation in either direction can make the difference between very slippery or merely wet pavements.

TABLE V

Ranking of Severe Hazards by Persons Interviewed

Sites	Number of Persons Interviewed	Number Making Estimate	Snow and High Winds	Snow and Sleet	Snow Over Ice	Ground Blizzard	Extremely Deep Snow	Snow and Extreme Cold
Cheyenne	43	43	1	3	2	5	4	6
Casper	45	45	1	6	3	2	4	5
Rapid City	62	55	1	3	2	4	5	6
Winona	21	20	2	1	4	6	3	5

end snows produce less internal disruption, but generally more external difficulties, and the reverse is true of snows that occur during the week.

THE FACTORS COMBINED

To summarize the impact of snow and associated weather conditions on human activity, probability matrixes have been constructed for the Western and Midwestern sites (Table VI). The data demonstrate the relative contribution to disruption of snow depth, wind, water content, and temporal variation.

Fundamentally, the matrix for the Midwestern sites illustrates that the probability of severe disruption increases with depth. High winds are shown to be an important catalyst in promoting the hazard at all snow depths. For example, the odds against a three-inch snow causing a crippling disruption are five to one; add wind and they drop to two and a half to one. Wet snows are not consistent in promoting additional havoc in the Midwest, but this is because most snows there are fairly wet. Expectably, weekend snows are generally less disruptive than their weekday counterparts. In the West the role of depth and wind are also apparent from the matrix. Furthermore, wet snows appear to cause significantly more difficulty than dry ones do.

THE ROLE OF ADJUSTMENT AND ATTITUDE

Most cities that lie within the "snow belt" (the area north of 35°N, excluding the Pacific states) have some form of snow-control program. Expenditures for this service range from the $22 million spent by New York City in 1963-1964 to the few hundreds of dollars appropriated annually by many of the smaller communities in the southern part of the belt. The total expenditures for snow control in the United States can only be estimated. The American Public Works Association has been using a figure of $100 million a year, but considers this to be much too low, especially since salt costs alone run to $44 million.[16] The following statement indicates the difficulties encountered in compiling figures for snow removal costs: "One of the main things we uncovered in our study was the general lack of basic operating and especially cost data. Surveys we made were generally inconclusive because data received were not comparable. We obviously were comparing apples with pears. The fact that data on snow opera-

---

[16] Written communication from Robert K. Lockwood, assistant director of Technical Services, American Public Works Association, May 4, 1965.

TABLE VI

Probability of Experiencing Disruption from Snow and Selected Associated Weather Conditions

Depth in Inches	No. of Snow Days	Depth Alone					Winds of ≥ 15 mph					Water Equivalents of ≥ .10/inch					Weekend Snows (time factor)				
		1st	2nd	3rd	4th	5th	1st	2nd	3rd	4th	5th	1st	2nd	3rd	4th	5th	1st	2nd	3rd	4th	5th
											MIDWESTERN SITES										
1 – 1.99	341	.00	.10	.25	.48	.17	.00	.20	.28	.44	.08	.00	.11	.30	.54	.05	.00	.08	.22	.48	.22
2 – 2.99	159	.02	.20	.31	.38	.09	.04	.32	.36	.28	.00	.02	.22	.39	.30	.07	.00	.21	.34	.40	.05
3 – 3.99	86	.04	.19	.44	.31	.02	.08	.41	.44	.07	.00	.06	.23	.39	.30	.02	.02	.16	.46	.34	.02
4 – 4.99	51	.04	.26	.39	.31	.00	.17	.58	.17	.08	.00	.08	.25	.37	.30	.00	.04	.29	.35	.32	.00
5 – 5.99	45	.07	.44	.44	.05	.00	.10	.70	.20	.00	.00	.12	.55	.30	.03	.00	.04	.45	.42	.09	.00
6 – 6.99	30	.20	.43	.23	.14	.00	.30	.40	.30	.00	.00	.27	.43	.20	.10	.00	.14	.47	.19	.20	.00
7 – 7.99	30	.27	.40	.30	.03	.00	.44	.38	.18	.00	.00	.38	.38	.21	.03	.00	.20	.42	.35	.03	.00
8 – 8.99	8	.13	.50	.37	.00	.00	.33	.67	.00	.00	.00	.25	.50	.25	.00	.00	—	—	—	—	—
9 – 9.99	12	.50	.33	.17	.00	.00	1.00	.00	.00	.00	.00	.60	.20	.20	.00	.00	.50	.25	.25	.00	.00
10 & over	65	.52	.42	.06	.00	.00	.64	.36	.00	.00	.00	.54	.42	.04	.00	.00	.46	.48	.06	.00	.00
											WESTERN SITES										
1 – 1.99	151	.00	.06	.11	.33	.50	.00	.08	.06	.44	.42	.00	.07	.21	.33	.39	.00	.05	.10	.40	.45
2 – 2.99	73	.03	.15	.22	.38	.22	.07	.11	.29	.32	.21	.05	.10	.15	.45	.25	.02	.08	.24	.34	.32
3 – 3.99	45	.02	.09	.39	.35	.15	.06	.18	.35	.35	.06	.00	.20	.20	.30	.30	.00	.15	.35	.40	.10
4 – 4.99	26	.04	.27	.19	.50	.00	.08	.42	.08	.42	.00	.00	.25	.50	.25	.00	.04	.18	.24	.54	.00
5 – 5.99	15	.20	.33	.27	.20	.00	.00	.38	.38	.24	.00	.25	.00	.50	.25	.00	.17	.33	.25	.25	.00
6 – 6.99	13	.00	.38	.38	.24	.00	.00	.20	.60	.20	.00	.00	.50	.00	.50	.00	.00	.20	.40	.40	.00
7 – 7.99	17	.18	.30	.30	.22	.00	.50	.33	.17	.00	.00	.38	.38	.24	.00	.00	.25	.38	.12	.25	.00
8 – 8.99	1	1.00	.00	.00	.00	.00	1.00	.00	.00	.00	.00	1.00	.00	.00	.00	.00	—	—	—	—	—
9 – 9.99	1	.00	1.00	.00	.00	.00	.00	1.00	.00	.00	.00	.00	1.00	.00	.00	.00	—	—	—	—	—
10 & over	13	.39	.39	.15	.07	.00	.67	.33	.00	.00	.00	.67	.33	.00	.00	.00	.25	.75	.00	.00	.00

tions are limited is understandable. Snow is treated as an emergency and record keeping has a secondary priority."[17] But costs are only one measure of man's attempt to counteract the snow hazard. Other important facets of control comprise organization, communication with the public, coordination among city agencies, and among state, city, and suburban agencies.

It is impossible within the scope of the present investigation to assess precisely the positive effects of public adjustment to the snow hazard. However, by analyzing and comparing the snow-control programs and the disruption patterns of the cities studied, a number of insights can be gained.

Snow- and ice-control operations at the Midwestern sites run the gamut from very good to marginal.[18] By present technological standards the programs of Milwaukee, Muskegon, and Winona rank high. The Green Bay program is better than average; that of Rapid City is definitely marginal. By Midwestern or Eastern standards, neither Casper nor Cheyenne is unduly concerned with snow and ice control.

Since the snow environments at Green Bay and Rapid City are basically similar, it is possible to gauge the effect that adjustment has on the impact of the hazard. Green Bay spends more money per capita, has an efficient alert system, and has a well-organized course of action that calls for operations to begin *during* the storm when accumulations reach two inches or more. On the other hand, Rapid City has no formal plan, and generally

postpones action until after the snowfall has ceased. Moreover, the city's police department is apparently unwilling to enforce snow-emergency regulations.

The more efficient snow-control operation at Green Bay has resulted in holding down higher-order disruptions to 2.59 per ten inches of snow, as compared with the figure of 3.21 for Rapid City (Table II). In percentage terms, Green Bay experiences less than 80 percent as much disruption. Whether or not this reduction can be attributed solely to snow-control differences is a question that can be answered only by the investigation of snow problems at many additional sites, or perhaps by a concentrated economic analysis of one or two cities. It is interesting that nearly half of those interviewed in Rapid City considered the city program to be woefully ineffective. The majority were in favor of immediate improvement, another indication of the general dissatisfaction with the current quality of snow-control service.

Newspaper coverage of storms in Milwaukee and Muskegon revealed that their alert and well-organized public works departments minimized the impact of snow on numerous occasions. Many first-order situations failed to materialize in Muskegon owing to the diligence of the city and county officials.

The Winona program presents an opportunity to measure community attitudes toward the disruptive impact of snow. Snow control in that city was viewed as "excellent" to "very good" by more than 80 percent of those queried. In addition, fewer than 10 percent felt improvements in the program were warranted. If these views can be accepted as factual, and not simply as statements of community pride, it would seem that Winonans are satisfied with the present level of snow-caused inconvenience which their city experiences.

---

[17] *Ibid.*

[18] The quality of a snow-control program can be evaluated on the basis of expenditures, alert systems, deployment of men and equipment, organization, public relations, and the degree of cooperation that exists among the various agencies necessary to its success.

The Winona case suggests that the "satis-ficer" notion is of considerable value in accounting for the curious relationship that exists between man and the snow hazard.[19] Perhaps the esthetic values of snow make us somehow reluctant to wage all-out war against it. If the "optimizer" approach were applied to the snow hazard, it would emphasize strategy designed to eliminate completely the negative impact of snow. Further evidence to support the applicability of the satisficer concept comes from the field of snow control. Innovations designed to improve snow control have lagged behind, and those that have emerged are being adopted very slowly. Essentially we are coping with snow in much the same way we did thirty years ago. Our attitudes are simply reflected in our actions. If demand existed for real innovations in snow control, they would be forthcoming. Most of the improvements developed thus far (radiant heat, snow melters, street flushing devices) have been rejected owing to their high cost and to the lack of knowledge concerning the losses attributable to snow.

Individuals spend considerably more to protect themselves and their property from the snow hazard than they spend as members of the public sector. Snow tires alone cost the citizens of Rapid City, Casper, and Cheyenne combined more than $600,000 annually.[20] Added to that are expenditures for tire chains, shovels, snow brooms and scrapers, sand, salt, and numerous ice-melting compounds. Since people are willing to funnel these amounts into personal snow control, it seems

reasonable to suppose that they would favor additional public expenditure. In fact, the majority of those queried did support the idea of program improvement. However, although an occasional clamor is heard after an unusually severe winter, memories tend to be short when the time for increased appropriations is at hand. This pattern is analogous to the attitudes that often prevail with respect to other hazards, particularly floods.[21]

Attitudes can promote or reduce disruption, largely through their effects on adjustment. Most of the persons queried in the seven cities tended to underestimate the hazard potential of snow, considering it to be more of a nuisance than a serious problem[22] — as, indeed, it is most of the time. In the case of minor storms, these attitudes probably lessen disruption; that is, people exhibit little concern for two, three, or four inches of snow and go about their business normally. On the other hand, they are apt to be grossly unprepared for a severe storm, and thus experience substantially more disruption.

THE ROLE OF PERCEPTION

Man's attitude toward the snow hazard can be partly explained in terms of his perception of the phenomenon, but this perception is difficult to measure. Awareness of any element varies not only among individuals and groups, but with the same individuals at different

[19] Herbert A. Simon, *Models of Man* (2nd ed., New York, 1957), pp. 196-200.

[20] This amount is derived from the number of car registrations and the percentage of vehicle owners who say they install snow tires. The estimate allows for a tire life of three years.

[21] See, for example, Henry C. Hart, "Crisis, Community, and Consent in Water Politics," *Law and Contemporary Problems*, Vol. 22 (1957), pp. 510-37.

[22] This statement does not apply to Muskegon, Milwaukee, and Green Bay, where extensive interviewing was not conducted. There is reason to believe that people hold the hazard in higher esteem in the Midwest, as evidenced by the existence of more sophisticated snow-control programs in that area.

points in time and space. "In any society, individuals of similar cultural background, who speak the same language, still perceive and understand the world differently."[23] "The specialized literature is replete with examples of difference in hazard perception" among the experts themselves.[24] Even with these drawbacks, the study of perception can be extremely valuable in identifying the geographical implications of the milieu, particularly that part of it which contains an uncertain hazard element.

In talking with people in the various cities a tendency was detected, especially in the West, to minimize the potential danger associated with snow. Statements such as these were common: "The legendary blizzard of 1949 was some sort of oddity that will probably never happen again."[25] "Snow doesn't bother or interfere with us or our business." "I view snow and ice as a challenge, something to break the monotony of the everyday routine." Perhaps the slogan emblazoned on the façade of the Engineering Building at the University of Wyoming is symbolic of prevailing attitudes. It reads: "Strive On, the Control of Nature Is Won, Not Given."

Perception of any hazard is based largely on experience. The slower pace of life in the Western cities may account in part for the rather low priority granted to the snow hazard there. This does not explain the views that prevail with respect to the "blizzard of 1949," or to the other storms since that have resulted in loss of life and widespread disruption. As many as three or four first-order disruptions may occur during the course of any winter season, yet the population remains largely apathetic and ill prepared, at least as a public body.[26] An examination of additional sites, particularly those with only small and highly variable amounts of snow, should provide greater insight concerning snow-hazard perception. "On the spot" interviews should also be useful.

FUTURE NEEDS

The snow hazard demands more attention. Additional research is needed, both in the physical parameters — accumulations, moisture content, wind velocities, and so on — and in the evaluation of local adjustments at the private and public levels.[27]

An even more pressing need is for improved public service in the field of snow control. A single storm can cost any of the cities investigated considerably more than they spend on snow removal each year. Organization, coordination, and public relations are integral parts of more effective snow-control programs. Disruption could be substantially reduced if more funds were available, and if present funds were more efficiently allocated.

23 David Lowenthal, "Geography, Experience, and Imagination: Towards a Geographical Epistemology," *Annals Assn. of Amer. Geogrs.*, Vol. 51 (1961), pp. 241-60; reference on p. 255.

24 Ian Burton and Robert W. Kates, "The Perception of Natural Hazards in Resource Management," *Natural Resources Journ.*, Vol. III (1964). pp. 412-41; reference on p. 424.

25 For a discussion of the problems associated with the blizzard of 1948-1949, see Wesley Calef, "The Winter of 1948-49 in the Great Plains," *Annals Assn. of Amer. Geogrs.*, Vol. XL (1950), pp. 267-92.

26 The political ideology in Wyoming and western South Dakota that stresses the role of the individual may be reflected in the inefficiency of public snow-removal programs. However, speculation along this line is difficult to substantiate.

27 The writer is currently engaged in further research on this matter at sites in the south-central and southeastern United States. An analysis of disruption patterns in these areas should provide answers concerning the benefits to be expected from the maintenance of various levels of snow-control programs.

An accurate benefit-cost analysis might produce guidelines for intelligent decisions on expenditures.

We are confronted by an interesting challenge. As a technically advanced urban society we have at our disposal the organizational and inventive abilities to deal successfully with snow, a menace that often severely hampers activity in our major centers. Why do we not use them?

39

Let Us Make Our

Cities Efficient

Eric Beecroft

It is an astonishing fact that, in a century dominated by the idea of productive efficiency, the uneconomic organization of our cities has caused so little concern. Today, however, there are signs that the cost of blight, congestion, ribbon development and suburban sprawl is understood better than ever before and that the public's courage is being screwed up to tackle urban redevelopment in a very big way.

The time is past when traffic congestion can be viewed as a minor inconvenience — as part of the price we must pay for all our other conveniences. It remains one of the greatest wasters of man-hours, a major impediment both to our industry and to our recreation. Precise estimates of loss in traffic are difficult to make; but in 1953 on the basis of Montreal experience, Mr. C.-E. Campeau, now Director of the Planning Department in

Reprinted from the Canadian Imperial Bank of Commerce *Commercial Letter* (October, 1955) by permission.

that City, concluded that loss from delays of trucking alone might be as high as $30 million annually. Mr. Campeau drew attention at the same time to the fact that traffic congestion in our central cities "results not so much from people living *in* the cities as from more people living *outside* them."

The basic remedies for congestion, therefore, are not the makeshift control and parking schemes which account for so great a part of the debating time of public bodies and of space in the press, but imaginative planning of the entire physical growth of the metropolis — in transport, industry and residential development.

In this age of high new capital investment, expanding economy and productive efficiency, industrialists try to plan a long way ahead in terms of the physical environment of their enterprise. They are attracted to cities which are taking some care to establish industrial zones, to assure adequate transport and warehousing facities and to provide economical and attractive home sites, recreation centers and other amenities of daily life. Cities having natural advantages for industry have found that long-term planning helps to exploit these advantages more fully and pays human dividends to employers and employees alike in satisfying a deeply-felt need for civic pride and good neighborliness.

Those directly concerned with the building industry are examining the causes of disorderly growth. The Canadian Construction Association has placed itself firmly behind "long-term community planning to achieve and maintain reasonable standards of housing and community development through the provision by appropriate governmental authorities of adequate planning controls, personnel and facilities, especially at the local level . . ."

As the general state of the Canadian eco-

nomy is examined with a view toward sustaining a high level of activity, the question "How are we to maintain the present rate of building?" is a vital one. Among builders as well as consumers, it is leading to a closer study of the economics of urban expansion. Hitherto this has tended to be a residual problem — a headache left over for local government — while house builders and housebuyers went single-mindedly about their immediate business. An uneasy feeling is now developing that the backlog of utility financing left to the taxpayers as such may compel a slowing up in the extension of municipal services and put the brakes on new building.

Indeed a great part of the new concern for city planning results from the bitter experience of city authorities in the past 15 years of fast growth. Everyone concerned with the housing of a rapidly-increasing population has been compelled to promote better planning of all the utilities upon which housing depends. The rates of growth shown in the accompanying table can be readily translated into a measure of the task imposed on the governments of our towns.

New housing has required not only the expenditure (mainly private) on land, building materials and labour, but a vast public investment in sewers, water supply, drainage, paved streets and power lines — not to mention schools, buses, fire and police protection and a great many other services. Beset by demands for such services from every quarter, municipal authorities have been forced by acute financial stringency to introduce orderliness and foresight into their programming of public works. Out of this experience, especially in the areas of most rapid growth, has come a determination to prevent the development of scattered residential areas which are costly to equip.

Let us look at the causes of "fringe development." In the absence of controlled growth, and faced by a grave shortage of housing, thousands of people have settled on unserviced land outside the built-up areas — in many cases outside the organized municipalities. Some just want to get away from the crowded city. Others of low income are attracted by cheaper land; many of them can build their own homes without conflicting with building codes. For many people, the lack of sewers and public water supply may seem, for the time being at least, to be minor handicaps compared to the high costs of urban life.

But, at time goes on, with the pressure of population, the sprawling suburbs become a trying problem for the public authorities; some of them eventually have to be serviced for more intensive use. In some areas, the land may be of such a character as to be unsuitable for underground utilities except at excessive cost. Others, suitable for industrial use, cannot be made available for that purpose without the removal of scattered homes already built. In still others, where a replotting is desirable for intensive residential development, the way may be blocked by existing uses. Still more expense is added by requirements for schools, fire and police protection, health services and other collective facilities. Providing such services for scattered communities represents a great financial waste; and, to make matters worse, under our antiquated system of municipal boundaries, the problem of providing the services often falls between two or more autonomous local governments, rural and urban.

It is not surprising that hundreds of municipalities are finally taking or considering measures to ensure that new developments should be compactly planned as successive extensions of the main urban area and that such areas of development should be selected for their most appropriate use. It follows that other less appropriate uses are forbidden, but this kind of negative control comes to be accepted where it is seen as a necessary means to promote a sound positive program of development. Effective planning controls are now preventing sporadic uneconomic development on the fringes of some of our cities. A great deal of wasteful spending on public services is saved, and to this extent, it becomes possible to finance a greater volume of residential and other development.

A science of land subdivision is finally being developed to enable us as property-owners and tax-payers to save financially by better planning. A well-planned neighborhood, for example, has a street system in which an important distinction is made between arteries, circulation streets, and local access streets. The less travelled streets require less heavy construction. The traditional "grid" system is expensive because every street is a "through" street and must be constructed as such. Economies can be effected because local access streets may need neither curbs nor sidewalks. In terms of a typical single-family house, such a saving is around $250-$300.

Costly street widenings are plaguing almost all our growing towns. If this is to be avoided in future, the major arteries must be laid out well in advance of urban growth. Planning must also provide that *traffic arteries* do not become used as *commercial* streets, cluttered with local shoppers and parking. The commerce of the country as a whole is gravely impeded by this confusion of local market traffic with through traffic flow.

Modern town planning, with judicious use of a master plan, is a prerequisite for the new form of shopping center, as it is for an efficient network of roads. Shopping centers require careful planning to spot the strategic locations of these little nuclei of trade. This characteristic of modern cities is probably here to stay — immensely preferable to the long ribbons of commercial frontage which are one of the most ugly and inefficient manifestations of unplanned urban growth. Ribbon development throttles commerce. Yet, in the absence of planning, our main highways are inevitably lined with stores, filling stations, hot dog stands and restaurants. Competition forces this kind of development, even though it is detrimental to our economy as a whole. Setback regulations are a partial remedy; by widening the ribbons, they accelerate traffic. But a more basic remedy is the modern planned neighborhood and shopping center, removed from the main traffic arteries.

One of the advantages of neighborhood planning then is that it frees "through" traffic and enables us to go to church and school and do much of our shopping without using arterial highways. Good neighborhood planning (as at Don Mills near Toronto, Wildwood in Greater Winnipeg, Fraserview in Vancouver, Manor Park in Ottawa, or the many new neighborhoods in Edmonton) attracts higher or moderate income families and holds them there, to the benefit of local business people and residents alike. For low income areas, good neighborhood planning is not only a desirable objective for the residents themselves; it is the best security against heavy public costs of protection for health, welfare, policing and fire. From the taxpayer's viewpoint, one of the most uneconomic features of the city is the blighted slum. Assessments are low and service costs are high.

Many of the older American cities, aided by federal legislation, are developing urban renewal programs of great magnitude to replace old, inadequate residential and commercial areas with new. Slum clearance is a part of a still larger program to provide not only decent low-rental housing but industrial and commercial facilities suited to modern needs, and civic centres, parks, recreation areas and throughways. In our own older and still-expanding cities, particularly Toronto, Montreal, Halifax, St. John's and Vancouver, a great need and opportunity is seen to make more efficient use of central space. Large projects are being conceived by both private investors and public authorities. Indeed it seems safe to predict that in the next 15 years: (1) urban redevelopment will be one of the largest fields of investment for private and public funds; and (2) it will be accomplished by bold and ingenious combinations of public and private initiative.

At first there may be painful struggles over the respective roles of public and private enterprise. Both may be hampered, not only by lack of precedents for dealing with such large and complex situations involving difficult issues regarding property rights and welfare problems, but by the absence of satisfactory enabling legislation. A great deal of patience and imagination will be required to devise appropriate legislation and administrative methods to reconcile the many technical, financial and social factors.

The city planning department can play a role that is very useful to all concerned. Its object should be to look at the scene as a whole in day-to-day teamwork with all the operating and financing agencies and, by so doing, to help city authorities to see the full significance of the separate projects of streets, housing, industries, commerce and transportation.

An immediate practical problem in redevelopment is the assembly of central area land. Such assembly of land has to be done on a large scale and with very careful planning. Otherwise the new development, by failing to generate new growth, may result only

TREND OF URBAN GROWTH IN TERMS OF HOUSING STOCK 1951-1955 *

Centre	Housing Stock in Units 1951	Estimate 1955	Annual Rate of Increase 1951-1955 %	No. of Years Required to Double at this Rate
Metropolitan Areas				
Calgary	40,235	50,671	5.77	12.0
Edmonton	46,395	59,614	6.27	11.0
Halifax	29,640	33,891	3.35	20.7
Hamilton	68,640	77,567	3.05	22.7
London	32,835	37,793	3.52	19.7
Montreal	334,705	394,138	4.09	17.0
Ottawa	66,265	74,282	2.85	24.3
Quebec	54,930	60,993	2.47	28.1
Saint John, N.B.	19,735	20,574	1.04	66.7
St. John's, Nfld.	12,995	14,598	2.91	23.8
Toronto	273,200	322,053	4.11	16.9
Vancouver	153,975	175,257	3.24	21.4
Victoria	31,620	35,405	2.83	24.5
Windsor	41,595	45,674	2.34	29.6
Winnipeg	95,955	106,906	2.64	26.3
Sub-Total	1,302,720	1,509,416	3.68	18.8
Other Major Cities				
Brantford	14,960	15,904	1.53	45.3
Fort William } Port Arthur }	19,550	21,005	1.79	38.7
Guelph	8,093	9,238	3.31	20.9
Kingston	13,349	14,121	1.40	49.5
Kitchener	16,700	19,050	3.29	21.1
Moncton	10,989	11,603	1.36	51.0
Oshawa	13,426	15,112	2.96	23.4
Peterborough	10,785	11,787	2.22	31.2
St. Catharines	17,485	18,173	0.96	72.2
Sarnia	11,100	12,920	3.80	18.2
Sault Ste. Marie	8,838	10,604	2.83	24.5
Shawinigan Falls	10,628	11,193	1.30	53.3
Sherbrooke, P.Q.	13,077	14,176	2.02	34.3
Sudbury	15,864	16,943	1.64	42.3
Sydney } Glace Bay }	21,418	22,037	0.71	97.6
Trois Rivières	14,079	15,178	1.88	37.9
Sub-Total	220,341	239,044	2.04	34.0
Total	1,523,061	1,748,460	3.45	20.1

* Based on 1951 Census and estimates of Central Mortgage and Housing Corporation.

in a waste of investment, public and private. This principle — *that the investment risk is minimized by the scale of the new projects and by carefully envisaging them in their long-term relationship to one another and to the entire environment* — is generally accepted. But the actual working out of a land assembly procedure may require some revisions in our traditional thinking. In practice, private investors are finding it difficult to acquire all of the land needed for a well-planned redevelopment project. They tend to look then to the public power to acquire land.

Since, in some Canadian jurisdictions, a municipality cannot acquire land except for a public purpose (a park or city hall, for example), it cannot assist an otherwise sound project by acquiring the land and leasing or reselling it to private developers. There appears also to be a limitation in present federal legislation. The National Housing Act, which authorizes the Government to share the costs of a city in buying up blighted areas, limits this authority to the assembling of blighted land for low-rental housing or for public purposes. This is good as far as it goes, but it is evident that, from the viewpoint of sound planning, low-rental housing is only one of the objects — however important — in urban redevelopment. And indeed low-rental housing projects may go forward much faster if they are viewed as a phase of the larger schemes of redevelopment.*

A challenge to investors and governments to tackle redevelopment on a large scale was thrown down by the Hon. H. R. Winters in a recent speech at Montreal at a large joint conference of the Community Planning Association of Canada and the American Society of Planning Officials. This problem, he said, could "never be solved lot by lot and piece by piece." The interest of private investors he thought would be enlisted by "the prospect of a scale of operation that will change the character of large areas." "I am not speaking," he added, "about streets or blocks, much less parts of them. This is not minor surgery but major operations. . . . Planning and the acquisition of land on the scale I have suggested may call for public action. But if redevelopment is more than a salvage operation, if the older parts of our cities have a vital role to play in the whole urban structure, then their redevelopment can properly be made the object of private investment too."

In the same speech, and in connection with new housing, Mr. Winters estimated that in the next 20 years, $25 billion would be in-

* *Editor's Note.* The *National Housing Act* has been amended substantially since to permit "the larger schemes of redevelopment".

The table opposite should not be taken as a prediction of future growth. The two right-hand columns, however, suggest the magnitude of the task which our municipal tax-payers undertook in servicing new housing. Even if the rate of housing construction were to drop considerably, the problem would remain acute. For besides the servicing of new areas, our municipalities are still burdened with the costs of much haphazard, uneconomic real estate development which is already completed or underway.

No one wants the rate of housing construction to diminish as a means of solving the economic plight of our tax-payer. It must be maintained if we are to have an adequate supply of decent housing. The remedy lies in seeing to it that our future residential sites are selected and subdivided not only with an eye to making them more attractive but on the basis of sound economic principles.

vested in raw land and residential structures and at least $2 billion in residential water and sewer mains and frontage roads (to say nothing of the trunk services required and the additions to central water and sewage disposal plant). This estimate included nothing for schools, churches, hospitals and other institutions. The impact of this investment on Canada over the next two decades would be enormous and would call for vital well-thought-out decisions as to the location of industry within cities, the location and layout of housing areas, the location and design of schools, the routing of roads, the extension of utilities and indeed all those matters which together determine the efficiency of our cities.

Mr. Winters then appealed to city planners to direct their thought to the problem of making the city a more efficient economic unit. There was a danger, he said, in breaking the problem down into parts (traffic, suburban sprawl, slum clearance). Unless the whole unit of the city was envisaged, the parts could not be dealt with soundly. There was also a danger that, by emphasizing beautification and social improvement, we would divert attention from the economic processes which form the basis of the city's existence.

Can we expect a conflict between the concept of the city as an economic unit and the concept of its beautification and social improvement? It seems rather academic to debate such a question at the present stage when many of our cities are both inefficient and ugly and, in some of their quarters, debasing to human character. If our ideals of economic efficiency, welfare and aesthetics are conceived in the broadest terms, we may expect no basic conflict.

It must be admitted that the City Beautiful idea which came into vogue a generation or two ago might have been more successful in practice if it had been accompanied by a determined attack of the city's rehabilitation as an economic unit. Similarly, we can probably expect that faster progress will be made toward elimination of slum-fostered evils if we enlarge our vision of the whole city as a field for enlightened investment.

Our cities have greatly increased their technical staffs to cope with their planning problems. In few places now are there any false conceptions of the professionatl planner as a destroyer of individual freedom. The demand for the planner is in fact outrunning the supply; and Canadian cities, once they have established planning departments, tend to retain or enlarge them. In most of our cities, where planning departments have been established for some time, they have been geared intimately into the technical teamwork of the administration so that they serve and are served by all departments in developing a coherent program for the physical development of the city. As part of the administrative system, the City planning staff acts as a kind of intelligence branch. Detailed plans of the whole city are made available to guide executives and elected officials in making important decisions. A master plan of development outlines a desirable program of public works to be carried out and makes possible systematic capital budgeting.

City planning also helps to bring into balance the various purposes for which cities exist. The inhabitants are both producers and consumers. As producers we are concerned with the total efficiency and productivity of the operating plant: public services and transportation must be economic and free of wasteful interruptions. As consumers, we all want a city that is spacious, beautiful and attractive to live in; we want as much luxury as possible for our home-buyer's or taxpayer's dollar. The ultimate decisions as to what we get in urban physical development, urban beauty and urban welfare are made by our elected bodies on the basis of the demands made by their constituents and the technical advice they receive from their staffs. We are making gradual progress in both these respects as urban growth is directly examined and better understood.

Sherbrooke District, Edmonton

As might be expected in a city having the most rapid rate of growth in Canada in the past five years, Edmonton is experimenting boldly in the planning of its physical development. It is becoming widely celebrated for its planned neighborhoods. Thirty of these neighborhoods have been completed since 1950 and more are planned.

One of these completed neighborhoods, Sherbrooke, is briefly described herein. In 1949, it was proposed to "develop" this area on the "grid-iron" basis. But this plan was cancelled and replaced by a new scheme. It was not easy to incorporate into the new subdivision 50 scattered houses which had been built in the previous 10 years; but, with 5 exceptions, this was accomplished.

A comparison of the design features of the old and the new plans shows some of the differences from the viewpoint of economics, appearance, conveience and safety. Mr. Dant points out that: "a considerable reduction in the lengths of both local streets and service lanes was possible, saving home-owners of the City many dollars of unnecessary street construction and maintenance cost. The land so saved was put into more fruitful use, adding to total investments and providing the City with increased real estate tax year by year. There were some slight increases in utility costs, as compared with the 'unplanned' scheme, and some added costs in curved curbing, but these were far outweighed by the above savings."

Perhaps the greatest saving is in the difficulties and expense to home-owners and taxpayers which, in the absence of such a subdivision plan, arise over the years as a result of failure to provide suitable sites for schools, churches, shops and play space, as well as safe traffic conditions.

The aesthetic and operating advantages of irregular street patterns are still being debated in Edmonton, but it seems unlikely that there will ever be a reversion to the "grid". In fact, it seems more likely that, for reasons of economy and better neighborhood living, the grid will lose its strong traditional appeal in all of the growing cities of the West.

There may be many imperfections in the new type of subdivision, and the future may witness many changes in the theory and practice of neighborhood planning. But the elected officials of the City of Edmonton and Mr. Dant and his associates in the City administration are to be congratulated for the bold and extensive pioneer work they have done in a field related so closely to the hearts and pocketbooks of millions of Canadians.

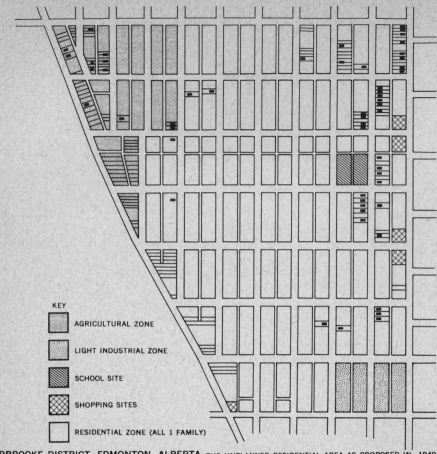

KEY

▨ AGRICULTURAL ZONE

▒ LIGHT INDUSTRIAL ZONE

▨ SCHOOL SITE

▨ SHOPPING SITES

☐ RESIDENTIAL ZONE (ALL 1 FAMILY)

SHERBROOKE DISTRICT, EDMONTON, ALBERTA THE UNPLANNED RESIDENTIAL AREA AS PROPOSED IN 1949

Unplanned Scheme

1. There is a complete absence of parks and recreation areas.
2. No church sites are provided.
3. Shopping areas are small and located on the perimeter instead of being central. No off-street parking is provided.
4. Only one school site is provided, and it is not centrally located.
5. All roads are of equal width and are potential "through" streets.
6. There is no variety in types of residential zones.
7. Some very long, narrow house lots are shown. These are uneconomical. Others are poorly shaped.
8. There is an unnecessary duplication of utility lanes in some places.
9. There are variations in the width of the main road. Half-jogs in the roads in some places are unsafe, and there are some dangerous junctions.
10. The light industrial zone has no place in a residential area.
11. Likewise the agricultural zone seems out of place, especially with houses allowed in it in excess of a ratio appropriate to such a zone.
12. Residential zones are all 1-family.

AND AS FINALLY DEVELOPED IN 1952

Planned Scheme

1. Sites are provided for parks, playing fields and recreational areas.
2. Church sites are provided in convenient locations.
3. There is a central shopping area, with off-street parking.
4. Two school sites are provided, reasonably accessible from all parts of the neighbourhood. The Catholic school is off-center because it also serves adjacent neighbourhoods.
5. "Through" arterial highways, of adequate width, are separated from local service roads by limited access planted strips. Thus both "local" and "through" traffic are safeguarded. There are feeder roads for bus routes. Local residential streets are designed in such a way as to discourage "through" driving, yet remain adequate for local purposes.
6. At the corners of the area, there are intersections designed to keep "through" traffic moving.
7. One-family housing is created in an aesthetic as well as a functional setting. Setbacks are arranged to allow for a "rhythmic variation". A buffer strip separates housing from an adjacent industrial zone.
8. There are also apartments and row housing in a variety of types.
9. A neighborhood "focus" of larger buildings and open space is included as an essential ingredient of a well-designed residential area.

COMPARATIVE STATISTICS

	UNPLANNED SCHEME		PLANNED SCHEME	
Internal Roads	37,960 lin. ft.	57.2 acres	27,600 lin. ft.	41.7 acres
Utility and Service Lanes	27,460 lin. ft.	12.6 acres	23,400 lin. ft.	10.7 acres
Public School Space		2.14 acres		6.0 acres
Catholic School Space		—		4.0 acres
Recreation League Area		—		2.0 acres
Parks		—		4.0 acres
Churches		—		1.5 acres
Shopping Area(s)	(scattered)	1.9 acres		1.5 acres
Agricultural Zone		19.0 acres		—
Light Industry		6.56 acres		—
Miscellaneous (planted islands, etc.)		—		11.6 acres
Residential				
1-Family Type	1,068 units	122.6 acres	896 units	112.0 acres
	3,400 people	—	3,584 people	
Row Housing	—	—	245 units	17.5 acres
			980 people	
Apartment Type	—	—	190 units	9.5 acres
			760 people	
Total	1,068 units	122.6 acres	1,331 units	139.0 acres

	UNPLANNED SCHEME	PLANNED SCHEME
TOTAL ACREAGE OF SCHEME	222 ACRES	222 ACRES
TOTAL POPULATION (residential)	3,400 PEOPLE	5,324 PEOPLE
GROSS DENSITY (i.e. total no. of dwelling units divided by total acreage of scheme)	4.8 dwelling units/acre	5.7 dwelling units/acre
NET RESIDENTIAL DENSITY (i.e. total no. of dwelling units or persons divided by total acreage of residential property and the roads and lanes which serve them)	26 persons/acre 6.27 units/acre	27 persons/acre 7 units/acre

Cumbernauld

New Town

L. H. Wilson

The building of new towns in post-war Britain has been a remarkable enterprise. At the present time work is in progress at various stages on fifteen towns and six further projects have recently been announced.

The towns are each under the control of a Development Corporation appointed under the New Towns Act 1946 and most of the capital is loaned by the Government although there are many opportunities for private enterprise to take part in the erection of some of the factories, houses and shops and such buildings as schools and churches are provided by the appropriate authorities. The Corporations are responsible for the planning and development of the towns to create self contained communities where people can live and work and spend their leisure in pleasant surroundings.

The towns fall into five functional groups. Eight of the towns, Basildon, Bracknell, Crawley, Harlow, Hemel Hempstead, Stevenage, Hatfield and Welwyn Garden City are linked to the London overspill problem and will provide homes and workplaces for over half a million people. The sites of these towns are some twenty to thirty miles from London. Three of the new towns in Scotland, East Kilbride, Cumbernauld and now Livingston are similarly related to the problems of Glasgow although in the case of the first two towns the sites are rather nearer to the city. Two towns, Skelmersdale and Runcorn are to be built to take overspill population from the Liverpool conurbation and the towns at Dawley and Redditch will have a similar relation to Birmingham. The remaining five towns are being built to serve the needs of local industry — Newton Aycliffe and Peterlee in County Durham, Corby in Northamptonshire, Cwmbran in Monmouthshire and Glenrothes in Scotland in the vicinity of a new coalfield in Fife. It has since been announced that this coalfield is to be closed and Glenrothes will, therefore, be developed to help in solving the acute overspill problem in Glasgow.

The first fourteen new towns were designated between 1947 and 1950 and the Development Corporations were given population targets, varying from 15,000 to 80,000 although many of these have since been increased. These towns have been planned on

Reprinted from *Plan*, Vol. 4, no. 2 (1963), pp. 70-85 by permission.

the basis of a number of residential neighbourhood units each complete with its own local shopping centre, schools and community and other public buildings.

Cumbernauld is the last new town on which construction work is in progress having been designated in 1956. It was one of the towns proposed in the Clyde Valley Regional Plan prepared in 1946 by Sir Patrick Abercrombie and Mr. (now Sir) Robert Matthew. It is being built to assist in the relief of congestion in Glasgow and the majority of the proposed total population of 70,000 will come from that city. In its siting it differs to a marked extent from all the other new towns so far developed and in its planning a number of principles have been introduced which are either new to or represent developments of recent practice. In their work the planners of Cumbernauld have had the advantage of being able to learn a great deal from the experiences of the other new towns.

Planning Aims

The main planning aim at Cumbernauld has been to achieve a unified coherent structure for the town with an urban character arising out of compact planning at a somewhat higher average density of development than in the other new towns. It should be stressed that this policy has been implemented on the basis of good standards of open space and compactness within the urban area has resulted from the placing of the major elements of open space on the periphery of the town. The neighbourhood unit concept of planning has been abandoned at Cumbernauld and instead of having a series of local centres in the main urban area there will be one town centre which will require to be developed at a relatively early stage. It is felt that the neighbourhood unit has little social significance, social contacts generally being confined to the residents in small groups of houses or being enjoyed by people of particular interests on a town scale.

Towns are essentially meeting places; at Cumbernauld it is considered that this function can only be fulfilled by recognising the rights of the pedestrian. Whilst planning for the motor car, therefore, freedom for the pedestrian has been achieved on the basis that the conflicting needs of vehicles and pedestrians can be satisfied only by maximum separation.

Much has been learnt from the other new towns particularly in terms of population and employment balance. New towns tend to attract a relatively young cross-section of the population with the result that children are in excess of the national average and older people represent a considerably smaller proportion. Efforts are being made to redress this state of unbalance by taking older people from Glasgow whenever possible. The population structure will also be helped if a wide range of employment can be achieved with particular emphasis on service industry including office employment and rather less manufacturing industry than has been apparent in the other new towns. The Cumbernauld proposals are for 45 percent of employment in manufacturing industry and 48 percent in offices and services, the remaining balance being taken up by construction, mining and agricultural employment.

Site

The site occupies a central position in the lowland industrial belt of Scotland between the deep inlets of the Firths of Clyde and Forth and contained to the north and south by upland areas. The trunk road from Glasgow to the north of Scotland passes the site of the

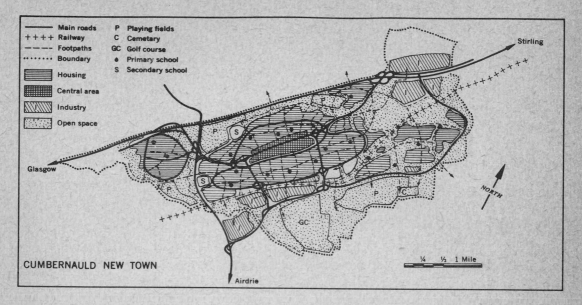

CUMBERNAULD NEW TOWN

Legend:
- Main roads
- ++++ Railway
- - - - Footpaths
- ······ Boundary
- Housing
- Central area
- Industry
- Open space

P Playing fields
C Cemetary
GC Golf course
• Primary school
S Secondary school

Glasgow

Stirling

Airdrie

NORTH

¼ ½ 1 Mile

new town where it is joined by the trunk road from England. The railway from Glasgow to the north runs through Cumbernauld Station and there are also rail connections to the main line to England. The area designated by the Secretary of State for Scotland comprises some 4,150 acres and is triangular in shape, five miles long from north east to south west and two miles across from the north west to south east at the widest point. The site is generally hilly and the area of land suitable for development is restricted by the presence of fireclay and coal workings, pockets of peat and steep slopes and part of the site is isolated by two deep glens. The main element on the site is a hill in the form of a broad hogsback between the valleys on the lines of the Glasgow trunk road and the Glasgow railway with a breadth of one mile and a length of two and a half miles. The altitude varies from about 260 feet above sea level in the valley to 485 feet at the highest point on the hilltop. There are steep and very broken slopes on the north west side of this hill and longer and more gentle slopes on the south east.

The watershed of Scotland crosses the site, the southern part draining to the Clyde and the northern part to the Forth. The whole site is exposed to the prevailing south west winds which blow down the valley and along the length of the site and many tree belts have been planted across the hill in the past to give shelter from these winds. The surface deposits are principally boulder clays.

The conditions and general characteristics of the site determine the areas suitable for development which, apart from the main hilltop, consist of a smaller hill to the south west, three areas to the north east and a series of sites to the south of the main hilltop on level land in the valley including one site, particularly suitable for industrial development, just outside the designated area.

Plan

It soon became clear that the main hilltop, with a gross area of about 930 acres for building, would provide the most suitable site for the major development of the new town since it is the only section of the area capable of being used for a large scale comprehensive scheme. The form of the hilltop, from which there are fine views in all directions and which can be seen from many points outside the area, with its clearly defined limits lent itself to the general conception of this part of the town as a compact urban centre containing a population of 50,000 with surrounding recreation areas, the whole set against the background of open hilly country. The town defines its own urban limits and its own green girdle of open space. The linear town form has many advantages, particularly in association with the linear central area. Apart from ensuring a more efficient and economical road and footpath system, the linear town allows the great majority of the population to live within a ten minutes walk of the town centre or of the open space. At Cumbernauld every part of the town can be in close touch visually and physically with the surrounding countryside.

The ultimate population of 70,000 will be achieved by the development of a series of satellite villages around the main hilltop each with its own local centre but relying on the central area of the town for the main shopping and recreational facilities. The overall pattern for the town can, therefore, be regarded as that of a cluster city in which there is one major urban centre surrounded by but separated from a number of smaller compact urban units of varying size the whole being linked together by an efficient road and footpath system. This process might well be extended in the future providing a very flexible approach to the ultimate size and detailed pattern of the town.

Housing

Housing design in Cumbernauld has been strongly conditioned by a number of factors including:

(a) attempt to achieve integration of dwelling design and layout
(b) need to achieve within ruling densities the maximum number of houses on the ground
(c) site conditions with slopes varying from almost level to very steep and with fine views out of the site
(d) the need to secure adequate daylighting and sunlighting standards
(e) privacy for main rooms and gardens
(f) flexibility in the use of space within dwellings
(g) maximum separation of pedestrians and vehicles
(h) the provision of one car storage space for every house plus parking space for visitors' cars

Net densities average about 80 persons per acre and vary on particular sites between 60 and 120 persons per acre with some small areas at a rather lower density. The solutions which have been evolved in response to these conditions have produced housing schemes far removed in form and character from most of the post war designs of local authorities and private enterprise developers in this country. The concept of streets lined with houses has been dropped in favour of designs in which the movement of vehicles and pedestrians and the planning of the individual dwellings to achieve good living conditions are highly integrated. The result is a strongly developed pattern of buildings and public and private spaces carefully related to the site conditions and with considerable attention being given to all the details of changes of level, pavings, planting, fencing, etc.

In higher density schemes it is possible to achieve separation of vehicles and pedestrians vertically but at the lower densities horizontal separation is being used at Cumbernauld. The general pattern is for the car to move outwards (in contrast to the pedestrian who moves inwards) to join a collector road forming part of the traffic distribution system. The effectiveness of a road pattern serving housing where high speeds are not the controlling factor can be measured by the delay or waiting time experienced at any point. At the start of his journey near the house where the pedestrian and the car meet the car should move slowly and fairly long waits are permissible. As the car moves through the hierarchy of roads, delays at peak flows are decreased until there is no delay at all at the town throughway junctions. Pedestrian movement varies according to the position in the town; on the main roads there is complete separation, at the house, pedestrian and car meet. Within housing areas the pedestrian is focussed inwards to the main town footpaths with access on foot to the shop, pub, primary schools and play areas. The object is to provide not only safe routes but safe areas for social life to develop. With segregation of traffic there are opportunities for increased social relationships within the housing group while the mobility of the car increases the range of social selection outside the group.

At Cumbernauld the housing layouts are generally based on a meshed system of roads and footpaths. Houses are approached by spur footpaths and garages are grouped in blocks alongside the roads at the ends of terraces. In some areas road access is provided to one side of the house and footpath access to the other. This involves quite separate patterns of roads and footpaths with complete separation. This form of layout has many advantages and it has been used at Cumbernauld with a wide frontage house with a through hall with an entrance door at either end. On another site the area is divided into units each containing about 200 houses surrounded by peripheral roads giving access to garaging areas and to a number of tree planted culs-de-sac driven into the housing areas to provide facilities for service traffic and visitors' cars only. The centres of the units are kept clear of traffic although of necessity there has to be a greater average distance between house and garage.

Car storage on housing sites is being dealt with in various ways including blocks of individual lock-ups in straight or curved terraces, garages attached to houses or at the ends of the gardens, car ports consisting of a roof and back wall, garages or car ports under the houses or blocks of flats and paved parking space reserved for particular cars. All these types are being used in various parts of the town according to site conditions and layout.

Privacy in houses and private gardens is being achieved not by the amount of space between buildings but by the design of the house and the space involving in particular the use of single aspect houses to prevent overlooking. These are of wide frontage type of houses which are single storey on the entrance side and two storey on the garden and sunny side. On steep sites split level designs are being used with living rooms on the first floor, particularly where there are fine views out of the site.

Great care is being taken with the landscaping of the areas with considerable use of pavings of various materials and textures together with the planting of trees and shrubs. Toddlers' play spaces occur at frequent intervals and provision is also being made for sites for playgrounds for older children.

Central Area

With a compact plan the central area of the town can be within easy distance of most of the houses and at Cumbernauld the main shopping provision will be concentrated in the centre. Local shopping needs are being satisfied by the provision of individual shops throughout the residential areas on the basis of one shop to about 300 houses; these shops will sell a wide variety of merchandise. Local centres will be provided in the satellite villages. In order to prepare a programme on which to base the design for the central area a study of shopping provision was made and particular notice was taken of shopping trends on the North American Continent. It is felt that the successful centre should be capable of adapting itself to unforeseen patterns of consumer goods distribution if it is to avoid obsolescence. Indeed the need for flexibility in the use of space and for protection for the shopper from weather leads to the design of very much larger building units of a more comprehensive nature each accommodating varying uses at different levels with the necessary circulation space contained within. In assessing the amount of shopping space required in the town, probable sales for each trade category were calculated and converted into the floor area required by assessing the sales per square foot for each trade. For this purpose figures were obtained from a sample group of one hundred towns with broad similarities to Cumbernauld. A total floor area of 620,000 sq. ft. for the town was calculated, divided to give 415,000 sq. ft. in the central area and the remainder for the local shops and village centres.

The amount of car parking space was calculated at some 3,000 car spaces with a possible rise in the future by another 2,000 spaces. Separation of pedestrians and vehicles is, of course, an essential requirement for a major centre and at Cumbernauld this will be achieved vertically by the provision of a multi deck centre with roads and car parks underneath. The site is south of and just below the ridge of the hill with road access from the major junctions on the radial roads and with pedestrian access from the main footpath system on the northern and southern slopes of the hill. In this way it is possible for the centre to take a linear form and to be planned on various levels. Road access will be by a dual carriageway running along the ridge of the hill and under the centre. The roads give access to car parks and also to areas where goods vehicles can load and unload. After leaving the car the driver and passengers are able to move to the pedestrian decks above by escalator or lift. Goods are taken directly from the loading docks into the storage areas of the shops or are conveyed by hoists to the shopping or storage levels above. A 'bus station is provided within the centre from which access can be gained to the upper floors. All the floor levels above the road and car parks are for the exclusive use of pedestrians and these decks are linked by steps and ramps and bridges to give easy communication throughout the centre. The upper floors are laid out in squares and promenades, some covered and enclosed to provide shopping halls, others open. All the facilities and amenities provided in a large town centre will be available in a compact yet spacious form and will include nearly ten acres of shopping floor space together with churches, hotel, restaurants, cinema, dance hall, public houses, business and professional offices, local and central government offices, town hall, technical college, library, clubs, etc. Above the centre there are terraces of flats and maisonettes where the residents can enjoy the advantages of being in the centre without the bustle and noise. Around the centre there is space for open terraces, tree planting, an arena for sports events, exhibitions and fairs and there are also sites for fire station and hospital.

Industry

Two main industrial areas have been provided, to the north and to the south of the main hilltop site and as well as providing sites for purpose built factories to be erected by the Corporation or by individual industrialists, the Corporation are building advance standard factories in units of 20,000 sq. ft. These have been specially designed to ensure maximum flexibility in the use of space and can be divided to form two smaller units or can be enlarged to provide a wide range of floor areas up to 60,000 sq. ft. The Corporation are also erecting three storey flatted factories within the housing areas to provide space for the small industrialist or as a staging post for the larger industrialist who wishes to train staff while his factory is being built. The units of accommodation in these buildings vary from 300 sq. ft to 3,300 sq. ft. on any one floor.

Community Services

Primary school sites are being provided in relation to the housing areas with access from the footpath system and sites are being reserved for secondary schools on the fringe of the hilltop where they can be situated in close proximity to a main road and 'bus service and their playing fields can be in the recreational area surrounding the town. Churches for the various denominations are being sited in convenient locations throughout the town although some of the denominations with only one church will have sites in the central area. Residents meeting rooms are being pro-

vided throughout the housing areas and there will also be provision for larger community halls although there will be a concentration of such facilities in the town centre.

Open Space and Recreation

A comprehensive scheme for the provision of open space of various kinds has been prepared on the basis that the whole of the peripheral areas of the town should form a continuous recreational and amenity system which will vary in use from place to place according to the demands of a particular development or to the requirements of the town as a whole; thus there are playing fields, woodland areas, parks and walks of various kinds and also reservation for a golf course. The open space system runs between the satellite villages and the main hilltop site and these are linked together by main pedestrian routes taken through the open spaces well away from all vehicular traffic. The aim has been that just as nobody on the main hilltop will live within much more than ten minutes walk from the town centre so no one will live more than ten minutes walk from the girdle of open space.

Landscaping has been considered as much more than being concerned with the design of the green spaces within the town. Everything within the town is landscape or, more properly, townscape. There must be as much shelter planting as possible on this exposed site with bold masses of trees on a scale large enough to contrast effectively with the bold mass of buildings and it is hoped that this interplay of trees and buildings may be one of the chief means of attaining ultimately a clear coherent pattern for the town as a whole. Except where openness is functionally required space within the town is regarded mainly as a site for trees contributing to shelter but also reinforcing a sense of enclosure that is one of the underlying qualities of urbanity.

Communications

The organisation of an efficient communications pattern in the town has been considered as a basic principle of the plan. The conflicting needs of vehicles and pedestrians can, of course, only be satisfied by maximum separation; this should be achieved to cause both the minimum unnecessary inconvenience but in general the car can be made to take the longer journey. The principle adopted at Cumbernauld is that if the car is to be accepted in the town then its reasonable requirements must be met; on the other hand it must be subjected to proper and adequate control.

A completely separate system of pedestrian paths is being provided throughout the town while conversely footpaths will not be placed alongside main roads. Local shops, primary schools, churches, pubs and other elements meeting the communal needs of the population are associated with these paths, many of which will pass through or terminate in the town centre. Where a path crosses a road other than a housing development road a bridge or underpass is being provided.

The town road system has been worked out after the preparation of traffic projections forecasting vehicular movements some twenty years ahead with an assumed rate of car ownership of one vehicle per family. Any study of traffic in Great Britain has to be made against a background of inadequate research and a great many of the assumptions in the Cumbernauld study had to be based on experiences in America. Desire line diagrams indicating ideal paths for traffic moving about the town were prepared and from these diagrams an ideal road pattern was evolved.

After a study of various alternatives based on this pattern, one eventually emerged as providing the best solution when considered in detail in relation to the comprehensive development of the whole hilltop area.

To ensure an easily recognisable communications pattern the multi purpose road was discarded and a traffic flow hierachy worked out with local development roads, collector roads, main town radial roads and trunk roads. The road plan for the main town area incorporates three radial roads running from the trunk roads up on to the hilltop where they are connected by radial link roads with junctions giving access to the central area and by a ring road and a spine road to the south of the centre serving the various housing areas. The major junctions have been designed to be grade separated although it will be possible to carry out the work in stages.

The pattern of roads and paths has been evolved as part of the general planning proposals for the town; it has not been imposed on the town to the possible detriment of detailed development proposals. The large scale of the road works will present considerable visual problems and it is felt that the only reasonable solution lies in the very careful treatment of cuttings and embankments or viaducts together with the planting of tree belts alongside the major roads.

Rail provision exists although the present station will have to be considerably enlarged. The station is well situated in relation to the town and there will be direct vehicular access to the ring road as well as a pedestrian route to the town centre.

Engineering Services

Various services are being provided, by the County Council in the case of main drainage and water and by the statutory bodies in respect of electricity, gas and telephones. The existence of the watershed requires the provision of two sewage disposal works with main trunk sewers running on either side of the watershed, along the foot of the main hill. A separate surface water drainage system is being provided with balancing ponds at either end of the main hill to deal with discharges under abnormal storm conditions. These ponds are being designed to be of amenity value in the town open space system. The fact that the site is situated on the watershed means that the existing streams are very small and, therefore, care has to be taken to avoid flooding in the lower reaches.

Agreement has been reached with the electricity and the telephone authorities to place underground all cables within the town area; decisions which have a marked effect on the total environment. It is also worth noting that Cumbernauld is close to the local television station and, therefore, no external aerials are required.

Planning Methods

From the beginning every effort has been made at Cumbernauld to achieve unity of design in the town with the integration of buildings, planning and townscape. One of the principal methods adopted to this end by the Chief Architect and Planning Officer was that of designing by teams drawn from the various professions involved. The whole of the technical staff of the Corporation has operated in his department and at all levels the office is organised in teams consisting of architects, planners, engineers, quantity surveyors and landscape architects. Projects are discussed at all stages and at all levels, each profession making its own contribution. It is not possible for any one profession to work in isolation on these problems and it is also felt that solutions arrived at as a result of team working are more likely to fit in to the overall conception of the town than by other methods.

The planning proposals for the new town are set out in a document called the 'basic plan' accompanied by various reports. It is intended that this should be a plan to guide but not to stifle the growth of the town and quite deliberately there has been no attempt to produce a master plan to fix future development once and for all. Most important of all there is an overriding need for a comprehensive approach to the detailed design of the whole town within the framework of the plan. With compact planning complete integration of all the space-consuming elements in the town is important and this involves a special technique in terms of planning procedure. Instead of reserving sites for individual buildings or uses it becomes necessary to settle the design form of the development at an early stage and to fix the site boundaries after this has been done. In this process the various architects engaged in the design of the individual buildings are briefed in terms of the requirements and problems to be dealt with and also on the character of the site in relation to the surroundings. All this involves great flexibility in the legal and technical processes involved. It is appreciated that these matters are comparatively simple in the context of a new town development where there is complete ownership of the land by the Development Corporation. On the other hand it does seem to be a problem which must be faced in the redevelopment of existing towns.

Conclusion

By March, 1963 some 1,800 houses had been completed and another 2,000 were under contract. Detailed designs have been produced for almost half of the ultimate number of houses required in the town and the design of the first stage of the central area has been prepared. Work is also complete on over half of the ring road and the first of the major interchanges, that at the junction of the northern radial and the ring road is now under construction.

Cumbernauld has been called the first of the Mark II new towns. In its design an attempt has been made to face up to the problem of the motor car but at the same time to create a town which will provide a good setting for the people who have to live and work there. British town planning has moved far from the garden city days and Cumbernauld represents, perhaps, a return to an earlier phase of town design, when towns achieved an urban quality which has so often been lacking in recent examples. Design, however, must look to the future and here is the crucial test of the success or otherwise of the Cumbernauld approach.